Good Dames

Good Dames

James Robert Parish

Editor
T. ALLAN TAYLOR

Research Associates
JOHN ROBERT COCCHI   FLORENCE SOLOMON

Photo Associate
GENE ANDREWSKI

SOUTH BRUNSWICK AND NEW YORK: A. S. BARNES AND COMPANY
LONDON: THOMAS YOSELOFF LTD

A. S. Barnes and Co., Inc.
Cranbury, New Jersey 08512

Thomas Yoseloff Ltd
108 New Bond Street
London W1Y OQX, England

Library of Congress Cataloging in Publication Data

Parish, James Robert.
    Good dames.

    Includes lists of films.
    1. Actresses—United States—Biography. I. Title.
PN2285.P33   791.43′028′0922 [B]   72-5172
ISBN 0-498-01111-9

PRINTED IN THE UNITED STATES OF AMERICA

To
GLENDA FARRELL
1904–1971

Contents

Acknowledgments

Agnes Moorehead chapter:
  Roy Buchanan, President of the Agnes Moorehead Club
    1410 Dauphine Street
    New Orleans, Louisiana 70116

  Ronald L. Bowers
  Georgia Johnstone

Angela Lansbury chapter:
  Pieter Jansen Van Vuuren

Thelma Ritter chapter:
  Monica Moran

Bruco Enterprises
James W. Buchanan
Mrs. Loraine Burdick
Cinemabilia Book Shop (Ernest Burns)
Classic Film Collector (Samuel K. Rubin)
Collectors Film Registry (Ted Riggs)
Filmfacts (Ernie Parmentier)
Film Fan Monthly (Leonard Maltin)

Mrs. R. F. Hastings
Charles Hoyt
Ken D. Jones
Kenneth G. Lawrence Movie Memorabilia (Arthur C. Peterson)
Doug McClelland
Albert B. Manski
Alvin H. Marill
Peter Miglierini
Muskingum College (Dr. L. A. Porter)
Jack A. Neal
Michael R. Pitts
Ronald Rainier
Screen Facts (Alan G. Barbour)
Mrs. Peter Smith
Charles K. Stumpf

Thanks also to Paul Myers and the staff of the theater collection at Lincoln Center Library for the Performing Arts, without whose congenial assistance this book would not be.

About the Contributors

Since the age of five, thirty-four year old Brooklynite JOHN ROBERT COCCHI has been viewing and collating meticulous data on motion pictures and is now regarded as one of the most energetic film researchers on the global scene. Professionally he is the chief film reviewer for *Boxoffice* magazine. He was research associate on *The American Movies Reference Book, The Fox Girls, The Cinema of Edward G. Robinson,* and the forthcoming *The RKO Gals.* He has written cinema history articles for such journals as *Film Fan Monthly* and *Screen Facts.*

T. ALLAN TAYLOR, the godson of the late Margaret Mitchell, was born in Greenwich Village, attended Wesleyan University, and is currently production manager of Engineering Index, Inc. He has functioned as manuscript editor on *The Fox Girls, The Paramount Pretties,* and *The Slapstick Queens.* Mr. Taylor is also a critique contributor on classical music to various record journals.

New York-born FLORENCE SOLOMON attended Hunter College and then joined Ligon Johnson's copyright research office. Later she was appointed director for research at Entertainment Copyright Research Co., Inc., and is currently a reference supervisor at A.S.C.A.P.'s Index Division. Miss Solomon has collaborated on such works as *The American Movies Reference Book, TV Movies, The Great Movie Series,* and the forthcoming *Guide to Actors' Television Work* and *The Great Spy Pictures.* She is the niece of the noted late sculptor Sir Jacob Epstein.

GENE ANDREWSKI, a native of Oklahoma City, has been a staunch part of the New York cultural scene for now well over a decade. A former editor of the *Paris Review,* he was coproducer of such off-Broadway shows as *Anything Goes* and *Valmouth.* More recently he converted his extensive private collection of film stills into a researching archive. Mr. Andrewski is the inventor of the popular game, *Movie Moguls.*

Good Dames

Eve Arden

Height: 5'9"
Weight: 139 pounds
Dark blonde hair
Green eyes
Birth sign: Taurus

For over forty years, Eve Arden has commanded tremendous respect as a polished situation comedienne. Her unique ability to arch an eyebrow and with perfect timing toss out a wisecrack made her an established entertainment personality by the age of twenty-one (1933). Whether on Broadway in The Ziegfeld Follies *(1934, 1936), in motion pictures (Stage Door, Mildred Pierce, Voice of the Turtle) or on radio-television ("Our Miss Brooks"), she excelled at epitomizing the acid-tongued, liberated miss, who deep at heart would much prefer a man by the home fire rather than engaging in a battle royale with a female rival in the business world. If she has any failing as a consummate performer, it is her inability to project convincing warmth in a characterization, a fault that blighted her attempts to play counter-type on television's* It Gives Me Great Feeling, *on stage in* Auntie Mame, *or on the screen in* The Dark at the Top of the Stairs.

Eve Arden (née Eunice Quedens) was born April 30, 1912, the only child of Charles Peter Quedens and Lucille (Frank) Quedens of Mill Valley, on the outskirts of San Francisco, California. When Eve was about five years old, her parents divorced, and she was raised by her mother and aunt.

About her mother, once a stock circuit actress, Eve later said, "She was very beautiful. I lost five years with a psychiatrist because of not being as beautiful as she."

Even as a child, Eve had definite theatrical ambitions. At the age of seven, she fancied herself an expert dialectician and was performing her favorite piece *No Kicka My Dog* for the Outdoor Art Club and any other audience that would tolerate her exaggerated rendition. She attended Mill Valley Grammar School and graduated from Tamalpais High School in 1928, where she had performed in such school productions as *Dulcy.*

There are at least three versions of how Eve initially broke into show business with Henry Duffy's San Francisco group: 1) she walked by the theater, stopped, and walked in, 2) as an employee in a fabric shop, she became acquainted with an interior decorator whose client was Duffy, and 3) "I was dumped by my mother and aunt at the Henry Duffy office in San Francisco and told to get a job acting, which I did." At any rate, Eve made herself known to Duffy and a month later he called on her to perform a walk-on part in *Alias the Deacon.* Because she was so tall and angular, it was almost impossible to cast Eve as the ingenue, so she usually portrayed the character roles in such productions as *The Patsy.*

Besides operating the Alcazar Theatre in San Francisco, Duffy owned the El Capitan Theatre in Hollywood, and the group would perform their repertory in both theaters. In 1929, Eve decided to remain in Los Angeles. By a fluke of luck, she was hired on a one picture contract by Columbia Pictures for their *The Song of Love* (1929), a sound feature, which was a talking vehicle to introduce vaudevillian Belle Baker to movie audiences. *The Song of Love* premiered at the George M. Cohan Theatre November 13, 1929, with patrons being charged two dollars admission (most reviewers thought it a bit steep price for an entertaining but unspectacular production). Columbia's picture was another backstage story of vaudevillians. Baker has an act with her husband Ralph Graves and their young son David Durand. She breaks up the family team so Durand can lead a normal life. He is sent to military school and she becomes a successful solo cabaret performer. Graves takes to drink and starts to play around with yellow-toned blonde songstress Eve (he was 6'2" which allowed for casting tall girl Eve "opposite" him). Eventually Baker and Graves are reunited through the enterprising efforts of their son, and all ends well. While

Eve Arden in 1934.

Variety tagged Eve ". . . the blonde come-between, a cinch part," the *New York Times* was more enthusiastic: "Eunice Quedens makes Mazie quite lifelike."

Columbia, a minor studio at the time, was not sufficiently impressed with Eve, nor could she land any movie assignments elsewhere at the time. Thus, she was happy to find a job with the Bandbox Repertory Theatre managed by Katherine Turney, who later became a screenwriter and playwright, and Katherine's husband. Eve was the fourth member of the troupe which traveled in an old Ford car along the west coast borscht belt circuit, playing the small hotels and low class desert resorts. It was a rangy gypsy life, but in the depression days she was fortunate to have any job, let alone one in her chosen profession. Her roles with the Bandbox group, such as Matilda in *On Approval* and Amanda in *Private Lives,* provided her with the opportunity to expand her scope as an actress.

Eve remained with the Bandbox company up to 1933, when she won her second film role, in the prestigious MGM musical *Dancing Lady,* starring Joan Crawford. It was another of Crawford's ladder-to-success vehicles in which, this time, she was a poor but resolute stripteaser, at the International Burlesque Theatre, determined both to land a big Broadway show assignment and to be a blushing virgin on her wedding day. Her rocky road to success is sprinkled with the temptation of wealthy Franchot Tone who might like to marry her, and the more resolute determinations of show director-producer Clark Gable. The elaborate backstage story debuted at the Capitol and Loew's Metro Theatres November 30, 1933. Eve's minor part occurs when star-struck Crawford arrives at Gable's Times Square audition office. As she timidly walks into the reception room, Eve and her dumbstruck agent Matt McHugh barge out from the inner office. In a syrupy southern accent and referring to the brush-off Gable and his assistant (Ted Healy) have just given her at the audition, Eve yells back into the room she has just left, "Gentlemen know how to speak to ladies." Then she beings berating her agent, "What a wise agent you are." All the while—and it is a lightning fast interplay—Crawford stands aside, gaping at the scene. Suddenly, blondized Eve, cloth hat, dangling earrings and all, drops her Dixie diction, and blurts out in a tough broad tone "I told you that southern accent would sound phoney." And out the door she goes.

Crawford sizes up the situation and waltzes into the audition area, displaying her own pseudo-southern drawl, hoping to land the lead in the new musical *Dancing Lady,* which, of course, she eventually does. Eve was not even billed for her on-again-off-again bit, and it is unlikely any viewers paid much heed to her,

particularly as the cast included such popular character performers as folksy Winnie Lightner, May Robson as Tone's aristocratic but deaf grandmother, and the Three Stooges with their knock-about routines, as theatre stagehands.

Once again, Eve's film role was a one-shot deal, and she was glad to accept producer Leonard Stillman's offer to appear in his new musical revue *Lo and Behold* (1933) which opened at the Pasadena Playhouse that fall and then transferred to the El Capitan Theatre for the remainder of its thirty-eight performance run. Others in this low-budget variety show were Kay Thompson, Tyrone Power, Teddy Hart and Charles Walters. As Eve later said, "I had always been an incorrigible mimic, so the author agreed to write in some numbers for me in the show." Along with the others, Eve hoped this showcase would lead to bigger things. Producer Lee Shubert saw the production and was sufficiently impressed with Eve's comic abilities to hire her to play in the first post-Florenz Ziegfeld (he died in 1933) *Ziegfeld Follies* with Billie Burke Ziegfeld as the titular producer of the new revue.

Arriving in Manhattan, Eve adopted the name of Eve Arden, reportedly the surname of which was inspired by a bottle of Elizabeth Arden's "Evening In Paris" perfume she carried in her purse, and the first name was borrowed from a novel she was then reading in which the heroine was named Eve.

Eve immediately went into rehearsals for *The Ziegfeld Follies of 1934,* which, after preliminary workouts on the road, opened at the Winter Garden Theatre on January 4, 1934. Eve was thirteenth billed in a cast which headlined Willie and Eugene Howard, Fannie Brice, and featured dancers Vilma and Buddy Ebsen and Cherry and June Preisser, along with songstress Jane Froman. Vernon Duke and E. Y. Harburg provided the majority of songs, with sketches by Fred Allen, David Turgend, David Freedman and H. I. Phillips. Eve had the non-glamorous assignment of supplying many of the necessary fill-in comedy spots. She appeared in "All Quiet In Havana" (as a bridge player and nightclub hostess), in "Barnyard Theatre, Inc." (as stooge Phoebe Colt to Fannie Brice's capering), in "Baby Snooks" (Eve was the mother and Victor Morley the dad), in "The Man Who Came Back" (as a mother with four sons) and in the finale song, "Time Is A Gypsy," she sang along with the entire company. The show lasted a satisfactory 182 performances with Eve paid $100 weekly. The reviewers were too busy reporting on the antics of the stars to really notice or appreciate Eve. One critic queried, "A tall blonde who may or may not be Betzi Beaton, does odd jobs and is eccentric." It was Eve.

In *The Ziegfeld Follies Of 1934.*

clubwoman song "Send For The Militia," in which Eve talk-sings about her vaunted liberation, emphasizing her delivery with her lorgnette. Helen Eager stated that, "The socialite delving lightly into Socialism, who shrieks loudly for the Militia, the Army, the Navy, and the Boy Scouts, when she is told to participate her theories, is cleverly interpreted in song by Eve Arden, thoroughly stopping the show." At age twenty-three Eve was finally making a professional impact.

Parade premiered at the Guild's 52nd Street Theatre, May 20, 1935. The titles of the skits clearly revealed the show's political bent: "The Last Jackass," "The Dead Cow," "Our Store," "The Happy Family," "Home Of The Brave," "The Plague," "Flight From The Soviet" (another Eve solo number) and the finale summing-up song, "No Time To Sing A Gay Song."

The critics reacted adversely to the show, calling it the "1935 blues" and snarling "Jimmy Savo is funny, Karl Marx isn't." Funnyman Savo earned his usual high plaudits, but it was Eve who consistently aroused the best comments from the reporters. "I call your attention to the various impersonations of Miss Eve Arden, a versatile, good-looking and intelligent satirist . . ." (Percy Hammond, *New York Herald Tribune*). "Eve Arden

Eve had almost a year's layoff before her next Broadway assignment in which the Theatre Guild hired her for a featured part in their "socially conscious" musical revue *Parade*. This show was designed to wrap up the Guild's seventeenth season. With its pointed jabs at politics and economics, this pioneer message production had first been considered for production by the more appropriate social-problem-oriented Group Theatre and the Theatre Union. When both organizations dropped the project, The Guild, in an altruistic moment of daring, signed on as sponsor. The show had sketches by George Sklar, Paul Peters and Jerome Moross, and the cast included Jimmy Savo as star, the feature singer-dancers Vera Marshe, Earl Oxford, Charles Walters and Dorothy Fox, and Leon Janney, Ezra Stone and Eve to handle the comedy relief odd jobs. When the show previewed at the Colonial Theatre, Boston (beginning May 6, 1935), there were many who accused the sting-and-bite filled production of being communist if not worse. America was just recovering from the depression and entertainment goers were not impressed with songs and skits detailing the beautiful possibilities of life and the wisdom of better property distribution. Helen Eager in the *Boston Traveler* was enthusiastic about Eve's rendition of the Mark Blitzstein satirical

In *Parade* (1935).

acquits herself well in several numbers, even when they are less than indifferent." (John Mason Brown, *New York Evening Post*). *Variety's* Ibee offered the corking booster: "Another standout comes with Eve Arden, a coast girl who wins rating as one of the cleverest of newcomers. Diction excellent, she displays versatility both in handling numbers and playing parts. . . . Miss Arden impresses so well that she is in for the rest of the performance. That producers were sure of her is shown by spotting her next to closing as a Russian aviatrix giving a comedy lecture with slides (the 'Flight From The Soviet' number). Dialect is just about right and Miss Arden is very easy to look at besides."

Parade lingered on for forty performances and then closed, at an estimated loss of $100,000.

Eve remained in New York jobless until she was hired again by Lee Shubert for *The Ziegfeld Follies of 1936* which opened at the Winter Garden Theatre (January 30, 1936) after tryouts in Boston and Philadelphia. This time she had moved up in the billing to number seven, midst a versatile cast which included Fannie Brice, Josephine Baker, Bob Hope, Gertrude Niesen, Judy Canova, Cherry and June Preisser and Ben Yost's Varsity 8. David Freedman supplied the sketches, and Vernon Duke and Ira Gershwin created the songs. Shubert heavily publicized the fact this was the first Broadway show to benefit from choreographer George Balanchine. Eve's varied numbers included: "The Economic Situation," (a solo specialty song), "Baby Snooks Goes Hollywood" (she was Mrs. Higgins to Brice's Snooks); "Of Thee I Spend" (a spoof on "Of Thee I Sing" set in the Office of the F.S.A. with Hope as Rexford Givewell and Eve as the efficient Miss Gherken) and "Amateur Night" (she was Lady DeVere at the broadcast studio show). In the specialty song "I Can't Get Started without You" Hope crooned to a sulky but amusing Eve, who is playing hard to get. She, Rodney McLennan, and Ben Yost's Varsity 8 were featured in the finale number "Dancing To Our Score" where Eve was garbed in a full-length gown and sported a long white fur cape.

This time around there was no question but that Eve was a major asset in the production. At a high $5.50 ticket tops, it ran a healthy 115 performances. Eve was well received by the reviewers: "The items in the Shubert *Follies* that I like best are those contributed by Miss Eve Arden, a young, gentle and savage comedienne, comely, humorous and a perfect revuer." (*New York Herald Tribune*). "Miss Arden is in most of the skits. She has her big moment with a humorous lyric 'The Economic Situation,' with a background of show girls. Number points out the difficulties of luring a man these days, what with his mind on the affairs of

the nation." (*Variety*). ". . . (She) has an alert sense of humor." (*New York Times*).

Due to *The Ziegfeld Follies of 1936* Eve was established as a top ranking revue artist, not yet a star, but a definite asset in the highly competitive variety show format cycle of 1930s Broadway. It was not long before columnists like the *New York Herald Tribune*'s gossip reporter was writing: "Miss Arden belongs with Miss (Adele) Astaire in that small group of actresses who can be funny and attractive at the same time."

In the summer of 1936 *The Ziegfeld Follies of 1936* closed for the summer, and when it reopened on September 14, 1936, Eve had left the show and was replaced by former burlesque queen supreme, Gypsy Rose Lee. Not only had Eve found her daily onstage comedy routines taxing, but her mother had become seriously ill. Shortly after Eve returned to California her mother died. "I was a child of a broken home," Eve later recalled. "I felt a tremendous sense of responsibility to my mother, whom I adored, and when she died, I was devastated."

But the exigency of earning a living soon brought Eve back to the realities of life and she began making the rounds of Hollywood studios, seeking possible screen work. Eve was asked to make a screen test at Universal, largely as background straight girl for the highlighting of some V.I.P.'s sweetheart. At the time, neither Eve nor her agent Arthur Landau (who had "discovered" and nurtured the career of Jean Harlow) realized how important the test was to be for her career.

Eve was given a role in Universal's *Oh, Doctor!* (1937), a remake of the studio's 1924 feature. Hypochondriac Edward Everett Horton is about to inherit $500,000 from his late mortician father, but if Horton should die before the end of six months, the funds will go to charity. A group of sharpies, including Eve, offer him $50,000 for the potential fortune, and he almost accepts, needing ready money for medical treatment. The middling hodgepodge comedy opened at the Palace Theatre June 18, 1937, on a double bill with *This Is My Affair*. The *New York Times* pegged the movie as ". . . story-telling that ranges all the way from bad to worse." Eve was not singled out by the critics for her performance.

When director Gregory La Cava was casting *Stage Door* (1937) at RKO, he remembered having seen Eve's screentest the previous year when working on *My Man Godfrey* at Universal. Subsequently she was fifteenth-billed in *Stage Door*, the revised version of the George Kaufman-Edna Ferber stage success. Eve played one of the stagestruck hopefuls residing at the Footlight Club theatrical boarding house in Manhattan's West 40's. The multi-faceted drama focused on con-

With Edward Everett Horton in *Oh, Doctor!* (Universal, 1937).

ceited debutante Katharine Hepburn and her wise-cracking, but warm-hearted, dancer roommate Ginger Rogers. Both girls attempt to make the big time in showbusiness while discovering life and love. When Hepburn is given the lead role in an important Broadway offering, fellow boarder Andrea Leeds, frustrated and disgusted at being bypassed after such dedicated patience, commits suicide. Director La Cava allowed the supporting players: including Constance Collier, Lucille Ball and Eve; to expand their characterizations as far as their brief scenes would allow. Eve's miniscule part called for her to be generally seen lounging about on the livingroom sofa-arm, wearing slacks and blouse,

With Phyllis Kennedy and Grady Sutton in *Stage Door* (RKO, 1937).

With Ben Blue in *Cocoanut Grove* (Paramount, 1938).

and tossing out an occasional tart remark.* Always wanting to ingenuously build on any given characterization, Eve had an inspiration in using cast member Whitey the alley cat (being paid $25 daily—more than Eve's salary) as a living prop, wrapped around her shoulders like a fur wrap. This theatrical trick focused audience interest on her brief appearances, even in the midst of such illustrious scene stealers as were in the cast. *Stage Door* premiered at Radio City Music Hall, October 7, 1937 and was a big, rousing hit. Eve re-

ceived little critical attention—Rogers and Oscar nominee Leeds garnered most of that—but audiences remembered long-legged sardonic Eve and her feline neckpiece. *Stage Door* set the basic standard for the typical Eve Arden role for decades to come; that of the smart remark observer who does not partake much within the framework of the story, but merely appears on call to drop a few caustic comments on the stars' latest doings.

Eve's flip screen style was a variation of the formula used by movie personalities Glenda Farrell, Helen Vinson et al, throughout the 1930s. It was Eve's coplayer from *Stage Door,* Lucille Ball, who later said: "She (Eve) and I competed for years—one of us would be the lady executive and the other would be the 'other woman.' They were the same roles, for we'd walk through a room, drop a smart remark, and exit. I called us 'the drop-gag girls.' I didn't dig it at all, for in such

---

* Some of Eve's best lines in the film were directed at her close pal, Henry the cat. Taking a gander at one of the girls' fur wraps, Eve wisecracks: "Get a load of that, Henry, that's where you'll wind up." Or later when dinner is announced, she makes a flip aside to her living neck piece: "Let's go in to the stew, Henry. You might find a mouse in it."

parts you lose your femininity."

On a freelance basis, Eve was able to keep working steadily in the late 1930s, when Hollywood production was at top form. The first of her three 1938 releases was Paramount's *Cocoanut Grove*. Its slender plot concerned Fred MacMurray's band being fired from its Lake Michigan excursion boat gig and making its tenuous way to California, where the group lands in the big time at Los Angeles's Cocoanut Grove Club. Clarinet-tooting MacMurray's love interest was provided by Harriet Hilliard, who played a school teacher turned torch vocalist. Tossed into the musical was Eve and her "brother" Ben Blue. They join the band on their California trek and at the Cocoanut Grove perform a wild burlesque of the adagio dance and an amusing travesty of contemporary ballroom dancing. Eve had just about one line of dialogue, although she was given a few sight gags more in the tradition of Joan Davis or Judy Canova. The gymnastic dancing was enough to capture reviewers' interest: ". . . a routine which manages to be amusing, even though everyone else in the country has one." (N. Y. Times) "Of the specialties, Blue-Arden open with a reverse apache which is rather lost on the customers, but okay. The hokum ballroomology later is clicko." (Variety) ". . . [she] has looks, style, personality, and a rare talent for clowning." (N. Y. Daily Mirror) Those good reviews and her past track record on stage and in film was enough to convince producers that Eve was one of the few talented character comediennes (i.e. those women too unusual in look, shape or age to be conventional ingenues) who could be counted on to offer the blessed comedy relief and audience pacification during slow stretches in any type of feature. More important Eve's years of revue work had refined her ability to improvise and make the most out of the special requirements of any given type of scene. Thus, the cinema director could rest assured that Eve, handed the sketchiest one-dimensional supporting movie role to portray, would do homework on her own and arrive on the soundstage full of ideas to carry her scenes across to the audience.

Eve was again the comedy relief in *Letter of Introduction* (1938), Universal's attempt at cashing in on the *Stage Door* brand of multiple drama. The film starred Andrea Leeds as a stage hopeful who is given a letter of introduction to a much-married stage-screen star Adolphe Menjou, who is later revealed as her father. He eventually agrees to co-star with her in a Broadway production. However, before the big moment of truth when he intends revealing to the theater audience his blood relationship to protegee Leeds, he collapses from drunkenness. Later in remorse he commits suicide. Ann Sheridan was cast as Menjou's sharp-

With Adolphe Menjou, Charlie McCarthy and Edgar Bergen, and Andrea Leeds in *Letter Of Introduction* (Universal, 1938).

tongued love, George Murphy was a wholesome hoofer interested in Eve, and Rita Johnson played Murphy's comely dance partner. In addition Edgar Bergen (along with his dummies Charlie McCarthy and Mortimer Snerd) lived at the same Broadway boarding house along with Leeds, Arden, and Johnson. Eve was cited for being a "grand character comedienne" in this "much too neat" story.

Back at RKO, Eve was part of the ensemble of *Having Wonderful Time* (1938), a genteel photoplay edition adapted from the Broadway play of life vignettes at a Jewish vacation camp in the Catskill Mountains. Harassed stenographer Ginger Rogers escapes the crowded family apartment and hot Manhattan to the supposed country pleasures and culture of Kamp-Free. There she encounters carefree lawyer Douglas Fairbanks, Jr. who is now waiting on tables for lack of anything better to do. Among the other camp guests are: Lee Bowman, Fairbanks's most persistent competition for socially-conscious Rogers; jealous camp roommate Lucille Ball; Rogers's ex-fiance Jack Carson; nitwit master of ceremonies Red Skelton (in his film debut); and Rogers' city girl friend Peggy Conklin. Eve had a more definite characterization this time around, although, as the prim miss with radical notions on life, she was garbed in matronly outfits and wore unbecoming spectacles. The bland *Having Wonderful Time* was a passable crowd pleaser at Radio City Music Hall, despite the critics harping on the whitewashing of the characters' ethnic backgrounds: "It's too bad they couldn't have come from the Bronx instead of Hollywood," said *New York Times*' Frank Nugent.

Eve was certainly capable of obtaining a stock studio

contract at this time with one of the major lots, but she valued her professional independence too much to be hamstrung at any one company. Actually she fared as well or better than such similar silver screen "types" as Lucille Ball, Ann Miller, or Helen Broderick, all under RKO contracts in the 1930s.

In 1939, Eve performed in five freelance cinema assignments. At Warner Bros., she appeared in Kay Francis's studio swansong, *Women in the Wind* (1939), a programmer less distinguished than Twentieth Century-Fox's similar *Tailspin*. The contrived salute to

With Sally Sage, Rosella Towne, William Gargan, Ida Rhodes, and Maxie Rosenbloom in *Women In The Wind* (WB, 1939).

With Peggy Conklin in *Having Wonderful Time* (RKO, 1938).

Universal sold *Big Town Czar* (1939) to the public on the theory that a feature film written by and headlining columnist Ed Sullivan as the narrator, had to be exciting. It was not particularly. The crime-does-not-pay melodrama focused on gang chieftain Barton Mac-Lane, corrupted by his tenement upbringing, who finds his kid brother (Tom Brown) quitting college to become part of the racketeering deal. Eve provided a light romantic angle as Brown's love interest. It was one of the few occasions in her early screen career where she not only had a man of her own to trade dialogue with on a person-to-person level but also a male who was emotionally interested in her. With her full, over-the-neck hairdo, and softer makeup she passed as an adequately appealing young woman. At appropriate mo-

aviatrix found Francis seeking money to provide medical attention for her invalid brother by entering the big Air Derby. Sheila Bromley was her spiteful rival. Eve's role was coverall pilot Kit Campbell, who takes a bad spill in a plane accident before Francis wins the Derby. It was such a hackneyed film that even Eve's occasional arch remarks could not help much. *Women in the Wind* sneaked into the Palace Theatre on the bottom half of a double bill with *The Oklahoma Kid,* a James Cagney western.

With Barton MacLane in *Big Town Czar* (Universal, 1939).

ments, Eve was forced to mouth assorted platitudes to underline Sullivan's didactic feelings on the virtues of justice. Frank S. Nugent (*New York Times*) approved of Eve's performance: ". . . [she] does her best to give some substance to a basically unsubstantial part." *Big Town Czar* opened at Loew's Criterion Theatre on May 8, 1939. The supporting bill, *The Warning,* a British propaganda release, received more enthusiastic critical attention.

The Forgotten Woman (1939) was a conventional fable of a good girl trying to stay right when sent to prison for four years on the strength of circumstantial evidence which had been distorted by a crusading district attorney. Sigrid Gurie, fresh from major roles in *The Adventures of Marco Polo* and *Algiers* portrayed the wrongfully jailed heroine, who hopes to retrieve custody of her baby, now under the guardianship of the repentent district attorney. It was no better fare than Paramount's similar *Prison Farm,* featuring Shirley Ross. *Variety's* reviewer singled out Eve: ". . . as the girl's pal and comforter, [who] reveals distinct possibilities in light comedienne roles." The *New York Herald Tribune* confirmed: Eve Arden acts as an effective foil for Miss Gurie."

With Ray Walker in *The Forgotten Woman* (Universal, 1939).

In *Eternally Yours* (1939), Eve slipped down to tenth-billing as mere set dressing in this account of respectable Loretta Young marrying charming but irresponsible magician David Niven, but temporarily leaving him when he refuses to settle down and persists in making his world-wide jaunts. In one of the picture's opening scenes, a comely Eve is seen at Young's shower, where the two engage in a discussion of women's rights pre and post marriage. Later Eve turns up in London with her husband (Walter Sande), and visits Young backstage at the theater where the latter and Niven are performing. Breezy Eve tells Young: "You see the world on toes, I answer doorbells."

Eve once again had good luck at RKO. She was felicitously cast in (*The Marx Brothers*) *At The Circus* (1939) directed by Edward Buzzell. She was Peerless Pauline, the human fly in Kenny Baker's struggling circus, and the moll of crafty James Burke, a scoundrel determined to gain possession of the tent show. When Baker's $10,000 cash reserve is stolen, Chico and Harpo Marx call in professional shyster Groucho Marx. The slow-moving, quick-tongued attorney eventually deduces that Eve has control of the missing money. Groucho visits her dressing room where she is then walking upside down on the ceiling. The amazed minion of the law quips: "If this is a spirit reading, I'd like something good in the fourth at Belmont." While Eve is preoccupied with her practice routines, Groucho searches her belongings and locates the cash. She quickly scampers down from the heights and flirts with him on the couch. Nothing will stop her from extricating the cash from Groucho's clutches, not even his sudden flipping open of a cigarette case to offer her peanut brittle. When she has flattened him on the divan, he inquires: "Your father wasn't by any chance an octopus, was he?" Eve regains the money and tucks it in her bra top. Retorts Groucho: "The thing I like about you is that money doesn't go to your head." Which leads to the film's biggest laugh getter. Groucho approaches the camera for an aside, and ponders: "There must be some way of getting that money without getting in trouble with the Hays Office."

Then Groucho lures Pauline back up on the ceiling, hoping the money will fall out during her upside down walk. She consents only if Groucho will join her. He hesitates: "No. I'd rather not. I have an agreement with the houseflies. The flies don't practice law, and I don't walk on the ceiling." But Groucho gives in to the inevitability. He changes into a pair of oversized tights, puts on his suction shoes, and joins Eve for a rendezvous on the ceiling, commenting: "I never thought we'd be hanging around together." After a gymnastic

With Groucho Marx on the set of *At The Circus* (MGM, 1939).

topsy-turvy rumba between the two opponents, the money falls to the ground. However, Eve jumps down, grabs it and makes a hasty exit, leaving Groucho stuck to the ceiling. The movie pulsates through several additional situations, including dowager Margaret Dumont's benefit affair, the attempted arson at the circus, and Harpo's coming to the rescue atop a wild ostrich.

At The Circus was Eve's first effort in the genre of slapdash, madcap comedy. Like Dumont who graced several Marxian melees, Eve was required to be the butt of the brothers' humor, primarily being the foil to Groucho's repartee and retorting largely in physical acts and pantomime gestures rather than with conventional dialogue. She performed her tasks admirably and was outstanding in her essentially vicarious, if athletic, role. Kate Cameron in her three star *New York Daily News* review observed that her fly-walking with Groucho ". . . is one of the most amusing scenes in the comedy." Robert Coleman (*New York Daily Mirror*) noted that Eve was "attractively villainous," one of the few times anyone associated her with attributes of beauty.

Unfortunately, *At The Circus* in general did not meet the critical and financial mark of the Marx Brothers' earlier efforts. It was panned as being a watered down version of their prior *At The Racetrack,* lacking the split timing rhythm and comedy of that masterpiece or of earlier pictures they made.

For any discerning follower of show business, a few double takes were to be gathered when *Variety* re-viewed the latest Nils T. Granlund Revue at the Shubert Theatre in Brooklyn in April, 1939, where a black-haired Eve Arden was performing a "dirty" veil-dance. The tradepaper reported: "Her talent lies strictly in her sparsely-clad chassis." Needless to say, it was not *the* Eve Arden, born Eunice Quedens.

On June 29, 1939, Eve married New York-based insurance agent Edward G. Bergen (descendant of Edward G. Bergen, one of the planners of Brooklyn), who had come to California on a selling trip. He not only sold Adolphe Menjou a $200,000 insurance policy, but asked Eve to marry him. They were wed in Reno, Nevada. It was the first marriage for each.

While veteran stage producer Max Gordon was in Hollywood preparing his RKO screen project *Abe Lincoln in Illinois* (1940), he happened to visit the MGM soundstage where Eve was performing with Groucho Marx in *At the Circus.* Gordon had been shaping a new Broadway musical *Very Warm for May* and decided Eve would be suitable for a lead role. Not overly happy with the shape of her screen career to date, and wanting to be near her husband, she accepted the offer. While in New York she and Bergen had an apartment at 10 Park Avenue.

Very Warm for May by Jerome Kern and Oscar Hammerstein II was directed by Vincente Minnelli. It tried out in Wilmington, Delaware, Washington, D.C., and Boston, before making its Broadway bow at the Alvin Theatre, November 11, 1939. The musical concerned playwright Hiram Sherman, who prods rich socialite Winnie Spofford (Eve), to finance a summer barn theater production of his latest esoteric "play." Eve is soon bitten by the glamorous show business bug and goes along with the enthusiasm of her children (Richard Quine, Frances Mercer) for stage careers. Eve participated in the Act I finale song "In Other Words" and performed one solo number "Seventeen," but it was the tune "All The Things You Are" that emerged as a popular standard. Eve's best acting moments were in the play within the play in which she sits and talks with friends, carrying on an endless vapid conversation.

Despite the Kern-Hammerstein II score and the Albertina Rasch choreographed dances, the critics were severely disappointed with the show. Eve came out on top with the reviewers again: "Eve Arden carries off the chief comedy honors with her portrayal of a silly society leader. A real comedienne is this girl. She looks like Miriam Hopkins and reminds one of Edna May Oliver in her style of work." (*Women's Wear Daily*). "Eve Arden is smartly amusing in the Ilka Chase tradition. . . ." (*New York Daily News*)

Very Warm for May failed to lure audiences. Members of the cast were to appear on NBC commercial television October 11, 1939, but Actors' Equity Association demanded that additional salary be paid the performers, so producer Gordon cancelled the appearance. He did send Eve out in December, 1939 to deliver talks to women's groups to boost sales. In January, 1940, Gordon cut the top prices for tickets from $4.40 to $3.30, but it did not help. The show folded after 59 performances, at a loss of most of its $150,000 investment. (MGM, who had optioned the screen rights to *Very Warm for May,* filmed the project as *Broadway Rhythm* (1944). Among those in the supporting cast of this losing musical were: June Allyson, Don Loper and Max Showalter. Despite this setback the stage was still Eve's first love: ". . . even if Mary Martin does get all Oscar Hammerstein's hits and I get all his flops."

Eve did not have to be convinced very much to remain in New York to star in the musical revue *Two For The Show* (Booth Theatre, February 8, 1940), which was a follow up to the previous year's *One For The Money,* with sketches and lyrics again by Nancy Hamilton. Besides Eve, the cast included Richard Haydn, Betty Hutton, Keenan Wynn, and Alfred Drake, and the production was staged by Joshua Logan. Eve's primary contributions consisted of amusing imitations of assorted entertainment world celebrities, including Marlene Dietrich, whom she rather savagely satirized in *Destry Has Ridden Again.* Also outstanding was another skit, *To A Skylark,* purporting to reveal the electric nature of Gertrude Lawrence as she attempts to rest backstage between acts of her latest Broadway show, *Skylark.* Eve was lauded as one ". . . who is always vivid, throws herself into the broad comedy with lovely abandon." (*New York World Telegram*) ". . . (The) handsome Miss Arden, who is an excellent comedienne when given half a chance." (*New York Herald Tribune*). "Say a little something for Eve Arden, the rangy blonde. . . . Mr. Wynn and she offer an amusing sketch ("Painless Distraction") in a dentist's operating room, somehow interpolating a movie plot into the gruesome business of repairing teeth." (*New York Times*).

Two For The Show lasted a modestly successful 124 performances, but Eve withdrew from production in mid-May 1940 due to ill health and was replaced by Grace Coppin. The strain of doing the imitations took its toll on her voice. She returned to Hollywood and to movie making.

Meanwhile, the backlog of features in which Eve had performed before her Broadway sojourn were released in quick succession in 1940. Warner's *A Child Is Born* appeared in January, 1940 at Loew's Criterion Theatre. Eve was eleventh-billed as Miss Pinty, the role handled

by Mary Phillips in *Life Begins* (1932), the studio's earlier treatment of the controversial 1920's stage success. Its subject matter (various women's reactions to pregnancy and child birth) and presentation (breezy unraveling of assorted interrelated vignettes) were typical of standard Warner Bros. fare: slickly handled domestic melodrama with a slight tinge of social conscience. The simple sets of a hospital ward and the Warner Bros.' stock company of actors and actresses blended together to effectively create a pseudo-realistic cut of lower-class American life. The performers under Lloyd Bacon's efficient direction were not required to express penetrating characterizations, but rather offer expansions of their catalogued screen personalities. Wistful Geraldine Fitzgerald was the unwilling murderess transferred from prison to the city hospital to have her child with her earnest husband, Jeffrey Lynn, constantly at her side. Other types in the ward were tough vaudevillian Gladys George, thrilled with her new twin babies, Gloria Holden, distraught by having given birth to her third still-born child, homey Spring Byington, returning for the yearly ritual of yet another baby (her seventh) and Nanette Fabray, given no peace by her in-laws. The hospital staff (more efficient but less sympathetic than MGM's Blair General Hospital in the *Dr. Kildare* series) consisted of nurses Gale Page and Eve, matron Esther Dale, and doctors Henry O'Neill and John Litel. Eve's subordinate role as the brassy nurse was an undemanding small part that a few years back would have been given to Warner contractee Jane Wyman. However the studio was grooming Wyman, ever so slowly, for bigger assignments and Eve got the part. More than one reviewer questioned the necessity of having remade this once daring drama.

Slightly Honorable (1940) was a crime clean-up actioner featuring snappy Pat O'Brien as a middle-aged lawyer who, with his younger partner (Broderick Crawford), sets out to break the racket syndicate headed by graft tycoon Edward Arnold. Nightclub singer Ruth Terry falls for O'Brien, which allows for romantic and musical interludes. Tough, but nice broad Claire Dodd (another forerunner variation of Eve's screen mold) is knifed as a reward for being Arnold's moll, Eve is Miss Atar, secretary to O'Brien, whose cool and cynical attitudes to the action provide minor chuckles. *Slightly Honorable* offered a new screen first for Eve: she is murdered! She is found slumped over her desk, stabbed in the back with the same knife that killed Dodd. The *New York Times* complained ". . . though the plot congeals, it never thickens, . . ." The *New York Daily News'* 2½ star review had kind words for Eve: "Claire Dodd and Eve Arden stand out from among the rest of the cast for their very capable performances, Miss Dodd

With Pat O'Brien and Broderick Crawford in *Slightly Honorable* (UA, 1940).

in a dramatic part and Eve Arden in a delightful comedy role."

At plush MGM in *Comrade X* (1940), Eve emoted in her first grade A feature since *Stage Door*. The studio made no bones about trying to duplicate the success of its previous *Ninotchka*. But neither director King Vidor, nor screen writers Ben Hecht-Charles Lederer, nor leads Clark Gable and Hedy Lamarr were up to the light comedy proficiency of that previous model film starring Greta Garbo and Melvyn Douglas. Foreign correspondent Gable is sneaking politically embarrassing stories about Russia out of the country. Hotel porter Felix Bressart discovers his ruse and demands Gable smuggle his trolley conductor daughter (Lamarr) out of Russia. She is a loyal communist which makes Gable's task all the more difficult. Eve appeared as American journalist Jane Wilson, displaying an abundance of aggressiveness in her job, and furious like the other

With Sig Rumann, Leon Belasco, and Clark Gable in *Comrade X* (MGM, 1940).

newsmen that Comrade X (Gable) is miraculously able to get the uncensored true news out of Moscow. She was complimented for her "neat bit of wisecracking." Her brief moments throughout the earlier portions of the film allowed for little character development. One wonders if the scripters thought at all about what Eve's character might do for entertainment in her spare time. *Comrade X* was a popular success, aided a great deal by public enthusiasm for Lamarr, especially in her extensive sequences garbed in a mock Soviet style nightgown.

Back at RKO, Eve had a supporting role in the remake of *No, No, Nanette* (1940) in which she played Winnie, one of the sirens with whom gay blade, oldster Roland Young is philandering on the side without the knowledge of his blustery wife, Helen Broderick. It is Miss Fix-it, Anna Neagle, who saves uncle Young's marriage by arranging that Eve, Tamara, and Dorothea Kent get the material needs they want from Young. While theatrical producer Victor Mature takes a shine to Neagle, she prefers artist Richard Carlson. Despite its Radio City Music Hall sendoff (December 19, 1940) *No, No, Nanette* was not a winner. Having updated the story line to 1940 style, old guard British producer-director Herbert Wilcox permitted the film to lumber ponderously and cast too much of the spotlight on his actress wife Neagle. The hit songs of the stage show, "Tea For Two" and "I Want To Be Happy" were submerged as totally incidental within this revamped version. *Variety* analyzed: "Miss Neagle" and the youngsters, Richard Carlson, Victor Mature and Eve Arden show to no advantage against such a trio of comedy vets (Young, Broderick, and the acid-tongue maid portrayal by Zasu Pitts).

With Richard Carlson in *No, No Nanette* (RKO, 1940).

Eve's most productive year on the screen was 1941 with nine releases. It would be the last span of any major experimentation with Eve's screen image before it settled into its final lucrative rut.

She hopped over to Culver City for a feature role in MGM's lush *Ziegfeld Girl* (1941) the middle item in that studio's trilogy tribute to America's greatest glorifier of girls, Florenz Ziegfeld. The gentle backstage story focused on the problems, fame, and reevaluations of three divergent gals (Judy Garland, Hedy Lamarr, Lana Turner) who become part of the famed revue show produced at the New Amsterdam Theatre for Broadway consumption. The storyline was glib and the ambience was far removed from the glamour and excitement of the more real *Ziegfeld Follies;* however, customers got their money worth as hick vaudevillian Garland made the big time, Lamarr realized the worth of her violinist husband (Philip Dorn) and Turner discovered that millionaire Ian Hunter was not half the man truck driver James Stewart was. When the screen was not ablaze with production numbers or morality lessons, the camera would focus on brief vignettes of behind-the-scenes situation. Eve was utilized as the experienced showgirl who knew all the ropes—from the inside outward—and had lots of advice for the fledgling showgirls. Sitting astride a dressing room table, she expounded upon the rights and wrongs of classy trouper life, if one wanted to stay successful and on top. It was a well punched out bit, demonstrating that Eve might have done well as a MGM contractee, for that studio was adept at handling specialty players.

In Ernst Lubitsch's *That Uncertain Feeling* (1941) a remake of his silent *Kiss Me again,* prosperous insurance man Melvyn Douglas believes himself settled into a pleasant home life routine after six years of marriage to aristocratic Merle Oberon. Of course this is not so. Melodramatic psychiatrist Alan Mowbray insists her bouts of hiccups are due to marital dissatisfaction, which soon leads the couple to the divorce courts and a later happy finale. Eve was Sally, the proficient secretary to Harry Davenport, Douglas' divorce attorney. When Douglas moves out of his home, he requests Eve to accompany him on public dates to make his wife jealous. Good old Eve is satisfied to take vicarious second best, if it will get her out of her office routine for even a short time. Her role was the same part Clara Bow had performed in the 1925 feature.

Warner Bros. next cast Eve as the lead (her first and last such top-billed spot for fifteen years) in the minor comedy *She Couldn't Say No* (1941). Although she is an attorney (she wears spectacles to prove she is scholarly), Eve nobly works as secretary to her unsuccessful lawyer fiancé Roger Pryor. She submerges her knowl-

With Harry Davenport and Melvyn Douglas in *That Uncertain Feeling* (UA, 1941).

edge for the sake of his love and a far-off marriage date. While he is away from the office one day, Clem Bevans arrives and demands the attorney in charge to handle his pending land title case. Eve just cannot say no, which results in her and Pryor being on opposite sides in a combined real estate action and breach of promise suit. The finale, of course, has Eve and Pryor marriage-bound. It was a programmer that did not require Eve's presence; it might just as well have gone to Joan Leslie, Warner studio starlet.

Wanda Hale in her 2½ star *New York Daily News* write up of *She Couldn't Say No* stated: "She is natural, poised and delivers her lines excellently. And though she deserves better things, it is a pleasure to see a good actress in a B picture." On the other hand, the *New York Herald Tribune* summarily dismissed the film and Eve: ". . . (Her) presence is required only to add some

With Roger Pryor in *She Couldn't Say No* (WB, 1941).

romantic interludes, . . ." *She Couldn't Say No* opened at the Palace Theatre January 16, 1941, rightly relegated to the bottom half of the bill with the second run showing of *Chad Hanna*. With typical inanity, Warner's publicity-advertising departments promoted the picture as a risqué sex comedy, using such "catch" lines as: "She doesn't say YES. She didn't say WHOA! She wouldn't say MAYBE and *She Couldn't Say No.*" On several occasions Eve has stressed that she was so embarrassed by the coy Warner's trailer for *She Couldn't Say No,* which played her up as a flirtatious man-handler, that she never went to see the finished picture. (On another occasion, she told the press, "When I was on the screen in my first part (referring to her "official" film debut in *Oh, Doctor*), someone in the audience shouted, 'Woo, woo. She's terrific.' I ran out of the

With Joan Bennett in *She Knew All The Answers* (Columbia, 1941).

theater and never saw the rest of the picture.") Her disapproval of herself on the screen in any of her finalized performances reveals the dichotomy of this ambitious performer. Eve was practical enouge to realize that she was not the conventional merchandise for Hollywood stardom, but also that she was too much of a competitive and feminine woman to truly accept what had become her professional stock-in-trade roles.

The title of Columbia's ambling *She Knew All the Answers* (1941) refers to Joan Bennett, a go-getting nightclub chorine who has designs on conservative Wall Street businessman Franchot Tone. Eve found some potential in her role as Sally Long, the fan-dancer roommate of Bennett. When not preoccupied in manipulating her own social schedule with four beaux, Eve is on hand to assist Bennett pursue Tone. Whether listening with visible belief to Bennett's tall tale of how she has obtained a new fur coat, or when pretending to be her roommate's crippled sister, Eve milks her part for all its inherent worth. She coats her performance with her by-now standard veiled sarcasm that expertly pushes her delivery across to audiences. True to the demands of formula movie-making, Eve as a supporting player, is left on the sidelines at Bennett's fade-out wedding to Tone. It was not only the *Brooklyn Eagle* reporter who thought: ". . . Miss Arden is smart. She steals the (Radio City) Music Hall's picture." Bennett and Eve, joined by Preston Foster, were heard on the *Lux Radio Theatre* (CBS) version of *She Knew All the Answers* on January 11, 1943.

San Antonio Rose (1941) was just another of Universal's myriad of mindless but pleasant wartime musicals—lowbudgeted, unpretentious, and lowbrow fun. Eve and Jane Frazee (in the third of her fifteen Universal stints) were a singing sister team who find themselves stranded at the deserted Plantation Club and join

up with Robert Paige and his band to turn the empty nightspot into a paying proposition despite interference by gangsters. Of the nine songs, the perennial "Hut Nut Song" sung by Frazee was the obvious hit of the production.

In Columbia's quickie *Sing for Your Supper* (1941) Eve was a dance hostess employed in Jinx Falkenberg's dime-a-dance joint. Charles 'Buddy' Rogers was the club's bandleader, with mad Bert Gordon as a band member and Don Beddoe as manager of the hostesses. All the critics wondered why Eve, "mistress of the tart retort," had so little to do, as this humdrum romantic comedy obviously needed every little bit of bolstering it could find.

Warner Bros.'s *Manpower* (1941) was an important turning point in Eve's cinema career. Not that her brief assignment was out of the usual, she was a tough dance hall hostess—but for one of the first times her screen role seemed especially written for her, rather than another nonedescript assignment which she had to amplify and mold to her particular talents. This time

With Shemp Howard, Jane Frazee, and Robert Paige in
San Antonio Rose (Universal, 1941).

With Jinx Falkenberg and Benny Baker in *Sing For Your Supper* (Columbia, 1941).

around she was a brassy blonde (in *Ziegfeld Follies of 1934* she was platinum blonde, in *Parade* a brunette, in *Ziegfeld Follies of 1936* a redhead, in *Stage Door,* a fluffy golden blonde, and in *Letter of Introduction* a brownette). This Raoul Walsh-directed actioner starred Edward G. Robinson and George Raft as power lines-men pals who each desire clip joint hostess Marlene Dietrich. Eve's projection of the brittle observer was here encased in the guise of a hardened gal who could match and outdo the witticisms of such fellow club dames as Joyce Compton and Lynn Baggott. Eve was selfconfident as always, but in addition she exuded an unusual character facet: satisfaction that her looks were sufficiently appetizing to keep her in mild clover. For this reason she would brook no nonsense from her club associates. She snaps at interfering Compton: "Stay in your own backyard, Scarlett. I can handle laughing

With Lucia Carroll, director Raoul Walsh, Marlene Dietrich, Lynn Baggott and Joyce Compton in *Manpower* (WB, 1941).

boy." Nightspot owner Bartan MacLane warns employee Eve: "You leak a lotta words, Dolly (Eve). Someday, you're gonna talk yourself into something sinister." Nothing phases cool Eve. She reminds her boss: "Smiley, there's one grand consolation about workin' in this establishment—you can't get any lower."

In her few *Manpower* scenes Eve has several interchanges with former club thrush, Dietrich. These scenes helped solidify Eve's stereotyped screen image as the man-hungry woman who is overly cynical about finding love and marriage. Dietrich tells Eve of Robinson's marriage proposal:

Eve: "No kiddin', Fay—if that guy really wants to marry you, what're you waitin' for?"

Dietrich: "I don't love him."

Eve: "Jeepers! That line ain't been used for years. Wake up, honey—do you know what year this is? Do you want *everything?*"

Dietrich: "I don't like to give a good guy a bad shake."

Eve: "Listen, if any fella ever proposed to me, I'd only ask myself two things—(a) does he wear pants, and (b) does he have a job. Look around you, honey—this joint's a dead-end street. I'm twenty-five, look thirty-five and feel like fifty. Grab him, Fay, before he changes his mind."

In this role Eve is practical enough to realize that fading youth spells the end of the line, not that she allows herself to think beyond to the future, which is a most uncharacteristic trait for the typical Eve screen role in which she is the perfection of business efficiency and would have no difficulty reentering the business world at any stage of life. She tells Dietrich: "Look, honey, how many more years of *that* [hustling drinks at the club] do you think you got? The first two wrinkles you show, you're washed up. Then you're really on the short end."

In a complete change of pace, Eve returned to comedy playing the ultra-efficient business manager of Red Skelton in MGM's *Whistling in The Dark* (1941). Skelton was cast as the radio detective "The Fox," whom racketeer Conrad Veidt kidnaps, intending to make the airwaves sleuth devise a scheme for the perfect murder. With gag-buster Skelton hogging every camera scene with double takes, crosseyes, and other looney mannerisms, there was little room for swank, sophisticated Eve to enlarge upon her commonplace role.

In *Last of the Duanes* (1941) Eve had a "fat role as a saloon hostess" of the 1880s in the Pecos district of Texas. She took third billing to George Montgomery as a Texas Ranger who is determined to find the culprit who murdered his father, and Lynn Roberts as the

With George Montgomery in *The Last of the Duanes* (20th Century-Fox, 1941).

ingenue kidnapped by the cutthroats and finally rescued by Montgomery. In her first western, Eve is the unfortunate recipient of a bullet during a gun battle. *Variety* thought Eve "convincing."

Her final 1941 release was the minor RKO comedy *Obliging Young Lady,* a vehicle for eight-year-old Joan Carroll, who had recently made such a hit in the Broadway edition of *Panama Hattie.* Rambunctious Carroll is sent out of town while her wealthy parents dally with a divorce suit in court. Ruth Warrick is the family secretary accompanying Carroll, and she finds herself courted by reporter Edmond O'Brien. Eve turned up as one of the industrious reporters, trying to get a scoop on the family "scandal." Said Robert W. Dana (*New York Herald Tribune*): "The ever-reliable Eve Arden, as a rival reporter, adds a sophisticated note to

With Pierre Watkin in *Obliging Young Lady* (RKO, 1941).

what is on the whole a gentle comedy bordering on farce." Eve herself had one boisterous scene in which she impersonates a Memphis belle to try and wangle some information on the potential big story.

Meanwhile, Eve had accepted an offer to return to Broadway in a featured role in the musical comedy, *Let's Face It,* with book by Herbert and Dorothy Fields and songs by Cole Porter. Charles Walter, who had worked with Eve in *Lo and Behold,* was the choreographer. Danny Kaye, having triumphed in Broadway's *Lady in the Dark,* starred as a simplistic serviceman who never seems able to manage the money or time to marry health farm supervisor Mary Jane Walsh. When Eve (second-billed), Edith Meiser and Vivian Vance, as three bored middle aged wives, hire Kaye and two of his army buddies to be their dates for the weekend to stir up some jealousy in their philandering husbands, fireworks break loose.

During the Boston tryout (Colonial Theatre, October 9, 1941) Eve ventured into the field of guest columnist, writing a humorous piece for the *Boston Post,* with illustrations supplied by Al Hirschfeld.

Let's Face It! premiered at the Imperial Theatre, October 29, 1941, to resounding popular acclaim. Kaye's wife Sylvia Fine wrote two fast-talking patter numbers for Kaye to sing, "Melody In Four F" and "Fairy Tale," which were the novelty hits of the show. Eve had her share of song spots: with Meiser and Vance, she harmonized "A Lady Needs A Rest," with the group she crooned "Baby Games," and with Kaye she had "Let's Not Talk About Love" (the lyrics were a catalogue of jokes aimed at big shots). Others in the cast included Nanette Fabray, Billy Daniel and Jane Ball, with newcomer Carol Channing as Eve's understudy.

As the past-thirty wife (character leads always could play a range of age types and still be believable), Eve reaped impressive notices. "Miss Arden, who can be briskly and genuinely comic without even losing her cool beauty and engaging charm, is a player of great style and quality and she is a complete delight in a not-altogether appetizing role." (Richard Watts, Jr. *New York Herald Tribune*). "Miss Arden is more than a match for him [Kaye]. . . . [she] is a match for almost anybody. (Richard Lockridge, *New York Sun*). "She gives the role beauty, charm and humor." (*Women's Wear Daily*). So impressed were the critics by Eve, that in *Variety*'s annual New York Drama Critics' Poll, she was voted the best female lead in a musical of that season. Being one of the trio of erring wives, Eve had her expected barbed lines to archly deliver as only she seemed capable of doing. At one point, she berates her stage husband: "Of all the people in the world to lead

With Danny Kaye in *Let's Face It* (1941).

a double life—why, you haven't even got enough strength to lead a single life."

With her growing professional popularity, Eve began being interviewed more often. Yet she still played down her mounting success, relying on a backhanded asperity to counteract any tinges of self-praise. "Just imagine I, who am filled with human kindness, making a neat profit out of vitriol." When newsmen asked her what she thought about during a performance, she admitted that more often than not while she was battering out devastating invective, she was busy acting as company spotter, picking out friends of theirs seated in the audience.

After a summer layoff in 1942, *Let's Face It!* resumed performances on August 17, 1942 and played through for a total of 547 showings, besting Cole Porter's previous musical *Panama Hattie* (starring Ethel Merman) which had had a 501 performance run.

During 1942, Eve and her husband had built a home in the Outpost Drive section of Hollywood, high up on a mountain. Bergen, who had given up his insurance business to become a Hollywood-based literary agent, enlisted in the army that year and was away in the service for the duration of World War II. With much time on her hands, Eve indulged her favorite hobbies: antique collecting and interior decorating, as well as painting and sculpting. She was among the many cinema celebrities to donate their time to working at the assorted Los Angeles servicemen canteens.

Columbia's *Bedtime Story* (1942), which she had made before going into *Let's Face It!,* opened at Radio

Eve Arden in 1943.

With Helen Westley, Joyce Compton, and Fredric March in *Bedtime Story* (Columbia, 1942).

City Music Hall on March 19, 1942. It was yet another farce comedy concerning a professional wife (actress Loretta Young) who wants to retire from the stage and vegetate on a Connecticut farm. However, her producer husband Frederic March has other ideas. When Young divorces March, hard-boiled musical comedy star Eve is hired to replace Young in the stage play and to carry out a ruse as March's paramour to arouse Young's smoldering jealousy.

Still on freelance, Eve had a subordinate role in Republic's *Hit Parade of 1943,* pure escapist fare with the most negligible story content. Country-bred Susan Hayward has songwriting ambitions, and is disgruntled when song publisher John Carroll steals her compositions. Later he steals her heart, much to Gail Patrick's chagrin. Eve is Hayward's big city cousin, full of wise sayings and jaded views, who "strolls about with

With Susan Hayward in *Hit Parade Of 1943* (Republic, 1943).

a sour puss and an ever ready wise crack." Seven new songs were injected into this major league attempt by Republic. To bolster the movie's marquee draw there were guest appearances by the bands of Count Basie, Freddy Martin, and Ray McKinley.

When Paramount filmed *Let's Face It* (1943), Eve was the only major performer from the stage show recruited for the movie version. It is most likely if she had not already been in Hollywood, another actress would have been assigned "her" role. Since the studio's contract gagster Bob Hope was no Danny Kaye, all of Cole Porter's score was dropped except "Let's Not Talk About Love," which became a solo spot for Eve. Effervescent Betty Hutton inherited the role of Winnie Potter, the health farm supervisor who is foolish and patriotic enough to wish to wed bumbling soldier Hope, even after he and two of his servicemen buddies become involved in the shenanigans of a weekend date with three frustrated matronly wives (Eve, Zasu Pitts, and Phyllis Povah). Sammy Cahn and Jules Styne composed two new ditties to fit the personality of Hutton and the movie's non-musical, comedy-oriented cast. No one seemed to take any note that Eve, then thirty-one years old, was made to be a contemporary of the older Pitts and Povah, and was given fifty-six-year-old Raymond Walburn as her cinema husband. *Let's Face It* proved to be one of Hope's less felicitous screen vehicles of the war years, even though he still could do no wrong at the nation's boxoffice.

Columbia's *Cover Girl* (1944) was Eve's first Technicolor movie. It starred pinup queen Rita Hayworth as a Brooklyn honky-tonk chorine who wins the cover contest of a national magazine and almost passes up her boss (Gene Kelly) to wed conniving Broadway producer Lee Bowman. Interspersed in the plot are several dull flashback scenes in which Rita, as her grandmother, almost makes the same errors her granddaughter would stumble into years later. Eve had a few good asides as the chic magazine editor, Cornelia "Stonewall" Jackson, ordered by publisher Otto Kruger to discover a new cover girl (which allowed for the well-publicized appearance of fifteen top American cover girls in bit roles in *Cover Girl*). The Columbia musical, which played Radio City Music Hall, proved to be one of Hayworth's biggest screen hits. The production abounded in elaborate dance numbers with Hayworth floating down assorted ramp runways, and Kelly's energetic hoofing was outshined only by his own toothy smile and the reflection of comedy sidekick Phil Silvers' oversized spectacles. There was a fine Ira Gershwin and Jerome Kern score (including "Long Ago And Far Away") to backstop the musical interludes. *Cover Girl* pulled in five Academy Award nominations with Morris Stoloff

With Cully Richards, Bob Hope, Dave Willock, Phyllis
Povah, and ZaSu Pitts in *Let's Face It* (Paramount, 1943).

With Rita Hayworth in *Cover Girl* (Columbia, 1944).

and Carmen Dragon winning Oscars for their scoring.

The Doughgirls (1944) proved to be the film that set the pattern for the bulk of Eve's remaining screen career. She had now reached the juncture in moviedom where film producers in casting a film would say "Get me Eve Arden. She can fill in the comedy relief." After *The Doughgirls,* Eve would reach the plateau in which producers would demand "Get me an Eve Arden type." (To date, Eve has never passed beyond stage three of the five phases of an actor's career: i.e. Who is Eve Arden, Get Me Eve Arden, Get Me An Eve Arden type, Get Me Eve Arden, Who is Eve Arden.)

The Joseph Fields play had been a terrific success on Broadway and had cost Warner Bros. $250,000 to acquire. Eve very much wanted to play Natalia Moskoroff, the celebrated Russian sniper visiting wartime Washington, D.C., the role handled by Arlene Francis on stage. Although Warner's contract player Faye Emerson had been scheduled for the comedy assignment, Eve made a pitch to producer Mark Hellinger and he and the studio agreed to cast her as Natalia *if* she would sign a seven year, three pictures per year contract with Warners. The agreement provided she could accept outside assignment. Eve reluctantly accepted the pact, but she admitted: "Whenever I get a yoke around my neck, I immediately start gnawing at it."

Even though *The Doughgirls* was purified for cinematic consumption, director James V. Kern imparted a solid breeziness to the production, in spite of the fact that the majority of the cast was less than pleased to be included in the photoplay. (Warner Bros. oomph girl Ann Sheridan had been begging studio mogul Harry Warner to allow her to go overseas on a USO tour. He suggested that if she made *The Doughgirls,* just maybe he would agree to her altruistic desire.)

Warners cast three of its top glamour girls in the leads of *The Doughgirls,* Sheridan, Alexis Smith and Jane Wyman. Newlyweds Wyman and Jack Carson arrive in bustling Washington, D.C. and manage to gain possession of their reserved honeymoon suite at the overcrowded hotel. But before they can enjoy the bliss of solitude, Wyman's former chorine buddies—Sheridan, who had been married to John Ridgely, and Smith, anxiously waiting for her intended spouse Craig Stevens to recover from measles—arrive on the scene and beg Wyman to allow them to share the suite. Scatterbrained Wyman readily agrees, believing falsely that it is only a temporary matter. Then Wyman and Carson learn that their recent marriage was not legal, and Carson refuses to go through the ceremony again until the unwanted guests depart. To add complications to the scene, Ridgely arrives with Russian sergeant Eve, who finds the apartment so congenial she refuses to return to the Russian embassy. Soon Wyman is forced to hock her jewels to pay the hotel bill, only to find that once this problem is solved, another guest has been added to the roster, bombastic radio commentator Alan Mowbray who has acquired legitimate rights to the suite, but permits the crowd to remain there. The finale finds resourceful Eve producing a Russian priest who performs a mass marriage for the three couples. Others dropped into the melee are Charles Ruggles, Carson's boss who takes a shine to dumb dora Wyman, and Irene Manning, the supposedly second wife of Ridgely.

The hit player of this uninspired potpourri of entrances and exits by an assortment of types confined to one setting was Eve. As the Russian guerilla soldier (her mother was also a soldier on the Russian Steppes), Eve has killed 397 Nazis. As a reward for her thoroughness as a sharpshooter she has been sent to America on a

With Alexis Smith, Ann Sheridan, Jane Wyman, and Francis Pierlot in *The Doughgirls* (WB, 1944).

goodwill mission. Replete with stark Russian soldiering uniform and a rifle on her shoulder, Eve sported a black, straight, close-cropped hairdo and projected a thick Russian accent similar to her stage dialect in *Parade.* In the film she was the one who took a short hike from Washington, D.C. to Baltimore and enjoyed a respite by viewing a double double feature, including "Mrs. Minovitch" starring Greer Garson. For further sport, this crack shot would like to shoot the pigeons gathered on the balcony of the hotel room, and has serious thoughts of practicing her sharp shooting from the gallery of the Senate house. When not otherwise engaged, she is busy organizing a communistic union of the hotel's maids and bellhops.

As the only unwanted guest in the hotel suite who has practical sense, Eve sometimes takes control of situations without first consulting the girls. She is the one who pawns Wyman's jewelry clips at the local pawnshop, which causes problems when Wyman must produce the clips for the donor's inspection. Much difficulty ensues in trying to explain to Eve that somehow (it is Sunday) she must retrieve the clips and substitute Wyman's diamond ring instead. What follows is the marvelously staged "impromptu" sequence in which Eve, finally comprehending the task at hand, sets off to hock the ring. To the tune of "The Volga Boatman" she proceeds down the hotel corridor chanting "Put the ring in, take the clips out. Put the ring in, take the clips out." As she stomps along, the song builds in its ridiculousness to its comic fadeout.

Eve had her quota of Russian-oriented quips. At one point, she taps a piano keyboard, and when it reverberates she comments: "Umm, two octaves, I'd better reduce." The role was not without its hazards, and Eve had a sore shoulder from toting the rifle around the set during the eight weeks of active production.

The Doughgirls was ranked above average in its commercial release, although straight-laced critics much preferred *The More The Merrier,* which also dealt with overcrowded living conditions in Washington, D.C. Eve received some of the most contrasting reviews of her career. ". . . armed with a bad Gregory Ratoff accent and even shoddier mannerisms, [she] seems to be doing her utmost to shove U.S. movie treatment of the Soviets back to the *Comrade X* level." (*PM*). Eve was described as "the vodka Dick-Tracy-in-drag" (*Variety*) who "bounds and struts about as a gale off the Caucasus" (*New York Times*). Most enthusiastic about Eve's performance was Howard Barnes (*New York Herald Tribune*): "Fortunately Eve Arden does a first-rate piece of acting. . . . She is altogether the best player in the lot, giving the photoplay a breezy continuity which is rarely contributed by the adaptation or the staging."

Although disliking the confining aspects of a studio term contract, Eve derived benefits from her Warners' contract that she could not obtain as a freelance player. Under a guaranteed salary from the studio, she had more latitude in foregoing bread-and-butter roles that she disliked but might have to accept otherwise from sheer financial necessity. Not that Warners always did right by her, for they were just as capable of wrongly utilizing her for a quick buck as any other studio. But this Burbank-based studio was the best spot for someone of Eve's calibre. Fiercely oriented towards dynamic women stars, Warners was noted for its strong dramatic features, presenting its female leads in showy theatrics. And nearly all these productions required the tempering quality of a strong second female lead, who could act as go-between for the distaff and male star, and perform the chores of a Greek chorus, reflecting upon and amplifying the characteristics and attitudes of the star players. This best friend role was automatically thrust at Eve at Warners and she milked the potentially stereotyped assignments for all they were worth.

It is a matter of conjecture whether Eve could have risen to star billing playing the assortment of ascorbic parts tossed at wisecracking Ann Sothern at MGM or Louise Allbritton and later to June Havoc and Celeste Holm at Twentieth Century-Fox. Such women players as these were more conventionally pretty than Eve and automatically rated the chance to strive for heroine-calibre roles. At least up to this time Eve had survived at the top of the heap in her genre. The careers of Helen Broderick, Glenda Farrell and others of a similar ilk had waned badly, and such similar specialty players as

Joan Davis (who could do as much with a pratfall and base voice retort as anyone then alive) had drifted into better success in radio.

Eve had four releases in 1945. She was fourth-billed in RKO's *Pan-Americana,* a seven-number musical, long on song and dance and short on enthusiastic entertainment. This routine salute to Latin American neighbors found the staff members of a Manhattan picture magazine embarking on a South American tour to select the prettiest girl from each nation for an elaborate musical revue to be staged in Washington, D.C. The contingent consisted of managing editor Eve (known as Hoppy), foreign editor Robert Benchley (also the narrator), feature writer Audrey Long and cameraman Phillip Terry. Terry and Long are supposed to eventually marry, but cynical and unattached Eve continually questions his matrimonial sincerity. The *New York Times* panned the film: "Eve Arden and Robert Benchley wander around trying to be funny, or at least slightly amusing, but they appear to be just plain bewildered most of the time."

Patrick the Great (1945)* at Universal was not much

With Audrey Long in *Pan-Americana* (RKO, 1944).

---

* A remake of *It's A Date* (1940), and the source for MGM's later edition, entitled *Nancy Goes To Rio* (1950).

With Tom Dugan, Alan Mowbray, and Constance Moore
in *Earl Carroll Vanities* (Republic, 1945).

better. It was the eleventh picture to co-star Donald O'Connor and Gloria Jean, and the first one in which she lands him. He is the eighteen-year-old son of waning Broadway musical comedy star Donald Cook, and wants a show business career himself, as does Jean, the dreamy-eyed Miss Fix-It. The subplot has Cook and his newfound love Frances Dee deciding to marry, leaving O'Connor free to accept the lead in a big important musical. The focus was entirely on the jivin' juveniles, and Eve only appeared occasionally to throw out a few one-liners.

Republic's *Earl Carroll's Vanities* (1945) was a mild clinker. Princess Constance Moore has arrived in New York to initiate a loan for her country. While in Manhattan she takes to visiting a Broadway nightclub, owned by Eve. When Dennis O'Keefe writes a new musical for producer Earl Carroll (Otto Kruger), the latter looks for talent at Eve's club. Stephanie Bachelor is the initial choice for the star part, but she sprains an

ankle, and Eve suggests Moore for the replacement. The musical film package is wrapped up with Moore playing in the show which is a success (of course), her country obtaining the needing financing (of course), and she and O'Keefe marrying (naturally). Eve's bright spot occurs when she and her club's vaudevillian master of ceremonies Pinky Lee perform the low brow comedy routine "The Last Man In Town."

Eve's final 1945 release *Mildred Pierce* offered her the best movie showcase in some time and she gave her definitive performance as the cinematic queen of the caustic remarks. Over the years, Eve has stated in interviews that at Warner Brothers, she played it very cool regarding studio politics, offering a friendly outgoing attitude to all celebrities involved. She knew her reputation as a masterly scene-stealer and audience-pleaser made any leading actress leery of allowing her in her films, and it would not take much cause to have her casting in a production vetoed by the star. Although

In *Mildred Pierce* (WB, 1945).

she was a natural choice for the role of Ida in *Mildred Pierce,* it was Eve's compatibility with star Joan Crawford that won her the assignment. Crawford was then staging a virtual comeback in a new type of screen image for her. Both Bette Davis and Ann Sheridan rejected the non-glamorous assignment, and Crawford convinced producer Jerry Wald to give her the title role in *Mildred Pierce* over Barbara Stanwyck. Since ace studio director Michael Curtiz was not especially happy about having stylized Crawford portray the sympathetic lead part, it was a ticklish situation for Crawford, and she needed to have a friendly, understanding cast working with her.

Mildred Pierce chronicles the rise of middle-class housewife Crawford from a divorcée (her ex-husband is sulky Bruce Bennett) who supports her two children (Ann Blyth and Jo Ann Marlowe) by first baking pies at home, then becoming a waitress (much to the shock of Blyth), and finally owning a chain of five restaurants. Along the way, she is crudely courted by Bennett's blustering ex-partner Jack Carson, but instead she succumbs to the blandishments of socially prominent loafer Zachary Scott and marries him, unwilling to comprehend that her reckless Blyth has been having an affair with Scott. Crawford finally sheds her self-sacrificing mother role when Blyth becomes involved in murder and the police, realizing she can no longer shield the grown-up child she has mercilessly spoiled. The pervading ambience of the seacoast area of southern California added reality to the tear-jerking tale of a woman who realized almost too late that in the final analysis she as a wife and mother can be responsible only to herself for her behavior.

Mildred Pierce proved extremely viable boxoffice material, promoted by the studio with the catchy slogan: "Please don't tell what *Mildred Pierce* did." Each of Eve's several scenes in the picture provided abundant evidence of the frozen screen image Eve had acquired along the way to her brand of movie success. For a change, her part was sufficiently well-written to offer a full depth analysis of the various characteristics which constituted her film personality. Contrary to what later Freudian screen historians-critics have suggested, there is no trace in the film of Eve having a latent lesbian relationship with her co-star Crawford, nor can this far-out possibility be substantiated in any of her performances to date without some outrageous theorizing.

Eve first appears in *Mildred Pierce* several minutes into the story, when Crawford wanders into Eve's tea-shop restaurant for a cup of tea and seizes the opportunity to ask Eve for a waitress job. With her adept ability at projecting the ultraefficient business woman,

Eve spouts a rushing stream of mundane dialogue and makes it very convincing:

Eve: "Study the prices. We furnish the uniform but it comes off your first check. Three-ninety-five. You get it at cost; keep it laundered. If you don't suit us, we charge you twenty-five cents on the uniform—that comes out of your check too. You keep your own tips." As she rattles off the data, Eve indoctrinates Crawford into procedures of the restaurant business, bustling about the premises with her uniquely efficient gait, charging about in her apparent unisex style.

Later, Crawford purchases her first restaurant, and the tables are turned—Eve now works for her, happy to have the burdens of ownership thrust on someone else's shoulders, particularly one as ambitious as the ever-striving Crawford. On the successful opening night, Crawford is aglow from her financial coup with the eatery, but even more bent on pleasing parasite Scott and providing pouty Blyth with any lavish object she desires. It is Eve who seemingly is the unselfish one, glad that her friend, and now employer, Crawford has made it.

Crawford: "It looks like we're in, Ida."

Eve: (Shuffling a packet of bills lovingly): "That's what it says here. (Ruffling money) "Isn't that a lovely noise?"

Later Crawford inquires: "You must be dead."

Eve: (Showing a wad of bills): "If I am—bury me with this."

Still later that evening, when Carson has left the restaurant in a huff, having informed Crawford of Scott's true nature and having unsuccessfully made a pitch for his own "romantic" cause, Eve the perpetual observer and audience informer archly remarks: "Laughing boy seems slightly burned at the edges. What's eating him?"

Crawford: "A small green-eyed monster."

Eve: "Jealous? Doesn't sound like Wally [Carson]. No profit in it . . . and there is a guy who loves a dollar."

Further on in *Mildred Pierce,* affluent Crawford indulgently purchases a sleek new sports model car for Blyth's birthday. Eve, the film's Greek chorus who is sufficiently detached emotionally to call a spade a spade, is disgusted at having had to effect the business transaction of acquiring the car for spoiled Blyth. Slapping the ownership papers and the car keys on Crawford's office desk: "A little eighteen-hundred-dollar birthday present for Miss Veda."

Crawford: "The car. It came."

Eve: "Yes. It's that shiny blue thing a block and a half long. . . ."

Crawford: "Do you think she'll like it, Ida?"

Eve: (Now at the desk) "If she doesn't she oughta

have her head examined for holes. Here—you have to sign this—in blood."

When Blyth and Scott next enter, Eve makes no bones about her feelings of antipathy. (To Blyth): "You're sitting on the statements from Laguna Beach. . . ." (Eve pries up the papers).

Blyth: "That's what I like about you, Ida. You're so informal . . . So delightfully provincial. . . ."

Eve: (Sweetly): "I like you too."

Scott: (Blyth has gone out to examine the car.) "Finished for the day?"

Eve: "Yeah" (as she prepares to exit). "Don't look now, junior . . . but you're standing under a brick wall."

Scott: "I don't get it."

Eve: "You will."

Fully aware of her hard-as-nails screen personality, Eve's Ida is not above ribbing her tough qualities, fully aware that other people will not grasp her self-digs. Meekish, middle-aged accountant Chester Clute arrives to prepare Crawford's extensive business statements. To Eve he says: "You always interrupt."

Eve: (Wolfishly): "It's because I want to be alone with you . . . come and let me bite you, you darling boy."

Further on in the feature, Crawford returns from a Mexican vacation. She is greeted at the office by Eve who has assumed full managership during the boss's absence. Her conversation with Crawford illustrates that she is considered by everyone, including herself, as just a workhorse without a fulfilling personal life. Eve (Ida) is resigned to her fate and will not devote the same effort to her private life as her business career. That she comprehends she would subconsciously be an odious castrating wife is implied in her prevailing attitude.

Eve: "Well, well . . . long time no see. How was Mexico?"

Crawford: "Nice. How is business?"

Eve: "Wonderful." (Indicating) "Want your desk back?"

Crawford: "No, thanks. On you it looks good." (Mixing a drink of liquor) "Here's to those who taught me how . . ." (Toasting) "Men!"

Eve: "That's the way it is, Mildred. It's a man's world. If you succeed, if you show signs of getting up in the world . . . then the knives come out. I never yet met a man who didn't have the instincts of a heel. (Pauses and shrugs) "I sometimes wish I could get along without 'em."

Crawford: (In a sudden moment of uncharacteristic concern for someone besides her daughters) "You've never been married, have you, Ida?"

Eve: "When men are around me they suddenly get allergic to wedding rings." (A rueful grimace) "I'm

the Big Sister type. You know. Good old Ida . . . you can talk with her man to man." (Reflective) "I'm getting very tired of men talking man to man with me. Think I'll have a drink myself."

Eve, the vitriolic soul, constantly tosses off cracks in the midst of her observations of others. (*Re* Blyth): "Personally, Veda has convinced me that alligators have the right idea. . . . They eat their young."

Being the uninvolved observer, Eve can speak her mind without fear of reprisal, saying what the lead players (and ultimately the movie audience) may feel, but are too polite to voice.

Eve: (To Scott): "I think Mildred is having business trouble."

Scott: (Smiling): "That can happen in the best of families."

Eve: (Puzzled) "Don't look now but you've got canary feathers all over."

Scott: (As he goes off to dance with Blyth): "Beauty calls. Excuse me."

Eve: "A pleasure."

At the finale, both Eve and Carson are left on the sidelines, while the liberated Crawford walks off into the sunrise with her ex-husband Bennett.

Carson: "I'm beginning to think I haven't got a chance [with Crawford]."

Eve: (Dryly): "You're just a pessimist."

Carson: "Say—how about you cooking some breakfast for me?"

Eve: "Ok. I'll give you some scrambled eggs . . . but that's all. I hate to wrestle in the morning."

The critics were generally enthusiastic about *Mildred Pierce,* which premiered at the Strand Theatre, September 28, 1945. "Eve Arden is her customary hardboiled self, and that's quite alright with us." (*New York Times*). "Miss Arden brings an insouciant and embittered accent to Mildred Pierce's pal which is always helpful in the continuity." (*New York Herald-Tribune*) Both Eve and Ann Blyth were nominated for best supporting actress Oscars, but lost out to Ann Revere who won for *National Velvet*. It was Eve's only Oscar nomination to date. The film was also nominated for best picture and best cinematography, but it was the picture's star, Crawford who won an Oscar as best actress of 1945.

If the movies failed to afford Eve with roles commensurate with her abilities, she had ample opportunity by performing in lead theater parts at the Griphon Players in La Jolla, California during the summer of 1945. She was Marion in *Biography,* Amytes in *The Road to Rome* and Mary Hilliard in *Here Today.* As salutory as it may have been for Eve, it did nothing to enhance her screen career, and she was soon back portraying her stock movie characterization.

Warner's *My Reputation* had been completed by March 1, 1944, but was not released until January, 1946, since it was caught in the bind of heavy World War II film production and delayed distribution as the escapist needs of the early 1940s tapered off with the armistice. The well-mounted tearjerker starred Barbara Stanwyck (in one of her very favorite roles) as a widow residing in suburban Chicago with two small sons. When she is introduced to army major George Brent matrimonial sparks fly, and within a short span of screen time, having survived the community's scorn of her relationship with Brent and deciding he is good for her sons, she agrees to wed him. Eve was sixth-billed as Ginna Abott, wife of the nondescript John Ridgely and bosom pal of troubled Stanwyck. Eve is the one who staunchly advises Stanwyck to cut loose and follow her romantic intuition. *My Reputation* was pegged by many as a "domestic sob story put together out of stock situations and old scraps of dialogue." (*New York Herald Tribune*).

The Kid From Brooklyn (1946) was RKO's Techni-color musical remake of Harold Lloyd's *The Milky Way*. It had mousey milkman Danny Kaye become a boxer and, by a fluke of luck, develop into a fight champion. He and his eventual gal, singer Virginia Mayo, decide upon a partnership in the dairy business as a better future. In this Samuel Goldwyn production, Eve had the non-demanding role of the cautious girl-friend of Kaye's flight manager Walter Abel. Bosley Crowther (*New York Times*) remarked: "Even the low-comedy cut-ups of Walter Abel, Lionel Stander and Eve Arden fail to inflate the blithesome spirit when they aren't conjoined with Mr. Kaye."

Having found boxoffice success with *Rhapsody in Blue* (the "life" of George Gershwin) Warners' produced an elaborate technicolor tin pan alley opus *Night and Day* (1946) starring Cary Grant in a pseudo biographical musical salute to song composer Cole Porter. Some reels into the storyline, Grant is overseas fighting in World War I and his wealthy admirer (Alexis Smith), now a Red Cross nurse, submits one of his song compositions to French singer Gabrielle (Eve) begging her to introduce the tune and help along the

With Barbara Stanwyck in *My Reputation* (WB, 1946).

With Walter Abel, Lionel Stander, Danny Kaye, and Vera-Ellen in *The Kid From Brooklyn* (RKO, 1946).

career of a talented composer. At first reluctant, Eve agrees to sing the song publicly, gallantly admiring Smith's devotion to Grant. To this day, cinema followers are divided in their opinions of Eve's impersonation of a French chanteuse. Some feel that her adopted Gallic accent and the uttering of such terms as "Bien possible" was as phony as could be. Others insist that she captured the flavor of the French songstress more than adequately. At the time, Eve's performance was accepted as better than sufficient, but there were too many specialty numbers (one including Mary Martin) following close upon one another, for anyone to take particular notice of Eve in this 128-minute production.

In 1946, Eve was named a star of tomorrow by the

Motion Picture Herald-Fame annual poll. This was seventeen years after her screen debut, and long after she had been pigeon-holed as the top notch supporting player! Other stars of tomorrow that year were Joan Leslie, Zachary Scott, Butch Jenkins, Yvonne DeCarlo and Robert Mitchum, none of them exactly fresh to the screen!

From the overweight but somewhat sublime *Night and Day,* Eve went to the ridiculous in Universal's seemingly ambitious costume romance biography *Song of Scheherazade* (1947), a most unlikely technicolor fable of the adventures of mid-nineteenth century Russian composer Rimsky-Korsakoff (Jean Pierre Aumont) in Morocco where he is overwhelmed by pretty dancer Yvonne DeCarlo. Eve received fourth billing in her first real period picture, playing the fashionable

With George Murphy in *The Arnelo Affair* (MGM, 1947).

With Brian Donlevy in *Song Of Scheherazade* (Universal, 1947).

widow mother of DeCarlo, who exists exceedingly well while her daughter dances incognito in a waterfront cafe. As Madame de Talevera, Eve paraded about in black frilled lace, elaborate headgear, and waving the obligatory fan. *Song of Scheherazade* pranced into Loew's Criterion Theatre February 26, 1947, and was roasted by the outraged critics, as being "unintentional half-hearted comedy with a superior score." *Variety* noted: "Adding to ludicrous spots are a variety of accents, topped by the Broadwayese and twentieth century flippancy tossed into the 1865 period by Eve Arden."

In MGM's *The Arnelo Affair* (1947) Eve was utilized as audience bait, pushed into the sluggish story on occasion to lighten the lugubrious proceedings. Frances Gifford, the neglected wife of successful attorney George Murphy, gets involved with unsavory John Hodiak, a nightclub owner, and finds herself involved in murder. Radio wonder boy Arch Obeler went far amiss in directing this film, completed in the early summer of 1946.

Eve's other two 1947 feature releases* were much better product. In Warner's *The Unfaithful* (1947), an unofficial, updated remake of Somerset Maugham's *The Letter,* Eve portrayed a nasty version of her usual caustic wisecracking observer. She played Paula, the ex-wife of Douglas Kennedy and the cousin of Zachary Scott. Scott returns to his southern California home to discover that his wife Ann Sheridan had knifed a male intruder. Attorney-friend Lew Ayres learns the murder victim was far more than a casual stranger to Sheridan, who had needed someone to fill her days and nights when she was a lonely war bride. Eve's opening scene occurs in her home at a party celebrating her divorce from Kennedy. Dressed in a smart cocktail ensemble with heavily padded shoulders and wearing her hair in a bun, she is first spotted standing atop a table in her living room in a deliberate Auntie Mame pose and the obvious center of interest. She jokes to her assembled friends: "In twenty minutes I was a free woman. Do I hear any bidders. My hair is my own. My teeth are my own. Almost everything is my own." Once again, Eve is the flippant man-hungry predatory female, whose tough exterior seems to belie a heart of gold. The only difference is that in this production it does not!

As *The Unfaithful* proceeds, Eve never has a good word about her cousin-in-law, and is eager to dish the dirt with her friends, especially after Sheridan has been involved in the puzzling homicide case. Later, sitting in a restaurant with her catty pals Peggy Knudsen and Joan Barker, Eve glimpses Sheridan arriving, and thinks it is a marvelous occasion to repeat every unpleasant tale she can recall about Sheridan. Her friends do not partake, and the frustrated Eve barks: "It's a shame to waste two perfectly good mouths on you." Eve cannot resist coming to Sheridan's table and feigning friendship: "Naturally, I am on your side." When she and her girlfriends are brushed off and leave, Ayres comments to Sheridan: "Those witches. They ought to be measured for brooms."

Eventually Sheridan is acquitted of the murder charge. One of the more salutary results of the arduous trials is that Eve undergoes a dramatic change of heart and discovers she has a strong degree of tolerance and understanding for Sheridan. Thus even in this picture Eve ends up a good dame after all.

---

* She was also in the Columbia short subject *Famous Hollywood Mothers* (1947) along with such other industry celebrities as Rosalind Russell, Eleanor Powell, Bebe Daniels, Gale Storm, and Brenda Marshall.

With Peggy Knudson, Ann Sheridan, and Jane Harker in *The Unfaithful* (WB, 1947).

The Unfaithful received a majority of complimentary reviews, but never made remarkable headway at the boxoffice. As Eve later recalled of her role: "[It] was a little different. I ran the gamut. I was mean, dumb, smart, kind. I was Ann's enemy. But at the end I was a reformed character." All reviewers had to say of Eve's appearance was: ". . . [she] has a moment or two as a wartime tramp." (*New York Herald Tribune*).

Eve's biggest screen part to that time occurred in Warners' filmization of John Van Druten's long running —it lasted 1,557 performances—stage success *Voice of the Turtle* (1947). Eve inherited the role of Olive Lashbrooke, played on stage by Audrey Christie and later in the run by Vicki Cummings. Filming on *Voice of the Turtle* began one day after Eve completed her *The Unfaithful* role. Since Margaret Sullavan was unavailable to recreate her lead part, Warners' contract star Eleanor Parker coiffed and made up to resemble Sullavan in appearance and coached to copy Sullavan's acting mannerisms as the retarded cute maiden who has an unfortunate love affair (producer Kent Smith jilted her because she became too serious) and is now leery of men.

Eve is the glib actress ("They wanted me to go out with *Tobacco Road*. . . . [But] Darling all those turnips!") who does not mind a one night stand here and there with a suitable man. She arrives to inspect Sullavan's new apartment, and decides to follow up a phone message from her old flame, Commodore Wayne Morris. Her rapid-fire telephone conversation is a classic of speedy storyline exposition and a gem of convincing dramatics by Eve:

"Hello . . . is Commodore Burling there? Ned? . . . This is Olive. Yes, I just called the hotel and they told me. When did you get into town? You did? You are?

When? You mean, you're just here till. . . . Well, I never got it. I've been on the road with a play, and I guess the mail got. . . . Oh, I can't. I'm terribly sorry, but I can't. How about lunch tomorrow? (Disappointed) Oh. No, I'm tied up the whole week-end. I've got someone to look after. Yes, I know. Darling, I know, I know, but. . . . (She is growing agonized). Oh, hell, I will! Yes, Yes, I will. I don't know how. I . . . but I will. What's the time now? Oh, my God, no, no, make it eight, will you? Eight at my hotel. Yes . . . lovely to talk to you. Good-bye now. (To Parker) There. There's an object lesson in how not to act with a man."

Eve quickly convinces Parker to substitute as a blind date with G.I. Ronald Reagan (on leave in 1944 Manhattan), someone Eve had met on one of her road tours. Parker agrees and before the evening is out, she and shy Reagan have developed a substantial rapport, and he stays overnight at her apartment because he cannot find any hotel accommodation.

Eve's most amusing visual scene in *Voice of the Turtle* occurs the following morning when she arrives bright and cheery at Parker's apartment, curious to know how her friend and Reagan got along. When Parker refuses to let her into the kitchen (Reagan has scooted in there), Eve strains and crains to peek inside, and the film realizes one of its few moments of duplicating the warmth and joy of the stage show.

Voice of the Turtle opened at the Warner Theatre December 25, 1947, while the stage edition was still playing on Broadway. No one was especially pleased with the film edition directed by Irving Rapper. To appease the censors, the cute risqueness had to be obliterated (i.e. in the play, the G.I. blind date and the would-be actress spend the night in bed together, in the film they very obviously do not). As *Time* magazine

With Eleanor Parker and Ronald Reagan in *The Voice Of The Turtle* (WB, 1947).

quipped, it was an "exchange of tattle for titillation." That Eleanor Parker was too slick and intelligent to capture the humanness of Margaret Sullavan's characterization all but destroyed the flavor of the film, and Ronald Reagan was too phlegmatic to be convincing as the gentle but decisive serviceman. Bue Eve got positive notices. The *New York Times* found her Olive "attractively portrayed and the *New York Herald Tribune* lauded: "Certainly Eve Arden gives her best to the part of the other girl. Several times there are genuine laughs as she expertly takes the last ounce out of the role. For television screenings, *Voice of the Turtle* is often retitled *One for the Books.*

For the past decade, Eve had been an active radio performer, appearing on several long running comedy/ variety shows. With her full-blown husky voice and expert sense of timing, she was a natural for the audio medium. She had made her radio debut on "The Ken Murray Show" (ABC) in 1936, followed by a stint on "The Russ Morgan Show" (NBC) in 1938. For a spell, Eve was a regular on "The Danny Kaye Show" (CBS) during the World War II years. but it was not until Eve replaced razor-sharp slapstick artist Joan Davis on Jack Haley's "Village Store" (NBC) in 1945, that she began gathering a noticeable radio following. While Eve worked well with jovial comedy song-and-dance man Haley, she found a better radio vis-a-vis when Jack Carson replaced Haley on the Thursday evening (9:30) "Village Store," as of September 11, 1947. Eve and her fellow Warner Bros. contract performer maintained a sharp but natural rapport on the program, each displaying a crisp and mordant wit with the given dialogue. Versatile Verna Felton and later Sharon Douglas supplied the backup comedy bits in the show. Reviewing the revised half hour variety outing, *Variety* reported: "Miss Arden remains the slightly acid but always attractive gal who periodically yanks the rug from under the star's feet, . . ."

Just when Eve was finishing the 1947–48 season on "Village Store," and planning a vacation from her radio chores, CBS sent her the pilot script to a new situation comedy "Our Miss Brooks." Originally Shirley Booth had been offered the show. (She and Eve had many parallels during their earlier show business careers, each possessing an unique ability to make a tart delivery amusing but inoffensive and add zest to any production she appeared in.) Eve was not enthusiastic about performing in another radio series, but agreed to audition the program in a limited summer run. Thus, on Monday, July 19, 1948 at 9 P.M., "Our Miss Brooks" made its debut. The cast consisted of Eve as Miss Brooks, Madison High School's man-hungry English teacher, Jeff Chandler as Philip Boynton, the bashful biology

instructor Eve adores, Gale Gordon as blustering Osgood Conklin, the authoritarian but occasionally nitwit high school principal, Gloria McMillan as Harriet his all-American, sweet daughter, Dick Crenna as the ultra high-voiced, low mentality student Walter Denton, pal to Eve and enamored of McMillan and the bane of Gordon's very existence, and Jane Morgan as the elderly but spry Mrs. Davis, Eve's landlady and willing abettor in assorted madcap capers. Larry Berns and Al Lewis were the show's directors.

Variety evaluated: "Here's another example of parlaying all the necessary show biz ingredients into an entertaining and adult half-hour of radio comedy."

"Eve Arden is cast in the lead role and it looks like CBS has found the right formula for integrating her talents into the audio medium. It's certainly a vast improvement over her "Sealtest" ("Village Store") career of the past season on NBC."

"Cast as a romantic English teacher who's on the make for a biology instructor, she accents all of the script's high points for a maximum of laugh payoff. She's surrounded by an equally competent cast."

A few radio critics were unimpressed by the essential stock situation comedy show, notably tough-to-please *New York Herald Tribune* reviewer John Crosby: "Although Miss Arden wisecracks indefatigably and courageously, still the program just isn't very funny."

Nevertheless, so successful was initial audience reaction to "Our Miss Brooks," that CBS induced Eve to sign a term contract to star in the radio series, and it premiered as a fall regular program on Sunday, September 10, 1948 in the 9:30–10 P.M. time spot, with scripts by Al Lewis and Lee Loeb, and Chandler, Gordon, Crenna, McMillan and Morgan repeating their audition roles. *Variety* was enthusiastic about this show which transformed the stereotyped dust-covered spinster teacher into a normal human being, very interested in life and in men in particular: "Miss Arden, zestfully enacting her title role as a smart cracking school marm who melts at the sight of a certain biology teacher, she found a characterization that gives happy range to her talents as a comedienne." Even John Crosby (*New York Herald Tribune*) admitted a partiality to the series as it progressed: "I'll have to revise those churlish remarks to some extent . . . it is a very amusing program . . . there just isn't anyone in the business who can handle feline dialogue as well as Miss Arden."

In 1948, with radio more than motion pictures suffering from the competing affects of widespread commercial television, it seemed initially peculiar that Our Miss Brooks, like such other new radio shows as "My Favorite Husband" (Lucille Ball) should have been relegated to that lesser audio medium. However, it was still at a time when the available name stars and leading character performers in Hollywood were uncertain of the television medium and the adverse affect of overexposure on the free home tube to their silver screen careers. Then too, the film studios deemed it wiser to prevent their contract players from appearing in that medium for the time being. Thus only such freelance movie players as Stu Irwin and June Collyer in "The Trouble with Father," and Jackie Gleason and Rosemary DeCamp in "The Life of Riley" were free to try their domestic comedy series on television initially. "Our Miss Brooks" would have to wait four years before Eve, then free of her Warners' contract, and CBS would agree to the switchover to the more costly and time-consuming television format.

Meanwhile, Eve's personal life was suffering emotional reverses. At the end of World War II, Bergen returned to Hollywood, and as Eve said: ". . . we made the ordinary discovery that we were both strangers." As of April 1947, they tried a trial separation. Eve explained: "Work takes up all your energies and it doesn't leave much time for anything else—including a husband." They were divorced on July 27, 1947. By the end of the next year, she had adopted two baby girls: Liza (born in 1946) and Connie (born in 1948). (Eve's radio series character name of Connie Brooks was named after her second adopted child.) (About this double adoption Eve said): "Having been an only child, I was determined not to have an only child. I think it's a lonely life, for one thing."

Eve had been continuing with her feature film work, still based at Warner Bros., under a revised two-picture-a-year contract at approximately $45,000 per film. Indicative of Eve's standing at the studio was an anonymously offered statement by a studio executive at the time: "There's no script, no budget, an indifferent director, and a fading star. But we've got Eve Arden, and the picture will make a buck." She had become an insurance policy for any producer for whom she worked, a complimentary but artistically unsatisfying situation. Eve complained to columnist Sheilah Graham: "I want to play parts like Rosalind Russell and Irene Dunn." She never did.

Whenever she had a break between films, Eve would visit Manhattan. "I love New York. It's the only city I love. I stay up in New York until 5:30 in the morning, have breakfast at noon, and go to the theater every night."

One Touch Of Venus (1948) was Universal's mild adaptation of the Kurt Weill Broadway (1943) musical which had starred Mary Martin and Kenny Baker and had run for 567 performances. Following the tradition of the popular movie the retitled production, *Here*

With Tom Conway in *One Touch Of Venus* (Universal, 1948).

Comes Mr. Jordan, and its less successful semi sequel *Down To Earth,* was changed from a stage musical into a whimsical potpourri fantasy about a department store window dresser (Robert Walker) who kisses a statue of Venus (Ava Gardner) which comes to life for twenty-four hours. More entertaining than the dreamy and dreary main story was the subsidiary plot involving Walker's friend Dick Haymes who eventually wins store clerk Olga San Juan, after Walker becomes agog over Gardner. Eve was on hand as the super-efficient ("qualified to take shorthand and body blows") secretary of wolfish store owner Tom Conway. She has eyes for all the men but wins none. She and peppy San Juan did their utmost, but they could not carry the whole show. *Variety* detailed: ". . . [she] gives another of her punch deliveries, smartly shaded to catch the full worth of every throwaway line and situation." Little appreciated at the time were the song numbers, especially Gardner's solo number "Speak Low."

Eve's next picture, *Whiplash,* was stylishly out of date when released by Warner Bros. in 1948. Dazed ex-prize fighter Dane Clark is engaged in a return boxing match and recalls while in the ring the circumstances that brought him to this predicament. He had been an unknown painter in Southern California, content to putter away at his creative true love, until he met mysterious Alexis Smith. He trails her to New York and is taken by good scout Eve to the Pelican Club where Smith sings. Clark finds out that Smith is married to wheelchair-ridden mobster Zachary Scott, who used to be a fighter himself. To be near her, Clark allows himself to be lured back into the boxing game, with nearly disastrous results. The film's best performance was

With Dane Clark in *Whiplash* (WB, 1948).

(The movie studios had returned to big musicals as a survival means against the smallbox television craze.) When crooner Lee Bowman gets too big for his britches and sheds his old pals, radio talent agent Jack Carson scouts the hinterlands for a replacement and finds widow Day as a likely candidate. He brings her, her song, and her uncle, Edgar Kennedy, back to Los Angeles and promotes her for the solo lead on a radio show with an all girl orchestra. Day becomes successful and discovers smiling Carson has more worth than just as a harassed agent. Adolphe Menjou appeared as the ulcerated advertising big shot, and S. Z. Sakall was the roly-poly sponsor. The plot was far from socko, but the Technicolor production directed smoothly by Michael Curtiz boasted fine singing by Day: "Canadian Capers," "I'll String Along With You," and the title

turned in by former Warners matinee idol Jeffrey Lynn as Smith's drunken doctor brother who discovers he still has a conscience. *Whiplash* dragged into the Globe Theatre December 26, 1948 to unremarkable results. The *Hollywood Reporter* observed: "Nor is Eve Arden her usual irrepressible self in the grim surroundings."

By 1949, Warners Bros. (playing it ultra conservative in the declining theatrical film market) like the other major Hollywood film studios, had rid itself of most of its contract stars and supporting players. But Eve's services were still indispensible and she remained on the Warners' roster, to boost and enhance whatever product the company churned out. *My Dream is Yours* (1949) was Doris Day's second feature, and its boxoffice success clearly demonstrated her growing status as one of Hollywood's brightest new stars and top attractions.

With Dennis Morgan and Jane Wyman in *The Lady Takes A Sailor* (WB, 1949).

tune. Fifth-billed Eve worked for Menjou's agency, which bankrolled Carson's talent search, and she was around often enough in a vicarious capacity to view and remark on ". . . the whole thing with guarded irony." Said the *New York Times:* "Those old and friendly Warner Brothers standbys, Jack Carson, Eve Arden and S. Z. Sakall give a little bounce now and again to a leaden script. . . ."

The Lady takes a Sailor (1949) had to rely heavily on the boxoffice draw of Jane Wyman—she had won a best actress Oscar the previous year for *Johnny Belinda*—and the supporting expertise of Eve. Wyman portrayed the prim director of the Buyer's Research Institute, who while sailing on Long Island Sound nearly capsizes in a sudden squall. She is rescued by Dennis Morgan, operator of a secret Navy undersea

With Jack Carson and Duncan Richardson in *My Dream Is Yours* (WB, 1949).

tank installation. The next morning he almost convinces her that all the confidential paraphernalia she thinks she saw the previous night was all part of a bad dream. Eventually she loses her executive post, but wins Morgan's heart, leaving her bemused fiancé Allyn Joslyn in the lurch. This time around male-less Eve was third billed as Susan Wayne, the successful cosmetician pal of Wyman. It was while resting at Eve's beach retreat that Wyman took her "fatal" sail. *The Lady takes a Sailor,* utilizing blatantly obvious indoor-outdoor studio sets, was subdued by the low grade direction of Michael Curtiz and its reliance on leaden slapstick as a substitute for wit and charm. Otis L. Gurnsey, Jr. (*New York Herald-Tribune*) championed Eve: "The fact still remains that almost any one can get a laugh by bumping his or head on a low beam; it takes an Eve Arden, however, to make a straight line sound funny."

Eve's "Our Miss Brooks" radio series returned for its second equally successful season on CBS on Sunday, September 11, 1949 at 6:30 P.M., having taken only a one week summer break. *Variety* wrote: "As a small-town schoolmarm, she puts a cutting edge on her delivery that's sharper than her actual lines. Last Sunday's show (11) was a standard campus mixup, involving a series of stock comedy characters. Although familiar in its wackiness, the show ran off with sustained snappiness for a big laugh payoff." According to a contemporary survey, "Our Miss Brooks" cost $7,250 per episode, while the more prestigious variety shows such as Bing Crosby's weekly stint tallied a $30,000 segment budget.

Evidently not wishing to use up one of her two yearly contractual pictures at Warners' Eve did not make a guest appearance in the studio's *It's a Great Feeling* (1949), a behind-the-kleig-lights story of commisary waitress Doris Day who makes good in the movies.

Considering the reduced amount of feature film production in 1950 Hollywood, Eve's three releases (each for a different studio) that year was an impressive feat. In Hal Wallis's Paramount tearjerker *Paid In Full* (1950), based on a true story, Lizabeth Scott had the

With Bob Cummings and Lizabeth Scott in *Paid In Full* (Paramount, 1950).

offbeat casting assignment of portraying a saintly soul, the good-intentioned sister of selfish Diana Lynn. Scott passes by advertising executive Bob Cummings so that Lynn may wed him. Having been the accidental cause of the death of Lynn's infant, Scott is determined to make amends. After Lynn and Cummings divorce, she weds him and insists upon having a child, knowing that with her hereditary medical problems, childbirth is fatal. Midst all this churning emotion, Eve and Frank Mc-Hugh supplied brief respites of comedy relief. The *British Monthly Film Bulletin* rightly called *Paid In Full* an "odd and baffling film," and it failed to live up to its boxoffice expectations. Because of Hal Wallis' delayed sale of his features to television, it is one of the few Eve performances not readily accessible to video viewers.

In Universal's Technicolor musical *Curtain Call at Cactus Creek* (1950), washed up actor Vincent Price leads a troupe of traveling repertory performers around the old west. His players consist of stage-struck stage-hand Donald O'Connor, frivolous ingenue Gale Storm and her mother, musical comedy actress Eve, an over-seasoned gal past her professional prime (Eve looked young enough to be Storm's contemporary). Eve handled one of the four song numbers, "Waiting at the Church." Mixed up in the proceedings was bank robber chief Walter Brennan, included for a fuller burlesque western flavor. (Indeed there are many parallels to the similar but classier 1960 film *Heller in Pink Tights*.) The "pedestrian" musical, tailored to the family trade, garnered few plaudits. *Variety* reported: "Miss Arden is well cast as the passe thesper, . . ."

Warner Bros. rummaged up *No, No, Nanette* for a third screen whirl in the revised *Tea For Two* (1950),

With Doris Day in *Tea For Two*.

starring the studio's musical team of Doris Day and Gordon MacRae. To retain the period flavor, the script resorted to the gimmick of having uncle S. Z. Sakall tell Day-MacRae's children the story of how their parents met in 1926. Day, a wealthy heiress until a Wall Street slump breaks her bank, invests $25,000 she really does not have in a Broadway-bound production, having been bitten by the show business bug. Her uncle (Sakall) still has money and good-naturedly agrees to provide the needed sum if she can say "no" to every question asked her for twenty-four hours. He hopes this might cure her of her proclivity for becoming involved with hairbrained schemes and romances. Having become a legitimate theatrical backer, she must deal with singer-songwriter MacCrae and the show's top dancer Gene Nelson, leading to obvious romantic complications. Bill Goodwin essayed the tightwad lawyer who keeps a firm lid on Sakall's dwindling bank account, and later, it is he who provides the required funds necessary to get the big show going. Eve is a girl on the prowl to marry Goodwin and, compared to the low-brow campy capers of comedian Billy De Wolfe (as the shoestring producer), Eve was a gem of sophistication. Popular in its day, *Tea for Two* has gained its own coterie of admirers for the better than usual selection of songs, especially the rendition of the title tune. The *New York Times* said of Eve: "And Miss Arden glides thru the picture dropping caustic comments with an air that seems to say make what you will of the innuendos, bub. Miss Arden is good at this sort of thing—very good, indeed."

During the summer of 1950, Eve returned to her first love, the theater, performing in the increasingly lucrative summer stock field. (For a long spell, Tallulah Bankhead had been the champ in this area, receiving

With Gale Storm and Donald O'Connor in *Curtain Call At Cactus Creek* (Universal, 1950).

Eve Arden and daughters Liza and Connie in 1950.

a guaranteed $5,000 weekly.) At an approximate $750 weekly, Eve was receiving far less than her current asking price per film in those days—$50,000–$75,000 per screen assignment—but it was a medium she loved and gave her an opportunity to work more closely with live audiences, in preparation for her entry into television. She chose to work in Ruth Gordon's Broadway comedy *Over Twenty-One* which had starred Irene Dunne in the film version. She portrayed Paula Wharton the sophisticated writer who attempts to help her journalist husband survive the rigors of military life. The *Newark Evening News* caught Eve's performance at the McCarter Theatre, Princeton, N.J.: "The statuesque blond's brassy humor, in the face of discouraging events was a lesson, in spirit as well as acting. Her excellent timing, flawless delivery of punch lines and amusing facial contortions were a pleasure to the entire audience."

After the summer tour, Eve returned to her "Our Miss Brooks" radio chores and to picture making.

Three Husbands (1950) was a direct steal from the successful motion picture *A Letter To Three Wives*, and most certainly did not benefit from any comparisons. It was a seedy affair that did nothing at the box office.

Urban San Francisco bachelor Emlyn Williams dies, leaving to his three best friends letters stating that one of their wives was unfaithful. This allows for extended flashbacks as each husband broods on his marital life and the possible truth of Williams' contention. Eve is married to rough-hewn Howard Da Silva, a gambler in the chips, and allows her spouse to believe she is playing around, hoping the gambit will restore his former interest in her. It evolves that Williams' scheme was merely a device to straighten out each of the three husbands who had forgotten how to appreciate their mates. His will divides the bulk of his estate among the couples. The *New York Times* conceded: "Mr. da Silva is a hard gent, whose sense of humor fits the role neatly, as does Miss Arden's conscious attempt at self betterment."

Eve's last full blown wise cracking lady role—and her final picture under her Warners' contract—was *Goodbye, My Fancy* (1951), which reteamed her with Joan Crawford. The studio had purchased the Fay Kanin stage winner (which starred Madeleine Carroll) for $55,000 and promptly diluted its astringent points for the tame screen version.

Chick Congresswoman Crawford is invited to Good Hope College to receive an honorary degree. She had been expelled from there years before for dating a young college professor (Robert Young) now the school's president. Obviously, the passing years have added a special glow to her campus days. She tries to convey this concept to her topnotch private secretary Woody (Eve), but the latter is too perceptive to be hoodwinked by sentimental hogwash.

Crawford: "You don't understand, Woody. I went to Good Hope."

Eve: "Oh, pardon me."

With Howard da Silva in *Three Husbands* (UA, 1951).

With Joan Crawford and Frank Lovejoy in *Goodbye, My Fancy* (WB, 1951).

Crawford: "Take a letter, please."

Eve: "Shall I type it on parchment?"

When the ever-practical Eve is packing at the hotel for the jaunt to the alma mater, she telephones room service, a bit of screen business which provides her with a characteristic double entendre filled with latent sexual connotations: "Say, what about that warm milk for 1202! . . . What? It doesn't have to be in a bottle! This is for a *big* girl!" (Not even Roscoe Karns in his amusing 1930s feature film assignments could have topped the delivery of that crack.)

After arriving at Good Hope, Crawford and Eve are ushered into the very dormitory room the Congresswoman once occupied as a student. The subsequent interplay between boss and employee—who are very good friends—reveals the emotionally frigid facade Eve's characters always adopt:

Crawford: "There is where it all started, Woody."

Eve: "I don't believe in looking at the past. I was born in Newark, N.J. Every time I go through on a train, I pull down the shade."

Crawford, revelling in the nostalgia of it all, and the possibility she might rekindle her romance with eligible widowed Young, finds no champion in Eve for her romantic fantasies.

Eve: "Agatha, when I was fourteen, I fell in love with the fellow who sold peanuts on our block. I'm not going to marry him."

Despite the frivolity of the college reunion, Crawford intends showing a movie to the graduating class about the horrors of war and dictator-controlled education. But she is told by school authorities that the documentary is too strong material for "unformed minds." While Crawford is cavorting about her high-toned business, Eve is required to handle most of the Congresswoman's dirty work. For example, Crawford is greatly perturbed when top *Life* magazine photographer-reporter Frank Lovejoy is assigned to cover her collegiate stay. She and the seemingly callous Lovejoy once had a brief romantic fling in World War II Europe and she would like to forget the episode and him because it was one of the few times when she revealed her womanly vulnerability. Crawford imperiously places a telephone call to Lovejoy's publisher Henry Luce, planning to order the executive to have Lovejoy removed from the assignment. But at the last minute Crawford has a change of mind (and heart). Eve, as always, is left to handle the potentially messy situation as Mr. Luce's office has just alerted the publisher that Crawford demands to speak with him. In typical Eve Arden fashion, Eve's Maida grabs the phone and says: "Hello? Mr. Luce? You'll be delighted to know we're renewing our subscription." End of sticky situation.

Yet Eve's Maida is not all efficiency and flip tactics. When Lovejoy presses her too hard about Crawford's do-gooder attitudes and her adolescent flirtation with Dean of College Young, Eve snaps back: "You don't think I just work for this woman, do you? I like her. I care what happens to her." One can almost believe it of Maida, thanks to Eve's knowing way with a cynical or soft-hearted bit of dialogue.

Later, she informs Crawford who has just announced

Eve Arden and her husband Brooks West in 1951.

bubblingly that she will wed Young: "Well, if that's what you want it's okay with me. I just want you to be happy." As if embarrassed by her show of warmth, Eve quickly recovers her cool, when Crawford suddenly remembers that Eve is human too and has her own personal life.

Crawford: "Isn't your date picking you up?"

Eve: "No, he had to shoe a couple of horses. I'm picking him up at the blacksmith's."

Still later, Crawford realizes how weak-willed Young really is, both as a father to Janice Rule and as a hold-out for academic freedom against the mediocre, ultra-conservative board of trustees. As she is packing her bags to leave, the flabberghasted Eve inquires what is happening.

Crawford: "Shut your mouth. You look like a fish."

Eve: "But I thought—."

Crawford: "That's your trouble . . . You think too much . . ."

Eve. "That's my trouble, all right. I think too much."

Near the finale, when Crawford has regained her perspective, she decides there is an important place in her overcrowded life for sensible Lovejoy. Eve, amazed by everything that has happened to alter the Congresswoman's outlook on life in such a short time, wonders to Lovejoy: "One weekend. A woman couldn't go crazy in one weekend, could she?"

Goodbye, My Fancy opened at the Holiday Theatre May 29, 1951 and had a respectable showing. Critics generally found Crawford too imperious and the Vincent Sherman-directed production too sterile. (This author, however, still relishes the earnest openness of Crawford's liberated characterization.) Fourth-billed Eve, in the role performed by Shirley Booth on stage, received her usual round of review approval. ". . . the lady's secretary, whom Eve Arden angularly performs, is a perfectly packaged wisecracker right out of the glittery Broadway bin" (*New York Times*). ". . . and Eve Arden pitches the acid comments in her own faultless style. . . ."

By now, thoroughly tired of her stock-in-trade character parts in movies, Eve refused to negotiate with Warner Brothers, or to allow her agent to accept any parts that required her to portray that usual self-contained, meaningless dame. Being the top screen comedienne—she was named the best comedienne in filmdom by the Motion Pictures Annual Poll for six consecutive years starting with 1948—was not enough for Eve. She said: "I'm sick of that wise-cracking blonde. It's got so bad that I never go to my own pictures, and even try to avoid looking at the rushes."

Besides the public was beginning to identify Eve with her brittle Connie Brooks radio characterization,

With Jeff Chandler on *Our Miss Brooks* (1952).

far removed from Eve's real offstage personality. Eve admitted she had a shy nature and that it caused problems on her occasional personal appearance tours: "They'd stand there and look at me expectantly. And brother, was I a letdown! I didn't get witchy . . . and I didn't gossip . . . And I couldn't come up with a wisecrack to save my life."

Having completed her 1950–1951 "Our Miss Brooks" radio season, Eve launched another summer stock tour, this time in George Oppenheimer's *Here Today* (a stock perennial for Faye Emerson and Tallulah Bankhead). The play concerns a prankish playwright (Eve) who rushes to Nassau to her ex-husband's romantic rescue. Having proven her box-office worth the previous season on the citronella circuit, Eve received $2,000 a week, $1,500 total for her four supporting players, and fifty percent over the manager's break-even figure at each theatre. Elliot Norton (*Boston Post*) reported: ". . . there is no point where Eve Arden is on the stage where it is not worth watching."

During the tour, Eve had a well-publicized (in the trade papers) run-in with some of the theatre managers, claiming they were padding the free ticket list and not presenting her with a true accounting. Most notably there was a published exchange of letters in *Variety* between Eve and the manager of the McCarter Theatre in Princeton, N.J.

A more constructive result of Eve's tour was actor Brooks West's appearance in *Here Today* as Eve's leading man. They had met the previous season. He was a graduate of the University of Texas, had done assorted Broadway assignments, and had gained some prominence playing opposite Marie Wilson on her early 1950s television series, "My Friend Irma." A

romance sparked between Eve and West, some ten years her junior, and they were wed in Bridgeport, Connecticut, at a friend's farm house. Her two adopted daughters were her flower girls at the ceremony.

Eve was back in Hollywood for the return of "Our Miss Brooks" fifth radio season on CBS, October 7, 1951. *Variety* noted: "Eve Arden's return to the air Sunday (7) as 'everybody's schoolmarm,' was only moderately amusing. There were a few choice gags in this preem segment, but scripting for the major part was labored, with only a mousey script brought forth. Story concerned Miss Brooks' return from a summer vacation spent in Paris, and her attempts to add a first year French course to the English course she already was teaching!

"Miss Arden was her usual alternately smooth and addlepated self, under the circumstances, with Jeff Chandler as routine support as a fellow teacher, and Gale Gordon very good as the badgered principal."

Even though Eve was earning a hefty $4,000 weekly in radio, she was not above admitting that as a performer she had some strange hang-ups. While, she stated, she had no difficulty whatsoever in memorizing her lines for the weekly radio series, or in handling warmup sessions with the live audiences for the "Our Miss Brooks" broadcasts, she had a persistent problem in remembering the cast members' real names when introducing them to the studio guests.

In the greatly reduced theatrical film market, Eve found it increasingly difficult to obtain satisfactory movie work, particularly in non-typecast assignments. In the multi-episode Twentieth Century-Fox confection *We're Not Married* (1952), justice of the peace Victor Moore has performed assorted marriage ceremonies before his license has become effective. Moore sends letters to five couples advising them of the illegality of their "wedded" unions. Eve and ex-playboy spouse Paul Douglas are Long Island suburbanites, a couple who communicate in monosyllables, having reached the marital stage of being "wedded, bedded and bored." He is so preoccupied with his fantasies of stepping out every night in a new amorous escapade, it is often hours later that he answers Eve's persistent questions. But when given the chance of freedom, Douglas realizes he is better off with the financial economy and the emotional security of being wed to Eve. So he burns Moore's letter. Of the five episodes, Eve's was the least gimmicky. But basically she was playing her old stock-in-trade, albeit this time a wife. The *New York World Telegram* reviewer observed: "The disdainful acid of Eve Arden's tongue helps the fun along." Eve was sixth-billed in this comedy which opened at the Roxy Theatre July 11, 1952.

In 1952, Eve and Brooks West adopted a son Duncan. Eve candidly admitted to the press that she had undergone psychoanalysis: "My real reason for getting my psyche explored was to avoid making major mistakes in raising our children."

Eve's fifth radio season for "Our Miss Brooks" began October 5, 1952 with Jeff Chandler still as her vis-a-vis. The opening episode dealt with she and her landlady getting rid of a house trailer they had purchased. Two days previously on Friday, October 3, 1952, Eve debuted a television series version of "Our Miss Brooks" on CBS (she had made her video bow on the same network's "Studio One" the previous year). The video cast of "Our Miss Brooks" was comprised of Gale Gordon, Richard Crenna, Gloria McMillan, and Jane Davis—all repeating their radio assignments. Robert Rockwell took over the assignment as Mr. Boynton Madison High School's most eligible bachelor. *Variety* penned: "Mix these (characters) and some subordinate characters with an improbable story line, spice with gags every other line in the script and dish it up with sharp timing—that's the payoff formula for the show."

Now that admirers of "Our Miss Brooks" could view as well as hear Eve, the series became even more popular, and won Eve a huge following. She did everything possible to avoid creating a stereotyped image of the weary, frustrated spinster teacher. Eve picked up a myriad of awards as "Our Miss Brooks," particularly from teachers' associations around the country. The alumni association of the Teachers College of Connecticut in 1952 cited Eve for her "contribution toward humanizing the American teacher." She received the radio industry's woman of the year award.

On the other hand, less easily pleased observers like Jack Gould (*New York Times*) wondered about Eve's actual service to the educational profession: "What that service could be defies any conceivable rationalization because "Our Miss Brooks" is strictly tired theatrics having no discernable relationship to the classroom."

Eve managed to make one feature in 1953, the low budget Republic domestic comedy *The Lady Wants Mink*. Filmed in murky Trucolor, Eve was third featured as Gladys Jones. She and her estranged suburban husband are neighbors of accountant Dennis O'Keefe and his wife Ruth Hussey. When Hussey takes it in her head to raise minks (O'Keefe will not buy her a fur coat), Eve and Demarest are harassed by the ranging minks, leading to O'Keefe-Hussey and their two children moving to a dilapidated farm. The *New York Herald-Tribune* acknowledged that Eve ". . . helps keep the matter rolling." But it was rambunctious Hope Emerson as the sloppy professional mink breeder who stole the little show.

Thus Eve was happy to return to her "Our Miss Brooks" tele-filming chores. Defending her new video image as a full-dimensional character, Eve said: "Sure Miss Brooks is just a make-believe teacher. Yet to me she's a warm, romantic, realistic, attractive woman. Teachers are like Miss Brooks. She's typical.

"I know many teachers now. I remember with affection those who taught me. I recall my third-grade teacher, umpteen years ago—Miss Ruth Waterman—she had dimples, big brown eyes, and was always smiling. I try to give Miss Brooks that same smiling quality."

Variety reviewed the opening show of "Our Miss Brooks" 's second television season on CBS, Friday night October 2, 1953 in the 9:30–10 P.M. spot. "It's a tricky device, that of making a story line show pop laughs with all the regularity and explosiveness of a standup comic a la Bob Hope, but Eve Arden has been doing it for years and what she puts on television for the seasonal first was more of the same, and better. In the crowded comedy field, she'll be poking around among the leaders of her set and sex.

"The punch lines go to Miss Arden, from whom all laughs flow. She's a past mistress of the type of humor and can time a gag with the precision of some of the best comedy minds. Uniquely too, she is lacking in warmth, humility and sympathy, the cardinal virtues of the successful mime, yet overrides these liabilities as a straight trader in laughs that seems to have caught on. It would have been fun to have had her as a school teacher."

For her work in the 1953–1954 television season on "Our Miss Brooks" Eve won an Emmy award, beating out Lucille Ball, Imogene Coca, Dinah Shore and Loretta Young. She would be nominated in other years, but would never win another to date.

On September 17, 1954, Eve, age forty-two, gave birth to her first child, Douglas, born at Cedars of Lebanon Hospital. That same year she and West purchased Ronald Coleman's former hideaway home on Hidden Valley Road in Thousand Oaks, California. They transformed the thirty-eight acre farm, with its badminton court, Japanese garden, and a yard full of prize zucchini, into a productive spread, raising sheep, horses, Herefords, pigs, goats, rabbits, hens and turkeys. The house proper was turned into elegant quarters, largely decorated by Eve and filled with her treasures gathered from years of antique hunting.

After completing her 1954–1955 television and radio (her seventh and last on the airwaves) seasons, Eve made a feature film version of *Our Miss Brooks* at her old studio alma mater, Warner Brothers. Unfortunately that company had much more success with movie renditions of such action teleseries as *The Lineup* and *Dragnet*. *Our Miss Brooks* should have been filmed at

With Ruth Hussey, Dennis O'Keefe, and William Demarest
in *The Lady Wants Mink* (Republic, 1953).

the height of the program's popularity in 1952–1953, when audiences might have been more willing to accept the overblown version of an essentially short domestic comedy sketch. The movie's weak premise revolved around Eve tutoring neglected rich youth Nick Adams, whose publisher father (Don Porter) takes a romantic interest in Eve. All of which makes square biology teacher Robert Rockwell jealous and precipitates assorted slapstick situations. None of the shenanigans tossed onto the big screen held up to audiences' changing tastes, and the film made a remarkably bad showing at the boxoffice.

Eve's *Our Miss Brooks* would continue on television through the 1956–1957 season, churning out a total of 154 episodes (she negotiated a sale to CBS-TV of the series, on a deferred payment basis). Eve's program first met substantial rating competition in the 1954 video season when it was pitted against Peter Lawford's series *Dear Phoebe* (NBC). Starting with the 1955 season, Eve's producer decided on a change of format.

She left Madison High (the script had the school being torn down to make way for a new state road) and went to teach at Mrs. Nestor's private elementary school in the San Fernando Valley. For her new love of life, there was first Bob Sweeney as Mr. Mundy, an available bachelor. Then there was William Ching as Clint Albright, the wolfish gym instructor, but soon he was dropped from the series. Ching was followed by Hy Averback who proved an unsubtle widower. Finally Gene Barry was hired on as Gene Talbot, the new gym instructor. But the new group all lacked the rapport between the old *Our Miss Brooks* stock company. Before mid-season, Jane Davis returned as her landlady, Gale Gordon was worked back into the series, and when Gene Barry asked to be released from the show, Robert Rockwell (he had floundered on freelance assignments) rejoined the series.

Eve completed the last filming of *Our Miss Brooks* at the Desilu Studio at the end of the 1956–1957 season, when the show had really sunk badly in the ratings, worn

Eve Arden and her Emmy Award for *Our Miss Brooks*, 1954.

With Jane Morgan, Robert Rockwell, Gloria McMillan, Richard Crenna, and Gale Gordon on radio's *Our Miss Brooks* (1954).

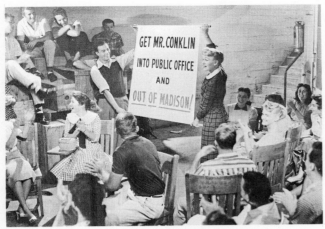

In *Our Miss Brooks* (WB), 1956.

out from lack of originality. Eve was sick of the program and made no bones about it: "Besides the old Madison High shows are going into syndication, the present show will be on all summers (in reruns) and RKO has just sold all those old movies to TV and I'm in most of them [six in actuality]. People are going to have to go to Siberia to escape me."

Re her movie career to date: "Too many people think of me as the caustic wisecracker, the expert squelcher. Most of my performances have had much more scope and depth than wisecracking comedy."

Even though she and Brooks West usually worked together in stock productions, she would tell the press about the secret of her marital success: "Separate careers is what keeps us together. He has his work (painting in particular) and I have my work and we have our own."

Eve fully intended avoiding performing in another television series. She played a nightclub engagement in Las Vegas, but she could not resist an offer by CBS to star in a new television series for the 1957–1958 season, for which Brooks West was associate producer. Based on Emily Kimbrough's reminiscences of her assorted lecture tours, *It Gives Me Great Pleasure*—filmed at Desilu—premiered September 17, 1957. Eve was a widow, Liza Hammond (the Liza derived from her eldest daughter's name) usually away on lecture tours, leaving her fumbling but well meaning mother Francis Bavier to care for the children (Gail Stone, the twelve year old sister of performer Rosemary Clooney, and Karen Greene played the pre-teen kids). *Variety* reported: "On two accounts this Eve Arden Tuesday night entry could be in for trouble. First off, it's regrettable that Miss Arden has become so stereotyped a TV personality, for this is a continuation of the barb-and-the-sally school of femme comedies which,

under new circumstances, essentially takes up where *Our Miss Brooks* left off.

"Having once established the premise the widowed writer of a best seller (*Summer's End*) 'turns chicken' and freezes when confronted with the prospects of hitting the gob circuit and addressing clubwomen (which would fit nicely into an anthology series as a single half-hour entry), one can't help wondering where does Miss Arden and her show go from there? The temptation to be repetitive will be irresistible.

". . . and Miss Arden, pro that she is, knows her way with a line or situation. But unfortunately it's all in the twice-told cliche manner tailored to the Arden touch." *TV Guide,* although not liking the show very much, evaluated her as "an actress of charm, restraint, style and grace" and found that her characterization was "impeccably perfect."

It was not long after the teleseries debuted that it was evident the series was in trouble. Producer Edmund Hartman was replaced by *Our Miss Brooks* alumnus Al Lewis. The show's title was changed to *The Eve Arden Show* and an attempt to add romantic interest to her existence was rung in, but to no avail. The presence of Warner Brothers veteran Allyn Joslyn as Eve's lecture tour employer was wasted. In the tradition of *I Love Lucy,* the production company Desilu had the series filmed live with an audience, using the three camera system to capture the best bits on film. Typical episodes found Eve competing on the lecture circuit with a high-powered French authoress, mistaken as a pin-up girl and involved with the queen of burlesque, and assorted other lowjinks as she traveled from town to town on the show's platform tour premise.

Eve explained to *TV Guide*'s reporter about her bad

With Nick Adams and Robert Rockwell in *Our Miss Brooks,* (WB, 1956).

Eve Arden and family in 1957.

luck: "The irony of it all is that I took a whole year to find a character I wanted to play. Then the blamed thing sold four days after the pilot was filmed. I was all for holding off until after the first of the year. Let some of these new fall shows weed each other out and then go on. But no. We knocked ourselves out filming five shows ahead before we went on the air.

"I don't mean we weren't ready. I mean we were still struggling when we went on—all getting used to each other. I like the show, but we're still struggling. That's how it feels to be putting on a new show after years of *Our Miss Brooks*—like struggling in public."

Re her new television characterization, a person who boasted a $10,000 wardrobe: "It seems an abrupt change to some people, but, really Liza is more nearly me than Connie was. After all, I'm a happily married career mother. And most people don't seem to realize I'm an introvert. It's true. When they open a freeway, I'm just not the ribbon-cutting type."

After twenty-six weeks, the series collapsed with its final episode aired in March, 1958. Besides its own inherent weaknesses, the show was up against the then-popular *Wyatt Earp* (ABC) series in the same 8:30–9:00 P.M. time spot.

For her television chores, Eve earned more than $5,000 plus a percentage, which did not prove much due to the short-lived nature of the series. But she still found this less than satisfactory video outing more interesting than her typical screen roles: "On television you can quiver a nostril once in a while."

Eve had several offers to return to the stage. Eve had turned down the lead in *The Marriage-Go Round* which finally Claudette Colbert accepted and rejected the Agnes Moorehead role in the tryout disaster *The Pink Jungle* starring Ginger Rogers. She did agree to head a West Coast tour of *Auntie Mame* which premiered at Russ Auditorium in San Diego on August 4,

1958 and closed December 13, 1958 at the Geary Theatre in San Francisco. The tour grossed the producers over $170,000. The cast included Willard Waterman, Benay Venuta, Madame Spivy and Brooks West as Beauregard Burnside. *Variety* reported: ". . . she gives it an earthy endearing flamboyance. She looks attractive onstage and projects with authority. What's more, with her expert timing, there's full mileage in the comic lines and takes. On the deficit side, the star might exude more warmth and a less dry approach. Withal, it's a winning performance of verve and style."

Then Otto Preminger offered Eve the role of Maida, the wisecracking girl Friday of impoverished attorney James Stewart in his new film, *Anatomy of a Murder*. Stewart played a lackadasical attorney who would rather fish with his friend Arthur O'Connell, a former lawyer turned alcoholic, than pursue his profession. Therefore even though his refrigerator is always filled with fish, Eve's salary is deeply in arrears. When army lieutenant Ben Gazzara is arrested for murdering a man, Stewart is hired to defend him, and successfully uses the defense that the defendant's wife (Lee Remick) had been raped by the murder victim and thus it was justifiable homicide. Eve warns easy-going Stewart: "Don't let him pay you off in purple hearts." The seemy side of the crime allowed the plausible use of forthright dialogue with the sex act and this urbane aspect was played up big in the promotion of the lethargic courtroom drama. Boston judge, Joseph N. Welch, making his film debut portrayed the presiding judge, and procecuting attorney George C. Scott helped save the picture from being a total entertainment bore. Eve was on-location with the production crew in Ishpeming, Michigan (on the upper peninsula) for eight weeks. Never one to sit idly by—and her role required little of her—

In *Auntie Mame* (1958).

With Arthur O'Connell and James Stewart in *Anatomy Of A Murder* (Columbia, 1959).

she took up mosaic work. Her husband Brooks West had a small featured role as a local comical lawyer. The feature debuted in a dual Manhattan opening at the Criterion and Plaza Theatres July 21, 1959, and did better than average business in its national distribution. *Variety* observed: "Eve Arden shows that her technique has not been seriously maimed by her stock work in television, . . ."

Eve guested on various television shows, such as *Meet Cyd Charisse* (December 29, 1959, NBC), and was a guest on such variety programs as *Red Skelton* (CBS), *Perry Como* (NBC) and *Dinah Shore* (CBS).

Her father, from whom she had long been estranged, died in 1959 at the age of 69. He was then living in Sonoma, California and had remarried.

When Warner Brothers filmed William Inge's long-running stage success *The Dark At The Top Of The Stairs* (1960) director Delbert Mann hired Eve to handle the role of Lottie, performed on the stage by Eileen Heckart and in stock by Joan Blondell, among others. The original concept of Inge's sensitive drama, had dealt with the assorted frustrations of a small-town family in the 1920s. On the screen, this frail emotional study, became a set of overbloated theatrics, particularly with Robert Preston's a la *Music Man* style of playing the coarse harness salesman who cannot quite adjust to the changeover to automobiles. When his wife Dorothy McGuire complains that his lack of adequate income and sulkiness prevents her from being in the mood for lovemaking, he strikes back by walking out on his family and intensifying his relationship with local hairdresser Angela Lansbury. However, they never go beyond the talking stage in their affair. Eve was McGuire's nagging sister, called in for a family conference in this time of crisis. Loudmouthed and ex-

tremely prejudiced ("I know what I know") and henpecking her weak but patient dentist husband (Preston reprimands her: "You wear the pants in your family, I'll wear mine"), Eve was definitely not up to the dramatic requirements of her assignment. She was allowed to caricature her role, overlooking all the subtleties inherent in her part as a woman who is ashamed to admit that she has not had sexual relations with her husband in over three years, bemoans the fact that she has no children, and nurtures a subconscious love for Rudolph Valentino. With her jazz age dress and long beads she strode around the set looking like a 1930s Miss Brooks, broadly tossing off double takes, and utilizing oversized gestures with her eyes, mouth and hands.

The Dark At The Top Of The Stairs had a big sendoff at Radio City Music Hall (September 22, 1960) and did extremely well in theatrical release. The critics were not impressed: ". . . Eve Arden is showy and shallow." (*New York Times*) ". . . (she plays) a little too metallically to let the character's misery show through completely. She is anti-Semitic and anti-Catholic, and Harriet Frank Jr. and Irving Ravetch, in writing the screenplay from Inge's play, have had the good judgment to let her absurd haranguing stand as it is, . . ." (*New York Herald-Tribune*) *Variety* was one of the few to feel: ". . . she could have done even more with her big scene if given the chance."

In the summer of 1960, Eve and Brooks West toured with George Axelrod's *Goodbye Charlie*. The forthright comedy about the female reincarnation of a bounder was softened up for stock audiences by omitting some of the shocking bits and by adding a new ending. The *Newark Evening News* said of her performance at the Papermill Playhouse in Millburn, N.J.: "with the experienced Miss Arden onstage batting every ball over the fence, as it were, the general effect was one of gamey glee."

The following summer, she and West were co-starred in the mature domestic comedy *The Marriage-Go-Round* on the stock circuit. Eve gave another of her "sparkling performances."

Eve was planning a fall 1962 video series, to be written by the team of Jerome Lawrence and Robert Lee, which would have had an international setting and be concerned with the generation gap problem. But the project fell through. (Ironically, *Our Miss Brooks* was doing well in television syndicated repeats). In a broadside talk with the press, Eve stressed: "You know, I hardly ever see anything I do anymore. And now the thought of watching my own face again gives me the shivers."

In the fall of 1963 Eve was mentioned to star in Howard Teichmann's satire on trade unionism *Rainy*

With Robert Preston and Dorothy McGuire in *The Dark At The Top Of The Stairs* (WB, 1960).

Day In Newark, but she withdrew from the project which opened and closed within six performances on Broadway in October, 1963, with a cast headed by Eddie Mayehoff, Zachary Scott, Mary McCarty and Dody Goodman.

She took a two-year hiatus from show business to live in London and an Italian countryside villa with her family. Back in the theater in 1965, after a brief stint of playing the mother-in-law role in *Barefoot In The Park* in Atlanta, Georgia in the early spring, Eve and Brooks West toured that summer first in *Plain and Fancy* and then in Samuel Taylor's *Beekman Place.* The latter play was a sophisticated soufflé which had starred Arlene Francis on Broadway. Eve proved that she was still a top drawing name in the summer circuit.

Eve's most recent theatrical feature film to date, *Sgt. Deadhead* was released on showcase October 22, 1965. Like many other one time active cinema performers (Dorothy Lamour, Buster Keaton, Elsa Lan-

chester, Mickey Rooney, Brian Donlevy, et al.) she found it expedient to accept American International Pictures' offer to play a comedy relief role. But she came off better than most who had "fallen" to such screen jobs. Her role provided an opportunity to let other screen producers know that she was still actively around, and very ready, willing and able to continue working. *Sgt. Deadhead* was a lamebrained space age comedy with Frankie Avalon as a non-commissioned soldier who is accidentally launched into space and returns a snotty, extrovert hero. Eve was the WAF leader at the U.S. Air Force's Smedley Missile Base, commanded by Fred Clark, with Cesar Romero, Gale Gordon and Reginald Gardiner as a trio of military inspectors on hand to observe the missile launching and retrieval. Wearing a dark haired, bangs-styled wig, Eve contributed some broad, smart-aleck acting as she pursued and harassed Clark around the base, and attempted to soothe the adolescent romance of WAF Deborah

With Gale Gordon in *Sergeant Deadhead* (American-International, 1965).

them (a potential TV series producer) I was not just Connie Brooks, the part went to somebody else. Sometimes I wondered whether there was a place for me." After performing in two unsold pilots* and guesting on the "Man from U.N.C.L.E." show ("Minus X Affair," NBC, April 8, 1966, with Eve as a professor who has developed a drug to sharpen the senses), she accepted the offer by producer Desi Arnaz to star in a wacky series *The Mothers-In-Law,* a variation of the *I Love Lucy* format, with the emphasis strongly on slapstick.

There was much speculation at the time (pre-debut, September 10, 1967, NBC) how Eve and costar balladeer Kay Ballard would get along together, being the opposite types of performers. On the promotional tour to publicize *The Mothers-In-Law* to the television critics around the country, Eve was rather tense at the requisite talk show sessions. Said one of her managers: "Give her the script and the dialog. Her sense of humor

Wally and Avalon. Eve performed one of the six song numbers, a cute mini-production number "You Should've Seen the One that Got Away" in which she told the girls in the barrack "I thought I had him on the hook, but then he took another look." Then she prances into the shower room and back again, offering an entertaining bump-grind-strutting shuffle dance, as she continues her song of "The game of love I love." Those who reviewed *Sgt. Deadhead,* released on a double bill with the same studio's *Ski Party,* referred to Eve as the "spectacular Air Force lieutenant."

The following year, Eve agreed to star in the Chicago national company of *Hello, Dolly!* which opened there at the Shubert Theatre June 13, 1966. She replaced lead Carol Channing who had departed for Hollywood to make *Thoroughly Modern Millie. Variety* reported: "After four performances in the starring role, Miss Arden was still a bit stiff. She occasionally lapsed behind Gower Champion's presto direction, and her lack of familiarity with the lines sometimes slowed the pace. However, the role is essentially a caricature, and Miss Arden's straight on portrayal does it justice."

Eve found the four-month stint in *Hello, Dolly!* extremely taxing. "I'd wake up every morning thinking, 'I'll never make it.' My knee was swollen up like a football, but I'd make it out of bed and to the theater, change costume. Then I'd hear the music and climb up the stairs and just before curtain I'd get into place and . . ." She was given the annual Sarah Siddons Award for best female performer of the year in Chicago.

Eve had been negotiating for a new television series for some time, and had found the going rough to obtain the proper vehicle. "By the time I got there to convince

Eve Arden in 1967.

___

* One of these costarred Eve with Bobby Daren, she playing a wealthy American lady from Ohio luxuriating on the French Riviera at Port d'Or. It was televised as "Who's Watching the Fleshpot" (NBC, March 7, 1966), an episode of "Run for Your Life."

is private. She is a shy person." Eve and Ballard soon adjusted to one another, when it was acknowledged finally that, next to Arnaz, Eve was in command. Deborah Walley, who played her daughter on the show, said: "There's an air about her. If she suggests something, you'll do your damndest to do it. She's a little like a queen and I'm afraid of her and the same goes for everybody."

The format of *The Mothers-In-Law,* initially written by *I Love Lucy* alumnae Bob Carroll, Jr. and Madelyn Davis, had Eve Winston Hubbard and her lawyer husband Herbert (Herbert Rudley) living next door to Kay Buell (Ballard) and her husband Roger (Roger Carmel), a television writer. Eve's daughter, Deborah Walley, marries Ballard's son, Terry Fege, and the young couple move into the garage apartment behind their parents' home. Naturally the two mothers-in-law cannot

help themselves from meddling, causing chaos in all three homes, usually with Eve and Ballard at each others' throats, and exploiting their contrasting origins (i.e. Yankee-American versus Italian-American) to the fullest extent. Very often, the two "girls" find themselves performing song numbers—for little reason at all—with the live studio audiences always surprised that Eve can really sing and dance at all. (Ballard had proven her singing worth during years of club and recording work.)

Eve at first was uncertain of the show's success. She told Rex Reed: "I read one script and didn't think it could work. The lines weren't funny. But when we did it, I laughed until I cried. Now I can't wait to see how it comes across in that little black box."

The series, premiering Sunday evening at 8:30 P.M. on September 15, 1968, did sufficiently well to return

With Kaye Ballard in the *All Fall Down* episode of *The Mothers-In-Law* (NBC-TV, September 24, 1967).

for a second season. The only major cast change was the substitution of Richard Deacon for Roger Carmel, when the latter demanded too high a salary increase. Both Eve and Ballard sported more chic wardrobes and more attractive wigs in the second season, pushing their alleged middle-class American images to the point of ridiculousness. The half-hour color series devoted most of the twenty-three episodes of its new season to the predicaments forthcoming from Deborah Walley's pregnancy. She eventually gives birth to twins. By mid-season, the series showed tattered signs of wear and the meddlesome attitudes of Eve and Ballard soon became oppressively tiresome. Having exhausted its potential, the series was not renewed at the end of the second season. Having been in competition with the second half of the *Ed Sullivan Show* (CBS-TV) both seasons had not helped *The Mothers-In-Law* in the decisive rating games.

Eve thereafter relaxed her schedule to concentrate more fully on her family, trying to make up for the time her career had submerged that of her husband. She has said: "I saw it coming [re Brooks West taking over responsibilities for the farm and family] and I guess it was selfish of me. But there was so much to be done at the farm. Somebody had to be there." Eve also began work on a book: "Everybody is laughing at me but I will finish it. It started as a travel book dealing with our experiences in Europe. But it's become more than that. That trip (1963–1965) represented the greatest feeling of freedom I've ever had in my life. We hoped to stay a year and we stayed one-and-a-half years. I don't expect people to do the same thing, necessarily, but I would like to see them set their sights high, to know what they want, and then do it." To date, her book has not been published.

Eve, who had guested on such assorted television dramatic series as *Run For Your Life* (ABC), *Bewitched* (ABC), *Laugh-In* (ABC), *The Man From U.N.C.L.E.* (NBC) and her first video western guest starring appearance on *Laredo* (November 18, 1965, NBC), finally made her telefeature debut in ABC's *In Name Only* (November 25, 1969) which bore tremendous resemblance to Eve's 1952 feature *We're Not Married*. This time Eve played Aunt Thelma, a chic matron, who assists Michael Callen and Ann Prentiss in their matrimonial arrangement service. In actuality, she was no more than a name guest star appearing as a glamorous secretary, who had a few smart lines to drop in this generally juvenile multi-episodic show. The program also featured Paul Ford, Elsa Lanchester, Christopher Connelly and Elinor Donahue.

Eve's next professional appearance was as Mrs. Baker in the national touring company of Leonard Gershe's

With Ellen Endicott-Jones and Wendell Burton in *Butterflies Are Free* (1970).

Butterflies Are Free which had debuted on Broadway (Booth Theatre, October 29, 1969) with Eileen Heckart in the lead role and was still running in Manhattan. She was the widowed matron from Scarsdale who first disapproves of the move that her blind son (Wendell Burton) makes to an East Greenwich Village apartment. Later in the play, after several confrontation scenes, she approves of his independence and encourages him further in his resolve, finding it the best thing for his well-being. The tour opened May 21, 1970 at the Nartford Theatre, Hollywood and was staged by Milton Kalsilas. Then it moved to Chicago in June, 1970 for an extended run. The role of the overly possessive mother—a relatively short assignment compared to the juvenile leads—was not a part easily handled by any type good actress, and the critics recognized this even in their mixed reviews. ". . . She is sturdily competent as the doting and driving mother but her particular talents seem irrelevant to the role at hand, whose ambiguities nearly defeated the splendid Eileen Heckart on Broadway." (*Chicago Daily News*). ". . . From the time she walked onstage to provide the first-act curtain, [she] took over as a knowing professional. Her role . . . could be a disaster. Miss Arden somehow invests it with vitality and interest." (*Chicago Tribune*). "She is furthermore the victim of a natural warmth and comedic mannerisms when the mother must be bitchy, badgering and sulky." (*Chicago American*). Nevertheless, audiences approved and Eve had a most successful run with the show there. When the production went on the real city-to-city road tour, the producers had the surprise casting of Gloria Swanson to take over Eve's assignment. (Swanson would return to Broadway September 7, 1971 as the new star of the then-still-running New York edition. Heckart would costar with Goldie Hawn in the Columbia movie version released in 1972.)

After several months back on the ranch and travel in Europe, Eve and Brooks West were signed for a pre-Broadway tour of Lee Thuna's new comedy *Natural Ingredients* (a.k.a. Silverpate). The comedy dealt with a married couple separating just before their twenty-fifth anniversary, she to a painting spree on Majorca and he to his new car and nubile secretary. Said *Variety:* "Clearly satisfying her tv public with her quip delivery and at least a dozen living color costumes changes, Miss Arden appears to accept her vehicle for what it's worth. All things considered there's no ground for complaint." The tour concluded at the Cape Playhouse in Dennis, Massachusetts, September 4, 1971. Plans for a New York opening were cancelled.

Eve made another bid for video stardom by starring in a telefeature pilot for a projected series about an ex-schoolteacher-turned-detective. *A Very Missing Person* (ABC, March 4, 1972) presented Eve as a flamboyant amateur private eye Hildegarde Withers,* who starts her new profession by trying to find a missing heiress and winds up solving a murder case. The ninety-minute mystery had a contemporary New York City background, but the plot was old hat. Neither sensibly modern in approach nor vintage nostalgia, *A Very Missing Person* failed to generate sufficient home viewer interest to make it a likely candidate for teleseries treatment. The Universal-made program also made the mistake of allowing Eve to be her usual *Our Miss Brooks* oncamera self, thus robbing Hildegarde Withers of any potential novelty of its own.

A charming, respected member of the multi-media California entertainment industry, Eve continues to appear in video commercials (Roast and Boast), on television game shows (she displayed a keen knowledge of cinema history on ABC's *Movie Game,* and guesting on variety programs. (Ironically in her October 1972 outing on the *Dean Martin Show* she was restrained to the point of anonymity, refraining from her usual barrage of antics that have made her a perennial audience pleaser.) On stage, in May of 1973, she starred at the Off Broadway Theatre in San Diego, California in a new comedy *Under Papa's Picture,* which did good boxoffice business.

Now that her family is nearly all grown up,** Eve devotes herself to her husband, their "franch" (her and Brooks West's description of their combination farm and ranch) and her creative hobbies—that is, in between professional appearances.

Beneath her extroverted surface image, Eve is still beset by personal insecurities that have been a problem for her since childhood. (It is these "weaknesses" that make Eve a very human person, unlike her screen stereotype who drops undiluted venom without a guilt pang.) Nevertheless, Eve seems to have adjusted to her noteworthy status as a star character comedienne rather than the more desirable category of a luminary per se. "I've had my problems but I've also had so many fulfillments. So many people just don't see it that way. They forget the real joy of living." Evidently, Eve fully believes and practices her favorite motto: "Today is the first day of the rest of my life."

---

* In the mid-1930s RKO had an unheralded but popular series devoted to the adventures of Stuart Palmer's Hildegarde Withers, first played on screen by Edna May Oliver, then by Helen Broderick.

**Liza was married in Spain in the spring of 1971 and recently gave birth to a daughter. Connie is a performing member of the New Shakespeare Company in San Francisco; Duncan enlisted in the Army, intending to be a career soldier, and recently wed; 6'4" Douglas has completed high school.

Filmography: EVE ARDEN
Feature Films

AS: Eunice Quedens

THE SONG OF LOVE (Columbia, 1929) 76 M.
Producer, Edward Small; director, Erle C. Kenton; supervisors, Harry Cohn, Howard Grey, Henry McCarthy; story, Howard Green, McCarthy; screenplay, Green, Dorothy Howell, Norman Houston; songs, Mack Gordon and Max Rich; Gordon, Rich and George Weist; Gordon, Rich and Maurice Abrahams; Bernie Grossman; camera, Joseph Walker; editor, Gene Havlick; assistant director, Sam Nelson.
Belle Baker (Anna Gibson); Ralph Graves (Tom Gibson); David Durand (Buddy Gibson); Eunice Quedens (Mazie); Arthur Housman (Acrobat); Charles Wilson (Traveling Salesman).

DANCING LADY (MGM, 1933) 94 M.
Executive producer, David O. Selznick; associate producer, John W. Considine, Jr.; director, Robert Z. Leonard; based on the novel by James Warner Bellah; screenplay, Allen Rivkin, P.J. Wolfson; music director, Lou Silvers; choreography, Sammy Lee, Eddie Prinz; songs, Burton Lane and Harold Adamson; Richard Rodgers and Lorenz Hart; Jimmy McHugh and Dorothy Fields; camera, Oliver T. Marsh; costumes, Adrian; special effects, Slavko Vorkapich; editor, Margaret Booth.
Joan Crawford (Janie Barlow); Clark Gable (Patch Gallagher); Franchot Tone (Tod Newton); Fred Astaire (Himself); Nelson Eddy (Himself); May Robson (Dolly Todhunter); Winnie Lightner (Rosette Henrietta La Rue); Robert Benchley (Ward King); Ted Healy (Steve); Moe Howard, Jerry Howard, Larry Fine (The Three Stooges); Gloria Foy (Vivian Warner); Art Jarrett (Art); Grant Mitchell (Jasper Bradley, Sr.); Maynard Holmes (Jasper Bradley, Jr.); Sterling Holloway (Pinky, the Author); Florine McKinney (Grace Newton); Bonita Barker, Dalie Dean, Shirley Aranson, Katharine Barnes, Lynn Bari (Chorus Girls); Jack Baxley (Barker); Frank Hagney (Cop); Pat Somerset (Tod's Friend); Charlie Williams (Arrested In Burlesque House); Ferdinand Gottschalk (Judge); Eunice Quedens (Marcia); Matt McHugh (Marcia's Agent); Charlie Sullivan (Cabby); Harry C. Bradley, John Sheehan (Author's Pals); Stanley Blystone (Traffic Cop); Charles C. Wilson (Club Manager); Bill Elliott (Cafe Extra); Larry Steers, C. Montague Shaw (First Nighters).

AS: EVE ARDEN
OH, DOCTOR! (Universal, 1937) 67 M.
Associate producer, Edmund Grainger; director, Ray McCarey; based on a play by Harry Leon Wilson; screenplay, Harry Clark, Brown Holmes; art director, Jack Otterson; music director, Lou Forbes; special effects, John P. Fulton; camera, Milton Krasner; editor, Bernard W. Burton.
Edward Everett Horton (Ned); Edward Brophy (Meg); Donvale Leighton (Helen); Eve Arden (Shirley Truman); William Hall (Rodney); Catherine Doucet (Martha); William Demarest (Marty); Thurston Hall (Doc); Minerva Urecal (Death Watch Mary); Wilson Benge (Butler); James Donlan (Mr. Stoddard); Kitty McHugh (Nurse); Cornelius Keefe (Ship's Officer); Ben Taggart (Policeman); Edward Le Saint (Dr. Evans); Lloyd Ingraham (Dr. Bower); Henry Roquemore (Auto Salesman); Frank B. Hammond (Patient); Carol Halloway (Woman); Heinie Conklin, Charley Sullivan (Men).

STAGE DOOR (RKO, 1937) 92 M.
Producer, Pandro S. Berman; director, Gregory La Cava; based on the play by Edna Ferber, George S. Kaufman; screenplay, Morrie Ryskind, Anthony Veiller; art director, Van Nest Polglase, Carroll Clark; music, Roy Webb; assistant director, James Anderson; makeup, Mel Burn; costumes, Muriel King; camera, Robert De Grasse; editor, William Hamilton.
Katharine Hepburn (Terry Randall); Ginger Rogers (Jean Maitland); Adolphe Menjou (Anthony Powell); Gail Patrick (Linda Shaw); Constance Collier (Catherine Luther); Andrea Leeds (Kaye Hamilton); Samuel S. Hinds (Henry Sims); Lucille Ball (Judy Canfield); Pierre Watkin (Richard Carmichael); Franklin Pangborn (Harcourt); Elizabeth Dunne (Mrs. Orcutt); Phyllis Kennedy (Hattie); Grady Sutton (Butcher); Jack Carson (Milbank); Fred Santley (Dukenfield); William Corson (Bill); Frank Reicher (Stage Director); Eve Arden (Eve); Ann Miller (Annie); Jane Rhodes (Ann Braddock); Margaret Early (Mary); Jean Rouverol (Dizzy); Norma Drury (Olga Brent); Peggy O'Donnell (Susan); Harriet Brandon (Madeline); Katherine Alexander, Ralph Forbes, Mary Forbes, Huntley Gordon (Players In Play); Lynton Brent (Aide); Theodore Von Eltz (Elsworth); Frances Gifford (Aspiring Actress).

COCOANUT GROVE (Paramount, 1938) 85 M.
Producer, George Arthur; director, Alfred Santell; story-screenplay, Sy Bartlett, Olive Cooper; songs, Ralph Freed and Frederick Hollander; Frank Loesser and Burton Lane; Harry Owens; "Jock". Loesser and Lane; Alfred Santell and Lane; Bert Kalmer and Yacht Club Boys; Yacht Club Boys; camera, Leo Tover; editor, Hugh Bennett.
Fred MacMurray (Johnny Prentice); Harriet Hilliard (Linda Rogers); The Yacht Club Boys (Themselves); Ben Blue (Joe De Lemma); Eve Arden (Sophie De Lemma); Billy Lee ("Half-Pint"); Rufe Davis (Bibb Tucker); Harry Owens (Hula Harry); Dorothy Howe (later Virginia Vale) (Hazel De Vore); George Walcott (Tony Wonder); Red Stanley ("Dixie"); Roy Gordon (Robert Grayson); Charles Lane (Weaver); Jimmy Conlin (Motel Proprietor); Paul Newlan (Tourist in Trailer Camp); Dorothy Dayton (Dancing Coach); Frances Morris (Receptionist); Max Wagner (Brakeman); Archie Twitchell, Phillip Warren (Radio Station Technicians); Jack Hubbard (Radio Station Attendant); Ellen Drew (Radio Station Receptionist); Cliff Clark (Auctioneer); Ronnie Rondell (Headwaiter); Stanley Andrews (Truant Officer); Jack Gardner (Father); Larry Harris (Boy with Father); Dix Davis (Boy Who Fights "Half-Pint"); Dolores Casey (Check Girl); William Davidson (Hewtrey); Murray Alper (Concessionaire); Egon Brecher (Pawnbroker); Jack Pennick (Bus Driver); Gloria Williams, Ethel Clayton (Women); Louise Seidel, Helaine Molar, Sheila Darcy, Cheryl Walker, Carol Parker, Gwen Kenyon, Lola Jensen, Nora Gale, Yvonne Duval, Barbara Jackson, Joyce Matthews, Ruth Rogers (Girls).

LETTER OF INTRODUCTION (Universal, 1938) 100 M.
Producer-director, John M. Stahl; story, Bernice Boone; screenplay, Sheridan Gibney, Leonard Spigelgass; camera, Karl Freund; editor, Ted Kent.
Adolphe Menjou (John Mannering); Edgar Bergen and Charlie McCarthy (Themselves); Andrea Leeds (Kay Martin); George Murphy (Barry Paige); Eve Arden (Cora); Rita Johnson (Honey); Ernest Cossart (Andrews); Ann Sheridan (Lydia); Jonathan Hale (Woodstock); Frank Jenks (Joe); Walter Perry (Backstage Doorman); Frances Robinson (Hat Check Girl); Constance Moore (Autograph Seeker); Eleanor Hansen (Stagestruck Girl); Raymond Parker (Call Boy); May Boley (Mrs. Meggs); Armand Kaliz (Jules, the Barber); Russell Hopton (Proc-

ess Server); Stanley Hughes (Kibitzer); William B. Davidson (Mr. Raleigh); Kathleen Howard (Aunt Jonnie); Esther Ralston (Mrs. Sinclair); Irving Bacon, Ray Walker (Reporters); Leonard Mudie (Critic); Doris Lloyd (Charlotte); Frank Reicher (Doctor); Morgan Wallace (Editor); Inez Courtney (Woman At Party); Richard Tucker (Gossip); George Humbert (Musician on Stage); Frank Reicher, Theodor Von Eltz, Chester Clute (Doctors); Natalie Moorhead (Mrs. Raleigh); Craufurd Kent (Mr. Sinclair); Bill Elliot (Backgammon Man); Sam Hayes (Announcer); Wade Boteler (Policeman); Donald Barry, Philip Trent (Men at Party); Dick Winslow (Elevator Boy); Rolfe Sedan (Fitter); Alphonse Martell (Maitre d'Hotel); Sharon Lewis (Bridge Player); Edith Craig, Kitty McHugh (Girl Singers); Claire Whitney (Nurse); Sandy Sanford (Fireman); John Archer, Allen Fox (photographers); Charlie Sherlock, Don Brodie (Reporters); Kane Richmond (Man); Dorothy Granger (Woman at Party).

HAVING WONDERFUL TIME (RKO, 1938) 70 M.

Producer, Pandro S. Berman; director, Alfred Santell; based on the play by Arthur Kober; screenplay, Kober; music director, Roy Webb; songs, Sam Stept and Charles Tobias and Bill Livingston; camera, Robert de Grasse; editor, William Hamilton.

Ginger Rogers (Teddy); Douglas Fairbanks, Jr. (Chick); Peggy Conklin (Fay); Lucille Ball (Miriam); Lee Bowman (Buzzy); Eve Arden (Henrietta); Dorothea Kent (Maxine); Richard "Red" Skelton (Itchy); Donald Mee (U.P. Rogers); Jack Carson (Emil Beatty); Clarence H. Wilson (Mr. G.); Allan Lane (Mac); Grady Sutton (Gus); Shimen Ruskin (Shrimpo); Dorothy Tree (Frances); Leona Roberts (Mrs. Shaw); Harlan Briggs (Mr. Shaw); Inez Courtney (Emma); Juanita Quigley (Mabel); Ann Miller (Vivian); Kirk Windsor (Henry); Ronnie Rondel, Hooper Atchley (Subway Riders); Dean Jagger (Charlie); George Meeker (Fresh Subway Rider); Steve Pendleton (Waiter).

WOMEN IN THE WIND (Warner Brothers, 1939) 63 M.

Producer, Mark Hellinger; associate producer, Bryan Foy; director John Farrow; based on the novel by Francis Walton; screenplay, Lee Katz, Albert De Mond; assistant director, Marshall Hageman; camera, Sid Hickox; editor, Thomas Pratt.

Kay Francis (Janet Steele); William Gargan (Ace Boreman); Victor Jory (Doc); Maxie Rosenbloom (Stuffy McInnes); Sheila Bromley (Frieda Boreman); Eve Arden (Kit Campbell); Eddie Foy (Denny Carson); Charles Anthony Hughes (Bill Steele); Frankie Burke (Johnnie); John Dilson (Sloan); Spencer Charters (Farmer); Vera Lewis (Farmer's Wife); William Gould (Palmer); Gordon Hart (Chairman at Air Races); Ila Rhodes (Joan); Roselie Towne (Phyllis); Sally Sag, Alice Connors, Marian Alden, Iris Gabrielle, Diana Hughes (Aviatrixes); John Harron (Process Server); John Ridgely, Mat Carr, Richard Bond, Jack Mower, Frank Mayo (Salesmen); Lucille Denever, Marie Astaire (Women); Steven Darrell, David Kerman (Photographers); Eddie Graham (Microphone Man); Milton Kibbee (Bartender); Wilfred Lucas (Official); Frank Faylen (Mechanic); Emmett Vogan (Radio Announcer); George O'Hanlon (Bellboy).

BIG TOWN CZAR (Universal, 1939) 61 M.

Producer, Ken Goldsmith; director, Arthur Lubin; story, Ed Sullivan; screenplay, Edmund L. Hartmann; assistant director, Vaughan Paul; songs, Frank Skinner; camera, Ellwood Bredell; editor, Phillip Cahn.

Barton MacLane (Phil Daley); Tom Brown (Danny Daley); Eve Arden (Susan Warren); Ed Sullivan (Himself); Frank Jenks (Sid Travers); Jack LaRue (Mike Luger); Jerry Marlowe (Nick); Walter Woolf King (Burgess); Esther Dale (Ma Daley); Oscar O'Shea (Pa Daley); Gordon Jones (Chuck Hardy); Irving Bacon (Real Estate Man); Frances Robinson (Florist Clerk); Raymond Parker (Student); Oscar Polk (Arthur); Horace MacMahon (Punchy); James Flavin (Mitchell); Clyde Dilson (Morgan); Charles R. Moore (Ray); Walter Young (Lawyer); John Sheehan (Ray Norman); Cully Richards (Herman); Tom Rutherfurd (Red); Carleton Young (Thompson); Roy Mason, Don Rowan (Strangers); Alan Davis (Barnard); Buster Phelps (Boy); Frank Melton (Hotel Clerk); Martin Turner (Mickey); Jimmie Lucas (Stooge); Heinie Conklin (Tenant); Jenifer Gray (Telephone Operator); Miki Morita (Butler).

THE FORGOTTEN WOMAN (Universal, 1939) 68 M.

Associate producer, Edmund Grainger; director, Harold Young; story, John Kobler; screenplay, Lionel Houser, Harold Bucman; art director, Jack Otterson; music director, Charles Previn; camera, Stanley Cortez; editor, Charles Maynard.

Sigrid Gurie (Anne); Donald Briggs (David Burke); Eve Arden (Carrie); William Lundigan (Terry); Paul Harvey (Courtney); Donnie Dunagan (Terry, Jr.); Elizabeth Risdon (Margaret); Charles Wilson (Gray); John Hamilton (Dr. May); Ray Walker (Marty); George Humbert (Proprietor); Selmer Jackson (Man); Joe Downing (Stu); Alan Edwards (Banker); Grace Hayle (Fat Woman in Beauty Shop); Norman Willis (Bradshaw); Virginia Brissac (Mrs. Kimball); Claire DuBrey (Foxie); Louise Lorimer, Pauline Haddon (Women); Betty Roadman, Frances Morris (Matrons); Sam McDaniel (Porter); Mariska Aldrich (Homely Woman); Charles Sherlock, William Thorne, Charles McMurphy (Policemen); Bess Flowers (Beauty Shop Operator); Claire Whitney (Woman Reporter); Jack Gardner, Ben Lewis (Reporters); William Worthington, Larry Steers (Doctors).

ETERNALLY YOURS (United Artists, 1939) 95 M.

Producer, Walter Wanger; director, Tay Garnett; story, Gene Towne, Graham Baker; screenplay, John Meehan; art director, Alexander Golitzen; music, Werner Janssen; song, I. Wolfe Gilbert and Jannsen; assistant director, Charles Kerr; camera, Merritt Gerstad; editor, Otho Lovering.

Loretta Young (Anita Halstead); David Niven (Tony Halstead); Hugh Herbert (Benton); Billie Burke (Aunt Abbey); C. Aubrey Smith (Bishop Hubert Peabody); Raymond Walburn (Harley Bingham); Zasu Pitts (Carrie Bingham); Broderick Crawford (Don Barnes); Virginia Field (Lola De Vere); Eve Arden (Gloria); Ralph Graves (Mr. Morrissey); Lionel Pape (Mr. Howard); Walter Sande (Ralph); Leyland Hodgson (Captain Vickers); Fred Keating (Master of Ceremonies); The Kettering Triplets (Gloria's Baby); Eleanor Stewart, Evelyn Woodbury, Patricia Stillman, Doreen McKay, Luana Walters, (Girls at Shower); Hillary Brooke (Blonde on Stage); Dennie Moore (Waitress); Mary Field (Maid); John Rice, Claude Payton (Scotland Yard Men in Plane); Larry Harris, Dickie Jackson (Boy Boxers); Edwin Stanley (Lawyer); Franklin Parker (Croupier); Billy Wayne (Stage Manager); Jack Greene, Dick Allen (Detectives); Jack Perrin, Broderick O'Farrell (Ship's Officers); Granville Bates (Ship's Captain); Tay Garnett (Pilot); Walter James (Police Official); Frank Jaquet (Doctor); Paul Le Paul (Butler); Ralph Norwood (Headwaiter); May Beatty (Gabby Dowager); Douglas Wood (Phillips); Al Hill (Heckler).

AT THE CIRCUS (MGM, 1939) 87 M.

Producer, Mervyn LeRoy; director, Edward Buzzell; screenplay, Irving Brecher; art director, Cedric Gibbons, Stan Rogers; sound, Douglas Shearer; songs, Harold Arlen and E.Y. Harburg; music director, Franz Waxman; camera, Leonard M. Smith; editor, William H. Terhune.

Groucho Marx (Attorney J. Cheever Loophole); Chico Marx (Antonio Pirelli); Harpo Marx (Punchy); Florence Rice (Julie Randall); Kenny Baker (Jeff Wilson); Nat Pendleton (Goliath); Margaret Dumont (Mrs. Dukesbury); Eve Arden (Peerless Pauline); Fritz Feld (Jardinet); Barnett Parker (Whitcomb); Jerry Merenghi (Little Professor Atom); Charles Gemora (Gibraltar); Granville Bates (Judge); Irving Bacon (Telephone Operator); John Dilson (Defense Attorney); Herbert Ashley (Detective Bludge); Irene Colman (Girl on Stand in Courtroom); James Burke (John Carter); Emory Parnell (Ringmaster); Barlowe Borland (Thorndyke); Henry Sylvester (Court Clerk); Frank Orth (Waiter); Willie Best (Redcap); Forbes Murray (Captain); Harry Hayden (Conductor); Murdock MacQuarrie (Attendant); Sidney Miller, Mickey Daniels, George Bockasts, Eugene Jackson (Quartet); Byron Foulger (Meek Defendant); Mariska Aldrich (Mannish Woman); Matt McHugh (Taxi Driver); Buck Mack (Checker Player); Paul Berne (Vaudeville Entertainer); Amanda Randolph (Singer); John Binns (Old Man); Frank Darien (Telegrapher).

A CHILD IS BORN (Warner Brothers, 1940) 79 M.

Producer, Jack L. Warner, Hal B. Wallis; associate producer, Sam Bischoff; director, Lloyd Bacon; based on the play *Life Begins* by Mary McDougal Axelson; screenplay, Robert Rossen; camera, Charles Rosher; editor, Jack Killifer.

Geraldine Fitzgerald (Grace Sutton); Jeffrey Lynn (Jed Sutton); Gladys George (Florette); Gale Page (Miss Bowers); Johnny Davis (Ringer Banks); Spring Byington (Mrs. West); Henry O'Neill (Dr. Lee); John Litel (Dr. Bratt); Eve Arden (Miss Pinty); Gloria Holden (Mrs. Kempner); Johnny Downs (Johnny Norton); Fay Helm (The Woman); Louis Jean Heydt (Mr. Kempner); Nanette Fabares (Gladys Norton); Hobart Cavanaugh (Mr. West); Jean Sharon (Mrs. Banks); George Irving (Dr. Cramm); Esther Dale (Matron); Ed Gargan (Guard); Edgar Dearing (Sergeant); Marie Blake (Gladys); Maris Wrixon (Information Girl); Sibyl Harris (Flower Woman); Creighton Hale (Elevator Operator); Buzz Buckley (Little Tot); George O'Hanlon (Young Husband); John Ridgely (William Hopper); Owen King, Charles Marsh, Carlyle Moore, Jr. (Internes); Garry Owen, Sidney Bracy (Drugstore Clerks); Frank Mayo (Policeman); Winifred Harris (Mrs. Holt); Nella Walker (Mrs. Twitchell); Marie Wells, Dorothy Adams, Frances Morris (Nurses); Georgia Caine (Mrs. Norton's Mother); Virginia Brissac (Mr. Norton's Mother).

SLIGHTLY HONORABLE (United Artists, 1940) 85 M.

Producer-director, Tay Garnett; based on the novel *Send Another Coffin* by F. G. Presnell; screenplay, John Hunter Lay, Robert Tallman, Ken Englund; art director, Alexander Golitzen; music, Werner Janssen; song, George R. Brown and Jule Styne; camera, Merritt Gerstad; editor, Otho Lovering.

Pat O'Brien (John Webb); Broderick Crawford (Russell Sampson); Edward Arnold (Vincent Cushing); Ruth Terry (Ann Seymour); Bernard Nedell (Pete Godena); Alan Dinehart (D.A. Joyce); Claire Dodd (Alma Brehmer); Douglass Dumbrille (George Taylor); John Sheehan (Mike Daley); Addison Richards (Inspector Melvyn Fromm); Cliff Clark (Captain Graves); Eve Arden (Miss Atar);

Phyllis Brooks (Sarilla Cushing); Ernest Truex (P. Hemingway Collins); Douglas Fowley (Charles Madder); Janet Beecher (Mrs. Cushing); Evelyn Keyes (Miss Vlissenger); Willie Best (Elevator Operator); Eddie Chandler, Bud Jamison (Cops); Robert Middlemass (Senator Barry); Frank Dee (President of Senate); George Magrill, Tay Garnett (Reporters); Art Baker (Radio Announcer); Charles K. French (Pallbearer); Howard Hickman (Senator Sam Scott); Irving Wickes (Photographer); Irene Colman (Curvy Brunette); Muriel Barr (Girl on Couch); Al Hill (Bartender); Marjorie "Babe" Kane (Switchboard Operator); Jack Greene, Dick Rush (Detectives); Bernard Matis, Gerald Pierce (Delivery Boys); Richard Keene (Fingerprint Man); Al Hill, Jr. (Newsboy); Zack Williams (Black Preacher); Wheaton Chambers (Guest); Jack Baxley (Detective With Godena).

COMRADE X (MGM, 1940) 90 M.

Producer, Gottfried Reinhardt; director, King Vidor; story, Walter Reisch; screenplay, Ben Hecht, Charles Lederer; special effects, Arnold Gillespie; camera, Joseph Ruttenberg; editor, Harold F. Kress.

Clark Gable (McKinley B. Thompson); Hedy Lamarr (Theodora); Oscar Homolka (Vasiliev); Felix Bressart (Vanya); Eve Arden (Jane Wilson); Sig Rumann (Emil von Hofer); Natasha Lytess (Olga); Vladimir Sokoloff (Michael Bastakoff); Edgar Barrier (Rubick); John Piccori (Laszlo).

NO, NO NANETTE (RKO, 1940) 96 M.

Producer-director, Herbert Wilcox; based on the play by Frank Mandel, Otto Harbach, Vincent Youmans, Emil Nyetray; screenplay, Ken Englund; songs, Youmans, Irving Caesar, and Harbach; music director, Anthony Collins; camera, Russell Metty; editor, Allen Williams.

Anna Neagle (Nanette); Richard Carlson (Tom); Victor Mature (William); Roland Young (Mr. Smith); Helen Broderick (Mrs. Smith); ZaSu Pitts (Pauline); Eve Arden (Winnie); Tamara (Sonya); Billy Gilbert (Styles); Stuart Robertson (Stillwater, Jr./Stillwater, Sr.); Dorothea Kent (Betty); Aubrey Mather (Betty); Mary Gordon (Gertrude); Russell Hicks (Hutch); Benny Rubin (Max); Margaret Armstrong (Dowager); George Nelson (Messenger Boy); Lester Dorr (Travel Agent); John Dilson, Joey Ray, Cyril Ring (Desk Clerks); Torben Meyer (Furtlemertle); Sally Payne (Maid); Rosella Towne (Stewardess); Victor Wong (Houseboy); Bud Geary (Taxi Driver); Chris Franke (Hansom Driver); Keye Luke, Ronnie Rondell (Men); Muriel Barr, Marion Graham, Georgianna Young (Show Girls); Frank Puglia, Paul Irving, Maurice Cass (Art Critics); Julius Tannen (Passenger on Ship); Minerva Urecal (Woman at Airport); Mary Currier, Jean Fenwick, Joan Blair, Dora Clemant (Women at Smith Home).

ZIEGFELD GIRL (MGM, 1941) 131 M.

Producer, Pandro S. Berman; director, Robert Z. Leonard; story, William Anthony McGuire; screenplay, Marguerite Roberts, Sonya Levien; music, Herbert Stothart; music director, Georgie Stoll; art director, Cedric Gibbons, Daniel B. Cathcart; songs, Gush Kahn and Nacio Herb Brown; Edward Gallagher and Al Shean; Joseph McCarthy and Harry Carroll; Ralph Freed and Roger Edens; Walter Donaldson; Harold Adamson and Donaldson; camera, Ray June; editor, Blanche Sewell.

James Stewart (Gilbert Young); Judy Garland (Susan Gallagher); Hedy Lamarr (Sandra Kolter); Lana Turner (Sheila Regan); Tony Martin (Frank Merton); Jackie Cooper (Jerry Regan); Ian Hunter (Geoffrey Collins); Charles Winninger (Pop Gallagher); Edward Everett Horton (Noble Sage); Philip Dorn (Franz Kolter); Paul Kelly (John Slayton); Eve Arden (Patsy Dixon); Dan Dailey, Jr. (Jimmy Walters); Al Shean (Al); Fay Holden (Mrs. Regan); Felix Bressart (Mischa); Rose Hobart (Mrs. Merton); Bernard Nedell (Nick Capalini); Ed McNamara (Mr. Regan); Renie Riano (Annie); Mae Busch (Jenny); Josephine Whittell (Perkins); Sergio Orta (Native Dancer); Jean Wallace, Myrna Dell, Leslie Brooks, Georgia Carroll, Louise La Planche, Nina Bissell, Virginia Cruzon, Alaine Brandes, Frances Gladwin, Patricia Dane, Irma Wilson, Anya Tarana, Madeline Martin, Vivien Mason (Ziegfeld Girls).

THAT UNCERTAIN FEELING (United Artists, 1941) 89 M.

Producer-director, Ernst Lubitsch; based on the play *Divorcons* by Victorien Sardou; adaptation, Walter Reisch; screenplay, Donald Ogden Stewart; camera, George Barnes; editor, William Shea.

Merle Oberon (Jill Baker); Melvyn Douglas (Larry Baker); Burgess Meredith (Sebastian); Alan Mowbray (Dr. Vengard); Olive Blakeney (Margie Stallings); Harry Davenport (Attorney Jones); Eve Arden (Sally); Sig Rumann (Mr. Kofka); Richard Carle (Butler); Jean Fenwick (Nurse); Mary Currier (Maid).

SHE COULDN'T SAY NO (Warner Brothers, 1941) 63 M.

Associate producer, William Jacobs; director, William Clemens; based on the play by Benjamin M. Kays; screenplay, Earl Baldwin; Charles Grayson; camera, Ted McCord; editor, Harold McLeron.

Eve Arden (Alice Hinsdale); Roger Pryor (Wallace Turnbull); Cliff Edwards (Banjo Page); Clem Bevans (Eli Potter); Spencer Charters (Hank Woodcock); Ferris Taylor (Judge Josiah Jenkins); Vera Lewis (Pansy Hawkins); Irving Bacon (Abner); Chester Clute (Ezra Pine); George Irving (Henry Rockwell); Zeffie Tilbury (Ma Hawkins); George Guhl (Barber); Frank Mayo (Town Marshal); Ann Edmonds (Rockwell's Secretary); Drew Roddy, Sonny Bupp (Boys); Creighton Hale (Jasper); Al Lloyd (Man); Inez Gay (Mathilda); Jessie Perry, Jean Maddox, Paulette Evans, Alexis Smith (Gossips); Leo White, Paul Panzer, Glen Cavender (Jurors).

SHE KNEW ALL THE ANSWERS (Columbia, 1941) 84 M.

Producer, Charles R. Rogers; director, Richard Wallace; based on the story *A Girl's Best Friend Is Wall Street* by Jane Allen; screenplay, Harry Segall, Kenneth Earl, Curtis Kenyon; assistant director, Norman Deming; camera, Henry Freulich; editor, Gene Havlick.

Joan Bennett (Gloria Winters); Franchot Tone (Mark Willows); John Hubbard (Randy Bradford); Eve Arden (Sally Long); William Tracy (Benny); Pierre Watkin (George Wharton); Almira Sessions (Elaine Wingate); Thurston Hall (J.D. Sutton); Grady Sutton (Ogleby); Luis Alberni (Inventor); Francis Compton (Tompkins); Dick Elliott, Selmer Jackson (Brokers); Roscoe Ates (Gas Station Attendant); Chester Clute (Butter and Egg Man); Frank Sully (Cop); Ed Conrad (Waiter); Patti McCarty (Hatcheck Girl); William Benedict (Singing Telegraph Boy); Fern Emmett (Woman Applicant); Pauline Starke (Prim Woman); Don Beddoe (Barber); Patricia Hill (Manicurist); Onest Conley (Shine Boy); George Hickman (Elevator Operator); Byron Foulger (Man); Alice Keating (Telephone Operator); George Beranger (Head Waiter); Tom Metletti (Milkman); Edward Earle (Harassed Man).

SAN ANTONIO ROSE (Universal, 1941) 64 M.

Producer, Ken Goldsmith; director, Charles Lamont; story, Jack Lait, Jr.; screenplay, Hugh Wedlock, Jr., Howard Snyder, Paul Gerald Smith; choreographer, Nick Castle; songs, Jack Brooks and Norman Berens; Don Raye and Gene DePaul; Leo Killion, Ted McMichael and Jack Owens; Bob Wills; Henry Russell, Don Raye, and Hughie Prince; Frank Skinner; camera, Stanley Cortez; editor, Milton Carruth.

Robert Paige (Con Conway); Jane Frazee (Hope Holloway); Eve Arden (Gabby Trent); Lon Chaney, Jr. (Jigsaw Kennedy); Shemp Howard (Benny the Bounce); Mary Lou Cook (Mona Mitchell); Joe McMichael (Harry); Ted McMichael (Ted); Judd McMichael (Phil); Richard Lane (Willoughby); Elaine Condos (Elaine); Louis DaPron (Alex); Charles Lang (Ralph); Roy Harris (Jimmy); Peter Sullivan (Don); Richard Davies (Eddie); Beatrice Roberts (Woman); Luis Alberni (Nick Ferris); Tim Ryan (Gus); Charles Irwin (Radio Announcer); Hal K. Dawson (Farnsworth); Billy Newell (Headwaiter); Rolfe Sedan (Henry); Ferris Taylor (Keller); Jason Robards, Sr. (Radio Station Man); Cyril Ring (Man at Bar); Major Sam Harris (Fitzgerald); Charles McAvoy (Bartender).

SING FOR YOUR SUPPER (Columbia, 1941) 65 M.

Producer, Leon Barsha; director, Charles Barton; story-screenplay, Harry Rebuas; assistant director, Leon Barsha; music director, Morris Stoloff; art director, Lionel Banks; songs, Sammy Cahn and Saul Chaplin; camera, Franz F. Planer; editor, Arthur Seld.

Jinx Falkenburg (Evelyn); Buddy Rogers, Larry); Bert Gordon (Russian); Eve Arden (Barbara); Don Beddoe (Wing); Bernadene Hayes (Kay); Henry Kolker (Hayworth); Benny Baker (William); Dewey Robinson (Bonzo); Luise Squire (Mildred); Larry Parks (Mickey); Lloyd Bridges (Doc); Harry Barris (Jimmy); Walter Sande (Irv); Berni Gould (Art); Red Stanley, Perc Launders, Harry Lang (Musicians); Don Porter (Tim); Virginia Pherrin (Helen); Jessie May Jackson (Mary); Dona Dax (Dorothy); Patricia Knox (Sue); Sig Arno (Raskalnifoff); Eve Carlton, Franchon Estes, Valeri Gratton, Betty Brooks, Dorothy Trail (Hostesses); Earle Hodgins (Yokel); Judith Linden (Ticket Girl); Ed Bruce (Jerk); Glenn Turnbull (Gawky Fellow); Dink Freeman (Seaman); Earl Bunn (Counter Man); Mildred Gover (Nancy).

MANPOWER (Warner Brothers, 1941) 105 M.

Executive producer, Hal B. Wallis; producer, Mark Hellinger; director, Raoul Walsh; screenplay, Richard Macaulay, Jerry Wald; music, Adolph Deutsch; songs, Frederick Hollander and Frank Loesser; art director, Max Parker; special effects, Byron Haskin, H.F. Koenekamp; camera, Ernest Haller; editor, Ralph Dawson.

Edward G. Robinson (Hank McHenry); Marlene Dietrich (Fay Duval); George Raft (Johnny Marshall); Alan Hale (Jumbo Wells); Frank McHugh (Omaha); Eve Arden (Dolly); Barton MacLane (Smiley Quinn); Walter Catlett (Sidney Whipple); Joyce Compton (Scarlett); Lucia Carroll (Flo); Ward Bond (Eddie Adams); Egon Brecher (Pop Duval); Cliff Clark (Cully); Joseph Crehan (Sweeney); Ben Weldon (Al Hurst); Carl Harbaugh (Noisy Nash); Barbara Land (Marilyn); Barbara Pepper (Polly); Dorothy Appleby (Wilma); Roland Drew, Eddie Fetherston, Charles Sherlock, Jeffrey Sayre, De Wolfe Hopper, Al Herman (Men); Ralph Dunn (Man at Phone); Harry Strang (Foreman); Nat Carr (Waiter); Isabel Withers (Floor Nurse); Joan Winfield, Faye Emerson (Nurses); James Flavin (Orderly); Chester Clute (Clerk); Dorothy Vaughan (Mrs. Boyle); Billy Wayne (Taxi Driver); Nella Walker (Floorlady); Brenda Fowler (Saleslady); Joyce Bryant (Miss Brewster); Gayle Mollott, Muriel Barr (Models); Joe Devlin (Bartender); Pat McKee (Bouncer);

Georgia Caine (Head Nurse); Beal Wong (Chinese Singer); Harry Holman (Justice of the Peace); Murray Alper, Charles Sullivan, Fred Graham, Elliott Sullivan, William Newell, Dick Wessel (Linemen); Eddy Chandler, Lee Phelps (Detectives).

WHISTLING IN THE DARK (MGM, 1941) 76 M.

Producer, George Haight; director, S. Sylvan Simon; based on the play by Laurence Gross, Edward Childs Carpenter; screenplay, Robert MacGunigle, Harry Clork, Albert Mannheimer; camera, Sidney Wagner; editor, Frank E. Hull.

Red Skelton (Wally Benton); Ann Rutherford (Carol Lambert); Virginia Grey (Fran Post); Conrad Veidt (Joseph Jones); Rags Ragland (Sylvester); Eve Arden (Buzz Baker); Don Douglas (Gordon Thomas); Don Costello (Moose Green); Paul Stanton (Jennings); William Tannen (Robert Graves); Reed Hadley (Beau Smith); Lloyd Corrigan (Harvey Upshaw); Henry O'Neill (Phillip Post); George Carleton (Deputy Commissioner O'Neill); Mariska Aldrich (Hilda); Will Lee (Herman); John Picorri (Gatekeeper); Joe Devlin (Taxi Driver); Ruth Robinson (Mrs. Robinson); John Wald (Announcer's Voice); Ken Christy (Inspector); Betty Farrington (Mrs. Moriarity); Paul Ellis (Captain); Dora Clement (Mrs. Upshaw); James Adamson (Attendant); Inez Cooper (Stewardess); Emmett Vogan (Producer); Barbara Bedford (Local Operator); Lester Dorr (Dispatcher) Mark Daniels (Co-Pilot); Leon Tyler (Gerry); Mel Ruick (Engineer); Dorothy Adams (Mrs. Farrell); Jenny Mac (Mrs. Kendall); John Dilson (Vanderhoff); Billy Bletcher (Effects Man); Larry Steers (Studio Manager); Ronnie Rondell (Waiter); Brick Sullivan, Al Hill, Robert Homans (Policemen).

THE LAST OF THE DUANES (20th Century-Fox, 1941) 57 M.

Producer Sol M. Wurtzel; director, James Tinling; based on the novel by Zane Grey; screenplay, Irving Cummings, Jr., William Conselman, Jr.; camera, Charles Clarke; editor, Nick DeMaggio.

George Montgomery (Buck Duane); Lynne , Roberts (Nancy); Eve Arden (Kate); Francis Ford (Luke Stevens); George E. Stone (Euchre); William Farnum (Major McNeil); Joseph Sawyer (Bull Lessomer); Truman Bradley (Captain Laramie); Russell Simpson (Tom Duane); Don Costello (Jim Bland); Harry Woods (Morgan); Andrew Tombes (Sheriff); William Pagan, LeRoy Mason, Lane Chandler, Ethan Laidlaw (Bland's Gang); Paul Sutton (Tired Man); Lew Kelly (Old Timer); Jack Stoney, Tom Moray, Syd Saylor (Men); Arthur Aylsworth (Older Man); Ann Carter (Cannon's Child); J. Anthony Hughes (Cannon); Paul Burns (Horseshoe Player); Erville Alderson (Zeke); Harry Hayden (Banker); Tom London (Deputy); Tim Ryan (Bartender); Walter McGrail, Russ Clark (Ranger Guards).

OBLIGING YOUNG LADY (RKO, 1941) 80 M.

Producer, Howard Benedict; director, Richard Wallace; story, Arthur T. Harmon; screenplay, Frank Ryan, Bert Granet; camera, Michael Musuraca; editor, Henry Berman.

Joan Carroll (Bridget); Edmond O'Brien (Red Reddy); Ruth Warrick (Linda Norton); Eve Arden (Space O'Shea); Robert Smith (Charles Baker); Franklin Pangborn (Professor Gibney); Marjorie Gateson (Mira Potter); John Miljan (George Potter); George Cleveland (Hotel Manager); Luis Alberni (Riccardi); Charles Lane (Detective); Fortunio Bonanova (Chef); Andrew Tombes (Conductor); Almira Sessions (Maid); Pierre Watkin (Markham); Florence Gill (Hallyrod); Sidney Blackmer (Attorney); Virginia Engels (Bonnie); George Watts (Judge Knox);

Hal K. Dawson (Pullman Bore); Dudley Dickerson (Dining Car Waiter); Snowflake Toones (Porter); Dora Clement (Aunt Lucy); John Dilson (Uncle Joe); Charles Peck (Johnny); Cecil Weston (Aunt); Ruth Cherrington (Dowager); Isabelle La Mal (Wife); James Carlisle (Husband); Gloria Whitney, Jean Acker, Walter Anthony Merrill, John Sylvester (Cousins); Jimmy Conlin (McIntyre); George Chandler (Skip); Max Wagner (Jerry); George Lloyd (Court Bailiff); Vera Marshe (Helen); Harry Harvey (Court Clerk); Jed Prouty (Judge Rufus); Frank M. Thomas (Keenan); John Farrell (Bottle); Ralph Sanford (Pudgy); Emory Parnell, Ted Oliver, Eddie Parker, Mickey Simpson (Motor Cops); Murray Alper (Station Wagon Driver); Benny Rubin, Ernie Stanton, Nora Cecil, Count Cutelli, Dot Farley, Ronnie Rondell, Marian Darlington, Tex C. C. Gilmore, Mary Lawrence, Eddie Borden (Bird Lovers).

BEDTIME STORY (Columbia, 1941) 85 M.

Producer, B.P. Schulberg; director, Alexander Hall; story, Horace Jackson, Grant Garrett; screenplay, Richard Flournoy; art director, William Mull; camera, Joseph Walker; editor, Viola Lawrence.

Fredric March (Lucius Drake); Loretta Young (Jane Drake); Robert Benchley (Eddie Turner); Allyn Joslyn (William Dudley, Jr.); Eve Arden (Virginia Cole); Helen Westley (Emma Harper); Joyce Compton (Beulah); Tim Ryan (Mat); Olaf Hytten (Alfred); Dorothy Adams (Betsy); Clarence Kolb (Collins); Andrew Tombes (Pierce); Grady Sutton (Bert-Costume Designer); Emmett Vogan (Mike-Set Designer); Byron Foulger (Desk Clerk-Reno); Spencer Charters (Gas Station Proprietor); William Newell (Proprietor's Son); Torben Meyer (Dinglehoff); Pierre Watkin (Echols); Chester Clute (Room Clerk); Harry Strang (Electrician); James Flavin (Room 625); Stanley Brown (Tommy); Duke York (Hotel Worker); Frank Darien (Theater Patron).

HIT PARADE OF 1943 (Republic, 1943) 90 M.

Producer, Herbert J. Yates; associate producer, Albert J. Cohen; director, Albert S. Rogell; screenplay, Frank Gill, Jr.; additional dialogue, Frances Hyland; songs, Jule Styne and Harold Adamson; J.C. Johnson and Andy Razaf; music director, Walter Scharf; choreographer, Nick Castle; art director, John B. Goodman; camera, Charles Van Enger; editor, Frank Gross.

John Carroll (Rick Farrell); Susan Hayward (Jill Wright); Gail Patrick (Toni Jarrett); Walter Catlett (J. MacClellan Davis); Eve Arden (Belinda Wright); Melville Cooper (Bradley Cole); Albert Whiteman (Pops); Louis Williams (Louie); Mary Treen (Janie); Count Basie & Orchestra With Dorothy Dandridge, (Freddie Martin & Orchestra); Ray McKinley & Band); Golden Gate Quartette Three Cheers, Music Maids (Themselves); Jack Williams (Harlem Sandman); Chinita Marin (Tam-Boom-Ba Number); Wally Vernon (Vaudeville Actor); Warren Ashe (Master Of Ceremonies); Tom Kennedy (Westinghouse); Addison Richards (Producer); Gary Breckner, Ken Niles (Announcers); Astrid Allwyn (Joyce); Paul Newlan (Doorman); Bud Jamison, Grandon Rhodes (Escorts); Philip Van Zandt, Joey Ray (Orchestra Leaders); Cordell Hickman (Small Black Boy); Earle Dewey (Cook); Olaf Hytten (Waiter); Edwin Mills (Page Boy); Sunshine Sammy Morrison (Heaven Air Pilot); Madeline Gray, Hooper Atchley (Couple in Cab); Milton Kibbee (Pastry Man); Sally Cairns (Blonde); Nicodemus Stewart (Willie).

LET'S FACE IT (Paramount, 1943) 76 M.

Associate producer, Fred Kohlmar; director, Sidney Lanfield; based on the musical by Dorothy Fields, Herbert

Fields, and Cole Porter, from the play *The Cradle Snatchers* by Norma Mitchell, Russell G. Medcraft; music director, Robert Emmett Dolan; songs, Porter; Sammy Cahn and Jule Styne; art director, Hans Dreier, Earl Hedrick; camera, Lionel Lindon; editor, Paul Weatherwax.

Bob Hope (Jerry Walker); Betty Hutton (Winnie Potter); Dona Drake (Muriel); Cully Richards (Frankie Burns); Eve Arden (Maggie Watson); ZaSu Pitts (Cornelia Pigeon); Marjorie Weaver (Jean Blanchard); Raymond Walburn (Julian Watson); Phyllis Povah (Nancy Collister); Joe Sawyer (Sgt. Wiggins); Dave Willock (Barney Hilliard); Nicco and Tanya (Dance Team); Andrew Tombes (Judge Henry Pigeon); Arthur Loft (George Collister); Grace Hayle (Mrs. Wigglesworth); Evelyn Dockson (Mrs. Taylor); Kay Linaker (Canteen Hostess); Andria Moreland, Brooke Evans (Milk Maids); Barbara Pepper (Daisy); Joyce Compton (Wiggins' Girl); Marie Windsor (Marie); George Meader (Justice of the Peace); Noel Neill, Yvonne DeCarlo (Girls); Cyril Ring (Head Waiter); William B. Davidson (Man In Boat); Janet Shaw (Girl In Boat); Fred Giermann (Officer on Sub); Elinor Troy (Elinor); Lena Belle (Lena); Ann Adams (Ann); Evelyn Frey (Evelyn); Helena Brinton (Helena); Tommye Adams (Tommye); Barbara Brooks (Barbara); Lionel Royce (Submarine Commander); Eddie Dunn (Cop); Marjorie Deanne (Dancer); Emory Parnell (Colonel); Bud Geary (Sergeant); Harry Morgan (Waiter).

COVER GIRL (Columbia, 1944) 107 M.

Director, Charles Vidor; story, Erwin Gelsey; adaptation, Marion Parsonnet, Paul Gangelin; screenplay, Virginia Van Upp; songs, Jerome Kerns and Ira Gershwin; music director, M.W. Stoloff; orchestrations, Carmen Dragon; camera, Rudolph Mate, Allen N. Davey; editor, Viola Lawrence.

Rita Hayworth (Rusty Parker/Maribelle Hicks); Gene Kelly (Danny McGuire); Lee Bowman (Noel Wheaton); Phil Silvers (Genius); Jinx Falkenburg (Jinx); Leslie Brooks (Maurine Martin); Eve Arden (Cornelia "Stonewall" Jackson); Otto Kruger (John Coudair); Jess Barker (Coudair-As a Young Man); Anita Colby (Anita); Curt Bois (Chem); Ed Brophy (Joe); Thurston Hall (Tony Pastor); Jack Norton (Drunk); Robert Homans (Doorman); Eddie Dunn (Cop); Ilene "Betty" Brewer (Autograph Hound); Johnny Mitchell (Pianist); Virginia Wilson (Dancer); Shelley Winters (Girl); Barbara Pepper (Chorus Girl); Stanley Clements (Elevator Boy); Constance Worth (Receptionist); Frances Morris (Coudair's Secretary); Billy Benedict (Florist Boy); COVER GIRLS: Jean Colleran (*American Magazine*); Francine Counihan (*American Home*); Helen Mueller (*Collier's Magazine*); Cecilia Meagher (*Coronet*); Betty Jane Hess (*Cosmopolitan*); Dusty Anderson (*Farm Journal*); Eileen McClory (*Glamour*); Cornelia B. Von Hessert (*Harper's Bazaar*); Peggy Lloyd (*Mademoiselle*); Betty Jane Graham (*McCalls*); Cheryl Archer (*Look*); Karen X. Gaylord (*Liberty*); Susann Shaw (*Vogue*); Martha Outlaw (*Redbook*); Rose May Robson (*Women's Home Companion*); William Sloan (Naval Officer).

THE DOUGHGIRLS (Warner Brothers, 1944) 102 M.

Producer, Mark Hellinger; director, James V. Kern; based on the play by Joseph A. Fields; screenplay, Kern, Sam Hellman; additional dialogue, Wilkie Mahoney; assistant director, Phil Quinn; art director, Hugh Reticher; special effects, William McCann; camera, Ernest Haller; editor, Folmer Blangsted.

Ann Sheridan (Edna); Alexis Smith (Nan); Jack Carson (Arthur); Jane Wyman (Vivian); Irene Manning (Mrs. Cadman); Charlie Ruggles (Stanley Slade); Eve Arden

(Natalia Moskoroff); John Ridgely (Julian Cadman); Alan Mowbray (Brackenridge Drake); John Alexander (Warren Buckley); Craig Stevens (Tom Dillon); Barbara Brown (Mrs. Cartwright); Francis Pierlot (Mr. Jordan); Donald MacBride (Judge Franklin); Mark Stevens (Lt. Harry Keary); Joe De Rita (The Stranger); Regis Toomey (Timothy Walsh); Walter De Palma (Justice of the Peace); John Walsh (Bellhop); Grandon Rhodes, Tom Quinn (Clerks); Fred Kelsey (Man With Suitcase); Dink Trout (Young Husband); John Hamilton (Businessman); Almira Sessions, Minerva Urecal (Hatchet-Faced Women); Earle Dewey (Fat Man); Dolores Conlin, Dorothy Reisner, Helen Gerald, Joan Breslaw, Yolanda Baiano, Julie Arlington (School Girls); Harry Tyler (Angular Man); Marie de Becker, Anita Bolster (Maids); Joan Winfield (Slade's Secretary); Oliver Blake (Porter); Elmer Jerome (Elderly Waiter); Lou Marcelle (Announcer's Voice); Warren Mills, Dick Hirbe, William Frambes (Bellboys); Ralph Sanford (Workman); Jack Mower, John O'Connor (Technicians); Larry Rio (Attendant in Baths); Carlyle Blackwell, Jr. (Messenger); Nick Kobliansky (Father Nicholai); Will Fowler (Lieutenant).

PAN-AMERICANA (RKO, 1944) 84 M.

Executive producer, Sid Rogell; producer-director, John H. Auer; story, Frederick Kohner, Auer; screenplay, Laurence Kimble; music director, C. Bakaleinikoff; choreographer, Charles O'Curran; songs, Mort Greene and Gabriel Ruiz; Bob Russell and Marguerita Lecuona; art director, Albert S. D'Agostino, Al Herman; camera, Frank Redman; editor, Harry Marker.

Phillip Terry (Dan); Audrey Long (Jo Anne); Robert Benchley (Charlie Corlcer Narrator); Eve Arden (Hoppy); Ernest Truex (Uncle Rudy); Marc Cramer (Jerry); Isabelita (Lupita); Rosaria and Antonio, Miguelito Valdes, Harold And Lola, Louise Burnett, Chinita Marin, Chuy Gastillion, Padilla Sistes, Chuy Reyes & His Orchestra, Nestor Amaral & His Samba Band (Themselves); Bill Garvin (Sancho); Frank Mrasco (Miguel); Armando Gonzales (Carlos) Rita Corday, Patti Brill, Rosemary La Planche, Greta Christensen, Virginia Belmont (Pan-American Girls); Bette Jane Greer (Miss Downing); Nina Bara (Miss Argentina); Alma Beltran (Miss Guatemala); Ruth Lorran (Miss Honduras); Velera Burton (Miss Dutch Guiana); Aldonna Gauvin (Miss Uruguay); Carmen Lopez (Miss Paraguay); Goya Del Valle (Miss Panama); Betty Joy Curtis (Miss Bolivia); Luz Vasquez (Miss Mexico); Valerie Hall (Miss El Salvador); Joan Beckstead (Miss Peru); Leif Argo (Pedro); Fernando Ramos (Jose); Hugh Hendrikson (Juan); Tom Costello (Brazillian Ambassador); Albano Valerio (Mexican Ambassador).

PATRICK THE GREAT (Universal, 1945) 88 M.

Producer, Howard Benedict; director, Frank Ryan; story, Jane Hall, Frederick Block, Ralph Block; screenplay, Bertram Millhauser, Dorothy Bennett; music, Hans J. Salter; art director, John B. Goodman, Abraham Grossman; choreographer, Louis DaPron; camera, Frank Redman; editor, Ted J. Kent.

Donald O'Connor (Pat Donahue, Jr.); Peggy Ryan (Judy); Frances Dee (Lynn Andrews); Donald Cook (Pat Donahue, Sr.); Eve Arden (Jean Mathews); Thomas Gomez (Max Wilson); Gavin Muir (Prentis Johns); Andrew Tombes (Sam Bassett); Irving Bacon (Mr. Merney); Emmett Vogan (Alsop); Cal Rothenberg, Robert Coleman, John Truel, Joe "Corky" Geil; Walter Carter, Bobby Scheerer, (Jivin' Jacks); Grace Costello, Shirley Mills, Peggy Brant, Dolores Diane, Jean Davis, Patsy O'Connor (Jivin' Jills); Isabelle LaMal (Grand Dame); Robert Emmett Keane (Henry Ames); Joel Allen (Actor); Lee

Phelps (Prop Man); Ernie Adams (Constable); Billy Benedict (Joey); Douglas Wood (Sir Orville Armstrong); Sidney Miller (Tony); Eddie Dunn (Plumber); Buster Brodie (Bellboy); Harry Harvey, Neely Edwards (Waiter); Ray Walker (Orchestra Leader); George Chandler (Bellhop); George Lloyd (Fisherman).

EARL CARROLL VANITIES (Republic, 1945) 91 M.

Associate producer, Albert J. Cohen; director, Joseph Santley; story, Cortland Fitzsimmons; screenplay, Frank Gill, Jr.; music director, Walter Scharf; songs, Walter Kent and Kim Gannon; choreographer, Sammy Lee; art director, Russell Kimball, Frank Hotaling; camera, Jack Marta; editor, Richard L. Van Enger.

Constance Moore (Drina); Dennis O'Keefe (Danny Farrell); Alan Mowbray (Grand Duke Paul); Eve Arden (Tex Donnolly); Pinky Lee (Pinky Price); Otto Kruger (Earl Carroll); Mary Forbes (Queen Mother Elena); Stephanie Bachelor (Claire Elliott); Parkyakarkus (Waiter); Leon Belasco (Dashek); Robert Greig (Vonce); Jimmy Alexander (Leading Man); Sarah Selby (Mrs. Thayer); Milton Graff (Mr. Thayer); Joan Blair (Mrs. Weems); Chester Clute (Mr. Weems); Tommy Ivo (Boy Dancer); Liliane and Mario (Dance Specialty); Woody Herman & His Orchestra (Themselves); Jimmy Kelly (Fat Man); Charles Dorety, Tom Dugan (Waiters); Donald Kerr (Assistant Dance Director); Rex Lease (Truck Driver); Edward Gargan (Policeman); Charles Sullivan (Cab Driver); Margia Dean (Chorus Girl); Charles Coleman (Doorman); Stanley Price (Sandwich Man); Guido Lombardo (Bartender).

MILDRED PIERCE (Warner Brothers, 1945) 113 M.

Producer, Jerry Wald; director, Michael Curtiz; based on the novel by James M. Cain; screenplay, Ranald MacDougall, Catherine Turney; music, Max Steiner; art director, Anton Grot; special effects, Willard Van Enger; camera, Ernest Haller; editor, David Weisbart.

Joan Crawford (Mildred Pierce); Jack Carson (Wally Fay); Zachary Scott (Monte Beragon); Eve Arden (Ida); Ann Blyth (Veda Pierce); Bruce Bennett (Bert Pierce); George Tobias (Mr. Chris); Lee Patrick (Maggie Binderhof); Moroni Olsen (Inspector Peterson); Jo Ann Marlowe (Kay Pierce); Barbara Brown (Mrs. Forrester); Charles Trowbridge (Mr. Williams); John Compton (Ted Forrester); Butterfly McQueen (Lottie); Garry Owen (Policeman on Pier); James Flavin, Jack O'Connor (Detectives); Clancy Cooper, Tom Dillon, Charles Jordan (Policemen); Robert Arthur (High School Boy); Joyce Compton, Lynne Baggett (Waitresses); Ramsey Ames (Party Guest); Leah Baird (Police Matron); John Christian (Singing Teacher); Joan Winfield (Piano Teacher); Jimmy Lono (Houseboy); Mary Servoss (Nurse); Manart Kippen (Doctor Gale); David Cota (Pancho); Chester Clute (Mr. Jones); Wallis Clark (Wally's Lawyer).

MY REPUTATION (Warner Brothers, 1946) 96 M.

Producer, Henry Blanke; director, Curtis Bernhardt; based on the novel *Instruct My Sorrows* by Clare Jaynes; screenplay, Catherine Turney; music Max Steiner; music director, Leo F. Forbstein; art director, Anton Grot; special effects, Roy Davidson; camera, James Wong Howe; editor, David Weisbart.

Barbara Stanwyck (Jessica Drummond); George Brent (Scott Landis); Warner Anderson (Frank Everett); Lucile Watson (Mrs. Kimball); John Ridgely (Cary Abbott); Eve Arden (Ginna Abbott); Jerome Cowan (George Van Orman); Esther Dale (Anna); Scotty Beckett (Kim Drummond); Bobby Cooper (Keith Drummond); Leona Mariole (Riette Van Orman); Mary Servoss (Mary); Cecil Cunningham (Mrs. Thompson); Janice Wilson (Penny Boardman); Ann Todd (Gretchen Van Orman); Nancy Evans (Baby Hawks); Oliver Blake (Dave); Charles Jordan (Butcher); Darwood Kaye (Billy "Droopy" Hawks); Fred Kelsey (Conductor); Marjorie Roshelle (Phyllis); Bruce Warren (Man in Bar); Harry Seymour (Hotel Desk Clerk); Frank Darien (Elevator Operator); Leah Baird (Woman); Hugh Prosser (Les Hanson); Helen Eby Rock (Mrs. Hanson); Alan Ward, Dan Dowling, Tom Quinn, Elyse Browne, Rosalie Roy (Party Guests); Dickie Humphreys, Marilyn Kaye, Shirley Doble, Dale Cornell (Jitterbugs); Deacon McDaniel (Johnson); Dick Elliott (Tipsy Man); Dick Winslow (Orchestra Leader).

THE KID FROM BROOKLYN (RKO, 1946) 114 M.

Producer, Samuel Goldwyn; director, Norman Z. McLeod; based on the play *The Milky Way* by Hugh O'Connell, Lynn Root, Harry Clork; screenplay by Grover Jones, Frank Butler, Richard Connell; new adaptation, Don Hartman, Melville Shavelson; choreographer, Bernard Pearce; music director, Carmen Dragon; songs, Sammy Cahn and Jule Styne; Sylvia Fine; camera, Gregg Toland; editor, Daniel Mandell.

Danny Kaye (Burleigh Sullivan); Virginio Mayo (Polly Pringle); Vera-Ellen (Susie Sullivan); Steve Cochran (Speed McFarlane); Eve Arden (Ann Westley); Walter Abel (Gabby Sloan); Lionel Stander (Spider Schultz); Fay Bainter (Mrs. E. Winthrop LeMoyne); Clarence Kolb (Mr. Austin); Victor Cutler (Photographer); Charles Cane (Willard); Jerome Cowan (Flight Announcer); Don Wilson, Knox Manning (Radio Announcers); Kay Thompson (Matron); Johnny Downs (Master of Ceremonies); Karen X. Gaylord, Ruth Valmy, Shirley Ballard, Virginia Belmont, Betty Cargyle, Jean Cronin, Vonne Lester, Diane Mumby, Mary Simpson, Virginia Thorpe, Tyra Vaughan, Kismi Stefan, Betty Alexander, Martha Montgomery, Joyce MacKenzie, Donna Hamilton, Helen Kimball, Jan Bryant (The Goldwyn Girls); Robert Strong, Billy Newell, Tom Quinn (Photographers); Billy Bletcher (News Photographer); Billy Wayne, George Sherwood, George Chandler, Donald Kerr (Reporters); Charles Sullivan (Timekeeper); Frank Moran (Fight Manager); Tom Kennedy (Referee); Thomas Patrick Dillon (Policeman); J.W. Cody (Indian Chief); Syd Saylor (Taxi Driver); Billy Nelson (Danny Kaye Second); Eddie Hart (Knockdown Timekeeper); Eric Witon, Alexander Pollard (Butlers); Hal K. Dawson (Hotel Clerk); Snub Pollard (Man for Reaction to Lion); Jack Norton, Torben Meyer, William Forrest (Guests); John Indrisano (Boxing Instructor); Dorothy Ellers (Vera-Ellen-Singing Double); Betty Russell (Virginia Mayo-Singing Double).

NIGHT AND DAY (Warner Brothers, 1946) 128 M.

Producer, Arthur Schwartz; director, Michael Curtiz; adaptation, Jack Moffitt; screenplay, Charles Hoffman, Leo Townsend, William Bowers; choreographer, LeRoy Prinz; music director, Leo F. Forbstein; songs, Cole Porter; additional music, Max Steiner; special effects, Robert Burke; assistant director, Frank Heath; camera, Peverell Marley, William V. Skall; editor, David Weisbart.

Cary Grant (Cole Porter); Alexis Smith (Linda Lee Porter); Monty Woolley (Himself); Ginny Simms (Carole Hill); Jane Wyman (Gracie Harris); Eve Arden (Gabrielle); Victor Francen (Anatole Giron); Alan Hale (Leon Dowling); Dorothy Malone (Nancy); Tom D'Andrea (Bernie); Selena Royale (Kate Porter); Donald Woods (Ward Blackburn); Henry Stephenson (Homer Cole); Paul Cavanagh (Bart McClelland); Sig Ruman (Wilowsky); Carlos Ramirez (Specialty Singer); Milada Mladova,

Estelle Sloan, George Zoritch, (Specialty Dancers); Adam & Jayne DeGatano (Specialty Team); Mary Martin (Herself); James Dobbs, John Compton (Students); Boyd Davis (Dead); John Alvin (Petey); Harlan Briggs (Doorman); Clarence Muse (Caleb); Frank Ferguson (Tina's Father); JoAnn Marlowe (Tina); George Meader (Minister); Virginia Sale (Minister's Wife); Creighton Hale, Paul Gustine (Men in Theater); James Dodd (Red); Ellen Lowe (Nurse); Emile Hilb (Orchestra Leader); George Riley (O'Halloran); Peter Camlin (French Lieutenant); Claire Meade, Charles Williams (Customers); Gordon Richards (Cochran); Howard Freeman (Producer); Bobby Watson (Director); John "Red" Pierson (First "Peaches"); Chester Clute (Music Publisher); Joyce Compton, Helen O'Hara, Susanne Rosser (Chorines); Eddie Kane (Headwaiter); Herman Bing (Second "Peaches"); Laurie Shermain (Interne); Gene Garrick (Soldier); George Kirby (Cab Driver); Eva Novak, Paula Rae, Ruth Matthews, Betty Blair, Valerie Ardis, Edna Morris (Nurses); Buddy Gorman (English Page Boy); Cyril Ring (Husband); Vivian Oakland (Wife); Pat Gleason (Dance Director); Joe Kirkwood, Jr., Gene Stanley (Classmates of Cole Porter); Henry Hastings (Bartender); Barbara Slater, Gloria Anderson (Tall Showgirls); Don Roy (Band Leader).

SONG OF SCHEHERAZADE (Universal, 1947) 106 M.

Producer, Edward Kaufman; associate producer, Edward Dodds; director, Walter Reisch; story inspired by the music of N. Rimsakoff; screenplay, Reisch; music adaptor-director, Miklos Rozsa; lyrics, Jack Brooks, choreographer, Tillie Losch; art director, Jack Otterson; camera, Hal Mohr; editor, Frank Gross.

Yvonne De Carlo (Cara de Talavera); Brian Donlevy (Captain); Jean Pierre Aumont (Rimsky-Korsakoff); Eve Arden (Madame de Talavera); Philip Reed (Prince Mischetsky); Charles Kullman (Dr. Klin); John Qualen (Lorenzo); Richard Lane (Lieutenant); Terry Kilburn (Lorin); George Dolenz (Pierre); Elena Verdugo (Fioretta); Robert Kendall (Hassan); Rex Ravelle (Sultan); Mickey Simpson (Orderly); Sol Haines (Giant); Florence Rozen (Little Sister); William Brooks, Leonard East, Edward Kelly, Russ Vincent, Peter Varney, Charles Roberson, Tom Skinner, Warren W. McCollum, Ernie Mishens, Marvin Press, Fred K. Hartsook, Gordon Arnold, Bill Cabanne, Don Garner, George Holmes (Students); Milio Sheron (Basso); Patricia Alphin (Native Girl); Joan Shawlee (French Girl); Theodora Lynch (Soprano); Dick Alexander (Attendant); Mary Moore (Spanish Girl); Ralph Brooks (Junior Officer); Emmett Vogan, Jr. (Coachman).

THE ARNELO AFFAIR (MGM, 1947) 86 M.

Producer, Jerry Bresler; director, Arch Oboler; story, Jane Burr; screenplay, Oboler; music, George Baseman; art director, Cedric Gibbons, Wade Rubottom; camera, Charles Salerno; editor, Harry Komer.

John Hodiak (Tony Arnelo); George Murphy (Ted Parkson); Frances Gifford (Annie Parkson); Dean Stockwell (Ricky Parkson); Eve Arden (Vivian Delwyn); Warner Anderson (Sam Leonard); Lowell Gilmore (Avery Border); Michael Brandon (Archie Twitchell) (Roger Alison); Ruthe Brady (Dorothy Alison); Ruby Dandridge (Maybelle); Joan Woodbury (Claire Lorrison); Griff Barnett (Mr. Adams); Constance Weiler (Wrapper); Barbara Billingsley (Clark Weil); George Carleton (Attendant); Lillian Bronson (Secretary); Bill Shaw (Salesman); Shimen Ruskin (Driver); Milton Kibbee (Passerby); Thaddeus Jones (Mr. Porterville); Erin O'Kelly (Nurse).

THE UNFAITHFUL (Warner Brothers, 1947) 109 M.

Producer, Jerry Wald; director, Vincent Sherman; story-

screenplay, David Goodis; art director, Leo S. Kuter; music, Max Steiner; music director, Leo F. Forbstein; camera, Ernest Haller; editor, Alan Crosland, Jr.

Ann Sheridan (Chris Hunter); Lew Ayres (Larry Hannaford); Zachary Scott (Bob Hunter); Eve Arden (Paula); Jerome Cowan (Prosecuting Attorney); Steven Geray (Martin Barrow); John Hoyt (Det. Lt. Reynolds); Peggy Knudsen (Claire); Marta Mitrovich (Mrs. Tanner); Douglas Kennedy (Roger); Claire Meade (Martha); Frances Morris (Agnes); Jane Barker (Joan); Joan Winfield (Bill Girl); Jay Eaton, Tristram Coffin (Men Guests); Jack Mower (Plainclothesman); Jean DeBriac (Maitre D'); Lois Austin (Middle Aged Woman); Ross Ford (Young Man); Eve Whitney (Young Woman); Mary Field (Receptionist); Dorothy Christie (Mrs. Freedley); Ray Montgomery (Male Secretary); Monte Blue (Businessman); Paul Bradley (Mr. Tanner); John Elliott (Judge); Maude Fealy (Old Maid); Cary Harrison (Seedy Man); Betty Hill (Woman Reporter); George Hickman, Bob Alden (Newsboys); Charles Marsh, Bob Lowell, Dick Walsh (Reporters); Charles Jordan (Attendant).

THE VOICE OF THE TURTLE (Warner Brothers, 1947) 103 M.

Producer, Charles Hoffman; director, Irving Rapper; based on the play by John Van Druten; screenplay, Van Druten; art director, Robert Hass; music director, Leo F. Forbstein; camera, Sol Polito; editor, Rudi Fehr.

Ronald Reagan (Sgt. Bill Page); Eleanor Parker (Sally Middleton); Eve Arden (Olive Lashbrooke); Wayne Morris (Comm. Ned Burling); Kent Smith (Kenneth Bartlett); John Emery (George Harrington); Erskine Sanford (Storekeeper); John Holland (Henry Atherton); Nino Pipitone (Headwaiter); Helen Wallace, Sarah Edwards (Women); William Gould (Man); Frank Wilcox (Stanley Blake); Ross Ford (Soda Clerk); Bunty Cutler (Girl at Telephone); Dick Bartell (Ticket Agent); Jack Lee (Director); Doris Kemper (Woman in Delicatessen); Nicodemus Stewart (Elevator Boy); Janet Warren, Tristram Coffin, Lois Austin, (Theatre Party); Philip Morris (Doorman); Alan Foster (Vendor); Brian O'Hara (Box Office Clerk); Joan Lawrence (Bill's Ex-Girl Friend); Ernest Anderson (Elevator Man); Juanita Roberts (Hat Check Girl); Peter Camlin (French-speaking Man); Suzanne Dulier (French-speaking Woman); Bernard DeRoux (French-speaking Waiter); Darlen Mohilef, Norma Fenton (Girls); Peter Gowland, Robert Spencer (Boys); Francine Bordeaux (French Girl); Douglas Kennedy (Naval Officer); Noel Delorme (French Hat Check Girl).

ONE TOUCH OF VENUS (Universal, 1948) 82 M.

Producer, Lester Cowan; associate producer, John Bech; director, William A. Seiter; based on the play by S. J. Perelman, Ogden Nash, Kurt Weill; new screenplay, Harry Kurnitz, Frank Tashlin; new songs, Ann Ronell; art director, Bernard Herzbrun, Emerich Nicholson; camera, Frank Planer; editor, Otto Ludwig.

Robert Walker (Eddie Hatch); Ava Gardner (Venus, Goddess of Love/Venus Jones); Dick Haymes (Joe); Eve Arden (Molly Grant); Olga San Juan (Gloria) Tom Conway (Whitfield Savory); James Flavin (Corrigan); Sara Allgood (Mrs. Gogarty, Landlady); Hugh Herbert (Mercury); Arthur O'Connell, Kenneth Patterson, Ann Nagel, Russ Conway, Jerry Marlowe, Ralph Brooks, Mary Benoit, Joan Miller (Reporters); Josephine Whittell (Dowager); George J. Lewis, Eddie Parker (Detectives); John Valentine (Stammers); Phil Garris (Counter Man); Ralph Peters (Taxi Driver); Pat Shade (Newsboy); George Meeker (Mr. Crust); Dick Gordon (Guest); Martha Montgomery (Pretty Girl); Yvette Reynard, Pat Parrish (Girls); Helen Francell, Harriet Bennett (Women).

WHIPLASH (Warner Brothers, 1948) 91 M.

Producer, William Jacobs; director, Lew Seiler; based on the story by Kenneth Earl; adaptation, Gordon Kahn; screenplay, Maurice Geraghty, Harriet Frank Jr.; music director, Lea F. Forbstein; songs, Dick Redmond; Mack David, Foster Curbelo, and John Camacho; art director, Charles H. Clarke; camera, Peverell Marley; editor, Frank Magee.

Dane Clark (Michael Gordon); Alexis Smith (Laurie Durant); Zachary Scott (Rex Durant); Eve Arden (Chris); Jeffrey Lynn (Dr. Arnold Vincent); S.Z. Sakall (Sam); Alan Hale (Terrence O'Leary); Douglas Kennedy (Tex Sanders); Fred Steele (Duke Carney); Robert Lowell (Trask); Don McGuire (Harkus); Clifton Young (Gunman); Sam Hayes (Announcer); Mike Lally (Ring Announcer); Howard Mitchell (Fight Announcer); Ralph Volkie (Referee); Donald Kerr (Vendor); Rudy Friml (Orchestra Leader); Jimmy Dodd (Bill-Piano Player); George Nokes, Norman Ollestad (Boys); Charles Marsh (Hotel Clerk); I. Stanford Jolley (Artist); Kate Lawson (Woman on Steps); Maude Prickett (Mrs. Gruman); Jack Worth (Doorman); Richard Walsh (Asst. Stage Mgr.); Tommy Garland (Rocky); Harvey Perry, Jim O'Catty (Handlers); John Daheim (Kid Lucas); Ray Montgomery, Harry Lewis (Press Men); John Harmon (Kid McGee); Wally Scott (Drunk); Cliff Herd (Waiter); Howard Negley (Policeman); Larry McGrath (Manager); Joey Gray, Aldo Spoldi, Ceferino Garcia, Georgie Goodman, John Salvata, Artie Sullivan, Henry Vroom, Rito Funay, Wally Rose, Larry Anzalone, Paul Baxley, Buddy Wright (Fighters); Bob Perry (Timekeeper); Sam Shack, Charles Sullivan, Cy Malis, Sailor Vincent, Gene Delmont, George Suzanne, Joe LaBarba, Ray McDonald (Seconds).

MY DREAM IS YOURS (Warner Brothers, 1949) 101 M.

Producer-director, Michael Curtiz; story adaptation, Allen Rivkin, Laura Kerr; screenplay, Harry Kurnitz, Dane Lussier; cartoon sequence, I. Freleng; songs, Harry Warren and Ralph Blane; art director, Robert Haas; music director, Ray Heindorf; camera, Ernest Haller, Wilfred M. Cline; editor, Folmar Blangsted.

Jack Carson (Doug Blake); Doris Day (Martha Gibson); Lee Bowman (Gary Mitchell); Adolphe Menjou (Thomas Hutchins); Eve Arden (Vivian Martin); S.Z. Sakall (Felix Hofer); Selena Royle (Freda Hofer); Edgar Kennedy (Uncle Charlie); Sheldon Leonard (Grimes); Franklin Pangborn (Sourpuss Manager); John Berkes (Character Actor); Ada Leonard (Herself); Frankie Carle (Himself); Ross Wesson (Hilliard); Duncan Richardson (Freddie Manners); Sandra Gould (Mildred); Jack Kenny (Cab Driver); Iris Adrian (Peggy); Jan Kayne (Polly); Bob Caron (Jeff); Lennie Bremen (Louis); Paul Maxey (Bald Man); Marian Martin (Blonde); Frank Scannell (Car Salesman); Belle Daube (Elderly Actress); Louise Sarayder (Actress); Chili Williams (Fan Club President); Patricia Northrop (Gary Mitchell Fan); Mary Bradley, Juin Whipple, Eve Whitney, Joan Lawrence, Maynard Holmes, Rodney Bell, Joan Vons, George Neise, Chester Clute, Danny Dowling, Bridget Browne (Party Guests); Art Gilmore (Radio Announcer); Edward Colman (Radio Voice); Rudy Friml (Orchestra Leader); Don Brodie (Engineer); Tristram Coffin (Head Waiter).

THE LADY TAKES A SAILOR (Warner Brothers, 1949) 98 M.

Producer, Harry Kurnitz; director, Michael Curtiz; story, Jerry Gruskin; screenplay, Everett Freeman; art director, Edward Carrere; music, Max Steiner; assistant director, Sherry Shourds; camera, Ted McCord; editor, David Weisbart.

Jane Wyman (Jennifer Smith); Dennis Morgan (Bill Craig); Eve Arden (Susan Wayne); Robert Douglas (John Tyson); Allyn Joslyn (Ralph Whitcomb); Tom Tully (Henry Duckworth); Lina Romay (Raquel Riviera); William Frawley (Oliver Harker); Fred Clark (Victor Sangell); Charles Meredith (Dr. McKewen); Craig Stevens (Danvers); Tom Stevenson (Institute Guide); Ray Montgomery (Lab Man); Ruth Lewis (Miss Clark); Ruth Lee (Miss Brand); Sonia Bryden (Arlette); Walter Shumway (Dr. Coombe); Henrietta Taylor (Dr. Anna Sparton); Emil Rameau (Dr. Mittenwald); Leslie Kimmell (Conrad Updike); John Halloran (Homer Benton); Harry Cheshire (Judge Vardon); Ken Britton (Davis); John Morgan, Len Hendry, Russ Conway (Constables); Josephine Whittell, Ken Patterson (Reporters); Ray Erlenborn (Photographer); John McGuire (Coast Guard Officer); Robert Malcolm (Chief of Police); Frank Cady (Mr. Crane); George Spaulding (Admiral Morell); Jack Lee (Captain Cutter); Joe McTurk (Waiter); Bridget Brown (Hat Check Girl); Hallene Hill (Flower Woman); Richard Ryan (Apt. House Clerk); Stanley Prager (Taxi Driver); Wendy Lee (Telephone Operator); Phyllis Godfrey (Hilda); Jack Boyle (Interne); Lute Crockett (Doctor); Nina Prescott (Tyson's Secretary).

PAID IN FULL (Paramount, 1950) 98 M.

Producer, Hal B. Wallis; director, William Dieterle; based on a story by Dr. Frederic M. Loomis; screenplay, Robert Blees, Charles Schnee; art director, Hans Dreier, Earl Hedrick; music, Walter Lang; Victor Young; camera, Leo Tover; editor, Warren Low.

Robert Cummings (Bill Prentice); Lizabeth Scott (Jane Langley); Diana Lynn (Nancy Langley); Eve Arden (Tommy Thompson); Ray Collins (Dr. Fredericks); Frank McHugh (Ben); Stanley Ridges (Dr. Winston); Louis Jean Heydt (Dr. Carter); Kristine Miller (Miss Williams); Laura Elliot (Tina); Ida Moore (Dorothy); James Nolan (Charlie Malloy); Geraldine Wall (Miss Ames); Rolland Morris (Bunny Howard); Jane Novak (Mrs. Fredericks); Carole Mathews (Model); Carol Channing (Mrs. Peters); Dorothy Adams (Emily Burroughs); Arlene Jenkins, Christine Cooper (Secretaries); Byron Barr (Man at Bar); Marie Blake (Tired Woman); Jimmie Dundee (Truck Driver); Gladys Blake (Talkative Woman); Douglas Spencer (Crib Man); Dewey Robinson (Diaper Man); Charles Bradstreet (Marc Hickman); Harry Cheshire (Minister).

CURTAIN CALL AT CACTUS CREEK (Universal, 1950) 86 M.

Producer, Robert Arthur; director, Charles Lamont; story, Stanley Roberts, Howard Dimsdale; screenplay, Dimsdale; art director, Bernard Herzbrun, John F. DeCuir; camera, Russell Metty; editor, Frank Gross.

Donald O'Connor (Edward Timmons); Gale Storm (Julie Martin); Walter Brennan (Rimrock); Vincent Price (Tracy Holland); Eve Arden (Lily Martin); Chick Chandler (Ralph); Joe Sawyer (Jake); Harry Shannon (Clay); Rex Lease (Yellowstone); I. Stamford Jolley (Pecos).

TEA FOR TWO (Warner Brothers, 1950) 97 M.

Producer, William Jacobs; director, David Butler; suggested by the play *No, No, Nanette* by Frank Mandel, Otto Harbach, Vincent Youmans, Emil Nyetray; screenplay, Harry Clork; choreographer, LeRoy Prinz; songs, Anne Caldwell and Youmans; Caesar, Roger Wolfe Kahn and Joseph Meyer; Al Dubin, and Harry Warren; Caesar and Youmans; Ira and George Gershwin; Arthur Francis and Youmans; art director, Douglas Bacon; music director, Ray Heindorf; camera, Wilfred M. Cline; editor, Irene Morra.

Doris Day (Nanette Carter); Gordon MacRae (Jimmy

Smith); Gene Nelson (Tommy Trainor); Patrice Wymore (Beatrice Darcy); Eve Arden (Pauline Hastings); Billy De Wolfe (Larry Blair); S.Z. Sakall (J. Maxwell Bloomhaus); Bill Goodwin (William Early); Virginia Gibson (Mabel Wiley); Crauford Kent (Stevens); Mary Eleanor Donahue (Lynne); Johnny McGovern (Richard); Michael Miller, Norman Ollestad (Boys); Carol Coombe, Daria Massey (Girls); Harry Harvey (Crochety Man); George Baxter (Backer); Herschel Dougherty (Theatre Manager); Abe Dinovitch (Taxi Driver); Elizabeth Flourney (Secretary); Buddy Shaw (Piano Mover); John Hedloe (Chorus Boy); Jack Daley (Truck Driver); Art Gilmore (Radio Announcer).

THREE HUSBANDS (United Artists, 1950) 78 M.
Producer, G. Goldsmith; director, Irving Reis; based on a story by Vera Caspary; screenplay, Caspary, Edward Eliscu; music, Herschel Burke Gilbert; art director, Rudolph Sternad; camera, Frank Planer; editor, Louis H. Sackin.
Emlyn Williams (Maxwell Bard); Eve Arden (Lucille McCabe); Howard da Silva (Dan McCabe); Sheppard Strudwick (Arthur Evans); Ruth Warrick (Jane Evans); Vanessa Brown (Mary Whittaker); Robert Karnes (Kenneth Whittaker); Luise Erickson (Mathilda Clegg); Billie Burke (Mrs. Whittaker); Jane Darwell (Mrs. Wurdeman); Benson Fong (George, The Butler); Frank Cady (Elevator Operator); Dorothy Wolbert (Cleaning Woman); Ralph Peters (Policeman); Martha Mitrovitch (Secretary); Jill Kraft (Receptionist); Jerry Hausner (Bartender); Dorothy Vaughan (Maid); John Dierkes (Warden); Alvin Hammer (Seedy Little Man); Richard Flato (Waiter); Jonathan Hale (Wurdeman); William Simpson (Barry); Maurice Marsac (French Man); Gay Gayle (French Girl); Stanley Prager (Sharpy).

GOODBYE, MY FANCY (Warner Brothers, 1951) 106 M.
Producer, Henry Blanke; director, Vincent Sherman; based on the play by Fay Kanin; screenplay, Dvan Goff, Ben Roberts; art director, Stanley Fleischer; music director, Ray Heindorf; assistant director, Frank Mattison; camera, Ted McCord; editor, Rudi Fehr.
Joan Crawford (Agatha Reed); Robert Young (Dr. James Merrill); Frank Lovejoy (Matt Cole); Eve Arden (Woody); Janice Rule (Virginia Merrill); Lurene Tuttle (Ellen Griswold); Howard St. John (Claude Griswold); Viola Roache (Miss Schackleford); Ellen Corby (Miss Birdeshaw); Morgan Farley (Dr. Pitt); Virginia Gibson (Mary Nell Dodge); John Qualen (Prof. Dingley); Ann Robin (Clarisse Carter); Mary Carver (Jon Wintner); Creighton Hale (Butler); Tony Merrill (Clay); James Griffith (Somers); Frank Hyer (Man); Jay Merrick (G.I.); Frank McFarland (Colonel); John Alvin (Jack White); Eddie Johnson (Bellboy); Frank Conlon (Frank); John Hedloe (Telephone Man); Harlan Briggs, George Bunny (Janitors); Billy McClean (Russ Hughes); Janet Stewart (Student); Charles Conrad, Phil Tead (Reporters); Isabelle Withers (Typist); Glen Turnbull (Photographer); Lucius Cook, Fredrick Howard, Larry Williams (Congressmen).

WE'RE NOT MARRIED (20th Century-Fox, 1952) 85 M.
Producer, Nunnally Johnson; director, Edmund Golding; story, Gina Kaus, Jay Dratler; adaptation, Dwight Taylor; screenplay, Johnson; music, Cyril J. Mockridge; art director, Lyle Wheeler, Leland Fuller; music director, Lionel Newman; camera, Leo Tover; editor, Louis Loeffler.
Ginger Rogers (Ramona Gladwyn); Fred Allen (Steve Gladwyn); Victor Moore (Justice of the Peace Bush); Marilyn Monroe (Annabel Norris); David Wayne (Jeff Norris); Eve Arden (Katie Woodruff); Paul Douglas (Hec-

tor Woodruff); Eddie Bracken (Wilson Boswell Fisher); Mitzi Gaynor (Patricia Reynolds); Louis Calhern (Frederic Melrose); Zsa Zsa Gabor (Eve Melrose); James Gleason (Duffy); Paul Stewart (Attorney Stone); Jane Darwell (Mrs. Bush); Alan Bridge (Detective Magnus); Harry Goler (Radio Announcer); Victor Sutherland (Governor Bush); Tom Powers (Attorney General); Maurice Cass (Organist); Maude Wallace (Autograph Hound); Margie Liszt (Irene Daughter on Radio); Richard Buckley (Mr. Graves); Blyth Daly (Secretary); Mike Lally, Mary Newton, Alvin Greenman, Eddie Firestone (People in Radio Station); Phyllis Brunner (Wife); Murray Pollock (Groom); James Burke (M/Sgt. Nuckols); Fred Datig, Jr. (Soldier); Robert Dane (M.P. at Railroad Station); Gregg Martell (Soldier); Jerry Miley (Station Master); Dick Cogan (Telegraph Agent); Robert Forrest, Bill Hale (M.P.'s); Richard Reeves (Brig Guard); George Wallace (Shore Patrolman); John Close (Major); June Bright (Secretary); Byron Foulger (License Bureau Clerk); Harry Antrim (Justice of the Peace); Lee Marvin (Pinky); Ralph Dumke (Twitchell); Marjorie Weaver (Ruthie); O.Z. Whitehead (Postman); Harry Harvey (Dr. Ned); Selmer Jackson (Chaplain Hall); Helen Stanley (Mary); Carol Brewster (Bridesmaid); Al Thompson (Minister); Jack Davidson (Best Man at Wedding); Marvel Andre (Governor's Secretary); Forbes Murray (Mississippi Governor); Noreen Nash (Miss O'Brien, Freddie's Secretary); Wilbur Mack (Minister).

THE LADY WANTS MINK (Republic, 1953) 92 M.
Producer, Herbert J. Yates; associate producer-director, William A. Seiter; story, Leonard Neubauer, Lou Schor; screenplay, Dane Lussier, Richard Alan Simmons; music, Stanley Wilson; art director, Martin Obzina; camera, Reggie Lanning; editor, Fred Allen.
Dennis O'Keefe (Jim Connors); Ruth Hussey (Nora Connors); Eve Arden (Gladys Jones); William Demarest (Harvey Jones); Gene Lockhart (Mr. Heggie); Hope Emerson (Mrs. Hoxie); Hillary Brooke (Mrs. Cantrell); Tommy Rettig (Ritchie Connors); Earl Robie (Sandy Connors); Mary Field (Janie); Isabel Randolph (Mrs. Frazier); Thomas Browne Henry (Mr. Swiss); Brad Johnson (Bud Dunn); Mara Corday (Model) Robert Shayne (Cecil); Wade Crosby, Slim Duncan, Michael Barton (Movers); Jean Fenwick (Faye); Jean Vachon (Doris); Vicki Raaf (Daisy); Mary Alan Hokanson (Marian); Angela Greene (Marge); Barbara Billingsley (Phyllis); Arthur Walsh (Motorcycle Postman); Howard J. Negley (Mr. Binyon); Max Wagner (Mr. Benson); Rodney Bell (Dave); Joseph Mell (Ralph); Sydney Mason (Newton); Frank Gerstle (Frank-Office Worker); Wayne Tredway (Mr. Murdock); Bobby Diamond (Melvin Potts); Dennis Ross (Augie); Gail Bonney (Landlady).

OUR MISS BROOKS (Warner Brothers, 1956) 86 M.
Producer, David Weisbart; director, Al Lewis; based on the radio-television series by Robert Mann; screenplay, Lewis, Joseph Quillan; music, Roy Webb; art director, Leo K. Kuter; camera, Joseph La Shella; editor, Frederick Y. Smith.
Eve Arden (Miss Brooks); Gale Gordon (Mr. Conklin); Bob Rockwell (Mr. Boynton); Richard Crenna (Walter Denton); Don Porter (Lawrence Nolan); Jane Morgan (Mrs. Davis); Gloria MacMillan (Harriet Conklin); Leonard Smith ("Stretch" Snodgrass); Nick Adams (Gary Nolan); Joe Kearns (Mr. Stone); Marjorie Bennett (Mrs. Boynton); June Blair (Miss Lonelyhearts); William Newell (Dr. Henley); Phil Van Zandt (Mr. Webster); Joe Forte (Butler); Leo Curley, David Alpert (Realty Men); Herb Vigran, Frank Mitchell (Reporters).

ANATOMY OF A MURDER (Columbia, 1959) 160 M.

Producer-director, Otto Preminger; based on the novel by John D. Voelker; screenplay, Wendell Mayes; art director, Boris Leven; music, Duke Ellington; assistant director, David Silver; camera, Sam Leavitt; editor, Louis R. Loeffler.

James Stewart (Paul Biegler); Lee Remick (Laura Manion); Ben Gazzara (Lt. Manion); Arthur O'Connell (Parnell McCarthy); Eve Arden (Maida); Kathryn Grant (Mary Pilant); George C. Scott (Claude Dancer); Orson Bean (Dr. Smith); Russ Brown (Mr. Lemon); Murray Hamilton (Paquette); Brooks West (Mitch Lodwick); Ken Lynch (Sgt. Durgo); John Qualen (Sulo); Duke Ellington (Pie Eye); Joseph N. Welch (Judge Weaver); Royal Beal (Sheriff Battisfore); Howard McNear (Dr. Dompierre); Ned Wever (Dr. Raschid); Jimmy Conlin (Madigan); Joseph Kearns (Mr. Burke); Don Ross (Duane Miller); Lloyd LeVasseur (Court Clerk); James Waters (Army Sergeant); Alexander Campbell (Dr. Campbell); Irv Kupcinet (Distinguished Gentleman); Mrs. Joseph Welch (Juror).

THE DARK AT THE TOP OF THE STAIRS (Warner Brothers, 1960) 123 M.

Producer, Michael Garrison; director, Delbert Mann; based on the play by William Inge; screenplay, Harriet Frank, Jr., Irving Ravetch; music, Max Steiner; assistant director, Russell Llewellyn; art director, Leo K. Kuter; camera, Harry Stradling, Sr.; editor, Flomar Blangsted.

Robert Preston (Rubin Flood); Dorothy McGuire (Cora Flood); Eve Arden (Lottie); Angela Lansbury (Marvis Pruitt); Shirley Knight (Reenie Flood); Frank Overton (Morris); Lee Kinsolving (Sammy Golden); Robert Eyer (Sonny Flood); Penney Parker (Flirt Conroy); Dennis Whitcomb (Punky Givens); Ken Lynch (Harry Ralston); Nelson Leigh (Ed Peabody); Emerson Treacy (George Williams); Ben Erway (Joseph Moody); Helen Brown (Mrs. Haycox); Jean Paul King, John Eiman, Mike Chain, Bobby Beekman, Butch Hengen (Boys); Helen Wallace (Lydia Harper); Peg LaCentra (Edna Harper); Paul Birch (Jonah Mills); Mary Patton (Mrs. Ralston); Paul Comi (Jenkins); Addison Richards (Harris); Robin Warga (Harold); Charles Seel (Percy Weems); Stoddard Kirby (Cadet).

SERGEANT DEADHEAD (American-International, 1965) 89 M.

Producer, James H. Nicholson, Samuel Z. Arkoff; co-producer, Anthony Carras; director, Norman Taurog; screenplay, Louis M. Heyward; art director, Howard Campbell; assistant director, Claude Binyon, Jr.; music, Les Baxter; songs, Guy Hemric; Jerry Styner; sound, Don Rush; choreographer, Jack Baker; camera, Floyd Crosby; editor, Ronald Sinclair, Fred Feitshans, Eve Newman.

Frankie Avalon (Sgt. O.K. Deadhead/Sgt. Donovan); Deborah Walley (Corporal Lucy Turner); Fred Clark (General Rufus Fogg); Cesar Romero (Admiral Stoneham); Eve Arden (Lt. Charlotte Kinsey); Gale Gordon (Captain Weiskopft); Harvey Lembeck (Pvt. McEvoy); Buster Keaton (Pvt. Blinker); John Ashley (Pvt. Filroy); Pat Buttram (President); Donna Loren (Susan); Tod Windsor (Sgt. Keeler); Norma Grabowski, Mike Nader (Air Police); Ed Faulkner (Radioman); Bobbi Shaw (Gilda); Romo Vincent (Tuba Player) John Heaston, Ed Reimers (Announcers); Patti Chandler (Patti); Salli Sachse (Sue Ellen); Luree Holmes (Luree); Sue Hamilton (Ivy); Bob Harvey (Bellhop); Jerry Brutsche (Newsman); Andy Romano, John Macchia (Marine Police); Mary Hughes, Astrid DeBria, Jean Ingram, Peggy Ward, Stephanie Nader, Lyzanne Ladue, Janice Levinson, Alberta Nelson (WAFS); Sallie Dornan (Secretary).

Agnes Moorehead

5'3½"
115 pounds
Titian hair
Blue eyes
Birth sign: Sagittarius

Ever since Agnes Moorehead made her distinguished screen debut in Orson Welles's Citizen Kane *(1941), followed by his* The Magnificent Ambersons, *audiences have associated her with heavy dramatics on the grand scale. For many, Agnes's performances represent the near epitome of screen theatrics, on a par in quality with top-ranking stars, even if most of her parts have been of the supporting player variety. Generally forgotten today is the fact she made her first professional mark as a versatile radio performer in 1930s New York and that most of her work was in the light comedy vein.*

Far more often than not, Agnes in her 62 feature films to date, has played offbeat roles far removed from the vitriolic screen image she maintains. She was a Damon Runyonesque food lover in The Big Street, *an elegant, sympathetic baroness in* Mrs. Parkington, *a thoughtful warden in* Caged, *and an arch judge in* Bachelor in Paradise. *But it has been her forceful film emoting in* Jane Eyre, Dragon Seed, Dark Passage, Hush . . . Hush, Sweet Charlotte, *and in* Sorry, Wrong Number *on radio that won her most acclaim and has remained longest in filmgoers' minds.*

*In addition to her prolific screen career, Agnes has made constant forays back to the stage (*Don Juan in Hell, Lord Pengo, Gigi*) and has been extremely successful with her long-touring one woman show,* The Fabulous Redhead. *To prove to one and all that she could be both glamorous and wryly comic, Agnes costarred for several seasons on television's successful series "Bewitched." Today, between her assorted acting chores, Agnes still finds time to conduct acting courses and to mingle with the public, revealing herself to be far removed from the termagant she enacts so effectively and so often onscreen.*

Of Protestant-Irish ancestry, Agnes Robertson Moorehead was born December 6, 1906, in Clinton, Massachusetts, the only child of Reverend John Henderson Moorehead, a Presbyterian minister. Her mother, Mary Mildred MacCauley, had been reared in rural Pennsylvania. Soon after the birth of Agnes, the Mooreheads moved to St. Louis, Missouri, where the Reverend had been assigned to a new pastorage.

Agnes' childhood was not as strictly supervised as one would suspect for a clergyman's daughter in the 1910s; it was a good deal more liberal than that of Marjorie Main, for example (born: February 24, 1890, near Acton, Indiana, the daughter of a pastor of the First Christian Church). Both of these personalities were more imaginative than most youths their age, and each would mature to become an actress and later play different stereotypes of the American pioneer woman at MGM in the 1940s.

Agnes recalls of her youth: "I was brought up on Grimm [Fairy tales] and I never had a trauma. I used to get all excited about things coming around the corner, but I wasn't scared. My mother says I was constantly pretending to be someone else. Once she found me crying in the corner because I had read *The Poor Little Match Girl* and was pretending to be cold and hungry too. She didn't stop me.

"I used to come home after school with great tales about people I saw in the street. I'd tell my father and he'd say 'Yes and then what did they do?' He never stopped me."

It became a familiar ritual in the Moorehead household for the mother to ask, "Well, Agnes, who are you today?"

As a child, Agnes would perform eagerly at church functions, singing such hymns as "The Lord Is My Shepherd." When she was ten, determined little Agnes persuaded her indulgent parents to allow her to become one of the local girls used for the ballet and chorus of the St. Louis Municipal Opera Company. Sometimes the girls would be used as extras and walk-ons at the Forest

Agnes Moorehead in the late 1920s.

Park Stock Company. This extra-curricular theater work lasted four years. Agnes loved every minute of it.

Contrary to the concept that all clergymen were stuffed shirts, Agnes has stated: "My father never discouraged me from the theater, but he never encouraged me. He said one thing and that was 'I want you to have an education first and then you can do what you want, try your wings.' "

Years later, publicity material regarding Agnes would mention that during her "childhood" she had played Little Eva in a Mississippi River showboat production of *Uncle Tom's Cabin,* rode an elephant in a circus act, and performed in a professional ice skating show. None of these unique activities can be verified by independent research, and Miss Moorehead has persistently refused to acknowledge or deny the same, simply stating every actress should have some mystery in her life and not be as straight forward as the proverbial girl next door.

Regarding her adolescent social life, Agnes remem-

bers: ". . . I never had a date by myself until I was in college. I was always chaperoned. There were parties, dances, and great sleigh parties but always there were older people with us, but not hampering us. Oh, we had a great time."

After completing high school in 1919, Agnes matriculated at Muskingum College in New Concord, Ohio, a coeducational institution founded by an uncle. While there, Agnes demonstrated her intellectual nature by majoring in biology. Not only did she perform in the glee club all four years, but she was an active member of the girls' athletic association and the Student Volunteer Group. And, of course, she participated in the class plays. She was Toinon Chepy in Louis N. Parker's *The Aristocrat* her junior year and played Margaret Lightfoot in Paul Kestler's historical drama *Friend Hannah* in her senior year.

Having received her B.A. from Muskingum,* Agnes remained at the College for an additional year of postgraduate work, majoring in education, speech, and English. The following year, she transferred to the University of Wisconsin at Madison, so she could be closer to home. Her father had by then been posted to Reedsburg, Wisconsin.

In the fall of 1925, Agnes began teaching public speaking and English at the Central High School in nearby Soldiers Grove, Wisconsin, and coaching the local drama group. She had made up her mind to embark on a professional acting career and had decided to save money to audition for and hopefully enter the American Academy of Dramatic Arts (AADA) in New York. In 1926, during time off from school, she performed on radio stations KSO and KMOX in St. Louis, but nothing promising developed from this fringe work.

Agnes arrived in New York in the fall of 1927 and was accepted as a student at the AADA. To support herself, since her parents never had really enough funds left over to help their daughter sufficiently, Agnes taught drama at the private, progressive Dalton School in Manhattan. While at the Academy, she appeared in such one-act dramas as Patricia Brown's *Gloria Mundi,* set in an insane asylum, Clare Krummer's *Chinese Love,* and Frank Craven's domestic study *The First Year.* In Frederick Lonsdale's *The Last of Mrs. Cheyney,* Agnes was aristocratic Mrs. Wynton; in Walter Hackett's fantasy-mystery *Captain Applejack,* she was a multi-accented thief; in Alice Duer Miller's comedy *The Springboard* she was Rhoda Brice; and in David Gray-Avery Hopwood's comedy *The Best People,* Agnes was

---

* In 1945, Muskingum would present Agnes with an honorary degree as a doctor of literature.

among those involved in New York's theatrical district. Agnes graduated with honors from the AADA in the spring of 1929. One of her classmates was Rosalind Russell.

It was not the most auspicious time to find work anywhere, let alone in the theatre. The entire country was gripped by the depression. She would later describe these financially difficult days in a byline article for *Guideposts* magazine (August, 1965):

> ... To make my money last, I ate almost nothing: hot water for breakfast, a roll for lunch, rice for dinner. It was hungry work, making the rounds of casting agents, mile after mile on the unyielding sidewalk, and I used to wonder fervently just how God was going to provide manna in this man-made wilderness.
>
> At last came the day when I was literally down to my last dime. I stood in front of an automat gazing hungrily at the plates of food behind their little glass doors. The trouble was that one of the agents had given clear instructions, 'Phone, don't come in,' which meant that five of my 10 cents would have to go into a telephone box instead of opening one of those little doors.
>
> With dragging feet I went into the drugstore next door and changed my worldly wealth into two nickels. I shut myself in the phone booth at the rear of the store, inserted one of my precious nickels—and then waited in growing alarm for the operator's voice. Half my fortune was in that phone, and nothing happened—the coin was not even returned to me!
>
> I jiggled the hook. I pounded the box, but it held tight to the coin that would have brought me a big white roll—and a pat of butter on the plate beside it. As always when I let myself think about food, a kind of desperation seized me. I thrust two fingers into the coin return, clawing the cold metal sides of the tube. They closed on a piece of paper.
>
> Though I didn't know it then, I had stumbled onto a familiar racket of those days. Pay phones were built in such a way that a piece of paper inserted from the bottom would trap the money in the chute. All I knew what as I drew out the paper, a little river of money streamed into my lap: dimes and quarters as well as nickels. In all, when I had finished my incredulous count, I had $4.25.
>
> I knew, of course, that the money belonged to the phone company—and I paid it back with interest as soon as I could. But I never doubted, also, that this money was manna direct from heaven. The oatmeal and rice it bought lasted until I got my first part.

For twenty-three old, determined Agnes, there were no obstacles too big to overcome. She had set her mind on a stage career, knew she had the abilities required, and would not allow any forces to sidetrack her from her ambition. By dint of perseverance, Agnes obtained small stage roles, often as the maid or near supernumerary, in second and third touring companies of such plays as *Marco Millions, Scarlet Pages, All the King's Horses,* and *Candlelight.* In Paul Harvey Fox and George Tilton's murder mystery *Soldiers And Women* (Ritz Theatre, September 2, 1929), Agnes was an understudy and substituted for Sarat Lahiri a week after the opening.

Agnes would later remark about her salad days in show business: "When I entered the theater, I became wholeheartedly a character performer. To me, character people are the actors." What she did not have to add was that she had shrewdly assessed her physical looks and knew that at best she was striking, and certainly not a conventional ingenue type.

Another facet of Agnes's personality which stood her in good stead during her fledgling period was her religious upbringing, which gave her the faith to continue where others might have quit. Says Agnes: "My life has been ruled by my beliefs ('working for the glory of God') and in matters of belief I am a Fundamentalist." Never content with reaching one level of artistic and/or intellectual achievement, Agnes has always been driven to further peaks. These aspects of her nature, while bettering her as a performer and person, have had the unfortunate result of coloring her professional work with an aura of seemingly egotistical self-determination. Such a quality was very often useful in the portrayal of her parts, but usually left the viewer with a wrong impression of Agnes, the real person behind her theatrical image.

While at the AADA, Agnes had met John Griffith Lee, the same age as she, and they had become good friends. They were married June 6, 1930, in New York. He would continue on with his stage and radio career, but in no degree ever obtained the steady prominence that Agnes did, which no doubt contributed to the eventual dissolution of the union.

With the helter-skelter nature of theater jobs, Agnes decided she would fare better by concentrating in radio. Having dabbled in the medium before, she did not find it too difficult to break into the field in Manhattan. She had a deep, resonant voice and the ability to project with good enunciation, no matter how she disguised her normal voice.

Her first major radio break occurred when she was hired in 1930 for a twenty-week stint on Phillips H. Lord's "Seth Parker Hour" (NBC), a folksy New England-set show that had great appeal for middle America. She was among the show's company who went on a nationwide personal appearance tour to meet the show's adoring public. With this big league background behind her, Agnes found it easier to obtain new audio assignments.

At one period in the early 1930s, Agnes was appear-

ing on as many as six radio shows a day. For her supporting parts, she would earn on the average of fifteen
to twenty dollars (total) per day.* It did not provide
fame or fortune, but it gave Agnes tremendous experience in a variety of roles.

It was in the early 1930s that Agnes had occasion to
work on several radio shows with Helen Hayes. Agnes
had the knack and the intelligence of becoming friendly
with her prominent co-workers, a habit which proved
smart business-ship in the years ahead. Miss Hayes
volunteered to arrange a motion picture interview for
Agnes with an East Coast talent agent. Agnes remembers the gentleman taking one look at her prominent
features, and then saying: "Broken nose, huh? Afraid
you're not the type." Any illusions Agnes may have had
about a film career at this time were shattered. She
went back to radio.

In the 1933–1936 period, Agnes expanded her radio
activities to vaudeville and for a long stretch appeared
with comedian Phil Baker in a theatre and club act entitled "Baker, Bottle, Bettle." She was the auxiliary
player, Mrs. Sarah Heartburn, a gal who could answer
two phone conversations at once and still manage to
get the messages almost right. (She would later play
this stooge role on Baker's long-running radio program
in the 1930s.)

It was about 1935 that Agnes first met Orson Welles
(then age twenty), who proved to be one of the most
influential persons in forming the course of her later
professional career. "We met on a soap opera and I
was immediately intrigued with him. He was very conservative, sat in a corner—constantly reading classics.
He had a marvelous voice. We became extremely good
friends."

It was not too long after that meeting that Agnes was
working with Welles (he being the narrator "voice")
on NBC's the "March of Time" and other radio programs. When in March, 1937, he was signed to play
millionaire playboy Lamont Cranston on the audio
thriller "The Shadow," Agnes was hired as secretary-

Ray Collins, Agnes Moorehead, and Orson Welles in a
performance of the "Mercury Theatre on the Air," circa
1938.

helper Margot Lane. The show was enormously popular
and ran for two years.

By mid 1937, boy-genius Welles hit upon the concept
of forming his own Broadway repertory theater that
would force-feed culture on the American scene. With
producer John Houseman (who helped form the avant-
garde Phoenix Theatre and had worked with Welles in
the Federal Theatre Project), he set about the monu-
mental task. After many false starts, Welles offered a
modern dress version of Shakespeare's *Julius Caesar*
at the Mercury Theatre (the renamed 622-seat Comedy
Theatre on 41st and Sixth Avenue) on November 11,
1937. Marc Blitzstein composed an entire score for the
show, to be played by the theater's tiny orchestra. The
cast consisted of Welles (Brutus), Joseph Cotten (Pub-
lius), Martin Gabel (Cassius), Hiram Sherman (Casca).
Since the two lead female roles, Calpurnia and Portia,
were played by Evelyn Allen and Muriel Brassler respectively, it has never been clarified what part Agnes
actually had in the original stage production. The show
proved a big hit and was later transferred to the National Theatre for a substantial run.

Meanwhile, Agnes continued with her radio work.
With her adeptness at portraying imperious indignity,
she was the perfect comedy foil for a host of radio
comedians such as Fred Allen, Phil Baker, Jack Benny
(she was on his first radio show), Ben Bernie, Bert
Lahr, and others. Vocally, Agnes could sum up all the
magnificent hautiness that made Margaret Dumont so
effective as the straight lady for the Marx Brothers' stage
and film shenanigans. Agnes was equally adept at soap
opera. She debuted on "Joyce Jordan, Girl Interne"
(February 1, 1937) and on "Way Down East" (March,
1938). With her knack for creating a variety of voice

---

* Agnes was a regular on such 1930s radio shows as
"The Adventures of Mister Meek" (comedy—as the first
maid); "The Aldrich Family" (comedy—as Mrs. Brown,
Homer's mother); "Bringing Up Father" (comedy—as
Maggie); "Bulldog Drummond" (mystery); "Dot and Will"
(serial drama—as Rosie); "East of Cairo" (adventure);
"The Gumps" (comedy-drama—as Min Gump); "Hilltop
House" (serial drama—as Mrs. Townsend); "Life Begins"
(serial drama—as Mrs. Riley); "Life Can Be Beautiful"
(serial drama—as Nellies Conrad); "Mystery House"
(mystery); "The Orange Lantern" (mystery); "Sherlock
Holmes" (mystery); "Terry and the Pirates" (adventure—
as The Dragon Lady); "This Day Is Ours" (serial drama—
as Catherine Allison); "Way Down East" (serial drama).

characterizations, she was an economical cast member to have around, and such shows as the "March of Time" took full advantage of her. Her record on that program was eight roles in one show. (Later in the series she would play such divergent international figures as Madame Chiang, Kai Shek, and Eleanor Roosevelt.)

In June, 1938, CBS hired Welles, Houseman, and the entire Mercury Theatre company as a package deal for a weekly program "The Mercury Theatre on the Air," with Welles functioning as producer, director, writer, narrator, star, and master of ceremonies ("Your obedient servant"). The show opened with "Treasure Island" and followed up with "Abraham Lincoln," "The 39 Steps," "Jane Eyre," "The Man Who Was Thursday," and "Julius Caesar." The most famous of this series' episodes was Howard Koch's adaptation of H.G. Wells' *The War of the Worlds* (October 30, 1938). This dramatization in documentary style was so realistic and vivid that it caused a near national panic when America tuned in and thought the Martians had really landed at Groves Mills, New Jersey.

The extraordinarily versatile Welles was not content with masterminding this one show for his Mercury Theatre group and had also launched "America's Hour" (CBS), a sixty-minute, Sunday night documentary show, presenting stories on various aspects of American life. There had been the *Columbia Workshop,* a dramatic series using the Mercury repertory group and the *"Orson Welles Almanac"* (CBS), an attempt at a comedy format which fizzled. By the 1938–1939 season, Welles-Mercury outfit was performing vignettes of this country's history in *Cavalcade Of America* (CBS). The March 15, 1939 broadcast consisted of excerpts from the life of the late film star Marie Dressler, with Agnes in the lead role. *Variety* reported: ". . . [she] turned in a superb performance, steadily changing from a diffident, youthful-voiced tyro to the celebrated and assured, but huge-hearted old woman. And her voice sounded quite like Miss Dressler's."

In the spring and summer of 1939, RKO Radio Pictures, under the executive leadership of George Schaefer, negotiated an amazing contract with Welles to be producer, director, writer, or actor (or any combination of these he desired) of one picture a year at $150,000 per film plus a percentage of the gross. One of the contract's other terms was that the members of the Mercury Theatre troupe should be given RKO contracts as well. Thus in the summer of 1939, Welles' group (including Agnes, Joseph Cotten, Everett Sloane, Paul Stewart, George Coulouris, Ray Collins, and Ruth Warwick) arrived in Hollywood. It had been decided that a screen version of Joseph Conrad's *Heart of Darkness* would be the Mercury Theatre production unit's first film project.

Some of the group, like Coulouris, were paid $1,000 weekly for five weeks with a renewal option to continue if it proved necessary. The salaries of the others, like Agnes, were less, but still substantial.

The Conrad project proved unsatisfactory to the RKO regime, and the Mercury troupe found itself off salary. To keep his people in money, Welles negotiated with CBS to broadcast the "Mercury Theatre on the Air" from the West Coast. This way, the group was employed and salaried.

It took Welles nearly a year before a proper project could be decided upon, one that was considered properly commercial by the RKO executives. During this waiting period, Welles' company were under orders not to accept any other possible film roles since he wanted his cast to be fresh movie faces when they finally appeared on the screen in his production. Only George Coulouris broke the structure, but Welles reasoned that since the actor had appeared in such heavy makeup in his roles in *All This and Heaven Too* and *The Lady in Question,* he would still be virtually a new movie face. Such was the Welles charisma, that the other Mercuryites sat back in silent patience with only their radio work to keep them professionally occupied.

The chosen picture, *Citizen Kane,* finally began its four month production, shooting on July 30, 1940. Filmed at a cost of $746,000, the feature was lensed in as much secrecy as was possible in studio-controlled, 1940 Hollywood. Before it was completed, word had leaked out that the picture was a shattering exposé of the life of newspaper chain publisher William Randolph Hearst. Welles' retort was: "It is not based upon the life of Mr. Hearst or anyone else. On the other hand, had Mr. Hearst and similar financial barons not lived during the period we discuss, *Citizen Kane* could not have been made."

Nevertheless, Hearst retaliated by banning newspaper ads of the film or Welles's name to appear in any of the Hearst papers. (He later relented in order to attack the picture.) By the time harried RKO executives opened *Citizen Kane* at the RKO Palace Theatre May 1, 1941, there was a good deal of public interest in this controversial feature. The critics who dared buck the Hearst interest were openly enthusiastic about the 119-minute, black and white picture, which proved to be the most technically and creatively innovative film Hollywood had seen in many years. *Citizen Kane* did well in urban centers, but failed badly in rural areas here and abroad. It would be many years before the feature finally showed a profit.

In the by-now familiar presentation of *Citizen Kane,* "News on the March" newsreel editor Philip Van Zandt orders newsreel reporter William Alland to find out all he can about newspaper mogul Kane: "You've got to tell us who he was. Maybe he told us all about himself on his deathbed. When Kane died, he said just one word, 'Rosebud.' Now what does that mean?" In his researching, Alland interviews four people who knew the private Charles Foster Kane (Welles), the world's sixth richest man, and head of an empire that includes 37 newspapers, 2 news syndicates, a radio network, ocean liners, factories, and so on.

It is through the memoirs of dead banker Walter Parks Thatcher (George Coulouris) that the viewer obtains his first introduction to Kane as an eight-year-old child in Colorado in 1871. In the remote town of Little Salem at a desolate wooden boardinghouse, Thatcher is seen talking to Mrs. Kane (Agnes) and her husband (Harry Shannon). A defaulting boarder had bequeathed her the Colorado Lode, and a fabulously rich ore strike there has made the Kane family tremendously wealthy. By terms of the agreement, the parents are to receive $50,000 yearly, with the rest in trust for the son, who will come into full control of the balance at the age of twenty-one. She has agreed to signing over control of the fortune and son to Coulouris' bank so the boy would be spared from his brutal and crude father and be taken away from the bleak Little Salem surroundings. When the boy (Buddy Swan), who had been romping in the snow with his sled, named Rosebud, is called to the house and told the news that he is wealthy and now will go East with Coulouris, his immediate reaction is to slam the sled into the banker.

In these few stark, deep-focus-filmed scenes, Agnes is shown as a barren woman, beaten by the elements of life. Dressed in her drab, functional wool dress and

With Harry Shannon, George Coulouris, and Buddy Swan in *Citizen Kane*.

dark shawl, she appears like a member of a Greek chorus, setting the stage for the later events, as the authority-hating young Kane is warped by the power of money into a tool of power himself and emerges a titanic egomaniac, possessing enormous worldly riches, but lacking what he wants most of all: love.

Agnes' brief appearance in *Citizen Kane* presented the actress in a screen type that she would play throughout the following decades. As a self-sufficient creature who could battle the elements successfully but had lost the struggle to nurture a growing personality, she typified a popular concept of the American pioneer woman. Hollywood would trade upon this immediate audience-reflex association and cast Agnes in such roles time and time again, using her as a change of pace from such other rural types as Anne Revere, Selena Royale, Jane Darwell, and Edna May Oliver.

As a member of the Welles' stock company in *Citizen Kane,* Agnes received her share of plaudits, but most of the critical attention went to Welles's virtuoso performance as actor, director, co-scriptor, producer, and so on. The feature was nominated for several Academy Awards, but members of the Academy Of Motion Pictures Arts And Sciences were no friends of hotshot Welles, who had crashed the inner circles of the film industry so easily and then proceeded to rock the safe political boat by infuriating the Hearst interests.

A side effect of the rhubarb over the release of *Citizen Kane* was to make Welles and his Mercury troupe, by association, *persona non grata* in many Hollywood social and business circles. In fact, the hands-off policy on the Welles team reached such a point in late 1941 that Hedda Hopper took up the championship of

With Harry Shannon and George Coulouris in *Citizen Kane* (RKO, 1941).

Agnes, who had ingratiated herself with this columnist supreme. In one of her syndicated columns Hopper asked the film industry at large about Agnes: "Why do you have an ax to grind with this girl? She hasn't done anything."

Through it all, Agnes has always remained loyal to Welles. She would later state: "Without a doubt, he is the most stimulating man I've ever met. I feel it is a disgrace, the way Hollywood and the press let him down, even turned against him. He's an authentic genius—and there are only one or two of these born in each era. He has many quirks. I admit it, but that is what makes him the talent he is. Those quirks give him that fantastic imagination. When you take that away from an actor, you've taken the thing that really makes him go, makes him different." She would still later reminisce about Welles and *Citizen Kane* on "It Was A Very Good Year" (July 26, 1971, ABC-TV).

Fortunately, before the 1941 holocaust over *Citizen Kane,* Welles had renegotiated an extended RKO contract for him and his troupe. The agreement called for another three pictures at the studio, which guaranteed the Mercury company additional performances.

It was a long wait, but finally Welles's next screen project *The Magnificent Ambersons* began production on October 28, 1941 and opened August 13, 1942. The property had been filmed before by Vitagraph in 1925 as *Pampered Youth,* and Welles had already presented the story on his "Mercury Theatre on the Air" (June 26, 1939). As a follow-up project to *Citizen Kane, The Magnificent Ambersons* suffered in contrast, not being devised on the same great scale. It was not a study of personal meglomania, but rather a general examination of a midwestern town in 1873, and in particular, a focus on the members of the once-prominent Amberson family and the people most closely affected by their actions.

The central character, but certainly not the only major focal point in *The Magnificent Ambersons,* is the enormous egotist, Georgie Minafer (Tim Holt). As a young adult he maneuvers his widowed mother (Dolores Costello) out of possible happiness with her long-standing beau, automobile inventor Eugene Morgan (Joseph Cotten), and out of self-pride refuses to wed Morgan's daughter Lucy (Anne Baxter). Later Costello dies unhappily, and her father (Richard Bennett) soon thereafter passes away. Holt and his "poor" Aunt Fanny (Agnes) whom he has terrorized since infancy, are impelled to sell the family mansion. Furthermore, she is forced to run a modest boardinghouse and he becomes a lawyer's assistant. As a final touch of irony, Georgie, now George, who has always hated cars (they remind him of Morgan), is involved in an automobile accident and taken to the hospital. Now humbled, he

With Joseph Cotten in *The Magnificent Ambersons* (RKO, 1942).

asks Cotton's forgiveness.

Before Welles could complete the editing of *The Magnificent Ambersons,* RKO sent him to Brasil to film *It's All True,* leaving the Tarkington story to be completed for release by executive committee decision. The resulting hacked-together feature pleased neither Welles nor the public. *The Magnificent Ambersons* made no concession to popular taste, and many wondered if a study of minor league aristocracy deserved such a resourceful and amplified production.

It was in this film that Agnes demonstrated the dramatic flare that so attracted Welles to her when they met in their radio days, years before. Here, Agnes revealed how totally different in nature she was from the other Mercury Theatre-ites. They all shared a love of the multi-media entertainment world, and each possessed an extremely well-modulated voice. However, next to Welles, Agnes was possibly the only member of the troupe who possessed a high-keyed personality. Like Welles, she had a dominant nature and would require strong direction to channel her tremendous energy so that it would emerge in accord with the film and not as an intriguing distraction.

Agnes was fifth-billed in *The Magnificent Ambersons* as poor unmarried Fanny, the sister of Dolores Costello's meek husband, Don Dillaway. In the context of the picture, she has always adored gentlemanly inventor Joseph Cotton but decided he and Costello were destined for each other. Thus, she retained her yearning love in quiet self-counsel. It is Fanny, so frustrated by her self-contained, passive existence, who is prone to violent outbursts of emotion when she can tolerate her voyeur role no longer. Goaded by her arrogant nephew George (Tim Holt) she shouts: "Oh, you're always picking on me! Always. Ever since you were a little boy!

With Ray Collins and Tim Holt in *The Magnificent Amber-sons*.

". . . You'd never treat anyone in the world like this, except old Fanny! 'Old Fanny,' that's what you say. 'It's only old Fanny, so I'll kick her . . . nobody'll resent me. I'll kick her all I want!' Then your're right. I've no one in the world since my brother died . . . nobody . . . nothing!"

As the film sweepingly progresses over the years, Fanny's unhappiness magnifies her worldly plight out of all proportion. The family fortune has been dissipated (some of it by her unwise investments). The once smug Holt has accepted an eight-dollar-a-week post in a lawyer's office, and they must bid a final goodbye to the shuttered Amberson home. The subsequent eight-minute scene, which was left uncut in the final screen version, moves over four rooms of the former grand house and provides Agnes with some of her best screen footage. Alone in the dark, deserted expanse with Holt, Agnes cries desperately: "I know what you're going to do! You're going to leave me in the lurch! . . . I knew your mother wanted me to watch over you and try to make something like a home for you, and I tried. I tried to make things as nice for you as I could. I walked my heels down looking for a place for us to live. I walked and walked over this town. I didn't ride one block on a streetcar."

With W.C. Fields on radio, circa 1942.

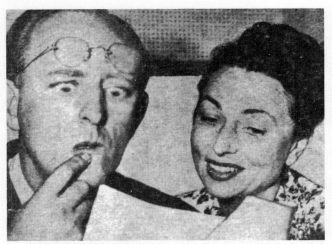

With Kay Kyser on radio, circa 1942.

The two humbled aristocrats end up in the boiler room, where repressed Fanny is fussing over the heater. She breaks into hysterics again: "It's not hot, it's cold. But I wouldn't mind if it was burning!" Holt pulls up the trembling woman and the camera rushes past them as they continue their frantic discussion about the possibility of her opening a modest boardinghouse in town and how in heaven's name they might finance this face-saving project.*

The critics were rightly enthusiastic about Agnes's performance as the jealous spinster, the "also" always on hand to accompany the main members of the family on sleigh rides, to tell Holt news about his mother's past and present, and to fetch and run for the others. Her few attempts to let down her own barriers of pride and inhibitions usually result in fumbled efforts at an easy-going manner that she does not possess (as in the wonderfully "impromptu" cake-eating scene in the kitchen—my favorite Moorehead moment in the film). The *New York Times* rated Agnes "splendid" in *The Magnificent Ambersons* and the *New York Herald-*

Tribune ranked her "brilliant." As a result of the critical plaudits, Agnes won the New York Film Critics' Award as best actress of the year. She was the only cast member of *The Magnificent Ambersons* to be nominated for an Academy Award, but she lost the best supporting actress Oscar to Teresa Wright's performance in *Mrs. Miniver* (the picture which also won the best picture Oscar over *The Magnificent Ambersons*). Hollywood was obviously not ready to forgive Orson Welles or his troupe.*

The same day *The Magnificent Ambersons* opened on the bottom half of a double bill in Manhattan, *The Big Street* (1942), Agnes' third film, debuted down the street at the RKO Palace Theatre. By the time *The Magnificent Ambersons* had gone into production, George Schaefer was out as RKO studio chief, and a new regime was installed at the studio. Charles Koerner, the new head of RKO production in Hollywood was no enthusiast of Welles and short-cutted the sanction about utilizing the Mercury Players in other RKO films. He and the executive board were determined to cut down the expensive losses sustained by the arrival of Welles and company at the studio. Thus Agnes found herself cast in *The Big Street.*

Based on a fanciful Damon Runyon story, *The Big Street* follows the rapid decline of a nifty Broadway cafe singer (Lucille Ball), a gold-digging bitch who

With Eugene Pallette in *The Big Street* (RKO, 1942).

---

* According to Charles Hingham in his book *The Films Of Orson Welles* (1970), among the several scenes deleted or altered for the final release print of *The Magnificent Ambersons* were those in reel seven, section four, in which Joseph Cotten sometime after Tim Holt's automobile accident visits Agnes at her boardinghouse. "They discuss George and his accident. A phonograph record plays in the background: a comedy duet about the loss of a city. Fanny and Eugene discuss the almost certain wedding of Lucy and George, and the change in George. As Eugene leaves the boardinghouse, the various people there are seen in mirrors. He goes out and gets into his car. Above him he sees, as he looks back, Fanny in the doorway, and the skyline of the great city. End."

---

* As recently as 1965, Orson Welles spoke of remaking the last half of *The Magnificent Ambersons,* using the same cast members who would have aged naturally and now not require the artifice of makeup to create the illusion.

becomes humanized after suffering a crippling fall at the hands of gangster club owner Barton MacLane. Her staunch supporter is Mindy's Restaurant busboy Henry Fonda (playing his naive role perfectly) who withstands all her scorn, pays her hospital bills, and magnanimously wheels her all the way to Florida in her wheelchair, so she can make one last stab at nailing her millionaire admirer. Ball does not get her man, but Fonda does provide her with a magnificent nightclub part which she thoroughly enjoys, and then she dies happily.

Agnes fitted in rather nicely in this mawkish comedy-drama, which is far more highly regarded today than when it was originally released. Agnes played Violette, a gal with a tapeworm stomach, who is always nibbling. She is the one realist among the sentimental guys-and-dolls crowd. Her secondary role had her advising Fonda mouthing such lines as: "What's the sense of having high blood pressure over a dame you can't get near. . . ." After she weds Nicely Nicely Johnson (Eugene Pallette), she and her rotund spouse move to Miami to open a boardinghouse and a barbecue stand. Marriage and the climate evidently agree with her because Agnes' Violette mellows and tries to be a helpful pal to the self-sacrificing Fonda and the humbled Ball. *The Big Street* would be Agnes's only screen fling in sentimental comedy, the one time she moved away from drama into the realm of lighthearted comedy. Her portrayal resulted in an oversized person, to be sure, but not a caricature, as she would later be in *Pardners* and *Who's Minding the Store?*

Agnes next appeared in *Journey into Fear* (1943), Welles's last picture for RKO at this period. The feature was originally released in November, 1942, but Welles persuaded the RKO studio executives to withdraw the release prints to make additional changes, and five months later it reopened to a new set of reviews. Based on an Eric Ambler mystery-thriller novel, the film was ostensibly directed by Norman Foster, although Welles supervised most of the overall concepts as well as co-scripting the screen adaptation with the picture's star, Joseph Cotten.

Journey into Fear, told within the framework of a letter from Joseph Cotten to his wife (Ruth Warrick), relates in flashback how American naval ordinance expert Cotten, sojourning in Istanbul before his return to America, suddenly finds himself a target in the international tug of power at the onslaught of World War II. After barely missing being the target of a murder attempt at the Le Jockey Club (where Dolores Del Rio is the featured dancer), he is advised by Turkish police chief Haki (Orson Welles) to leave the city by a steamer (a stinking Greek cattle boat) across the Black Sea to Batum. Aboard the vessel, he encounters socialist railwayman Frank Readick and his shrewish French wife Agnes. She is dressed very conservatively, with a shawl clinging around her plain face, her black hair piled high in ringlets. Earlier in the corridor she had screamed at Cotten to be quiet and not wake the cattle. Now she insists upon apologizing to him about her leftwing intellectual spouse. She says: "He talks like a fool but you should take no notice, monsieur. He was a brave soldier. He won this silver war badge." Later on, Readick reveals to Cotten that by pretending to be a socialist, he could maneuver his wife to leave him alone. "I discovered that my wife was a snob and even more stupid than I dreamed. . . . I, a capitalist by instinct, became a socialist by conviction." At this point the story moves on and beyond the haggling couple.

Agnes's role was not much in *Journey into Fear,* but she grabbed all the screen attention she could, sporting a stagey Gallic accent and projecting with the tremendous intensity of her piercing dark eyes her haughty busybodiness. It was as if she were compelled to draw the viewer's attention to her, before she faded from sight on the screen. The *New York Times* duly noted: "Agnes Moorehead adds another exacerbating portrait of a shrewish woman, . . ."

In the long stretches in between filmmaking Agnes had ample time to devote to performing on radio. Besides the "Mercury Theatre on the Air," she obtained comedy-foil work on the Jack Carson show. She was making dramatic guest appearances on assorted audio series, but none had the impact of her performance on CBS's "Suspense" radio program, when she played in Lucille Fletcher's "Sorry, Wrong Number" (May 25, 1943). This radio script, which has been called that medium's perfect actor's vehicle, was especially written for Agnes. It allowed her a full range of emotions, as she ". . . whimpers, cajoles and screams for twenty-five minutes without a stop." The one person tour-de-force centers on Mrs. Elbert Stevenson, a hyperneurotic invalid attempting to communicate with her husband, who claims to be working late again at the office. Through a crossed telephone wire, she overhears a conversation between two men plotting a murder. As the tale progresses to its inevitable homicide, she realizes that she is the intended victim. *Variety* reported of this broadcast: "Miss Moorehead's playing of this extraordinary role has rarely, if ever, been equalled on the air. From the woman's first faltering lines, through to scenes of growing dread to the final moments of gibbering semi-delirium, it was a blood-chilling performance of a brilliantly agonizing script." Noted film composer Bernard Herrmann, then married to Miss Fletcher, prepared a special musical score for the show.*

On July 1, 1942, RKO Studios' chief, Charles Koerner, had issued a public statement that after the completion of *The Magnificent Ambersons* and *Journey into Fear* (and the pending *It's All True*), there was no further need for Welles or his Mercury Productions on the studio lot. Agnes, who had had lots of experience in shifting for herself, made her availability known and shortly after was given a stock seven-year contract by MGM. This alliance with the studio that "had more stars than are in the heavens" would be the bridge that carried her further away from the intelligencia stigma of the Broadway-oriented Mercury troupe to the middle-brow-culture-clique of everyday Hollywood filmmaking. She would work with Welles and members of the Mercury Theatre in subsequent years, but never again would she have on film the relatively uncompromising dramatic roles provided in her trio of Welles's pictures.

Meanwhile, her marital life was not proving tranquil or successful. Unlike her husband, Agnes had firmly established herself in both pictures and the radio, a fact sure to drive a wedge between any union of two show business personalities. This domestic strife was an additional burden to her recent blacklisting in Hollywood which she had to contend with and overcome. As with most challenges, Agnes did succeed in the latter, and by the end of 1942 was an accepted member of the film industry community. She was not, by any means, on the highest plateau, but she was way up in the strata as a noted character star who now belonged to the MGM firmament of players.

Her first MGM assignment was in *The Youngest Profession* (1943) in which high schooler Virginia Weidler is head of Guiding Stars, Ltd., a group of autograph-hound teenagers, providing the necessary backdrop for brief guest appearances by studio stars Greer Garson, Walter Pidgeon, William Powell, Robert Taylor, and Lana Turner. This aspect of the feature was a pleasant diversion, but then the script shifted into a soap opera about Weidler's stern, busybody governess (Agnes) who engineers a romance between Weidler's lawyer-father (Edward Arnold) and his secretary (Ann

With Virginia Weidler and Jean Porter in *The Youngest Profession* (MGM, 1943).

Ayars). All of the action confounded Arnold's Red Cross-working wife, Marta Linden. The *New York World-Telegram* decided: "Agnes Moorehead continues her habit of becoming the dominant person of the picture in a minor role."

Agnes was next in RKO's *Government Girl* (1944). She was seventh-billed as Mrs. Wright, an influential Washingtonite who throws a party for a brilliant young production engineer (Sonny Tufts), now a $1 a year man. When Tufts appears at the gala evening soiree with his secretary (Olivia de Havilland) as his date, haughty Agnes is insulted. Her reaction is compounded when Tufts walks out early on the gathering. Agnes conspires with attorney Jess Barker to have Tufts hauled before an investigating commission headed by Senator Harry Davenport. The extended motorcycle finale chase (with Tufts and de Havilland astride a cycle) turned the satirical picture into pure slapstick. The film was ignored by most critics. The *New York Post* went on record as saying the cast was ". . . not to blame for a set of performances distinctly below their own standards."

Because Orson Welles was the star in, and ex-Mercury Theatre executive John Houseman one of the co-scripters of the Twentieth Century-Fox version of Charlotte Bronte's *Jane Eyre* (1944), Agnes's presence in the film was requested and MGM loaned her to portray the harridan Mrs. Reed, guardian of Jane Eyre (Joan Fontaine). Her character was required to be an exacting clever woman who despises and misuses her charge. It is Agnes who spits out to Henry Daniell: "This, Mr. Brocklehurst, is the child in question. She's the daughter of my late husband's sister, and has unfortunately been put into *my* hands." In the early course

---

* So popular would this performance become, that by September, 1945, Agnes had repeated it for a fourth time on *Suspense,* an audio industry record. She would always do the show fresh through, never memorizing her lines, for fear it would remove the spontaneity of her changing characterization. It was in 1947 that Decca Records obtained permission to tape the broadcast for an LP, which has remained a popular seller throughout the years, as has Agnes's subsequent recordings: *The Psalms of David, Our Common Heritage, Don Juan in Hell, The Rivalry, Nancy Hanks,* and *Barbara Fritchie.*

In *Jane Eyre* (20th Century-Fox, 1944).

of the somber tale, Agnes's Mrs. Reed dies and has her possessions auctioned off at sale. In her few screen moments, Agnes handled her characterization with excellent competence.

Jane Eyre was not the artistic success it might have been. While art directors James Basevi and Wiard B. Ihnen caught the exact moody ambiance of Thornfield Hall and the other gloomy settings of Bronte's romantic fiction, Welles portrayed Edward Rochester in such an oversized theatrical manner that it easily overshadowed the gentle performance of Fontaine, thus distorting the proper balance of the movie. It remained for Agnes, Ethel Griffies (as the keeper of Welles' mad wife) and Sara Allgood (as Agnes' governess) to supply the glossy $2 million feature with its early Victorian flavor.

By 1944, Agnes was the featured performer on what proved to be an extremely popular radio half-hour series, "Mayor of the Town" (Saturday night, 7:30 P.M., CBS) starring MGM contract luminary Lionel Barrymore as a cantankerous small-town official who devotes his time righting the real and imaginary indignities heaped upon his town and its people. Agnes was Marilyn, Barrymore's volatile housekeeper, who spends a good deal of her workday bickering with her resolute employer over an assortment of trivial and major matters. Conrad Binyon as the youngster, Butch, rounded out the cast, who were directed by Jack Van Nostrand. The family-geared program would last through the 1947–1948 season, adding to Agnes' popularity and her bank account.

United Artists' *Since You Went Away* (1944) was David O. Selznick's mammoth tribute to the American family on the homefront during World War II. Claudette

With Irving Bacon, Joseph Cotten, and Claudette Colbert in *Since You Went Away* (UA, 1944).

Colbert was top-featured as the ever-courageous mother of teenager Shirley Temple and her sister, the blooming Jennifer Jones. While her middle-aged husband is away on volunteer military assignment, Colbert takes in a boarder (Monty Woolley) to supplement the household budget. In addition, she participates in war factory work, and flirts ever so innocently with long-time friend and naval officer, Joseph Cotten. Agnes was the chief meanie in this tearjerker. As the bitchy Emily Hawkins, the acid-tongued cocktail acquaintance of Colbert, she mouths nasty innuendoes about everybody and everything. It was the dose of vinegar the sugary production so badly needed. That Agnes's character could also be humanly frivolous (e.g., leading the conga line at the airplane hangar dance) provided Emily Hawkins with a good degree of dimension.

The role itself was a variation of the cinema type portrayed throughout the 1940s by the very adept Eve Arden. The difference in these two actresses' approach to such a part is that whenever Agnes is required to make a flip remark on screen, it comes across in total seriousness as a reflection of her character's basic, unregenerated meanness. Her piercing eyes and overall body movements provide the viewer with no other interpretation. In contrast, Eve Arden, who early in the game acquired the knack of looking through and beyond the person she is addressing, can toss off the most devastating remark, and it emerges as a pert observation, juicy and smart, but essentially nonvicious. The off-the-cuff phrasing and rising-and-falling vocal pitch emphasize the observer quality to Arden's projection, which make her barbs clinical, hypothetical, and very impersonal.

Back at MGM, Agnes was among the Occidental contractees utilized to portray Orientals in the lush picturization of Pearl Buck's *Dragon Seed,* which opened at Radio City Music Hall, July 20, 1944. Set in 1937 in a little village near Nanking, the movie traces the effect of the Japanese invasion on the local inhabitants, particularly patriarch Walter Huston, his wife Aline MacMahon, their second son Turhan Bey, and his wife Katharine Hepburn, an idealistic but realistic Chinese woman. Agnes portrayed the badgering, devious peasant wife of third cousin Henry Travers. (It was such a small role that it would be unfair to make comparisons with other screen Oriental semi-villainesses like Gale Sondergaard's Eurasian in *The Letter* and Ona Munson's Madame Gin-Sling in *The Shanghai Gesture.*) Agnes's typically strong performance was all but lost in the overwoven tribute to wartorn China. It was MacMahon as the understanding matriarch who won an Academy Award nomination. *Dragon Seed,* with all its propaganda excesses, was enormously pop-

With Henry Travers in *Dragon Seed* (MGM, 1944).

ular with World War II American and Allied audiences, although critics were rather cynical about the distortions of the novels and the distinctly western acting styles of the majority of the cast.

Agnes' fifth 1944 release was another propaganda story, *The Seventh Cross,* set in 1936 Nazi Germany. Seven prisoners escape from a concentration camp. As each man is recaptured, he is put to death on one of the erected crosses in the compound's exercise yard. The seventh cross remains empty, as Spencer Tracy makes good his escape. Agnes was briefly seen as Mme. Marelli, a theatrical costumer, who is one of the few to risk danger by showing compassion to Tracy. She supplies him with a change of clothes.

It was at this time that Agnes told her friend Hedda Hopper: "On the stage you have to elbow your way through your career. Here it doesn't much matter whether you're a star or a bit player. There's always someone near by ready and willing to give you encouragement. At least, that's been my experience."

It was Agnes' next picture *Mrs. Parkington* (1944), which afforded her an offbeat casting assignment, and it remains her favorite screen role. As Agnes recalls: ". . . [it] came to me only because I put up a fine battle to get it. After playing a series of women who were either strained, neurotic or mousy, I was eager for a good, normal role, and this was it. So I went to producer Leon Gordon and asked for it.

" 'I don't think Aspasia (Conti) is an Agnes Moorehead kind of role,' he said. 'But there's a drunken duchess I'd love to have you play.

'Why not test me for Aspasia?' I said, 'Then if you don't like the test, I'll play your drunken duchess.'

"I got the test and then I started scurrying around. I found that Greer Garson was wearing a dark wig, so I got a blonde one. Then I had a sheer nightgown fixed up, as the test was a bedroom scene. Fortunately, my French was fine, and the day after the test Leon told me the part was mine."

Mrs. Parkington was yet another expensive and luxurious woman's picture to showcase the popular team of Greer Garson and Walter Pidgeon. Filled with clichés of idealized romance, there was little that was genuine in the picture or in Tay Garnett's direction. Its story starts in 1938 as tottering Garson gathers her family together to decide how to keep her pompous son-in-law Edward Arnold out of jail. In an extended flashback, she thinks back to 1872 when she was a boardinghouse keeper's daughter in Leaping Rock, Arizona and met Pidgeon. The rising tycoon is enchanted with Garson and takes her to New York as his bride. Pidgeon enlists his former mistress, the Baroness (Agnes), to coach westerner Garson on the art of dress and manner.

With Spencer Tracy in *The Seventh Cross* (MGM, 1944).

For her performance as the elegant social arbiter, Agnes was approved of by the critics. ". . . [she] does a brilliant job as the ex-mistress of the tycoon who grows to love Mrs. Parkington." (*New York Herald-Tribune*). The Hollywood Foreign Correspondents and *Radio Life* chose her as best (supporting) actress of the year, and she received her second Academy Award nomination. This time she lost out to Ethel Barrymore who won the best supporting Oscar for *None but the Lonely Heart.*

Her seventh and final release of 1944 was United Artists' *Tomorrow the World,* based on the Broadway play, which had lasted 499 performances during the

With Walter Pidgeon and Greer Garson in *Mrs. Parkington* (MGM, 1944).

1943 season. The script tells the story of German youth Skippy Homeier (from the Broadway cast), brought to America after his parents die in a concentration camp to live with his uncle, college chemistry professor Fredric March and his spinster sister Agnes. The film is a pointed propaganda tract on how easily foreign "poison," in this case Homeier as an unregenerated Hitler Youth, can be insinuated into wholesome American households. As the picture progresses, malicious Homeier almost wrecks havoc with March's romance with Jewish schoolteacher Betty Field, as well as setting up problems with March's innocent, motherless daughter, Joan Carroll. Unfortunately, what had been a vivid document on stage, became too bland in the screen presentation. The *New York Times* complimented Agnes on her "acceptable jaundiced performance" as the one who looks skeptically on the seemingly innocent Homeier.

In four years in Hollywood, Agnes had appeared in prominent supporting roles in twelve feature films, an impressive track record, but seemingly no chore for a determined lady with enough energy for twice the number of screen parts, not to mention her weekly radio chores and other multi-media publicity work. At age thirty-eight, Agnes obviously had made her mark within the industry and on the public's consciousness.

Her next picture, *Keep Your Powder Dry* (1945),* came near the tail end of World War II and was stale both in presentation and in casting. Three girls enlist

---

* Agnes was also in the MGM short subject *Victory in Europe* (1945) which also featured Margaret O'Brien. The brief 5½ minute story tells of a mother and daughter who hear of the loss of the head of their family, just as the town begins its celebration of the European victory.

in the WACS for different reasons. Lana Turner wants to prove herself worthy to fulfill terms of a lucrative inheritance, and Laraine Day, a general's daughter, intends to carry on the family's military tradition. Finally, Susan Peters wants to do her patriotic bit while her husband is serving with the armed forces overseas. Agnes functioned as the commanding officer. Needless to say, military discipline does wonders for the heroines.

Much better cinema fare was the sentimental *Our Vines Have Tender Grapes* (1945), set in a small Scandinavian farming community in Wisconsin. Agnes was fifth-billed as Bruna Jacobson, the wife of Edward G. Robinson and the mother of little Margaret O'Brien. It is through the child's idealistic eyes that the feature gains its point of view. Surrounded by such natural scene stealers as Robinson and O'Brien, Agnes was restrained and sympathetic, and enjoyed the opportunity to display a foreign-accented vocabulary.

In *Her Highness and the Bellboy* (1945), Agnes did a modern dress variation of her Mrs. Parkington role. She played countess-companion of visiting royalty Hedy Lamarr, the latter being courted by naive hotel employee Robert Walker. The Cinderella-like story featured extended screen scenes of crippled June Allyson pining in her apartment because Walker has seemingly forsaken her. But she need have no fears since Walker soon discovers that his tenement sweetheart is really a princess at heart. Lamarr rediscovers newspaperman Warner Anderson, a former love-of-her-life, and renounces her royal duty for matrimony. The *New York Herald-Tribune* penned: "Agnes Moorehead, who can do no wrong, comes near to making sense out of her role as the princess' guardian."

Agnes had been suggested for the role of the sixty-year-old grandmother in *The Green Years* (1946), but the assignment was given to MGM contractee Gladys Cooper. Orson Welles wanted Agnes for a lead role in *The Stranger* (1946) which Welles directed and starred in for the new International Pictures Company. United Artists did the releasing. However, the production executives decided the Welles-Loretta Young vehicle required a third star name, so Edward G. Robinson was hired and the part rewritten as Inspector Harper of the Commission of War Crimes.

During 1946 Agnes was off the screen, but busy at work on the MGM studio lot, making *The Beginning or the End,* which was not released until February, 1947. This movie dealt in a semi-documentary fashion with America's development and utilization of the atomic bomb during World War II. Agnes was handed the role of a German scientist who had escaped to Sweden and then aided the Allies. After filming her scenes, MGM's legal department discovered that no official release had

With Margaret O'Brien and Edward G. Robinson in *Our
Vines Have Tender Grapes* (MGM, 1945).

With Hedy Lamarr in *Her Highness and the Bellboy*
(MGM, 1945).

been obtained from the real-life scientist who was still
very much alive. With no such permission forthcoming,
Agnes's scenes were excised from the release print.

In the post-World War II film production slowdown
in Hollywood, MGM did not require Agnes's full-time
services, and she was allowed to negotiate a contract for
two pictures a year with Warner Bros. to insure she
would be kept busy filmmaking.

Her first Warners' picture was the nearly first-rate
Dark Passage (1947), a Humphrey Bogart-Lauren Bacall thriller, in which escaped San Quentin convict Bogart is picked up and hidden by Bacall in her San
Francisco hills apartment. Everything seems safe enough
(Bogart had plastic surgery to disguise his facial appearance) until Bruce Bennett, who has been having
an affair with Bacall, begins questioning her strange,
secretive behavior. Even more troublesome is Bennett's

With Conrad Binyon and Lionel Barrymore on radio's "Mayor Of The Town," 1946.

portrait of bitchery; . . ." The *Baltimore Sun* ranked this screen creature as ". . . one of the most poisonous termagents the screen has presented in some time." It remains one of Agnes's best-remembered film performances.

Her other 1947 picture was the arty United Artists failure *The Lost Moment,* based on Henry James's esteemed *The Aspern Papers.* It boasted a virtuoso acting job by Agnes, who played a 105-year-old woman (enhanced by an expert makeup job) stashed away in her somber Venetian home with her schizophrenic relative Susan Hayward. American publisher Robert Cummings discovers that Moorehead is the now-aged woman to whom a long-dead, famous poet once wrote a series of love letters, and that after all these years she may still possess the original missives in her home. Director Martin Gabel attempted to instill some new twists into James's brooding psychological story, but they proved to be empty gestures, particularly after the feature had been edited to the bare bones in order for it to be pushed out onto the market. The studio publicity department tried to work miracles with the cinematic bomb it knew it had. It concocted a distorted publicity campaign which ballyhooed the film as "Beneath these eyes, a deathless secret of the past. Behind these walls,

shrewish wife (Agnes) who just happens (by scripting machinations) to have known Bogart and his murdered wife. Later, Bogart confronts the passionate virago and she admits to being the real killer, but then just as it looks as if Bogart's problems are solved, he lurches toward her in anger, and she falls backward out of a window to her death.

Dark Passage was one of the few occasions to date that allowed Agnes to portray on the screen a woman close to her own age without disguising costumes, makeup or foreign accents. At this time Agnes told an interviewer of the one constant factor present in her meeting people who knew her only from her screen work: "My age. Because of having played so many character parts, I'm expected to be older than I am." *Dark Passage* remedied this problem to a great degree. Here was a jealous, sex-starved characterization that the electric Dame Judith Anderson would have been proud to play in her heyday. In her few scenes, Agnes proved adept at matching dynamo Bogart in personality projection. Charles Higham and Joel Greenberg in their book *Hollywood in the Forties* (1968) find that her ". . . prying, vicious Madge Rapf is a definitive

With Humphrey Bogart in *Dark Passage* (WB, 1947).

In *The Lost Moment* (Universal, 1947).

no love has lived for years." The *New York Herald-Tribune* reported: "Chief among the supporting cast is Agnes Moorehead, unrecognizable in heavy old-age make-up, re-casting the cracked voice and palsied hand of extremely advanced years, and immobilized among the memories of a long-dead romance."

After many years absence from the stage, Agnes was asked by Orson Welles to appear opposite him in *Macbeth,* which he staged for ANTA as part of Utah's centennial celebration at Salt Lake City. He wanted Agnes to repeat her leading assignment in the movie he made of this stage production for Republic in 1948, but Jeanette Nolan was substituted in the role when Agnes' filmmaking schedule would not permit the loan-out.

MGM's *Summer Holiday,* which had finished production in October, 1946, at last saw distribution in June, 1948, the studio being in no rush to release a picture in which they had so little faith. This Technicolor musical version of Eugene O'Neill's *Ah! Wilderness* has always had a divided critical reception, many critics being unwilling to concede the stylishness of Rouben Mamoulian's leisurely direction. The story line centers on Mickey Rooney in Danville, Connecticut, in 1906. He has just graduated from the local high school and is experiencing a most difficult time passing through the traumas of approaching manhood as he prepares to enter Yale University. In the introductory song number, "It's Our Home Town," started by Rooney's newspaper-publisher-father Walter Huston, all the members of the Miller household join in singing a few refrains as in *Meet Me in St. Louis.*

Agnes, in her first color feature, is prissy Cousin Lillie who for years has been trying to woo erstwhile reporter

Uncle Sid (Frank Morgan) away from the bottle and into the path of stability and matrimony. She is a practical and often unbending woman who yearns for a homelife like that of her in-laws, Huston and Selena Royle. That Agnes' characterization here is far removed from the emotionally repressed Aunt Fanny of *The Magnificent Ambersons* is demonstrated in the "Stanley Steamer" production number. In this sequence a gleeful Mickey Rooney is finally allowed to drive the family car and takes his relatives on an outing. Unlike the parallel sequence in *The Magnificent Ambersons* in which Agnes' Aunt Fanny remains a constrained, withdrawn soul, in the *Summer Holiday* family ride, she joins into the group glee with relish. At the Fourth of July picnic, Agnes' Lillie is a welcome asset, having helped in preparing the food and seen to its distribution at the picnic grounds. She concentrates on keeping liquor-loving Morgan from getting too tipsy (she does not fare well) by repeatedly offering him different pastries (he keeps bypassing her offers). By the end of the picture, Agnes has forgiven Morgan for "that woman in New York," and they sit in a swing-chair in the garden, talking of their tranquil, loving future together.

One of the chief complaints lodged against *Summer Holiday* was that Rooney (by then age 24) was too old to be playing the cavorting teenager, and that his interpretation was only a variation of his standard Andy Hardy delineation. Nonetheless, the movie musical boasts a sumptuous use of color, art direction, and photography, combining to create not just a picture postcard of nostalgia, but an appropriate atmosphere for describing a boy's coming-of-age. Needless to say, 1948 filmgoing audiences in general were not entranced with *Summer Holiday,* and its poor reception did much to make director Mamoulian an unwanted Hollywood figure.

A complete change of pace was *The Woman in White,* which had been completed February 9, 1947, but was held up for theatrical release by Warner Bros. until May, 1948. It was a painstaking reproduction of Wilkie Collins's mystery novel about rural England of the 1850s. It was well cast with Warners' contractees. Agnes was fifth-billed as Countess Farco, the cold and impenetrable wife of Italian count Sydney Greenstreet, one of the chief villains of this melodrama. That Greenstreet is obsessed with a pet monkey, is a voyeur (he delights in watching a woman undress), and has an unreasoning covetnous for a much-sought gem drives Agnes to despair, and she eventually stabs him in the back with a dagger. The *New York Herald-Tribune* was of the opinion: "Agnes Moorehead is both sinister and lunatic as the woman who knows about him (Green-

In a performance of "Sorry, Wrong Number" on "Suspense," circa 1947.

With Mickey Rooney, Walter Huston, Jackie "Butch" Jenkins, Gloria De Haven, and Selena Royle in *Summer Holiday* (MGM, 1948).

Agnes made her first western, *Station West* (1948), for RKO, a Dick Powell melodrama about gold robbers in the Old West, which was sold to the public as "Sometimes a man has to double-cross the woman he loves." The woman in this case was Jane Greer, a dance hall proprietress who turns out to be the pivotal force in running the town. Powell was an army undercover man sent to ferret out who was responsible for murdering the soldier convoy assigned to guard a gold shipment. Agnes was on hand, briefly, as the sturdy owner of a gold mine. The film also included Burl Ives as the laconic hotel keeper and Regis Toomey as Powell's assistant. The picture came and went with little notice.

Her fourth and final release of 1948 was her best screen assignment in some time, a part which properly channeled her histrionic intensities, Warners' *Johnny Belinda*. On the surface, the project seemed a most un-

street) but loses her mind in an effort to stop it." Had the rich period drama come ten years earlier on the scene, it might have been successful. However by 1948, costume thrillers were decidedly out of fashion.

It was in 1948 that Agnes (known as "Aggie" to her friends) purchased the fourteen-room Beverly Hills home that formerly belonged to composer Sigmund Romberg. (She has since renamed it the Villa Agnese.) With her $1,750-plus weekly (forty weeks out of the year) paycheck from MGM and her other money-earning appearances (such as enacting *The Little Foxes* on radio's *Theatre Guild on the Air* [January 4, 1948] with Thomas Mitchell and Zachary Scott), Agnes could well afford to live in such luxury.

With Dick Powell and Tom Powers in *Station West* (RKO, 1948).

With Sydney Greenstreet in *The Woman in White* (WB, 1948).

likely subject: set on stark Cape Breton Island, it focuses on a deaf-and-dumb girl (Jane Wyman) who is conceded a misfit by her basic farmer father (Charles Bickford) and her aunt (Agnes). When the new doctor (Lew Ayres) arrives in the village, he takes a strong interest in Wyman and teaches her to communicate by sign language. When the local heavy, fisherman Stephen McNally, rapes Wyman, it is assumed first that Ayres is the culprit. The ensuing strife displays all the pettiness of mankind as typically found in any cross section of humanity. An upbeat ending made the film viable box office. The *New York Herald-Tribune* noted of this remarkably vibrant film: "Charles Bickford as the girl's father and Agnes Moorehead as her aunt are gaunt and Gothic but innately kindly."

Jane Wyman won an Oscar for her performance,

With Jane Wyman, Lew Ayres, and Charles Bickford in *Johnny Belinda* (WB, 1948).

while Agnes who had been nominated in the best supporting actress category, lost out to Claire Trevor who won for *Key Largo*. Most likely, having been typecast from the start of her film career as a strong dramatic actress weighed against Agnes in the Academy Award sweepstakes. Whatever she essayed on the screen she did with such apparent ease that it seemed her screen portrayals were merely extensions of herself. Being a go-getting kind of actress, Agnes had never earned a reputation as an underdog, so she could never count on a backwash of sympathy votes to bolster her showing in the Academy voting.

It was also during 1948 that *Sorry, Wrong Number,* so closely associated with Agnes, was filmed by Hal Wallis's production unit at Paramount with Barbara Stanwyck in the lead role. Many years later Agnes told film history writer Ronald L. Bowers: "Of course I wanted to play the Stanwyck part in *Sorry, Wrong Number*. It had been written for me by Lucille Fletcher, and I must have done it on radio about 18 times. I went to Hal Wallis at Paramount when they were casting it to put my hat in the ring, but he said he owed Barbara a picture and that I could have a supporting role. I said no. I'm not bitter about it. Let the chips fall where they may and go on from there. . . . They played my recording constantly on the set."*

---

* It was in 1948 that Agnes made a plea to disc jockeys of the nation to stop playing the Decca recording of her "Sorry, Wrong Number." She was afraid the constant airing of the program would kill her future live performances. It did not. On the tenth anniversary of the radio show "Suspense" (September 15, 1952), Agnes repeated her performance of the tour-de-force live for the sixth time. *Time* magazine once said of Agnes's rendition of the play: ". . . [she] has perfect timing, [and] can control her voice as expertly as a radio engineer can control sound." "Sorry, Wrong Number" would have a video outing on "Climax" (November 4, 1954, CBS) with Shelley Winters in the lead.

Agnes' 1949 releases were big pictures, but her roles were merely stock-in-trade for her. In *The Stratton Story* (1949), she was the back-country mother of James Stewart. From childhood on, he dreams of being a baseball player, and after being discovered by has-been veteran player Frank Morgan, he goes on to join the major leagues with the Chicago White Sox. Having married June Allyson, everything seems rosy until a hunting accident costs him one of his legs. But both restrained Agnes and sweet Allyson stand staunchly behind him and silently urge him to overcome the physical and mental obstacle. He does, and returns to active participation in the professional sport he loves so much. *Variety* recorded that both actresses: "Sensitively portray the silent torment of the womenfolk."

MGM's *The Great Sinner* attempted to distill Dostoievski's *The Gambler* (with elements of *Crime and Punishment* and autobiographical data thrown in) into cultural and classy screenfare for the masses. It emerged a lugubrious costume drama misfire, hindered by pretentious dialogue and the obvious direction by Robert Siodmak. Writer Gregory Peck, on the lookout for new material, finds himself at the gaming tables of 1880s Wiesbaden where he encounters stylish Ava Gardner. Other participants in this screen debacle were Melvyn Douglas as the suave casino owner, luckless gambler Frank Morgan who commits suicide, and Ethel Barrymore, the aged mother of Walter Huston. The latter arrives at the resort bearing a silver coffin in case death should overtake her there. Having lost her fortune in a run of bad gambling luck, she sinks into death at the gaming tables. Agnes had a few brief scenes as a cackling pawnshop crone who finds her amusement as the feckless aristocracy are forced to rely on her resources when their checkbooks run dry. One of the few startling images in the film is that of Agnes intently examining a bit of new merchandise under an oversized magnifying glass.

By 1950, Agnes's MGM contract had expired (*Show Boat,* released in 1951 would be last film under her term agreement with the studio), and in the post television slump in Hollywood, studios were reluctant to sign players to long-term contracts. So, Agnes, adept at being an independent soul, began freelancing, having built a sufficiently strong reputation as a top supporting player to survive very nicely in the wheeler-dealer system of 1950s Hollywood. Unlike such similar types as Judith Anderson, Anne Revere, Marjorie Main, Selena Royle, Gale Sondergaard, Patricia Morison, and others who drifted off into stage work, semi-retirement, or were blacklisted by the McCarthy hearings, Agnes remained the personification of the screen pioneer woman in the 1950s. Throughout the decade she would

With James Stewart and June Allyson in *The Stratton Story* (MGM, 1949).

With Gregory Peck in *The Great Sinner* (MGM, 1949).

often play this stereotyped role unless she could grab an opportunity to play a fancy-dress lady or an offbeat type, the latter two categories leading her to accept some embarrassing assignments in the years to come. Probably the strongest motivating force behind Agnes's choice of screen parts in these years was to earn sufficient money to carry on her other professional activities: her stage work, and, later in the 1950s, her dramatic coaching.

In *Without Honor* (1950), an odd, short (68 minutes) feature dealing with marital indiscretions, Agnes was cast as the wife of Franchot Tone who was having a love affair with the wife (Laraine Day) of Bruce Bennett. Complicating the matter is Bennett's younger brother (Dane Clark) who had made passes at Day before she chose Bennett. This unattractive picture al-

With Laraine Day in *Without Honor* (MGM, 1950).

most went without notice, save for Agnes's characterization ". . . acting a wronged wife who exhibits poised pity toward her rival [and who] manages to capture the true style of this piece" (*New York Herald-Tribune*).

From this trash, Agnes moved into the noteworthy *Caged* (1950), Warners' theatrical, but dramatically valid, study of sordid life in a woman's prison. The unrelenting story centers on Eleanor Parker (deglamorized for the role) who is a first offender and who becomes more hardbitten and unrepentant as her prison surroundings corrupt her basic innocence. Among the other types at the penitentiary are kindly matron Jane Darwell, sadistic, corrupt matron Hope Emerson, psychopathic prisoner Gertrude Michael, prostitute jailee Jan Sterling, and Agnes as the understanding, but politically hampered prison superintendent. At the end of the picture as Parker is released from prison, it is the knowledgeable Agnes who advises her assistant: "Keep her file active. She'll be back."

In her second-billed part, Agnes made the most of the dramatic opportunities presented in the screenplay, co-authored by Virginia Kellogg who had deliberately spent time as a prison inmate to obtain the real flavor of her study. Agnes neatly balanced her characterization as a warmhearted woman who by the very nature of her profession must maintain a rigid objectivity (pointed up by her functional, unfeminine garb and light makeup). The *New York Times* ranked Agnes as ". . . splendid in the role of the humane warden who earnestly tries to give the prisoners a decent life but is thwarted by venal and indifferent political interference." The format of *Caged* has been repeatedly reused in subsequent features, such as *Woman's Prison*.

In 1950, she was asked to join with Charles Boyer, Cedric Hardwicke, and Charles Laughton (he also directed the showcase) in a tour of *Don Juan in Hell,* a dramatic reading of the third act of George Bernard Shaw's play *Man and Superman.* The project appealed to Agnes for several reasons. She respected the property ("The content is so timely") and the other co-stars. She firmly believed in an actor going back on the boards to refresh his acting techniques in front of a live audience. The womanly nature of Agnes reveled at the opportunity of appearing to the public in a new professional guise, as a well-dressed lady. (Her stage costume consisted of a lavender evening gown with, as Hedda Hopper described it, ". . . her flaming red hair swept upward to a ballerina's coronet of brilliance. . . .")

The group called themselves The First Drama Quartette and prepared an extensive road tour under the auspices of Paul Gregory. The performance was staged in concert version without benefit of scenery and costume trapping (the men wore evening clothes), using stools, music racks and large leatherbound scripts as their only props. Said Agnes, "Our technique is by no means new. It dates all the way back to the old Greek poets, who took their works straight to the people, reading to the audiences what they had written. But it is the hardest technique I've ever tried."

After playing several successful American engagements, the group went abroad, appearing in England in June and July of 1951. The *London Evening Chronicle* reported: "Four people talking brilliantly brought something new to the English theatre. A triumph of words over scenery. Charles Laughton's performance as the Devil was magnificent. Charles Boyer's performance as Don Juan is unequalled. Cedric Hardwicke's performance treated with the sly shades of Shavian wit. Agnes Moorehead as Donna Anna was superb. . . ." On October 22, 1951, one year after the tour began, the First Drama Quartette performed the concert reading at Carnegie Hall, then moved to the Century Theatre (November 20, 1951) for 36 sold-out performances, returned to the hinterlands, reemerged on Broadway at the Plymouth Theatre (April 6, 1952) for a short stint, and then went back on the road.

In the decidedly masculine play, Agnes portrayed the daughter of Don Juan (both as a young woman and as a 77-year-old), who has just arrived in hell. There she encounters the living statue of her Spanish-nobleman-father (Hardwicke) killed in a duel with Don Juan (Boyer). In the presence of the devil (Laughton) they discuss life, love, and metaphysics. Everywhere the production played, it rated high praise and would gross over $1 million before concluding the tour. In New York, Cue lauded the cast for making ". . . the English lan-

With Eleanor Parker in *Caged* (WB, 1950).

guage leap and sizzle into revolutionary brilliance."*

In between her road engagements, Agnes made time to appear in four 1951 releases, a mixed bag of screen ventures. *Fourteen Hours* (1951) was based on the real life case of John Ward who stood on the ledge of Manhattan's Gotham Hotel for over half a day in July, 1938, and then leaped to his death. Richard Basehart had the lead role of the emotionally disturbed Robert Cosick. Agnes was his erratic, hysterical mother. ("Don't listen to the doctors. The doctors are wrong. You're *not* sick! Please come in—oh, Bobby . . . baby. . . .") The film emerged as synthetic drama with the most fully realized performance by Paul Douglas as the do-gooder traffic cop who attempts to rescue Basehart from the ledge. Agnes received her by now obligatory critical due: ". . . [she] gives another of her acute, unbalanced performances as the boy's self-pitying mother."

When the film was adapted for the "Twentieth Century-Fox Hour" (December 28, 1955, CBS-TV), Sylvia Sidney inherited Agnes's role.

With Howard da Silva, Paul Douglas, James Millican, and Martin Gabel in *Fourteen Hours* (20th-Fox, 1951).

---

* Agnes would continue to tour with the vehicle on and off through 1955. Vincent Price would replace Laughton as the Devil. In 1955, Agnes directed a version of *Don Juan in Hell,* with Kurt Kaznar (the Devil), Ricardo Montalban (Don Juan), Reginald Denny (Statue) and Mary Astor (Donna Ana). Said Mary Astor in her autobiography *My Story* (1959): "I liked Agnes Moorehead—'Aggie,' as we called her. A fine actress, now she proved to be an excellent director. . . . Aggie stressed the importance of playing it like a quartette, with great precision of movement, with harmony. It is all memorized, contrary to the general impression, and the pages are turned for emphasis, or 'punctuation.' Each character stands or sits on a definite word cue, so there is no inharmonious popping up and down."

With Joe E. Brown in *Show Boat* (MGM, 1951).

The third picturization of *Show Boat* reached Radio City Music Hall on July 9, 1951. Costing $2.4 million, it was a splashy moneymaker, decked out in rich color, with sumptuous sets and costumes, and over-orchestrated renditions of Jerome Kerns's score. In a caricature of her screen shrew, Agnes was the harsh wife of Andy Hawks (Joe E. Brown), captain of the Cotton Blossom show boat. Reported one New York journal: "Agnes Moorehead plays the domineering Parthy Hawks like somebody sinister from the Greek drama."

In RKO's *The Blue Veil* (1951), adapted from a popular French film, Jane Wyman starred as a World War I widow who turns to governess-nursing to earn a salary and to fill her lonely life. After thirty years of such ministrations to generations of youngsters, she finds herself reduced to being a charwoman in a New Jersey grammar school. Forgotten and alone, she is rescued finally by one of her ex-charges, long since a parent himself. In one of the many segments in the script, Agnes portrayed Fleur Palfrey, the wealthy matron of a country estate and the mother of two difficult sons who come under Wyman's supervision. The best acting in this tearjerker was offered by Joan Blondell as a fading musical comedy star, and she won an Academy Award nomination for her performance.

Agnes's last release of the year was the absurd *The Adventures of Captain Fabian,* a poor man's version of *Saratoga Trunk,* scripted by Errol Flynn who starred as a helpful ship's captain who rescues former servant, Micheline Presle. She has had to beat a hasty retreat after causing a ruckus in nineteenth century New Orleans. Eventually Presle weds simpering Vincent Price and goads him into murdering his wealthy uncle (Victor Francen). Agnes's black, French-accented Aunt Jesebel was almost as ludicrous as Flora Robson's similar role in *Saratoga Trunk.* The *New York Times* bemoaned:

In *The Blue Veil* (RKO, 1951).

With Charles Boyer in *Don Juan in Hell,* circa 1951.

from the Paramount programmer unit, filmed in techni-color and geared for the general action market. Power-ful landowner Agnes intends to stake her niece Susan Morrow to a spree of city life. To finance the venture, she hires tough logging boss John Payne to supervise the cutting of timber on her land. All of which leads to Payne's ne'er-do-well brother (Richard Arlen) mis-appropriating Agnes's fund and setting into motion a timber blaze which climaxes the feature. For local flavor there was Roscoe Ates as the stuttering camp cook and William Demarest as a dedicated logger. *Variety* whote: "Demarest and Miss Moorehead hoke up their performances for chuckles. . . ." And, one might ask, why not?

During the filming of *The Stratton Story,* Agnes had met actor Robert Gist, who had a small role in that film. In early 1953, Agnes age 47, and Gist, age 35, were married. The union did not prove a happy one, and in July, 1954 they were separated, because, she stated, he was dating other women. They would be

"And poor Agnes Moorehead, as her faithful octaroon sidekick, chews on a pipe beligerently and looks for all the world like Al Capp's Mamy Yokum. This indirectly provides the only honest touch in a long, laborious and confusing comic strip."

Meanwhile, Agnes's marital life had been going more publicly sour. On May 18, 1951, she obtained an inter-locutory divorce degree from her husband John Lee. She testified that he drank heavily, and that once he hurled a glass of beer at her and beat her with his fist; the divorce became final a year later. In 1951, she would adopt an infant boy, Sean, who is now completing his schooling abroad.

In 1952, Agnes earned $60,000-plus, largely from her work in low-class quickie movies. *Captain Black Jack* (1952), filmed abroad as had been *The Adventures of Captain Fabian,* found Agnes third-billed as Mrs. Biric, seemingly the silliest lady in the Riviera social set. In reality, she is the queen of an international dope smuggling ring, who is posing as an undercover law enforcer. On the other hand, Herbert Marshall, pretending to be a physician, is really a detective. The film, posing as melodrama, was pure trash.

The Blazing Forest (1952) was a tall timber yarn

In *Don Juan in Hell,* circa 1951.

With Patricia Roc in *Captain Black Jack* (Classic, 1952).

divorced March 12, 1958. He has since become an active TV director.

At least Agnes's four 1953 releases were generally well-mounted productions. MGM's *The Story of Three Loves* (1953) was a lavish omnibus film in which assorted types recollect their misfated love matches. In the opening episode, "The Jealous Lover," Agnes played the brief part of the aunt of Moira Shearer. The latter is a dancer with a heart ailment who becomes infatuated with imperious but urbane choreographer James Mason. He drives her on to perform an exhausting dance for him, and she succumbs to a heart attack. Had the three segments of this feature been less whimsical, the intended wistful qualities of the director would have been more apparent. Nevertheless, the film had a good Radio City Music Hall send-off and performed well in general distribution.

With William Demarest in *The Blazing Forest* (Paramount, 1952).

Also for MGM, Agnes appeared in *Scandal at Scourie* (1953), the swan song teaming of Greer Garson and Walter Pidgeon. (Agnes had been good friends with Garson since their *Mrs. Parkington* association.) Middle-aged and childless Protestant couple Garson (she being Ulster Protestant and boasting an Irish brogue) and Pidgeon decide to adopt a waif (Donna Corcoran) who comes into their home at Scourie, Canada, a drab Catholic community. Townspeople rise up in arms at the possibility of a Catholic child being reared in a Protestant home, and their fury is whipped into a storm when it is suspected the girl may be the one who set fire to a Catholic orphanage and later to the local school. Agnes was relegated to a short role near the

With Moira Shearer in *The Story of Three Loves* (MGM, 1953).

opening of the picture as Sister Josephine, one of the nuns in charge of transporting a group of orphans (including Corcoran) to a new home. Agnes seemed at ease in her religious garments, performing in a dignified if overly-intense manner, which was a relief compared to the over-noble performance of angelic Garson and pillar-of-the-community Pidgeon. The film did little box office business.

Paramount's *Those Redheads from Seattle* (1953) had the distinction of being the first 3-D color musical. The storybook plot had a mother (Agnes) and her four daughters (Rhonda Fleming, Teresa Brewer, Cynthia Bell, Kay Bell) head to the Yukon to join their newspaper publisher father. They arrive in Dawson, Alaska, to find he has been killed, and they must shift for themselves. Agnes becomes a dressmaker, and before long, the girls are paired off with local citizenry. The film was pleasant but innocuous fun. The *New York*

With Cynthia Bell, Teresa Brewer, Rhonda Fleming, and Frank Wilcox (framed picture) in *Those Redheads from Seattle* (Paramount, 1953).

Herald-Tribune wryly noted: ". . . and no doubt to avoid letting Miss Moorehead pack up the picture and carry it away from everybody else, her characterization was allowed to fade into ineffectualness long before the picture ended."

The aim of MGM's *Main Street to Broadway* (1953) was admirable. Twenty-five per cent of the film's proceeds was earmarked for the Council of the Living Theatre to help rekindle interest in theatergoing. This project appealed to MGM studio boss Dore Schary, and he alloted $1 million to the budget and recruited an assortment of "prominent" Broadway names to sparkle the story. Unfortunately what resulted was a slipshod backstage story of budding playwright Tom Morton fumbling to make a go of his career and falling in love with actress Mary Murphy. To fill out the plot, there

With Tallulah Bankhead in *Main Street to Broadway* (MGM, 1953).

was Morton's landlady Gertrude Berg who constantly offered motherly advice and hoosier hardware salesman Herb Shriner who took a shine to Murphy and New York. Agnes, who was then in between engagements of the fifth tour of *Don Juan in Hell,* played an unscrupulous, lace-edged theatrical agent, who is a shrewd New Yorker out to make a sharp deal.

The following year, 1954, was the watershed of Agnes's career. She had so enjoyed performing in *Don Juan in Hell* that its producer Paul Gregory sought another vehicle for her. In 1952, she was slated for a tour of *My Life and Hard Times,* but that did not jell. However, in early 1954, Agnes organized a one-woman tour which she eventually titled *The Fabulous Redhead* (As she once said of herself: "I live in a mass of clean clutter. Temper. Why not, I have red hair?"). The program consisted of selected readings from the Bible, Rupert Brooke, Rosemary Benet, Guy De Maupassant, Sir Thomas Hood, Ring Lardner, Edna St. Vincent Millay, Marcel Proust, Osgood Sitwell, James Thurber, and of course, Lucille Fletcher's "Sorry, Wrong Number."

When the production, at the time titled *An Evening with Agnes Moorehead,* played the Academy of Music in Brooklyn (March 13, 1954), the *Brooklyn Daily Eagle* reported Agnes was: "Displaying an assured, attractive personality and a sense of humor which you could never guess from her many neurotic roles in films, as well as a distinguished titian-hair beauty which is hidden generally under character makeup. . . ." The reviewer went on to observe, she ". . . doesn't actually read her program, for she has almost all of it committed to heart, glancing only occasionally at her book." In describing one of her selections, it was noted: "Miss Moorehead, giving Queen Elizabeth's imperious letter to the Bishop of Pike in 1573, sounded like the rolling of drums in her opening phrase, 'Pr-r-roud Pr-r-r-relate'. . . . when she finished the brief note, the actress said 'Elizabeth!' and grinned at the audience, and the audience couldn't help grinning back. There's showmanship in her act."*

At this time in her career Agnes decided to give herself a new professional status which was soon ratified by both Hollywood television producers and by the public at large. After a decade and a half in movies, twenty years in radio, and several seasons of extensive show-touring the country, she felt qualified to be elevated to the rank of the multi-media grande dame. The transformation was not an egomaniacal change of personality, for those who know her in private life have *always* found her a most worldly but extremely down-to-earth individual with an intense concern for the welfare of others. Rather it was a change in approach to her on-screen image. No longer was she the striving actress seeking to reach a higher plateau. She had risen as far as it was possible for a character star. Now she could offer her name and appearance to grace a film, television show, or stage presentation as a celebrity of the first rank. Gone were the determined but hesitant performances of the 1940s in which her growing reputation depended on a disciplined handling of each assignment.

And Agnes had much to say on many subjects.

About touring: "An actor is a wandering minstrel, and must sell his talent to the whole country. Touring is a real eye-opener because culture is not, as some think, only in New York City or on the West Coast. There are marvelous audiences all over the country. I always say you haven't played an audience until you've played Stillwater, Oklahoma."

On awards: "It's an immensely gratifying thing to realize that a majority of people in your industry have voted for you. But I'm just as happy knowing that I have the respect of the fellow members of my profession. I just want the opportunity to get good parts and do them justice.

". . . I'd rather get memorable roles than live on remembered awards which others don't remember.

"The greatest award an actor or actress can achieve is the chance to do another good part. That old saw about an actor being only as good as his last role ought to be changed to 'as good as his next role.' If there isn't any next role, you're no good."

On radio: "I loved radio. More than television, it appealed to the imagination. It demanded of the player far more psychological detail, because one had to characterize solely through a voice."

Agnes' screen career from the mid-1950s onward has been characterized for its variety of roles rather than for any substantial dramatic depth. This syndrome has hit such other such still-functioning character stars as Angela Lansbury, Eve Arden and Thelma Ritter. Each in their own distinctive way has earned a box office reputation as an audience-drawer, but what with the cutback in story line feature filmmaking, they have found themselves reaching out for oddball screen or television roles just to break the monotony of the stereotyped movie image that has won them their fame and its accompanying fortune. Of all the American-based female character stars, none has worked harder than Agnes to appear before the public in a series of

---

* Since then, Agnes has offered her one-woman show in over 400 cities in the United States and abroad. In recent years, she has revised and revived the virtuoso show as both *The Fabulous Redhead* and also under the title *Come Closer, and I'll Give You an Earful.*

new surface roles of great variety.

The philosophical premise of *Magnificent Obsession* (1954), a faithful remake of the Irene Dunne-Robert Taylor soap opera from Lloyd C. Douglas's novel, was that humans should endeavor to perform random good deeds without letting anybody know about it. To explicate this creed, Douglas had woven a saturnine tale which proved again to be a commercial box office hit in the women's picture revival of the 1950s. Rich playboy Rock Hudson is indirectly responsible for both the death of Jane Wyman's husband and for later causing her blindness. He decides to pick up the medical career he had once dropped and becomes the proficient surgeon who restores her sight. Agnes functioned as Wyman's companion and nurse, who bolsters her employer's courage during the rugged stretches of physical and emotional uncertainty. It was Agnes's only release of the year, but the picture ranked as one of the biggest moneymakers of 1954.

Agnes returned to her hearty pioneer type in Twentieth Century-Fox's cinemascope color actioner *Untamed* (1955). In this South African western, Tyrone Power refused to wed Susan Hayward whom he meets on a horse buying trip to County Cork, Ireland, because he fears it might curtail his work as a Boer commando in the pending Anglo-Boer hassle in South Africa. She later weds John Justin, and, after the potato famine that devastates Ireland, travels with him, their baby, and nurse Agnes to Capetown, South Africa. Justin is killed in a Zulu raid, but Power rescues the others. Later, after a tug of power with bandit leader Richard Egan (who also hankers for Hayward), Power emerges victorious and weds Hayward. The *New York Times* noted: "Only Agnes Moorehead as an Irish nanny sneers and snorts at the entire goings-on."

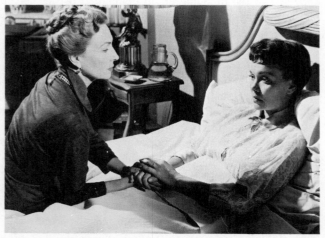

With Jane Wyman in *Magnificent Obsession* (Universal, 1954).

Also for Fox, Agnes appeared in *The Left Hand of God* (1955) as the wife of E. G. Marshall, a mission doctor at a poor village in the China of the 1940s. American flyer Humphrey Bogart, who had been forced down in China during the war and had spent three years as a military advisor to war lord Lee J. Cobb, turns up at the village in the garb of a Roman Catholic priest. (He had tired of Cobb's wanton way of life and made good his escape.) It is blunt, stern Agnes who perceives: ". . . there seems to be so much in him that wasn't intended to be a priest." Evidently repressed Catholic nurse Gene Tierney agrees, for she is emotionally attracted to Bogart, and at the finale, she follows after him into the sunset. With the Bogart marquee name, the pseudo-Oriental flavor, and the hints of promised but undelivered action, the film went over well with the public.

It was in 1956 that Agnes had seven releases, each revealing her in a different variation of her standard screen image. She was reunited by producer Ross Hunter and director Douglas Sirk with Jane Wyman and Rock Hudson in *All That Heaven Allows,* another turgid tale of troublesome love. Small New England-town widow Wyman, with a son and daughter at school, is debating whether to marry conservative, older Conrad Nagel or to be foolish and defy conventions by wedding rugged gardener Hudson, fifteen years her junior. Agnes is Sara Warren, one of Wyman's few true friends, who agrees with Wyman's query to Hudson: "Isn't it enough that we love each other?" It is noisy Agnes who reports all the town gossip on the romance to distraught Wyman. In addition she brings the whole situation fully into the open by giving a big party for Wyman and Hudson. This film pulled out every heartrending ploy in the screenwriter's canon, and with the aid of plush music and color, managed to do nearly as well as *Magnificent Obsession* at the consumer market.

Meet Me in Las Vegas (1956) came at the declining end of MGM's musical revival. It boasted Cyd Charisse as an elegant dancer unhappy about having to perform in the raucous gaming capital. She discovers that she is a good luck charm for Dan Dailey, a rancher and sometimes gambler. The *New York Times* rated Agnes "full of explosive charm" as Dailey's boisterous, fun-loving mama, Miss Hattie.

The Conqueror (1956), RKO's $6 million epic directed by Dick Powell, is ranked as one of the most absurd films of any year, with an entirely miscast roster of players. John Wayne, in slant-eyed makeup but still spouting his own drawling diction, was the twelfth century Mongol leader Genghis Khan who hungers for world power. He still is man enough to desire Tartar princess Susan Hayward (of whom he declaims in ade-

With Richard Egan, Susan Hayward, and John Justin in
Untamed (20th-Fox, 1955).

With Humphrey Bogart in *The Left Hand of God* (20th-
Fox, 1955).

With Rock Hudson and Jane Wyman in *All That Heaven
Allows* (Universal, 1956).

With Cyd Charisse and Dan Dailey in *Meet Me in Las Vegas* (MGM, 1956).

noidal monotones, "for good or ill, she is my destiny"). Agnes was fourth-billed as Hunlun, Wayne's wizened widowed mother who worries that her son's love for Hayward will bring destruction to the Mongols. The *Christian Science Monitor* was one of the few sources to be gracious about Agnes or anything about the film: "In spite of the script, Agnes Moorehead manages to inject a spirit of foreboding tribal maternalism into the role. . . ." The oversized Oriental western still made its due at the boxoffice, thanks to Wayne's legion of fans who came to cheer, hoot, or both.

The Revolt Of Mamie Stover (1956) almost achieved the impossible, by diluting William Bradford Huie's popular novel about a San Francisco whore who becomes the chief brothel attraction in Honolulu during World War II into a conventional romance about a not-so-moral taxi dancer (Jane Russell) who is almost inspired to redemption by well-bred novelist Richard Egan who lives in comfort on an Oahu hilltop home. Agnes, decked out in an auburn-haired wig, seemed to have a field day as the matronly owner of "The Bungalow" where Russell entertained the enthusiastic armed forces. It was as difficult to perceive that Agnes was an efficient madam as to understand why military men were lined up for blocks, eager to pay Russell big money just to talk with her. But this was 1957, and the censors had to be appeased.

Agnes was in more gracious surroundings at MGM in *The Swan* (1956), Grace Kelly's next-to-last film, which premiered at Radio City Music Hall. It was a somewhat precious Ruritanian romance that the public did not buy. Filmed on location at Asheville, North Carolina, the film managed to convey the elegance of 1910 Edwardian splendor. Matriarch of a crownless

central European family, Jessie Royce Landis attempts to marry off her virginial daughter (Kelly) to a blasé crown prince (Alec Guinness, in his first American-made movie). As Guinness's testy Queen Mother, Agnes caused more than one reviewer to note her characterization added "a touch of Westphalian ham" to the proceedings. She may have been arch and clamorous, but she looked splendiferous in her regal wardrobe.

With the same amount of energy she would have devoted to a serious drama, Agnes threw herself wholeheartedly into the Dean Martin-Jerry Lewis vehicle *Pardners* (1956), a loose remake of the Bing Crosby-Martha Raye *Rhythm on the Range*. Agnes played the wife of Lewis. When her husband is killed by varmints, she travels east with her son and becomes an enormously wealthy New York businesswoman. Years later, her son (also played by Lewis) goes west with the son of Dean Martin (also played by Martin) and cleans up the sagebrush town of local crooks. In her later sequences as the waspish grand lady, Agnes's emoting was as broad as Lewis's telegraphed visual comedy antics. Like the preceding eleven Martin-Lewis screen efforts, this Vistavision and color picture made a healthy financial return.

The Opposite Sex (1956) was an unsuccessful musical remake of *The Women,* which relied too heavily on

With Jane Russell in *The Revolt of Mamie Stover* (20th-Fox, 1956).

With Milton Frome and Jerry Lewis in *Pardners* (Paramount, 1956).

With Ann Miller, June Allyson, and Dolores Gray in *The Opposite Sex* (MGM, 1956).

With Brian Aherne and Alec Guinness in *The Swan* (MGM, 1956).

the nostalgia value of a cast of once-prominent sex sirens to bolster the now-clichéd account of clawing and cawing females. Agnes inherited the Mary Boland role as the brassy, much-married countess. The play's once famous fight scene was also watered down to a meaningless quality. In this battle royale version, it is dewy-eyed June Allyson who holds back husband-switching Ann Miller, while regal Agnes restrains catty Dolores Gray.

Agnes was almost as busy in 1957 as in the preceding year with four pictures in distribution. In *The True Story of Jesse James* (1957), at least the fourteenth movie dealing with the famed outlaw, Agnes was Mrs. Samuels, Jesse's victimized mother. The feature utilized a psychological approach, as several individuals who "knew" the real Jesse (Robert Wagner) recall their associations with him. It was overdirected in much too strong an approach by Nicholas Ray, whose experience handling the prairie fiasco *Johnny Guitar* had taught him little. The *New York Daily Mirror* described Agnes as ". . . an offkey hysterical mother" which came off badly in comparison to the bland performances of Hope Lange as Jessie's loving, worried wife, the wholesomeness of Jeffrey Hunter as Frank James, and the egotism of Robert Wagner's performance.

Agnes next appeared in another fictionalized screen biography, this one a purported account of 1920s American stage actress *Jeanne Eagels* (1957), but it was really a showcase of sorts for Columbia's latest sex goddess Kim Novak. Jeff Chandler was Novak's love interest, a carnival operator who gives the stagestruck girl her first break and then stands gallantly in the background as she rises to theatrical success and then speedily declines from addiction to drink (and the unmen-

With Kim Novak in *Jeanne Eagels* (Columbia, 1957).

tioned dope). Agnes was presented as Mme. Neilsen, the New York City acting coach who decides after a quick look at wriggling Novak "This girl has talent" (a ludicrous misjudgment) and becomes her devoted mentor. Said the *New York Daily Mirror*: ". . . [Agnes] acts loftily, [probably at directorial instigation] that she seems like a creature of the haut monde rather than one of footlight and greasepaint."* *Variety* corroborated: "Miss Moorehead is far too dramatic and artificial in her early scenes, later settling down for more realistic and sympathetic performance." Few movie biographies have ever been so candid in their introductory screen credits as *Jeanne Eagels* was. In the picture's opening credits, the disclaimer read: "All events in this photoplay are based on fact and fiction."

The $5½ million blockbuster *Raintree County* (1957) was a chronicle of the Old South from 1859 through the Civil War, focusing in particular on the predatory Elizabeth Taylor who tricks sensitive Montgomery Clift away from Eva Marie Saint and maneuvers him into marrying her. She soon finds that being the wife of an Indiana abolitionist school-teacher is not suitable to her cockeyed ideals. Agnes was the plain-spoken wife of Walter Abel and the proud mother of sensitive Clift. She is aghast to discover the changes in her intellectual adult son when near the opening of the picture he returns home, having completed his education. She rebukes him: "Whatever did they learn you at that school? You learned to guzzle beer? You learned to smoke tobacco?" Shortly thereafter within the storyline, Agnes blurs into the background of the main

With Robert Wagner and Hope Lange in *The True Story of Jesse James* (20th-Fox, 1957).

---

* An irony since at the time Agnes was devoting a good deal of her efforts to coaching, at the University of Wisconsin, later at the University of Southern California, and with private pupils taught from her home studio.

action, a stern figure parading through mechanical scenes, speaking a word or two, and then drifting off into the sidelines.

It took several releasings of *Raintree County* before the roadshow picture, filmed in the new but unperfected Camera 65 widescreen process, showed any substantial return on its huge investment. No matter what the publicists or indulgent critics opined, *Raintree County* was in no way the anticipated successor to *Gone With the Wind*.

Agnes was among the stars and leading character people corralled for cameo assignments in Warners' *The Story Of Mankind* (1957). The film's lofty premise was geared to a high tribunal in heaven arguing the merits of allowing mankind to continue its existence. The advocates were the Devil (Vincent Price) versus the Spirit of Man (Ronald Colman). To prove their point, they recall various high and low points of mankind's history, which allowed for the battery of screen names to appear in shallow vignettes of global history, aided

In *Raintree County* (MGM, 1957).

With Reginald Gardiner, Cesar Romero, and Major Sam Harris (elderly noble) in *The Story of Mankind* (WB, 1957).

by a most liberal use of stock footage. At long last, Agnes was allowed to portray on-camera royalty; she was Queen Elizabeth I engaged in animated conversation with William Shakespeare (Reginald Gardiner) about what to do with the Spanish envoy (Cesar Romero) whose country is verging on war with Britain. Agnes looked magnificent, but she was both "quivering with resolution" (*New York Herald-Tribune*) and "borders on hysteria" (*New Yorker*) which did not set well with the critics.

Meanwhile, Agnes hankered to return to the theater. She was intrigued by radio writer Norman Corwin's Broadway-bound play *The Rivalry,* based on the Abraham Lincoln-Stephen Douglas debates of 1858. The project had its genesis in 1955 in a concert reading form under the title *Tonight! Lincoln versus Douglas,* with Mala Powers and Jeff Morrows in two of the leads. The revised version featured Agnes as Mrs. Douglas, Raymond Massey (Lincoln) and Martin Gabel (who replaced Brian Donlevy as Douglas) in the concertized stage rendering which used no setting and few props. There were no intermissions in the program. The show would tour seventy-two cities between 1957 and 1958. *Variety* viewed a performance in Seattle, Washington, September 24, 1957 and reported: "It is in the asides and shorter scenes featuring Agnes Moorehead as Mrs. Douglas that Corwin brings the rivalry to life. The actress fairly steals the show in a charming performance as the shrewd but very feminine Adele Cutts Douglas." When *The Rivalry* reached Boston and played that city's Symphony Hall (January 19, 1958), one local reviewer recorded: "Handsome and graceful, she has a melodious voice and a perfect command of the stage. She lightens and brightens and stirs *The Rivalry* with a feeling of human warmth."

It was decided *The Rivalry,* which *Variety* termed "interesting, moving, but not exciting" was not then right for Broadway, and the cast disbanded. It would be brought to Broadway in February, 1959, with Nancy Kelly, Richard Boone, and Martin Gabel in the leads, but it folded after 8 performances. In 1965, a teletape would be aired of the Cleveland Playhouse production of *The Rivalry.*

The following year (1959) Paul Gregory persuaded Agnes to play opposite Ginger Rogers in Leslie Stevens's *The Pink Jungle.* Originally Eve Arden had been wanted for Agnes's role of the world-weary cosmetician who after death returns to earth as a ghostly shade to watch over her beauty empire which her son (Leif Erickson) is tired of managing. He has nominated humble beautician (Rogers) to become the new company manager. Directed by Joseph Anthony, the show began as a straight chic comedy in the view of *Lady in the Dark,*

and opened at the Alcazar Theatre, San Francisco, on October 14, 1959. But very soon it was evident to all involved, the heavily-budgeted show was in deep trouble. Vernon Duke was whisked in to add a belated musical score to brighten the proceedings, and all sorts of gimmicks were added to the play.

In *The Pink Jungle,* Agnes appeared in a variety of disguises, from a telephone operator to a tearoom waitress and including such roles as a Central Park policewoman and a speedwriting secretary. When the show reached Boston after a Detroit stay, the *Boston Daily Globe* reporter wrote: "With her crisp, sardonic style of comedy and her voice that cuts like a knife, [Agnes] really steals the show. . . ." Despite the Jean Louis costumes, Rogers' dancing and singing, and the aplomb of Agnes, the production never gelled. One critic quipped: ". . . inconsequential as a powder puff and as artificial as a penciled eyebrow." Producer Gregory decided to cancel the Philadelphia engagement, which had had an excellent advance sale order, and dropped plans for a New York opening. The backers suffered a $180,000 loss, even though in each of the three cities the show played it had been performed to a practically full house. Throughout production, there were continual rumors of traumatic clashes between Agnes and Rogers's mother Lela, the latter feeling her daughter was losing the limelight due to Agnes's strong performance.

Agnes then returned to the screen after a two-year absence. *The Night of the Quarter Moon* (1959) concerned itself with miscegenation and its repercussions. Its story was built around socially prominent San Franciscan Agnes who institutes annulment proceedings to have the marriage of her son (John Drew Barrymore)

With Edward Andrews, Dean Jones, John Drew Barrymore, and Jack Kosslyn in *Night of the Quarter Moon* (MGM, 1959).

to quadroon (Julie London) erased. That Barrymore
is a Korean War veteran who has suffered a nervous
breakdown and has been temporarily committed to an
asylum by Agnes makes it a unique legal case which
the press follows with great interest. A "highlight" of
the trial is when London must remove most of her
clothing in full court to demonstrate that Barrymore
had seen her wearing a beach bikini and fully knew the
color of her skin. Had the picture not contrived to be
controversial, realistic and commercial (weaving Nat
King Cole into the script as London's uncle so he can
perform musical numbers), it might be better remembered today. Agnes as the highhanded mama who is the
loser in the contest to retain her son's loyalty, was rated
"competent" by *Variety,* but it was James Edwards as
the black lawyer who scored with the most effective
performance.

The Tempest (1959) was produced largely on location in Yugoslavia by Italian producer Dino De Laurentis, who was attempting to duplicate the grandeur of
his earlier *War and Peace.* What resulted in the $2
million film was a distorted epic-style account of Pushkin's *The Captain's Daughter.* Set in 1775 Russia, it
had Viveca Lindfors as Queen Catherine II who exiles
a captain of the royal guards (Geoffrey Horne) to a
remote post in the Russian steppes. On the way, he
saves a Cossack from freezing to death. The man
(Van Heflin) in question becomes the self-titled Czar
Peter III who leads the peasants and soldiers against
the forces of Catherine II. Horne arrives at Ft. Bjelo-
gorsk which is commanded by inept Robert Keith.
Also present there are Keith's spirited wife (Agnes
Moorehead) and their daughter (Silvana Mangano,
wife of producer De Laurentis), a tempestuous creature
who soon wins Horne's attention. It is not long before
the outpost is under siege from Heflin's troops. Keith
is hanged for failing to submit, and Agnes is summarily
disposed of—as she huddles over the dead body of her
husband, a Cossack rebel splits open her skull. *The
Tempest* was hardly a success. In retrospect, one barely
recalls a horde of soldier-extras passing this way and
that across the wide screen and interludes of incredible
personal conflicts and passions, but none of the gripping
dramatics or pageantry of olden Russia was caught by
the camera.

Agnes's penchant for screen theatrics was well exer-
cised in her next outing, *The Bat* (1959), a Vincent
Price horror piece of the Gothic school. Based on the
Mary Roberts Rinehart play of the 1920s and the 1926
feature film, it cast Agnes as a successful mystery
writer who rents a gloomy mansion only to find its
banker-owner, who embezzled $1 million, has been
murdered. Subsequently several parties seek the hidden

In *The Bat* (AA, 1959).

loot, including a one-claw, no-face bat creature. This
provided the framework for the mild shock show
which became a contest between Price and Agnes—
who could ham the most. *Variety* thought her performance ". . . somewhat over-active, [but] is at least
interesting." The ghoul tale was double-billed with the

Agnes Moorehead, circa 1960.

remake of *The Mummy* and made its money on the lucrative action and kiddie theatrical film market.

When asked if luck had played any part in her career to date, Agnes replied: "I have never had a 'lucky break' of the kind you hear about in pictures and on the stage. I've gotten every job I ever had either by asking for it or by evolving into it from what I was already doing."

As a change of pace, Agnes moved over to the Walt Disney film factory to perform in the remake of *Polly-anna* (1960), a sweet confection that boasted a charming performance by youngster Hayley Mills and fine cameos by a horde of well-remembered character performers. The saccharine tale finds Mills coming to the country village of Harrington in 1912 to live with her spinster aunt Jane Wyman. It is only a few reels before irrepressible do-gooder Mills has dramatically altered the lives of all those about her. One of her "victims" is grouchy hypochondriac Mrs. Snow (Agnes) who exudes more self-pity than Mills does ribbon candy

sweetness. Under the girl's benevolent influence, Agnes soon ceases her continual shopping for casket linings and finds herself joyfully capering at a local ball.

It was often difficult to perceive the logic in Agnes's choice of movie roles, other than screen exposure and the lucrative salary involved. There had to be better alternatives than such ventures as the shapeless Allied Artists mystery entry *Twenty Plus Two* (1961). This film found David Janssen, a stolid tracer of missing heirs, zipping around the country in his quest to solve a twelve-year-old case which was tied into a blackmail caper and the murder of movie star Bradford Dexter's secretary. Agnes was on camera briefly as the wealthy dowager, Mrs. Delaney, mother of Dina Merrill.

There was more reason for Agnes accepting her part in Bob Hope's *Bachelor in Paradise* (1961). It afforded her an opportunity to play a farce characterization as the female judge who attempts to maintain order in her overcrowded courtroom as she hears conflicting testimony on three divorce suits in which book-writing wolf

With Hayley Mills in *Pollyanna* (BV, 1960).

With David Janssen in *Twenty Plus Two* (AA, 1961).

Bob Hope is listed as chief culprit. Her judicial stern-
ness lent the proper comic reality to the untidy finale
of this lesser Hope vehicle, which also found Lana
Turner floundering as the comedian's love interest.
Agnes stated about her comedy judge characterization:
"You distort the basic truth—that's the principle of
comedy; then you find your own particular humor in
the situations." On another occasion, she mentioned
that the key to her Judge Peterson was the swivel chair
she used on the presiding platform in her courtroom
scenes.

Jessica (1962) at least afforded Agnes a trip abroad
in this Sicilian-located attempt at a modern rendering
of *Lysistrata*. Its improbable premise had Angie Dickinson as an American nurse wed to an Italian medical
student. When he is killed in an automobile crash, she
determines to live in his peasant village, functioning as a
glorified midwife. Her shapely arrival in Forja D'Agro

With Maurice Chevalier in *Jessica* (UA, 1962).

is greeted with glee by the townsmen, particularly as she
jaunts about town straddling a motor scooter wearing
shorts and a tight bodice. But the local women are not
impressed. In particular, the female pillars of the community, grandmother Agnes (stern and old-fashioned)
and youthful Sylva Koscina (up-to-date but conservative) lead the town's femmes in revolt by refusing to
perform wifely duties, figuring that soon there will be
no pregnancies in the village and thus no need for
Dickinson's presence. With Noel-Noel as a gardener
and Maurice Chevalier as an ever-smiling priest, the
inexplicable mixture of accents becomes even more
ludicrous than the script. At least, the scenery was
handsomely photographed in color.

The plethora of bad films that Agnes graced did
provide her with income to maintain her drama workshop, which often operated out of her Beverly Hills
home. Her academic philosophy was: "No [drama
cannot be taught], but one can be guided in technique,
in speech, body movement, interpretation, and the cold
reading of a part."

And to renew herself as a practitioner of the live
theater, Agnes agreed to costar with Joseph Cotten,
Patricia Medina, and Thomas Mitchell in Paul Gregory's production of *Prescription Murder* (a.k.a. *RX
Murder*), a three-act thriller by William Link and Richard Levinson. The pre-Broadway tour opened January
15, 1962, at the Curan Theatre in San Francisco and
closed in Boston, May 26, 1962, never reaching Broadway. Agnes had the brief role as the aristocratic wife
of psychiatrist Cotten who is strangled by her husband
before the end of act I because he is interested in
having Medina as his fulltime mistress.

When asked why she had accepted such a relatively
small role, Agnes admitted she did it as a favor to
Gregory and that she believed even the smallest role
should be played by the best talent available. As she
stated: "Well, someone has to die or there wouldn't
be any play. Besides I think it's better that way. I
would rather do that than become an old hag later in
the play and have the audience wish for me to get
killed." Third-billed, Agnes received her customary
good reviews. "Miss Moorehead in a relatively brief
appearance does well as the bored, middle-aged woman
with a sharp tongue and a jealous streak." And what
pleased Agnes most about the assignment was that she
looked stunning in her Don Loper stage wardrobe.*

---

* The project would eventually be translated into a Uni-
versal-produced telefeature (February 27, 1968, NBC) with
Nina Foch in Agnes's role.

Having tasted the theater again, Agnes was willing to play a featured role in Paul Gregory's production of *Lord Pengo* (Royale Theatre, November 19, 1962). Based on events in the life of the legendary art merchant Joseph Duveen, Charles Boyer portrayed a 1930s culture connoisseur who has one objective in his middle-aged life. He is determined to transform and elevate America's taste in art, no matter what swindle he has to perform in order to obtain his personal goal. Agnes was Miss Swanson, Pengo's faithful critic and ever-loving secretary. Brian Bedford played Boyer's recalcitrant son who finally agrees to carry on the family profession, and Henry Daniell portrayed a millionaire American industrialist who is the pawn in Pengo's plot of tangible immortality. Agnes's big scene came in the last act when she breaks into tears, wondering what is going to happen to her employer in the years to come.

When the classy, Vincent J. Donahue-directed production tried out in Philadelphia, the *Philadelphia Inquirer* noted Agnes ". . . gives pungency to each of her rather limited sides of dialogue." After a Detroit sojourn, the show reached Broadway. As the loyal secretary, Agnes was approved for her "gruff integrity" (*New York Times*). But the production as a whole was greeted with negative reviews, one critic terming the show a "two and a half hour still life." It closed after 17 performances.

At the time, Agnes told Broadway theatre critic Whitney Bolton of her professional creed: "I was brought up, as most actors are brought up, that your obligation is two-fold—to those in a cast with you, and to the men and women who have paid money to see you. You may be ill, tired, vexed, distracted, but bored you may not and must not be, disdainful of your audience you must not be. That is your boss, out there. Night after night there sits your obligation and I wish these kids would learn and, more importantly, respect it."

About characterization and interpretation Agnes told writer Ronald L. Bowers: "An actor must think as the role thinks, not as he thinks. It is this schizophrenic ability that sets the actor apart. As for those actors who go to an analyst, the analyst takes away one of these two parts and ruins the actor."

On the qualities of an actor: "An actor needs the strength of an Amazon and the skin of a crocodile . . . [As] an active actor ('an inactive one is a dead one'), you must be constantly refueling yourself."

Before returning to California, Agnes presented a one-woman performance entitled *The Reminiscences of Wanda Landowska* at Manhattan's 92nd Street YMCA (February 24, 1963). She would repeat this skillful performance on television's "Camera Three" (March 17, 1963, CBS).

MGM's roadshow cinerama attraction *How the West Was Won* premiered in March, 1963, alleging to be a

With Debbie Reynolds, Kimm Charney, Carroll Baker, Bryan Russell (foreground), and Karl Malden (at the stern) in *How the West Was Won* (MGM, 1963).

tribute to the spirit of the nineteenth century American pioneer, but proved to be a 165-minute paeon to commercial low-brow taste. In the opening scene in 1829, Agnes was the sardonic wife of westward mover Karl Malden. While rafting down the Ohio River with their family (including daughters Carroll Baker and Debbie Reynolds), their flatboat overturns on the rapids, and the parents are killed, paving the way for the story to follow the adventure-filled lives of the girls and their subsequent families.

With Charles Boyer and Brian Bedford in *Lord Pengo* (1962).

In *How the West Was Won*.

Agnes was again hired to work with Jerry Lewis in his Paramount release *Who's Minding the Store?* (1963), in which Agnes capered as the fashionable store owner who browbeats her henpecked husband (John McGiver) and ignores the desires of her curvaceous daughter Jill St. John. In order to separate St. John from inept poodle-sitter Lewis, Agnes gives the numbskull man a job in her store as a jack-of-all-trades and advises store manager Ray Walston to give Lewis a tough time. In the course of the slapstick picture, Lewis wreaks havoc on the establishment, department by department, his vacuum cleaner fracus being the last straw. The film was no classic like the Marx Brothers' *The Big Store* or Charles Chaplin's *Modern Times,* but it was diverting, visual shenanigans. That Agnes emerged as a stock caricature of a bossy chic mama could be blamed on both Frank Tashlin's indulgent direction and to Agnes's broad performance.

With the lack of any intriguing new play projects,* Agnes in 1964 turned to television as a full time source for practicing her craft. She had been no stranger to the medium, having performed on most of the major series since the mid-1950s, including "Schlitz Playhouse," "Playhouse 90," "Matinee Theatre," "Gunsmoke," "Adventure in Paradise," "Wagon Train," "Rawhide," "Suspicion," "G. E. Theater," "Studio One," "Cameo Theater," "Burke's Law," "The Rifleman," "The Greatest Show on Earth," "The Rebel," "Channing," and others. On the majority of these video assignments, she played the sturdy pioneer type or the self-willed aristocrat. One of her better roles was as Madame DeFarge on *A Tale of Two Cities* (March 27, 1958, CBS). At the time Agnes said of her role in this video special: "I'm a French Carrie Nation, but it isn't liquor I'm after. You must have one purpose and never deviate. I'm a terribly determined person, just like DeFarge. I look on acting as a running battle, day after day." The *New York Times* reported of her performance in this Eric Portman-Rosemary Harris starrer: "She seldom was truly menacing and vindictive. The hysterical note was present, but not the coldly frightening determination for revenge."

On "The Shirley Temple Storybook" (October 27, 1958, NBC), Agnes scampered about as the nasty

In *The Fabulous Redhead,* circa 1964.

witch in the segment entitled "Rapunzel." The *New York Times* observed: "She glared fiercely, manipulated her talon-like fingers menacingly, hissed imprecations and must have temporarily scared the mischief out of thousands of youngsters. . . ."

One of Agnes's first rate television roles was on "The Twilight Zone" (CBS) in the episode "The Invaders" (January 21, 1961), scripted by Richard Matheson. In the course of the show, there was almost no dialogue, as the story traces the effect of a tiny space ship crashing into the attic of a rude shack owned by lonely Agnes. When two robot-like miniature men emerge from the craft, the action is set into play.

Then in 1964, Agnes made her debut as a television series regular* on "Bewitched" (September 14, 1964, ABC). The show costarred Elizabeth Montgomery as a pert witch named Samantha who weds a normal middle-class American, Darrin Stephens (Dick York, replaced in the 1970–1971 season by Dick Sargent), and must restrain her wealth of hokus-pokus in order to live a somewhat normal suburban life. Nevertheless, she is often tempted to twitch her nose and perform a minor

---

* Agnes informed one reporter at the time: "Perhaps the reason there are less and less exciting players is that there are less and less exciting plays. There is a tendency for writers to try to give the audience merely a violent, shocking impression. As a result there is no more really excellent dramaturgy.

"If you have a great play, there is so much more you can do with it. Still, an actor has so much conjuring to do. Imagine how much harder it is to work with a bad play."

---

* She had made a prior unsold series pilot "Poor Mr. Campbell" with Edward Andrews, circa 1961.

miracle. Agnes was situated as the elegant Endora, mother of Montgomery, who has no use for her mortal son-in-law. She persistently refuses to remember his name, and at the slightest provocation will pull some prank on the usually patient Darrin. Agnes's warlock husband who made occasional appearances on the show was played by Maurice Evans. Others in the half-hour color comedy were Mabel Albertson and Robert Simon as Darrin's parents, George Tobias as the neighbor Abner Kravitz, Alice Pearce as his wife (when she died in early 1965, she was replaced by Sandra Gould), David White as Darrin's boss Larry Tate, and Kasey Rogers as his wife. Then there were flibberty-gibbet Aunt Clara (Marion Lorne) and fey Uncle Arthur (Paul Lynde) and later to instill new life into the long-running series, Samantha and Darrin had a daughter Tabatha, and, more recently, a son Adam. Popping up on occasion as a ghostly baby sitter is Yoo-Hoo (Alice Ghostly), better known as Esmeralda. The series was created by Paul Henning, who guided such series as "The Beverly Hillbillies," "Green Acres," and "Petticoat Junction" to success. Producer and often director of "Bewitched" is William Asher, husband of star Montgomery.

Agnes recalls how she got roped into the treadmill of television series work, in particular on "Bewitched." "I was trapped. I was sent the pilot film script. I looked it over and it was charming and had no violence in it; it was clean and had a smile in it, and a little fantasy and a little romance, so I said, 'This won't sell,' and since they offered me a good sum to make the pilot, I did it. Then I went out on the road to do my one-woman show, and when I came back they told me it was sold . . . and I was committed to it."

Of the opening Thursday evening installment (9:00–9:30), the *Hollywood Reporter* wrote: "Primarily, this hokus-pokus has a magnetic trio in delightful Elizabeth Montgomery and Dick York as newlyweds, and the insatiable villain in irresponsible Agnes Moorehead, and a plethora of hanky-panky-tanky by two witches (mother Moorehead and daughter Montgomery) gesturing, twitching, staring and finger-flicking to make things and persons appear and disappear and do tricks. It's all a lot of nonsense taken in stride, and when it's all over one is left with the feeling 'I wonder what they'll be up to next week?' "

From the start, *Bewitched* proved an enormous success with television-watching America and is currently still running in prime time as one of the top series (with daily syndicated reruns which adds a lot of residual salary to the fancy fees earned by Agnes, Montgomery, and the others). Agnes was nominated for Emmy Awards for her chic, acid-tongue performance

as Endora in the 1965 through 1968 yearly contests, but it was for her dramatic performance in an episode of "Wild West West" (CBS) entitled "Night of the Vicious Valentine" (February 10, 1967) that Agnes received an Emmy for outstanding performance by an actress in a supporting role in a drama. In the series' segment, she was Emma Valentine, the very regal Washington hostess involved in a series of murders.

Meanwhile, Agnes continued to make occasional feature films. In *Hush . . . Hush, Sweet Charlotte* (1964), a grandly conceived follow-up to *Whatever Happened to Baby Jane?*, Bette Davis was again cast as a pathetic creature whose life has been ruined by the selfish whims of others. In the opening flashback (set in the 1920s) of the horror picture, she is planning to run away with married man Bruce Dern, but her domineering father (Victor Buono) orders Dern to break off the relationship. Very soon thereafter at a big ball given at Buono's mansion, Davis returns from a stroll in the garden, her dress covered with blood. Dern's mutilated body is found, and it is assumed that she is the culprit, although Buono's political connections sidetrack a trial. Years later (1964) demented Davis exists alone in her ghostly house, with only bedraggled white trash Velma Cruther (Agnes) as her servant-companion. A new highway is to be constructed through the property and the house has been condemned, but determined Davis will not leave the mansion where so many ghosts roam unburied. She sends for her cousin Olivia de Havilland, a stately lady who arrives on the scene, and the plot soon reveals that she and a local doctor, Joseph Cotten, have hatched a nefarious little plan. Another in Hollisville involved in the plot is deathly ill Mary Astor, the widow of Bruce Dern. She has long

With Bette Davis in *Hush . . . Hush, Sweet Charlotte* (20th-Fox, 1965).

wanted to confide certain information regarding that horrific night long decades ago, and now approaching her end, is relieved to pass on data to British insurance investigator Cecil Kellaway, a most ready listener.

In her raggedy dress, with her face smudged with dirt and her hair constantly in disarray, Agnes lopes about the Hollis house, doing Davis's bidding and taking careful note of the new arrival, de Havilland. It is not long before she is in dire conflict with the polite but determined cousin. She tells her "I take my orders from Miss Charlotte and not you. I can see right through you." The cards are stacked against Agnes. She visits Kellaway and tells him that peculiar things are transpiring up at the house. In her sing-song southern drawl, she hysterically whimpers, "I ain't gonna ever see her [Miss Charlotte] again. I knows it. I just knows it." She does return to the mansion to rescue her employer from de Havilland's clutches, but is confronted by the cousin. As Agnes backs down the staircase, she trips and falls down the stairs, only to be clobbered to death by de Havilland.

With the spate of several other once-famous movie stars making horror film comeback, *Hush . . . Hush, Sweet Charlotte* was not the surprise package its predecessor had been. It did well at the box office, but the novelty was missing. Judith Crist wrote in the *New York Herald-Tribune* ". . . and Agnes Moorehead— well, Agnes Moorehead almost, just almost walks off with the show as the whiny 'po white trash' Velma." Agnes was nominated for her fourth Academy Award, but this time lost out to Lila Kedrova who won a best supporting actress Oscar for *Zorba the Greek*.

On first viewing, Agnes's performance in this Davis vehicle rankles with scene-stealing and seems out and out camp, contrived to be comic relief midst the setting of murder, mayhem, and deceit. But on further screenings, it becomes apparent that Agnes's exaggerated histrionics (shuffling about, her arms akimbo and eyes rolling, as she speaks in an ever-so-slow, syrupy Dixie accent) is a needed bridge between Davis's interpretation of the looney Charlotte Hollis and the refined, coldly calculating interpretation of Parisian-visitor de Havilland. Which makes Bosley Crowthers' opinion in the *New York Times* seem superficial and unfair. "And Agnes Moorehead as her [Davis's] weird and crone like servant is allowed to get away with some of the broadest mugging and snarling ever done by a respectable actress on the screen. If she gets an Academy Award for this performance—which is possible, because she's been nominated for it—the Academy should close up shop!"

After making a guest appearance in a short run as Madame Arcardi in *High Spirits* at the Dallas State

With Olivia de Havilland in *Hush . . . , Hush, Sweet Charlotte.*

Fair, Agnes returned to the screen in the gooey *The Singing Nun* (1966), having bowed out of the role of Doris Day's landlady in *Do Not Disturb* (1965).* *The Singing Nun* was MGM's hastily merchandised effort to cash in on the craze of Belgian recording star, Sister Dominique, whose albums were selling fast and furious throughout America. The phony biography presented an unconvincing Debbie Reynolds in the title role of a guitar-strumming Soeur Sourire, who leaves the Dominican convent near Antwerp for an assignment at the Samaritan House in a depressed area of Brussels. There angelic Greer Garson is the (theatrical) mother superior, and Agnes is Sister Cluny, performing as the hard-hearted, crotchety nun won over by the ever-smiling Reynolds. Added into the froth were scenes of Reynolds riding a motor scooter in her nun's habit and a special guest appearance by Ed Sullivan as himself, coming to Brussels to tape a session of Reynolds's singing to use on his Sunday night video show. Heaven help the cultural level of America, but the picture made money. During the production, Agnes and Reynolds, who had worked together in *How the West Was Won*, became close friends, in a mother-daughter type relationship. After that, there was nothing the well-heeled Reynolds was not wont to do for her pal, including lending Agnes the use of her $40,000 trailer-dressing room on occasion.

Agnes continued with her *Bewitched* assignment. Although the series was a consistent high placer in the Nielsen video ratings, Agnes claimed she did not care:

---

* In the fall of 1966, Robert Aldrich was preparing *The Mummified Mummy* to feature Agnes, but it did not come about.

With Debbie Reynolds in *The Singing Nun* (MGM, 1966).

ber 6, 1966), did readings on "The Hollywood Palace," was a panelist on "Hollywood Squares," did two "Mr. Blackwell Presents" variety shows, repeatedly made the rounds of the talk shows, acted on "The Men from Shiloh" and in "Barefoot in the Park," made an episode of "Lancer," two appearances on "Night Gallery," and in 1970 did a voice-over commercial for "The Wonderful World of Walt Disney," a series she has also acted on in recent seasons. With her "name" status, Agnes also ventured into the hectic world of guesting in telefeatures, the specially made feature films for television consumption. On *The Ballad of Andy Crocker* (November 18, 1969, ABC) she was the rich, gun-shooting mother of Joey Heatherton; in *Marriage Year One* (October 15, 1971, NBC) she played the youngish grandmother of immature Sally Field, in *Suddenly Single* (October 19, 1971, ABC) she was the confidant of Hal Holbrook.

As a favor to Debbie Reynolds, Agnes made a guest appearance in Reynolds's shocker theatrical film *What's the Matter with Helen?* (1971), scripted by Henry Farrell who had written *Whatever Happened to Baby Jane?* Reynolds and Shelley Winters are the mothers of teenagers convicted in a midwestern thrill killing in the

"Ratings? Ratings. I just don't think about them. I really don't . . . no, not even when the show went on the air. Oh, you hear things here and there, but you have to do the best job of acting you can, just do the job, and not become obsessed with that sort of thing." About the show's popularity: "It's really kind of frightening you know. It is wonderful and one is very grateful to be in a show that people enjoy, but the thing that frightens me is the tremendous amount of responsibility. To keep up the quality week after week, you have to work hard at it."

Of television in general: "I don't watch much television, I find it hard to get involved in a show. I'm so interested in the technical aspects—but this summer (1967) I began watching one show: it's called *Mission: Impossible*—and do you know it was really good—really good."

Agnes, always filled with an abundance of energy and anxious to play other parts as opposed to her type-casting in "Bewitched" ("It's great to get off the broom-stick once in awhile!"), has turned up in a wide assortment of video roles in recent years. She guested on "Batman," replaced Bette Davis as the Red Queen on NBC's "Alice through the Looking Glass" (Novem-

In *Bewitched,* (CBS-TV, 1967).

With Shelley Winters in *What's the Matter with Helen?*
(UA, 1971).

1930s. These two women band together to make a new life for themselves in California, with Reynolds running a dance-acting school for would-be Shirley Temples. Winters, harassed by bad memories of her husband's untimely end years before, turns more and more to the consolation of radio evangelist Sister Alma (Agnes) who preaches the pure love of god, at three broadcasted daily services. Later in the film, distraught Winters appears at Agnes's cathedral, devoted to the open hand of god, and is rebuked by the charlatan spiritual leader when she attempts to gain eternal forgiveness by confessing to a crime she has been recently involved in with Reynolds. *What's the Matter with Helen?* was pushed out onto the saturation showcase market in mid-summer, 1971, and did not fare too well. The problems of the title figure (Winters) were obvious from the start, and director Curtis Harrington wrongly evoked mirth at the 1930s rather than extolling nos-

talgia. The best that could be said of Agnes in her brief assignment was that she was stately.

Now in the prime of her mature professional career, Agnes is wont to be accepted as a queen bee wherever she goes, and she likes that just fine. "Bewitched" dribbled to an end in the 1971–1972 video season, so she returned to a multitude of media activity, including the lead in a Nashville, Tennessee-filmed horror picture *Dear Dead Delilah* (1972), more guest appearances on telefeatures such as *Rolling Man* (ABC, October 9, 1972). *Don Juan in Hell* was put on tour again, including a brief Broadway stand in early 1973. Then Agnes flew to London to play a featured role in the Universal telefeature version of *Dr. Frankenstein,* starring James Mason, David McCallum, and with Michael Sarrazin as the famed mongrel monster. Back in the States, she joined the cast of the Los Angeles Civic Light Opera's *Gigi,* a musical which debuted in

July, 1973. The stage version heavily relied on the 1958 MGM movie musical for its roster of Alan Jay Lerner and Frederick Loewe songs, and in presentation suffered by comparison. Agnes, as archly sarcastic Aunt Alicia, gave a hammy performance, but considering the tedium of the elaborate legitimate production, it was considered a godsend. Agnes joined with cast members Alfred Drake, Daniel Massey, Maria Karnilova, and Karen Wolfe, in the new Broadway production of *Gigi,* which opened in the fall of 1973.

Her "spare" time is devoted to teaching private acting courses and coaching. She freely admits: "I haven't time to cook and keep house. But that doesn't mean I'm not a good cook, especially when it comes to creative dishes." Of her television work, she claims: "This is the treadmill. This is TV. Mad, hectic, no time to relax. Every second counts. This is not an era of convictions."

Although her work of recent years has not taxed her abilities, Agnes maintains: "You have to keep on developing and maturing and being sincere in your work and just go right on whether audiences or critics are taking your scalp off or not."

Agnes owns a 320-acre farm, Kitchen Middens, between Zanesville and Cambridge, Ohio, property deeded to her grandparents by Presidents Monroe and Tyler. She thinks one day she might retire there with her mother, who still lives in the semiwilds of Wisconsin.

There are times when Agnes ponders on her way of life: "It's really the loneliest sort of life. Sure, it's terribly exciting but when I'm making a film or traveling in stock, how long am I in one place to make good friends? I did become good friends with Debbie Reynolds. . . . Mostly it's just cold hotels. But that's the wandering minstrel's life. I'd love to just stay home and be married again, to have someone take care of me, but I've never been that fortunate."

Of her future in the profession: "But if I didn't do that (*Gigi*), I'd go out and do something else. I'd pick up my grip and go teach a seminar or coach. I can't just sit around. I can't be bothered with that." About the unknown challenges of her craft: "After all my years in this business, nothing can frighten me one whit and nothing does!"

So Agnes, now in her late sixties, continues on in the entertainment world. In 1971 she invested in United General Theatres which plans to distribute 16mm. G-rated feature films in the United States. She has been a board member of the Screen Actors Guild and is an active participant of the Episcopal Actors Guild. And she continues to win awards: in April, 1970 she was called to Washington, D.C. by the governor of Massachusetts to receive one of two gold plaques presented to "outstanding natives" of that state. (The other award went to famed heart specialist Dr. Dudley White.) A year later Agnes was given the first Maude Adams Award at Stephens College, Missouri. Maude Adams, one of the distinguished stars of American theater, was also head of the Stephens College Theater Department from 1937–1950.

Agnes' fondest wish: "To be called a 'pro' is the nicest compliment you can pay an actress, or an artist. I hope to deserve that to the day I retire, if I retire from the world of show business."

FILMOGRAPHY: AGNES MOOREHEAD
FEATURE FILMS

CITIZEN KANE (RKO, 1941) 119 M.

Producer-director, Orson Welles; screenplay, Herman J. Mankiewicz, Welles; art director, Van Nest Polglase, Perry Ferguson; gowns, Edward Stevenson, music, Bernard Herrmann; special effects, Vernon L. Walker; camera, Gregg Toland; editor, Robert Wise, Mark Robson.

Orson Welles (Charles Foster Kane); Joseph Cotten (Jedediah Leland); Dorothy Comingore (Susan Alexander); Agnes Moorehead (Kane's mother); Ruth Warrick (Emily); Ray Collins (Jim Gettys); Erskine Sanford (Carter); Everett Sloane (Bernstein); William Alland (Thompson, The Reporter); Paul Stewart (Raymond); George Coulouris (Thatcher); Fortunio Bonanova (Matiste); Gus Schilling (Headwaiter); Philip Van Zandt (Rawlston); Georgia Backus (Miss Anderson); Harry Shannon (Kane's Father); Sonny Bupp (Kane's Son); Buddy Swan (Kane at the Age of Eight); Al Eben (Mike); Charles Bennett (Entertainer); Lew Harvey (Newspaper Man); Bruce Sidney (Newsman); Tom Curran (Teddy Roosevelt); Ed Peil, Charles Meakin (Civic Leaders); Mitchell Ingraham, Francis Sayles (Politicians); Edith Evanson (Nurse); Louise Franklin (Maid); Irving Mitchell (Dr. Corey); Arthur Kay (Orchestra Leader); Tudor Williams (Chorus Master); James Mack (Prompter); Gohr Van Vleck, Jack Raymond (Stagehands); Herbert Corthell (City Editor); Shimen Ruskin, George Sherwood (Hirelings); Milton Kibbee, Louis Natheaux, Alan Ladd, Louise Currie, Eddie Coke, Walter Sande, Art O'Connell, Richard Wilson, Katherine Trosper (Reporters); Bob Dudley (Photographer); Eddie Cobb (Inquiring Reporter); John Dilson, Walter James (Ward Heeler); Major McBride (Shadowgraph Man); Suzanne Dulier (French Maid); Harry Vejar (Portuguese Laborer); Captain Garcia (General); Art Yeoman (Speaker); Philip Morris (Politician); Albert Frazier (Gorilla Man); Tim Davis (Copy Boy); Jack Morton (Butler); Karl Thomas (Jetsam); Glenn Turnbull (Flotsam); Donna Dax (Housemaid); Myrtle Mischell (Governess); Joe North (Secretary).

THE MAGNIFICENT AMBERSONS (RKO, 1942) 88 M.

Producer-director, Orson Welles; based on the novel by Booth Tarkington; screenplay, Welles; art director, Mark-Lee Kirk; gowns, Edward Stevenson; music, Bernard Herrmann; special effects, Vernon L. Walker; editor, Robert Wise.

Joseph Cotten (Eugene Morgan); Tim Holt (George Minafer Amberson); Dolores Costello (Isabel Amberson); Anne Baxter (Lucy Morgan); Agnes Moorehead (Fanny Minafer); Ray Collins (Jack); Erskine Sanford (Bronson); Richard Bennett (Major Amberson); Don Dillaway (Wilbur Minafer); Orson Welles (Narrator); Charles Phipps (Uncle John); Ray Collins (Jack); Dorothy Vaughan, Sam Rice, Elmer Jerome (Attendees At Funeral); Olive Ball (Mary); Nina Guilbert, John Elliott (Guests); Kathryn Sheldon (Matron—Mrs. Foster's); Anne O'Neal (Mrs. Foster); Georgia Backus (Matron); Henry Roquemore (Hardware Man); Hilda Plowright (Nurse); Mel Ford (Fred Kinney); Bob Pittard (Charles Johnson); Ken Stewart (Man at Club Room); Lillian Nicholson (Landlady); Billy Elmer (House Servant); Harry Humphrey, Lew Kelly, Maynard Holmes, Ed Howard (Citizens); Gus Schilling (Drug Clerk); Bobby Cooper (George Amberson as a Boy); John Maguire (Young Man); William Blees (Youth at Accident); James Westerfield (Cop at Accident); Heenan Elliott (Laborer); Nancy Gates (Girl); Jack Santoro (Barber); Philip Morris (Cop).

THE BIG STREET (RKO, 1942) 88 M.

Producer, Damon Runyon; director, Irving Reis; based on the story "Little Pinks" by Runyon; screenplay, Leonard Spigelgass; music director, C. Bakaleinikoff; song, Mort Greene and Harry Revel; art director, Albert S. D'Agostino; choreographer, Chester Hale; special effects, Vernon L. Walker; camera, Russell Metty; editor, William Hamilton.

Henry Fonda (Little Pinks); Lucille Ball (Gloria); Barton MacLane (Cass Ables); Eugene Pallette (Nicely Johnson); Agnes Moorehead (Violette); Sam Levene (Horse Thief); Ray Collins (Professor B); Marion Martin (Mrs. Venus); William Orr (Decatur Reed); George Cleveland (Colonel Venus); Louise Beavers (Ruby); Juan Varro (Lou Adolia); Millard Mitchell (Gentleman George); Hans Conreid (Louie—Headwaiter); Vera Gordon (Mrs. Lefkowitz); Harry Shannon (Doctor); John Miljan (McWhirter); Don Barclay (M.C.); Julius Tannen (Judge Bamberger); Eddie Dunn (Mulvaney); Bert Hanlon (Philly the Weeper); Bob Perry (Toupee); Anthony Blair (O'Rourke); Art Hamburger (Joel Duffle); Addison Richards (Doctor Mitchell); Ozzie Nelson & Orchestra (Themselves); (Chet) Chester Huntley (Radio Announcer); Sammy Stein, Johnny Indrisano, Warren Jackson, Tony Merlo, George Magrill, Peter Duray, Arnold Virt, Jack Chefe, Joe Niemeyer, Don Kerr (Mugs At Mindy's); Walter Soderling (Doctor—Mindy's); Frank Moran, James O'Gatty (Mugs); Bill Halligan (Detective); Ralph Peters (Florist); Marie Windsor (Girl); Don Kerr (Mobster); Little Charles Hall (Caviar Waiter); Joe Scadato (Spanish Joe); Mim Doyle (Nurse); Donald Kirke (Surgeon); John Miller, Wayne McCoy, Jimmy Dime, Ross Forrester, Jim Toney, Lee Moore (Truck Drivers); George McKay (Sergeant); Charles Cane, Lou Wood (Cops); Dewey Robinson, Elliott Sullivan (Tramps).

JOURNEY INTO FEAR (RKO, 1942) 89 M.

Producer, Orson Welles; director, Norman Foster, Welles; based on the novel by Eric Ambler; screenplay, Joseph Cotten, Welles; music, Roy Webb; music director, C. Bakaleinikoff; art director, Albert S. D'Agostino, Mark-Lee Kirk; gowns, Edward Stevenson; special effects, Vernon L. Walker; camera, Karl Struss; editor, Mark Robson.

Joseph Cotten (Howard Graham); Dolores del Rio (Josette Martel); Orson Welles (Colonel Haki); Ruth Warrick (Stephanie Graham); Agnes Moorehead (Mrs. Mathis); Jack Durant (Gobo); Everett Sloane (Kopeikin); Eustace Wyatt (Dr. Haller); Frank Readick (Mathis); Edgar Barrier (Kuvetli); Jack Moss (Peter Banat); Stefan Schnabel (Purser); Hans Conried (Magician at Le Jockey); Richard Bennett (Captain); Shifra Haran (Mrs. Haller); Robert Meltzer, Herbert Drake, Bill Roberts (Bits).

THE YOUNGEST PROFESSION (MGM, 1943) 82 M.

Producer, B. F. Zeldman; director, Edward Buzzell; story, Lillian Day; screenplay, George Oppenheimer, Charles Lederer, Leonard Spigelgass; music, David Snell; art director, Cedric Gibbons; camera, Charles Lawton; editor, Ralph Winters.

Virginia Weidler (Joan Lyons); Edward Arnold (Mr. Lawrence Lyons); John Carroll (Hercules); Jean Porter (Patricia Drew); Marta Linden (Mrs. Edith Lyons); Dick Simmons (Douglas Sutton); Ann Ayars (Miss Susan Thayer); Agnes Moorehead (Miss Featherstone); Marcia Mae Jones (Vera Bailey); Raymond Roe (Schuyler); Scotty Beckett (Junior Lyons); Jessie Grayson (Lilybud); Walter Pidgeon, Robert Taylor, Greer Garson, William Powell, Lana Turner (Themselves); Beverly Tyler (Thyra Winters); Patricia Roe (Polly); Marjorie Gateson (Mrs.

Drew); Thurston Hall (Mr. Drew); Aileen Pringle (Miss Farwood); Dorothy Christy (Wally); Nora Lane (Hilda); Mary Vallee (Mary); Gloria Tucker (Gladys); Jane Isbell (June); Hazel Dawn (Hazel); Beverly Boyd (Beverly); Gloria Mackey (Gloria); Ann MacLean (Ann); Shirley Coates, Mary McCarty (Girls); William Tannen (Hotel Clerk); Ann Codee (Sandra's Maid); Eddie Buzzell (Man in Theater); George Nelson (Delivery Boy); Alice Keating (Governess); Harry Barris (Man); Herberta Williams (Hortense); Sara Haden (Salvation Army Lass); Ray Teal (Taxi Driver); Polly Bailey, Margaret Bert, Violet Seton, Hazel Doblman (Governesses); Dorothy Morris (Secretary).

GOVERNMENT GIRL (RKO, 1944) 94 M.

Producer, Dudley Nichols; associate producer, Edward Donahue; director, Nichols; story, Adela Rogers St. John; screenplay, Nichols; art director, Albert S. D'Agostino; music, Leigh Harline; music director, C. Bakaleinikoff; special effects, Vernon L. Walker; camera, Frank Redman; editor, Roland Gross.

Olivia de Havilland (Smokey); Sonny Tufts (Browne); Anne Shirley (May); Jess Barker (Dana); James Dunn (Sgt. Joe); Paul Stewart (Branch); Agnes Moorehead (Mrs. Wright); Harry Davenport (Senator MacVickers); Una O'Connor (Mrs. Harris); Sig Ruman (Ambassador); Jane Darwell (Miss Trask); George Givot (Count Medinsky); Paul Stanton (Mr. Harvester); Art Smith (Marqueenie); Joan Valerie (Miss MacVickers); Harry Shannon (Mr. Gibson); Emory Parnell (The Chief); Ray Walker (Tom Holliday); J.C. Fowler (Man); Russell Huestes, Larry Steers, James Carlisle, Bert Moorhouse, Fred Norton, Demetrius Alexis, Larry Williams, Chester Carlisle, Harry Denny, Tom Costello, Ronnie Rondell (Businessmen); Olive Morgan (Officer); Harold Miller (Naval Officer); Major Sam Harris (American General); Warren Hymer, Harry Tenbrook (M.P.s); Karl Miller (Janitor); Cy Ring (Lt. Commander); Bruce Edwards, Lawrence Tierney, Ralph Dunn, Al Hill, David Newell, George Ford (F.B.I. Men); Frank Moran (Tough Sergeant); Chef Milani (Hotel Waiter); J. Louis Johnson (Mrs. Wright's Butler); June Booth (Secretary); Edward Fielding (Mr. Benson); Joe Bernard (Workman); Ian Wolfe (Hotel Clerk); Ivan Simpson (Judge Leonard); Virginia Gardner (Branch's Girl); Tom Burton, Harry Clay, Steve Winston (Reporters); George Riley (Cop); James Kirkwood, Fred Fox, Babe Green, Frank McClure, Harry Bailey, Donald Hall, Louis Payne, Wally Dean (Senators).

JANE EYRE (20th Century-Fox, 1944) 95 M.

Producer, William Goetz; director, Robert Stevenson; based on the novel by Charlotte Bronte; screenplay, Aldous Huxley, Stevenson, John Houseman; art director, James Basevi, Wiard B. Ihnen; special effects, Fred Sersen; camera, George Barnes; editor, Walter Thompson.

Orson Welles (Edward Rochester); Joan Fontaine (Jane Eyre); Margaret O'Brien (Adele); Peggy Ann Garner (Jane—as a Child); John Sutton (Dr. Rivers); Sara Allgood (Bessie); Henry Daniell (Brocklehurst); Agnes Moorehead (Mrs. Reed); Aubrey Mather (Colonel Dent); Edith Barrett (Mrs. Fairfax); Barbara Everest (Lady Ingraham); Hillary Brooke (Blanche); Ethel Griffies (Grace Pool); Eily Malyon (Mrs. Sketcher); Ivan Simpson (Mr. Woods); Erskine Sanford (Mr. Braggs); John Abbott (Mason); Elizabeth Taylor (Helen); Mae Marsh (Leah); Mary Forbes (Mrs. Eshton); Thomas Louden (Sir George Lynn); Yorke Sherwood (Beadle); Ronald Harris (John); Charles Irwin (Auctioneer); Gwendolen Logan, Moyna Macgill (Dowagers); Gerald Oliver Smith (Footman At

Gateshead); Jean Fenwick, Bud Lawler, John Meredith, Leslie Vincent, Roseanna Murray, Marion Rosamond, Dan Wallace (Guests); Billie Seward, Ruth Brady, Adele Jergens (Girls at Party); Colin Campbell (Proprietor); Eustace Wyatt (Dr. Carter); David Clyde (Guard); Billy Bevan (Bookie); Tempe Pigott (Fortune Teller) Alec Craig (Footman); Frederick Worlock (Waiter); George Kirby (Old Gentleman); Alan Edmiston (Dealer); Arthur Gould-Porter (Young Man).

SINCE YOU WENT AWAY (United Artists, 1944) 172 M.

Producer, David O. Selznick; director, John Cromwell; screenplay, Selznick; production designer, William L. Pereira; music, Max Steiner; choreographer, Charles Walters; special effects, Jack Cosgrove; camera, Stanley Cortez, Lee Garmes; editor, Hal C. Kern.

Claudette Colbert (Anne Hilton); Jennifer Jones (Jane Hilton); Joseph Cotten (Anthony Willett); Shirley Temple (Bridget 'Brig' Hilton); Monty Woolley (Colonel Smollett); Lionel Barrymore (Clergyman); Robert Walker (William G. Smollett II); Hattie McDaniel (Fidelia); Agnes Moorehead (Emily Hawkins); Guy Madison (Harold Smith); Keenan Wynn (Lt. Solomon); Lloyd Corrigan (Mr. Mahoney); Gordon Oliver (Marine Officer); Jane Devlin (Gladys Brown); Ann Gillis (Becky Anderson); Nazimova (Zosia Koslawska); Dorothy Garner ('Sugar'); Andrew McLaglen (Former Plowboy); Jill Warren (Waitress); Terry Moore (Refugee Child); Warren Hymer (Patient at Finger Ladder); Robert Johnson (Black Officer); Dorothy Dandridge (His Wife); Johnny Bond (AWOL); George Chandler (Cabby); Irving Bacon (Bartender); Jackie Moran (Johnny Mahoney); Addison Richards (Major Atkins); Barbara Pepper (Pin Girl); Byron Foulger (Principal); Harry Hayden (Conductor); Edwin Maxwell (Businessman); Florence Bates (Hungry Dowager); Theodore von Eltz (Desk Clerk); Neil Hamilton (Tim Hilton-Photograph); Doodles Weaver (Convalescent); Eilene Janssen (Sergeant's Child); Ruth Roman (Envious Girl); William B. Davidson (Taxpayer).

DRAGON SEED (MGM, 1944) 145 M.

Producer, Pandro S. Berman; director, Jack Conway, Harold S. Bucquet; based on the novel by Pearl S. Buck; screenplay, Marguerite Roberts, Jane Murfin; music, Herbert Stothart; art director, Cedric Gibbons, Lyle R. Wheeler; special effects, Warren Newcombe; camera, Sidney Wagner; editor, Harold F. Kress.

Katharine Hepburn (Jade); Walter Huston (Ling Tan); Aline MacMahon (Mrs. Ling Tan); Akim Tamiroff (Wu Len); Turhan Bey (Lao Er); Hurd Hatfield (Lao San); Frances Rafferty (Orchid); Henry Travers (Third Cousin); Agnes Moorehead (Third Cousin's Wife); Robert Lewis (Captain Sato); J. Carroll Naish (Japanese Kitchen Overseer); Jacqueline DeWit (Mrs. Wu Lien); Paul E. Burns (Fourth Cousin); Anna Demetrio (Neighbor Shen); Lionel Barrymore (Narrator); Ted Hecht (Major Hoagi); Abner Biberman (Captain Yasuda); Leonard Mudie (Old Peddler); Arthur Dulac, Richard Wang, Prince Walm, Baldo Albert (Japanese Soldiers); Beal Wong, Victor Wong, Pete Katchenaro (Japanese Officers); Charles Lung (Japanese Diplomat); John Bleifer, Phil Van Zandt (Japanese Guards); Winifred Woo (Jade's Child); Philip Ahn (Leader Of City People); Frank Eng, Richard Yee (Students); Paul Fung, Spencer Chan (Farmers); Lee Tung Foo (Innkeeper); Claire DuBrey (Hysterical Woman).

THE SEVENTH CROSS (MGM, 1944) 110 M.

Producer, Pandro S. Berman; director, Fred Zinnemann; based on the novel by Anna Seghers; screenplay, Helen

Deutsch; music, Roy Webb; art director, Cedric Gibbons, Leonid Vasian; camert, Karl Freund; editor, Thomas Richards.

Spencer Tracy (George Heisler); Signe Hasso (Toni); Agnes Moorehead (Mme. Marelli); Felix Bressart (Schlamm); Hume Cronyn (Paul Roeder); Herbert Rudley (Franz Marnet); Jessica Tandy (Liesel Roeder); Kurt Katch (Leo Herman); Fay Wall (Elsa Hermann); George Zucco (Fahrenberg); Alexander Granach (Zillich); William Challee (Fischer); John Wengraf (Kommisar Oberkamp); George Macready (Bruno Sauer); Katherine Locke (Mrs. Sauer); John Meredith (Dutch Sailor); Ludwig Donath (Wilhelm Reinhardt); Paul Guilfoyle (Fiedler); Frank Jaquet (Herr Schmitt); Lotte Stein (Frau Schmitt); Charles Arnt (Herr Binder); Connie Gilchrist (Frau Binder); Steven Geray (Dr. Lowenstein); George Suzanne (Bellani); William Edmunds (Aldinger); Martin Berliner (Beutler); Konstantin Shayne (Fuellgrabe); Ray Collins (Wallau); Paul E. Burns (Pelzer); Steven Muller (Hellwig Anders); Lionel Royce (Karl Anders); Norbert Muller (Max Anders); Karen Verne (K Leni); Frederick Giermann (Inspector); Hans Herbert (Schoolmaster); Eily Malyon (Fraulein Bachmann); Helen Weigel (Janitress); Larry Olsen (Ludi Roder); Lisa Golm (Mrs. Hinkel); Irene Seidner (Mrs. Grossner); Lotte Palfi (Anna); Gisella Werbiseck (Old Woman); Eileen Jansen (Girl in Orchard); Gigi Petreau, Gary Taylor, Jim Hawkins (Roeder's Children); Leon Tyler (Fritz); Bobby Blake (Small Boy); Hugh Beaumont (Truck Driver); Egon Brecher (Sexton); Herbert Holcomb, Holger Bendixon, Fred Nurney, Otto Reichow, Hans Von Morhart (Gestapo); Leon Tyler, Hugh Maguire (Hitler Youths); Captain John Van Eyck (S.A. Man); Hallene Hill (Mrs. Kaupfen); Mitchell Lewis, Earl Schenck, Wes Howard, Joe Yule, James Dime, Tony Carson, Henri Reineque, Louis Hart, Alex Schonberg, Michael Macy (Prisoners—Concentration Camp); Art Fowler, Clifford Rathjen, Allen Fox, George Magrill, Holger Bendixon, Brent Shugar (Guards—Concentration Camp).

MRS. PARKINGTON (MGM, 1944) 124 M.

Producer, Leon Gordon; director, Tay Garnett; based on the novel by Louis Bromfield; screenplay, Robert Thoeren, Polly James; music, Bronislau Kaper; art director, Cedric Gibbons, Randall Duell; camera, Joseph Ruttenberg; editor, George Boemler.

Greer Garson (Susie Parkington); Walter Pidgeon (Major Augustus Parkington); Edward Arnold (Amory Stilham); Frances Rafferty (Jane Stilham); Agnes Moorehead (Aspasia Conti); Selena Royle (Hattie Trounsen); Gladys Cooper (Alice, Duchess De Brancourt); Lee Patrick (Madeleine); Dan Duryea (Jack Stilham); Rod Cameron (Al Swann); Tom Drake (Ned Talbot); Helen Freeman (Helen Stilham); Cecil Kellaway (Edward, Prince Of Wales); Hugh Marlowe (John Marbey); Tala Birell (Lady Nora Ebbsworth); Peter Lawford (Thornley); Fortunio Bonanova (Signor Callini); Mary Servoss (Mrs. Graham); Gerald Oliver Smith (Taylor); Ruthe Brady (Bridgett); Byron Foulger (Vance); Wallis Clark (Captain McTavish); Ann Codee (Mme. Dupont); Frank Reicher (French Doctor); George Davis (French Policeman); Harry Cording (Humphrey); Celia Travers (Belle); Kay Medford (Minnie); Hans Conried (Mr. Ernst); Edward Fielding (Rev. Pilbridge); Alma Kruger (Mrs. Jacob Livingstone); Rhea Mitchell (Mrs. Humphrey); Ivo Henderson (Albert); Charles Pecora (Headwaiter); Mary Zavian (Can-Can Girl); Myron Tobias (Boy); Eugene Borden (Drunk); Charles Cane, Al Hill, Bert Le Baron, Al Ferguson, Richard Thorne (Miners); Franco Corsaro (Gypsy Fiddler); Marcelle Corday (Mme. De Thebes); Bertha Feducha, Symona Boniface (Pitter); Noreen Nash (Bridget); Billy Bletcher,

Harry Tyler, Vernon Dent, Bud Jamison (Quartette); Margaret Burt, Naomi Childers (Nurses); Harry Adams, Nolan Leary, John Bohn, Leonard Mellin, John Phipps, Billy Engle, Fred Rapport, Maurice Brier (Waiters at Ball); Wilson Benge, William O'Brien, Walter Rode, George Calliga (Caterers at Ball); Wyndham Standing (Butler); Brandon Hurst (Footman).

TOMORROW THE WORLD (United Artists, 1944) 86 M.

Producer, Lester Cowan; associate producer, David Hall; director, Leslie Fenton; based on the play by James Gow, Arnaud D'Usseau; screenplay, Ring Lardner, Jr. Leopold Atlas; art director, James Sullivan; camera, Henry Sharp; editor, Ann Bauchens.

Fredric March (Mike Frame); Betty Field (Leona Richards); Agnes Moorehead (Jessie); Skippy Homeier (Emil Bruckner); Joan Carroll (Pat Frame); Edith Angold (Frieda); Rudy Wissler (Stan); Boots Brown (Ray); Marvin Davis (Dennis); Patsy Ann Thompson (Millie); Mary Newton (School Principal); Tom Fadden (Mailman).

KEEP YOUR POWDER DRY (MGM, 1945) 93 M.

Producer, George Haight; director, Edward Buzzell; screenplay, Mary C. McCall, Jr., George Bruce; music, David Snell; art director, Cedric Gibbons, Leonid Vasian; camera, Ray June; editor, Frank E. Hull.

Lana Turner (Valerie Parks); Laraine Day (Leigh Rand); Susan Peters (Ann Darrison); Agnes Moorehead (Lt. Colonel Spottiswood); Bill Johnson (Captain Bill Barclay); Natalie Schafer (Harriett Corwin); Lee Patrick (Gladys Hopkins); Marta Linden (Captain Sanders); June Lockhart (Sarah Swanson); Edith Leach (Mary Carter); Jess Barker (Junior Vanderhausen); Michael Kirby (Captain John Darrison); Henry O'Neill (Brig. General Rand); Tim Murdock (Captain Mannering); Sondra Rodgers (WAC Hodgekins); Marjorie Davies (WAC Polhemus); Rex Evans (Marco Cummings); Pierre Watkin (Mr. Lorrison); Shirley Patterson (WAC Brooks); Bobo Rockefeller (WAC McBride); George Peters (Lieutenant); George Dudley (Sergeant); Stanley Andrews (Army Colonel); Frances Morris, Elizabeth Russell (WAC Sergeants); Geraldine Wall (Judo Instructor); Jesse Graves (Elevator Man); Anne Loos, Roberta Ridley (WACs on Drill Field); Clyde Fillmore (Brig. General Bratten); Early Cantrell (WAC Company Commander).

OUR VINES HAVE TENDER GRAPES (MGM, 1945) 105 M.

Producer, Robert Sisk; director, Roy Rowland; based on the novel *For Our Vines Have Tender Grapes* by George Victor Martin; screenplay, Dalton Trumbo; music, Bronislau Kaper; art director, Cedric Gibbons, Edward Carfagno; special effects, A. Arnold Gillespie, Danny Hall; camera, Robert Surtees; editor, Ralph E. Winters.

Edward G. Robinson (Martinius Jacobson); Margaret O'Brien (Selma Jacobson); James Craig (Nels Halverson); Agnes Moorehead (Ma Jacobson); Jackie 'Butch' Jenkins (Arnold Hanson); Morris Carnovsky (Bjorn Bjornson); Frances Gifford (Viola Johnson); Sarah Haden (Mrs. Bjornson); Louis Jean Heydt (Mr. X Farrasen); Greta Granstedt (Mrs. Farrasen); Arthur Space (Pete Hanson); Elizabeth Russell (Kola Hanson); Dorothy Morris (Ingaborg Jensen); Charles Middleton (Kurt Jensen); Arthur Hohl (Dvar Svenson); Abigail Adams (Girl); Johnny Berkes (Driver); Rhoda Williams (Marguerita Larsen); George Lloyd (Farmer).

HER HIGHNESS AND THE BELLBOY (MGM, 1945) 112 M.

Producer, Joe Pasternak; director, Richard Thorpe;

screenplay, Richard Connell, Gladys Lehman; music, Georgie Stoll; choreographer, Charles Walters; art director, Cedric Gibbons, Urie McCleary; special effects, Warren Newcombe; camera, Harry Stradling; editor, George Boemler.

Hedy Lamarr (Princess Veronica); Robert Walker (Jimmy Dobson); June Allyson (Leslie Odell); Rags Ragland (Albert Weaver); Agnes Moorehead (Countess Zoe); Carl Esmond (Baron Zoltan Faludi); Warner Anderson (Paul MacMillan); Ludwig Stossel (Mr. Tuft); Konstantin Shayne (Count Tradiska); Ann Codee (Countess Tradiska); Emil Rameau (Mr. Korb); Ferdinand Munier (Mr. Fabler); Tom Trout (Hack); Ben Lessey (Himself); Gladys Blake (Pearl); George Cleveland (Dr. Elfson); Olga Fabian (Mrs. Korb); Edward Gargan (Cop); Audrey Totter (Mildred); Grace Hampton (Mrs. Chuddwater); William Halligan (Police Captain Perie); Virginia Sale (Aunt Gertrude Odell); Constance Weiler (Newsstand Girl); Mayo Newhall (Henri); Mary Icide, Florence Pepper, Ann Adams (Glamazons); John Piffle (Santa Claus Footman); Donna Dax, Erin O'Kelly, Vera Lee (Page Girls); James Carlyle (Doorman); Brick Sullivan (N.Y. Cop); Otto Mazetti (Nixie); Betty Blythe, Zoie Karabanova, Greta Gould, Fernanda Eliscu, Laura Treadwell (Diplomat's Wives); Dutch Slickenmeyer (Obie); Sylvia Andrews (Tired Woman); Marie Melish, Bertha Feducha, Symona Boniface, Wanda Perry, Margaret Bert, Marjorie Whalley (Maids); Charles Morton (Santa Claus); Ed Agresti, Larry Arnold, Tom Tamarez (Attaches).

THE BEGINNING OR THE END (MGM, 1947) 112 M.

Producer, Samuel Marx; director, Norman Taurog; story, Robert Considine; screenplay, Frank Wead; art director, Cedric Gibbons; music, Daniele Amphiteatroff; camera, Ray June; editor, George Boemler.

Brian Donlevy (Maj. Gen. Leslie R. Groves); Robert Walker (Col. Jeff Nixon); Tom Drake (Matt Cochran); Beverly Tyler (Anne Cochran); Hume Cronyn (Dr. J. Robert Oppenheimer); Hurd Hatfield (Dr. John Wyatt); Joseph Calleia (Dr. Enrico Fermi); Godfrey Tearle (President Roosevelt); Victor Francen (Dr. Mafre); Richard Haydn (Dr. Chisholm); Jonathan Hale (Dr. Vannevaar Bush); John Litel (M.K. T. Keller); Henry O'Neill (Gen. Thomas F. Farrell); Agnes Moorehead (German Scientist —Role Deleted); Warner Anderson (Capt. Wm. S. Parsons, U.S.N.); Barry Nelson (Col. Paul Tibbetts, Jr.); Art Baker (President Truman); Ludwig Stossel (Dr. Albert Einstein); Frank Ferguson (Dr. James Conant); John Hamilton (Dr. Harold C. Vrey); Nella Walker (Grace Tully); John Gallaudet (Dr. Leo Szilard); Moroni Olsen (Dr. Arthur Compton); Martin Kosleck (Dr. O.E. Frisch); Jim Davis (Pilot at Tinien); Henry Hall (Gen. Brehon Somervell); William Wright (Col. John Lansdale); James Bush (Dr. Ernest O. Lawrence); William Bishop (2nd Lt.—Electronics Officer); Patricia Medina (English Girl— Laboratory Assistant); Ed Cassidy (Rafferty); Harry Tyler, Eddy Waller (Men); Carlyle Blackwell (Armed Officer); Blake Edwards (C.I.C. Man); Kirk Alyn (Scientist).

DARK PASSAGE (Warner Bros., 1947) 106 M.

Producer, Jerry Wald; director, Delmer Daves; based on the novel by David Goodis; screenplay, Daves; art director, David Weisbart; music, Franz Waxman; camera, Sid Hickox; editor, Weisbart.

Humphrey Bogart (Vincent Parry); Lauren Bacall (Irene Jansen); Bruce Bennett (Bob); Agnes Moorehead (Madge Rapf); Tom D'Andrea (Sam, Cabby); Clifton Young (Baker); Douglas Kennedy (Detective); Rory Mallinson (George Fellsinger); Houseley Stevenson (Dr. Walter Coley); Bob Farber, Richard Walsh, Ian MacDon-

ald (Policemen); Clancy Cooper (Man on Street); Lennie Bremen (Ticket Clerk); Mary Field (Mary); Michael Daves, Deborah Daves, John Arledge (Children); Ross Ford (Ross—Driver); Pat McVey (Taxi Driver); Tom Fadden (Waiter at Cafe); Shimen Ruskin (Watchman); Tom Reynolds (Hotel Clerk); Ramon Ros (Waiter); John Arledge (Lonely Man).

THE LOST MOMENT (Universal, 1947) 89 M.

Producer, Walter Wanger; director, Martin Gabel; based on the novel *The Aspern Papers* by Henry James; screenplay, Leonardo Bercovici; art director, Alexander Golitzen; music, Daniele Amfitheatrof; camera, Hal Mohr; editor, Milton Carruth.

Robert Cummings (Lewis); Susan Hayward (Tina); Agnes Moorehead (Juliana); Joan Lorring (Amelia); Eduardo Ciannelli (Father Rinaldo); John Archer (Charles); Frank Puglia (Pietro); Minerva Urecal (Maria); William Edmunds (Vittorio); Martin Garralaga (Waiter); Eugene Borden (proprietor); Nicolas Khadarik (Singer); Julian Rivero (Story Teller); Lillian Molieri, Donna De Mario (Pretty Girls); Wallace Stark (Sketch Artist); Pete Cusanelli (Fruit Vendor); Chris Drake (Young Man).

SUMMER HOLIDAY (MGM, 1948) 92 M.

Producer, Arthur Freed; director, Rouben Mamoulian; based on the play *Ah! Wilderness* by Eugene O'Neill; screenplay, Frances Goodrich, Albert Hackett; music director, Lennie Hayton; songs, Ralph Blane and Harry Warren; camera, Charles Schonenbaum; editor, Albert Akst.

Mickey Rooney (Richard Miller); Gloria DeHaven (Muriel); Walter Huston (Nat Miller); Frank Morgan (Uncle Sid); Jackie 'Butch' Jenkins (Tommy Miller); Marilyn Maxwell (Belle); Agnes Moorehead (Cousin Lillie); Selena Royle (Mrs. Miller); Michael Kirby (Arthur Miller); Shirley Johns (Mildred Miller); Hal Hackett (Wint); Anne Francis (Elsie Rand); John Alexander (Mr. Macomber); Virginia Brissac (Miss Hawley); Howard Freeman (Mr. Peabody); Alice MacKenzie (Mrs. Macomber); Don Garner (Gilbert Ralston); Ruth Brady (Crystal); Emory Parnell (Bartender); Wally Cassell (Salesman); Jack Baxley (Gus); Walter Soderling (Mr. Lipscott); Ann Kimball (Katherine); Jack Clifford (Passerby); Charles Bates, Donald Mayo (Boys); Margaret Bert (Mrs. Nichols); Oliver Blake (Scorekeeper); Jack Lipson (Klaumeyer); Terry Moore (Hat Check Girl); Louise Colombet, Blanche Rose, Margaret Fealey, Nell Spaugh (Old Painting Characters); Francis Stevens (Farmer); Audrey Betz (Fat Woman); Henry Sylvester, David Dunbar, Larry Lathrop (Spirit of '76).

THE WOMAN IN WHITE (Warner Bros., 1948) 109 M.

Producer, Henry Blanke; director, Peter Godfrey; based on the novel by Wilkie Collins; screenplay, Stephen Morehouse Avery; music, Max Steiner; art director, Stanley Fleischer; music director, Leo F. Forbstein; camera, Carl Guthrie; editor, Clarence Kolster.

Alexis Smith (Marian Halcombe); Eleanor Parker (Laura Fairlie/Anne Catherick); Sydney Greenstreet (Count Fosco); Gig Young (Walter Hartright); Agnes Moorehead (Countess Fosco); John Abbott (Frederick Fairlie); John Emery (Sir Percival Gylde); Curt Bois (Louis); Emma Dunn (Mrs. Vesey); Matthew Boulton (Dr. Nevin); Anita Sharp-Bolster (Mrs. Todd); Clifford Brooke (Jepson); Barry Bernard (Dimmock); John Goldsworthy (Station Agent); Connie Leon (Village Woman); Randy Hairston (Young Boy); Tony Marsh (Coach boy); Creighton Hale (Underservant); Harold DeBecker (Attendant); Crauford Kent (Rector); Hilda Plowright

(Woman Attendant); Edgar Norton (Night Clerk); Melody Lichtenfeld, Michael Ryan (Children).

STATION WEST (RKO, 1948) 91 M.

Producer, Robert Sparks; director, Sidney Lanfield; based on the novel by Luke Short; screenplay, Frank Fenton, Winston Miller; music, Heinz Roemheld; songs, Mort Greene and Leigh Harline; camera, Harry J. Wild; editor, Frederick Knudtson.

Dick Powell (Haven); Jane Greer (Charlie); Agnes Moorehead (Mrs. Caslon); Burl Ives (Hotel Clerk); Tom Powers (Captain Iles); Gordon Oliver (Prince); Steve Brodie (Stellman); Guinn 'Big Boy' Williams (Mick); Raymond Burr (Mark Bristow); Regis Toomey (Goddard); Olin Howlin (Cook); John Berkes (Pianist); Michael Steele (Whitey); Dan White (Pete); John Kellogg (Ben); John Doucette (Bartender); Charles Middleton (Sheriff); Suzi Crandall (Girl); Al Hill (Croupier); Jack Stoney, Stanley Blystone (Bouncers); Robert Gates (Sam); Robert Jefferson (Black Boy); Erville Alderson (Stage Agent); William Phipps (Sergeant); Marie Thomas (Dance Hall Girl); Joey Ray (Stickman); Leo McMahon (Rider with Kellogg); Bud Osborne, Ethan Laidlaw, Monte Montague, Lomax Study (Men).

JOHNNY BELINDA (Warner Bros., 1948) 101 M.

Producer, Jerry Wald; director, Jean Negulesco; based on the play by Elmer Harris; screenplay, Irmgard von Cube; music, Max Steiner; art director, Robert Haas; music director, Leo F. Forbstein; camera, Ted McCord; editor, David Weisbart.

Jane Wyman (Belinda McDonald); Lew Ayres (Dr. Robert Richardson); Charles Bickford (Black McDonald); Agnes Moorehead (Aggie McDonald); Stephen McNally (Locky McCormick); Jan Sterling (Stella Maguire); Rosalind Ivan (Mrs. Foggety); Dan Seymour (Pacquet); Mabel Paige (Mrs. Lutz); Ida Moore (Mrs. McKee); Alan Napier (Defense Attorney); Monte Blue (Ben); Douglas Kennedy (Mountie); James Craven (Interpreter); Jeff Richards (Floyd McQuiggen); Richard Walsh (Fergus McQuiggen); Joan Winfield (Mrs. Tim Moore); Ian Wolfe (Rector); Holmes Herbert (Judge); Jonathan Hale (Dr. Gray); Ray Montgomery (Tim Moore); Blayney Lewis (Dan'l); Barbara Bates (Gracie Anderson); Frank Hagney, Larry McGrath, Colin Kenny, Lew Harvey, Al Ferguson (Men Reciting Lord's Prayer); Alice MacKenzie (Farm Woman); Snub Pollard, Franklyn Farnum (Jury Men); Frederick Worlock (Prosecutor); Creighton Hale (Bailiff); Charles Horvath (Churchgoer).

THE STRATTON STORY (MGM, 1949) 106 M.

Producer, Jack Cummings; director, Sam Wood; story, Douglas Morrow; screenplay, Morrow, Guy Trosper; music director, Adolph Deutsch; art director, Cedric Gibbons, Paule Groesse; camera, Harold Rosson; editor, Ben Lewis.

James Stewart (Monty Stratton); June Allyson (Ethel Stratton); Frank Morgan (Barney Wile); Agnes Moorehead (Ma Stratton); Bill Williams (Gene Watson); Bruce Cowling (Ted Lyons); Eugene Bearden (Western All Stars Pitcher); Bill Dickey, Jimmy Dykes (Themselves); Cliff Clark (Higgins); Mary Lawrence (Dot); Dean White (Luke Appling); Robert Gist (Larnie); Mervyn Shea (White Sox Catcher); Mitchell Lewis (Conductor); Michael Ross (Pitcher); James Nolan, Peter Crouse (Reporters); Florence Lake (Mrs. Appling); Anne Nagel (Mrs. Piet); Barbara Wooddell (Mrs. Shea); Alphonse Martel (Headwaiter); Holmes Herbert (Doctor); Robert Graham, Eugene Persson (Boys); Charles S. Smith (Theatre Usher); Syd Saylor, George Melford, George Ovey, William H. Bailey, Cy Stevens, Polly Bailey, Vangie Beilby,

Mabel Smaney, Jessie Arnold, (People in Theater); Al Rosen (Vendor); Clarence Hennecke (News Vendor); Jim Drum, Charles Sullivan (Spectators); Kenneth Tobey (Detroit Player); Roy Partee (Western Pitcher); Pat Flaherty (Western Manager); Fred William (All Star Catcher); John 'Red' Burger (Ball Player); Brick Sullivan, Mike Pat Donovan (Umpires); James Gladd, Leonard Perme, Gerald Priddy, Harry Lowrey, Robert H. Sturgeon, Henry Sauer, William White, Allan Zarilla (Yankee Ball Team); Walter Berger (Yankee Pitcher); Ralph Kress (Southern All Stars Coach); Golden Holt (St. Louis Coach); William Allington (Western All Stars Coach); Ira Gordon, Al Mutart (All Stars Umpires).

THE GREAT SINNER (MGM, 1949) 110 M.

Producer, Gottfried Reinhardt; director, Robert Siodmak; based on the story *The Gambler* by Fyodor Dostoevski; adaptation, Ladislas Fodor, Rene Fueloep-Miller; screenplay, Fodor, Christopher Isherwood; assistant director, Marin Stuart; art director, Cedric Gibbons, Hans Peters; music director, Andre Previn; camera, George Folsey; editor, Harold F. Kress.

Gregory Peck (Fyodor Dostoevski); Ava Gardner (Pauline Ostrovski); Melvyn Douglas (Armand De Glasse); Walter Huston (General Ostrovski); Ethel Barrymore (Granny); Frank Morgan (Aristide Piard); Agnes Moorehead (Emma Getzel); Ludwig Stossel (Hotel Manager); Ludwig Donath (Doctor); Erno Verebes (Hotel Valet); Curt Bois (Jeweler); Martin Garralaga (Maharajah); Frederick Ledebur (De Glasse's Secretary); Jean Del Val (Croupier); Vincent Renno (Casino Inspector); William H. Hawes (Nervous Englishman); Andre Charlot (Distinguished Man); Sam Scar (Turk); Elsa Heims (Woman With Cigar); Joan Miller (Cold Sexy Woman); John Piffle (Fat Man); Emil Rameau, Elspeth Dudgeon (Fearful Old Couple); James Anderson (Nervous Young Man); Charles Wagenheim (Man with Ring); Gisella Werbisek (Greedy Woman); Leonid Kinsky (Band Leader); Ilka Gruning (Duenna); David McMahon (Station Master); Sue Casey (Pretty Girl); George Paris (Soldier); Wheaton Chambers (Priest); Dick Bartell (Cloakroom Attendant); William Stelling (Assistant Hotel Manager); Lotte Stein (Buxom Woman); Max Willenz (Policeman); John Cortay (Inspector); Betty Jane Howarth (Girl at Baccarat Table); Irene Seidner (Woman Vendor); Hans Hopf (Hurdy-Gurdy-Man).

WITHOUT HONOR (United Artists, 1950) 68 M.

Producer, Robert Hakim, Raymond Hakim; director, Irving Pichel; screenplay, James Poe; music, Max Steiner; camera, Lionel Lindon; editor, Gregg Tallas.

Laraine Day (Jane Bandle); Dane Clark (Bill Bandle); Franchot Tone (Dennis Williams); Agnes Moorehead (Katherine Williams); Bruce Bennett (Fred Bandle); Harry Lauter, Peter Virgo (Ambulance Attendants); Margie Stapp (Neighbor's Wife); Patricia Ann Ewing, Joan Dupius (Girl Scouts); Lester Dorr (Neighbor); Frank Marlowe, Harrison Hearne (Radio Men).

CAGED (Warner Bros., 1950) 96 M.

Producer, Jerry Wald; director, John Cromwell; story-screenplay, Virginia Kellogg, Bernard C. Schoenfeld; art director, Charles H. Clarke; music, Max Steiner; camera, Carl Guthrie; editor, Owen Marks.

Eleanor Parker (Marie Allen); Agnes Moorehead (Ruth Benton); Ellen Corby (Emma); Hope Emerson (Evelyn Harper); Betty Garde (Kitty Stark); Jan Sterling (Smoochie); Lee Patrick (Elvira Powell); Olive Deering (June); Jane Darwell (Isolation Matron); Gertrude Michael (Georgia); Sheila (MacRae) Stevens

(Helen); Joan Miller (Claire); Marjorie Crossland (Cassie); Gertrude Hoffman (Milie); Lynn Sherman (Ann); Queenie Smith (Mrs. Warren); Naomi Robison (Hattie); Esther Howard (Grace); Marlo Dwyer (Julie); Wanda Tynan (Meta); Peggy Wynne (Lottie); Frances Morris (Mrs. Foley); Edith Evanson (Miss Barker); Yvonne Rob (Elaine); Ann Tyrell (Edna); Eileen Stevens (Infirmary Nurse); June Whipple (Ada); Sandra Gould (Skip); Grace Hayes (Mugging Matron); Taylor Holmes (Senator Donnolly); Don Beddoe (Commissioner Walker); Charles Meredith (Chairman); George Baxter (Jeffries); Guy Beach (Mr. Cooper); Harlan Warde (Dr. Ashton); Bill Hunter (Guard); Barbara Esback (Matron); Gail Bonney, Doris Kemper, Lovyss Bradley, Eva Nelson, Rosemary O'Neill, Jean Calhoun, Nita Talbot, Tina Menard, Gladys Roach, Virginia Engels, Claudia Cauldwell, Helen Eby-Rock, Joyce Newhard, Pauline Creasman, Marie Melish (Inmates); Davison Clark (Doctor); Pauline Drake (Doctor's Wife); Bill Wayne (Ada's Father); Doris Whitney (Woman Visitor); Ruth Warren (Miss Lyons).

FOURTEEN HOURS (20th Century-Fox, 1951) 92 M.

Producer, Sol C. Siegel; director, Henry Hathaway; based on the book *The Man on the Ledge* by Joel Sayre; screenplay, John Paxton; art director, Lyle Wheeler, Leland Fuller; music, Alfred Newman; camera, Joe MacDonald; editor, Dorothy Spencer.

Paul Douglas (Dunnigan); Richard Basehart (Robert Cosick); Barbara Bel Geddes (Virginia); Debra Paget (Ruth); Agnes Moorehead (Mrs. Cosick); Robert Keith (Mr. Cosick); Howard da Silva (Lt. Moksar); Jeffrey Hunter (Danny); Martin Gabel (Dr. Strauss); Grace Kelly (Mrs. Fuller); Frank Faylen (Waiter); Jeff Corey (Sgt. Farley); James Millican (Sgt. Boyle); Donald Randolph (Dr. Benson); Willard Waterman (Mr. Harris); Kenneth Harvey (Police Operator); George MacQuarrie (Evangelist); Ann Morrison (Mrs. Dunnigan); Forbes Murray (Police Commissioner); George Putnam (Radio Announcer); Michael Fitzmaurice (TV Announcer); Russell Hicks (Regan); David Burns, Ossie Davis, Henry State, Harvey Lembeck (Cab Drivers); Brad Dexter, Shep Menken (Reporters); Joyce Van Patten (Barbara); Rennie McEvoy (Radio Man); Marvin Williams (Photographer); Frank Nelson (Frantic Guest); William Welsh, Jr.)Hotel Clerk); Ali Talton (Secretary); James Warren (Mr. Fuller).

SHOW BOAT (MGM, 1951) 108 M.

Producer, Arthur Freed; director, George Sidney; based on the novel by Edna Ferber and the play by Jerome Kern, Oscar Hammerstein II; screenplay, John Lee Mahin; music director, Adolph Deutsch; choreographer, Robert Alton; orchestrator, Conrad Salinger; songs, Kern and Hammerstein II; art director, Cedric Gibbons, Jack Martin Smith; camera, Charles Rosher; editor, Leonard W. Herman.

Kathryn Grayson (Magnolia Hawks); Ava Gardner (Julie Laverne); Howard Keel (Gaylor Ravenal); Joe E. Brown (Captain Andy Hawks); Marge Champion (Ellie May Shipley); Gower Champion (Frank Scultz); Robert Sterling (Stephen Baker); Agnes Moorehead (Parthy Hawks); Adele Jergens (Cameo McQueen); William Warfield (Joe); Leif Erickson (Pete); Owen McGiveney (Windy McClain); Frances Williams (Queenie); Regis Toomey (Sheriff Ike Vallon); Frank Wilcox (Mark Hallson); Chick Chandler (Herman); Emory Parnell (Jake Green); Sheila Clark (Kim); Ian MacDonald (Drunk Sport); Fuzzy Knight (Trocadero Piano Player); Norman Leavitt (George—Calliope Player); Anne Marie Dore, Christina Lind, Lyn Wilde, Marietta Elliott, Joyce Jameson, Bette Arlen, Helen Kimbell, Tao Porchon, Mitzie Uehlein,

Judy Landon, Nova Dale, Mary Jane French, Marilyn Kinsley, Alice Markham (Showboat Cast Girls); Michael Dugan, Robert Fortier, George Ford, Cass Jaeger, Boyd Ackerman, Roy Damron, Joseph Roach (Showboat Cast Boys); George Lynn (Dealer); Melford Jones (Pickaninny); Louis Mercier (Dabney); Lisa Ferraday (Renee); Al Rhein, Charles Regan, Carl Sklover (Ad Libs); Peter Camlin (Croupier); Gil Perkins (Player); Edward Keane (Hotel Manager); Allan Ray (Elevator Operator); Robert Stebbins (Bellhop); Jim Pierce (Doorman); Marjorie Wood (Landlady); Anna Q. Nilsson (Seamstress); Earle Hodgins (Bartender); Dan Foster (Deckhand); Ida Moore (Little Old Lady); Alphonse Martel (Headwaiter); Bert Roach (Drunk); Harry Seymour (Pianist).

THE BLUE VEIL (RKO, 1951) 113 M.

Producer, Jerry Wald, Norman Krasna; director, Curtis Bernhardt; story, Francois Campaux; screenplay, Norman Corwin; art director, Albert S. D'Agostino, Carroll Clark; music director, C. Bakaleinikoff; camera, Frank Planer; editor, George J. Amy.

Jane Wyman (Louise Mason); Charles Laughton (Fred K. Begley); Joan Blondell (Annie Rawlins); Richard Carlson (Gerald Kean); Agnes Moorehead (Mrs. Palfrey); Don Taylor (Dr. Robert Palfrey); Audrey Totter (Helen Williams); Cyril Cusack (Frank Hutchins); Everett Sloane (District Attorney); Natalie Wood (Stephanie Rawlins); Vivian Vance (Alicia); Carleton Young (Mr. Palfrey); Alan Napier (Prof. Carter); Warner Anderson (Bill); Les Tremayne (Joplin); Dan Seymour (Pelt); Dan O'Herlihy (Hugh Williams); Henry Morgan (Charles Hall); Gary Jackson (Robert Palfrey—As a Boy); Gregory Marshall (Harrison Palfrey); Dee Pollack (Tony); Roberta Lee (Actress); Athalie Daniell (Sue); Ruth Packard (Sue's Mother); Jo Gilbert (Miss Dunlop); Pat Joiner (Phyllis); Mack Williams (Detective); Irene Vernon (Stephanie—As an Adult); Bob Nichols (Fred Begley, Jr.); Richard Norris (Denis); Jane Liddell (Denis's Wife); Ann Moore (Sarah); Harry Strang (Traffic Cop); Hazel Keener (Nurse); Torben Meyer (Photographer); Lisa Golm (Elsa); Frank Gerstle (Doctor); Edith Leslie (Gussie); Sylvia Simms (Miss Quimby); Joy Hallward (Miss Golub); Genevieve Bell (Head Nurse); James Anderson (Jim Tappan); Frank O'Connor (Train Conductor); Muriel Maddox (Mrs. Tappan); Lillian Albertson (Mrs. Lipscott); Jim Hawkins (Tommy); Kathryn Sheldon (Mrs. Chalmers).

THE ADVENTURES OF CAPTAIN FABIAN (Republic, 1951) 100 M.

Producer, William Marshall; associate producer, Robert Dorfmann; director, William Marshall; based on the novel *Fabulous Ann Madlock* by Robert Shannon; screenplay, Errol Flynn; music, René Cloerec; assistant director, Marc Maurette; costumes, Arlington Valles; sets, Eugene Lourie, Max Douy; sound, Roger Cosson; camera, Marcel Grignon; editor, Henri Taverna.

Errol Flynn (Captain Michael Fabian); Micheline Presle (Lea Marriotte); Vincent Price (George Brissac); Agnes Moorehead (Aunt Jesebel); Victor Francen (Henri Brissac); Jim Gerald (Constable Gilpin); Helena Manson (Madam Pirott); Howard Vernon (Emil); Roger Blin (Phillipe); Valentine Camax (Housekeeper); Georges Flateau (Judge Jean Brissac); Zanie Campan (Cynthia Winthrop); Reggie Nalder (Constant); Charles Fawcett (Defense Attorney); Aubrey Bower (Mate).

CAPTAIN BLACK JACK (Classic, 1952) 90 M.

Executive producer, Walter Gould; producer-director, Julien Duvivier; screenplay, Duvivier, Charles Spaah.

George Sanders (Mike Alexander); Herbert Marshall (Dr. Curtis); Patricia Roc (Ingrid Dekker); Agnes Moorehead (Mrs. Birk); Dalio (Captain Nikarescu); Jose Nieto (Inspector Carnero); Howard Vernon (Captain of Schooner); Dennis Wyndham (Fernando Barris); Jose Jaspe (Jose).

THE BLAZING FOREST (Paramount, 1952) 90 M.

Producer, William H. Pine, William C. Thomas; director, Edward Ludwig; screenplay, Lewis R. Foster, Winston Miller; music, Lucien Cailliet; art director, Lewis H. Creber; camera, Lionel Lindon; editor, Howard Smith.

John Payne (Kelly Hanson); William Demarest (Syd Jessup); Agnes Moorehead (Jessie Crain); Richard Arlen (Joe Morgan); Susan Morrow (Sharon Wilks); Roscoe Ates (Beans); Lynne Roberts (Grace); Ewing Mitchell (Ranger); Walter Reed (Max); Jim Davis, Joey Ray, Joe Garcia, Brett Houston, Max Wagner (Lumberjacks).

THE STORY OF THREE LOVES (MGM, 1953) 122 M.

Producer, Sidney Franklin; art director, Cedric Gibbons, Preston Ames, Edward Carfango, Gabriel Scognamillo; choreographer, Frederick Ashton; music, Miklos Rozsa; camera, Charles Rosher, Harold Rosson; editor, Ralph E. Winters:

The Jealous Lover: director, Gottfried Reinhardt; screenplay, John Collier.

Mademoiselle: director, Vincente Minelli; story, Arnold Phillips; screenplay, Jan Lustig, George Froeschal.

Equilibrium: director, Gottfried Reinhardt; story, Ladislas Vajda, Jacques Maret; adaptation, Jan Lustig, George Froeschel; screenplay, John Collier.

The Jealous Lover: Moira Shearer (Paula Woodward); James Mason (Charles Coudray); Agnes Moorehead (Aunt Lydia); Jacob Gimpel (Pianist); Miklos Rozsa (Conductor); John Lupton (Studious Young Man); Jack Raine (Doctor); Lysa Baugher (Ballerina); Flo Wix, Towyna Daily, Colin Kenny, Major Sam Harris (Ad Libs); Ottola Nesmith (Usher); Reginald Sheffield (Production Manager); Anne Howard, Paula Allen (Chorus Girls); Ivan Hayes, Bruce Lansbury, Bruce Edwards (Chorus Boys).

SCANDAL AT SCOURIE (MGM, 1953) 89 M.

Producer, Edwin H. Knopf; director, Jean Negulesco; based on the story by Mary McSherry; screenplay, Norman Corwin, Leonard Spigelgass; music, Daniele Amfitheatrof; art director, Cedric Gibbons, Wade B. Rubottom; assistant director, Jack Greenwood; camera, Robert Planck; editor, Ferris Webster.

Greer Garson (Mrs. Patrick J. McChesney); Walter Pidgeon (Patrick J. McChesney); Donna Corcoran (Patsy); Agnes Moorehead (Sister Josephine); Arthur Shields (Father Reilly); Philip Ober (B. G. Belney); Rhys Williams (Bill Swazey); Margalo Gillmore (Alice Hanover); John Lupton (Artemus); Philip Tonge (Fred Gogarty); Wilton Graff (Mr. Leffington); Ian Wolfe (Councilman Hurdwell); Michael Pate (Rev. Williams); Tony Taylor (Edward); Patricia Tiernan (Nun); Victor Wood (James Motley); Ferdita Chandler (Sister Dominique); Walter Baldwin (Michael Hayward); Ida Moore (Mrs. Ames).

THOSE REDHEADS FROM SEATTLE (Paramount, 1953) 90 M.

Producer, William H. Pine, William C. Thomas; director, Lewis R. Foster; screenplay, Foster, Geoffrey Homes, George Worthing Yates; songs, Mack David, Jerry Livingston, Bob Merrill, Johnny Mercer, Hoagy Carmichael, Jay Livingston, Ray Evans, H.J. Rosenfeld, Louis W. Pritz-

kow; music, Leo Shuken, Sidney Cutner; choreographer, Jack Baker; camera, Lionel Lindon; editor, Archie Marshek.

Rhonda Fleming (Kathie Edmonds); Gene Barry (Johnny Kisco); Agnes Moorehead (Mrs. Edmonds); Teresa Brewer (Pat Edmonds); Guy Mitchell (Joe Keenen); Cynthia Bell (Connie Edmonds); Kay Bell (Nell Edmonds); Jean Parker (Liz); Roscoe Ates (Dan Taylor); John Kellogg (Mike Yurkil); Frank Wilcox (Vance Edmonds); Walter Reed (Whitey Marks); William Pullen (Rev. Petrie); Michael Ross (Mack Donahue); Ed Rand (Jacobs).

MAIN STREET TO BROADWAY (MGM, 1953) 97 M.

Producer, Lester Cowan; director, Tay Garnett; story, Robert E. Sherwood; screenplay, Samson Raphaelson; art director, Perry Ferguson; assistant director, James Anderson; music, Ann Ronell; song, Richard Rodgers and Oscar Hammerstein II; camera, James Wong Howe; editor, Gene Fowler, Jr.

Tom Morton (Tony Monaco); Mary Murphy (Mary Craig); Agnes Moorehead (Mildred Waterbury); Herb Shriner (Frank Johnson); Rosemary De Camp (Mrs. Craig); Clinton Sundberg (Mr. Craig); Florence Bates, Madge Kennedy, Carl Benton Reid, Frank Ferguson, Robert Bray (Fantasy Sequence); Tallulah Bankhead, Ethel Barrymore, Lionel Barrymore, Gertrude Berg, Shirley Booth, Louis Calhern, Leo Durocher, Faye Emerson, Oscar Hammerstein II, Rex Harrison, Helen Hayes, Joshua Logan, Mary Martin, Lilli Palmer, Richard Rodgers, John Van Druten, Cornel Wilde, Bill Rigney, Chris Durocher, Arthur Shields (Themselves).

MAGNIFICENT OBSESSION (Universal, 1954) 108 M.

Producer, Ross Hunter; director, Douglas Sirk; based on the novel by Lloyd C. Douglas; adaptation, Wells Root; screenplay, Sarah Y. Mason, Victor Heerman; music, Frank Skinner; art director, Bernard Herzbrun, Emrich Nicholson; camera, Russell Metty; editor, Milton Carruth.

Jane Wyman (Helen Phillips); Rock Hudson (Bob Merrick); Agnes Moorehead (Nancy Ashford); Barbara Rush (Joyce Phillips); Gregg Palmer (Tom Masterson); Otto Kruger (Randolph); Paul Cavanagh (Dr. Giraud); Sara Shane (Valerie); Richard H. Cutting (Dr. Dodge); Judy Nugent (Judy); Helen Kleeb (Mrs. Eden); Robert B. Williams (Sgt. Burnham); Will White (Sgt. Ames); George Lynn (Williams); Jack Kelly, Lee Roberts (Mechanics); Lida Gaye, Kathleen O'Malley (Switchboard Girls); William Leslie, Lance Fuller, Brad Jackson, Myrna Hansen (Customers); Alexander Campbell (Dr. Allan); Rudolph Anders (Dr. Fuss); Fred Nurney (Dr. Laradetti); Joe Mell (Dan); John Mylong (Dr. Hofer); Harold Dyrenforth (Mr. Jouvet); Norbert Schiller (Mr. Long); Paul Levitt (Anaesthetist); Mae Clarke (Mrs. Miller); Harvey Grant (Chris); Frederick Stevens (Cafe Owner); Helen Winston (Receptionist); Robert Herron (Taxi Driver); Greta Ullman (Flower Woman); Gail Bonney (Phyllis); Bill Malkin, Charles Victor, George Brand, Ray Quinn, Jack Gargan (Doctors).

UNTAMED (20th Century-Fox, 1955) 111 M.

Producer, Bert E. Friedlob, William A. Bacher; director, Henry King; based on the novel by Helga Moray; adaptation, Talbot Jennings, William A. Bacher; screenplay, Jennings, Frank Fenton, Michael Blankfort; art director, Lyle Wheeler, Addison Hehr; music, Franz Waxman; orchestrator, Edward B. Powell; camera, Leo Tover; editor, Barbara McLean.

Tyrone Power (Paul Van Riebeck); Susan Hayward (Katie O'Neill); Richard Egan (Kurt); John Justin (Shawn Kildare); Agnes Moorehead (Aggie); Rita Moreno (Julia);

Hope Emerson (Maria De Groot); Brad Dexter (Christian); Henry O'Neill (Squire O'Neill); Paul Thompson (Tachaka); Alexander D. Havemann (Jan); Louis Mercier (Joubert); Emmett Smith (Jantsie); Jack Macy (Simon); Trude Wyler (Madame Joubert); Louis Polliman Brown (Bani); Tina Thompson, Linda Lowell, Betty Diamond, Gary Diamond, Brian Corcoran (Maria's Children); Edward Mundy (Grandfather Joubert); Catherine Pasques (Miss Joubert); Christian Pasques (Young Joubert) John Dodsworth (Capt. Richard Eaton); Alberto Morin (Driver —Bree Street); Robert Adler (York); Philip Van Zandt (Schuman); Kevin Corcoran (Young Paul); Charles Evans (Sir George Gray); Eleanor Audley (Lady Vernon); John Caryle (Cornelius); Alan Marston (English Sailor); Leonard Carey (Hansen); Forest Burns (Commando); Walter Flannery, Kem Dibbs (Outlaws).

THE LEFT HAND OF GOD (20th Century-Fox, 1955) 87M.

Producer, Buddy Adler; director, Edward Dmytryk; based on the novel by William E. Barrett; screenplay, Alfred Hayes; assistant director, Ben Kadish; art director, Lyle Wheeler, Maurice Ransford; music, Victor Young; technical advisor, Frank Tang; special effects, Ray Kellogg; makeup, Ben Nye; camera, Franz Planer; editor, Dorothy Spencer.

Humphrey Bogart (Jim Carmody); Gene Tierney (Anne Scott); Lee J. Cobb (Mich Yang); Agnes Moorehead (Beryl Sigman); E. G. Marshall (Dr. Sigman); Jean Porter (Mary Yin); Carl Benton Reid (Rev. Cornelius); Victor Sen Yung (John Wong); Philip Ahn (Jan Teng); Benson Fong (Chun Tien); Richard Cutting (Father O'Shea); Leon Lontoc (Pao-Ching); Don Forbes (Father Keller); Noel Toy (Woman in Sarong); Peter Chong (Feng Merchant); Marie Taien (Woman in Kimona); George Chan (Li Kwan); Stephen Wong (Boy); Walter Soo Hoo, Henry S. Quan (Orderlies); Doris Chung (Nurse); Moy Ming (Old Man) Stella Lynn (Fao Chu); Robert Burton (Rev. Marvin); Soo Yong (Midwife); Kam Tong (Moslem); Sammee Tong (Servant).

ALL THAT HEAVEN ALLOWS (Universal, 1956) 89 M.

Producer, Ross Hunter; director, Douglas Sirk; story, Edna Lee, Harry Lee; screenplay, Peg Fenwick; art director, Alexander Golitzen, Eric Orbom; music, Frank Skinner; music director, Joseph Gershenson; camera, Russell Metty; editor, Frank Cross.

Jane Wyman (Cary Scott); Rock Hudson (Ron Kirby); Agnes Moorehead (Sara Warren); Conrad Nagel (Harvey); Gloria Talbott (Kay); William Reynolds (Ned); Virginia Grey (Alida); Charles Drake (Mick Anderson); Hayden Rorke (Dr. Hennessy); Jacqueline de Wit (Mona Plash); Donald Curtis (Howard Hoffer); Leigh Snowden (Jo-Ann); Nestor Paiva (Manuel); Forrest Lewis (Mr. Macks); Alex Gerry (George Warren); Merry Anders (Mary Ann); Tol Avery (Tom Allenby); Helene Heigh (Ann); Vernon Rich (Bill); Paul Keast (Mark Plash); David Janssen (Freddie Norton); Gia Scala (Manuel's Daughter); Eleanor Audley (Mrs. Humphrey); Paul Smith (Tom); Jim Hayward (John); Alan De Witt (Stationmaster); Rosa Turich (Rozanna); Anthony Jochim (Mr. Adams); Joseph Mell (Mr. Gow); Helen Andrews (Myrtle); Lillian Culver (Mrs. Taylor); Donna Jo Gribble (Miss Taylor).

MEET ME IN LAS VEGAS (MGM, 1956) 112 M.

Producer, Joe Pasternak; director, Roy Rowland; screenplay, Isobel Lennart; art director, Cedric Gibbons, Urie McCleary; songs, Nicholas Brodszky and Sammy Cahn;

orchestrator, Albert Sendrey, Skip Martin; music director, George Stoll; choreographer, Hermes Pan; camera, Robert Bronner; editor, Albert Akst.

Dan Daily (Chuck Rodwell); Cyd Charisse (Maria Corvier); Agnes Moorehead (Miss Hattie); Lili Darvas (Sari Hatvany); Jim Backus (Tom Culdane); Oscar Karlweis (Lotzi); Liliane Montevecchi (Lilli); Cara Williams (Kelly Donavan); George Chakiris (Young Groom); Betty Lynn (Young Bride); Slate Brothers (Themselves); Pete Rugolo (Conductor); John Brascia (Specialty Dancer); John Harding (Worried Boss); Benny Rubin (Croupier); Jack Daly (Meek Husband); Henny Backus (Bossy Wife); Jerry Colonna, Paul Henreid, Lena Horne, Frankie Laine, Mitsuko Sawamura (Themselves); Dabbs Greer (Mr. Smith-Johnson); Frank Kumagai (Gus); June McCall (Smith's Girl); Marc Wilder (Prince Charming); Allan Wood, Allan Ray (Bellboys at Sands); Michael Dugan, James Farrar, Jim O'Neil, Anthony Merrill (Guests at Sands); Lillian Powell (Nervous Woman); Al Rhein (Roulette Dealer); Casse Jaeger, William Chatham (Dancing Partners— "Frankie And Johnny" Number); Gisele Verlain, Perry Sheehan, Bob Dix, Ronald Green (Players At New Frontier); Phil Arnold (Blackjack Player); Katherine Sheldon, Kate McKenna (Old Ladies); Roscoe Ates (Scotty); Lee Tung Foo (Lee); Peter Lorre (Impatient Player); Gloria Rhoads (Passing Girl); Pat Denise (Specialty); Hank Worden, Chuck Courtney, Phil Rich, Guy Wilkerson, Billy Dix (Ranch Hands); Lennie Bremen, Joey Ray (Croupiers—New Frontier); Frank Wilcox, John Eldredge (Owners).

THE CONQUEROR (RKO, 1956) 111 M.

Presenter, Howard Hughes; associate producer, Richard Sokolove; producer-director, Dick Powell; screenplay, Omar Millard; assistant director, Edward Killy; music, Victor Young; choreographer, Robert Sidney; costumes, Michael Woulfe, Yvonne Wood; art director, Albert D'Agostino, Carroll Clark; camera, Joseph LaShelle, Leo Tover, Harry Wild, William Snyder; editor, Stuart Gilmore.

John Wayne (Temujin); Susan Hayward (Bortai); Pedro Armendariz (Jamuga); Agnes Moorehead (Hunlun); Thomas Gomez (Wang Khan); John Hoyt (Shaman); William Conrad (Kasar); Ted de Corsia (Kumick); Leslie Bradley (Targutai); Lee Van Cleef (Chepei); Peter Mamakos (Bogurchi); Leo Gordon (Tartar Captain); Richard Loo (Captain Of Wang's Guards); Richard Keane (Customer); David Hoffman (Potter); Bob Lugo (Wang Khan Guard); Ray Spiker, Charles Horvath (Thugs); Henry Escalente, Max Wagner, Bernie Gozier (Tartar Generals); Alex Montoya (Chieftain); Boy Foy (Juggler); Sylvia Lewis (Solo Dancer); Jarma Lewis, Pat McMahon (Girls in Bath); George E. Stone (Sibilant Sam); Phil Arnold (Honest John); Torben Meyer (Scribe); Arva Burrus, Dolly Summers, Joanne Arnold (Drape Girls); John George (Drummer Boy); Weaver Levy (Mongol); Carl Vernell (Merkit Captain); Fred Graham (Subaya); Gregg Barton (Jalair); Ken Terrell (Sorgan); Jeanne Gerson (Hochin).

THE REVOLT OF MAMIE STOVER (20th Century-Fox, 1956) 92 M.

Producer, Buddy Adler; director, Raoul Walsh; based on the novel by William Bradford Huie; screenplay, Sydney Boehm; art director, Lyle R. Wheeler, Mark-Lee Kirk; songs, Paul Francis Webster and Sammy Fain; Tony Todaro and Mary Johnston; music director, Lionel Newman; music, Hugo Friedhofer; assistant director, Joseph E. Richards; special effects, Ray Kellogg; camera, Leo Tover; editor, Louis Loeffler.

Jane Russell (Mamie Stover); Richard Egan (Jim);

Joan Leslie (Annalea); Agnes Moorehead (Bertha Parchman); Jorja Curtright (Jackie); Michael Pate (Harry Adkins); Richard Coogan (Eldon Sumac); Alan Reed (Gorecki); Eddie Firestone (Tarzan); Jean Willes (Gladys); Leon Lontoc (Aki); Kathy Marlowe (Zelda); Margia Dean (Peaches); Jack Mather (Bartender); Boyd "Red" Morgan (Hackett); John Halloran (Henry); Naida Lani, Anita Dano (Hula Dancers); Dorothy Gordon, Irene Bolton, Merry Townsend, Claire James, Sally Jo Todd, Margarita Camacho (Dance Hall Girls); Richard Collier (Photographer); Kayoka Wakita (Japanese Girl); Arthur Grady (Young Soldier); Frank Griffin (M.P.); Jay Jostyn (Doctor); Charles Keane (Detective); Sherwood Price (Sailor).

THE SWAN (MGM, 1956) 107 M.

Producer, Dore Schary; director, Charles Vidor; based on the play by Ferenc Molnar; screenplay, John Dighton; art director, Cedric Gibbons, Randell Duells; music, Bronislau Kaper; assistant director, Ridgeway C. Meller; camera, Joseph Ruttenberg, Robert Surtees; editor, John Dunning.

Grace Kelly (Princess Alexandra); Alec Guinness (Prince Albert); Louis Jourdan (Dr. Nicholas Agi); Agnes Moorehead (Queen Maria Dominika); Jessie Royce Landis (Princess Beatrix); Brian Aherne (Father Hyacinth); Leo G. Carroll (Caesar); Estelle Winwood (Symphorosa); Van Dyke Parks (George); Christopher Cook (Arsene); Robert Coote (Captain Wunderlich); Doris Lloyd (Countess Sibenstoyn); Edith Barrett (Beatrix's Maid); Jenifer Raine (Alexandra's Maid); Arthur Lovejoy (Albert's Valet); Stan Fraser, John Sheffield, Michael Ferris (Footmen); Ottola Nesmith (Housekeeper); Leslie Denison (Head Groom); David Thursby (Head Gardener); Harry Joe Canutt (Mounted Hussar); Jean Heremans (Officer); Dawn Richards (Woman Guest).

PARDNERS (Paramount, 1956) 82 M.

Producer, Paul Jones; director, Norman Taurog; based on *Rhythm on the Range* by Marvin J. Houser; adaptation, Jerry Davis; screenplay, Sidney Sheldon; art director, Hal Pereira, Roland Anderson; music, Frank De Vol; songs, Sammy Cahn and James Van Heusen; assistant director, Michael D. Moore; camera, Daniel Fapp; editor, Archie Marshek.

Dean Martin (Slim); Jerry Lewis (Wade Kingsley); Lori Nelson (Carol Kingsley); Jeff Morrow (Pete Rio); Jackie Loughery (Dolly Riley); John Baragrey (Dan Hollis); Agnes Moorehead (Matila Kingsley); Lon Chaney, Jr. (Whitey); Milton Frome (Hawkins, The Butler); Richard Aherne (Chauffeur); Lee Van Cleef (Gus); Stuart Randall (Carol's Cowhand); Scott Douglas (Selvin); Jack Elam (Pete); Bob Steele (Shorty); Mickey Finn (Red); Douglas Spencer (Smith); Philip Tonge (Footman); Valerie Allen, Elaine Riley, Ann McCrae (Dance Hall Girls); Emory Parnell (Colonel Hart); Don House, Frank Cordell, Robert Garvey, Keith Wilson, Emily Belser, Stanley Blystone, Hank Mann, Bobby Barber (Townspeople); Dorothy Ford (Amanda); Frances Mercer (Sally); William Forrest (Hocker); James Parnell (Bank Teller); Mary Newton (Laura); Gavin Gordon, Robert Brubaker, Tony Michael, Johnstone White (Businessmen); Len Hendry (Western Cowboy); Charles Stevens (Indian).

THE OPPOSITE SEX (MGM, 1956) 117 M.

Producer, Joe Pasternak; director, David Miller; based on the play *The Women* by Clare Booth; screenplay, Fay and Michael Kanin; choreographer, Robert Sidney; music director, George Stoll; songs, Nicholas Brodsky and Sammy Cahn; assistant director, George Rhein; art director, Cedric Gibbons, Daniel B. Cathcart; camera, Robert Bronner; editor, John McSweeney.

June Allyson (Kay); Joan Collins (Crystal); Dolores Gray (Sylvia); Ann Sheridan (Amanda); Ann Miller (Gloria); Leslie Nielsen (Steve Hilliard); Jeff Richards (Buck Winston); Charlotte Greenwood (Lucy); Agnes Moorehead (Countess); Joan Blondell (Edith); Sam Levene (Mike Pearl); Bill Goodwin (Howard Fowler); Alice Pearce (Olga); Barbara Jo Allen (Dolly); Sandy Descher (Debbie); Carolyn Jones (Pat); Jerry Antes (Leading Man Dancer); Alan Marshal (Ted); Jonathan Hole (Phelps Potter); Harry James, Art Mooney (Themselves); Jim Backus (Psychiatrist); Dick Shawn (Singer); Celia Lovsky (Lutsi); Harry McKenna (Hughie); Janet Lake (Girl on Train); Ann Morriss (Receptionist); Luana Lee (Telephone Girl); Madie Norman (Amazon); Jo Gilbert (Woman Attendant); Don Dillaway (Box Office Man); James Farrar, Estelle Etterre (Ticket Buyers); Lillian Powell (Woman in Audience); Dean Jones (Assistant Stage Manager); Wayne Taylor (Counter Boy); Harry Harvey, Jr. (Delivery Boy); Charlotte Lawrence (Manicurist); Kay English (Aristocratic Woman); Gordon Richards (Butler); Joe Karnes (Pianist); Joseph Corey (Army Officer); Joe McTurk (Vendor); Jesse Kirkpatrick (Stage Manager); Jack Daly (Drunk); Dudley Dickerson (Pullman Porter); Juanita Moore (Maid); Gabriel Curtis (Maitre D'); Lela Bliss (Wealthy Matron); George Cisar (Orchestra Leader); Sue George (Debutante); Richard Grant (TV Stage Manager); Karine Nordman (Helene); Barrie Chase, Ellen Ray (Specialty Dancers).

THE TRUE STORY OF JESSE JAMES (20th Century-Fox) 92 M.

Producer, Herbert B. Swope, Jr.; director, Nicholas Ray; based on the screenplay by Nunnally Johnson; new screenplay, Walter Newman; music, Leigh Harline; assistant director, Joseph E. Richards; costumes, Mary Wills.

Robert Wagner (Jesse James); Jeffrey Hunter (Frank James); Hope Lange (Zee); Agnes Moorehead (Mrs. Samuels); Alan Hale (Cole Younger); Alan Baxter (Remington); John Carradine (Reverend Jethro Bailey); Rachel Stephens (Anne); Barney Phillips (Dr. Samuels); Biff Elliott (Jim Younger); Frank Overton (Major Cobb); Barry Atwater (Attorney Walker); Marian Seldes (Rowena Cobb); Chubby Johnson (Askew); Frank Gorshin (Charley); Carl Thayler (Bobby); John Doucette (Hillstrom); Robert Adler (Sheriff Trump); Clancy Cooper (Sheriff Yoe); Sumner Williams (Bill Stiles); Tom Greenway (Deputy Leo); Mike Steen (Deputy Ed); Jason Wingreen (Peter); Aaron Saxon (Wiley); Anthony Ray (Bob Younger); Clegg Hoyt (Tucker Bassham); Tom Pittman (Hugie); Louis Zito (Clell Miller); Mark Hickman (Sam Wells); Adam Marshall (Dick Iddell); Joseph Di Reda (Bill Ryan); J. Frederik Albeck (Jorgensen); Kellogg Junge, Jr. (Archie, Age 4); Kay Kuter (Fleming); Bing Russell (Jayhawker Sergeant); Kendall Scott (Man); James F. Stone (Flower); Edmund Cobb (Bantock); Howard Negley (Burnside); Paul Webber (Telegraph Operator); Jeane Wood (Mrs. Younger); Mike Ross (Mr. Younger); Sally Corner (Widow Keevey); Fay Roope (Tom Trope); Gene Roth (Engineer); Jason Johnson (Engineer); George Comfort, Sr. (Singer); Ruth Robinson (Mary, Age 5); Ray Ferrell (Tim, Age 6); Alex Campbell (Judge).

JEANNE EAGELS (Columbia, 1957) 108 M.

Producer-director, George Sidney; story, Daniel Fuchs; screenplay, Fuchs, Sonya Levien, John Fante; art director, Ross Bellah; music director, Morris Stoloff; music, George Duning; assistant director, Charles S. Gould; camera, Robert Planck; editor, Viola Lawrence, Jerome Thomas.

Kim Novak (Jeanne Eagels); Jeff Chandler (Sal Satori); Agnes Moorehead (Mme. Neilson); Charles Drake (John Donahue); Larry Gates (Al Brooks); Virginia Grey (Elsie Desmond); Gene Lockhart (Equity Board President); Joe de Santis (Frank Satori); Murray Hamilton (Chick O'Hara); Will Wright (Marshal); Sheridan Comerate (Actor—Confederate Officer); Lowell Gilmore (Rev. Dr. Davidson); Juney Ellis (Mrs. Davidson); Beulah Archuletta (Mrs. Horn); Florence MacAfee (Mrs. McPhail); Snub Pollard (Quartermaster Bates); Joseph Novak (Patron); Bert Spencer (Dr. McPhail); Michael Dante (Sgt. O'Hara); Myrtle Anderson (Jeanne's Maid); Ward Wood (Stage Manager); George Neise (Traveling Salesman); Patricia Mowry (Hefty Bathing Beauty); Judd Holdren (Actor); Myna Cunard (Neilson Maid); Eleanor Audley (Sob Sister); Raymond Greenleaf (Elderly . Lawyer); Tommy Nolan, John Celentano (Satori Sons); Doris Lloyd (Mrs. Corliss); Carlyle Mitchell (Equity Spokesman); James Gonzales (Equity Man); Lillian Culver (Equity Board Woman); Alyn Lockwood (Rosalie Sartori); Leon Tyler (Bellhop); Eugene Sherman (Reporter); Frank Borzage (Director); Lou Borzage (Assistant Director); Jack Ano (Soldier); Jean Vachon (Middle Aged Woman).

RAINTREE COUNTY (MGM, 1957) 187 M.

Producer, David Lewis; associate producer, Millard Kaufman; director, Edward Dmytryk; based on the novel by Ross Lockridge, Jr.; screenplay, Kaufman; assistant director, Ridgeway Callow; music, Johnny Green; art director, William A. Horning, Urie McCleary; song, Paul Francis Webster and Green; special effects, Warren Newcombe; camera, Robert Surtees; editor, John Dunning.

Montgomery Clift (John Wickliff Shawnessy); Elizabeth Taylor (Susanna Drake); Eva Marie Saint (Nell Gaither); Nigel Patrick (Professor Jerusalem Webster Stiles); Lee Marvin (Orville "Flash" Perkins); Rod Taylor (Garwood B. Jones); Agnes Moorehead (Ellen Shawnessy); Walter Abel (T.D. Shawnessy); Jarma Lewis (Barbara Drake); Tom Drake (Bobby Drake); Rhys Williams (Ezra Gray); Russell Collins (Niles Foster); DeForrest Kelley (Southern Officer); Myrna Hansen (Lydia Gray); Oliver Blake (Jake, Bartender); John Eldredge (Cousin Sam); Isabelle Cooley (Soona); Ruth Attaway (Parthenia); Eileene Stevens (Miss Roman); Rosalind Hayes (Bessie); Don Burnett (Tom Conway); Michael Dugan (Nat Franklin); Michael Dante (Jesse Gardner); William Challee, Frank Kreig, Joe Brown (Spectators); Phil Chambers (Starter); James Griffith (Bourbon Voice); Burt Mustin (Grandpa Peters); Dorothy Granger (Madam Gobert); Owen McGiveney (Blind Man); Jack Daly (Photographer); Bill Walker (Old Black Man).

THE STORY OF MANKIND (Warner Bros., 1957) 110 M.

Producer, Irwin Allen; associate producer, George E. Swink; director, Allen; based on the book by Hendrik van Loon; screenplay, Allen, Charles Bennett; art director, Art Loel; music, Paul Sawtell; assistant director, Joseph Don Page; costumes, Marjorie Best; camera, Nick Musuraca; editor, Roland Gross.

Ronald Colman (Spirit of Man); Hedy Lamarr (Joan of Arc); Groucho Marx (Peter Minuit); Harpo Marx (Isaac Newton); Chico Marx (Monk); Virginia Mayo (Cleopatra); Agnes Moorehead (Queen Elizabeth); Vincent Price (Devil); Peter Lorre (Nero); Charles Coburn (Hippocrates); Cedric Hardwicke (High Judge); Cesar Romero (Spanish Envoy); John Carradine (Khufu); Dennis Hopper (Napoleon); Marie Wilson (Marie Antoinette); Helmut Dantine (Antony); Edward Everett Horton (Sir

Walter Raleigh); Reginald Gardiner (Shakespeare); Marie Windsor (Josephine); Cathy O'Donnell (Early Christian Woman); Franklin Pangborn (Marquis de Varennes); Melville Cooper (Major Domo); Francis X. Bushman (Moses); Jim Ameche (Alexander Graham Bell); Dani Crayne (Helen of Troy); Anthony Dexter (Columbus); Austin Green (Lincoln); Bobby Watson (Hitler); Reginald Sheffield (Caesar).

NIGHT OF THE QUARTER MOON (MGM, 1959) 95 M.

Producer, Albert Zugsmith; director, Hugo Haas; screenplay, Frank Davis, Franklin Coen; songs, Sammy Cahn and James Van Heusen; Charlotte Hawkers; Nat "King" Cole; music supervisor, Albert Glasser; art director, William A. Horning, Malcolm Brown; assistant director, Ridgeway Callow; camera, Ellis Carter; editor, Ben Lewis.

Julie London (Ginny Nelson); John Drew Barrymore (Roderic "Chuck" Nelson); Nat King Cole (Cy Robbin); Anna Kashfi (Maria Robbin); Dean Jones (Lexington Nelson); James Edwards (Asa Tully); Agnes Moorehead (Cornelia Nelson); Arthur Shields (Capt. O'Sullivan); Cathy Crosby (The Singer); Edward Andrews (Clinton Page); Ray Anthony (Hotel Manager); Jackie Coogan (Sgt. Bragan); Charles Chaplin, Jr. (Neighbor); Billy Daniels (Headwaiter); Robert Warwick (Judge); Marguerite Belafonte (Hostess); Joseph Cordovan (Boy in Woods); Bobi Byrnes (Girl in Woods); Jack Kosslyn (Dr. Parkson); Katharine Scott (Amanda); Frank Gorshin (Boy); George E. Stone, Ken Patterson (Detectives); Helene Marshall (Miss Kirby); Arthur Marshall (Stranger); Peter G. Vaiches (Sid Joss); Charles Horvath (Carter); John Harding (Major Folsey); Patricia Lloyd (Police Matron).

THE TEMPEST (Paramount, 1959) 121 M.

Producer, Dino DeLaurentiis; associate producer, Ralph B. Serpe; director, Alberto Lattuada; based on *The Captain's Daughter, The Revolt Of Pugacev* by Alexander Pushkin; screenplay, Louis Peterson, Ivo Perilli, Alberto Lattuada; set director, Mario Chiari; music, Piero Piccioni; assistant director, Aldo Buzzi, Dragoljub Stojanovic, Milo Kjukanovic; costumes, Maria De Matteis; camera, Aldo Tonti; editor, Otello Colangeli.

Silvana Mangano (Nasha); Van Heflin (Pugachov); Viveca Lindfors (Catherine The Great); Geoffrey Horne (Peter Griniev); Oscar Homolka (Savelic); Robert Keith (Captain Miranov); Agnes Moorehead (Vassilissa); Helmut Dantine (Svabrin); Finlay Currie (Count Griniev); Vittorio Gassman (Prosecutor); Laurence Naismith (Major Zurin); Claudio Gora (Minister); Aldo Silvania (Pope Gerasim); Nevenka Mikulic (Akulina); Milivoi Zivanovic (Surveyor); Jovan Gec (Captain Dimitri); Niksa Stefanini (Beloborodov); Janez Vrhovec (Sokolov); Claudio Gora (Minister); Maria Cristina Gajoni (Girl); Milivoje Pepovic Mavid (Pugachov Chief); Milutin Jasnik (Bashir Prisoner); Guido Celano (Peasant); Marjia Crnobori (Woman On Cart); Fulvia Franco (Palaska); and: Tonio Selwart, Dragutin Felba, Pera Obradovic, Mirdo Sreckovic.

THE BAT (Allied Artists, 1959) 80 M.

Producer, C.J. Tevlin; director, Crane Wilbur; based on the play by Mary Roberts Rinehart, Avery Hopkins; screenplay, Wilbur; art director, David Milton; music, Louis Forbes; assistant director, Clifford Broughton; camera, Joseph Biroc; editor, William Austin.

Vincent Price (Dr. Malcolm Wells); Agnes Moorehead (Cornelia Van Gorder); Gavin Gordon (Lt. Anderson); John Sutton (Warner); Lenita Lane (Lizzie Allen); Elaine Edwards (Dale Bailey); Darla Hood (Judy Hollander);

John Bryant (Mark Fleming); Mike Steele (Jack Bailey); Riza Royce (Mrs. Patterson); Robert B. Williams (Detective).

POLLYANNA (Buena Vista, 1960) 133 M.

Producer, Walt Disney; associate producer, George Golitzen; director, David Swift; based on the novel by Eleanor H. Porter; screenplay, Swift; art director, Carroll Clark, Robert Clatworthy; assistant director, Joseph Behn; music, Paul Smith; special effects, Ub Iwerks; camera, Russell Harlan; editor, Frank Gross.

Hayley Mills (Pollyanna); Jane Wyman (Aunt Polly); Richard Egan (Dr. Edmond Chilton); Karl Malden (Rev. Paul Ford); Nancy Olson (Nancy Furman); Adolphe Menjou (Mr. Pendergast); Donald Crisp (Mayor Karl Warren); Agnes Moorehead (Mrs. Snow); Kevin Corcoran (Jimmy Bean); James Drury (George Dodds); Reta Shaw (Tillie Lagerlof); Leora Dana (Mrs. Paul Ford); Anne Seymour (Mrs. Amelia Tarbell); Edward Platt (Ben Tarbell); Mary Grace Canfield (Angelica); Jenny Egan (Mildred Snow); Gage Clark (Mr. Murg); Ian Wolfe (Mr. Neely); Nolan Leary (Mr. Thomas); Edgar Dearing (Mr. Gorman).

TWENTY PLUS TWO (Allied Artists, 1961) 102 M.

Producer, Frank Gruber; director, Joseph M. Newman; based on the novel by Gruber; screenplay, Gruber; music, Gerald Fried; assistant director, Lindsley Parsons, Jr.; camera, Carl Guthrie; editor, George White.

David Janssen (Alder); Jeanne Crain (Linda); Dina Merrill (Nikki); Agnes Moorehead (Mrs. Delaney); William Demarest (Slocum); Brad Dexter (Dane); Jacques Aubuchon (Peschette); Robert Strauss (Romainger); George N. Neise (Collinson); Fredd Wayne (Toomey); Mort Mills (Harbin); Will Wright (Attendant); Robert H. Harris (Stanley); Wolfe Barzell (Old Frenchy); John Goddard (Erlinger); Carleton Young (Colonel); Ella Ethridge (Mrs. Woodson); Billy Varga (Mark); Chester Jones (Butler); Gertrude Astor (Julia Joliet); David Greene (Drunk Sailor); Teri Janssen (Stewardess); Fred E. Sherman (Brute Lodge Manager); Robert Gruber (Bellboy).

BACHELOR IN PARADISE (MGM, 1961) 109 M.

Producer, Ted Richmond; director, Jack Arnold; story, Vera Caspary; screenplay, Valentine Davies, Hal Kanter; music, Henry Mancini; song, Mancini and Mack David; art director, George W. Davis, Hans Peter; camera, Joseph Ruttenberg; editor, Richard W. Farrell.

Bob Hope (Adam J. Niles); Lana Turner (Rosemary Howard); Janis Paige (Dolores Jynson); Jim Hutton (Larry Delavane); Paula Prentiss (Linda Delavane); Don Porter (Thomas W. Jynson); Virginia Grey (Camille Quinlaw); Agnes Moorehead (Judge Peterson); Florence Sundstrom (Mrs. Pickering); Clinton Sundberg (Rodney Jones); Alan Hewitt (Backett); Reta Shaw (Mrs. Brown); John McGiver (Austin Palfrey); Lee Goodman (Leland Quinlaw); William Zuckert (W. P. Matthews); Roberta Shore (Rosemary's Secretary); Sean Peters (Peter Pickering); Edward Rossen (Steve Delavane); Dick Whittinghill (Bruce Freedman); Jack Pepper (Floor Man); Lee Krieger (Court Clerk); Robert B. Williams (Fireman); Olan Soule (Waiter); Jerry Doggett (himself); Arlene Wakefield (Reporter); Vince Scully (Announcer).

JESSICA (United Artists, 1962) 105 M.

Producer-director, Jean Negulesco; based on the novel *The Midwife of Pont Clery* by Flora Sandstrom; screenplay, Edith Sommer; assistant director, Ottavio Oppo; art director, Giulio Bongine; music, Mario Nascimbene; camera,

Piero Portalupi; editor, Hanzo Lucidi.

Angie Dickinson (Jessica); Maurice Chevalier (Father Antonio); Noel Noel (Old Crupi); Gabriele Ferzetti (Edmondo Raumo); Sylva Koscina (Nunzia Tuffi); Agnes Moorehead (Maria Lombardo); Marcel Dalio (Luigi Ruffi); Danielle DeMetz (Nicolina Lombardo); Antonio Cifariello (Gianni Crupi); Kerima (Virginia Toriello); Carlo Croccolo (Beppi Toriello); Georgette Anys (Mamma Parigi); Rossana Rory (Rosa Masudino); Alberto Rabagliati (Pietro Masudino); Angelo Galassi (Antonio Risini); Marina Berti (Filippella Risino); Manuela Rinaldi (Lucia Casabranca); Gianni Musy (Filippo Casabranca); Joe Pollini (Rosario).

HOW THE WEST WAS WON (MGM, 1963) 165 M.

Producer, Bernard Smith; director, John Ford (The Civil War); George Marshall (The Railroad); Henry Hathaway (The Rivers, The Plains, The Outlaws); suggested by a series of articles in *Life* magazine; screenplay, James R. Webb; art director, George W. Davis, William Ferrari, Addison Vehr; assistant director, George Marshall, Jr., William McGarry, William Shanks, Robert Saunders, Wingate Smith; music, Alfred Newman; songs, Newman and Ken Darby; Newman and Johnny Mercer; Newman and Sammy Cahn; camera, William H. Daniels, Milton Krasner, Charles Lang, Jr., Joseph LaShelle; editor, Harold F. Kress.

Carroll Baker (Eve Prescott); Lee. J. Cobb (Marshal); Henry Fonda (Jethro Stuart); Carolyn Jones (Julie Rawlings); Karl Malden (Zebulon Prescott); Gregory Peck (Cleve Van Valen); George Peppard (Zeb Rawling); Robert Preston (Roger Morgan); Debbie Reynolds (Lilith Prescott); James Stewart (Linus Rawlings); John Wayne (General Sherman); Spencer Tracy (Narrator); Eli Wallach (Charlie Gant); Richard Widmark (Mike King); Brigid Bazlen (Dora); Walter Brennan (Colonel Hawkins); David Brian (Attorney); Andy Devine (Peterson); Agnes Moorehead (Rebecca Prescott); Raymond Massey (Abraham Lincoln); Russ Tamblyn (Reb Soldier); Mickey Shaughnessy (Deputy); Thelma Ritter (Agatha Clegg); Kimm Charney (Sam Prescott); Byron Russell (Zeke Prescott); Lee Van Cleef (Marty); Charles Briggs (Parker); Tudor Owen (Harvey); Barry Harvey (Angus); Jamie Ross (Bruce); Jay C. Flippen (Huggins); Clinton Sundberg (Hylan Seabury); Joe Sawyer (Ship's Officer); Polly Burson (Stock Player); Beulah Archuletta (Indian Squaw); John Larch (Grimes); Claude Johnson (Jeremiah); Bill Henry (Staff Officer); William Wellman, Jr. (Second Officer); Bob Morgan, Chuck Roberson (Officers); Ken Curtis, Red Perkins (Union Soldiers); Ben Black Elk, Sr. (Indian Chief); Danny Sands (Trapeze Man); Rofolfe Acosta, Dean Stanton, Jack Lambert (Henchmen); Jack Pennick (Corporal Murphy).

WHO'S MINDING THE STORE? (Paramount, 1963) 90 M.

Producer, Paul Jones; director, Frank Tashlin; screenplay, Tashlin, Harry Tugend; music, Joseph J. Lilley; assistant director, Ralph Axness; costumes, Edith Head; camera, Wallace Kelley; editor, John Woodcock.

Jerry Lewis (Raymond Phiffier); Jill St. John (Barbara Tuttle); Ray Walston (Quimby); John McGiver (Mr. Tuttle); Agnes Moorehead (Mrs. Phoebe Tuttle); Francesca Bellini (Shirley); Peggy Mondo (Lady Wrestler); Nancy Kulp (Mrs. Rothgater); Isobel Elsom (Dowager); John Abbott (Roberts); Kathleen Freeman (Mrs. Glucksman); Mary Treen (Woman in Mattress Department); Richard Deacon (Tie Salesman); Richard Wessel (Cop); Jerry Hausner (Smith); James Gaines (French Little Boy); Quinn O'Hara (Elevator Operator); Byron Foulger (Manager, Bargain Department); Richard Collier (Customer); Mike Ross (Janitor); Barbara Pepper, Felice Richmond (Women in Bargain basement); Fritz Feld (Gourmet Manager).

HUSH . . . HUSH, SWEET CHARLOTTE (20th Century-Fox, 1964) 133 M.

Producer, Robert Aldrich; associate producer, Walter Blake; director, Aldrich; based on the novel by Henry Farrell; screenplay, Farrell, Lukas Heller; music, Frank DeVol; song, Mack David and DeVol; assistant director, William McGarry, Sam Strangis; costumes, Norma Koch; choreographer, Alex Ruiz; art director, William Glasgow; sound, Bernard Fredricks; camera, Joseph Biroc; editor, Michael Luciano.

Bette Davis (Charlotte Hollis); Olivia de Havilland (Miriam Deering); Joseph Cotten (Dr. Drew Bayliss); Agnes Moorehead (Velma Cruther); Cecil Kellaway (Harry Willis); Victor Buono (Big Sam Hollis); Mary Astor (Mrs. Jewel Mayhew); William Campbell (Paul Marchand); Wesley Addy (Sheriff Luke Standish); Bruce Dern (John Mayhew); George Kennedy (Foreman); Dave Willock (Taxi Driver); John Megna (Boy); Ellen Corby, Helen Kleeb, Marianne Stewart (Gossips); Frank Ferguson (Newspaper Editor).

THE SINGING NUN (MGM, 1966) 98 M.

Producer, John Beck; director, Henry Koster; story, John Furia, Jr.; screenplay, Sally Benson, Furia; songs, Soeur Sourire and Randy Sparks; assistant director, Kevin Donnelly; music, Harry Sukman; camera, Milton Krasner; editor, Rita Roland.

Debbie Reynolds (Sister Ann); Ricardo Montalban (Father Clementi); Greer Garson (Mother Prioress); Agnes Moorehead (Sister Cluny); Chad Everett (Robert Gerade); Katharine Ross (Nicole Arlien); Ed Sullivan (Himself); Juanita Moore (Sister Mary); Ricky Cordell (Dominic Arlien); Michael Pate (Mr. Arlien); Tom Drake (Fitzpatrick); Larry D. Mann (Mr. Duvries); Charles Robinson (Marauder); Monique Montaigne (Sister Michele); Joyce Vanderveen (Sister Elise); Ann Wakefield (Sister Brigitte); Pam Peterson (Sister Gertrude); Marina Koshetz (Sister Marthe); Nancy Walters (Sister Therese); Violet Rensing (Sister Elizabeth); Inez Petroza (Sister Consuella).

WHAT'S THE MATTER WITH HELEN? (United Artists, 1971) 101 M.

Executive producer, Edward S. Feldman; producer, George Edwards; director, Curtis Harrington; screenplay, Henry Farrell; music, David Raksin; art director, Eugene Lourie; assistant director, Claude Binyon, Jr.; sound, Al Overton, Jr.; camera, Lucien Ballard; editor, William H. Reynolds.

Debbie Reynolds (Adele); Shelley Winters (Helen); Dennis Weaver (Lincoln Palmer); Agnes Moorehead (Sister Alma); Michael MacLiammoir (Hamilton Starr); Sammee Lee Jones (Winona Palmer); Robbi Morgan (Rosalie Greenbaum); Helene Winston (Mrs. Greenbaum); Swen Swenson (Gigolo); Logan Ramsey (Cop).

DEAR DEAD DELILAH (Southern Star, 1972) 90 M.

Executive producer, Jack H. Music; producer, Jack Clement; associate producer, Susan Richardson; director-screenplay, John Farris; camera, William R. Johnson.

With: Agnes Moorehead, Will Geer, Michael Ansara, Dennis Patrick, Patricia Carmichael, Anne Meacham.

Angela Lansbury

5'8"
135 pounds
Blonde
Blue eyes
Birth sign: Libra

Even before she was twenty-three-years old, British-born Angela Lansbury was portraying mature screen snits (Gaslight) and middle-aged screen harridans (If Winter Comes) with a perfection of powerhouse technique that earned her respect within the film industry and won her a devoted audience. Twenty years later, in the mid-1960s, she had acquired an unwanted reputation as the American cinema's favorite archetype possessive mother. On screen, she could suffocate an overgrown child with misguided love (All Fall Down), uncoil her offspring's mind with warped political ambitions (The Manchurian Candidate), or selfishly feed her daughter to the money machines for personal aggrandizement (Harlow); at home, she was the devoted mother of three children.

But Angela was not content in her well-paying screen niche and returned to the Broadway stage on several occasions to remind audiences she was far more versatile than she seemed in motion pictures. Few person-alities have ever made the transition from top character film star to leading lady, let alone in the splashy manner Angela did with Mame *(1966). "Overnight," she had become the 1960s most sparkling toast of Broadway, and in a sympathetic lead role to boot! Since then, she has played a see-saw game with the public's affection.* Dear World *and* Prettybelle *were stage flops, and her starring roles in the movies* Something for Everyone *and* Bedknobs and Broomsticks *went by the boards generally unappreciated. However, she wisely accepted the lead in the London premiere version of the four-teen-year-old musical* Gypsy, *and her performance won enthusiastic endorsements from the critics and public alike. Angela is now back on the top of the show busi-ness heap where she so rightly belongs.*

Angela Bridget Lansbury was born in London, England, October 16, 1925, the daughter of Edgar Isaac Lansbury, a lumber merchant, and Monya MacGill,* a stage actress. Her mother's previous marriage to Reginald Denham had produced a daughter Isolde, four years Angela's senior.

As a toddler, Angela was close to Isolde and they would perform dances and imitations for the family. They were later separated when Isolde went to live with her father (she would later become an actress herself and and at one time was married to performer Peter Ustinov). When Angela was five (1930), her mother gave birth to identical twin boys, Edgar and Bruce.

Even as a youngster, Angela was unusually uncon-cerned with her physical appearance. "I never thought I was pretty. I was always self-conscious. I had a very beautiful mother. She's still beautiful. Maybe the psy-chiatrists would say that's why I felt that way about myself. I like the way I look now (1966) more than I did when I was younger. I think I've grown into myself. I found a style that's right for me. In the past, I always felt I had to look like someone else."

Since Angela's paternal grandfather, George Lans-bury, was a famous politician of the 1920s–1930s and leader of the opposition Labour Party from 1931–1935, Angela got a good taste of politicking in her childhood.

---

* Born Chattie McIldowie, she adopted the stage name of Monya MacGill, making her professional theatrical de-but as Joanne in *Dear Brutus* in 1918 at Wyndham's Theatre, London, followed by roles in such productions as *As You Like It* (1920), *Chiba* (1921), *Othello* (1921), *If Four Walls Told* (1922), *Success* (1923), *The Fairy Tale* (1924). In later years, she would return to the stage in America, as in the Broadway version of *The Boy Friend* (1954) playing Lady Brockhurst. Miss MacGill's father had been the director of the Belfast Opera House, and her two brothers (James and Dennis) were stage actors, as well as a granduncle who toured America in Shakespearean repertory under the stage name of Robert B. Mantell. She was the first of three wives of actor-writer-director Reginald Denham (born January 10, 1894) who made his London stage debut in September, 1913, in *Joseph and His Brethren.*

Angela Lansbury at the age of twenty-one.

She would often accompany her grandfather to political rallies and return home to mimic the various speakers she had heard. At times, she would fantasize about becoming a politician herself, but on other occasions she would change her mind and consider the possibility of being a concert pianist.

It was when Angela was nine that she was so struck by a performance of *Pygmalion* that she saw the show an additional two times and decided show business was for her.

The Lansburys were financially quite comfortable and spent as much time as possible at their farm in Berrik-Salmone, near Benson, which they purchased in 1931. But in 1934, Angela's father died and the family's life style had to change. After a recuperative trip to Italy with the children, Mrs. Lansbury moved the family residence to a more modest home in Hampstead, on the outskirts of London. Angela was enrolled at the South Hampstead High School for Girls, whose headmistress, Muriel Potter, was the sister of writer Stephen Potter, who had been Mr. Lansbury's best friend.

Of this period Angela recalls: "I was a morose little girl at times. I was very sensitive, very easily hurt, and I would cry when my mother left me to go to the theatre. And I would retreat into make-believe. From the time I was eight until I was twelve, I'd go for days pretending to be other people. I was also terribly stubborn. And I'd do all sorts of things just to make people laugh."

With the onslaught of World War II, most of the London school children were evacuated to the country to avoid the bombing raids. Angela hated the thought of being sent away to boarding school and persuaded her mother to allow her to study at home with a tutor. At this time, she and her mother decided she should embark on a series of courses of dancing, diction, and singing since she had firmly decided a stage career was her destiny. After six months of this catch-as-catch-can instruction, Angela's mother enrolled her daughter, via a scholarship, in the Webber-Douglas School Of Singing and Dramatic Art in Kensington. Angela's first stage role at the school was as a lady-in-waiting in a class production of *Mary of Scotland.*

By the summer of 1940 the bombing raids on London and the environs had increased, and Mrs. Lansbury thought it better to follow the advice of a distant cousin from Brawley, California, and evacuate herself and the children to America.

The Lansburys arrived in New York in the late summer of 1940 and for a time stayed with their sponsors, Wall Street businessman Charles T. Wilson and his wife, at their Lake Mahopac, New York summer home.

That September, through the auspices of the American Theatre Wing, Angela auditioned for the Feagin School of Drama and Radio in Manhattan. Her test consisted of a scene from *Romeo and Juliet.* She was accepted at the school on a scholarship, and arrangements were made for her to board at the East 94th Street house of Mr. and Mrs. George W. Perkins. Angela recalls herself as a cheeky, self-sufficient youth: "I was fifteen and very grown up. English girls *are,* for the most part." By the fall of 1941, Angela had moved in with her mother in a forty-two-dollar-a-month one-room apartment on Morton Street in Greenwich Village, with the twin boys at Choate School in Wallingford, Connecticut.*

At the Feagin School, Angela drifted naturally into character roles since she was a bit on the chubby side, playing such roles as the sixty-year-old Lady Wishfort in Congreve's *The Way of the World* and occasionally taking a lead assignment as in *Lady Windermere's Fan.* Angela remembers: "I never had any trouble making an ass of myself. I had a sort of comedienne thing about me. I was never the ingenue type—luckily, since there were too many girls who looked like ingenues. But I would have been a character actress in any case. It was my bent from the beginning."

One of Angela's classmates at the Feagin School was Arthur Bourbon, who encouraged her to develop her knack of mimicry into an act. She prepared a full-blown imitation of Beatrice Lillie singing Noel Coward's "I Went to a Marvelous Party," and Bourbon arranged an agent's audition for her. This led to her being offered a job in Montreal in the summer of 1942, at a little club called the Samovar, at a sixty-dollar-a-week salary. The job lasted six weeks, and Angela always maintains it taught her a great deal about the ways of the world.

Since Mrs. Lansbury had joined a Canadian variety show tour with Anna Neagle that was entertaining the R.C.A.F. units there, Angela was officially in charge of her brothers and herself. After packing the twins off to Choate, she received a letter from her mother who had gone to Los Angeles to crash the movies. Mrs. Lansbury was not having much luck in the film world, but living on the West Coast was cheaper (she paid twenty-eight dollars a month for a one-room apartment). She suggested Angela join her, and she did. They each made the rounds of the studios but with no success. Then at Christmas time, both mother and daughter obtained jobs at Bullock's Wilshire Department Store. Mrs. Lansbury

---

* They would both later graduate from U.C.L.A. Edgar would become a stage scenic designer and later a Broadway producer, while Bruce has been both a CBS television production executive and a playwright.

was assigned to the toy department but was soon fired, because she spent too much time playing with the games. Agnes had better luck. After a time in the wrapping department (at eighteen dollars weekly), she was made a salesgirl in the cosmetics department (at twenty-six dollars weekly). At one point, the store offered to enroll Angela in the buyer's training program, but her fumbling sense of mathematics put an end to that scheme. She remained a salesgirl.

It was in June, 1943, that Michael Dyne, a struggling young actor friend of Angela's, who was auditioning for the title part in MGM's *The Picture of Dorian Gray* (1945), told her the studio needed a youngish English girl to round out the cast. Angela took the afternoon off from work and went out to the MGM studios in Culver City where the casting director was suitably impressed by Angela's personality and referred her to an interview with director George Cukor, then preparing to direct *Gaslight* (1944).

Cukor agreed to test Angela for the role of the Cockney maid in *Gaslight,* since this film was scheduled to go into production before the forthcoming *The Picture of Dorian Gray.* The test was made during Angela's vacation week from Bullock's. Angela performed a scene from the original British play that was not to be in the film version. Her co-player was actor Hugh Marlowe, in the role to be played by Charles Boyer in the movie. Angela recalls: "I can't say I was frightened. I was terribly interested in how it was all done."

Although Angela proved satisfactory in the *Gaslight* test, the film's production executives decided she was still too young for the role. However, studio mogul Louis B. Mayer saw the test and voted to put Angela under contract (a seven-year term agreement with options, starting at $500 weekly on the forty-week pay scale).

MGM, and culture-conscious Louis B. Mayer in particular, had always been drawn to English performers. In fact, the bulk of the British-Irish player colony in Hollywood was under MGM contract or frequently worked at the studio, including in the 1935–1945 period Greer Garson, Freddie Bartholomew, C. Aubrey Smith, Vivien Leigh, Robert Coote, Elizabeth Taylor, Gladys Cooper, Dame May Whitty, Peter Lawford, Roddy MacDowall and Terry Kilburn. With that studio so fond of the British drawing room and outdoors drama as source material for its yearly product, it was a natural decision that Angela, who at age eighteen showed such high natural potential as an actress, should become part of the MGM stock company. The studio had long ago learned the value of having strong supporting players to bolster their productions, and it was cheaper in the long run to have such character players on hand under exclusive contract for the needed time. This was still the time of luxury in the industry, bolstered to an unprecedented annual production schedule by the demands of World War II audiences for escapist entertainment.

With Angela under contract, director Cukor decided he might as well make use of her, and she was assigned to the role of the parlor maid, Nancy Oliver, in *Gaslight* (1944). Patrick Hamilton's play had first been produced in London to great acclaim and then opened on Broadway in December, 1941, under the title *Angel Street,* where it ran up a most impressive stay of 1,293 performances. Meanwhile, MGM acquired new screen rights to the property and prevented the distribution of the British-made film version (1940)* which starred Anton Walbrook.

In the revamped MGM screenplay, the story's action is spread out over several years, whereas in the play it had occurred within a twelve-hour period. Its plot begins in 1870s England when the niece (Ingrid Bergman) of a murdered opera singer is sent to Italy to recuperate from the terrors of the event. She remains in Rome to study opera. Later as a mature young woman, she encounters and marries suave pianist Charles Boyer. After a brief Italian honeymoon, he suggests they return to London to reopen #10 Thornton Square, the house left to her by her murdered aunt. She would rather not, since the Victorian house is filled with unpleasant memories, but he insists. Before long, he has undermined her self-confidence by accusing her of forgetfulness and minor thefts. Under the growing pressure of his accusations and icy manner, she grows continually more hysterical, unsure of her every action or his motivation. Then stubborn Scotland Yard detective Joseph Cotten enters the scene with suspicions that Boyer is linked to the unsolved murder of her aunt fifteen years before. He later takes the distraught Bergman into his confidence, and a trap is set for the devious Boyer.

Woven into the main plot of the psychological confrontation between well-bred Bergman versus cunning Boyer is Angela as the pouting downstairs maid (played in the Broadway stage version by Elizabeth Custis). When the Thornton Square house is reopened, Angela is hired to assist middle-aged housekeeper Barbara Everett in the running of the bric-a-brac-laden residence. In her introductory interview with her would-be employers, Boyer immediately decides this predatory Cockney could be useful in his sinister plan against Bergman. That Angela's Nancy is a snit with no respect for her well-defined station in life is soon made clear by her flirtatious attitude to Boyer, her rebellious ap-

---

* Not released in the United States until 1952.

proach to Everett, and her condescending manner to the growingly more uncertain Bergman. As Boyer becomes more obsessed with his efforts to locate gems secreted somewhere in the house, his relationship with Angela fluctuates back and forth between comrade-in-arm, servant, and vague romantic interest. Angela soon decides she has milked her camaraderie with Boyer to the fullest and settles for the customary policeman on the beat to satisfy her romantic needs.

The smooth period thriller opened at the Capitol Theatre, May 4, 1944, while the stage version was still playing down the street. The critics and the public endorsed the romanticized MGM *Gaslight,* which found both Boyer and Bergman at the height of their screen popularity. Angela made her mark in her screen debut. Kate Cameron in her three-and-one-half star *New York Daily News* review wrote: "A newcomer named Angela Lansbury gives a wonderful performance in the role of the cockney maid." Even more enthusiastic was the *New York Post*'s Archer Winston: ". . . [she] calls to mind one of Bette Davis's most famous efforts in *Of Human Bondage.*" Angela was nominated for an Academy Award, along with such more experienced performers as Agnes Moorehead (*Mrs. Parkington*), Jennifer Jones (*Since You Went Away*), Aline MacMahon (*Dragon Seed*), but they all lost to Ethel Barrymore who won the best supporting actress Oscar for *None but the Lonely Heart.*

The most astonishing element of Angela's performance in *Gaslight* is that she was not even eighteen when she played the role of the approximately 25-year-old Nancy Oliver (in fact Angela celebrated her eighteenth birthday on the set with a cast party, and her smoking scenes had to be delayed by law until she

reached her legal maturity). It was not just that her physical maturity and slight plumpness along with carefully manipulated costuming, hairstyling, and makeup made her seem ten years older, it was her unrelenting confidence in her characterization that came across as both natural and almost too convincing. One has only to compare Angela's film debut with the amateurish performances of such later similar-aged players as Sandra Dee, Diane Varsi, Janice Rule, Katharine Ross, or countless others to further appreciate the inborn talent Angela possessed from the start. As Angela would later say: "I happened to see *Gaslight* not long ago on television. I was amazed. I thought, My God, how did I have all that assurance. I have much less assurance now. In those days, I suppose, I went ahead on trust."

It was a strange bit of carelessness that led MGM to next cast Angela in *National Velvet* (1944). Having scored so well in *Gaslight,* it might have been assumed she would have at the very least been handed similar assignments and not turned back to a silly supporting role as the boy-crazy older sister of Elizabeth Taylor.

National Velvet had been in the works at MGM for several years. In 1941 it was considered as a costarring vehicle for Spencer Tracy and new contractee Shirley Temple, but the latter's galloping adolescence made her too old for the role in question. With the success of such animal pictures as *Lassie Come Home,* the studio felt new impetus to put its horse story into active production and did so in early 1944. Set in rural England, the Brown household consists of father Donald Crisp, a butcher by trade, mother Anne Revere, who in her youth once swam the English channel, older daughter Angela, dreamy daughter Taylor, young son Butch Jenkins, and the baby of the family, Juanita Quigley. When a local farmer auctions off a gelding, Taylor wins the raffle. With the aid of ex-jockey Micky Rooney (whom the Browns have befriended), she trains the steed to run in the annual Grand National steeplechase race. Because the chosen jockey expresses doubt about National Velvet's winning ability, Taylor demands to ride the horse herself. She wins the Pi run, but is disqualified when her true sex and age are discovered. However, it does not matter, for she has accomplished her mission and is well satisfied.

Angela's relatively slight role in *National Velvet* was just set dressing. She is the rebellious daughter, physically mature beyond her mid-teen years (she definitely needed a bra). She thinks it is just super to wear nail polish to school on the last day of the term and is equally unconventional at home as in her independent attitude at the dinner table or later at night when she goes to bed with her clothes still on, planning to sneak out for a late evening date.

With Charles Boyer in *Gaslight* (MGM, 1944).

With Donald Crisp, Mickey Rooney, Elizabeth Taylor, and Anne Revere in *National Velvet* (MGM, 1944).

National Velvet was exceedingly popular in its initial release, and later spawned a short-lived video series.

Far more impressive was Angela's sole 1945 release, Albert Lewin's *The Picture of Dorian Gray*. Lewin, a long-time MGM scenarist-associate-executive at MGM and more recently an independent producer with United Artists before returning to MGM, had a penchant for bringing offbeat classics to the screen. As if charged with a noble cause, his purpose always seemed greater than the sum of his or his associates' screen talents, as in *The Moon and Sixpence*. There was much concern whether Oscar Wilde's elegant little novel *The Picture of Dorian Gray* (published in 1891) could be adapted to the screen without offending the still-strict Hays Office or public taste. With compromises all along the line, the feature was filmed in black and white (save for color inserts of the diabolical painting) and released in March, 1945.

Although manufactured at the MGM facilities, *The Picture of Dorian Gray* emerged with a distinct low-budget quality about it. Narrated by Cedric Hardwicke, it recounted the strange events that befall 1890s London dandy Dorian Gray (Hurd Hatfield) once his portrait is painted by pompous artist Lowell Gilmore. Already attracted to the world of the corrupt by his hedonistic nature, Hatfield desires that the oil painting should grow old and not he. No sooner is his wish seemingly granted than he meets witty degenerate George Sanders (popping off brittle epigrams with sneering aplomb) who proceeds to lead Hatfield into a ravenously depraved existence. The devil has come for his due, and sensualist Hatfield is the perfect victim.

One of the two women who come into Hatfield's in-

dulgent life is Sibyl Vane (Angela) a virginal East End music hall singer. She is drawn to the handsome Hatfield, whom she knows only as Prince Charming. At first he is intrigued by her innocent lower-class ways and her enchantment with his world of upper-class sophistication. It is insidious Sanders who suggests Hatfield put Angela to the test by seducing her and then later leads the would-be degenerate into treating the girl cruelly. Hatfield at one point realizes how heartless he has been and seeks to apologize to Angela, but he learns that she has killed herself.

The other female influence in his life is Donna Reed, the screenplay's invented role of Gilmore's sweet niece. As she matures, she is increasingly attracted to stiff Hatfield, not realizing he is the one who has killed her uncle in a fit of rage or that he has accidentally shot Sibyl Vane's brother (Richard Fraser) who has traced his sister's long-ago debaucher to his country home. To balance the story for homogeneous entertainment, Peter Lawford is around to adore the docile Reed and protect her from Hatfield.

The general public was not really ready for a visual presentation (and one filled with mawkish pomposity at that) of Wilde's thesis that man's ignoble acts are often masked to the world, but that they eventually come crashing down upon him. This premise is dem-

Angela Lansbury and her mother Moyna MacGill in 1945.

With Hurd Hatfield in *The Picture of Dorian Gray* (MGM, 1945).

In *The Picture of Dorian Gray.*

With Billy Bevan and Hurd Hatfield in *The Picture of Dorian Gray.*

onstrated in Hatfield's case, when after many years of remaining the masklike youth, he finally decides to destroy the hideous portrait which has been absorbing his sundry corruptions over the decades. He stabs wildly at the canvas with a knife, with amazingly moralistic results.

Once again, it was Angela who emerged the creative success of the picture. ". . . I very much like Angela Lansbury as Sibyl Vane. Some people are liable to laugh at her and to think of her as insipid, but I think she is touching and exact in her defenseless romanticism and in a special kind of short-lipped English beauty, appropriate to the period and to Sibyl's class, and evocative of milkmaids in Eighteenth-century pornographic prints. (James Agee in *The Nation*). In the long run, his critical evaluation of Angela's work here was far more in keeping with the reality of her performance, than the interpretation offered by Bosley Crowther in the *New York Times:* "Angela Lansbury wears a quaint little costume as a music-hall-singing Sibyl Vane and wears an even more ridiculous pose of purity which provokes Dorian's bestiality."

In the stylized setting of Lewin's gaslight era picture, Angela was one of the few genuine characters, a frail creature seen at her most pathetic as she chants the lovely tune "Goodbye Little Yellow Bird,"* wistfully yearning for what life is destined to deny her.

---

* When Manhattan's Gallery Of Modern Art held an Albert Lewin film festival in 1966, Angela made an appearance and sang "Yellow Bird." At the time she stated: "I love 'Yellow Bird.' It is very close to my heart. I am touched when out of the blue people remember it. They seem to identify it with very specific times in their lives. I myself feel very emotional when I hear 'Yellow Bird,' but then I'm a very emotional person, and I cry at the drop of a hat. . . . I can't cry at things I consider truly sad."

Angela received a Golden Globes award for her acting in *The Picture of Dorian Gray* and received a second Oscar nomination. However, she lost the best supporting actress award to Anne Revere's performance in *National Velvet. Dorian Gray* would be remade in 1970 with a homosexual-sexploitation slant, starring Helmut Berger in the lead role, with Marie Liljedahl as Sybil.

In two years in the movies, Angela had made three films, two of which (*Gaslight* and *The Picture of Dorian Gray*) provided her with contrasting roles that would be among the four best assignments of her feature films to date. At this point in her life, Angela did not have the temperament to push at her career in the manner she would display in later years. She found working at MGM comfortable: "I came in at the end of a very lush period. L. B. Mayer was always terribly nice to me. He always seemed interested in how the family was getting along. He wanted to put my brothers under contract, but Mother wouldn't have it, and we both felt that it wouldn't be fair to do that to the boys. I was always able to go and chat with L. B. Mayer— mostly about the family or about the movies. I suppose I was an enigma to him." On another occasion, Angela would more perceptively remark: "Louis B. Mayer and I got along like a house afire. He never chased me around his desk or tried anything with me. Of course, he never gave me any good parts either."

One role Angela wanted very much was that of Bessie Watty in Warner Bros. *The Corn Is Green* (1945). She requested that MGM allow her to be considered for a loan-out, but the studio decided the part was not suitable for the image* they vaguely had in mind for Angela and refused her request. It was one of the big disappointments of her early movie years.

It was in 1945 that Angela married screen actor Richard Cromwell.* She was only nineteen and he

---

* A MGM publicist who had been with the studio in the 1940s once said: "Angela couldn't play ladies, and that was the era of the ladies. She was very young, but looked mature. That was because she was so chubby. She ate all the time, chocolate bars, fig newton cookies. She wasn't a compulsive eater—she was a hungry eater."

* Richard Cromwell was born Ray Radabaugh in Los Angeles, January 8, 1910. From his first screen role (*Tol'able David*, 1931) he made his mark as the sensitive young man type a la Phillips Holmes. As the decade moved on, he continued in the same stereotype but in smaller assignments, such as *Hoopla, Lives of a Bengal Lancer,* and *Jezebel.* By the 1940s his screen career was on the decline, and he was reduced to second and third male leads in programmers. He became a novelist and short story writer, and in 1953 made a small fortune for his creation of ceramic objects, including face masks of movie people. He died October 11, 1960, of cancer, in Hollywood.

thirty-five. Angela admits it was a mistake: "The marriage lasted nine months, and, thank goodness, did a great deal for me. I learned the meaning of marriage and a lot of other things, and I had a better idea of what it was all about when I was married again."

In late 1945, Angela initiated legal proceedings to become an American citizen, which she did in 1951.

The following year proved to be Angela's most productive and representative on the screen. World War II was just over, and screen musicals which had so enlivened the war morale effort were still in vogue.

The Harvey Girls (1946) delved its Technicolor way into the Old West for its premise, following in the tradition of Broadway's outstanding musical comedy success *Oklahoma.* Set in the 1890s, the movie highlights the adventures of Judy Garland who arrives in Sandrock, New Mexico aboard the "Atchinson, Topeka And Santa Fe." She has come to be the mail-order bride of Chill Wills, but learns it was all a joke contrived by gambler John Hodiak and that Wills is the town's drunk. Hard put for finances, she accepts a post with the Fred Harvey restaurant chain, whose starched-aproned girls are supervised and chaperoned by no-nonsense Marjorie Main. Wide-eyed, virginal Judy is more than distressed to find Sandrock such a wide open town, what with crooked Judge Preston Foster and the Alhambra Saloon presided over by icy dance hall queen Angela and her pack of girls. It soon becomes a personal battle for Garland to emerge victorious over Angela's tainted life style, for both women find Hodiak mighty attractive.

For a cardboard villainess, Angela proved particularly adept in *The Harvey Girls.* Parading in her spiffy working hours evening gowns or decked out in her black, short tights outfit with a wide brimmed hat, she is elegantly in command of the situation. As the Mae West of the saloon, she is a worthy rival to the town's clean-up campaign being instigated by Garland.

The finale requires the good elements of Sandrock to emerge victorious. After the Alhambra girls attempt to break up the wholesome dance social organized by the Harvey Girls, Foster sets fire to the Harvey restaurant. Hodiak undergoes a change of heart and turns over his saloon as a temporary headquarters for the Harvey eatery. And Angela . . . well, like any good "other woman" she stoically takes the hint and packs up her possessions and her girls, heading further westward. Her parting good gesture is to convince Hodiak he should remain in town with Garland.

Said the *New York Times:* ". . . and Angela Lansbury, pouty and pomaded, looks dazzling as the queen of the den." Graced with a fine music score by Johnny Mercer and Harry Warren and picture postcard sets,

the feature went to gross an eventual $4.35 million.

Angela's next picture, a decided contrast, was the low-keyed *The Hoodlum Saint* (1946). This black and white entry attempted (unsuccessfully) to make a dramatic star of swimming queen Esther Williams. When Army major William Powell returns to St. Louis after World War I, he is full of enthusiasm for the opportunities seemingly lying ahead. He attempts to return to his old journalist post, but America's life style has changed, and he had to alter his standards or sink into poverty. He later emerges as the cynical head of a corrupt power utility combine and makes a fortune. Then the stock market crash hits and he is again broke. Along the way, Powell romanced Williams, niece of a newspaperpaper publisher, who is aghast at his morals or lack of them. Not so upset is blonde torch singer Angela, unperturbed by Powell's lack of acceptable values.

On one occasion Powell has taken a cynical interest in St. Dismas, the good thief who reforms wrongdoers. When he is ill in the hospital, Angela is talked into an intriguing scheme to have Powell's poolroom cronies (Rags Ragland, Frank McHugh, Slim Summerville, James Gleason) take up a well-organized collection for St. Dismas and then to abscond with the fund. She queries, "Isn't it sort of risky to be fooling around with religion?" and she is right. Powell finds himself morally regenerated and suitable for Williams' serious attention.

As Dusty Milland, the other woman, Angela functioned well, once again projecting as a well-seasoned creature, far older than her real-life years. She had the opportunity to sing such standards as "Sweetheart," "How Am I to Know" and "If I Had You," and exuded a believable sensuality as she sought to draw Powell to her side. But the film as a whole was tedious and pat, well-intentioned but crammed full of unwieldy dialogue.

Angela had not been included in the studio's all-star musical revue *The Ziegfeld Follies of 1946* (in production since 1944), but she was among those in the less-than-satisfactory elephantine extravaganza *Till The Clouds Roll By* (1946) which speciously purported to be the biography of song composer Jerome Kern. As played by Robert Walker, Kern's life seemed to be the very height of vapidness, hopefully the fault of scriptwriters and director, and not reality. The film's framework is established when at the opening of the Broadway musical *Show Boat,* composer Kern thinks back on his long road to success. He recalls having had to go to England in the early 1900s, determined to outsmart the big-shot New York producers who insisted the only good song hits came from abroad. While wandering through London one evening, he stops in a music hall, and lo and behold, there is Angela performing a num-

With Judy Garland in *The Harvey Girls* (MGM, 1946).

With William Powell in *The Hoodlum Saint* (MGM, 1946).

ber ("How'd You Like to Spoon with Me") on a gigantic swing. Howard Barnes of the *New York Herald-Tribune* decided Angela's musical interpretation was "strictly Hollywood 1946."

Because Angela was categorized as a character actress at MGM,* she was billed in *Till the Clouds Roll by* in the same guest performer, lower case "also" capacity as Gower Champion, Ray McDonald, Cyd Charisse, and June Allyson (who was most effective in her rendition of "Cleopatterer"). The film's star cluster included Dinah Shore, Van Johnson, Tony Martin, Lena Horne, Frank Sinatra, Lucille Bremer, Kathryn Grayson, and Judy Garland who stole the limelight as Marilyn Miller, performing "Who?" and "Sunny."

At one point Angela wisely observed about herself: "I have a period face. And I have a wasp waist which is rather ideal for costume drama. I always have felt right in costumes. . . ." Because of her figure, face, her British breeding and her histrionic abilities, Angela was seriously considered for Twentieth Century-Fox's attempted historical blockbuster *Forever Amber* (1947), but it was Peggy Cummins and then Linda Darnell who played the role. Angela shunned off the disappointment with the quip: "Whatever would I have used for bosoms?"

But then Albert Lewin, who had been so impressed with Angela in *The Picture of Dorian Gray,* requested her on loan-out for his United Artists' production of

---

* In the early 1960s she would state: "There's always been joy, exuberance and fun in movie acting, but I have never been blinded by it. I had an opportunity to do all the things that would have led me to the glamorous side of a screen career, but I didn't want that."

The Private Affairs of Bel Ami (1947), purportedly based on the Guy de Maupassant costume drama of an 1880s Parisian scoundrel. As the second-billed Clotilde de Marelle, Angela is the parlor maid who has aspirations for a higher social station in life. When she encounters raffish Sanders, her heart is lost to the opportunity, although she later has occasion to regret her attraction ("what a brute you are"). But she is trapped by her inexplicable attachment for her cruel lover and masochistically resigns herself to her destiny ("as if I could ever stop loving you").

The essential fault with *The Private Affairs of Bel Ami* was the conceptual belief that 112 minutes of keyhole peeking at boulevardier Sanders's conquests and rejection of various femmes would hold the viewer spellbound. There is momentary interest in pathetic Folies dancer Marie Wilson, journalist's wife Ann Dvorak, publisher's wife Katherine Emery and her daughter Susan Douglas, all of whom succumb to leering Sanders's epigrammatic wit (Frances Dee is the only one who rejects him), but not enough to sustain the picture which sinks into repetitious variation and a hearty air of ennui. The period trappings would have been adequate enough for a "Playhouse 90" television special, but the entire production had an inescapable

In *Till the Clouds Roll By* (MGM, 1946).

With George Sanders in *The Private Affairs of Bel Ami* (UA, 1947).

seediness about it. This shabbiness was reflected by the presence of imposing screen personalities (Dee, Wilson, Dvorak, and particularly Warren William as the politician) struggling once more with inferior roles and materials.

In retrospect, Angela's role in *The Private Affairs of Bel Ami* was atypical. With her hair done in a bun, she was most comely, and her grasping nature was detailed with some sympathy. In her wild cafe dance with Sanders, in her intuitive knowledge that Sanders seeks more than she can provide ("What is it then you want in life?"), or when she slumps in despair as Sanders informs her of his forthcoming wedding to another (shattering her dreams of children they might have had in marriage together), Angela displayed a fine sense of full-bodied theatrics.

One of the advertising posters for this film showed Angela lying prone on the floor, gripping Sanders's leg as he walks out on her. The actress's friends tagged her "The Clutch."

Like her contemporary, Keenan Wynn, or the older Agnes Moorehead or veterans Frank Morgan, Lewis Stone, Glady Cooper and Ethel Barrymore, Angela was now considered by MGM as a stabilized, reliable supporting star, on hand to bolster the box office strength

of major productions. There was no longer—if there ever in fact had been—any pretentions of grooming her for the bigger and better things that her performances warranted. She had made an overt decision, both by attitude of mind (allowing herself to coast along until assigned a role and then digging into her characterization no matter how shallow the part) and body (not reducing down to a svelt, star-type figure) to accept the short shrift being handed her. MGM executives were too preoccupied with shepherding its stable of female stars like Lana Turner, Greer Garson, and Elizabeth Taylor to devote more than a paternalistic pat on the head to one like Angela who took everything in her stride so seemingly gracefully.

If Winter Comes (1948), a remake of a 1923 Fox film, was hogwash soap opera that had neither the clarity of a reasoned screenplay nor the conviction of fine direction to present its turgid tale in the needed grand manner. Instead it backed off into quietude at inappropriate moments as if ashamed of the sham it was weaving for the gullible public. In Penny Green, England, 1939, an idealistic textbook author, Walter Pidgeon, cannot make a proper go of his marriage to his demanding, snobbish wife (Angela, madeup and coiffed to be in her mid-thirties). Good-heartedly he engages local girl Janet Leigh to be a companion for elderly villager Dame May Whitty when her son is drafted into the army. When the youth is killed in service, Pidgeon and Leigh spend the night trying to comfort her, but Whitty dies from the shock. Later the villagers learn that Leigh is pregnant and assume that Pidgeon is to blame, as does Angela who divorces him. The ostracized girl commits suicide. At the investigation it remains for Deborah Kerr, who had loved Pidgeon

With Walter Pidgeon in *If Winter Comes* (MGM, 1948).

With Henry Blair and Margaret O'Brien in *Tenth Avenue Angel* (MGM, 1948).

for some time but had married a wealthy playboy instead (now dead), to testify in Pidgeon's behalf and later to declare her devotion to him.

In her third-billed role (a part played by Margaret Fielding in the silent version), Angela was approved for being ". . . quite believable and proper as the distrusting wife." (*New York Times*). It seemed a role Angela could perform in her sleep.

Tenth Avenue Angel (1948) marked the beginning of the end for Margaret O'Brien at MGM. She was going on eleven and had run the gamut of studio vehicles to exploit her precocious dramatics. This synthetic weeper was so inconsequential that even MGM dumped it onto the distribution market with very little build-up. Here, moppet O'Brien (playing an eight-year-old) is the daughter of unemployed pianist Warner Anderson and Phyllis Thaxter. She has been spoon-fed idealistic pap about the wonders of life, a philosophical cure-all indulged in by her impoverished parents. "Sweet" O'Brien's prime interest is to marry her schoolteacher aunt (Angela) to George Murphy. But no one has told the innocent that Murphy, a former taxi driver, has not really been on a world cruise but actually has just been released from prison. Thus the real reason O'Brien cannot persuade "Uncle" Murphy to wed Angela is his shame of his jail record. When O'Brien learns of Murphy's past, her world is shattered. She loses faith in her relatives and in her mentor, blind, local newspaper seller Rhys Williams. However, the indulgent screenwriters were able to back out of the plot corner by having O'Brien take pity on her mother, who is fighting a life and death battle after a premature childbirth. She invokes the blessing of God by journey-

ing to a local stockyard and inducing a cow to kneel in prayer with her (another cure-all spun to her by her family) and all ends happily.

Angela's first class screen production in a long spell was Frank Capra's *State of the Union* (1948), based on the Pulitzer Prize-winning Broadway play (765 performances) by Howard Lindsay and Russell Crouse. Originally Gary Cooper and Claudette Colbert had been slated to star in the feature, but contractual disputes resulted in Spencer Tracy and Katharine Hepburn being substituted in this Liberty Pictures production for MGM release.

The politically-oriented plot finds idealistic plane manufacturer Tracy being groomed for the Republican presidential nomination, bolstered by such staunch party supporters as Angela, the shrewd forty-six year old daughter of a newspaper tycoon, and by old-line politico Adolph Menjou. The latter will only offer his expertise and backing if Tracy's estranged, down-to-earth wife (Hepburn) is persuaded to pose as his happily married spouse to make him more appealing to the American voter.

As the campaign gathers momentum, Tracy finds himself sacrificing all his standards for the sake of the party platform, a situation he dislikes but accepts as the thought of actually becoming president seems more appealing. All along, Angela has nurtured a growing love for Tracy, which arouses Hepburn's jealousy and leads her at a political dinner to lambast those corrupt associates of Tracy who have led him astray. Tracy sees the moral light, and on a national political radio broadcast he apologizes to the public for his essential dishonesty and withdraws from the race.

The movie version of *State of the Union* did not pack the punch of its stage original, wherein the playwrights had meticulously updated the political references on an almost daily basis. Since the picture appeared in 1948, the year of a real presidential race, MGM was not about to offend any important national figures, and the screenplay was diluted accordingly in its barbs. Nevertheless, with the Tracy-Hepburn box office lure and the reputation of the Broadway play version behind it, this picture made a good showing in distribution.

As for the middle-aged woman who cares more for Tracy to win the campaign than for her to win his heart, Angela was excellent as the mild villainess. It was a more mature, full-bodied version of a screen role Eve Arden in the 1940s or Helen Vinson in the 1930s might have played. However, Angela's portrayal was a more well-rounded characterization due both to the screenplay delineation and to Angela's ability to be both a caustic foil and a sexually-oriented human being at the same time. *Time* magazine printed: "Only Lansbury,

With Lewis Stone in *State of the Union* (MGM, 1948).

whom Metro has long dieted on lean parts, does any real acting. As the adderish lady publisher, she sinks in a fine fang." *Variety's* only criticism of her performance as the maneuvering figure behind political bigwigs was her ". . . frequently unintelligible speech." Maybe it was the rapid-fire delivery approach of director Capra (trying to match the smooth quick dialogue rapport between Tracy-Hepburn) or her efforts to make a full assault on eliminating her English accent that stumped Angela in this, her second screen role as an American. Unlike the play (in which Kay Johnson had performed the Kay Thorndyke role), Angela's screen character too often was required to be haughty and platonic, making it rather difficult to believe in her power over Tracy. It was stretching a point to have the studio's advertising campaign publicize Angela as ". . . the sleek blonde armful who tries to break up a romance."

With Spencer Tracy and Van Johnson in *State of the Union*.

When it was announced that MGM was preparing a new version of Alexander Dumas's *The Three Musketeers* (1948), Angela made it known that she wanted to portray the evil Milady de Winters, but it had already been decided that the George Sidney production would be geared to box office luster rather than good casting, and Lana Turner was assigned to the costume drama in the desired part. There was lilting color to highlight the lush settings and costumes, but little else to recommend in the final picture. Angela donned royal robes as the fifth-billed Queen Anne of Austria, wife of France's King Louis XIII (Frank Morgan). She has imprudently bestowed two diamond studs on her British duke-lover, John Sutton, which D'Artagnan (Gene Kelly and his three musketeers Van Heflin, Gig Young, and Robert Coote) is commissioned to retrieve, overcoming the obstacles of dastardly Cardinal Richelieu (Vincent Price) and his wily accomplice, Turner.

The MGM ads proclaimed Angela "Dazzling as her gilded palace. For her men dared a thousand perils." However, the *New York Herald-Tribune* criticized her for ". . . looking more the plump courtesan than the queen." Regardless, in her finery Angela was resplendent, and she demonstrated a far greater flare for over-sized characterization in this historical tapestry than either Turner or June Allyson, the latter cast as the ill-fated Constance Bonancieux, the wife of D'Artagnan's landlord and a confidential servant of Angela who is poisoned by a spiteful Turner.

By 1948 the film industry was engulfed by the competing television medium, and to combat the tough rival, MGM reshuffled its executive lineup, in particular, bringing in Dore Schary as executive vice president in charge of production as he had been at RKO. Sixty-three-year-old studio head Louis B. Mayer found himself being pushed aside as out of touch with current trends in the business. It was at this point that Angela, as she phrases it ". . . began to get lost in the shuffle." By now "I found being under contract terribly confining." It seems that after five years in the business, Angela was realizing at long last the tarantula nature of the profession, and that if she wished to continue in the craft, she could no longer tread water as had been her practice under the Mayer regime. But her career stagnation had already set in.

It was at a party given by Hurd Hatfield at his Ojai Valley home in 1947, that Angela met Peter Pullen Shaw, an Irish-born theatrical designer who had become a William Morris theatrical agent.* Angela said, "We

---

* He would later become an executive assistant to Robert Weitman and Benjamin Thau at MGM in the mid-1950s, and a decade later he would return to William Morris in an executive capacity.

With John Sutton in *The Three Musketeers* (MGM, 1948).

had a very slow sort of courtship. Peter had a little boy, David. And I'd been burnt." But eventually (August 12, 1949), Angela and Shaw were married at the Chapel of St. Columbia's Church House, Lennox Gardens, London.

Meanwhile, Angela was tossed into a thankless role in the antiseptic *Red Danube* (1949), one of Dore Schary's message pictures, which paid token acknowledgment to the rising rift between the free world and the iron curtain countries. Set in 1945, British army colonel Walter Pidgeon is transferred from Rome to Vienna, along with his staff, including adjutant Peter Lawford, subaltern Angela, and private Melville Cooper. They are billeted at a convent supervised by mother superior Ethel Barrymore. Pidgeon is ordered to cooperate with the United Nations' forced repatriation of Soviet citizenry who have found themselves in the free world and would prefer to remain in detention camps than return to their iron curtain homelands. Pidgeon follows orders down the line, although he intellectually finds the policies of his Soviet counterpart (Louis Calhern) suspect. After Lawford brings the case of escaped Soviet Ballerina Janet Leigh to his attention (she eventually kills herself rather than be sent back to Russia), Pidgeon has a change of heart and refuses to carry out his "inhuman" orders. He is relieved of his command, but by the finale, he has been reassigned to humanize the army in England.

Angela was almost too sparkling as the plain Jane junior subaltern, dressed in uniform throughout the picture. Her secondary role required her to portray the efficient worker and maintain a chipper attitude, even though she is carrying a crush for Lawford. There was not much to be said for her window dressing role, other than she ". . . fits pertly into the part of a subaltern assisting Pidgeon in his work" (*Variety*).

With Henry Wilcoxon in *Samson and Delilah* (Paramount 1949).

It was producer-director Cecil B. DeMille who made cinematic use of Angela's screen potential, left untapped by MGM. He cast her in his major historical extravaganza *Samson and Delilah,* released by Paramount in 1949. In the $3.2 million technicolor epic, Angela is the aristocratic Semadar, of the Philistine nobility in 1100 B.C. in the land of Dan on the isle of Crete. When shepherd Samson (Victor Mature) kills a marauding lion and saves the life of the Saran of Gaza (George Sanders), he is granted permission to court Angela. But at a tribal feast, the Philistine Ahtur (Henry Wilcoxon) objects to Angela's suitor. Stirred on by her wily younger sister (Hedy Lamarr), the wedding banquet turns into a wild fight as the guests revile the Danite. In the course of the melee, Angela is an accidental victim. She is pinned to a wall by a spear that pierces her body (a visual sight long remembered by Lansbury fans).* *Samson and Delilah,* certainly no dramatic triumph, still proved to be a gaudy box office bonanza and to date, after several lucrative reissues, has grossed $11.5 million.

Bosley Crowther of the *New York Times,* seemingly no friend of Angela, observed again in his review of her in *Samson and Delilah:* ". . . [she] is a plump and pouting doll, . . ." With her golden hair in regal curls and her bare-midriff wedding outfit, Angela had the opportunity to show all of Hollywood that she was no mere dowdy character actress.

With Robert Coote and Walter Pidgeon in *The Red Danube* (MGM, 1949).

---

* Angela has said: "People ask me to this day if it hurt. With DeMille, everything was that real. I feel sorry for actors who never worked with him. He was an experience. Taught me how to throw a javelin. 25 yards and I can still hit a bull's eye."

In her Hollywood years, Angela had performed on occasion on radio but never with any tremendous impact. She was heard on such programs as "The Theatre Guild of the Air" (ABC) in *Gold* (March 16, 1947) with Raymond Massey, in 1949 with Philip Friend in *Pride And Prejudice* (NBC), on "The Theatre Guild of the Air's" *The Voysey Inheritance* (November 12, 1950) with Douglas Fairbanks, Jr., and on the same series' *Dear Brutus* (May 4, 1952) with David Niven.

It was in 1950, after making *Kind Lady* (1951), her last picture under her MGM contract, that Angela and her husband made a trip to England to see if the work scene there might be more favorable. But after three months they returned to Hollywood, where each of them continued to experience difficulty in escalating their careers.

The psychological melodrama *Kind Lady* was released in August, 1951 with Ethel Barrymore in a rare screen leading role. It was based on the Edward Chodorov play of 1934 which had starred Grace George, and it had been filmed the following year by MGM with Aline MacMahon in the title part. The new version of the thriller was again set in 1900s London, with kindly, elderly spinster Barrymore taking unscrupulous artist Maurice Evans under wing. He is actually a confidence man who has set his sights on gaining control of her valuable art treasure. His scheme is to cut her off from her friends and relatives in the outside world by convincing everyone she is senile. To assist in his plan, he insinuates cockney Angela into Barrymore's household as a maid, with her unprincipled husband Kennan Wynn as the new handyman. Evans is almost successful in his plot, but bank clerk John Williams becomes suspicious of the situation, leading to Evans's undoing.

As the callous accomplice, cold-blooded enough to help Evans do Barrymore in for the sake of money, *Variety* rated Angela ". . . excellent in the matter-of-fact way she goes about her part in the villainy."

Thus at age twenty-six, Angela found herself forced to compete strenuously for screen work in the freelance Hollywood world of 1951. She was in a peculiar artistic situation. Most people in the industry who associated her name as a top character actress assumed she was far older than her real chronological age. Her performances in *Gaslight, The Picture of Dorian Gray* and *State of the Union* seemed a generation ago when Hollywood was still Hollywood. And now there was a lack of prime character roles, even for those performers who had stayed on top of the scene by ingratiating themselves with studio and independent producers and casting agents. For Angela, who had finally decided it was time to act her age on screen, it meant accepting assignments that were far from the cream of the crop.

With Sherlee Collier, Keenan Wynn, and Maurice Evans in *Kind Lady* (MGM, 1951).

As a maturing ingenue, her name had a minimum of box office lure.

Mutiny (1952) was an expensively mounted United Artists production, dealing with the War of 1812. American naval officer Mark Stevens is ordered to escort a $10 million gold shipment from the French, designated to assist America's fight against the British. Aboard his barricade-breaking ship are First Officer Patric Knowles, himself a cashiered British navy captain, and Angela, Knowles's greedy sweetheart, who soon sides with the rebellious crew anxious to abscond with the gold. Angela appeared to enjoy this lightweight romp. She photographed well in Technicolor, managing to look pretty as well as very indignant at times. Again she dominated, without seeming to be bossy. While

With Patric Knowles in *Mutiny* (UA, 1952).

Variety thought most of the cast wooden, it said of Angela: ". . . [she] is attractive and reads her lines crisply, . . ."

In early 1952, Angela gave birth to her first child, Anthony. By early summer, she ventured into the summer stock circuit, where on the basis of her movie name (matronly matinee audiences never forget their past favorites), she could command $1,000 weekly. Angela toured the citronella showtops for six weeks in Louis Verneuil's Washington-set comedy *Affairs of State* and in the Howard Lindsay-Russell Crouse *Remains to Be Seen,* which had starred Janis Paige on Broadway for 198 performances.

In stock Angela played the lead in *Remains to Be Seen,* but in the MGM movie (1953), studio contractee star June Allyson portrayed her part, Jody Revere, a midwestern band singer. Park Avenue apartment house manager Van Johnson wires Allyson to come to New York to attend to the estate of her murdered uncle, a man she despised so much she refuses his sizable bequest to her. It is not long before she is scampering about (in two songs and a dance) with Johnson, himself a frustrated jazz drummer.

Involved in the case are Louis Calhern as the deceased's mercenary attorney, shady house doctor John Beal, and Angela, the brunette "other woman." Allyson takes an immediate dislike to strong-willed Angela, the latter standing to gain a portion of the dead man's estate if Allyson withdraws her claim (Angela had interested the deceased in a scheme for financing her bogus international language program). To spite Angela, Allyson decides to accept the inheritance and then distribute it to real charities. But Angela is not so easily dismissed. There is a secret door panel connecting her

With June Allyson in *Remains to Be Seen* (MGM, 1953).

apartment in the adjacent building to that of the deceased's where Allyson has taken up residence. The miniature anti-climax has Angela appearing at Allyson's apartment one night, putting her into a trance, and leading her to a high balcony, intending that the girl should fall to her death. But it is Angela who ends up being murdered and stuffed into a closet by the story's true villain. *Remains to Be Seen* came at the tail end of the once-popular Allyson-Johnson screen teaming, and the feature was pushed out onto the market, in some situations as the bottom half of double bills.

The most productive and satisfying event that occurred to Angela in the 1953–1955 period was the birth of her daughter Deirdre in 1953. In the helter-skelter movie world of the 1950s, Angela was not making much headway. In fact, in this phase of her professional career, she was accepting anything that would bring in money, regardless of how much she despised the work.

Life at Stake (a.k.a. *Key Man*) (1954) was a cheapie production, typical of the tawdry fodder shoved off by independent companies for a quick buck in the declining double bill theatrical market. Glamorous, blonde Angela and her husband (Douglass Dumbrille) dupe penniless building contractor Keith Andes into a phony building deal. Their gambit is to heavily insure partner Andes and then have him murdered. Even when Andes discovers their ruse, he cannot convince the police or anyone of his plight, and he is forced to fend for himself to stay alive. Neither the tongue-in-cheek humor nor the black-heartedness of the melodrama sustained this B picture with its ludicrous climax which sees the villains disposed of in a most preposterous manner.

Angela acknowledges her two 1955 releases as the lowest point of her screen career. *A Lawless Street* (1955) was not a bad entry in the Randolph Scott-Harry Joe Brown co-produced western series of features, but the sagebrush tale offered little histrionic opportunity for Angela. She is the dance hall entertainer in Medicine Bend, Colorado, who has wearied of her husband's (Scott) preoccupation with his job as marshal of the rugged community. She leaves him, and chastised Scott decides to retire. But trouble is pending, and his conscience will not allow him to leave a situation uncompleted, particularly when a hired gunman has already tried to eliminate him. The inevitable rally of the good versus Warner Anderson and his mob occurs, with Scott emerging victorious. The recalcitrant Angela returns to hubby, who now can start a less hazardous career in peace. The finale finds the couple riding off into the Technicolor sunset together. One can only imagine what thoughts were coursing through Angela's mind as she endured the ignomy of filming this scene.

Over at Universal, Angela obtained a supporting

Angela Lansbury in 1954.

With Warner Anderson in *A Lawless Street* (Columbia, 1955).

role in Tony Curtis's latest swashbuckling juvenilia *The Purple Mask* (1955), a Cinemascope-color variation of *The Scarlet Pimpernel*. The story is set in 1802 Paris where Angela runs a millinary shop which is a front for espionage activities against the Napoleonic regime. Starlet Coleen Miller is employed in Mme. Angela's establishment and is amazed to discover that seeming fop Curtis is really the rapier-wielding Purple Mask who rescues condemned nobles from the guillotine. Others trapped into this escapist fare were George Dolenz as Miller's father and a Royalist leader, John Hoyt as the minister of police, and Dan O'Herlihy as Bonaparte's secret agent. The *New York Herald-Tribune* thought ". . . the movie may keep American girlhood in swoon for a while," but neither it nor the other reviewers had much to say about Angela's wallflower role.

Angela's career perked up in 1956 with *The Court Jester,* her first major feature in five years. Gordon Gow in his book *Hollywood in the Fifties* (1971) ranks this "The best [Danny] Kaye movie of the decade, . . ." The combination of Kaye's tongue-twisting dialogue and visual gags, a fine supporting cast, regal costuming, and setting displayed in Vistavision and color combined harmoniously to offer a diverting romp in a period when most screen comedy was staid and lackluster. As a spoof on swashbuckling screen fare, *The Court Jester* is set in medieval England where dastardly Cecil Parker has usurped the throne, disposing of all the royal family save the infant prince. The latter has been bundled off to the forest, where the Black Fox gang have banded together to restore the rightful heir to the throne. Naturally, it is dimwitted, timorous Kaye who is selected to infiltrate the palace and spy on the regal goings-on.

Posing as a court jester, Kaye gains entrance to the imposing castle and suddenly finds himself in great demand. Princess Angela has refused to wed a powerful Scot war lord, and being bored with her tedious existence, would not mind a royal dalliance with Kaye. Once her spellbinding witch-maid Mildred Natwick casts a spell on buffoon Kaye, he forgets his hoydenish forest maiden love (Glynis Johns). Unwittingly Kaye assists Sir Basil Rathbone in eliminating some of his court rivals which does not endear the jester to King Parker. In fact, to eliminate him, Parker rushes Kaye through the knighthood induction ceremony within a speedy twelve-hour period, so he can be entered and disposed of in a pending tournament.

This burlesque of the age of chivalry and ladies fair had a modest array of songs (five) to spell the high-keyed hokum and the film did nicely in its distribution. For Angela, fourth-billed as Princess Gwendolyn, it was a much-needed opportunity to remind Hollywood she was still very much around, available, and in good physical shape for a veteran character actress now at the ripe age of thirty. Her assignment in *The Court Jester* was reminiscent of her costumed appearances in *The Three Musketeers* and *Samson and Delilah*. What was unique about Angela's performance in this Kaye vehicle was that somewhere in her career she had developed a flipness to her delivery which came from within her and not from the Norman Panama-Melvin Frank screenplay. This characteristic separated her from the run of wishy-washy picture postcard heroines or over-energetic second female leads who usually lacked humor in their portrayals.

Please Murder Me (1956) ranks as an important milestone in Angela's screen career, although few at

With Danny Kaye in *The Court Jester* (Paramount, 1956).

With Mildred Natwick in *The Court Jester.*

the time were either aware of the poverty row picture or would connect the Angela in this picture with her earlier nasty young miss of *Gaslight* or the later diabolical mother in *The Manchurian Candidate* (1962). Here Angela had to combine a cold-blooded screen bitchiness so often portrayed by Lizabeth Scott in the 1940s with a neurotic possessiveness often seen in

With Coleen Miller, Donald Randolph, and Stephen Bekassy in *The Purple Mask* (Universal, 1955).

screen portrayals of Barbara Stanwyck in the 1950s. In *Please Murder Me,* attorney Raymond Burr is hired to defend Angela, accused of murdering her husband (Dick Foran), who was Burr's best friend. Being in love with Angela prompts Burr to fight harder to prove her innocence, which he does, only to learn from a delayed letter from the now-dead husband that Angela was guilty after all. Burr had been planning to leave town with her, but Angela has her own plans. The finale leaves Burr very much dead, and she very much trapped by a conveniently running tape recorder.

It was in the 1956–1957 period that Angela became extremely active on television, for the simple reason "It paid awfully well and didn't take me away from home." It was the era of the anthology drama series,

In *Please Murder Me* (DCA, 1956).

both live and on film, and there was a terrific need for accomplished performers, those with a "name" but who for one reason or another would not charge *too* demanding a salary and could function professionally under the hurried-up production timetable of the video medium. After a few initial outings on such live variety shows as the "George Gobel Show" (1955, NBC), Angela plunged fully into the dramatic guest starring gambit. For example, on "Star and the Story" she was in the episode "The Force of Circumstances" (April 11, 1956), on "Screen Director's Playhouse" in "Claire" (April 25, 1956) as George Montgomery's second wife who must cope with a malevolent cat, and on "Celebrity Playhouse" (NBC) in "Empty Arms" (May 29, 1956) opposite William Bishop. In "Studio 57"'s (ABC) "The Brown Leather Case" (June 14, 1956) the *Hollywood Reporter* noted: "John Sutton and Angela

Lansbury, the boy-girl duo, perform competently despite the staticy nature of the script." In "Climax"'s (CBS) "Bury Me Later" (September 6, 1956), she played opposite Boris Karloff. Then there was "Celebrity Playhouse"'s "Deborah" (April 7, 1957) with Zachary Scott, and on "Climax"'s "The Devil's Brood" (December 5, 1957) Angela was the daughter of an Australian sheep rancher who encounters law breakers John Erickson and Stephen McNally.

Perhaps the most profound and unexpected turn of events in Angela's professional career was British director Peter Glenville's offer for Angela to have a top-featured role in the Broadway version of *Hotel Paradiso* (1957). She was tempted because: "I adore comedy. Such a change after the harpies and heavies Hollywood cast me in. This play was offered me on a platter."

The French bedroom farce *Hotel Paradiso* (or *L'Hotel du Libre Exchange*) by Georges Feydeau and Maurice Desvallieres was first performed at the Palais Royal Theatre in Paris in 1886 and was thereafter acknowledged to be the forerunner of all subsequent sex farces, even to *Up in Mabel's Room*. *Hotel Paradiso* had been revived over the years and in 1956 had enjoyed a nice run with a cast headed by Alec Guinnes and Irene Worth. Because the vaguely similar *The Matchmaker* had done so well on the Broadway stage at this time, it was decided to prepare *Hotel Paradiso* for the American theater, with Glenville again staging his adaptation.

Hotel Paradiso opened in Washington, D.C. at the National Theatre for a three-week engagement on March 16, 1957. Set in 1910 Paris, the farce concerns middle-aged builder Bert Lahr, tired of his fierce bag of a wife (Vera Pearce), arranging an evening rendezvous with Angela, the mildly over-sexed wife of his best friend, architect Arthur Treacher (replaced during tryouts by John Emery). Their assignation is to take place at the nefarious inn called the Hotel Paradiso, a seemingly out-of-the-way spot. No sooner does the

With Bert Lahr and director Peter Glenville at a rehearsal for *Hotel Paradiso* (1957).

Angela Lansbury with her children Deirdre and Anthony, 1957.

theatre." (*N.Y. Times*). A large chunk of the critical praise went to stammering master farceur Lahr, who had not enjoyed such a fruitful stage role in many years. Angela, as the arm-throwing Marcelle, took Broadway by mild surprise. With a perfection of her comedy manner from *The Court Jester* (and her years of experience in and around Restoration comedy), Angela could utter potentially flat lines in deadpan. "Well sir, you may be rather plain—but you certainly have a way with women," says Angela to the confounded Lahr, giving the right inflection to her reading, which invested the dialogue with innuendoes and plot references that turn the words into laugh makers. The years had taught Angela to effectively combine charm with a keen sense of satirical humor.

Walter Kerr reported in the *New York Herald-Tribune:* "Angela Lansbury, ravishing in that flat-top hair-do that made the Gibson Girl glorious, sweeps on [and off, a thousand times] in yards and yards of fluffy pink, dives at an enemy like a cat caught in a windmill, and generally demonstrates that she is a very crisp chick with a snappish line." Even the less easily impressed Thomas Dash of *Women's Wear Daily* observed: "Angela Lansbury, looking supple, shapely and sensuous, is capital as a frantic lady who regrets her febrile adventure into extra-marital amour." It was George Oppenheimer of *Newsday* who prophetically expressed: "She endows slapstick humor with both decorativeness and dignity and remains strikingly beautiful even when she has a man's high hat pulled over her face. Miss Lansbury is quite a dish and I trust she will be served to us frequently in the future."

Hotel Paradiso ran for only 108 performances, a modest showing which should have been hyped into a longer stand with a more ingenious advertising campaign behind the production.*

Performing on Broadway served Angela well in several ways. She learned much about her acting craft that moviemaking chores had overlooked. John Lahr in his biography of his late father, *Notes on a Cowardly Lion* (1969), would quote Angela as saying: "He taught me about the signposts and props that hold up a funny situation and how you build it. The rules have to do with movement. I can never forget him. He'd come off stage worrying like a bird dog. He defended and protected those comedy moments which he knew were sure laughs like a soldier with a bayonet. And we learned; none of us ever dreamed of breaking the rules. We learned therefore, how to get our own laughs! Now

nervous Lahr arrive at the hotel, then he encounters one problem after another, which hinders any attempt to make love to the willing but timid Angela. If it is not a peeping Tom bellboy boring a hole through the wall (and almost through Lahr's derriere), there is somebody else at the door seeking help or refuge from pursuing parties. Thus the entire evening is spent dashing in and out of rooms avoiding Lahr's wife and friends and knowing servants (like maid Sandre Lee) who just happen to find themselves at the inn. The only thing poor frustrated Lahr gets to embrace at the hotel is a hot water bag, and all Angela has to show for her marathon chase about the hotel is soot on her nose and a dazed look.

Hotel Paradiso, with its combination of stylized theatrical performances, double takes, and slapstick would have done justice to a Marx Brothers outing, and it endeared itself to the theater-going public. It was a hit in Washington. *Variety* noted: "Miss Lansbury is a fine foil as his [Lahr's] almost paramour."

Hotel Paradiso rolled into New York at the Henry Miller Theatre on April 11, 1957, where it was acclaimed as "enormously amusing in a vein of sheer

---

* Peter Glenville would eventually translate *Hotel Paradiso* into a screen farce (1966) with Alec Guinness and Gina Lollabrigida. It flopped badly.

on the stage with *Mame* or Shelagh Delaney's *A Taste of Honey,* if I didn't get a laugh or someone else missed a laugh, I know what to tell them."

Another aspect of Angela's New York stay with *Hotel Paradiso* was her introduction to the social world of Shubert's Alley. As a top-featured personality in a respectable main stem production, she now had entres to all the fashionable celebrity spots haunted by theater denizens, participating for the first time in a social swirl that had been unavailable to her as just a Hollywood figure. Angela rented a Fifth Avenue duplex for her Manhattan stay and it soon became a new show business gathering spot. The social aspect to her new theatre career was an ego-satisfying experience. Angela was beginning to realize just how stifled she had been (and allowed herself to become) while at MGM and in the dog days of the early 1950s when nothing professionally worthwhile had materialized for her.

Nevertheless, after the run of *Hotel Paradiso* the homebody spirit of Angela's nature made her more than happy to return to the Malibu home (24818 Pacific Coast Highway) where the Shaws had now moved.

With her restored marquee name, Angela found it far easier to obtain movie assignments in prestigious films. She took up where she had left off with *State of the Union,* nearly ten years prior, in top character roles. While it was still frustrating to a degree (the star bug had not quite bitten Angela) to be the polished support behind lead players, it was comforting to receive high salaries for offering her expertise to bolster major pictures.

The Long Hot Summer (1958) in cinemascope and color is the best of the multi-episoded features produced by Jerry Wald at Twentieth Century-Fox in the 1950s. Based on an amalgam of William Faulkner's short stories and novels, director Martin Ritt (who had panned rich gold for Fox with his steaming *Peyton Place*) turned to the South to explore the latent sensuality and passions in rural Frenchman's Bend, Mississippi, run by gargantuan Orson Welles. His fumbling son Anthony Franciosa, wed to pert Lee Remick, is a weakling suffocating in his father's enormous shadow, while the spinster daughter (Joanne Woodward) is spunky enough to stand up to domineering Welles, but can find no worthwhile man of her own, that is, until alleged barnburner Paul Newman wanders into town. The roughneck proves both a match for empire-wielding Big Daddy Welles and virile enough for love-hungry Woodward.

Angela was sixth-billed as Minnie, who runs the local hotel and who for years has been the discreet mistress of sixty-year-old Welles. Her on-screen scenes were brief, but she invested them with an authority and warmth

that was entirely credible, as was her impersonation of a forty-year-old woman who is a little thick around the waist but still fetching. It is Angela who keeps hammering away with her magnolia accent at the obstreperous Welles to make an honest woman of her. At the big summer charity bazaar she persuades him to wed her, and the finale finds them in togetherness on the veranda at Welles's homestead with the other couples suitably paired off for an upbeat ending. *Variety* penned: "Angela Lansbury was inspired casting for Welles' romantic vis-a-vis, she gives it humor and tenderness." The *New York Times* described Angela as ". . . a good old fleshy doll."*

In complete contrast was Angela's other 1958 release, MGM's *The Reluctant Debutante,* based on William Douglas Home's two-year-running London hit, which had had a modest Broadway stay in 1956. Its farcical premise was a sideswipe at the British social scene in general, and in particular, the rigmarole involved in the debutante syndrome. As handled by Vincente Minnelli, it was a stylish Metrocolor widescreen pastiche, short on substance, but adroitly played by fellow Britishers Rex Harrison, his actress wife Kay Kendall, and Angela. The movie presents the high-born Harrison-Kendall team welcoming their stepdaughter Sandra Dee home from a whirl of American education. They are aghast to learn she has fallen madly in love with drummer John Saxon, an obvious breach of etiquette, since they fully intend she should in due course

With Paul Newman, Orson Welles, and Joanne Woodward in *The Long, Hot Summer* (20th-Fox, 1958).

---

* *The Long Hot Summer,* one of the heftier money-makers of the year, was eventually translated into a mid 1960s video series with Ruth Roman playing a modified version of Angela's role.

With Orson Welles in *The Long, Hot Summer*.

wed stuffy Peter Myers, a member of Her Majesty's Horse Guard. While Dee is pushed into a round of coming-out parties on the London social scene, her parents maneuver, in often slapstick fashion, to keep the maturing young lady away from Saxon.

Angela, fifth-billed as Mabel Claremont (Brenda Forbes's Broadway role) is not about to let such a good catch as Myers get away from her equally eligible daughter (Diane Clare), and she embarks on a strategic campaign to woo the bachelor to Clare's side. Whether lounging in bed in her elegantly furnished boudoir and ever so politely talking to her competitor (Kendall) while picking her nose or making snide remarks at fashionable parties, Angela etched a full-bodied caricature of the bitchy aristocrat, determined to come out first in this contest. If it can be called winning, she does. After Harrison-Kendall discover Saxon is a true-blue Italian duke, fumbling Myers is thrown to the wind and

With Kay Kendall and Rex Harrison in *The Reluctant Debutante* (MGM, 1958).

hastily snapped up by scheming Angela for her child. Reported Kate Cameron in her three-star *New York Daily News* review: "The performances of Angela Lansbury and Peter Myers are the only ones that come up to expectation and give the audience cause for hearty laughter."

Angela had no 1959 theatrical features in release, but she was in evidence on television. On the annual Academy Awards show (April 6, 1959, NBC), she, Dana Wynters, and Joan Collins sang "It's Bully." The satirical song sung by the trio of Anglo movie players referred to the "alarming" number of Britishers receiving Oscar nominations in the American-based yearly award fest. It was strange to think that Angela, who had first made her impact on American film audiences in the 1940s, should be coupled with two mid-1950s English screen imports, seemingly a generation away in movie orientation. Yet there was only five and eight years (respectively) difference in their chronological age.

In mid-1960, Angela agreed to return again to the stage. ". . . I said no at first [to producer David Merrick]. I couldn't imagine how to arrange it domestically. I didn't want to leave Malibu for New York in the winter. I wanted to hole in, garden, cook, and just generally be at home. Then I had a call from the director [Tony Richardson] who said what a wonderful part it was—the part of the girl's irresponsible mother. Then Merrick came out. He's a very persuasive man, but I made very steep demands. He met them. So then I had to do it, and I got terribly enthusiastic." Part of Angela's enthusiasm for *A Taste of Honey,* which had just enjoyed a recent London stage success with Avis Binnage as the mother and Frances Cuka as the daughter, was that the American edition would have a pre-Broadway engagement in Los Angeles. It would offer Angela an excellent showcase to demonstrate to the short-sighted Hollywood producers what they had been overlooking in her all these years.

Rehearsals commenced in August, 1960, in Los Angeles, and the play opened there September 6, 1960, at the Biltmore Theatre. The two-act serious comedy had been written by nineteen-year-old Shelagh Delaney of Lancashire, England, and concerned a similarly-aged girl living in a railroad flat in Lancashire. She is affection-starved and receives no love from her selfish, slutty forty-year-old mother (Angela) who has no qualms about ditching her daughter to marry a drunken playboy (Nigel Davenport). The girl thinks she has found romance with a black sailor, but he leaves her pregnant, and it remains for a homosexual boy to offer her the mothering she never received from Angela. Richardson's offbeat direction had Bobby Short's jazz

In *A Taste of Honey* (1960).

combo playing onstage throughout the performance, giving mood to Delaney's wry and wistful dialogue. The various audience asides gave the potentially drab study a relevant intimacy. *Variety* reported of Angela's Los Angeles performance: "As the irresponsible mother who believes she owes her daughter, she plays principally for laughs, and gets them." The *Hollywood Reporter* wrote: "Angela Lansbury, playing with genial ease against the steel tension of Miss (Joan) Plowright, is objectively despicable, but so rich a treat she cannot be despised."

A Taste of Honey moved to Cincinnati for two weeks and then opened on Broadway October 11, 1960, at the Lyceum Theatre. Neither the jaded theater critics nor sedate playgoers were quite prepared for Delaney's racy dialogue or its bitter treatment of unsavory characters who emerge as human and not just ugly like the seedy set of the play.

The critics were favorably impressed by Angela's acting range: ". . . [she] plays the mother with quicksilver that does not conceal the seaminess of her life" (*New York Times*). *Variety* praised: "Miss Lansbury is excellent as the trollop without maternal feelings, a boozer, a pushover but herself a victim of her own badness. The part may be the screen gal's finest legit opportunity to date." Whitney Bolton in the *New York Morning Telegraph* lauded: "Angela Lansbury fairly drenches the role of the mother in perfection of characterization. She is tart, sweet, engulfing consideration and contemptuous disdain all in one, a mercurial misfit swinging between her heat for men and her chill for her child. This is [a] performance in full color and a heady flavor."

One intriguing aspect of Angela's *A Taste of Honey* performance was the merging of her theatrical acting with her own developing theater personality. Both blended into a new whole which reflected a seasoned maturity to Angela's histrionic approach. This transformation was particularly in evidence in her many asides in which she spoke of herself and life to the audience in a chummy, off-handed manner. That the chatty asides broke the spell of reality was jarring but almost forgivable for the added dimension it added to Angela's characterization.

The moody daughter asks: "You never go to the pictures?"

Angela: "I used to but the cinema has become more and more like the theatre, it's all mauling and muttering, can't hear what they're saying half the time and when you do it's not worth listening to. Look at that advertisement [pointing to a newspaper in front of her]. It's pornographic. In my opinion such a frank and open display of the female form can only induce little boys of all ages to add vulgar comments by pencil. I ask you, what sort of an inflated woman is that? She's got bosom, bosom, and still more bosom. I bet every inch of her

With Joan Plowright and Nigel Davenport in *A Taste of Honey*.

chest is worth its weight in gold. Let's have a look at you. I wonder if I could turn you into a mountain of voluptuous temptation?"

The daughter later prods her mother about her past:

Angela: "I was married to a Puritan—do you know what I mean?"

"And when I met your father I was as pure and unsullied as I fondly, and perhaps mistakenly, imagine you to be. It was the first time and though you can enjoy the second, the third and even the fourth time, there's no time like the first. . . . I'm off now. I've got to go and find my husband [Davenport]. Now don't sit here sulking all day."

By act II, scene II, Angela returns to the flat where Plowright is now living with her homosexual friend, Alexander Ray. Davenport has ditched Angela, and she has no where better to stop off for the present time. She is not disturbed by her past, present, or the unlikely prospects for the future. In her egocentricity, her little world revolves firmly around her every whim, a characteristic of the ghoul-mothers Angela would make famous in her screen roles of the 1960s.

Angela: "Anybody at home? Well, I'm back. You see, I couldn't stay away, could I? There's some flowers for you, Jo. The barrows are smothered in them. Oh! How I carried that lot from the bus stop I'll never know. The old place looks a bit more cheerful doesn't it? I say, there's a nice homey smell. Have you been doing a bit of baking? I'll tell you one thing, it's a lovely day for flitting."

The play ends on a sad note, as daughter has become more like mother, she too becoming more selfish, to a degree that she probably will never be able to enjoy marriage. She has also learned to repress any expression of affection by humor, a modus operandi once reserved just for her relationship with her mother. The girl still has a heart and a bit of soul, but one wonders for how long.

A Taste of Honey would run for 376 performances on Broadway, with Angela leaving the cast in the spring of 1961 and replaced by Hermione Baddeley, who would head the road company.* The Broadway version did not return a profit.

During the New York run, Angela again sublet a Fifth Avenue apartment, this time bringing her children Anthony and Deirdre to be with her while her husband remained on the West Coast. Despite the satisfaction offered Angela on the stage, she did not

---

* A British-made film version of *A Taste Of Honey* would appear in 1962 with Dora Bryan as the mother and Rita Tushingham as the daughter. It had a modest art house release in the United States.

find the work all that easy: "I like acting in movies better than on the stage, because you don't have to keep on and on with it. I'm a traitor to the cause. I don't indulge myself in the enjoyment of acting. I have a tremendous sense of duty about the theatre. For instance, I have a strong sense of guilt about being late. I become all professional as soon as I leave my home— as soon as I have my coat and am on my way. I feel I have to be early. And if I don't put the makeup on just right, I worry about it all night. I have a great sense of responsibility."

About performing: Some nights, in playing a part on stage, I can give the part more validity than I can on other nights. It's pushing all the way, however, and especially when the audience has mass ennui. Everything I do is the same in every performance. It's set. But there are some nights when I have an extra impetus, especially if I feel I'm ringing bells with the audience. If I give it that extra push some night, it may not always mean it's a better performance. I go on technique. You get it set

and it goes along. If you try to do too much, the more you do, and the more you try to win an audience, the more it turns away. You can't live it night after night. Creative interpretation counts for a great deal, but if you maintain that you can't say a line until you *feel* it, to me that seems to be lack of discipline. Born actors are like sponges. They go through life soaking up idiosyncracies and storing them up in themselves—all the little bits and pieces of what people are and what people do. When I act, it's completely apart from *me*. It's like putting on a suit of clothes that doesn't belong to me but fits me.

Angela had two screen releases in 1960, both very much in her character star mold. In the overblown adaptation of William Inge's *The Dark at the Top of the Stairs* (1960), Warner Brothers provided a lush budget for director Delbert Mann to physically open up the Oklahoma 1920s setting of the successful Broadway play. What had been a touching, if theatrical, account on stage became magnified slop on screen. In the film's context, harness salesman Robert Preston finds the

With Robert Preston in *The Dark at the Top of the Stairs*
(WB, 1960).

advent of the assembly line automobile forcing him to adapt to a new business field, but he is too emotionally at loose ends to concentrate on new job prospects. His wife (Dorothy McGuire) is bogged down by their souring seventeen-year-old marriage. She now finds sex with him a burden, and her mind is too preoccupied with coping with Preston's restlessness, money worries, and the upbringing of her over-sensitive children; shy young Richard Eyer, and overly introspective, maturing Shirley Knight.

Preston has been making hesitant advances to Mavis (Angela), a widow who runs a beauty parlor in her home. When the understanding, lonely Angela almost blatantly offers herself to Preston, he replies, "I never cheated on Cora once since I've been married." Angela is touched by his loyalty to his wife, and eases off her gentle attack. After Preston has walked out on McGuire and says he will not return, she sends for her sister (Eve Arden) and her mousey brother-in-law (Frank Overton). They have few words of consolation for McGuire, and she decides to visit Angela and learn for herself what her "competition" is really like. Not giving her name, McGuire arrives at Angela's home shop, setting the stage for one of the film's few honest screen moments. As Angela, her black-colored hair fixed in a bun, gives McGuire a manicure, they sound each other out, soon revealing themselves to one another.

Angela: "Well, I suppose we were bound to meet someday."

A few minutes later she concludes their discussion with: "I'm not blonde, Mrs. Flood, but I'm hard." Then with a shake of her head and a waggle to her square jaw, she advises McGuire: "Do your job, pay attention to him. . . . there's something waiting, someone like me."

Compared to the Music Man style shouting-emoting of Preston and the arch playing of Arden, Angela was a paragon of restrained performing as the forthright Mavis. The *New York Times* decided: ". . . Angela Lansbury makes a prepossessing widow who is just too noble for anybody's good," but most critics agreed ". . . [she] plays one of her better and more sympathetic roles" (*Variety*). *The Dark at the Top of the Stairs* opened at Radio City Music Hall and immediately proved a satisfactory crowd pleaser, if not an artistic success.

The salary must have been very attractive to lure Angela to accept a role in Paramount's *A Breath of Scandal* (1960). It was a low ebb for once-distinguished director Michael Curtiz to transfer Ferenc Molnar's threadbare play into a $1 million Vistavision-color fiasco which further substantiated the American

With Tullio Carminati in *A Breath Of Scandal* (Paramount, 1960).

cinema's inability to properly showcase the talents of Italian import Sophia Loren.

The draggy costume picture is localed in 1905 Austria where Princess Loren has been banished from the court because of her scandalous behavior following the death of her seventy-two-year-old husband. Loren's parents (Maurice Chevalier and Isabel Jeans) win a royal reprieve for their wayward daughter on provision that she wed staid Prussian prince Carlo Hinterman. It is a loveless proposition in Loren's eyes, but not considered as such by somewhat older Angela, a chic courtesan, who has been counting on Hinterman as her own special bird of prey.

It was now *de rigeur* for Angela's movie character to mouth snappy *bon mots* about her screen rivals. At the royal palace, where the amoral Angela is more than at home (about the emperor she gossips: "I've known him since he was sixty-five."), she remarks about the newly-restored Loren: "It's a pity her looks aren't matched by her virtue." Meanwhile, Loren spends an innocent night alone with American mining engineer John Gavin, which leads to further whispering about her reputation (Angela hastens to inform the Emperor of all the alleged details) with Loren eventually deciding Gavin is more than enough man for her, title or not. The *New York Herald-Tribune* reported of Angela's appearance in *A Breath of Scandal:* "It is Miss Lansbury's task to be disagreeable in the role. She certainly succeeds." After her padded, mature look as the wageearner in *The Dark at the Top of the Stairs,* it must have been a small comfort to Angela to be decked out in fine period formal apparel in *A Breath of Scandal.*

Season of Passion (1961), shot on location in Australia in 1960, was an artistic venture sluffed off by its distributor, United Artists, as a commercial disaster even before its delayed New York opening in February, 1962, having played around the country in spotted engagements. Based on Ray Lawler's quietly dramatic play *Summer of the Seventeenth Doll.** The low-keyed feature starred Ernest Borgnine and John Mills as two lusty middle-aged Australian cane cutters who for sixteen years have spent their annual lay-off season in Sydney with their devoted gals. This year, barmaid Anne Baxter must find a new friend for Mills, since his steady has gone off and married, so she induces a skeptical widow, manicurist Angela, to be the substitute. From the start, nothing goes properly. Mills and Borgnine have arguments, and being with the more rigid Angela is not the same for Mills. Eventually, Angela packs up and leaves, and Mills barges off to pick grapes instead of returning to the cane fields. Borg-

With Anne Baxter and Ernest Borgnine in *Season of Passion* (UA, 1961).

---

* The play had been a London hit, but only had a brief stay on Broadway in January, 1958, with Madge Ryan as Pearl.

nine at last realizes he is no longer a carefree young man and decides to settle down in Sydney and wed Baxter.

Even in this occasionally touching drama, Angela had to play the one unsympathetic character in the proceedings. For example, she cannot resist replying to Baxter's query about a new outfit the latter has purchased: "It's not my taste, but it suits you." Vain through and through, it is Angela who, primping in front of the mirror, complains about her new hairdo: "That new girl doesn't know how to handle it." Although at first she is leery of entering on such a casual romance, Angela adjusts to the sexual situation rather quickly when she decides that Mills might be good marriage bait (the furthest idea from his mind, particularly since he still pines for his lost love). It is Baxter's nosey but perceptive landlady who tags Angela "droopy drawers," a name which suits the pretentious creature.

Both Baxter and Borgnine seemed miscast in their assignments, and Mills was too low-keyed in his interpretation. Once again, it was Angela who made the biggest impression. *Variety* evaluated: "Miss Lansbury brings a comic and sometimes sad dignity to bear on the role of the woman who is caught up in some odd proceedings, doesn't like them very much, but is not persuaded till the end of the film that this alfresco summer romance is not for her."

It was in *Blue Hawaii* (1961) that Angela standardized her possessive mother screen characterization. Angela would later evaluate: "From the artistic point of view, I love these parts. You see, I lack guts in my own life. I lack fire and meanness so I love playing it in screen roles. I am rather a sensitive person, and I think you have to be a sensitive person to play it nasty. It isn't true that you have to be one to play one. I have seen some real bitches in Hollywood play soft sentimental roles so beautifully I wept."

Blue Hawaii returned Elvis Presley to the far more lucrative format of teeny-bopper musicals, after venturing into the realm of straight dramatics in two mediocre pictures. Producer Hal B. Wallace effectively employed the lush tropical isle as a backdrop (largely via rear view projection) for the concocted yarn of army draftee Presley, the scion of millionaire Roland Winters, returning to Honolulu after military service. His determined mama insists he should enter the family's lucrative pineapple business, but he prefers a more carefree existence as a tourist agency associate, romancing young female tourists and singling out nubile half-French, half-Hawaiian Joan Blackman as his special girl. Needless to say, snobbish Angela turns up her pug nose at the thought of her precious son wedding Blackman, but finds she has little to say in the matter. But for Angela, sonny can do no wrong. When he returns home

With Elvis Presley and Roland Winters in *Blue Hawaii* (Paramount, 1961).

from a night in jail after being involved in a luau riot, Angela gushes: "Oh, my baby's back from the big house." Later, Angela's transplanted southern matron character asks her dominated husband about the turn of character in Presley: "Oh, daddy, what'd we do wrong?" Winters archly replies: "Offhand, I'd say we got married."

With its fourteen tunes, palms, pineapple plantations, and native festivals, *Blue Hawaii* proved one of Presley's richest box office successes in this period. Angela received outstanding notices from the critics who appreciated her giving her professional all to such an undemanding picture. ". . . Miss Lansbury's antics give the picture much of its slightly salty good humor." (*New York Herald-Tribune*). ". . . connoisseurs will relish Angela Lansbury as his Mom, with an Atlanta accent dripping over the screen like barbecue butter."

MGM had sunk a good deal of change into the glossy Vincente Minnelli-directed remake of *The Four Horsemen of the Apocalypse* (1962), convinced it could duplicate the success of the Rudolph Valentino silent version by updating the account to World War II and providing handsome mountings. But Glenn Ford was no Valentino, and passing time had made Vicente Blasco Ibanez's romantic novel more than trite. Worst of all, after completing production, MGM executives discovered that Swedish actress Ingrid Thulin, while visually aristocratic on screen, was too thick-accented to be properly understood by western-world audiences. Thus Angela was hired to dub in the role of Marguerite Laurier, wife of Free-French journalist Paul Henried, who falls in love with Argentinian playboy Ford. More than one reviewer noted that in this "pompous and idiotic fiction" Thulin's lip movements and the voice supposedly coming from her mouth did not jive.

The time was long overdue for Angela to again bite into a meaty script, supervised by a powerhouse director. *All Fall Down* (1962) directed by John Frankenheimer was Angela's first such screen opportunity in nearly two decades. Based on the James Leo Herlihy novel and William Inge's refashioned and decidedly tempered screenplay, *All Fall Down* was intended to hit close at middle-class America and the once-sacred institution of the American mother. Because of its own internal compromising, partly due to the morality codes of the early 1960s and to the distillation of characterization created by box office lure casting, the feature missed the sizzling impact it so obviously intended to create.

The story is conveniently framed through the naive eyes of Brandon de Wilde, the sixteen-year-old son of Cleveland couple Karl Malden and Angela. Malden is an ineffectual real estate broker, and Angela is a strong-willed, prattling woman filled with exaggerated conventional ambitions and gratification desires. De Wilde's older brother Berry-Berry (Warren Beatty) is a wanton stud for whom Angela has a rash, overpossessive love

With Karl Malden in *All Fall Down* (MGM, 1962).

("my first born," "my baby"). He has been capering about the country, a melancholy drifter, servicing bored and lonely women. Beatty returns home to find nothing has changed, but the arrival of mama's friend from Toledo, thirtyish unmarried Eva Marie Saint, prompts the mumbling prodigal to stick around. He is as fascinated by her vulnerability as by her precious 1936 Packard touring car.

As the one-sided romance between Beatty and Saint progresses, Angela becomes sharp with her friend for supposedly breaking the sacred bond of her suffocating love for dear Berry-Berry. Through it all, Malden sticks to his jigsaw puzzle playing and lonely drinking, a despondent, broken man. And de Wilde continues to eavesdrop through dumbwaiters, writing in his diary of the bewildering family life.

The catharsis, for de Wilde at least, is when Saint becomes pregnant and Beatty typically refuses responsibility for his action. In despair, she drives off and is killed in a car crash. This traumatic event forces de Wild to finally mature and face the fact that his older brother is merely a self-indulgent shell of a man, a bastard unworthy of admiration or any understanding. For Beatty, Angela, and Malden, life goes on much as before.

As the florid, prying mother, Angela is the one everyone in the big old Willart house avoids with a passion. It does not escape her that she has failed her husband and sons in some fuzzy manner, but she is too foolish and vain to explore her actions to their core. Her *raison d'etre* is herself.

All Fall Down had many cinematic and creative faults, but the majority of critics raved over Angela's performance: ". . . what makes it worth seeing is the work of Angela Lansbury. She plays Berry-Berry's mother as a woman with the brain of a flea, the heart of a whale, the tongue of a toad, the devotion of a dog, the cunning of a serpent, the innocence of a noisy old parrot" (*Time* Magazine). "Angela Lansbury and Karl Malden are true to the Inge image of American parenthood" (*British Films and Filming*). ". . . [she] is allowed to convert her usual ninny's role into a maddening, querilous, nagging but pitiable human being" (*London Sunday Times*).

It was in her next film, also for director John Frankenheimer, that Angela reached the peak of her screen career. Created from Richard Condon's sturdy novel *The Manchurian Candidate* (1962) is a prophetic account of an American sergeant (Laurence Harvey) who returns from the Korean War, a congressional medal of honor winner. In reality, Harvey and his platoon had been captured by the Communists and brainwashed at the Pavlov Institute in Russia. The conditioned Harvey has been trained to kill upon memory response order. Only Army intelligence major Frank Sinatra and corporal James Edwards recover sufficiently from the brainwashing ordeal to compare notes, and then they insist the army commence an investigation. It develops Harvey has been placed by the Russians in the hands of an American operative, none other than his mother (Angela), the wife of his extreme right-wing U.S. senator stepfather (James Gregory). The final tension is built on Sinatra's effort to piece together and prevent the Communist scheme, which is to have Harvey shoot the presidential candidate at a Madison Square Garden rally, affording Angela's puppet-like husband the opportunity to grab the party nomination.

This time Angela's dominating figure is pure evil through and through.* She is a voracious, brutal creature, all the more dangerous for her worldliness and unswerving conviction to herself, above and beyond her loyalty to the Communist ideology. (She even tells her

With Eva Marie Saint, Warren Beatty, and Karl Malden in *All Fall Down*.

---

* In 1966, Angela told interviewer Rex Reed: "I've always done two type of things: first, things like *The Harvey Girls* and *Harlow* which I could do competently with my hands tied behind my back, but which appealed to huge masses of people. And second, roles which taxed me emotionally and physically and broke my heart with pride, but only appealed to a small rather special audience. Roles like Annabel in *All Fall Down* and that heartbreaking woman in *The Dark at the Top of the Stairs*. And of course my musical debut on Broadway in *Anyone Can Whistle*. The first breakthrough was the fiendish mother in *Manchurian Candidate*. Imagine! I was only 37 and playing Larry Harvey's mother. I've played so many old hags most people think I'm 65 years old. I didn't want to play all those nasty ladies but in Hollywood you're either a member of the working group or not, and if not you're very easily forgotten."

Angela Lansbury in 1962.

With James Gregory in *The Manchurian Candidate* (UA, 1962).

the plot to. . . . to sweep us into the White House with powers that will make martial law look like anarchy."

The Manchurian Candidate, steeped in the tradition of Alfred Hitchcock, mesmerized filmgoers who accepted its premise as far-out but intriguing. The obvious loopholes in the story were ignored by most viewers. After all, how realistic does entertainment have to be? There were divergent opinions about Angela's dynamic, intense performance: "She laps up her own witty lines with the appetite of a charming tarantula" (*New York Herald-Tribune*). "Angela Lansbury is Walt Disney's evil queen in the raging flesh, a performance that has been widely praised, I am convinced, because this highly-skilled actress is the only one currently working the set-chewing dodge" (*Washington Post*).

Angela was nominated for a best supporting actress award; had her part been slightly enlarged, she certainly would have been best actress award material. This time she lost out to Patty Duke, who won the Oscar for her performance as the young Helen Keller, recreating her stage role from *The Miracle Worker.*

At this peak in her screen career it would logically seem that Angela should have progressed onward to loftier acting assignments, but each new feature was a

son that the Reds ". . . will be pulled down and ground into the dirt for what they did to you and what they did in so grotesquely underestimating me.") Everyone and everything is a tool to serve her needs. She maneuvers her brainwashed son ("Raymond, why do you always have to look as if your head were about to come to a point?" Another time she says, "Raymond really can be a royal pain.") as easily as her child-like political husband (she refers to him as "hon" and he calls her "babe"), a man who rants about card-carrying Communists (before a big investigatory session, Angela advises him not to think, but just to shout "Point of order!"). For Angela, "a latter-day Lady Macbeth," anyone who disagrees with her is a de facto Communist pure and simple.

Ian and Elisabeth Cameron in their book *Dames* (1969) write about Angela in *The Manchurian Candidate:* "There can be few actresses around who could carry this part, but Miss Lansbury has both the skill and the appearance for it; the face is remarkable—slightly puffy, with a large forehead and small chin, features which seem only to focus attention on the glittery, predatory eyes and the hard little mouth that looks as if she is keeping her lips pursed in determination. One can easily believe that this could be behind

With James Gregory in *The Manchurian Candidate.*

downward swing. Juicy roles such as she had in *All Fall Down* and *The Manchurian Candidate* did not materialize every day. Now typecast the vicious screen mother, it was as difficult for Angela to break out of her new stereotype as it has been to overstep her pigeon-holed character woman status back at MGM. No creative producer was yet willing to back Angela's conviction that the full scope of her onscreen personality had yet to be tapped. Thus Angela had a rather depressing career choice: accept *deja vu* roles which rehashed past characterizations, or parlay to win the offbeat assignments other more famous personalities had rejected because the productions themselves seemed initially so unpromising.

In the Cool of the Day (1963) was a misfire from its title onward, an outmoded attempt at dimensionless soap opera. Produced by John Houseman (who had supervised *All Fall Down*) at Elstree studio in England and on continental location, its plot has book publisher Peter Finch touring Greece with his acid-tongue wife Angela (she blames him for the automobile accident which killed their child and scarred her face—with a quick sweep of her hand she uplifts a lock of hair to show others the telltale blemishes) and the consumptive wife (Jane Fonda) of a colleague (Arthur Hill). It is not long before Angela has tired of viewing the ruins of the Acropolis ("a glorified junk yard" she calls it) and triumphantly packs herself off to the French Riviera for some fun with a British businessman ("He's from Birmingham—he sells electrical equipment all over Europe"). She knows it will not work out, but at this point something is better than nothing. Having dished out her venom to Finch, she moves on to Fonda. She tells the bemused woman "He is all yours" and sweeps out, leaving Finch and Fonda, guilty and moody, to mope about their doomed love.

In the Cool of the Day proved an embarrassment to almost all concerned, save the Greek travel bureau, and it came and went quickly in its distribution. It did not require much effort for Angela to walk off with the picture, in which for once she played a woman her own age. "She stirs up the only fun in the generally sour proceedings" (*Variety*). "It is Miss Lansbury, as a vicious vulgarian and the epitome of fed-up tourists, who steals the picture—lock, stock, barrel and Greece. At least we can applaud some cool, professional witchery" (*New York Times*). "Only Angela Lansbury, bursting through the surrounding primness as an intolerable, nagging wife, brings a welcome touch of bravura to the proceedings" (*British Films and Filming*).

On a rare sojourn into television, Angela gave a good account of herself on the series "The Eleventh Hour" (ABC) in the episode "Something Crazy's Going on in

In *In the Cool of the Day* (MGM, 1963).

the Back Room" (April 3, 1963). She was the mother of troubled teenager Don Grady, who had been sent to Dr. Jack Ging for psychiatric help regarding his uncontrollable fits of physical destructiveness. Ging suggests holding a family therapy session which leads to a confrontation between Angela, her husband Martin Balsam, daughter Tuesday Weld, and Grady.

Angela succinctly phrased why she accepted the top starring role in the Broadway-bound musical *Anyone Can Whistle* (1964): "I always fancied I had a sexy singing voice, but no one would let me use it. When 'Whistle' was offered to me, I grabbed it."

Playwright Arthur Laurents and composer Stephen Sondheim, who had created together *West Side Story* and *Gypsy,* reteamed to make *Anyone Can Whistle* (originally called *Side Show*). They sought a variant approach by adapting the theatre of the absurd to the musical comedy format in order to present their philosophical theme that in the modern world it is often difficult to distinguish between sane and insane people. The story is set in "a not too distant town" run by mayoress Cora Hoover Hooper (Angela). She and the town council concoct a fake miracle in order to bring new revenue to the impoverished citizens and, more importantly, to themselves. The lucrative fakery is set into motion without a hitch, except for the threat of the patients at the Cookie Jar, the local sanitarium where anyone with individuality has been incarcerated and tranquilized. Lee Remick, head nurse at the asylum, is none too stable herself. In fact, she has to don a red wig and a fake French accent in order to cavort as the lady from Lourdes who is both investigating the miracle of the fountain and determined to liberate the asylum inmates. The man of the story is practicing idealist

With Lee Remick in *Anyone Can Whistle* (1964).

Harry Guardino. He is attracted to Remick, and Angela is romanced by sinister town comptroller Gabriel Dell, which leads to a proper balance.

Rehearsals began January 20, 1964, for *Anyone Can Whistle,* and its out-of-town tryouts commenced in Philadelphia at the Forrest Theatre, March 2, 1964. To shape up for her first stage musical Angela somewhat kiddingly stated: "I plan to trot around the Central Park reservoir every morning. You know, like the professional boxers do, until I can get to the point where I can gallop. Come and watch me. You have to go into training like an athlete. To act fast is okay; but to sing and dance and act fast, that requires . . . the timing of a squash player. No I don't play squash. How silly! Bouncing your bottom off all those walls!"

Anyone Can Whistle premiered at the Majestic Theatre, New York, April 4, 1964, a week after it began paid previews at the theater. Everyone admitted it was an interesting experiment, but as the *New York Times* complained: ". . . it's unconstitutional to omit imagination and wit." From the moment Angela ap-

peared on stage, carried in a four-man litter, she jumped about, singing and dancing. She did her utmost to bolster life into the play, but the songs, with their heavy syncopated beat and unmelodious ring, were no help. It was not until the third act that star Angela had a soft-shoe dance that managed to rouse the audience to genuine applause.

Despite the mechanically ingenious sets, the cast's efforts, and the intellectually-geared book, *Anyone Can Whistle* just did not have it, and it folded after 9 performances with a loss of its $350,000 investment. Ironically, the original cast album was recorded by Columbia Records the day after the show closed.

George Oppenheimer of *Newsday* summed up the valiant try by Angela: "That skillful comedienne, Angela Lansbury, scores heavily in two numbers and in several scenes. However, Mr. Laurents has allowed her to press far too hard for her comic effects, so that she becomes after a while, a caricature on one monotonous note."

A short time after *Anyone Can Whistle* came and went, Angela was represented on the screen by *The World of Henry Orient* (1964), the Easter show at Radio City Music Hall. This picture was an offbeat story by Nora Johnson, daughter of longtime screenwriter-producer Nunnally Johnson, that took the industry by pleasant surprise. Its lighthearted premise turns on the silly adolescent behavior of two fourteen-year-old girls (Tippy Walker and Merrie Spaeth) who attend a fashionable Manhattan private school. Walker's unhappily married parents, assertive Angela and meek Tom Bosley, are always away on European jaunts, which leads the teen-ager into a closer friendship with Spaeth. It is the latter's divorced mother (Phyllis Thaxter) and her amusing friend (Bibi Osterwald) who

With Merrie Spaeth, Phyllis Thaxter, Bibi Osterwald, and Tom Bosley in *The World of Henry Orient* (UA, 1964).

In *The World of Henry Orient.*

shower Walker with needed kindness. During one of the girls' escapades in Central Park, they come upon oddball concert pianist Peter Sellers, attempting to make love to attractive suburbanite Paula Prentiss. The girls become infatuated with the wolfish pianist and dog his every footstep with a relentlessness that infuriates Sellers and scares off Prentiss. The duo's merry adventures are brought to an abrupt halt when Angela and Bosley return to Manhattan. Angela, who has been having a casual affair with young pianist Peter Duchin, finds herself contacting Sellers when she thinks the missing Walker might be rendezvousing with him. It is only a few scenes away for self-indulgent Angela to plunk herself into an affair with Sellers, which costs her both husband and daughter. Meanwhile, the girls abandon their fantasy pursuits, for they now have discovered boys.

The World of Henry Orient did better than expected in general release and even managed to be selected as the United States entry at the annual Cannes Film Festival. For her role as the wealthy, dominating Mrs. Boyd, Angela received her customary top drawer notices. "[Director George Roy] Hills's facility with actors is reflected in Angela Lansbury's intelligent and expressive performance. . . ." (*British Monthly Film Bulletin*). "Angela Lansbury is both seductive and bitchy as the terrible Mrs. Boyd" (*New York Herald-Tribune*).

Two ventures which did not come to pass might have boosted Angela's career above the well-paid but creatively meaningless assignments the movie producers were dishing out to her. In mid-1964 she was signed

---

* The movie would be adapted into a short-running Broadway musical, *Henry, Sweet Henry* (1967) with Carol Bruce in Angela's role.

by David Merrick to star in the London company of *Hello, Dolly!*, but he was adamant that her version should be showcased in the Drury Lane Theatre. The theater was booked, and by the time the producer renegotiated for the London engagement, Angela was committed to new movie ventures. Then in early 1965 Angela was contracted to a package deal to star in the London stage, the American stage, and the movie version of Jay Allen's play *The Prime of Miss Jean Brodie*. When done on Broadway, the part brought Zoe Caldwell great acclaim, and Maggie Smith won an Oscar for her performance in the film version.

Meanwhile on October 21, 1964, Angela made her first appearance in more than a decade on a television variety show. She guested on Danny Kaye's NBC program, singing, dancing and clowning to generally good results.

Angela had four 1965 motion picture releases. Producer-director George Stevens had been planning *The Greatest Story Ever Told* (1965) for several years, and after many false starts, the $20 million production was filmed in 1964 and released in February, 1965. Weighing in at a hefty 222 minutes, it was a topheavy study that had no predominating dramatic point of view, sacrificing its potential biblical ambience to the scanning of the widescreen camera and to the ludicrous inclusion of a horde of miscast name personalities in quickflash cameos. Angela was billed thirty-second as Claudia, Pontius Pilate's wife. *Variety* aptly reported: "Angela Lansbury is a mere flash in the Panavision, literally a face glimpsed on the stairway beckoning Pontius Pilate (Telly Savalas) to come hear her advice. She has no lines but seems to be saying 'Ponti, sweets, don't get involved in this case!' " By the time the roadshow film epic was subsequently reissued in 1967, it was chopped down to a still-unwieldy 141-minute version, with the embarrassing cameo performances by John Wayne, Shelley Winters, and many others gone. Angela's bit remained.

More fortuitous was her presence in Warner Bros.' *Dear Heart* (1965), based on a Tad Mosel teleplay that had starred Eileen Heckhart. It was no coincidence that Delbert Mann, who favored directing stories of the heart, should have helmed this picture as well as the previous *The Dark at the Top of the Stairs* and that Angela, who had performed so well for him before, should be hired for this project. *Dear Heart* emerged as a rare warm-hearted comedy in an age of cynicism. Its premise found smalltown postmistress Geraldine Page arriving in New York for a business convention and meeting greeting card salesman Glenn Ford, also staying at the same hotel. Their fumbling romance is almost aborted by Ford's relationship with a widow (Angela)

With Glenn Ford in *Dear Heart* (WB, 1964).

from Altoona, Pennsylvania, who has a father-needing beatnik son (Michael Anderson, Jr.). Ford is about to tie himself down to Angela and has come to Manhattan to find an apartment for them, but as expected, eventually realizes Page is a far more suitable prospective spouse.

As the third-billed Phyllis, Angela again played an unsympathetic part, this time in the form of a threat to the future of romanticism, since her prime aim in snagging Ford is to acquire an "absence of responsibility." She does not mind lying to Ford for expediency (saying her son is thirteen when he is a troublesome eighteen), nor can she hold her tongue after a quick appraisal of the new apartment Ford has selected for them (in sharp contrast to Page who glows with happi-

Angela Lansbury and co-star Geraldine Page at a publicity party for *Dear Heart.*

ness for Ford at the wonderful potentials of the place). Angela's big moment is the staircase scene where she informs her husband-to-be that she has done quite enough in the past for friends and relatives back home. She gives a long recital and concludes by saying "and Phyllis is tired of doing." Thus there is little room, if any, for sympathy on her part regarding the emotional quandry Ford feels in transferring to his company's main office and having to reside and work in the New York jungle. Not that Angela's Phyllis is unobservant by any means. The knowing look she tosses at Barbara Nichols, who had spent a night with Ford, deserves special mention. Judith Crist in the *New York Herald-Tribune* praised Angela's grasping widow performance: ". . . her part is short and sour in the perfect Lansbury fashion."

Because *Tom Jones* had been a box office bonanza, it was assumed a distaff version done in the identical jocular, sexually-kidding vein would duplicate the original's grosses. Not so. *The Amorous Adventures of Moll Flanders* (1965) starred Kim Novak as a female tramp who strides from bed to bed up the social ladder in this twisted version of Daniel DeFoe's novel of Eighteenth century England. At one point in the picture, she is employed as a maid in the London household of Lady Blystone (Angela). There she is mistaken by highwayman Richard Johnson as the mistress of the house. Angela allows her employee to continue the ruse, because it suits the purpose of Angela and her pal (Vittorio De Sica).

The episodic *The Amorous Adventures of Moll Flanders* did not make it with audiences. There were amusing performances by George Sanders as the worldly banker who weds Novak, and Lilli Palmer as a crooked gal about town, but neither they nor Angela could carry a picture where so much depended on Novak displaying a tongue-in-cheek quality which she most obviously did not possess. British, *Films and Filming* reported: "Angela Lansbury works wonder with little good dialogue or situations as the impoverished Lady Blystone."

Not since the rivalry of two British-made versions of *Oscar Wilde* to beat one another to theatrical distribution had there been such a fuss over two movie producers rushing to complete and distribute their screen version of the same story. Joseph Sargent's Electronovision *Harlow,* made in eight days, opened and disappeared in May, 1965, followed two months later by Joseph E. Levine's $4 million version of *Harlow.*

Levine's *Harlow* was an unslick, exploitive version of Irving Shulman's sexually-oriented biography of 1930s film star Jean Harlow. Since the book was as suspect in its psychological interpretation as it was in

In *The Amorous Adventures Of Moll Flanders* (Paramount, 1965).

the presentation of facts, it was no surprise that the feature film was a further exploration of the realm of triteness. The color picture was as ludicrous as the same producer's *The Carpetbaggers,* which had also offered moviegoers a thoughtless recreation of life in early Hollywood. This *Harlow* glossed over hard facts, reducing everything to basic, juvenile emotions, as Carroll Baker enacted the fabled girl's rise from movie extra to Mack Sennett slapstick comedies to her lush days at MGM (here called Majestic). Typical of this version's childish dialogue was Baker screaming to her mother (Angela): "Oh Mamma, all they want is my body!" Or later when Angela muses about her soon-to-be legendary daughter: "I knew you were too young for this business."

With Kim Novak in *The Amorous Adventures of Moll Flanders.*

Harlow did squeeze $3 million in box office grosses from the public, due to its saturation publicity campaign (billed as "The picture they said couldn't be made"), certainly not from word of mouth of those who had viewed the Paramount release. Angela as Mama Jean Bello was asked to lend credence to the role of a grasping stage mother, who with her second husband (Raf Vallone) pushes and shoves the daughter into stardom so that they can continue their lazy and selfish existence, living off the girl's salary. Just to add spurious sexual overtones to this facet of *Harlowe*'s life, there are the scenes where Baker attempts to seduce her stepfather, or at another point prods Angela to talk of her sex life. At first Angela is embarrassed by the query, but upon active contemplation purrs that her sexual life with Vallone is quite satisfactory indeed. The film ends with Mama and everyone agreeing that Harlow did not die of uremic poisoning (the real cause) but from an overdose of life.

From an interpretative point of view, Angela's characterization of the mama was far more theatrical than the low-keyed performance by Ginger Rogers in the Electronovision version, the latter actress offering one of the few professional touches to that quickie black-and-white rendition. Leo Mishkin of the *New York Morning Telegraph* appropriately noted of the Paramount *Harlow* ". . . although Angela Lansbury and Raf Vallone try their best to make something out of the curious roles of the mother and stepfather, they too both seem oddly out of focus, or perhaps the word is off-balance, in the total structure."

Much more fun was Angela's campy appearance in the teleseries "The Man from U.N.C.L.E." (NBC) in the "The Deadly Toy Affair" (November 2, 1965) in which she portrayed a madcap actress.

After the warmup experience of *Anyone Can Whistle,* from which Angela had emerged unscathed, she was eager to return to Broadway in a more conventional musical that not only would give her a star part but also be a hit. *Mame* (1966) (originally called *My Best Gal*) proved to be the vehicle. Long before Angela was announced (December 15, 1965) for the plum role, she made her bid for the part. It was one of the few occasions where agents, relatives, and friends did not have to nag her to go after the assignment. At first, the producers sought Rosalind Russell to recreate her stage and film role from the projected musical's original straight version *Auntie Mame.* But she said: "I don't like to eat last week's stew." Then Mary Martin said yes, and then no. Ethel Merman did not want to sign a long-term stage contract. Now the field was wide open, and Angela flew to New York to audition for director Joshua Logan. No sooner had she learned she was a

Carroll Baker, Raf Vallone, and Red Buttons in *Harlow* (Paramount, 1965).

prime contender for the lead than Logan left the project and was replaced by Gene Saks. Angela had to launch her campaign all over again, auditioning for the new director and waiting for the results. It was rare occasion that saw Angela devoting so much energy to winning a part. ". . . [Acting] has never been the driving thing with me. . . . I am strictly practical and won't lift a finger unless I get paid for it . . . I don't indulge myself in the enjoyment of acting." Eventually it was determined that Angela was the proper choice for the vehicle, budgeted at $500,000.

Rehearsals began February 21, 1966, with the out-of-town tryout tour playing Philadelphia (Shubert Theatre, April 4, 1966). The *Philadelphia Bulletin* reported: "She dances with grace and something close to abandon and looks like a million dollars." Then *Mame* moved to Boston for a run at the Shubert Theatre (April 29, 1966). Alta Maloney in the *Boston Traveler* penned: "What a surprise Miss Lansbury is, though, even to those who have recognized her quality as an

actress. She not only makes Mame her own, with a very special sort of warmth, but she can sing with the best of them, and is a real hoofer. . . . One reason she's so good is that she's a conscientious ensemble worker and she has much talent surrounding her. . . . Her voice has quality—sometimes shaky, sometimes quivery, sometimes light—but always in character, and ever the sure, deft instrument of a superb comedienne. She's a shimmering joy and makes *Mame* a quicksilver delight."

Mame sprang on Broadway at the Winter Garden Theatre, May 24, 1966, boasting a $9.50 ticket top. It came at the tail end of the 1965–1966 period and proved to be the biggest hit of the season. The *Auntie Mame* book by Jerome Lawrence and Robert E. Lee combined with Jerry Herman's songs to offer Angela a marvelous showcase. Once again, it was the story of Mame of Beekman Place who in 1928 suddenly finds herself saddled with the supervision of her nephew (Frankie Michael as little Patrick, Jerry Lanning as

With composer Jerry Herman at a press conference for *Mame* (1966).

Patrick the adult). With the assistance of her bosom rival pal, actress Vera Charles (Beatrice Arthur), her life-tasting secretary Agnes Gooch (Jane Connell), and her new southern gentleman husband Beauregard Jackson Pickett Burnside (Charles Braswell), Angela sets out to prove that "Life is a banquet and most poor sons of bitches are starving to death." Angela's solo songs reflected her character's changing attitudes on life, as she moves from the carefree hedonist who now must guide her charge Patrick to adulthood ("If He Walked into My Life"), to her ability to bounce back from frequent reversals ("It's Today"), and to her zest for risking the unknown challenges of life ("Open a New Window"). In the tradition of Jerry Herman's *Hello, Dolly!* score, there was the overpowering title song *Mame,* pointing up the uniqueness of the effervescent, flamboyant female.

In the course of *Mame,* Angela performed a tango, a cakewalk, and the charleston, and had twenty-four costume changes ranging from gold lamé pajamas to

In *Mame.*

riding outfit. Angela explained: "The quick changes have to look easy to the audience. I mean, you have to come out on stage with a new costume and not look like you are going to bust a gut. People get rather distressed if they feel you are breaking your neck to make a change. But I think the costumes are a great help to my performance."

Stanley Kaufman wrote in the *New York Times:* "The star vehicle deserves its star, and vice is very much versa. No one can be surprised to learn that Angela Lansbury is an accomplished actress, but not all of us may know that she has an adequate singing voice, can dance trimly, and can combine all these matters into a musical performance.

"In short, Miss Lansbury is a singing-dancing actress, not a singer or dancer who also acts (somewhat surprisingly, there is even more character color in her singing than in her spoken dialogue). In this marathon role she has wit, poise, warmth, and a very taking cool. The visceral test, I suppose, is whether one is jealous of little Patrick growing up with an aunt like that. I was green."

For her performance in *Mame,* Angela was awarded a Tony as the best musical actress of the year.

Angela was now the celebrity in residence in New York and was very much in demand for interviews. Everyone wanted to know where the "real" Angela with her shingle bob hairdo and total chic had been hiding all these years.

". . . the thing that made me know I could play *Mame* was something I knew about myself, just as we all know certain things about ourselves. I have a tremendous amount of energy and vitality, and that's basic to *Mame*. Just as basic as performing the role on stage every night. There are certain things that I must hit in every performance. I absolutely must not miss on 'If He Walked into My Life' which is my big number. If I missed on that, I would lose the audience. They would have no sympathy for what happens in the next scene . . . where Mame really steps in and shows the Upsons for what they are."

Concerning her *Mame* success Angela told interviewer Rex Reed: "When I did *Anyone Can Whistle,* a magnificent failure—the crowd yelled bravo, too. But that was the insypoo New York crowd. They're marvelous, but they fizzle out after six weeks. I'm out to get the taxi drivers, shop ladies and people on the street. Even teen-agers are paying $9.50 a seat to see *Mame*. They love this dame. I hope the way I play her she's more than just a song and dance woman. She's all the women I've played. I'm like a sponge. Everything I see is ducated away in my pores. I've known a lot of Mames in my day and underneath they all cry 'Need me!' It's

taken me 41 years, but I've finally found a role that is the sum total of everything I know and everybody's digging me for the first time."

It got so, everywhere Angela went she was greeted as *Mame* and not herself. There was even the Heublein cocktail ad in 1966 that she posed for, which proclaimed "put the spirit of *Mame* in your party." Later in the *Mame* run, Angela would say: ". . . people . . . want me to be Mame, to be all of the time what I was for two hours on stage each night; a little rocket of happiness. However, there are several realities, and one must live with them. One reality is that I am not Mame and I'm living with it, so must other people, the people who can only take from you. It's really rather difficult to explain."

After playing 418 performances of *Mame* (and recording the Columbia LP cast album which became a gold record best seller), Angela left the Broadway version, March 30, 1967, and was replaced by Janis Paige.* Angela headed the national touring company, playing with the show for an eighteen-week period in Los Angeles and San Francisco. Once again, a prime motive for her doing the show on the West Coast was to let the film industry know in person just how zestful her *Mame* performance actually was. Moreover, Warner Bros.-Seven Arts had paid $3 million plus 30 per cent of the film grosses after costs for the screen rights to the musical. Angela wanted a crack at the movie version. But the producers backed away from her, preferring to chance their investment on the slapstick queen of television, Lucille Ball, and the latter began filming of the much-delayed movie musical in January of 1973.

Meanwhile, *Mister Buddwing,* made in 1965 on location in New York, was finally shoved into distribution in October, 1966, MGM realizing it had a fiasco on its hands. It was Angela's third collaboration with director Delbert Mann. This would-be suspense yarn was another film in the amnesia thriller cycle of *Mirage* and *36 Hours*.

The premise of *Mister Buddwing* has James Garner awakening in Central Park to discover he has lost his money and memory. The only clues on his person are a telephone number in his pocket and an inscribed signet ring on his hand. He dials the digits on the slip

_____
* Other Broadway *Mames* would be Celeste Holm, Jane Morgan, and Ann Miller. The London company starred Ginger Rogers; and on the road Mame was played by (among others) Edie Adams, Eve Arden, Giselle McKenzie, Elaine Stritch, Susan Hayward, Janet Blair, Juliet Prowse, Gretchen Wyler, Patricie Munsel, Charlotte Fairbanks, and Sheila Smith (Angela's Broadway *Mame* understudy).

With James Garner in *Mister Buddwing* (MGM, 1966).

Interestingly, the critics who had not minded Angela intruding her own personality into her stage performance of *A Taste of Honey* or such screen roles as *Season of Passion* (where she grossly submerged her character's nature for too big an offering of Angela) were unhappy with her work in *Mr. Buddwing*. It was one of the few occasions where Angela received unfavorable notices, even in an overall bad film. Judith Crist (*New York Herald-Tribune*) said: "Forget her. The script does." *Variety* reported: "Angela Lansbury's opening cameo is overdone."

One of Angela's now rare television appearances was on Perry Como's "Kraft Music Hall" (November 21, 1966, NBC) in which she reprised some of her *Mame* songs.

During her lush days as the top drawing Broadway musical star of *Mame,* Angela had said: "I hope . . . that because of *Mame* I will be able to go back to the movies and possibly move into a new era of roles for a woman of my age . . . roles of a leading nature. . . ." Angela was offered the starring role in the film version of *The Killing of Sister George* (1969), a part Bette Davis dearly wanted, but she refused, saying: ". . . crazy as it sounds, I don't want to destroy the image I've created for myself in *Mame*. Later that year, Angela would comment: "As far as the movies are concerned, I've had it. I've done a lot of puttering around in Hollywood and the movie people never were really interested in what I could or couldn't do."

Meanwhile, the still-toast of Broadway returned to New York to appear in *Cue* Magazine's Salute to A.S.C.A.P. (September 30, 1967) and continued with her socially oriented charity work, such as the chairmanship of the Mothers' March on Birth Defects. On April 6, 1968, Angela was on the Academy Award show. She sang and danced to the nominated title tune from *Thoroughly Modern Millie*. Said *Films in Review:* "She can both sing and dance, even made that mediocre song endurable, despite a half dozen unnecessary male dancers who flitted about her." On April 21, 1968, Angela was among those Broadway luminaries appearing on the NBC-televised Tony Award show. She seemed much more in command of the situation in her outing there.

With the phenominal success of *Mame,* the team of playwright Jerome Lawrence and Robert E. Lee and Jerry Herman (who worked on both the book as well as composing the songs) prepared a musical version of Jean Giraudoux's *The Madwoman of Chaillot,** titled

but gets a wrong number, being connected with a woman named Gloria (Angela) who thinks he is someone picked up by her drunken husband and has called her because the husband says that she "puts out." Garner comes to her apartment, introduces himself as Mr. Buddwing (an amalgam of the brand name on a can of beer and the inspiration from a jet plane flying overhead). She is dressed in a sloppy nightgown and looks like a middle-aged floozy, with frizzy hair and bags under her eyes. Angela soon takes pity on the confused man, offers him a cup of coffee, and stakes him to $5. Later on, Garner encounters student Katharine Ross, actress Suzanne Pleshette and alcoholic blonde Jean Simmons, all of whom remind him of different aspects of his wife Grace. By the finale, he has pieced together the mystery. It would not be until 1969 that *Mister Buddwing,* under the title *Woman without a Face,* would drop onto the British theatrical market to equally unimpressive results.

When *Mister Buddwing* was produced, it was decided to hold a special press conference to demonstrate that Angela's screen appearance herein was not for real. She showed the reporters the special sponge rubber "fattener" utilized to gain the sloppy figure.

---

* The straight dramatic version starring Martita Hunt had won the N.Y. Drama Critics Circle Award as the best foreign play of the 1948–1949 Broadway season.

With Milo O'Shea in *Dear World* (1969).

Dear World, which producer Alexander H. Cohen capitalized at $600,000. Angela signed a two-year contract which gave her, as part of her salary, ten per cent of the weekly gross and a two-week vacation every six months.

Dear World was concocted on the belief that playgoing audiences might wish to enjoy precious philosophical thoughts while watching a musical. The show evolved as a strange mixture of "poetic and comic fable set in the twilight zone of the not-quite-true." A group of promoters meet at the Cafe Chez Francis in Paris, planning to tear up the city to unearth a wealth of oil which they believe to be located in the subterranean vicinity. Their nefarious plot comes to the attention of the cafe's bizarre owner (Angela), a person who seems insane. She prefers to exist as if it were still 1903, the last good year for her, and dresses in outrageous ragged versions of once high styles, using pure starch instead of

face powder. She calls together her friends, the Madwoman of Montmarte (Jane Connell) and the Madwoman of the Flea Market (Carmen Mathews), and they decide to rid the world of greedy corrupts. At a mad tea party in her cellar abode, she gathers together representatives of the earth's despoilers and after condemning them all, she lures the materialistic people into a bottomless pit.

Rehearsals for *Dear World* began September 30, 1968, and opened in Boston at the Colonial Theatre, November 11, 1968, for a five-week engagement. The show itself was found drastically wanting, but Angela as the old crone, decked out in a red wing, blackened eyes, a big flopping hat, and utilizing a jerky step and a hesitant speech, received impressive notices. *Variety* reported: ". . . Miss Lansbury brings a robust sense of drama, comedy and timing to the role. She is onstage almost all the time but when she isn't the whole affair

In *Dear World.*

seems pale by comparison."

Despite the healthy box office advance sales, there were creative problems in Boston. First, director Lucia Victor was replaced by Peter Glenville, and he in turn was superseded by director Joe Layton. It was rumored that Angela asked to close the production, but there was nearly a $2 million advance sale for the Broadway engagement, and she was persuaded it would be an uneconomical decision. At another point it was mentioned that Gene Saks might become the show's new director and that his wife Beatrice Arthur might be the new star.

Dear World, in two acts and thirteen numbers and with a new $12.50 high for tickets, was scheduled to open at the Mark Hellinger Theatre, December 26, 1968, but instead went through a series of 49 paid previews before finally opening February 6, 1969. There was general disappointment from all corners about the overblown effects on the intimate Giraudoux play, the expansive Oliver Smith set, and in particular, that Angela who had gained a reputation as the stylish *Mame* should be buried beneath so many rags a la Baby Jane. *Variety* analyzed: "Miss Lansbury is spectacular, and when she has a song or a few dancing steps to do, the performance comes alive. She's eloquent and captivating as she sings and leads the likable riffraff of the Paris streets. . . .

"As the story progresses, however, Miss Lansbury has to become more emphatic, and she loses some of the boobyhatch vagueness of the eccentric Countess. She's also left on the end of a limb by the implausible plotting, which fails to explain how she leads the venal members of the oil-seeking ring of autocrats to the fatal tunnel, or why they obligingly enter it."

Of Angela who sings "I Don't Want To Know" (about the tawdry present), "And I Was Beautiful," and "Each Tomorrow Morning" (her philosophy), Clive Barnes of the *New York Times* wrote: "The minor miracle is Miss Lansbury and whether or not the musical itself is worth seeing—for it is extraordinarily tedious—no connoisseur of musical comedy can afford to miss Miss Lansbury's performance. It is lovely. . . . there is wild poetry in every mincing genteel gesture. Her dancing is exquisite. She moves like a camp version of Bernhardt, and her acting and singing perfectly expresses a character seen in precise musical comedy terms."

For her performance in *Dear World,* Angela was named Harvard's Hasty Pudding Woman of the Year, and more importantly, won her second Tony Award. A Capital original cast LP album was made of the show, but by February, 1969, Angela wanted out. Producer Cohen is said to have stated no, not until the weekly take had dropped to $51,000. There were also backwash rumors that cast members regarded Angela as a virago on the pre-tryout tour and that the star was feuding with the cast. Angela denied it all.

Dear World, which *Time* magazine labeled a "$750,-000 bomb" and a "smoldering rubble of tedium," closed on May 31, 1969, after 132 performances at a loss of $720,000.* Later that year, Angela would inform columnist Earl Wilson concerning *Dear World:* "Playing that 'lovely old crock' as somebody called me in *Dear World* was pretty depressing for six months." On another occasion, she talked of the unglamorous rigors of starring in a Broadway musical: "When you're in a musical you don't do anything but stay home and rest to protect your voice. You come alive about 5 P.M. and you go to bed at 3. You can's smoke or drink or eat or shop or stay out because you'll start missing shows and audiences will get disgruntled. You don't have any life at all."

After the commercial failure of *Dear World,* Angela was easily persuaded to accept Broadway producer-director Harold Prince's offer for the starring role in his initial feature film, *Something for Everyone* (1970). Filmed on location at the Meuschwanstein castle in Bavaria in late summer 1969, the color feature premiered the following July, billed as a black comedy.

Something for Everyone was adapted from Harry Kressing's delightful novel, *The Cook.* Unfortunately,

---

* Producer Cohen had fought with Warner Bros.-Seven Arts to prevent the distribution of or at least delay the opening of their straight dramatic version of *The Madwoman of Chaillot,* starring Katharine Hepburn. That film version did open on October 12, 1969, to mixed notices and did poorly in distribution.

With director Hal Prince on the set of *Something for Everyone* (National General, 1970).

York, wed the *nouveau riche* Heidelinde Weis in order to restore the Ornstein fortune. When the new bride discovers her husband passionately embracing York, the schemer solves the matter by crashing the car in which he is chauffeuring her and her parents. He naturally is the only survivor. Now the newly rich Angela greedily decides to wed the unprincipled York, but her grossly fat daughter (Jane Carr) has her own plans.

Something for Everyone, which cost an expensive $2 million, earned a R rating from the motion picture industry's self-rating department for its undisguised presentation of deviant sexual behavior. In its initial art house release, the picture drew strong critical and audience attention, but then petered out on the general

the feature emerged as too much of an oversized caricature. Its plotline found ambitious but impoverished Michael York cycling through Bavaria, where he chances upon and admires the stately Castle Ornstein. He learns its owner, the widowed countess Angela, can no longer afford to maintain the magnificent structure and has moved with her young adult children to the nearby servant's house on the estate. York insinuates himself in the Ornstein household by pushing Angela's drunken footman under a passing train and taking his place. Later he denounces the unfriendly butler (Wolfried Lier) to the authorities as the son of a once prominent Nazi official. Now as butler, he converts the strawberry-eating Angela to his scheme to have her son (Anthony Corlan), who is more than infatuated with

In *Something for Everyone.*

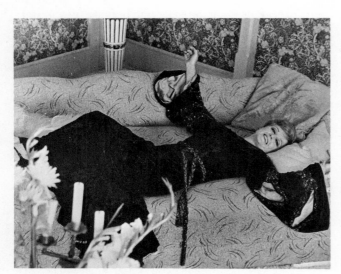

With Michael York in *Something for Everyone.*

market, too rich a dish for the mass public. One critical poll decided: "Miss Lansbury is splendid. Stylishly marvelously decadent as she devours strawberries and cream or strides elegantly about her castle in slinky, grotesquely unbecoming dresses" (*Los Angeles Examiner*). On the other hand, the *British Monthly Film Bulletin* determined (when the picture retitled *Black Flowers for the Bride* opened in London in July, 1971): "Nearly all of the scenes in his [director Prince's] pop *Teorema* [many of them extremely funny] linger on for one joke or one reaction shot too many, so that ultimately only the pleasures of certain performances remain: ... Angela Lansbury, camping it up outrageously as she disdainfully laments the age of 'the American tourist and the plastic dirndl.' "

With the unsatisfactory results of her first starring film vehicle, a proposed second project for the Cinema Center producing company, *The Widowed,* based on a script by Alvin Sargent and to be directed by Alan Padula never materialized. And plans for Angela to costar with Marcello Mastroianni in the film version of *Tchin-Tchin,* which originally was to have been filmed while she was in *Dear World* were finally abandoned.

Angela returned to California where she accepted the lucrative offer from the Walt Disney studio to star in a live-animated musical fantasy, *Bedknobs and Broomsticks* (1971), which was filmed at the Burbanks studio during the summer of 1970. It was an important project, paid well, and would give Angela a screen introduction to the family market who never saw her adult features or Broadway plays. In many ways, the film can be considered a step up in her professional career.

Thus, it was little wonder that Angela was again lured back to the Broadway stage with *Prettybelle,* based on the novel *Rape of Prettybelle* by Jean Arnold, with book and lyrics by Bob Merrill and lyrics by Jule Styne. Angela said, "I find that I must go back to the stage as often as I can. The work agrees with me—and I'm a person who needs to be doing something all the time. It can be anything—a garden project, or my home, or going to Ireland."

About studying for a role, she explained: "Finding out about a character and deciding what I'm going to take on as far as physical and emotional attributes, is part of the fun.

"I just do it automatically. I don't go to the lengths that some people I know go to to create a character. They spend a lot of time on research and background. I find that by getting that explicit I lose something on the way."

Rehearsals for Alexander H. Cohen's production of *Prettybelle* commenced December 28, 1970, and the show opened in Boston at the Shubert Theatre, February 17, 1971, staged by Gower Champion. Its story concerns southern belle Prettybelle Sweet (Angela), a patient in a mental hospital. As therapy, she is asked to write her memoirs. Because she is obsessed with sex, she writes of "rape and resurrection," detailing how after the death of her cruel sheriff husband, she decides to have an affair with a member of each minority group he had so maligned. Her amorous escapades nearly destroy the social fabric of her ingrown small Dixie town. Others in the cast were Mark Dawson as the burly ghost of her law enforcer husband, Renee Lupen as her fat, ugly daughter, Charlotte Rae as her senile mother-in-law, Jon Cypher as a sadistic bigot who hates and mutilates women, and Peter Lombard as a do-gooder revolutionary.

Angela, in her best press interview style, described *Prettybelle* as: "It's a charming study of a woman's dilemma and how she decides to solve it. I would say

Playbill for *Prettybelle* (1971).

Prettybelle is a bit of every woman of the south. Her problems sum up a lot of situations women must feel. The story does not necessarily have to do with the question of civil rights. Prettybelle's an alcoholic schizophrenic, who behaves in many curious, funny and delightful ways." Evidently, Angela's penchant for the offbeat had surmounted any sense of what would make viable theatrics. Her experience playing the Madwoman should have taught her a valuable lesson.

Her most typical song in *Prettybelle* was the second act honky-tonk number "When I Drink"; her other rather lackluster tunes included "Manic Depressives," "To a Small Degree," "How Could I Know What Was Goin' On?," "In the Japanese Gardens," "I Met a Man," "The No-Tell Motel," and "I'm a Tree."

Variety generously reported: "Miss Lansbury is poised and beautiful, completely at home on that stage. She plays the looney lady's wide-eyed, blank stare with bewitching charm, yet gives the impression she's aware of exactly how to manipulate each moment for her own gain. She sings delicately and with sweetness and handles her rather limited dancing opportunity with agility and grace. She's a strong performer and a delight to watch."

Kevin Kelly of the *Boston Globe* summed it up more realistically: ". . . the test of her skill is that she never bores us even when the musical does. Yet is it a fairly forced performance, uneasy despite its easy victories."

Long before producer Cohen closed *Prettybelle* in

Boston on March 6, 1971, the rumors of a troubled show had spread throughout the industry. There were many treks by Angela fans to Boston to catch her performance in a show that seemingly would not make it to Broadway. Despite her run of bad luck on the stage, Angela had her devoted following. When Cohen cancelled the projected New York opening at the Majestic Theatre (scheduled for March 15, 1971) at a loss of its $500,000 investment, he simply stated: "I have decided that the show is not in shape for Broadway."

After an appearance on the 1971 Tony Awards show (March 28, 1971, ABC) in which Angela glided onstage and off in flowing chiffon and seemed too much the grand lady of the theater, she returned to California to concentrate on reshaping her domestic life, which she stated required a good year off from the show business world.* But by mid-1971, Angela had evidently changed her mind. It was announced she would star in *Sister*, a musical to be produced by her brother Edgar Lansbury and by Stuart Duncan, with a book by Paul Zindel and songs by Al Carmines. It would deal with the career of an Aimee McPherson-type evangelist and was a project that had been making the rounds for several years. *Sister* was originally slated for the 1971–1972 season, but by late 1971 it had dropped from sight.

Meanwhile *Bedknobs and Broomsticks* had its London premiere and *Variety* reported: "Buena Vista by promoting it as the successor to *Mary Poppins* invite comparisons all of which may not be entirely favorable, but what it may lack in the charm of the earlier picture it more than measures in inventiveness. Indeed, it is doubtful if special effects or animation have been ever bettered or used to greater advantage. Alone they are a reason for seeing the film."

The candy-coated premise of *Bedknobs and Broomsticks* is situated in the seaside English village of Pepperinge Eye during World War II. Prim spinster Eglantine Price (Angela) pops into view riding a motorcycle that spews forth yellow sulphur fumes. She has rushed into town to receive her latest delivery from the Emelius Browne College of Witchcraft. She is more than disconcerted that the local authorities have decided to billet three young evacuees from London at her large home, but she is told she must do her part. She reluc-

tantly agrees, although she admits, "Children and I don't get along." Before long, the Cockney waifs and she have become bosom pals, once she explains that she is practicing to become a good witch so that she can help the British war effort. With the aid of a magic bedknob, she and the children set out for London to find Professor Browne (David Tomlinson), only to learn that he is a humbug and cannot really help her with the final lesson in sorcery needed to complete the course. On their search for the missing book from which Tomlinson has copied his courses, they end up in the storybook (animated) isle of Naboombu where Angela locates the talisman enabling her to practice "substitutiary locomotion," the animation of inanimate objects. Later when a Nazi landing party invades Pepperinge Eye, Angela uses her substitutiary locomotion to summon up a ghostly medieval army which repels the raiders. In the ousting of the invaders, Angela's laboratory and formulas are destroyed, but that is all right, for as in true child-oriented morality, she wisely tells the children she always knew she was not meant to be a total witch and is happy to have done her part. She and Tomlinson admit their mutual love, and he joins up with the British army to serve in the war.

Angela, as a sort of younger version of an eccentric Elsa Lanchester, managed to combine an oversized performance with professionalism and avoided playing down to her juvenile audiences. She performed assorted double taking scenes nobly, as when she unwraps a parcel and lovingly announces "My first broom" or when she takes her first flight on her stick. For a musical film, there were surprisingly few songs (reduced to six in the final release print), and Angela the star only had two numbers. The Richard M. and Robert B. Sherman tunes, "The Age of Not Believing" (as she and the children prepare to embark for London on the magic bed) and "Sub-sti-tutiary Locomotion" (as she practices her spell on the inanimate objects), were at best pleasant, and certainly not memorable in the *Mary Poppins* tradition. At age forty-six, Angela looked remarkably unchanged from the days two and a half decades before, when she had performed in the similarly British-located *If Winter Comes*. There is one brief fantasy scene in which Angela, wearing show business tights, balances along a railroad track, looking chic and shimmering.

The New York *Times'* Vincent Canby had what proved to be a typical reaction to Angela's performance in *Bedknobs and Broomsticks*: ". . . [the picture] benefits from the presence of Miss Lansbury, who is neither an especially winning singer nor dancer, but who can't help projecting a certain healthy sensuality, even in the most proper Disney circumstances." While the semi-

---

* At the time of the London opening of *Bedknobs and Broomsticks* (October, 1971) there was much publicity about Angela's nineteen-year-old son Anthony, who had just shaken a three-year heroin habit. Said Angela: "It's over. I think he's marvelous because he kicked the habit himself." Anthony is in London planning to study drama for a year and then following his mother into acting.

With Roddy McDowall, Ian Weighall, and Cindy O'Callaghan in *Bedknobs and Broomsticks* (Buena Vista, 1971).

With David Tomlinson, Ian Weighall, Cindy O'Callaghan,
and Roy Smart in *Bedknobs and Broomsticks*.

In *Bedknobs and Broomsticks*.

animated feature went on to gross very respectable box office returns (via ultra high pressure selling on the part of Buena Vista), neither responsible show business observers nor the public refused to endorse this entry as a legitimate follow up to *Mary Poppins*. No matter how much the Disney organization bally-hooed the picture, it was not a classic.

After *Bedknobs and Broomsticks* Angela found herself at even greater professional loose ends than she had in the early 1950s post her MGM tenure. Thus she readily agreed to play one of the leads in the London version of Edward Albee's *All Over* (Aldwych Theatre, January 31, 1972), a rancorous drama that had failed to win a Broadway foothold in 1971. Despite the high calibre performances by Angela, Peggy Ashcroft and Sheila Hancock, the Peter Hall-directed theater piece did not grab public favor, largely theorized *Variety* because: "high-pitched as the emotional tone is, the impact is dulled by characters that are skeletal and remote. Albee attempts to confront us with the force of language more than people, however mean and ritualized he says they are."

Angela was obviously adrift when she returned to the States in mid-1972, for she found no better offers than to recap her *Mame* chores in a summer stock tour. Her zigzagging career of peaks and lows was definitely stuck in another gully.

When it became clear that Ethel Merman would not replay her famed "Mama Rose" role in the London premiere of the 1950s Broadway musical *Gypsy*, it was first rumored that Elaine Stritch would accept the Wagnerian role of musical comedy. However, that idea

fizzled and lo and behold it was Angela who emerged as the bright star of the project (co-produced by her brother Edgar). *Gypsy* had a dazzling opening at the Piccadilly Theatre in London's West End on May 29, 1973, with Angela receiving a more enthusiastic critical reception than she had in New York for her last big stage success, *Mame*. The next morning, the headlines read, "Everything's coming up Angela." The *London Daily Mail* insisted, "The London musical stage belongs to only one woman from this very second; a rose by any other name is now Angela Lansbury!" As *Variety's* British correspondent analyzed her gutsy stage outing, "It is a marathon, high-voltage performance and, coupled with the star's personality represents the production's biggest asset."

Angela revelled at being "back home" as the toast of London, but she was equally enthusiastic about bringing *Gypsy* back to the United States, where in 1974 it enjoyed a national tour before its scheduled Broadway showcase.

Having dramatically overcome her post-*Mame* professional slump with *Gypsy*, Angela is again riding high in the show business world she knows and loves so well. Very essential to her growth as a performing luminary is a sentiment she has repeated on more than one occasion in recent years: "I'm a true Libran. I wait, I weigh, I see both points of view. I'm not at all moody. I'm very pleased and undogmatic. But I'm less afraid to stand up and think for myself than I used to be. I've discovered finally that I can trust my own opinions. Maybe that comes with success."

FILMOGRAPHY: ANGELA LANSBURY
FEATURE FILMS

GASLIGHT (MGM, 1944) 114 M.

Producer, Arthur Hornblow, Jr.; director, George Cukor; based on the play by Patrick Hamilton; screenplay, John Van Druten, Walter Reisch, John L. Balderston; music, Bronislau Kaper; art director, Cedric Gibbons; special effects, Warren Newcombe; camera, Joseph Ruttenberg; editor, Ralph E. Winters.

Charles Boyer (Gregory Anton); Ingrid Bergman (Paula); Joseph Cotten (Brian Cameron); Dame May Whitty (Miss Thwaites); Barbara Everest (Elizabeth Tompkins); Angela Lansbury (Nancy Oliver); Eustace Wyatt (Budge); Emil Rameau (Mario Guardi); Edmond Breon (General Huddulstein); Terry Moore (Paula—Age 14); Halliwell Hobbes (Mr. Mufflin); Heather Thatcher (Lady Dalroy); Lawrence Grossmith (Lord Dalroy); Charles McNaughton (Wilkins); Tom Stevenson (Williams); Harry Adams, Pat Malone (Policemen); Bobby Hale (Lamplighter); Leonard Carey (Guide); Joy Harington (Miss Pritchard); Wilson Benge, Florence Benson, Tom Hughes, Frank Baker (Pedestrians).

NATIONAL VELVET (MGM, 1944) 125 M.

Producer, Pandro S. Berman; director, Clarence Brown; based on the novel by Enid Bagnold; screenplay, Theodore Reeves, Helen Deutsch; music, Herbert Stothart; art director, Cedric Gibbons, Urie McCleary; special effects, Warren Newcombe; camera, Leonard Smith; editor, Robert J. Kern.

Mickey Rooney (Mi Taylor); Donald Crisp (Mr. Brown); Elizabeth Taylor (Velvet Brown); Anne Revere (Mrs. Brown); Juanita Quigley (Malvolia Brown); Butch Jenkins (Donald Brown); Angela Lansbury (Edwina Brown); Reginald Owen (Farmer Ede); Terry Kilburn (Ted); Alec Craig (Tim); Eugene Loring (Mr. Taski); Norma Varden (Miss Sims); Arthur Shields (Mr. Hallan); Dennis Hoey (Mr. Greenford); Aubrey Mather (Entry Official); Frederic Worlock (Stewart); Arthur Treacher (Man with Umbrella); Harry Allen (Van Driver); Billy Bevan (Constable); Barry Macollum (Townsman); Alec Harford (Valet); Gerald Oliver Smith (Cameraman); Matthew Boulton (Entry Clerk); Jack Lee (Assistant Checker); Major Douglas Francis (Track Official); William Bailey, Rose Langdon (Bookies); Donald Curtis (American); Charles Irwin (Starter).

THE PICTURE OF DORIAN GRAY (MGM, 1945) 110 M.

Producer, Pandro S. Berman; director, Albert Lewin; based on the novel by Oscar Wilde; art director, Cedric Gibbons, Hans Peters; music, Herbert Stothart; song, William Hargreaves and Dan O'Brien; camera, Harry Stradling; editor, Ferris Webster.

George Sanders (Lord Henry Wotton); Hurd Hatfield (Dorian Gray); Donna Reed (Gladys Hallward); Angela Lansbury (Sibyl Vane); Lowell Gilmore (Basil Hallward); Peter Lawford (David Stone); Richard Fraser (James Vane); Lydia Bilbrook (Mrs. Vane); Miles Mander (Sir Robert Bentley); Billy Bevan (Malvolio Jones); Moyna Macgill (Duchess); Lisa Carpenter (Lady Henry Wotton); Sir Cedric Hardwicke (Narrator); William Stack (Mr. Erskine); Natalie Draper (Mrs. Vandeleur); Anita Bolster (Lady Harborough); Lilian Bond (Kate); Sir Sidney Lawford (Davenant); Dorothy Ford (Woman); Guy Bates Post (Victor—Butler); Crauford Kent (Friend); Jimmy Conlin (Piano Player); Carol Diane Kappler (Gladys—

As a Child); Rex Evans (Lord Gerald Goodbody); Renee Carson (Young French Woman); Lee Powell (Station Master); Edward Cooper (Ernest Harrowden); Frederic Worlock (Francis, Servant); Tom Pilkington (Ant Man); John George (Hunchback).

THE HARVEY GIRLS (MGM, 1946) 104 M.

Producer, Arthur Freed; associate producer, Roger Edens; director, George Sidney; based on the book by Samuel Hopkins Adams and the story by Eleanore Griffin, William Rankin; screenplay, Edmund Beloin, Nathaniel Curtis, Harry Crane, James O'Hanlon, Samson Raphaelson; additional dialogue, Kay Van Riper; choreographer, Robert Alton; songs, Johnny Mercer and Harry Warren; art director, Cedric Gibbons, William Ferrari; music director, Lennie Hayton; special effects, Warren Newcombe; camera, George Folsey; editor, Albert Akst.

Judy Garland (Susan Bradley); John Hodiak (Ned Trent); Ray Bolger (Chris Maule); Preston Foster (Judge Sam Purvis); Virginia O'Brien (Alma); Angela Lansbury (Em); Marjorie Main (Sonora Cassidy); Chill Wills (H.H. Hartsey); Kenny Baker (Terry O'Halloran); Cyd Charisse (Deborah); Selena Royle (Miss Bliss); Ruth Brady (Ethel); Catherine McLeod (Louise); Jack Lambert (Marty Peters); Edward Earle (Jed Adams); Virginia Hunter (Jane); William 'Bill' Phillips, Norman Leavitt (Cowboys); Mitchell Lewis (Sandy); Stephen McNally (Goldust McClean); Bill Hall (Big Joe); Al Rhein (Dealer); Lee Phelps, John Merton, Tom Quinn (Players); Charles Ragan (Dealer); Ray Teal (Conductor); Jim Toney (Mule Skinner); Vernon Dent (Engineer); Paul Newlan (Station Agent); Shirley Patterson, Dorothy Tuttle, Maryedith Durrell, Eleanor Payley, Dorothy Gilmore, Lucille Casey, Virginia Davis, Mary Mullen, Joan Carey, Ruth Merman (Harvey Girls).

THE HOODLUM SAINT (MGM, 1946) 93 M.

Producer, Cliff Reid; director, Norman Taurog; screenplay, Frank Wead, James Hill; art director, Cedric Gibbons, Harry McAfee; music, Nathaniel Shilkret; special effects, Warren Newcombe; editor, Ferris Webster.

William Powell (Terry Ellerton O'Neill); Esther Williams (May Lorrison); Angela Lansbury (Dusty Willard); James Gleason (Sharp); Lewis Stone (Father Nolan); Rags Ragland (Fishface); Frank McHugh (3-Fingers); Slim Summerville (Eel); Charles Trowbridge (Uncle Joe Lorrison); Louis Jean Heydt (Mike Flaherty); Charles Arnt (Cy Nolan); Addison Richards (Reverend Miller); Tom Dugan (Muggsy); Emma Dunn (Maggie); Mary Gordon (Trina); Ernest Anderson (Sam); Paul Langton (Burton Kinston); Al Murphy (Benny); Byron Foulger (J. Cornwall Travers); Will Wright (Allan Smith); Billy Engle, Al Thompson, Capt. Fred Somers, Harry Tenbrook, William A. Janssen, Sam Finn, Sol Davis, Phil Friedman (Muggs); Charles Judels (Waiter Captain); William B. Davidson (Annoyed Man); Hope Landin (Spinster); Eddie Dunn (Gateman); Fred "Snowflake" Toomes (Pullman Porter); Jack Norton (Drunk); Dwayne Hickman (Johnny Ryan); Ruth Robinson (Mrs. Cohn); Charles Wagenheim (Mr. Cohn); Paul E. Burns (Mr. Smith); Harry Hayden (Mr. Samuels); Forbes Murray (Prosperous Man); Budd Buster (Jitney Driver).

TILL THE CLOUDS ROLL BY (MGM, 1946) 120 M.

Producer, Arthur Freed; director, Richard Whorf, Vincente Minnelli (Judy Garland numbers); story, Guy Bolten; adaptation, George Wells; screenplay, Myles Connolly, Jean Holloway; choreographer, Robert Alton; music director, Lennie Hayton; orchestrator, Conrad Salinger; art director, Cedric Gibbons; songs, Jerome Kern and Oscar

Hammerstein II; Kern and P.G. Wodehouse; Kern and Edward Laska; Kern and Herbert Reynolds; Kern, Otto Harbach, and Hammerstein II: Kern and Harbach; Kern and B.G. DeSylva; Kern and Ira Gershwin; Kern and Dorothy Fields; special effects, Warren Newcombe; camera, Harry Stradling, George J. Folsey; editor, Albert Akst.

Robert Walker (Jerome Kern); Judy Garland (Marilyn Miller); Lucille Bremer (Sally); Joan Wells (Sally—As a Girl); Van Heflin (James I. Hessler); Paul Langton (Oscar Hammerstein); Dorothy Patrick (Mrs. Jerome Kern); Mary Nash (Mrs. Muller); Harry Hayden (Charles Frohman); Paul Maxey (Victor Herbert); Rex Evans (Cecil Keller); William "Bill" Phillips (Hennessey); Dinah Shore (Julie Sanderson); Van Johnson (Band Leader); June Allyson, Angela Lansbury, Ray McDonald (Guest Stars); Maurice Kelly, Cyd Charisse, Gower Champion (Dance Specialties); Ray Teal (Orchestra Conductor); Wilde Twins (Specialty); Byron Foulger (Frohman's Secretary); William Halligan (Captain Andy); Tony Martin (Ravenal); Kathryn Grayson (Magnolia); Virginia O'Brien (Ellie); Lena Horne (Julie); Caleb Peterson (Joe); Bruce Cowling (Steve); Frank Sinatra, Johnnie Johnston (Finale); Lucille Casey, Mary Jane French, Beryl McCuthcheon, Alice Wallace, Irene Vernon, Gloria Joy Arden, Mickey Malloy, Alma Carroll, Wesley Brent (Showgirls); John Albright (Call Boy); Armand Tanney, Rube Schaeffer (Trapeze Men); James Finlayson (Candy Vendor); Ann Codee (Miss Laroche); Lilyan Irene (Barmaid); Robert Cory (Barker); George Kirby, Bobby Hale, Tom Pilkington, Al Duvall (Barkers); Stanley Andrews (Doctor); Ernest Galon (German Spectator); Bert Morehouse, Don Anderson, Charles Bradstreet (Cafe People); Reginald Simpson (Headwaiter); Paul Gordon (Unicycle Clown); Jim Grey, Douglas Wright (Bull Clowns); Arnaut Brothers (Bird Act).

THE PRIVATE AFFAIRS OF BEL AMI (United Artists, 1947), 119 M.

Producer, David L. Loew; associate producer, Ray Heinz; director Albert Lewin; based on the novel *Bel Ami* by Guy de Maupassant; screenplay, Lewin; art director, Frank Sylos; song, Jack Lawrence and Irving Drutman; camera, Russell Metty; editor, Albrecht Joseph.

George Sanders (Georges Duroy); Angela Lansbury (Clotilde de Marelle); Ann Dvorak (Madeleine Forestier); Frances Dee (Marie de Varenne); John Carradine (Charles Forestier); Susan Douglas (Suzanna Walter); Hugo Haas (Monsieur Walter); Marie Wilson (Rachel Michot); Albert Basserman (Jacques Rival); Warren William (Laroche-Mathieu); Richard Fraser (Philippe de Cantel); David Bond (Norbert de Varenne); John Good (Paul de Cazolles); Leonard Mudie (Potin); Judy Cook (Hortense); Katherine Emery (Madame Walter); Lumsden Hare (Mayor of Canteleu); Karolyn Grimes (Laurine de Marelle); Olaf Hytten (Keeper of the Seals); Wyndham Standing (Count de Vaudrec); Jean Del Val (Commissioner); Charles Trowbridge (Lawyer); Alex Pollard (Forestier Butler); Betty Fairfax (Louise, Maid); Rudy Germaine (Georges' Butler).

IF WINTER COMES (MGM, 1947) 97 M.

Producer, Pandro S. Berman; director, Victor Saville; based on the novel by A.S.M. Hutchinson; screenplay, Marguerite Roberts, Arthur Wimperis; music, Herbert Stothart; art director, Cedric Gibbons, Hans Peters; camera, George Folsey; editor, Ferris Webster.

Walter Pidgeon (Mark Sabre); Deborah Kerr, Nona Tybar); Angela Lansbury (Mabel Sabre); Binnie Barnes (Natalie Bagshaw); Janet Leigh (Effie Fright); Dame May Whitty (Mrs. Perch); Rene Ray (Sarah "Low Jinks");

Reginald Owen (Mr. Fortune); John Abbott (Mr. Twyning); Hugh Frech (Lord Tybar); Nickolas Joy (Pattigrew); Dennis Hoey (Tiny Wilson); Victor Wood (Mr. Fargus); Hugh Green (Freddie Perch); James Wethered (Harold Twyning); Virginia Keiley (Rebecca "High Jinks"); Owen McGiveney (Uncle Fouraker); Pat Aherne (Grimes, The Chauffeur); James Fairfax (George); Alex Fraser (Clint); Phyllis Morris (Mrs. Fargus); Joe Strauch (Fat Youth); Herbert Wyndham (Higgins, The Salesman); David Martin Jones (Garnett, The Chauffeur); Ruth Sanderson (Mabel's Bridge Partner); Ian Wolfe (Doctor); David Dunbar (Milkman); Richard Glyn (General Gart); Winston Severn (Hitler); Norman Leavitt (Cyril Cottswood); Wyndham Standing (Aged Gentleman); Elspeth Dudgeon (Mrs. Ward); Jack Merivale (Inspector Broster); Cyril Smith (Truck Driver); Stanley Fraser (Sergeant Local Depot); John Powers (Constable); Major Sam Harris (Clerk in Book Store); Olaf Hytten (Officer); Cyril Thornton (Jury Foreman).

TENTH AVENUE ANGEL (MGM, 1948) 74 M.

Producer, Ralph Wheelwright; director, Roy Rowland; story, Angna Enters, Craig Rice; screenplay, Harry Ruskin, Eleanor Griffin; art director, Cedric Gibbons, Wade Rubottom; music, Rudolph G. Kopp; camera, Robert Surtees; editor, Ralph E. Winters, George Boemler.

Margaret O'Brien (Flavia Mills); George Murphy (Steve Abbott); Angela Lansbury (Susan Bratten); Phyllis Thaxter (Helen Mills); Rhys Williams (Blind Mac); Warner Anderson (Joseph Mills); Audrey Totter (Gloria Slack); Henry Blair (Rad Ardley); Dickie Tyler (Jimmy Madson); Connie Gilchrist (Mrs. Murphy); Tom Trout (Daniel Oliver Madson); Cameron Mitchell (Ted Foley); Marissa O'Brien (Jane Dighton); Walter Soderling (Mr. Cassitto); Cy Kendall (Higgins); Paul Burns (Pop); Barry Nelson (Al Parker); Richard Lane (Vendor); Claire Dubrey (Mrs. Madson); Robert Emmett O'Connor (O'Callan); Della Clark (Mrs. Klein); Charles Bates, Gary Gray (Children); Nolan Leary (Fruit Vendor); Tom Dillon (Doctor) Lane Chandler (Doorman); Mike P. Donovan (Engineer); George Magrill (Brakeman); Ray Teal (Cowboy); Lee Phelps (Police Officer); Ben Mosselle (Emile); Angi O. Poulos (Mr. Challupaki); Jane Green (Woman); Heinie Conklin, John W. Dillon, Henry Sylvester (Aldermen); Jesse Arnold (Woman at Block Party).

STATE OF THE UNION (MGM, 1948) 124 M.

Producer, Frank Capra; associate producer, Anthony Veiller; director, Capra; based on the play by Howard Lindsay, Russell Crouse; screenplay, Veiller, Myles Connolly; music, Victor Young; art director, Cedric Gibbons, Urie McCleary; camera, George J. Folsey; editor, William Hornbeck.

Spencer Tracy (Grant Matthews); Katharine Hepburn (Mary Matthews); Van Johnson (Spike McManus); Angela Lansbury (Kay Thorndyke); Adolphe Menjou (Jim Conover); Lewis Stone (Sam Thorndyke); Howard Smith (Sam Parrish); Maidel Turner (Lulubelle Alexander); Raymond Walburn (Judge Alexander); Charles Dingle (Bill Hardy); Florence Auer (Grace Draper); Pierre Watkin (Senator Lauterbach); Margaret Hamilton (Norah); Irving Bacon (Buck); Patti Brady (Joyce); Carl Switzer (Bellboy); George Nokes (Grant, Jr.); Tom Fadden (Waiter); Tom Pedi (Barber); Art Baker (Leith, Radio Announcer); Rhea Mitchell (Jenny); Charles Lane (Blink Moran); Boyd Davis, Howard Mitchell (Doctors); Arthur O'Connell, Bob Skelton, Drew Demorest, Barry Regan, Ed Randolph (Reporters); Henry Sylvester (Butler); Netta Parker (Nurse); Sig Frolich (Page Boy); Maurice Cass (Little Man); Franklyn Farnum (Man); Stanley Andrews

(Senator); Dave Willock (Pilot); Edwin Cooper (Bradbury); Norma Brown (Cigarette Girl); Mahlon Hamilton (Business Man); Garry Owen, Judy Brent (Brooklyn Couple); Eddie Phillips (Television Man); Jerry Schumaker, Joe Gilbert (Newsreel Camermen); Roger Moore, Lew Smith, Gene Coogan, Douglas Carter, Charles Sherlock, Wilson Wood, George Barton, Harry Anderson, Charles Colean, Stanley Price, Fred Zendar, Jack Boyle (Photographers); Helen Eby-Rock (Business Woman); Ann Beck (Receptionist).

THE THREE MUSKETEERS (MGM, 1948)) 132 M.

Producer, Pandro S. Berman; director, George Sidney; based on the novel by Alexandre Dumas; screenplay, Robert Audrey; art director, Cedric Gibbons, Malcolm Brown; music, Herbert Stothart; special effects, Warren Newcombe; camera, Robert Planck; editor, Robert J. Kern, George Boembler.

Lana Turner (Milady Countess deWinter); Gene Kelly (D'Artagnan); June Allyson (Constance Bonacieux); Van Heflin (Athos); Angela Lansbury (Queen Anne); Frank Morgan (Louis XIII); Vincent Price (Richelieu, Prime Minister); Keenan Wynn (Planchet); John Sutton (Duke of Buckingham); Gig Young (Porthos); Robert Coote (Aramis); Reginald Owen (de Treville); Ian Keith (de Rochefort); Patricia Medina (Kitty); Richard Stapley (Albert); Robert Warwick (D'Artagnan, Senior); Byron Foulger (Bonacieux); Marie Windsor (Lady-In-Waiting); Ruth Robinson (D'Artagnan's Mother); Dickie Dubins, Charles Bates, David Blair (D'Artagnan's Brothers); Tom Tyler, Michael Kostrick (Travelers); Gordon Clark, Gregg Barton, Leonard Penn, Fred Coby (Musketeers); Kirk Alyn, John Holland (Friends of Aramis); Francis McDonald (Fisherman); Wilson Benge (Valet); Paul Maxey (Major Domo); Jean L. Heremans (Cardinal Guard); Carl Saxe, Gil Perkins (Guards); Frank Hagney (Executioner of Lyons); Dave Sharpe (Double for D'Artagnan); Mickey Simpson (Executioner); David Thursby (Innkeeper).

THE RED DANUBE (MGM, 1949) 119 M.

Producer, Carey Wilson; director, George Sidney; based on the novel *Vespers in Vienna* by Bruce Marshall; screenplay, Gina Kaus, Arthur Wimperis; art director, Cedric Gibbons, Hans Peters; camera, Charles Rosher; editor, James E. Newcom.

Walter Pidgeon (Colonel Michael "Jooky" Nicobar); Peter Lawford (Major John "Twingo" McPhimister); Angela Lansbury (Audrey Quail); Janet Leigh (Marie Buhlen); Ethel Barrymore (Mother Superior); Louis Calhern (Colonel Piniev); Francis L. Sullivan (Colonel Humphrey "Blinker" Omicron); Melville Cooper (Private David Moonlight); Robert Coote (Brigadier C.M.V. Catlock); Alan Napier (General); Roman Toporow (Second Lieutenant Maxim Omansky); Kasia Orzazewski (Sister Kasimira); Janine Perreau ("Mickey Mouse"); Konstantin Shayne (Professor Serge Bruloff); David Hydes (Lieutenant Guedalia-Wood); Audrey Long (Countess Cressanti); Margo Von Leu (Lani Hansel); Tito Vuolo (Italian Billposter); Argentina Brunetti (Italian Woman); Lotus Thompson (Woman Private); John Royce (Sergeant); Henry Kulky (Lieutenant); Emil Rameau (Proprietor); Carol Savage (Private Jemima); Doris Lloyd (Mrs. Omicron); Richard Fraser (Pilot); Geoffrey Alah (Major); Sigmund Halperon (German); Kenneth Hunter (Brigadier General).

SAMSON AND DELILAH (Paramount, 1949) 127 M.

Producer-director, Cecil B. DeMille; based on a treatment by Harold Lamb of the story of Samson and Delilah in the Holy Bible and the novel *Judge and Fool* by Vladimir Jabotinsky; screenplay, Jesse L. Lasky, Jr., Frederic M. Frank; music, Victor Young; art director, Hans Dreier, Walter Tyler; camera, George Barnes; editor, Anne Bauchens.

Hedy Lamarr (Delilah); Victor Mature (Samson); George Sanders (Saran of Gaza); Angela Lansbury (Semadar); Henry Wilcoxon (Ahtur); Olive Deering (Miriam); Fay Holden (Hazel); Julia Faye (Hisham); Rusty Tamblyn (Saul); William Farnum (Tubal); Lane Chandler (Teresh); John Miljan (Lesh Lakish); William Davis (Garmiskar); Francis J. McDonald (Story Teller): Laura Elliot (Spectator); Victor Varconi (Lord of Ashdod); John Parrish (Lord of Gath); Frank Wilcox (Lord of Ekron); Russell Hicks (Lord of Ashkelon); Boyd Davis (Priest); Davison Clark (Merchant Prince); George Reeves (Wounded Messenger); Frank Reicher (Village Barber); Pedro de Cordoba (Bar Simon); Charles Evans (Manoah, Samson's Father); Frank Mayo (Master Architect); Lloyd Whitlock (Chief Scribe); Crauford Kent (Court Astrologer); Harry Woods (Gammad); Ed Hinton (Makon at Feast/Double for Samson); Carl Saxe (Slave); Nils Asther, Colin Tapley, James Craven (Princes); Marjorie Pragon (Snake Dancer); Fred Graham, Wesley Hopper, Budd Fine, Joe Dominguez, Larry Steers, Howard Gardiner, Harry Templeton (Priests); Leoncio Madero (Pottery Worker); Ethan Laidlaw, John Halloran, Ray Teal (Tax Collectors); Eric Alden, Sally Rawlinson, Joyce Miller (Guests); Al Ferguson (Villager); Lester Dorr, Wheaton Chambers, Larry Thompson, Jack Clifford (Victims); Tom Tyler (Philistine Captain at Gristmill); Ray Bennett (Overseer at Gristmill); George Magrill (Courtier); Bob Kortman (Vendor); Fred Kohler, Jr., Dick Foote (Soldiers—Temple); Ted Mapes (Captain Killed by Jawbone); Leo J. McMahon (Charioteer); Bert Moorhouse, Keith Richards, Rodric Redwing (Spectators); Perry Ivins (Herdsman); Byron Foulger (Man); Charles Dayton, Angelo Rossitto (Midgets at Arena); Henry Willis (Saran's Charioteer).

KIND LADY (MGM, 1951) 78 M.

Producer, Armand Deutsch; director, John Sturges; based on the story by Hugh Walpole and the play by Edward Chodorov; screenplay, Jerry Davis, Chodorov; music, David Raskin; art director, Cedric Gibbons, William Ferrari; camera, Joseph Ruttenberg; editor, Ferris Webster.

Ethel Barrymore (Mary Herries); Maurice Evans (Henry Springer Elcott); Angela Lansbury (Mrs. Edwards); Keenan Wynn (Edwards); Betsy Blair (Ada Elcott); John Williams (Mr. Foster); Doris Lloyd (Rose); John O'Malley (Antique Dealer); Henri Letondal (Monsieur Malsquaise); Moyna Macgill (Mrs. Harkley); Barry Bernard (Mr. Harkley); Sally Cooper (Lucy Weston); Arthur Gould-Porter (Chauffeur); Sherlee Collier (Aggie Edwards); Phyllis Morris (Dora); Patrick O'Moore (Constable Orkin); Keith McConnell (Jones); Leonard Carey (Postman); Victor Wood (Doc); Wilson Benge, Robert Hale (Carol Singers); Alex Frazer (Book Clerk); Bob Evans (Man); Ida McGill, Queenie Leonard (Women); Malcolm Keen (Mr. Blakeley); Patrick Whyte (Foreman); James Logan (Workman); George Cathrey (Delivery Man); Stanley Fraser (Tailor); Stanley Mann, Vesey O'Davoren, Colin Kenny, George Kirby (Pedestrians).

MUTINY (United Artists, 1952) 77 M.

Producer, Maurice King, Frank King; director, Edward Dmytryk; story, Hollister Noble; screenplay, Philip Yordan, Sidney Harmon; music, Dmitri Tiomkin; camera, Ernest Lazlo; editor, Frank Sullivan.

Mark Stevens (James Marshall); Angela Lansbury (Leslie); Patric Knowles (Ben Waldridge); Gene Evans (Hook); Rhys Williams (Redlegs); Robert Osterlon (Faversham); Peter Brocco (Sykes); Norman Leavitt (Hackett); Gene Roth (Potter); Walter Sande (Stone); Clayton Moore (Peters); Morris Ankrum (Radford); Todd Karnes (Andrews); Louis Jean Heydt (Captain Herwig); Robin Hughes (Lt. Vaughan); Crane Whitley (Colonel Rogers); Emerson Treacy (Council Speaker); Harry Antrim (Chairman Parsons).

REMAINS TO BE SEEN (MGM, 1953) 88 M.

Producer, Arthur Hornblow, Jr.; director, Don Weis; based on the play by Howard Lindsay and Russell Crouse; music director, Jeff Alexander, art director, Cedric Gibbons, Hans Peters; camera, Robert Planck; editor, Cotton Warburton.

June Allyson (Jody Revere); Van Johnson (Waldo Williams); Louis Calhern (Benjamin Goodwin); Angela Lansbury (Valeska Chauval); John Beal (Dr. Glenson); Dorothy Dandridge (Herself); Barry Kelley (Lt. O'Flair); Sammy White (Ben); Kathryn Card (Mrs. West); Paul Harvey (Mr. Bennett); Helene Millard (Mrs. Bennett); Peter Chong (Ling Tan); Charles Lane (Examiner Delapp); Larry Blake (Detective Minetti); Morgan Farley (Kyle Manning); Howard Freeman (Clark); Frank Nelson (Fleming); Robert Foulk (Officer Miller); Dabbs Greer (Julius); Emmett Smith (Buck); Thomas P. Dillon (Frank); Dave Willock (Driver); Don Anderson (Attendant); Gregory Gay (Head Waiter); Erno Verebes, Frank Scannell (Waiters); Shep Menken (Man); Veronika Pataky, Fernanda Eliscu (Women); Dick Simmons (M.C.); Fred Welsh (Taxi Driver).

KEY MAN (a.k.a. A LIFE AT STAKE) (Gibraltar, 1954) 77 M.

Producer, Hank McCune; director, Paul Guilfoyle; screenplay, Russ Bender; music, Les Baxter, McCune; camera, Ted Allan.

Angela Lansbury (Doris Hillman); Keith Andes (Edward Shaw); Douglass Dumbrille (Gus Hillman); Claudia Barrett (Madge); Jane Darwell (Mrs. Piltz); Gavin Gordon (Sam Pearson); Charles Maxwell (Lt. Hoff); Bill Henry (Myles Norman); Kathleen Mulqueen (Mary); Dan Sturkee (Policeman).

A LAWLESS STREET (Columbia, 1955) 78 M.

Producer, Harry Joe Brown, associate producer, Randolph Scott; director, Joseph H. Lewis; based on the novel *Marshall of Medicine Bend* by Brad Ward; screenplay, Kenneth Gamet; art director, George Brooks; music, Paul Sawtell; camera, Ray Rennahan; editor, Gene Havlick.

Randolph Scott (Calem Ware); Angela Lansbury (Tally Dickinson); Warner Anderson (Hamer Thorne); Jean Parker (Cora Dean); Wallace Ford (Doctor Amos Wynn); John Emery (Cody Clark); James Bell (Asaph Dean); Ruth Donnelly (Molly Higgins); Michael Pate (Harley Baskam); Don Megowan (Dooley Brion); Jeanette Nolan (Mrs. Dingo Brion); Peter Ortiz (Hiram Hays); Frank Hagney (Dingo Brion); Don Carlos (Juan Tobrez); Charles B. Williams (Willis); Frank Ferguson (Abe Deland); Harry Tyler (Tony Cabrillo); Harry Antrim (Mayor Kent); Jay Lawrence, Reed Howes, Guy Teague (Townsmen); Pat Collins (Gambler); Hal K. Dawson (Hotel Clerk); Frank Scannell (Bartender); Edwin Chandler (Man); Stanley Blystone (Rancher).

THE PURPLE MASK (Universal, 1955) 82 M.

Producer, Howard Christie; director, Bruce Humberstone; based on the play *Le Chevalier du Masque* by Paul Aumont, Jean Manoussi; adaptation, Charles Latour; screenplay, Oscar Brodney; art director, Alexander Golitzen, Eric Orbom; music director, Joseph Gershenson; camera, Irving Glassberg; editor, Ted J. Kent.

Tony Curtis (Rene); Colleen Miller (Laurette); Dan O'Herlihy (Brisquet); Gene Barry (Captain Laverne); Angela Lansbury (Madame Valentine); George Dolenz (Marcel Cadonal); John Hoyt (Rochet); Donald Randolph (Majolin); Robert Cornthwaite (Napoleon); Stephe Bekassy (Baron De Morleve); Paul Cavanagh (Duc de Latour); Myrna Hansen (Constance); Allison Hayes (Irene); Betty Jane Howarth (Yvonne); Carl Miletaire (Edouard); Gene Darcy (De Morsanne); Robert Hunter (De Vivanne); Richard Avonde (Roger); Glase Lohman (Raoul); Diane Dubois (Sabine); Jane Easton (Marie); Richard Richonne, Donald Lawton (Passersby); Everett Glass (Father Brochard); Jean De Briac (Count De Chauvac); Adrienne D'Ambricourt (Madame Anais); Eugene Borden (Napoleon Officer); Louis Bourell (Workman); Olga Andre (Customer); Peter Camlin (Colonel); George Baxter (Official); Ralph Faulkner (Opponent); Lomax Study, Richard Flato (Orderlies); Joseph Romantini, Charles Bastin (Gendarmes); Albert Godderis (Servant); George Bruggeman (Officer).

THE COURT JESTER (Paramount, 1956) 101 M.

Producer-director-screenplay, Norman Panama, Melvin Frank; choreographer, James Starbuck; songs, Sylvia Fine; Sammy Cahn; music conductor, Victor Schoen; art director, Hal Pereira, Roland Anderson; camera, Ray June; editor, Tom McAdoo.

Danny Kaye (Hawkins); Glynis Johns (Maid Jean); Basil Rathbone (Sir Ravehurst); Angela Lansbury (Princess Gwendolyn); Cecil Parker (King Roderick); Mildred Natwick (Griselda); John Carradine (Gracomo); Robert Middleton (Sir Griswold); Michael Pate (Sir Locksley); Herbert Rudley (Captain of the Guard); Noel Drayton (Fergus); Edward Ashley (Flack Fox); Alan Napier (Sir Brockhurst); Lewis Martin (Sir Finsdale); Patrick Aherne (Sir Pertwee); Richard Kean (Archbishop); Hermine's Midgets (Themselves); Larry Pennell (Novice Knight); Tudor Owen (Friar); Charles Irwin (Griswold Aide); Leo Britt (Sir Bertram); Russell Gaige (Chamberlain) Ray Kellog (Court Official); Eric Alden (King's Man); William Augustus Fuller, Joel Smith (Forestry Officer); Robert E. Smith (Priest) Robert Hart, Burnell Dietach, Chad Dee Block, Leo Wheeler (Specialty Dancers); Robert E. Smith (Forester); Michael Mahoney (Soldier); Phyllis Coghlan (Hairdresser); Claude Wuhrman, Harry Lloyd Nelson (Knights); John Irving (Gate House Guard); Roy G. Gunther (Pageboy); Frank Meservey, Ronald R. Rice, Roger Lee McKee (Knight Recruits); Lee Belser (Court Lady).

PLEASE MURDER ME (Distributors Corporation Of America, 1956) 78 M.

Producer, Donald Hyde; director, Peter Godfrey; screenplay, Al C. Ward, Hyde; art director, Nick Remisoff; camera, Allen Stensvold; editor, Kenny Crane.

Angela Lansbury (Myra Leeds); Raymond Burr (Craig Carlson); Dick Foran (Joe Leeds); John Dehner (District Attorney); Lamont Johnson (Carl Holt); Robert Griffin (Lou Kazorian); Denver Pyle (Lt. Bradley); Alex Sharpe (Sergeant); Lee Miller (Policeman); Madge Blake (Jenny); Russ Thorson (Judge).

THE LONG, HOT SUMMER (Twentieth Century-Fox, 1958) 117 M.

Producer, Jerry Wald; director, Martin Ritt; based on the stories "Barn Burners," "The Spotted Horses" by William

Faulkner and the novel *The Hamlet* by Faulkner; screenplay, Irving Ravetch, Harriet Frank, Jr.; assistant director, Eli Dunn; art director, Lyle R. Wheeler, Maurice Ransford; music, Alex North; song, Sammy Cahn and North; camera, Joseph LaShelle; editor, Louis R. Loeffler.

Paul Newman (Ben Quick); Joanne Woodward (Clara Varner); Anthony Franciosa (Jody Varner); Orson Welles (Will Varner); Lee Remick (Eula Varner); Angela Lansbury (Minnie); Sarah Marshall (Agnes Stewart); Richard Anderson (Alan Stewart); Mabel Albertson (Mrs. Stewart); J. Pat O'Malley (Ratliff); William Walker (Lucius); George Dunn (Peabody); Jess Kirkpatrick (Armistead); Val Avery (Wilk); I. Stanford Jolley (Houstin); Helen Wallace (Mrs. Houstin); Byron Foulger (Harris); Victor Rodman (Justice of the Peace); Terry Rangno (Pete Armistead); Ben Adler (Ambulance Driver); Pat Rosemond (Black Girl); Nicholas King (John Fisher); Lee Erickson (Tom Shorty); Ralph Reed (J.V. Bookright); Steve Widders (Buddy Peabody); Jim Brandt (Linus Olds); Brian Corcoran (Harry Peabody); Eugene Jackson (Waiter).

THE RELUCTANT DEBUTANTE (MGM, 1958) 94 M.

Producer, Pandro S. Berman; director, Vincente Minnelli; based on the play by William Douglas Home; screenplay, Home; art director, A.J. d'Eaubonne; assistant director, William McGarry; music arranger, Eddie Warner; camera, Joseph Ruttenberg; editor, Adrienne Fazan.

Rex Harrison (Jimmy Broadbent); Kay Kendall (Sheila Broadbent); John Saxon (David Parkson); Sandra Dee (Jane Broadbent); Angela Lansbury (Mabel Claremont); Peter Myers (David Fenner); Diane Clare (Clarissa Claremont); Sheila Raynor (Maid); Charles Cullum (English Colonel); Ambrosine Phillpotts (Secretary).

THE DARK AT THE TOP OF THE STAIRS (Warner Brothers, 1960) 123 M.

Producer, Michael Garrison; director, Delbert Mann; based on the play by William Inge; screenplay, Harriet Frank, Jr., Irving Ravetch; music, Max Steiner; assistant director, Russell Llewellyn; art director, Leo K. Kuter; camera, Harry Stradling, Sr.; editor, Flomar Blangsted.

Robert Preston (Rubin Flood); Dorothy McGuire (Cora Flood); Eve Arden (Lottie); Angela Lansbury (Mavis Pruitt); Shirley Knight (Reenie Flood); Frank Overton (Morris); Lee Kinsolving (Sammy Golden); Robert Eyer (Sonny Flood); Penney Parker (Flirt Conroy); Dennis Whitcomb (Punky Givens); Ken Lynch (Harry Ralston); Nelson Leigh (Ed Peabody); Emerson Treacy (George Williams); Ben Erway (Joseph Moody); Helen Brown (Mrs. Haycox); Jean Paul King, John Eiman, Mike Chain, Bobby Beekman, Butch Hengen (Boys); Helen Wallace (Lydia Harper); Peg LaCentra (Edna Harper); Paul Birch (Jonah Mills); Mary Patton (Mrs. Ralston); Paul Comi (Jenkins); Addison Richards (Harris); Robin Warga (Harold); Charles Seel (Percy Weems); Stoddard Kirby (Cadet).

A BREATH OF SCANDAL (Paramount, 1960) 98 M.

Producer, Carlo Ponti, Marcello Girosi; associate producer, Gene Allen; director, Michael Curtiz; based on the play *Olympia* by Ferenc Molnar; screenplay, Walter Bernstein; assistant director, Mario Russo; music, Alessandro Cicognini; songs, Robert Stolz and Al Stillman; Sepp Fellner, Karl Schneider, and Patrick Michael; camera, Mario Montuori; editor, Howard Smith.

Sophia Loren (Olympia); John Gavin (Charlie); Maurice Chevalier (Philip); Isabel Jeans (Eugenie); Angela Lansbury (Lina); Tullio Carminati (Albert); Roberto Risso (Aide); Carlo Hinterman (Rupert); Milly Vitale (Can-Can Girl); Adrienne Gessner (Amelia); Frederich Ledebur (Count Sandur).

SEASON OF PASSION (United Artists, 1961) 93 M.

Producer, Leslie Norman; associate producer, Cecil Ford; director, Norman; based on the play *Summer of the Seventeenth Doll* by Ray Lawler; screenplay, John Dighton; assistant director, Alex Ezard; music, Benjamin Frankel; camera, Paul Beeron; editor, Gordon Hales.

Ernest Borgnine (Roo); Anne Baxter (Olive); John Mills (Barney); Angela Lansbury (Pearl); Vincent Ball (Dowd); Ethel Gabriel (Emma); Janette Craig (Bubba); Deryck Barnes (Spruiker); Tom Lurich ("The Atomic Bomber"); Al Thomas, Al Garcia, Frank Wilson (Cane Cutters); Dana Wilson (Little Girl); Jessica Noad (Nancy).

BLUE HAWAII (Paramount, 1961) 101 M.

Producer, Hal B. Wallis; associate producer, Paul Nathan; director, Norman Taurog; story, Allan Weiss; screenplay, Hal Kanter; assistant director, Mickey Moore; art director, Walter Tyler; choreographer, Charles O'Curran; music director, Joseph J. Lilley; camera, Charles Lang, Jr.; editor, Warren Low.

Elvis Presley (Chad Gates); Joan Blackman (Maile Duval); Nancy Walters (Abigail Prentace); Roland Winters (Fred Gates); Angela Lansbury (Sarah Lee Gates); John Archer (Jack Kelman); Howard McNear (Mr. Chapman); Flora Hayes (Mrs. Manaka); Gregory Gay (Mr. Duval); Steve Brodie (Mr. Garvey); Iris Adrian (Mrs. Garvey); Darlene Tompkins (Patsy); Pamela Akert (Sandy); Christian Kay (Beverly); Jenny Maxwell (Ellie); Frank Atienza (Ito O'Hara); Lani Kai (Carl); Jose De Varga (Ernie); Ralph Hanalie (Wes).

THE FOUR HORSEMEN OF THE APOCALYPSE (MGM, 1962) 153 M.

Producer, Julian Blaustein; associate producer, Olallo Rubio, Jr.; director, Vincente Minelli; based on the novel by Vicente Blasco Ibanez; screenplay, Robert Ardre, John Gay; assistant director, Erich Von Stroheim, Jr.; choreographer, Alex Romero; costumes, Rene Hubert, camera, Milton Krasner; editor, Adrienne Fazan, Ben Lewis; special effects, A. Arnold Gillespie, Lee LeBlanc, Robert R. Hoag.

Glenn Ford (Julio Desnoyers); Ingrid Thulin (Marguerite Laurier; Charles Boyer (Margelo Desnoyers); Lee J. Cobb (Julio Madariaga); Paul Henried (Etienne Laurier); Paul Lukas (Karl Von Hartrott); Harriet MacGibbon (Dona Luise Desnoyers); Karl Boehm (Heinrich Von Hartrott); Yvette Mimieux (Chi-Chi Desnoyers); Kathryn Givney (Elena Von Hartrott); Stephen Bekassy (Colonel Kleinsdorf); Nestor Paiva (Miguel); Albert Remy (Francois); Richard Franchot (Gustav Von Hartrott); Brian Avery (Franz Von Hartrott); Robert Stevenson (Clerk); Louise Vincent, Fifi Dorsay, Lilian Chauvin, Elizabeth Harrower, Richard Fatlo (French Prisoners); Tom Hernandez (Headwaiter); Angela Lansbury (Voice of Marguerite Laurier).

ALL FALL DOWN (MGM, 1962) 111 M.

Producer, John Houseman; director, John Frankenheimer; based on the novel by James Leo Herlihy; screenplay, William Inge; music, Alex North; art director, George W. Davis, Preston Ames; assistant director, Hal Polaire; sound, Franklyn Milton; camera, Lionel Lindon; editor, Frederick Steincamp.

Eva Marie Saint (Echo O'Brien); Warren Beatty (Berry-Berry Willart); Karl Malden (Ralph Willart); Angela Lansbury (Annabel Willart); Brandon deWilde (Clinton Willart); Constance Ford (Mrs. Mandel); Barbara Baxley (Schoolteacher); Evans Evans (Hedy); Jennifer Howard (Myra); Madame Spivy (Bouncer); Colette Jackson (Dorothy); Albert Paulsen (Captain Pamirez); Robert Sorrells

(Waiter in Sweet Shop); Carol Kelly (Flame); Paul Bryar (Manager of Sweet Shop); Anton Van Stralen, Walter Roberson, Henry Kulky (Sailors); Murray Kay (Bus Driver); W.C. Greenfield (Clerk); Edna Sweeting (Waitress); Buffy Dee (Police Lieutenant); Kay Masters (April Storm); James Callahan (Gas Station Attendant); William Challee, Harry Hines, Burt Mustin (Bums); Mike Ross (Vinnie Agricola); Charles Whitley (Bartender); Fuchia Hayes (Stripteaser); Ella Ethridge, Caryl Lincoln, Estelle Etterre, Mary Benoit (Club Women).

THE MANCHURIAN CANDIDATE (United Artists, 1962) 126 M.

Executive producer, Howard W. Koch; producer, George Axelrod, John Frankenheimer; director, Frankenheimer; based on the novel by Richard Condon; screenplay, Axelrod; assistant director, Joseph Behm; music, David Amram; production designer, Richard Sylbert; sound, Joe Edmondson; camera, Lionel Lindon; editor, Ferris Webster.

Frank Sinatra (Bennett Marco); Laurence Harvey (Raymond Shaw); Janet Leigh (Rosie); Angela Lansbury (Raymond's Mother); Henry Silva (Chunjin); James Gregory (Senator John Iselin); Leslie Parrish (Jocie Jordan); John McGiver (Senator Thomas Jordan); Khigh Dhiegh (Yen Lo); James Edwards (Corporal Melvin); Douglas Henderson (Colonel); Albert Paulsen (Zilkov); Barry Kelley (Secretary of Defense); Lloyd Corrigan (Holborn Gaines); Madame Spivy (Berezova).

IN THE COOL OF THE DAY (MGM, 1963) 88 M.

Producer, John Houseman; director, Robert Stevens; based on a novel by Susan Ertz; screenplay, Meade Roberts; art director, Kenneth Adam; music, Francis Chagrin; camera, Peter Newbrook; editor, Thomas Stanford.

Peter Finch (Murray Logan); Jane Fonda (Christine Bonner); Angela Lansbury (Sibyl Logan); Arthur Hill (Sam Bonner); Constance Cummings (Mrs. Gellert); Nigel Davenport (Len Graham); Alexander Knox (Frederick Bonner); John Le Mesurier (Doctor); Alec McCowen (Dickie Bayliss); Valerie Taylor(Lily Kendrick); Andreas Markos (Andreas).

THE WORLD OF HENRY ORIENT (United Artists, 1964) 115 M.

Producer, Jerome Helman; director, George Roy Hill; based on the novel by Nora Johnson; screenplay, Nora Johnson, Nunnally Johnson; assistant director, Michael Hertzberg, Roger Rothstein; music, Elmer Bernstein; costumes, Ann Roth; camera, Boris Kaufman; editor, Stuart Gilmore.

Peter Sellers (Henry Orient); Paula Prentiss (Stella); Angela Lansbury (Isabel Boyd); Tom Bosley (Frank Boyd); Phyllis Thaxter (Mrs. Gilbert); Tippy Walker (Valerie Boyd); Merrie Spaeth (Marian Gilbert); Peter Duchin (Joe Byrd); Bibi Osterwald (Boothy); John Fiedler (Sidney); Al Lewis (Store Owner); Fred Stewart (Doctor); Philippa Bevans (Emma); Jane Buchanan (Kafritz).

DEAR HEART (Warner Brothers, 1963) 114 M.

Producer, Martin Manulis; director, Delbert Mann; based on the story by Tad Mosel; screenplay, Mosel; assistant director, Carter DeHaven, Jr.; music, Henry Mancini; song, Mancini, Jay Livingston, and Ray Evans; camera, Russell Harlan; editor, Folmar Blangsted.

Glenn Ford (Harry Mork); Geraldine Page (Evie Jackson); Angela Lansbury (Phyllis); Barbara Nichols (June); Michael Anderson (Patrick); Patricia Barry (Mitchell); Charles Drake (Frank Taylor); Neva Patterson (Connie); Ruth McDevitt (Miss Tait); Richard Deacon (Cruikshank); Joanna Crawford (Zola); Mary Wickes (Miss

Fox); Alice Pearce (Miss Moore); Ken Lynch (The Masher); Peter Turgeon (Peterson); Nelson Olmsted (Herb); James Bell (Chester); Billy Benedict (Stu); Donald Kerr (Drunk); Jeanne Arnold (Rita); Tom Palmer (Weinstock); Patsy Garrett (Millicent); Dorothy Abbott (Veronica); John Wilson (Maurice); Barbara Luddy (Miss Carmichael); Pauline Myers (Florist); Tad Mosel (Man in Lobby); Charles Alvin Bell (Zanzibar); Martin Bolger (Fred).

THE GREATEST STORY EVER TOLD (United Artists, 1965) 195 M.

Producer, George Stevens; associate producer, George Stevens, Jr., Antonio Vellani; director, Stevens; based on the Bible, ancient scripts, the writings of Henry Denker, and the book *The Greatest Story Ever Told* by Fulton Oursler; screenplay, James Lee Barrett, Stevens, and the creative association of Carl Sandburg; music, Alfred Newman; assistant director, Ridgeway, Callow, John Veitch; costumes, Vittorio Nino Novarese; special camera effects, J. McMillan Johnson, Clarence Stefer, A. Arnold Gillespie, Robert R. Hoag; sound, Franklin Milton, William Steinkamp, Charles Wallace; camera, William C. Mellor, Loyal Griggs; editor, Harold F. Kress, Argyle Nelson, Frank O'Neill.

Max Von Sydow (Jesus); Dorothy McGuire (Mary); Robert Loggia (Joseph); Charlton Heston (John The Baptist); Michael Anderson, Jr. (James The Younger); Robert Blake (Simon The Zealot); Burt Brinckerhoff (Andrew); Jamie Farr (Thaddaeus); John Considine (John); David Hedison (Philip); Peter Mann (Nathanael); Gary Raymond (Peter); David McCallum (Judas Iscariot); Roddy McDowall (Matthew); Tom Reese (Thomas); David Sheiner (James The Elder); Ina Balin (Martha of Bethany); Janet Margolin (Mary of Bethany); Michael Tolan (Lazarus); Sidney Poitier (Simon of Cyrene); Joanna Dunham (Mary Magdalene); Carroll Baker (Veronica); Pat Boone (Young Man at the Tomb); Van Heflin (Bar Armand); Sal Mineo (Uriah); Shelley Winters (Woman of No Name); Ed Wynn (Old Aram); John Wayne (The Centurian); Angela Lansbury (Claudia); Telly Savalas (Pontius Pilate); Johnny Seven (Pilate's Aide); Martin Landau (Caiaphas); Harold J. Stone (General Varus); Paul Stewart (Questor); Nehemiah Persoff (Shemiah); Joseph Schildkraut (Nicodemus); Victor Buono (Sorak); Robert Busch (Emissary); John Crawford (Alexander); Russell Johnson (Scribe); John Lupton (Speaker of Capernaum); Abraham Sofaer (Joseph of Arimatheaea); Chet Stratton (Theophilus); Ron Whelan (Annas); Jose Ferrer (Herod Antipas); Claude Rains (Herod The Great); John Abbott (Aben); Michael Ansara (Herod's Commander); Rodolfo Acosta (Captain Of Lancers); Dal Jenkins (Philip); Philip Coolidge (Chuza); Marian Seldes (Herodias); Donald Pleasence (Dark Hermit); Richard Conte (Barabbas); Frank DeKova (Tormentor); Joseph Sirola (Dumah); Cyril Delevanti (Melchior); Mark Lenard (Balthazar); Frank Silvera (Caspar); and Members of the Inbal Dance Theatre of Israel.

THE AMOROUS ADVENTURES OF MOLL FLANDERS (Paramount, 1965) 123 M.

Producer, Marcel Hellman; director, Terence Young; based on the novel by Daniel DeFoe; screenplay, Denis Cannan, Roland Kibbee; production designer, Syd Cain; assistant director, David Adderson; music, John Addison; camera, Ted Moore; editor, Frederick Wilson.

Kim Novak (Moll Flanders); Richard Johnson (Jemmy); Angela Lansbury (Lady Blystone); Vittorio De Sica (The Count); Leo McKern (Squint); George Sanders (The Banker); Lilli Palmer (Dutchy); Peter Butterworth

(Grunt); Dandy Nichols (Orphanage Superintendent); Noel Howlett (Bishop); Barbara Couper (Mayor's Wife); Daniel Massey (Elder Brother); Derren Nesbitt (Younger Brother); Ingrid Hafner (Elder Sister); June Watts (Younger Sister); Judith Furse (Miss Glowber); Anthony Dawson (Officer Of Dragoons); Roger Livesey (Drunken Parson); Jess Conrad (Muhock).

HARLOW (Paramount, 1965) 125 M.

Producer, Joseph E. Levine; director, Gordon Douglas; based on the book by Irving Shulman in collaboration with Arthur Landau; screenplay, John Michael Hayes; assistant director, Dave Salven; music, Heal Hefti; gowns, Edith Head; art director, Hal Pereira, Roland Anderson; camera, Joseph Ruttenberg; editor, Frank Bracht, Archie Marshek.

Carroll Baker (Jean Harlow); Martin Balsam (Everett Redman); Red Buttons (Arthur Landau); Michael Connors (Jack Harrison); Angela Lansbury (Mama Jean Bello); Peter Lawford (Paul Bern); Raf Vallone (Marino Bello); Leslie Nielsen (Richard Manley); Mary Murphy (Studio Secretary); Hanna Landy (Mrs. Arthur Landau); Peter Hansen (Assistant Director); Kipp Hamilton (Girl at Pool); Peter Leeds (Director of '30s); Edy Williams (Mail Room One); Myron Healey (Rex Chambers).

MISTER BUDDWING (MGM, 1966) 100 M.

Producer, W. Douglas Laurence, Delbert Mann; director, Mann; based on the novel *Buddwing* by Evan Hunter; screenplay, Dale Wasserman; art director, George W. Davis, Paul Groesse; music, Kenyon Hopkins; assistant director, Erich Von Stroheim, Jr.; camera, Ellsworth Fredericks; editor, Frederic Steinkamp.

James Garner (Mister Buddwing); Jean Simmons (The Blonde); Suzanne Pleshette (Fiddle); Katharine Ross (Janet); Angela Lansbury (Gloria); George Voskovec (Shabby Old Man); Jack Gilford (Mr. Schwartz); Joe Mantell, Billy Halop (Cab Drivers); Raymond St. Jacques (Hank); Ken Lynch (Dan); Beeson Carroll (Policeman); Michael Hodge (Counterman); Charles Seel (Printer); John Tracy (Tony); Bart Conrad (Chauffeur); Wesley Addy, Romo Vincent, John Dennis, Nichelle Nichols,

James O'Rear, Kam Tong, Rafael Campos, Pat Li, Rikki Stevens (Dice Players); Fiddle Viracola (Smoky Eyed Girl); Dick Winslow (Musician); Emma Tyson (Jeannie); Evelyn King (Mother); Margo Ann Berdeshevsky (Beatnik).

SOMETHING FOR EVERYONE (National General, 1970) 110 M.

Producer, John Flaxman; director, Hal Prince; based on the novel *The Cook* by Harry Kressing; screenplay, Hugh Wheeler; art director, Herta Pischinger; assistant director, Eberhard Schroeder, music John Kander; camera, Walter Lassally; editor, Ralph Rosenblum.

Angela Lansbury (Countess Herthe von Ornstein); Michael York (Conrad Ludwig); Anthony Corlan (Helmuth von Ornstein); Heidelinde Weis (Annaliese Pleschke); Eva-Maria Meineke (Mrs. Pleschke); John Gill (Mr. Pleschke); Jane Carr (Lotte von Ornstein); Despo (Bobby); Wolfrid Lier (Klaus); Walter Janssen (Father Georg); Klaus Havenstein (Rudolph).

BEDKNOBS AND BROOMSTICKS (Buena Vista, 1971) 117 M.

Producer, Bill Walsh; director, Robert Stevenson; based on the book by Mary Norton; screenplay, Walsh, Don DaGradl; animation director, Ward Kimball; animation-live action design, McLaren Stewart; second unit director, Arthur J. Vitarelli; songs, Richard M. Sherman and Robert B. Sherman; special effects, Alan Maley, Eustace Lycett, Danny Lee; assistant director, Christopher Hibler; art direction, John D. Mansbridge, Peter Ellenshaw; camera, Frank Phillips; editor, Cotton Warburton.

Angela Lansbury (Eglantine Price); David Tomlinson (Emelius Browne); Roddy McDowall (Mr. Jelk); Sam Jaffe (Bookman); John Ericson (Col. Heller); Bruce Forsyth (Swinburn); Cindy O'Callaghan (Carrie); Roy Smart (Paul); Ian Weghall (Charlie); Tessie O'Shea (Mrs. Hobday); Arthur E. Gould-Porter (Capt. Green); Rick Traeger, Manfred Lating (German Sergeants); John Orchard (Vendor); Robert Holt (Voice of Codfish); Lennie Weinrib (Voice of Secretary Bird and Lion).

Thelma Ritter

5'1"
110 pounds
Brown hair
Brown eyes
Birth sign: Aquarius

*On screen, short and stocky, Thelma Ritter usually looked like something the cat mistakenly dragged in and sounded much like a beached Tugboat Annie. Her movie performances as the caustic, raspy-voiced domestic (*All about Eve, The Mating Season, Pillow Talk, *and* Boeing-Boeing) *seemed so effortless that one was never sure if she were playacting or being herself.*

But there was a long stage apprenticeship from the 1920s onward before Thelma made her motion picture debut in a bit assignment in The Miracle on 34th Street *(1947) and went on to claim six Academy Award nominations as best supporting actress, a record still unsurpassed.*

Thelma was equally adept at wry drama, as demonstrated in such films as Pickup on South Street *and on television in* The Catered Affair. *To keep in touch with the demands of live audiences, she returned to the Broadway stage in the musical* New Girl in Town *(1957) and won a Tony Award for her costarring role as the drunken Marthy. Right up to the end of her life (1969), Thelma was in constant demand as a top character star whose presence in any entertainment venture would bolster the project's vitality flow and box office gross.*

Thelma Ritter was born February 14, 1905, on Hart Street in South Brooklyn, N.Y., near the edge of the Williamsburg area, a geographic zone which then still had a tinge of respectability. Of Scottish-Dutch ancestry, she was the only child of Charles V. and Lucy (Hale) Ritter.* Mr. Ritter was the office manager of a shoe manufacturing firm. His job gave the family a tone of

---
* The surname was originally Ruyter.

status, if not material affluence. As a boy, Mr. Ritter had sung in various Brooklyn glee clubs, including the choir of the Episcopal Church of Garden City, Long Island, and remained an amateur singer throughout his life. But being Dutch, his upbringing made him overly timorous of a theatrical career and caused his entrance into the business world. As Thelma once put it: "He really was artistic, but fundamentally Dutch."

Thelma would reminisce in 1967: "Scarcely anybody today is being named Thelma. My mother read a novel by that name, in which the heroine was a tall, blonde Norwegian, and I suppose that appealed to her." Of her Brooklyn neighborhood, Thelma recalled: "It was a polyglot section and most of the kids were first-generation Americans. My grandmother's name was Hale, and they used to speak of her as 'Mrs. Hale, the American lady.'" (Her husband, Mr. Hale, had been born in Maine, enlisted in the Union army at age fourteen, and after the Civil War bought and operated a Brooklyn farm on Bedford Avenue.)

By the age of eight, extroverted Thelma was as adept in performing in public as at home. In thinking back on her adolescent days she has stated, "I was one of those poisonous child entertainers, who used to do monologues. I was the poor man's Cornelia Otis Skinner." She was, admitted Thelma, ". . . practically a personality in Brooklyn. The principal used to yank me out of class to perform for visitors." During her stay at Brooklyn's Public School #77, she would relish any opportunity to recite a favorite work such as "Mr. Brook Gets His Haircut," "The Statue of Liberty," and "The Story of Cremona." At age eleven, she played Puck in *A Midsummer Night's Dream* with a semi-professional group. Later, she attended Manuel Training High School where she was active in school theatricals. Whenever possible, she would perform walk-on bits in various local stock companies and do dramatic readings at the nearby Masonic Temple and other churches. Obviously, her show business craving was deep-rooted.

Money was not plentiful in the Ritter household, and Thelma worked summers at a nearby candy store. In

Thelma Ritter in 1924.

Thelma Ritter at the age of nineteen.

fact, she had to drop out of Manual Training High School to find employment and bolster the family's income. While working as a switchboard operator at a Chase Manhattan bank, she began saving the $600 needed to enter the American Academy of Dramatic Arts. She was determined to meet her goal of becoming properly trained for her chosen profession.

One can only imagine the drive that spurred on this sixteen-year-old girl bent on breaking out of the confines of her lower-middle-class life into the world of artistic achievement. Other classmates at the Academy were Allen Jenkins and Pat O'Brien, both of whom achieved stage and film popularity long before Thelma would make her mark in the entertainment field. She would have graduated in the spring of 1922 from the Academy, but her finances were so shaky that she had to leave the school and seek acting work long before she felt herself ready for the professional stage.

In the early 1920s there still existed a tradition and need for acting stock companies in many small to medium size American towns. If a would-be actor were industrious, there were plenty of opportunities to audition for and obtain a post with such a group. This type

of grass roots acting provided necessary experience and a modest salary. If a person proved professional and versatile, word got around, and it would not be long before the company manager of a more elite stock company in a bigger city would offer the fledgling player a chance to advance in the theater world, possibly out of character assignments into the sphere of occasional leading roles.

Thelma had her initial taste of such stock work in Brookfield, Massachusetts, with Louise Galloway's year-round organization. By early 1924, Thelma had joined the F. James Carroll Players in Newark, New Jersey. She later recalled about her stay in Massachusetts: "I was always the maid, the friend of the family, the passing pedestrian, or just *anything* that stood around and said nothing. I was in the theater three years before anyone [on stage] called me by name."

Once with the Carroll Players, Thelma began winning larger roles. She was Rickety Ann in Denman Thompson's four-act drama *The Old Homestead,* leading a local critic to report ". . . [she] makes herself up so effectively as a little girl that she positively is deceiving. She is none the less skillful in acting the part." In the following weeks, there was a new show every seven days, Thelma played in the bedroom farce *Twin Beds,* the melodrama *The Woman on the Jury,* the comedy *The Fashion Girl* (which saw female impersonator Tommy Martelle as the guest leading "lady"), the chiller *The Bat,* the farce *Fair and Warmer, The Cat and the Canary, Three Weeks,* and the final production of the spring season, *The Love Test.*

Throughout her stay with the Carroll Players, Thelma was noted on stage and off as a master of the wisecrack, a reputation that would stand her in good stead in years to come. But beneath the smart talk, Thelma was as typical as any would-be company ingenue of the day. She was considered "comely" by 1920s standards, a forgotten image of the woman whose leathery countenance and salty characterizations would win her fame in later life. As a relative newcomer to the show business field, Thelma had much to learn from her fellow players. She later reminisced: ". . . (they) could be tough. They knew all the tricks. If you were playing a love scene, they'd inspect your collar for bugs or reach slowly into their pocket as though for a gun and pull out a handkerchief. Or they'd notice something on the floor and bend down to see what it was. If you had a laugh, they'd walk in front of you on your punch line."

In the summer of 1924, Thelma moved over to the Proctor Players, who toured the circuit of New Jersey and upstate New York with such productions as the farce *Parlor, Bedroom And Bath* and the perennial tearjerker *Madame X.* Among the company were Russell Hicks, Charles Dingle, and Joseph A. Moran.* At the time, Thelma was not very impressed by Moran: "He thought he was the world's gift to the American stage." But later, due to, as she phrased it, his "insidious campaign," she would change her mind and they would be married April 21, 1927.

Meanwhile in the fall of 1924, Thelma joined the Manhattan Players, a new stock group operating on the Poli Connecticut-New York theatre circuit, and based in Waterbury, Connecticut. Other players were Bella Cairnes, Harlan Briggs, and Kenneth Richards. Their first production was Anne Nichols's "comical connubial entanglement" *Just Married.* In the second female lead role, Thelma won plaudits from local reviewers: ". . . the snappy brown-eyed ingenue is stamped with a vivacity that blends with the type of entertainment that a Waterbury audience likes and upholds. . . . she has that spontaneous personality so pleasant in the woman which acts as a magnet and helps bring realization of an ability that is out of the ordinary." Next came roles in the melodrama *Guilty or Not Guilty,* the matrimonial drama *The First Year* (in which Thelma played the black maid Hattie), and in the musical *Irene,* Thelma had the opportunity to dance and sing. During the week of February 17, 1925, Thelma had another role which revealed her growing versatility. In Walton Butterfield's *Manhandled,* which became one of Gloria Swanson's best silent films, Thelma was Rose, a flapper extraordinaire. The Waterbury reviewer was enthusiastic about Thelma's performance: "Her lovable smile, her happy voice and her fine histrionic talent are not buried beneath the baby-talk, flapper role which she plays. Instead, she brings to the part so much art that she lifts it into a real creation. She is a real darling to local stock fame." The concluding production of the season was the comedy *Her Temporary Husband,* performed during the week of May 25, 1925.

In the world of stock theater it was essential that a performer keep constantly in touch with theater managers in the hopes that when a good opening occurred, he or she might be considered to fill the breach. Thelma, who was ingratiating by nature, had little difficulty in adapting to the demanded etiquette of her profession. She was always on hand at civic functions any hour of the day when not rehearsing, and this was remembered by the managers whose responsibility it was to make the stock company a vital part of the town in which they were playing in order to gain the needed audience support throughout the season.

---

* A Baltimorian, he had studied engineering at that city's Polytechnic Institute, and later received a B.A. degree from Johns Hopkins University.

Thelma's break came in June, 1925, when the ingenue of the Century Players in Erie, Pennsylvania, had to withdraw due to ill health, and a friendly manager recalled Thelma's availability. She made her debut with the Players on June 8, 1925, in the comedy *Adam and Eve,* with Walter Greaza as her leading man. As the *Erie Daily Times* reported about the city's new ranking ingenue: ". . . her achievements of several years past in cities of larger population than Erie indicate that her coming here will give Erie patrons of the Park the full benefit of the exchange. . . ."

Thelma's mother accompanied her to Erie, since no respectable ingenue could make inroads on local society without a proper chaperone at hand. As one local reporter described the scope of Thelma's public relations work: "They [she and her mother] are widening their acquaintances in Erie daily as they devote all their time, outside of 'stage hours' to the world of everyday folks and the golf links and aviation fields, with the lake bathing beaches finding them regular visitors." In short, Thelma's job required her to be on hand at public functions more than the town's mayor, and without the salary that post usually boasted.

Among the other shows that summer were *The Demi-Virgin, Ladies Night, The Unkissable Bride,* and *The Love Test.* Perhaps of most note to Thelma's career during that season was her debut in motion pictures, a fact often overlooked by followers of her career. A local business organization, the North Central Zone Association, decided to follow a new line of promotion for their district and hit upon the scheme of filming short subjects in the local area to highlight the progressiveness of the Erie shopping area. On July 16, 1925, a one-reel film was shot showing Thelma shopping in assorted Erie stores, giving the viewer a full picture of the variety of merchandise offered by Erie merchants.

In the fall of 1925, Thelma and her leading man Walter Greaza joined the Century Players in Bayonne, New Jersey, for the season, performing in *Little Miss Bluebeard, The Whole Town's Talking, The Girl in the Taxi, The Mad Honeymoon,* and others. All these plays were typical of the popular fare of the day and hardly innovative theater. Thelma's most far-reaching role was in *The Barrier,* based on a Rex Beach work, in which she played a half-breed.

Perhaps what separated Thelma most from the myriad of other stock ingenues was her sense of humor, which gave her theatrical dedication a unique soft tone. When the *Newark Times*'s reporter asked her what her favorite role was, she said, "Thelma Ritter in 'Nothing to do until tomorrow, on Sunday morning, one performance weekly.'" She was a great kidder even in those days of round-the-clock hard work.

Thelma finally made the big time when she won a small role in Dorrance Davis's *The Shelf* (Morosco Theatre, September 27, 1926). Starring Frances Starr and featuring Jessie Ralph, Donald Meek, and Lee Patrick, it concerned a European-bred woman of the world thrust into the life of a small American town (Kwainisport, population 15,000) who must learn how to age gracefully and find her new place in scall-scale society. The show tried out in Boston in February, 1927, and Thelma with a bit role as Mrs. Batterson garnered nice reviews. The *Boston Evening Transcript* reported: "For as fine a moment as any, however, the credit must go to Miss Thelma Ritter, who, as the young lady who accompanies Mrs. Chetwold [Leah Winslow] on her early morning missions of light, lends to a routine situation and pitifully few lines such a wealth of color and downright beauty as should make the heart of Mr. Davis turn humble and exceedingly grateful within him."

When *The Shelf* debuted in New York, noted Broadway critic Alexander Woollcott (*New York World*) was inspired to pen about Thelma: "In the first act, for a few moments, the stage was made lively and important by the passing presence of a beautiful performance. The name of the actress was Thelma Ritter." Unfortunately, the mild drama lasted only 32 performances. But it proved to Thelma, at least, that she had all the necessary talent for the big time and should continue in her chosen craft.

Even after Thelma and Joseph Moran were married, they found it difficult to establish a joint household. If they were to survive in the hectic theater world, they had to accept the best post offered, and it often required their taking separate assignments. On the occasions when they did make a stab at working together it usually was in vaudeville or an endless succession of one-night stands. There was no grand overnight success for either of them.

Thelma proved better than her husband in winning roles. She had a small part in the touring company of Ben Hecht-Charles MacArthur's *The Front Page* in 1929, but then she was forced to accept pedestrian stock work in the provinces. She and Moran made ends meet as best they could in the rough depression times when few were working, let alone in show business. As Thelma recalls about those bad times: "I hoped I was only dreaming or that I'd just fall down dead or something."

She was in a Boston edition of *Five Star Final* (Wilbur Theatre, October 12, 1931), directed by Irving Rapper and starring Arthur Byron. Thelma played both the ingenue Pearl and did a bit as an exchange telephone operator. The rehash of the Broadway success did nothing much to progress Thelma's career, but it was cer-

tainly better than her previous assignment touring with *Sisters of the Chorus* on the road.

Now a Broadway veteran—of one show—she found it easier to obtain auditions for upcoming mainstem vehicles. Thus she was cast as Sally Stewart in Dodson Mitchell's *In Times Square* (Stuyvesant Theatre, November 23, 1931). It was another backstage theater story, with homicide thrown in as a gimmick. Thelma and John S. Butler were the juvenile leads. All the stereotypes of the theater were present in the script: the theater owner, the leading lady with her has-been actor husband, an oldtime character actress, the half-mad Shakespearean player, the burly stage manager (played by author Mitchell), the barking doorman, and the murder victim, in this case a dope addict. The plot was so convoluted that the critics complained it tripped over its own complex story line. The *New York Evening Post* labeled Thelma and Butler as "two tiresome juveniles," perhaps the worst criticism thrown at Thelma to that time. The show quietly folded after eight performances.

By 1932, the year of the deep depression, both Thelma and her husband (she had toured in *Counsellor-in-Law* earlier in the year), were jobless, and they barely managed to pay for their small apartment in Sunnyside, a tenement Long Island suburb of Manhat-

In *In Times Square* (1931).

tan.* In an act of desperation to earn money, Moran began entering countless numbers of advertising contests, hoping that his natural ability to write slogans and jingles would pay off, which it did. He soon began winning prizes with increasing frequency and would sell the gifts for cash. A point was reached when he was entering an increasing number of competitions under different names and addresses. One national contest sponsor was displeased to learn that Moran, under various aliases, had won three top prizes, and it voiced its objection. The *New Yorker* magazine's "Talk of the Town" column picked up this human interest story, and its printed rendition of the facts brought Moran to the attention of Young and Rubicam, the big Manhattan-based advertising agency. They hired Moran at $30 weekly as an advertising copyright. Thelma recalls: "From that moment on, Joe was headed onward and upward. My star was rising too. . . . I got out of the theatre. Got out, did I say? I was starved out!"

With Moran's rising success at Young and Rubicam, he expanded his activities at the agency. Due to his background in the theater, he was requested to select actors for the assorted radio programs which his company's clients sponsored. Moran later remembered, "As I grew into the job, I found myself handling such stars as Lawrence Tibbett, Jack Benny, Burns and Allen, Kate Smith, and a host of others." By the late 1930s, he was a vice president of Young and Rubicam.

On the surface, Thelma moved gracefully into the role of a proud housewife: "Joe made a living and a career out of the air, and he brought us the security that enabled us to afford a family. I decided we were both through with show business and settled down to be a housewife." Joseph Anthony** was born February 4, 1937, and Monica Ann*** (nicknamed Nikki) was born July 9, 1940.

With Moran's business success, the family moved to 65 Greenway Terrace, Forest Hills, where they remained right up to the time of Thelma's death in 1969. As

---

* One of the building's tenants and a good friend of Thelma was Phyllis Loughton, who would later marry screen producer-director George Seaton.

** After attending Fordham University, Joseph joined the Marines. After his discharge he worked on the West Coast and then returned to New York City to enter the construction business. He is married and the father of two children.

*** Monica graduated from Stephens College in 1960. She appeared in summer stock and made her screen debut in *Take Her, She's Mine* (1963). In the off-Broadway production of *Fireworks* (1969) she played the lead and in 1971 was understudy to Sandy Dennis in the Broadway show *How the Other Half Live*. She is married to advertising executive Michael Shalette and has two children.

Thelma would later explain about her suburban living: "We're only a block and a half from the subway. We came here in 1937 to see the tennis matches and decided that it was a nice place to live. We moved here and haven't been to the matches since."

In the early years of World War II Thelma made her first reentry into show business. She and her husband wrote the *Treasury Star Parade* radio program commercials, devising little playlets and clever lines to spark the public into purchasing war bonds. It was enough of a taste of her old professional life to make Thelma reevaluate her full-time housewife chores. "I missed it [show business] and wanted to get back into it somewhere. For seven years all I heard was neighbors' gab about how the baby reacted to the formula and how much trouble it was getting a good maid. It was like living at the bottom of the well."

Her husband acceded to Thelma's reactivated professional wishes and introduced her to assorted radio casting directors and producers. In the first year (1944) she made $500 on the airwaves. But by the following year, she had become a fixture on such programs as "The Theater Guild on the Air," "U.S. Steel Hour," "Mr. District Attorney," "Big Town," "The Aldrich Family," "Lorenzo Jones" and would often perform in the commercials Moran prepared for the Eddie Cantor, Fred Allen, and Ed Wynn shows.

Thelma recalled of her radio work: "But I never could seem to make it on daytime radio. I had too much projection for them, I guess. I could never master the soap opera technique. They worked in monotone. When I said a line like 'Mother just died,' I must have sounded as though I meant it. I just wouldn't do." In another interview, she amplified on the subject: "No, I played in those nighttime murder mysteries. For a long stretch I was the dame being driven out of her mind, or an out-and-out looney. Finally, though I graduated. I became the murderer."

Thelma's next lucky break and the turning point of her professional career came in 1946. George Seaton had become a seasoned Hollywood director, and he came to New York to supervise location scenes being shot for his current Twentieth Century-Fox release, *Miracle on 34th Street* (1947). His wife, Phyllis, had kept in touch with her former neighbor Thelma over the years, and she and her husband thought it would be nice to have Thelma do a cameo role in the movie. He told the actress: "It isn't much of a part, but'll be fun, and maybe you'll bring me luck."

Thus at the age of forty-one and twenty-one years after her screen debut, Thelma was in a Hollywood-produced feature film. Her short scene cast her as a tired mother dragged to Macy's Department Store by her son who insists upon meeting Santa Claus (Edmund Gwenn). When Santa promises the youth a pair of skates, harassed Thelma launches into a tirade with the bearded do-gooder, since in the end she is the one who will either have to buy the gift or suffer her child's disappointment.

Fox studio mogul Darryl F. Zanuck was impressed by the rushes of the scene. The obvious humanity of Thelma's personality projected perfectly. Her nasal, raspy voice, her working-class look, and her ability to convey a universality of expressed emotion (a disgruntled soul rebelling against the seeming benevolence of big business) were just the bits of reality that the scene required. Zanuck contacted Seaton to build up Thelma's scenes and had her brought to Hollywood for the additional shooting.

One can only imagine the psychological effect this fast series of events had on Thelma. For years she had struggled with moderate success in the lesser realm of small-time stock work and now through a quirk of good luck she was wanted by Hollywood, albeit for a bit assignment. She was a middle-aged housewife and by now had no illusions about being a screen star. Her recent radio work had proven she was still an adept character performer whose versatility would provide her with plenty of secondary assignments, but always out of the limelight. Thelma later described her awed reaction to arriving at the Fox lot where Betty Grable, June Haver, and Gene Tierney were the ranking stars. "Nervous? I walked on this great big set—all those lights—the noise—seven or eight assistant directors running around. I told myself I'd just wait till it died down and sneak out. You know what? They were setting up a background for me!" This glamour-struck attitude of Thelma's would always play an important part in her film career, becoming the unmentioned force behind many of her filmmaking decisions, even in later years when she had become a world famous, top-ranking character star.

But there was a dual side to Thelma's personality: a matter-of-fact nature bred from years of struggles and an ability to call 'em as they are with the laugh-cry that characterizes so many of the professional comics. She could be jovially philosophical about her brief moment of glory. "Two days of the red carpet treatment and then back to the washing machine."

Miracle on 34th Street opened at the Roxy Theatre June 5, 1947, without much advanced ballyhoo. The movie trade was skeptical about the public's possible positive reaction to such a fanciful idea as a pixillated old Macy's Santa Claus who is convinced he is the real St. Nicholas and who is more than willing to go to court to prove his point. Surrounding this concept was the *de rigeur* conventional love tale, concerning Gwenn's

department store supervisor, widow Maureen O'Hara who has a progressive young daughter Natalie Wood and an attorney, John Payne, who is hired for the sanity trial. The finished movie became one of the big hits of the years, earning several Oscar nominations, and Thelma's unbilled bit was well appreciated by amused moviegoers. She later recalled having attended a performance of *Miracle* at the Roxy Theatre and having her pride quickly deflated when one housewife viewer said to her friend about the on-screen Thelma, "My God, look at the face on that one!" (*Miracle* would later be transformed into a mild stage musical *Here's Love* (1963); starring Lawrence Naismith, Janis Paige, and Craig Stevens.)

In relationship to her small role in *Miracle,* Thelma received outstanding audience acclaim. Zanuck decided to cast her in additional pictures, particularly when his staff producer-writer Joseph L. Mankiewicz asked for Thelma's service for a pending project *A Letter to Three Wives* (Radio City Music Hall, January 20, 1949). While this film was being prepared, Fox had Thelma return to the West Coast to appear as James Stewart's secretary in the realistic drama *Call North-*

Thelma Ritter in 1949.

side 777 (Roxy Theatre, February 18, 1948). The feature focused on reporter-sleuth Stewart who is told to investigate the human angle in an advertisement placed in his publisher's newspaper. A Polish scrubwoman (Kasia Orzesewki) has offered a $5,000 reward for information leading to the clearing of her son (Richard Conte), wrongfully jailed for a crime he did not commit. Stewart pursues the case and eventually proves the man's innocence. In the final release print, six of Thelma's seven scenes as Stewart's secretary were cut, and she can only be glimpsed in one police station sequence, telling Stewart that the police captain will now see him.

But *A Letter to Three Wives* was a different story. Thirteenth-billed as Sadie, an aggressively democratic maid of all work, Thelma appeared in the third episode of this brilliantly sardonic film. The feature deals in flashback with the unstable domestic lives of three women (Ann Sothern, Jeanne Crain, Linda Darnell) who wonder which one of their husbands has run off with the town tease. Darnell, from the wrong side of the tracks, reflects on how she married department store magnate Paul Douglas and ponders her perpetual fear, that her unrefined background may outweigh her beauty appeal for him. Thelma was worked into the movie as the cynical and overly loquacious pal of Darnell's mother (Connie Gilchrist). The two of them sit at the table talking for hours on every subject, unmindful that when a train roars by on the nearby tracks, the entire shanty shakes to its foundation. Thelma is the one who advises Darnell "Why don't cha show more of what you got. Wear some beads." Darnell snaps back, "What I got don't need beads."

Once again, Thelma's screen character required her

With Connie Gilchrist in *A Letter to Three Wives* (20th-Fox, 1949).

With Ann Sothern in *A Letter to Three Wives.*

to be a bedraggled working woman who sees through any sort of self-deception, including Gilchrist's perpetual tipsy state. Obviously, Thelma's Sadie could handle her own beer guzzling and, inebriated or not, had sharp powers of observation.

A Letter to Three Wives was a big commercial success, receiving healthy plaudits from a majority of the critics. The *New York Times* noted the film was "crowded with skilled performances" and that in particular ". . . the blatherskite performance of these two (Thelma and Gilchrist), punctuated with rowdy backhand swipes, gives a wonderful shanty-town setting to a vulgar yet pathetic romance." *Variety* accorded "Hilarious comedy support is lent by Thelma Ritter. . . ."

On the basis of her work in *A Letter to Three Wives,* Thelma signed a contract for three pictures a year with Twentieth Century-Fox. It was a sure indication that the studio had sizable plans for Thelma, or else they would not have bothered with such an agreement. As she would tell columnist Mike Connolly a few years later: "I was beginning to roll. But by this time it didn't mean to me what it would have years before. I was a housewife with two small kids. And our children were, and always have been, first with us, above anything and everything else. So, at this point, if Joe had said: "I wish you wouldn't go running off to Hollywood and leave me with two kids on my hands, I would have said, 'Fine—I'd just as soon pass it up.' " Be that as it may, Thelma would spend a good deal of time commuting back and forth across America, working in Hollywood approximately eighteen weeks per year.

For her third 1949 release, *City Across The River* (Capitol Theatre, April 7, 1949), Thelma was loaned out to Universal. In this low-budget entry she received second billing. The film was a study of juvenile delin-

With Peter Fernandez in *City Across The River* (Universal, 1949).

quency in New York City, and even though it avoided preaching, it was still a flabby drama. Thelma and Luis Van Rooten played the down-to-earth parents of Peter Fernandez, living in a Brooklyn tenement and despite being hard workers, having to rely on relief checks. They are dismayed to learn that their son and two of his street corner pals have killed a schoolteacher in an accidental brawl. Universal contract player Tony Curtis was cast as leader of the Amboy Dukes. Once again, it is Thelma who pierces through the good intentions of community center counselor Stephen McNally and investigating detective Jeff Corey, pointing out that seldom is there any lenient justice given to the poor. The reviewers agreed that Thelma and Van Rooten "excite pity" in their roles. It was a bread-and-butter assignment for Thelma, primarily giving her more screen exposure.

With Luis Van Rooten and Sharon McManus in *City Across The River*.

Back at Fox, Thelma played another domestic in *Father Was a Fullback* (Roxy Theatre, October 12, 1949). College football coach Fred MacMurray and his wife Maureen O'Hara are having a difficult time with their two exasperating growing daughters. The older daughter is shunned for being too "chintzy." Sourpuss maid Geraldine (Thelma) has a simple remedy: "She needs a good clip on the chops." As a realistic soul, she has as little use for the platitudinous behavior of either MacMurray or O'Hara as for the attitudes of busybody neighbor Jim Backus and prissy college alumnus Rudy Vallee. The harmless comedy focused more on domestic problems than on MacMurray's effort to provide the aroused alumni with a winning football team. (Thelma has so little faith in her employer's prowess as a coach that she bets on the opposing team.) About her role in *Father Was a Fullback,* the *New York Times* accorded: ". . . by virtue of her facile handling of crisp, colloquial lines, [Thelma is] superb in the role of the family servant." *Cue* voted laconic Thelma as ". . . the nicest thing about the picture."

Thelma still found time to continue with her radio assignments, (particularly on "Theatre Guild of the Air" (ABC)) such as performing with Van Heflin and Ida Lupino in the segment "Ladies and Gentlemen" (May 15, 1949). This particular radio presentation was based on a 1939 Helen Hayes stage play, which also provided the source for the Warner Brothers movie, *Perfect Strangers* (Strand Theatre, March 10, 1940). Thelm was third-cast as Lena Frassler, the pregnant housewife who finds herself part of the jury of twelve judging a man accused of killing his wife. Like the other jurors, she discovers that she is far from perfect and has lots of fences to mend herself. Most of the camera time

With Paul McVey, Margalo Gillmore, Howard Freeman, George Chandler, Ginger Rogers, Anthony Ross, and Charles Meredith in *Perfect Strangers* (WB, 1950).

in this comedy drama went to married man Dennis Morgan and divorcée Ginger Rogers, who during the two weeks of behind-locked-doors deliberating, fall in love and rally to prove the defendant's innocence. The *New York Times* noted Thelma "gets a laugh whenever she speaks." This critical remark sums up why she was cast in her one-dimensional role in *Perfect Strangers.*

Joseph L. Mankiewicz remembered Thelma for a role in his *All About Eve* (Roxy Theatre, October 13, 1950), which starred Bette Davis as the aging stage actress who meets professional and romantic competition from conniving young actress Anne Baxter. Although Baxter craftily flatters vain Davis with her dedication to the theater and total admiration of the older woman, it is sharp-as-nails Birdie (Thelma) who first notes the too-good-to-be-true quality of Baxter's supposedly plagued youth: ". . . (yeah) everything but the bloodhounds yappin' at her behind." Later she is quick to surmise that beneath Baxter's gooey niceness lies a cold-blooded meanness.

For the first time, Thelma's screen characterization had full-rigged dimensions. In the movie, she is a former vaudevillian, sensitive about her past status in the profession and quick to snap at her needling employer Davis: "As for bein' fifth-rate. I closed the first half for eleven years an' you know it." She still considers herself eminently feminine, with fond memories of her risqué youth. "Once George Jessel played my home town. For a gal, gettin' in to see him was easy. Gettin' out was the problem." She is not above tossing off a funny off-color remark: "I'll never forget that

With Fred MacMurray and Mike Mahoney in *Father Was A Fullback* (20th-Fox, 1949).

With Anthony Ross in *Perfect Strangers*.

Thelma Ritter with her Academy Award nomination from *All about Eve*.

With Bette Davis and Claude Stroud in *All About Eve* (20th-Fox, 1950).

blizzard the night we played Cheyenne. A cold nite. First time I ever saw a brassiere break like a piece of matzos." If someone by error jokes about her age, she becomes incensed: "I never played Ft. Sumter." She has no illusions about the glamour of fetching for a Broadway celebrity: "I haven't got a union. I'm slave labor."

As *All About Eve* progresses the see-saw battle royale between established Davis and up-and-coming Baxter, Thelma is on hand as a seasoned observer (although there are great gaps in the screenplay in which she just disappears). She may just comment "Oh, brother" at the various digging dialogue being bandied about by the warring ladies, but the twist of her lips and the squinting of her eyes fully convey that not one gesture or blood point has escaped her vigilant notice.

Once in a while, the scripter of *All About Eve* fed Thelma a good gag line, as when Davis is hostessing her big party, and Thelma quips: "The bed looks like a dead animal act. Which one is sables?"

The critics were enthusiastic about Thelma's *All About Eve* portrayal. ". . . [she] is screamingly funny as a wised-up maid until she is summarily lopped off." (*New York Times*). ". . . another wonderfully done performance by Thelma Ritter" (*Saturday Review of Literature*).

Thelma was nominated for her first Academy Award as best supporting actress of 1950, but lost out to Josephine Hull who had recreated her stage role for the film of *Harvey*. A major factor hindering Thelma's chances of winning the award was that another actress, Celeste Holm, was also nominated from *All About Eve,* which decidedly canceled out many of Thelma's potential votes.

With *All About Eve,* Thelma moved into the ranks of the big time character actresses. Hollywood had learned its lesson well in the 1930s—that personalities such as Edna May Oliver, Marjorie Rambeau, Dame May Witty, Jane Darwell, Constance Collier, Allison Skipworth, or, especially, Marie Dressler could carry even a mediocre picture at the box office. The public knew and accepted the stereotyped characterizations these actresses would be handed and greatly appreciated that they would perform their roles with a mastery touch of human warmth and/or tartness, alone worth the price of admission. However, by the late 1940s, all of the above people had either died or greatly reduced their screen activities, leaving a gap that relative newcomer Marjorie Main could not fill (particularly after she was dug into the rut of the *Ma and Pa Kettle* films). There were now such backstoppers as Lucile Watson, Selena Royale, and Evelyn Varden to play mother roles. In addition, Eve Arden, Lucille Ball, Janis Paige, Louise Allbritton, and still Glenda Farrell portrayed the smart-mouthed best friends. Finally Judith Anderson, Angela

Lansbury, and Agnes Moorehead played the vitriolic "other woman" chores. However, none of these actresses could handle a major human-warmth role with the proper credibility to win over a large following of rural America. The Hollywood studios then, as the television industry of today, insisted that no major financial investment should be placed in a female contractee who could not handle sympathetic assignments. "Heartless" male character performers were more fortunate, because they could at least aspire to horror film stardom or a flush career as a screen scoundrel.

Thus, when Thelma came along in the late 1940s and proved her marquee appeal to middle America, Fox was quick to promote her as "the" new leading second lead attraction, betting that she would more than recoup the publicity build-up investment by salvaging any picture she might be tossed into by the casting department. Fox made a big hoopla that Thelma was another Marie Dressler. (Marjorie Main had been the 1940s Dressler, but at least in that case there was some justification due to parallels in the two women's acting styles and because Main was actually teamed with Dressler's best vis-a-vis, Wallace Beery). At first Thelma politely accepted the studio's focus on her being a new Dressler: "It's always very complimentary to be called another somebody—just so they don't make it stick." But she had definite ideas about what type of screen image she wanted to avoid. She would later comment about Fox: "They once tried to build me up as a 'homebody.' They wanted pictures of me fixing dinner, vacuuming the floor and dusting the furniture. Like a sap I went for it.

"They had me cooking a frappe or something. Then they had me running the vacuum cleaner. It was fake and it was wrong, and when the pictures were finally

With Danny Davenport, Dennis Day, and William Lundigan in *I'll Get By* (20th-Fox, 1950).

developed, I killed them all." (Actually, not all the pictures were scrapped; there were several magazine spreads showing her in the domestic gambit.)

Thelma's third 1950 release was the tepid remake of *Tin Pan Alley,* this time called *I'll Get By* (Paramount Theatre, November 1, 1950). It starred June Haver and Gloria DeHaven as two singing sisters involved with struggling songplugger William Lundigan who had become a music publisher and his business pal Dennis Day. The unimaginative musical covers the 1939–1945 period, and its bevy of ten songs are given a variety of presentations as the story follows the would-be Tin Pan Alley song writers who enlist in the army during World War II and following their discharge, become successful Hollywood composers. Thelma was on hand to supply comedy relief as Miss Murphy, the acid-mouthed secretary of Lundigan-Day. *Variety* penned: "Thelma Ritter sharpens her footage for comedy."

She was back in form as Ellen McNulty in *The Mating Season* (Paramount Theatre, April 1, 1951) made on loan-out to Paramount. She was billed fourth as the proprietress of a Jersey City hamburger stand who has put her son (John Lund) through college and stood by in the shadows when he married the socially prominent Gene Tierney. When the couple move to Ohio, Thelma pays them a visit. She hitchhikes to the Midwest, arriving on the day Tierney is hostessing her first big party. Her daughter-in-law mistakes Thelma for a temporary maid, and Thelma goes along with the ploy, knowing it will give her a good opportunity to observe their domestic life. Everything works well until Tierney's posturing, bird-brained southern belle mother (Miriam Hopkins) appears on the scene, and the two mothers-in-law square off for a full-fledged contest of giving backseat advice.

With Gene Tierney in *The Mating Season* (Paramount, 1951).

With John Lund and Grayce Hampton in *The Mating Season.*

Of Thelma's *The Mating Season* performance, *New York Times*'s Bosley Crowther wrote:

That grand comedienne, Thelma Ritter, who neatly ate up the minor role of a gawky, outspoken domestic in *A Letter to Three Wives* and *All About Eve* finally is handed a portion into which she can get her working teeth. And what she does with the character that she is given to play in this pastiche is almost enough to make a silk purse out of routine merchandise. We said almost.

Cast as the plain, unpolished mama, . . . Miss Ritter rips into the character with all the gusto she might lavish on a steak, and the evidence of her satisfaction is very similar to what you might expect therefrom.

Wholesomely does she take hold of the rich and solid substance of a dame, who is one of the working people and makes no pretense to anything else. Out of this potion of homely character she bites big and nourishing chunks, and juicily chaws on them for all of their savoriness. Her manners are clumsy but forthright, her appearance is amiably absurd and her commenting while tortured in their grammar and accent, are frank and to the point. Miss Ritter endows a candid low-brow with impressively high ideals.

The *Christian Science Monitor* was equally laudatory: "Miss Ritter's sincerity as well as her dry and dour comicality invest the proceedings not only with authentic gaiety but with a kind of human dignity rarely encountered in such films."

For single-handedly carrying *The Mating Season* as a viable theatrical release, Thelma was again nominated for an Academy Award, but lost out in the best supporting actress category to Kim Hunter, who repeated her stage role from *A Streetcar Named Desire.*

Back at Fox, Thelma was short-shrifted when cast in

Thelma Ritter at the age of forty-six.

With Monty Woolley in *As Young as You Feel* (20th-Fox, 1951).

As Young as You Feel (Palace Theatre, August 2, 1951), a lackluster non-comedy considered as bland in its day as now when seen on television. Monty Woolley starred as the gentleman who on reaching the age of sixty-five, is automatically retired from the printing company for which he has worked many years. He is so incensed by the stupidity of this mandatory pension rule that he impersonates the president of the combine which owns the printing company and immediately tosses out all the age limitation rules. His new company dictate is picked up by the press, and he soon becomes a national celebrity. It ends with his employer rehiring him in his old job, and everyone living happily ever after. Others in the cast were Albert Dekker as Woolley's employer and Constance Bennett as the former's chic wife, Jean Peters as Woolley's granddaughter and David Wayne as her man, Allyn Joslyn as Woolley's son and Thelma as his resentful daughter-in-law (she is more concerned with the price of meat at the butcher's than in her father-in-law's goofy ideology). The picture was not much of a box office attraction. *Newsweek* found Thelma's characterization as a former singer with a high opinion of her alleged talents was ". . . through no fault of her own, something of a trial." *Variety* evaluated that the screen teaming of Thelma and Joslyn only achieved "mild results."

Thelma was still commuting back and forth from New York to the West Coast. She had reached a major status level in the Hollywood community in spite of the fact that she was really just a visiting performer and even though the combination of her screen image and her housewife background did not qualify her for hobnobbing with the upper crust cinema society. She was

wise enough about her screen characters and analyzed: "I'm not a funny woman like Joan Davis. I play real characters and I get my laughs from their hard-boiled or cynical reactions to given situations." She later elaborated on her stereotyped on-camera person: "With one cutting line, she destroys all the pretty pretensions of the phonies. She always says the thing people never can think of until it's too late."

At another point in 1951, she frankly told the press: "Let me tell you something, dearie. It's a darn good thing for me that I don't have any illusions about myself. They give me scrubwoman's clothes to wear, and then they put me in pictures with gals like Linda Darnell, Jeanne Crain, and Ginger Rogers. How can I look?"

Although Thelma respected and adored the new medium which had given her the popularity and luxury the stage never did, she refused to become addicted to a total moviemaking life. "All these movie people ending up on benzadrine or in the Menninger Clinic—not for me. Pictures are really killers. I've been in show business all my life and never worked like this before. A six-day week, too. Whew!"

Since her film schedule left many completely free weeks during the year, Thelma continued to accept radio assignments. In 1951, she celebrated her seventh consecutive year on the audio "Theatre Guild of the Air," and was heard in "Light up the Sky" (April 15, 1951) with Joan Bennett.

Charles Brackett who had produced and co-scripted *The Mating Season* at Paramount, moved over to Fox in mid-1951 to prepare *The Model and the Marriage Broker* (Roxy Theatre, January 11, 1952). He had Thelma cast as Mae Swazey, a lady who runs a matchmaking bureau for a most eccentric group of unsophisti-

With Frank Fontaine in *The Model and the Marriage Broker* (20th-Fox, 1951).

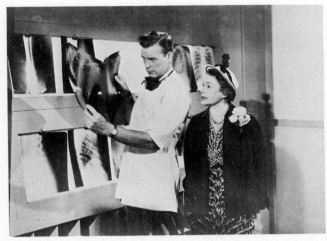

With Scott Brady in *The Model and the Marriage Broker.*

cated clients. Her friends and customers include Michael O'Shea, a wise observer who drops in for an occasional game of pinochle with Thelma; old maid Nancy Kulp; dumb Swede Frank Fontaine; and Helen Ford, an ex-sexy miss who wooed away Thelma's husband several years ago. When Thelma meets prim model Jeanne Crain, she talks her out of embarking on an affair with a married man and is inspired to match her with X-ray technician Scotty Brady. She is convinced they are a perfect couple and does the job gratis.

Bosley Crowther enthused in the *New York Times* about *The Model and the Marriage Broker:* "Miss Ritter is wonderfully human, . . . and her wry manipulation of her clients touching to behold.

". . . [she] runs away with [the] show, particularly when she is able to get free of the undertow. Her wise-up air, her cynicism disguising a heart of gold, her barrel-house voice, her sudden radiance have never been better employed."

The *New York Herald-Tribune*'s Otis L. Guernsey found: "Miss Ritter holds the whole story together with her stalwart performance. . . . There is the flavor of New York's sidewalks in her speech, and in the pungently slangy lines written for her, and the flavor of homely sophistication in her performance. She is an enjoyable 'character,' and at the same time she overcomes the resistance to her eccentric trade with the steady pressure of a convincing personality."

The public cottoned to this lighthearted handling of the potentially sad lonely hearts business. Many people consider this as Thelma's best movie role. She repeated the assignment on "Lux Radio Theatre" (CBS) co-starring with Jeanne Crain. When Fox adapted its backlog of features for its weekly television show "The Twentieth Century-Fox Hour" (CBS June 12, 1957),

Glenda Farrell inherited Thelma's role in the condensed "The Marriage Broker."

It was for Thelma's other 1952 release that she received her third Oscar nomination. *With a Song in My Heart* (Roxy Theatre, April 4, 1952) was a vehicle for Fox's hottest screen property, Susan Hayward, who did wonders with the highly fictionalized biography of tragedy-struck vocalist Jane Froman, the popular vocalist who gained a legion of admirers for her courageous physical comeback. The technicolor musical (twenty-six songs, with Froman doing the actual singing) traced Hayward from stage-radio singer in the mid-1930s to her volunteer U.S.O. tours during World War II and the fateful plane crash in Lisbon harbor in February, 1943, which partially crippled her for life. Thelma was nurse Clancy, a manufactured role, who treats Hayward in Lisbon and stays with the vocalist through the years as a companion-friend. As the cynical miss from Flatbush, Brooklyn, Thelma was typically hard-bitten and bighearted, urging Hayward on as she slowly recovers her body strength and finds new love with Pan American pilot Rory Calhoun. (Hayward's first marriage to vaudevillian David Wayne had disintegrated along the way to success, which provided additional elements of soap opera.) "Of the cast, Thelma Ritter is the only one who comes out with some dignity. . . ." (*New York Herald-Tribune*). The *Saturday Review of Literature* concurred in its opinion of Thelma: ". . . tough but human—as you might expect." Thelma repeated her *With a Song in My Heart* role with Hayward, Calhoun, and Wayne on the "Lux Radio Theatre" (February 9, 1953).

Once again, Thelma lost out on her Oscar bid from *With a Song in My Heart* when the Academy of Motion

With Susan Hayward in *With a Song in My Heart* (20th-Fox, 1952).

With Allyn Joslyn in *Titanic* (20th-Fox, 1953).

Pictures Arts and Sciences bestowed the best supporting actress award on Gloria Grahame for her performance in *The Bad and the Beautiful*.

Although no one knew it at the time, *With a Song in My Heart* ended the golden period of Thelma's tenure at Fox. Her remaining pictures at the studio would merely capitalize on her status as the 1950s leading progenitor of the woebegone soul who looked like something the cat dragged in but had an uproarious way of delivering a comedy line. Idiotically, Fox would not even leave well enough alone but insisted upon dressing her up to play her stock-in-trade in a more refined guise. As could be expected by all but the film executives involved, the gimmick did not add to her effectiveness as a character actress.

Titanic (Roxy Theatre, May 27, 1953) has a nitch in cinema history as the last major feature Fox produced for the small screen before Cinemascope filming swept the studio and the industry. *Titanic* was a glossy, high-class soap opera about the maiden and last voyage of the huge ocean liner which sunk on April 15, 1912, with the loss of over 1,500 lives. Among the passengers aboard the elegant luxury ship were stoic Captain Brian Aherne, wealthy Barbara Stanwyck, her estranged husband Clifton Webb, their son Harper Carter and daughter Audrey Dalton, Robert Wagner (a Dalton's love interest), defrocked priest Richard Basehart, and Thelma. She was fifth-billed as Mrs. Young, a brash Montana mining millionairess who knows how to enjoy life and get a good laugh out of most any situation. Her vulgar characterization was frivolous and inclined to vapidness as much as the other performances in this pulp fiction Grand-Hotel style tale. (There are many similarities in her uneasy performance with the problems

With Betty Grable in *The Farmer Takes a Wife* (20th-Fox, 1953).

Marjorie Main had in adapting herself to the crude, rich matron role in MGM's *The Law and the Lady*.) The actual human interest story of the ocean disaster would be handled more appropriately in the realistic, if clinical, British-made film *A Night to Remember*. Moreover, Thelma's disguised character of Molly Brown would reappear to better advantage in the musical *The Unsinkable Molly Brown*.

The Farmer Takes a Wife (completed July 15, 1952, but not released at the Globe Theatre until June 12, 1953) was a musical rehash of the once popular play and earlier film (1935), based on the Walter D. Edmonds novel *Rome Haul*. The story focused on a vibrant cook (Betty Grable) on the Old Hickory, an Erie canal barge boat owned by John Carroll. Because of his excessive drinking, she asks Thelma, head of a cooking school, to find her a new post. But Carroll, who loves Grable, promises not to drink and she stays on. Grable finally falls in love with farmer Dale Robertson who eventually wins Grable's heart and convinces her to return to farming with him. To accommodate the limited histrionic talents of Grable, the heroine was revamped to a more angelic, bland miss who emerges as nothing more than a pretty cook in starched uniforms with not a realistic thought in her wholesome-as-apple-pie mind. Since Grable was past her physical and box office peak, there was little to recommend in the staid musical. Thelma's standing gag had her as a man-chasing widow (a novelty for her on screen) who would not mind wedding eligible liquor salesman Eddy Foy, Jr. Gussied up in period costumes, Thelma looked like a handsome matron for a change, but she seemed suffocated under all her frills. Thelma would later refer to this role by snapping: "I've played in films when the

In *Titanic*.

With Betty Grable, Dale Robertson, and Eddie Foy, Jr. in *The Farmer Takes a Wife.*

studio costumed me up to the nines. Never again! You keep the fancy clothes, I'll settle for the jokes."

Fox finally gave Thelma some dramatic latitude in its much heralded, but often postponed melodrama, *Pickup on South Street* (Roxy Theatre, June 17, 1953),* directed by the now stylish Samuel Fuller. Intitally a project for Shelley Winters, then Betty Grable, Zanuck activated his pet picture of the month by casting the too-gentle ingenue, Jean Peters, in the female lead. She plays the prostitute girlfriend of Richard Kiley, who, unknown to her, carries in her wallet microfilms of a secret chemical formula which Communist agents desperately

With Richard Kiley in *Pickup on South Street* (20th-Fox, 1953).

———
* Remade as *Capetown Affair* (1968).

want. When her wallet is snatched by three-time convicted loser Richard Widmark, FBI agent Willis Bouchy follows the leads, hoping to capture the espionage gang operating in New York. Thelma was billed third as Moe, a raggedy secondhand dealer of ties who sells information on her underworld associates to the police in order to have enough money for a decent cemetery "plot and stone." She is first presented as a Damon Runyonesque sympathetic character—pitiful, lonely, kind, shrewd, and comic. But the situation soon changes. She will not sell information about Widmark's whereabouts to the Communists ("What do I know about Commies? I know one thing, I just don't like them."), but for cash she is willing to point out the way to Widmark's hideout to both the police and to Peters. As a result of her inadvertent assistance in the anti-Communist clean-up, Red agent Kiley returns to Thelma's waterfront shack and shoots her. As the *New York Times*'s reviewer pointed out: "There is something about the destruction of Miss Ritter that punches a hole in the film."

The impact of Thelma's performance did much to elevate the public's reception to this sadistic (for the time) and sex-ridden study of Manhattan's seamier characters, where right wins out over evil, not because gangster Widmark and slut Peters particularly detest the Communist cause, but because they fall in love and because Widmark wants to avenge stool pigeon Thelma's brutal death. *Punch* magazine observed: "The invaluable Thelma Ritter contributes one of her pawky heart-of-gold studies and is able to make it positively moving, . . ." *Variety* stated: ". . . the only halfway convincing figure in an otherwise unconvincing cast. . . . Miss Ritter is both pathetic and amusing, proving that it takes more than a bad script to defeat real talent." With Terry Moore and Stephen McNally, Thelma performed in an adaptation of *Pickup on South Street* on "Lux Radio Theatre" (June 20, 1954).

Thelma was nominated for her fourth Academy Award for her dramatic portrayal in *Pickup,* but once again was a loser. Donna Reed won the best supporting actress award of the year for *From Here to Eternity.* Thelma told the press with bittersweet cheer: "I'm the William Jennings Bryan of the acting profession, always nominated, never elected."

About this time Hollywood columnist Sheila Graham interviewed this atypical movie "star" and asked how she went about selecting her screen parts. Thelma admitted that she picked a role on its strength and appeal, adding "I don't care if it's small or not." The statement makes little sense when one considers the parts Thelma had agreed to in 1953 at Fox or the spate of caricature assignments she would "select" in future years.

Even though Thelma and her husband now were

With Richard Widmark in *Pickup on South Street*.

earning substantial salaries in their chosen fields, they did not forget their past financial struggles. As Thelma phrased it: "It's all the luck we never had in show business piling up for us in the movies.

"In those days we never even had one teaspoonful of gravy. We were kicked around all the time. Finally we decided that one of us would have to drop out and concentrate on the bread and beans. My Joe started in there at the office—at the bottom—and worked his way up. That's why all this means so much to us now."

Alfred Hitchcock borrowed Thelma's services for his Paramount suspense thriller *Rear Window* (Rivoli Theatre, August 4, 1954). She was billed fourth as Stella, the practical nurse who drops in daily to the apartment of news photographer James Stewart. Since an accident in which he broke his legs, Stewart must stay in a wheelchair and spends the bulk of the hot summer days studying the life-styles of his assorted

neighbors, whom he spies on from the rear window of his Greenwich Village apartment. He suspects one of his neighbors (Raymond Burr) has murdered his wife, and Stewart must convince his fiancée Grace Kelly and detective friend Wendell Corey of the validity of his supposition. Thelma's wisecracking presence (i.e., as she pops the thermometer into Stewart's mouth, she barks, "See if you can break a hundred") provided a sweet contrast to the tenseness of Stewart and the patronizing graciousness of Kelly. In the course of her daily visits, Thelma cannot resist a few tart remarks and withering glances about the immoral nature of Stewart's relationship with his frequent overnight guest Kelly. *Rear Window* was one of the top grossing films of the year, and Thelma received her share of credit for its success, despite her brief on screen footage. "Thelma Ritter is never one to be elbowed out of the way when there is good work to be done on the screen and she is

In *Rear Window* (Paramount, 1954).

Astaire. As she grows up, Caron becomes more and more frustrated in her attempts to learn the identity of her unknown benefactor whom she has called Daddy Long Legs since childhood. When she enrolls in an American college, it is Astaire's heart-of-gold but testy personal secretary Thelma who nags her detached boss into taking a personal interest in his ward. Several Cinemascope color reels later, and after much dancing and some singing (including the outstanding "Somethin' Got to Give"), Astaire and Caron realize they are wholesomely in love with one another and despite their age difference, plan to wed.

Thelma Ritter at the age of fifty.

wonderful as usual in the role of a kindly authoritative practical nurse with a wholesome interest in dismembered corpses." (*New York Times*).

Thelma's last picture under her Fox contract was *Daddy Long Legs* (Roxy Theatre, May 5, 1955), the third filming of the Jean Webster novel. Leslie Caron was now the French waif who is anonymously supported through adolescence by wealthy businessman, Fred

Thelma's supporting role as Miss Pritchard offered her no scope whatsoever. She spent most of her few scenes running in and out of Astaire's business suite crying into her handkerchief about Astaire's coolness toward Caron and bewailing the fact that she has had to answer each and every one of the many letters Caron had sent her sponsor. As in all 1950s screen comedies, everyone, including the comedy relief leads, had to be paired off by the film's finale. Thelma's love interest in *Daddy Long Legs* was Fred Clark. As Astaire's waspish business manager, he had even less of a cultivated sense of warm deportment than his boss. His barking and

With Wendell Corey, Grace Kelly, and James Stewart in *Rear Window*.

With Fred Clark and Fred Astaire in *Daddy Long Legs* (20th-Fox, 1955).

Thelma's raspy weeping were intended as yok-ful hilarity treats but frequently became merely cloying by their very artificial nature. At the film's wrap-up they exit together, and what is supposed to transpire afterwards was probably not decided by the screenwriters.

It seems likely Fox would have reteamed Thelma and Clark had Thelma elected to remain at the studio. She jokingly said about her departure from the lot, "I don't look so good in a toga. [This was the period of making historical epic films.] And there was nothing more for me to do at 20th-Fox, so after six years we called it a day." Coincidental or not, Thelma's leave-taking from the studio occurred just about the time Fox chief Zanuck left his executive capacity to enter independent production. From what transpired during the following years under the Fox regime of Buddy Adler and Jerry Wald, it is unlikely that Thelma would have fitted into the scheme of things. The studio's product was geared even more exclusively to the young at heart, and the bulk of contract players (Robert Wagner, Jeffrey Hunter, Bradford Dillman, Hope Lange, Diane Varsi, Suzy Parker, Joanne Woodward, Joan Collins, et al.) were under thirty. The decline in the theatrical film market was making it increasingly impractical for a studio to maintain a roster of character players in spite of their box office lure.

In 1954 Thelma had been asked if she would perform on television. She replied, "No, I don't mind doing some filmed guest shots for TV, but I won't do anything live." Obviously, Thelma had had her fill of the helter-skelter rat race which made live television much like the old days of stock repertory work.

She finally made her video debut on the CBS-TV hour color series, "The Best of Broadway" in its pro- duction of George Kelly's *The Show Off* (February 2, 1955), which starred Jackie Gleason in the title role. As the obnoxious windbag who marries Cathy O'Connell, the daughter of Thelma and Russell Collins, Gleason nearly drives his West Philadelphia in-laws insane with his perpetual bragging and blundering interference. Sidney Lumet directed the vehicle, which was pleasant enough entertainment but was distorted by the over-jovial blustering of funnyman Gleason. It was a safe and mild television debut for Thelma, who was becoming decidedly less adventuresome in her profession as the years went by. (In the 1944 MGM edition of *The Show Off* which starred Red Skelton, Marjorie Main played Thelma's role.)

Thelma's next video assignment was her most fruitful and best remembered television performance. On "Goodyear Playhouse" (NBC), she starred in Paddy Chayefsky's *The Catered Affair* (May 22, 1955), an hour drama concerning a Bronx Jewish mother living in a railroad flat who is determined her daughter shall have a glamorous big wedding, but strictly catered. For the mother, the wedding represented everything life had denied to her, and she would hear no arguments against her grandiose plans, neither from her hard-

With Leslie Caron in *Daddy Long Legs*.

working taxi driver husband (Pat Henning) who could not afford such extravagance, nor from her daughter (Kathleen Maguire), who is dismayed to learn the snowballing wedding plans are scaring off the groom and her impoverished friends. Jack Gould writing in the *New York Times* reported: ". . . as the mother, Miss Ritter often was a touching figure, perhaps more convincing as a wounded and tired woman, than as the administrator of a household."

The Catered Affair's author, Paddy Chayefsky, years later had high praise for Thelma's performance in his ". . . unfocused piece in which the first act was farce and the second was character-comedy and the third was abruptly drama. There aren't a dozen actresses who could make one piece out of all that; Miss Ritter, of course did."

For her "rich and profoundly moving performance," Thelma was nominated for an Emmy Award in the category of "Best actress in a supporting role" but lost out to Nanette Fabray, female foil of *Caesar's Hour* (NBC). In those years, the Television Academy of Arts and Sciences lumped together dramatic and comedy performances.

In 1956, MGM would adapt *The Catered Affair* into an Irish-oriented study, with Bette Davis offering a stylized piece of acting in the mother role.

The Late Christopher Bean (November 30, 1955) on the "Twentieth Century-Fox Hour" (CBS) proved to be Thelma's most publicized video appearance, largely because it had the press departments of both the network and the producing studio pushing the show. Presented on Broadway in 1932 and filmed by MGM in 1933 with Marie Dressler, it concerned an artist who after his death becomes famous and the New England country doctor and his family who years before had given him refuge. With the sudden spurt of interest in the painter, the physician becomes a focus of interest, but none more so than the family servant Abby (Thelma) who has possession of one of his best paintings and in fact knew the artist best of all—she had been married to him. Her costar in her third video outing was Gene Lockhart.

Thelma told the press about the production of this program: "It's an all-stage cast and it made the filming of the show so much easier.

"Stage people, for one thing, are used to handling props. Some actors who have worked only in films would hold a glass or any other object in their hands indefinitely if they were not told what to do with it. Stage-trained actors have so much intuition about these things. They don't wait to be told what to do. I think the American Academy of Dramatic Arts should have a class to teach young actors how to handle props. So

many of them get into movies and never learn."

About the subject matter of Sidney Howard's old-fashioned drama: "I've seen so much lust and violence and great, big fat problems written into plays that I think this is the kind of thing people might like for a change. It's just a tender love story and I don't think cutting it to an hour has hurt it. When it was written, thirty-five years ago, plays were more leisurely than they are today."

At this stage in her life, Thelma might have sat back and ignored further film work and only occasionally appeared in a video play of her choice, but it pleased her husband to see his wife finally in the limelight. Said Thelma: ". . . he's been like my stage mother ever since [her entry into films]. He gets a childlike pleasure out of my career. Showbusiness has spotted me with scar tissues. But Joe is as starry-eyed about it as he was at eighteen. He loves to see me get the red-carpet treatment in restaurants and theaters and in the studios when he visits Hollywood.

"Wanna know the truth? I'm just as hammy as he is!"

On a free-lance basis, Thelma accepted the fourth lead role as Molly Basserman in Jane Wyman's Paramount sudser, *Lucy Gallant* (Victoria Theatre, October

In *Lucy Gallant* (Paramount, 1955).

With Gloria Talbott and Charlton Heston in *Lucy Gallant*.

20, 1955). This women's picture concerns career girl Wyman who hastily leaves Manhattan to forget a broken love affair. When her train breaks down in a Texas oil town, she decides to remain there and soon opens a dress shop (which later in the film allows for endless fashion parades). She is attracted to hardheaded oil man Charlton Heston and has a see-saw struggle to become wealthy and eventually to wed her beau. Claire Trevor turned in her usual professional performance as a good-hearted tart, and Thelma and Wallace Ford were on hand as the jovial *nouveau riche* oil millionaires, who recalling their poverty salad days, do their best to live life to the hilt. Thelma functioned as the "wry and witty confessor to one and all." The *New York Times* decided the screen team of Thelma and Ford was "amusingly satirical." *Lucy Gallant* was no artistic achievement, but it was spottily entertaining as an obvious romance of early middle-aged love.

Producer-director George Seaton asked Thelma to bolster his Paramount production of *The Proud and Profane* (Astor Theatre, June 12, 1956), and Thelma readily agreed to join the on-location shooting in Puerto Rico and the Virgin Islands. Such occasional work as this kept Thelma's name in the limelight, added over $60,000 to her bank account, and could be treated as a professional lark.

It was more than coincidental that Deborah Kerr who had made such a hit in *From Here to Eternity* should be the female lead in this soap opera successor to that war picture hit. Sneering William Holden (with his hair dyed black and sporting a fierce moustache) is a lieutenant colonel in the marines, stationed on the Free French Isle of New Caledonia during World War II. Genteel Kerr is a pious war widow who has joined the Red Cross in order to visit the grave of her architect husband killed on Guadalcanal. Deciding to remain with the volunteer group in the South Pacific, she refuses any grisly work, preferring to handle such minor tasks as distributing cigarettes and giving French lessons. She is introduced to Holden and a clandestine

In *The Proud and Profane* (Paramount, 1956).

romance buds. Until she presses him to marry her, he does not bother to inform her he is married to an alcholic he has not seen in ten years. Later Kerr becomes pregnant and attempts suicide, and he is wounded in action. The climax is more than predictable.

Thelma was present (with a ". . . life-saving draught of humour . . ." stated one British film magazine) as

With Deborah Kerr in *The Proud and Profane*.

the lovable head of the Red Cross workers on the island, in charge of administering to the marines and looking out for the younger women assistants. For her role as "another of those indispensible onlookers with a barbed tongue and a heart of junket" (*Christian Science Monitor*), Thelma learned to drive a jeep as well as arranging for the screen debut of her son Joseph.* In one sequence in which Thelma jovially but tearfully bids farewell to a group of marines returning to dangerous combat action, she says "Good luck, son" to one of the extras boarding the plane. The soldier referred to was her child.

As a large-scale tearjerker, *The Proud and Profane* served its purpose, but its artlessness did not go unnoticed by reviewers or the public. With such a despicable male lead and an unsympathetic heroine who was blind to reality, there was not much to applaud in the proceedings. Thelma received her customary good notices for her by-now stock performance as the bystander always full of pepper and good advice, in this case for distraught Kerr and for lonely marine Dewey Martin. ". . . [she] manages to rise above the messy story." (*New York Herald-Tribune*).

Once again, it was on television that Thelma had a juicy role in a piece of offbeat casting on "Alfred Hitchcock Presents" (CBS). She starred in "The Baby Sitter" (May 6, 1956) as the employee who pries into the family of her socially prominent employers (Carmen Matthews and Theodore Newton). When the wife is found murdered, Thelma anxiously awaits the husband's proposal of marriage, followed by the typical Hitchcockian twist. In its brief 26½ minutes, it amply demonstrated how badly Thelma had allowed the cinema to shortchange her when both she and her studio employers refused to look beyond her proven worth as a comedy foil.

In June, 1956, Thelma was a guest participant on a few video quiz shows and returned to acting chores the following year on "The U.S. Steel Hour" (CBS) in *The Human Pattern* (January 2, 1957) by Irving H. Cooper. She portrayed the wife who ignores her husband (Frank McHugh) in order to focus all her attention on her high school football coach son (Michael Higgins). She has great social ambitions for him and is disconcerted when he falls for pedestrian teacher Lori March. It is her plan that sonny wed a rich but vulgar girl and secure a new job position so he can earn more

---

* Joseph was already part of the marine unit at Camp LeJeune, South Carolina. In fact, he was a member of the platoon under Sgt. Matthew C. McKeon's command who led his command into a coastal swamp, which cost the lives of six of his men.

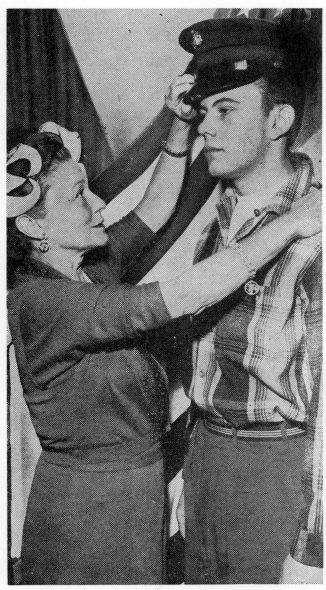

Thelma Ritter and her son Joseph in 1956.

Thelma had planned a Broadway return for some time, now that she could win an assortment of roles with little effort and command the billing and salary she had been unable to obtain in the 1920s and 1930s. She had considered the costarring role opposite her friend Nancy Walker in the musical comedy *Copper and Brass,* but dropped out of the project. Joan Blondell assumed the part, but she too left the show which opened October 17, 1957, at the Martin Beck Theatre and closed within 36 performances. But Thelma did accept the co-lead role opposite Gwen Verdon in *New Girl in Town* (46th Street Theatre, May 14, 1957), a musical derived from Eugene O'Neill's Pulitzer Prize play of 1921, which had been filmed by MGM in 1930 with Greta Garbo and Marie Dressler. The studio had long been planning a musical remake of the story, but finally gave up rights to the property.

In *New Girl in Town,* Thelma finally lived up to her decade-old tag as the new Marie Dressler when she undertook the role of Marthy, the waterfront drudge who

With Gwen Verdon in *New Girl in Town* (1957).

money "like his brother." She nags: ". . . a fella with your brains shouldn't be just a gym teacher all his life" and repeatedly reminds the young man "I worry about you twenty-four hours a day." The scripting verged on the banal, but Thelma's performance as the shrewish mama led one New York video critic to state: "Thelma Ritter persuaded us, against all our instinct and training. Now, there is an actress."

In mid-year, Thelma popped up on "Telephone Times" (ABC) in *Plot to Save a Boy* (June 6, 1957). She played a grief-stricken mother who redeems the young hood who accidentally killed her son.

before her looks had faded had been the sailors' delight. She is the one who greets weary prostitute Verdon when the latter returns to the safety of her father's (Cameron Prud'homme) tugboat home. Slouched drunkenly in a chair at the waterfront saloon, she tells Vardon in her slurred voice: "I got your number the moment you set foot in that door."

Verdon: "I got yours, too. You're me forty years from now."

Later Thelma confides to her on-again, off-again "man": ". . . how I hate the changeability of people. First I get used to you as a drunken friend and now I gotta start all over again and get used to you as a father."

Her Marthy may not look it now, but beneath her ramshackled appearances lies the remnants of a once hot number: "I was quite a thing, you know—gay, merry, up on me toes. It was a terrible strain. So I say to myself—'Marthy Ownes, is it worth it? Why don't you relax?' So I quit. I quit cold."

And yet Marthy still has memories of her sensuous past: "When it comes to tatoos I always claim, it ain't what you say, it's where you put it. I knew a sailor once who—oh, well, never mind. . . ."

With a book by George Abbott, songs by Bob Merrill,

Thelma Ritter in 1959.

and staged by Bob Fosse, *New Girl in Town* prettified the basic play to make it viable for commercial Broadway in the 1950s. Its lusty dancing and laundered characters detracted from the suggestions of the grim waterfront and blunted the sting of the original drama.

Thelma's role required her to put across three songs in the show; the first act comedy showstopper "Flings" sung by Thelma and two pals (in which they claim "Any hand which buys your sandwich, You can love."), "Yet My Friend, Aintcha" with Prud'homme, and the second act number "Play as You Go" with the dancers and chorus. Composer Merrill had readily agreed that Thelma was the perfect person for the part, but he wondered if she could vocalize. He later recalled: "So she came over [with an accompanist] and did a concert of the most obscure, off-beat Rodgers and Hart songs you ever heard in your life. Talk about chic! I thought, 'Wait till she hears what she's going to have to sing in this show.' "

New Girl in Town opened to resounding approval, with equal hosannas for Verdon and Thelma. ". . .[she] endows a rather inelastic role with a winning, raffish charm" (*Time* magazine). "Miss Ritter will win you as she toddles flat footedly on in Marthy's moth-eaten sweater, her fastidious fingers twitching sassily" (*New York Herald-Tribune*). "Miss Ritter, as the tatterdemalion waterfront belle, Marthy is a one-woman riot. Whether slyly outmaneuvering her 'squarehead' sweetie, Chris, getting a snootful and spilling the dirt about Annie at a lowbrow society ball, or just cracking over a line or singing a time, she invariably bullseyes. She's Broadway's gain and Hollywood's loss" (*Variety*). "And Thelma Ritter is Thelma Ritter and that's all to the good" (*Newsday*). Others termed her performance as the boozy saloon-ite as "consistently wonderful, dry and appealing," and "gifted in pantomime, timing, and humor."

Thelma topped her smash Broadway return by winning a Tony award as best musical star-actress of 1957. It was the first time two stars (Thelma and Verdon) from the same show won the coveted stage prize.

New Girl in Town ran for 431 performances. During the run, Thelma suffered from a throat hemorrhage and had to withdraw from the production for ten days. Her understudy Bibi Osterwald took over.

With her increased popularity, Thelma was much in the news now. Everyone wanted an interview with this brittle, middle-aged character star. The *Dallas Morning News* summed up Thelma: "She is primarily a personality, not an actress, but she appears to have inventoried her characters and to have subjected them to the control of intelligence and technique."

She told the press about the stigma that used to be

attached to being a stock repertory performer: "They used to be terribly prejudiced against stock actors. Why? Oh, the fact we did one play a week made us hacks. And because we did things fast. Yet when a Broadway actor came into stock we didn't exactly like him, either. He couldn't learn his lines fast enough."

On the new-styled method acting: "I hear a lot about it. I've been in show business since I was eight and by this time there are a couple of things I'd better know by instinct. I don't know enough about 'The Method.' I'd like to know more. Also, more about the method that produces a Ralph Richardson or a Fredric March."

About technique in general, she observed: "It's something you learn and then just put away. It's a basic thing—as an experienced pianist knows how to move his hands a certain way for a stretch of octaves. You take radio. It teaches you economy. You have to dramatize with your voice—no hands, no body, no face. On the old screen, movies were a little like television—you had to be compressed. With the wide screen, you have more leverage.

Thelma's typical day during her Broadway stay was a busy one. She long had become accustomed to reading a book a day (Charles Dickens was her favorite), then bulleting her way through novels, scripts, and plays at lightning pace to determine if there were any parts for her. A good deal of her time was devoted to the Board of Directors chores of the Girl Scouts of America and her activity on behalf of the American Cancer Society. At one point, Thelma was considered "a must in any fund-raising drive." In her spare time, she loved going canoeing and swimming with her family.

Thelma was lured back to the movies by Frank Capra for *A Hole in the Head* (Loew's State Theatre, July 15,

With Frank Sinatra, Eddie Hodges, and Edward G. Robinson in *A Hole in the Head* (UA, 1959).

1959). The property had first been a television play, then a Broadway comedy, and later would become a musical show. The story line was not much: forty-year-old widower Frank Sinatra operates a shabby Miami Beach hotel and is a loving but lackadaisical father to his eleven-year-old son, Eddie Hodges. In desperation for money, he asks his older brother (Edward G. Robinson) for a loan. New York businessman Robinson decides to view the preposterous situation first hand and arrives with his wife (Thelma) in Florida, leaving his less-than-bright son to run the business. It is not long before compassionate Thelma and narrow-minded dullard Robinson are attempting to get rid of Sinatra's kookie girl friend (Carolyn Jones) and marrying him off to proper widow Eleanor Parker. As the warm Italian aunt, Thelma utilized a broad accent and oversized gestures, matching Robinson in the creation of believable and lovable characters. The *New York Herald-Tribune* noted: "As entertainment, it owes most of its success to Miss Ritter and Robinson, whose sense of timing in dialogue exchanges is fascinating to watch."

In his autobiography, director Frank Capra recalls Thelma's morning ritual on the set of whispering into his ear: " '. . . I'm gonna stink, Sinatra's goinna stink, you're gonna stink, and *The Picture's* gonna stink! Wait and see." After the troublesome production was completed and previewed in the Bronx, Capra remembers: ". . . [suddenly] beads rattled, a woman's arms encircled my neck, a tear-stained face clamped on to mine, and Thelma Ritter's voice poured happy wet noises into my ear, "Oh Frank . . . It's so wonderful . . . so beautiful . . . I'm so proud to be a part of it . . . so proud . . . so proud . . .' "

Back in the Hollywood swing, Thelma continued to free-lance wherever the money was good. It was a cinch; her stereotyped characterizations offered no challenges. She was a howl as Doris Day's boozing maid in *Pillow Talk* (Palace, Murray Hills Theatres, October 6, 1959), the picture which not only changed Day's wholesome girl image, but set a new trend for rich money-making comedies (*Pillow Talk* has grossed over $7.5 million to date). The zippy script had brittle interior decorator Day, who wears a new Jean Louis extravagant dress creation in nearly every scene, forced to share a party line with girl-crazy songwriter Rock Hudson, who seemingly never gets off the telephone. When he learns his co-user's identity and how much she detests his wolfish habits, he pretends to be a naive, rich Texas cowboy and wins her love. The adult double entendres and interactions—1959 style—titillated the public beyond all of Universal's expectations, particularly when decked out with all of producer Ross Hunter's lavish production values. Rounding out the leading roles was

With Edward G. Robinson in *A Hole in the Head*.

Tony Randall, playing a Broadway producer for whom Hudson is writing a new score. As Day's disappointed suitor, he was handed many bright give-away, one-line jokes.

Thelma's limited screen time found her continually wobbling into Day's plush apartment, nursing a bad hangover. (Why she had to get drunk every night is never satisfactorily explained.) With an ice bag on her head, sipping tomato juice, and her feet up on a chair, she is too discomforted to perform many house-cleaning chores. (It did not matter, the apartment was always spotless.) She was primarily a script device to serve as a sounding board both for Day and for Hudson (she eavesdrops on his amazing phone calls). Her best scene occurs near the finale when she and Hudson find themselves engaged in a drinking contest, and she drinks her companion under the table. The *British Monthly Film Bulletin* rightly observed about *Pillow Talk:* "Thelma Ritter has regretably little to do; and her drunk scenes belong to the least likeable aspects of the script."

During the filming of *Pillow Talk,* Thelma was asked if she enjoyed making the picture, to which she aptly

With Doris Day in *Pillow Talk* (Universal, 1959).

With Rock Hudson in *Pillow Talk.*

replied: "If you're responsible in any way for a three million dollar project, you'd better not have any fun." As to viewing her own screen work: "I never see rushes. It doesn't pay me to see them. I don't think you can learn a thing, except just how bad you can be. . . . But to go to see yourself give a performance (half of which is going to be cut out) doesn't make any sense."

Thelma was nominated for a best supporting Oscar for her performance in *Pillow Talk.* This time she lost to Shelley Winters who won for her performance in *The Diary of Anne Frank.*

A projected stage version of Paul Galico's *Mrs. 'arris Goes to Paris* never materialized for Thelma, so she returned to the television fold to keep in the thick of things. In "Sarah's Laughter" (January 3, 1960) on "GE Theatre" (CBS), she and James Gregory appeared in an adequate half-hour drama depicting the efforts of a childless wife. On "NBC Startime," Thelma was seen to excellent dramatic advantage in "The Man" (January 5, 1960) as a too good-natured landlady who discovers herself locked alone in her house with a psychotic roomer (Audie Murphy). She even turned up on the "Perry Como Show" (NBC, October 26, 1960) to sing "I'm Staying Young."

Now aged fifty-five, Thelma was enjoying her off-camera moments more and more. For years, she and her husband had maintained a Fire Island retreat: "We don't use it just week-ends. We get out from our home in Forest Hills whenever we feel too beat by what's going on in town." Having multiple households occasionally caused problems, particularly when she was in Hollywood and had to maintain a hotel suite where she did her own housekeeping. Once, she recalled, "When I was running three houses, the place in Hollywood, the one in Forest Hills and the six-room place on Fire Island, I'd get a little confused. I'd reach for the mustard

in Forest Hills and it wouldn't be there and I'd say, 'I bought some just yesterday.' And I had—but in California.''

About her family life: "Joe and I are happy about the children's setup, and we're often baby-sitting for our son's baby daughter. We are new at being grandparents, but we are 'heavy' parents, and enjoy our kids. My career has never been as important as the children—though I've been acting since I was eleven [sic]."

When asked again about theater acting methods, she still maintained: ". . . I'm not for a single method of acting, but I believe a good performer will put himself across in his own particular fashion. . . . I'm for doing a good job, of course, without sacrificing any of the other terrific things in life and believe me, wifehood, housekeeping and motherhood are mighty important."

Thelma was always terribly proud to have attended the American Academy of Dramatic Arts (even for a year) and always did her utmost to promote the school and its functions. As part of the Academy's education program, a series of outstanding actors were interviewed on WNTA-TV in New York. Thelma's session was televised September 24, 1960. In the course of the program she talked about the essence of creating characterizations: "I expect the playwright or the author to do about half my work for me, if not most of it. Occasionally you get an incompetent or lazy playwright, who throws you a bone without any meat on it. In that event you have to use tricks. It's very unsatisfactory. It's like covering up a misshapen cake with a lot of icing. It may look all right, but it isn't; it isn't sound."

About success: "Well, of course, my close friends and family are not very reverent. Occasionally, when we go to the moving pictures and the manager recognizes me and lets us in for nothing, my stock zooms for the time being. And as far as the pinnacle is concerned, I've reached no pinnacle except that I'm doing the thing I think I can do best, that I love the most. That's a pinnacle, whatever it is."

The following year, The American Academy of Dramatic Arts saluted her at a dinner at the Astor Hotel (October 22, 1961), making her the first female recipient of the Alumni Award. Past winners included Edward G. Robinson, Garson Kanin, Kirk Douglas, Howard Lindsay, and Cecil B. DeMille.

Thelma was enticed back to filmmaking in the John Huston-directed *The Misfits* (Capitol Theatre, February 1, 1961), which was filmed on location in Nevada at a cost of over $3 million. Its story dealt with newly divorced Marilyn Monroe, who is staying at Thelma's Reno rooming house. Monroe meets independent but aging cowboy Clark Gable. The two are immediately attracted to one another, largely to each's unrealized

With Clark Gable and Marilyn Monroe in *The Misfits*
(UA, 1961).

potentials, and they move into the partially completed ranch home of Gable's pal, Eli Wallach. Gable is soon talked into joining Wallach and battered rodeo rider Montgomery Clift into rounding up misfit mustangs to be sold to a dog food manufacturer. Weirdish Monroe later persuades Gable to abandon the inhumane mission, which he reluctantly does, leaving the two of them to find their uncertain future together.

Thelma was cast as happy-go-lucky Isabella Steers, an eccentric landlady who has six clocks in her house, none of which work. On each anniversary of her divorce she deceives one potted yellow rose from her ex-husband. As she explains to Monroe, it has been nearly nineteen years since the divorce. "Of course, he never did send me the alimony. I wouldn't want to put a man out you know." Later on, Thelma, with sloppy kimona and frizzled hairdo, is seen wearing a cast on her

broken arm. Lightheartedly she chirps: "We celebrated my friend's [Monroe's] divorce and I misbehaved." It is Thelma who catches viewers off guard when she reflects: "Cowboys are the last real men in the world, but they're as reliable as jackrabbits." This line is one of the keys to Arthur Miller's screenplay.

Further into the picture, Thelma spots her ex-husband and his new wife in Reno and invites them to her home with all the genuine glee of a perfect hostess. Then she almost disappears from the story, because her almost superfluous function to the tale is finished.

The Misfits had a tragic production history, including Monroe's recurrent exhaustion collapses during filming and Gable's post-filming death (November 16, 1960) due to the physical strain endured on location. Thelma sat patiently on the sidelines during the protracted shooting, waiting for her brief on-camera scenes to be shot. No matter the size or quality of her role, she must have felt great satisfaction in being in such illustrious company on one of *the* most prestigious pictures of the year. As always, she had her own opinions about the picture and the cast. Of Gable, she said when she returned to New York: "Clark is one of the last great symbols of the picture industry, and with his prestige, I was prepared for him to take a pretty casual attitude toward his work. But he worked as if he needed the job, which I can assure you, he doesn't."

The Misfits continued its bad luck history at the box office. Many admired the performances of Gable and the seriousness of the picture's theme, but criticized that director Huston ". . . failed to instill an even tempo and there are some unaccountably awkward passages. . . ." (*Newsweek*). About Thelma, the reviewers were more enthusiastic: "In a supporting role, Thelma Ritter—still one of the most capable players in Hollywood—does a beautiful job as a friendly divorcee who finds all life a giggle" (*Cue*). ". . . Thelma Ritter in one of her thoroughly professional bitter-sweet performances" (*British Monthly Film Bulletin*).

Once curiosity seekers had caught Gable's last screen performance and the Monroe cult had seen *The Misfits,* it died at the box office, too sombre and disjointed for popular taste.

There was nothing earth-shaking about Thelma's next picture, *The Second Time Around* (Paramount Theatre, December 22, 1961), a comedy western starring rambunctious Debbie Reynolds as widow who comes to Charleyville, Arizona, in 1911 and finds employment and love. She is so aghast at the complacency of the townfolk and the orneriness of sheriff Ken Scott that she runs for the sheriff's post herself and is elected.

With Debbie Reynolds in *The Second Time Around* (20th-Fox, 1962).

The widescreen color film had Thelma as the disheveled ("hard-boiled softie") ranch owner who eventually hires Reynolds to work on her spread and continually advises the energetic easterner on the ways of western life. At one point, she tells the snappy miss: "If you don't weaken, you'll be getting drunk on Saturday night and setting fire to the barn." Here again, she was icing on a skimpy pastry of a film, supplying a sounding board for Reynolds and explaining her young friend's emotional state to the interested menfolk of Charleyville (e.g., "Yes, she's all right. There was a holdup in the bank").

In one of the script's few generous moments toward Thelma she has a short kitchen scene with Reynolds where she reveals an untapped sentimental nature: "It's goin' to be awful lonesome here without you." (Reynolds has threatened to pack up and go back East—which she cannot do, of course, without abruptly concluding the film.) But soon Thelma is back to her subordinate "They went thataway" assignment.

The easy-going picture passed muster at the box office, with the *New York Herald-Tribune* observing: ". . . as for Miss Ritter, she doesn't have to do much more than walk past in an old coat and a pair of jeans to make a scene look salty." *Variety* detailed that Thelma was just playing ". . . her customary character —an exterior of steel covering up a heart of pure goo."

It was another year before Thelma was on the screen again, this time in a purely dramatic role in John Frankenheimer's *Bird Man Of Alcatraz* (Trans-Lux Theatre, July 18, 1962), billed third as Elizabeth Stroud, mother of the film's star Burt Lancaster. Based on the true life case of Robert Stroud, the documentary-style drama finds Lancaster sentenced to twelve years imprisonment for accidentally killing another person. When in a fit of uncontrollable anger he fights with another prisoner, Warden Karl Malden, who had initially taken a liking to him, rules against any parole for him. Thelma appears as Lancaster's typically American mother, filled with an overpossesive love of her son. For this weather-beaten woman, he can do no wrong. She travels half-way across the country to see him, but because it does not happen to be a visiting day, she is denied permission to talk with Lancaster. He becomes infuriated by this situation and is egged into a fight with another prisoner (Telly Savalas), whom he kills.

Sentenced to death, it is determined Thelma who makes an appeal plea to U.S. President Woodrow Wilson and has the death verdict commuted to life imprisonment in solitary confinement. Time passes and one day Lancaster finds a fledgling sparrow in the exercise yard and is sufficiently touched by the bird's plight to care for it. From that episode develops his

With Burt Lancaster in *Bird Man of Alcatraz* (UA, 1962).

fanatical interest and absorption in ornithology. Eventually he prepares a classic textbook on the subject. One of his magazine articles comes to the attention of bird-lover and widow Betty Field. She suggests they go into business to merchandise bird medicine, and later she offers to marry him. At this point, Thelma, losing her grip on her middle-aged son, demands he choose be-

With Burt Lancaster in *Bird Man Of Alcatraz*.

tween her and Field. Lancaster sides with Field and marries her, despite his still being within prison. He spends the remainder of his years incarcerated, but at least his harsh life is made easier by his scholarly renown.

As the dauntless, jealous mother in *Bird Man of Alcatraz,* there were moments when Thelma brought horrifying reality to her truncated role, but too often she seemed "merely a weak and somewhat lacrymose character" (*New York Times*). The *New York Herald-Tribune's* reviewer was more generous toward Thelma: ". . . [she] gives it a reality that, if it cannot overcome the script's reluctance to define the relationship explicitly, makes the force undeniable."

For the sixth time, a record in itself, Thelma was nominated for a best supporting actress Academy Award. Unlike some of the other participants, she did not campaign for the Oscar sweepstakes. This time she was passed aside for Patty Duke who recreated her stage role from *The Miracle Worker*. Thelma's comment about losing was: "I feel it's a great honor just to have been nominated so many times, and truthfully speaking, only once have I ever felt a twinge of disappointment when someone else was named the winner. That was after I had been nominated for my role in *Pickup on South Street*. I really loved that picture, and it would have been an extra thrill to have won an Oscar for it." But Thelma could never take either herself or her Hollywood career too seriously. Nevertheless, she was always respectful, grateful, and conscientious about her screen work. She described her type of screen character: "Whenever a director would tell the cast 'Freshen your makeup,' somebody would hit me in the face with a pie."

The following year, 1963, was Thelma's most active period on the screen. She was among the many stars and leading character players corralled by MGM to star in its blockbuster three-panel Cinerama spectacle, *How the West Was Won* (Cinerama Theatre, March 27, 1963). Thelma's minimal contribution to this chronicle of American life in the West of the mid-1880s was in the Henry Hathaway-directed segment *The Rivers*. She was the lonely but cheery pioneer woman driving along in Robert Preston's wagon train to the new frontier. Thelma allows latecomer Debbie Reynolds, a saloon entertainer going to claim a mine left her by an admirer, to join her wagon party. On the journey, Reynolds falls for gambler Gregory Peck. It was a small bit for Thelma, but her presence added some degree of authenticity to this sprawling feature which went on to gross an amazing $24 million at the box office.

Of her cameo assignment in *How the West Was Won,* Thelma remarked: ". . . don't think the picture was any

In *How the West Was Won* (MGM, 1963).

snap. The directors were not brilliant young men who grope. Henry Hathaway, John Ford and George Marshall are seasoned, men of action. They *know* just what they want—and they are slave drivers. However, it's a pleasure to work yourself out for them, really, real excitement."

With Debbie Reynolds and Gregory Peck in *How the West Was Won.*

"I'm only in one sequence, but it is a tough one." About the location work required for the picture: ". . . when we were snowed out of Colorado, we headed for Lone Pine, California. All I have to say about this locale is that if the bomb fell upon it, it couldn't do any further damage! It is a thoroughly miserable, isolated place in the winter season."

What attracted Thelma to Universal's *For Love or Money* (RKO Palace and Trans-Lux Theatres, August 7, 1963) was ". . . for the first time in my career, I get to be beautifully dressed, and they made a gesture; they presented me with the wardrobe. It's so elegant, I don't know when I'll wear it." In the fragile comedy, plain-spoken, multi-millionaire San Francisco widow Thelma hires bachelor attorney Kirk Douglas at a $100,000 fee to insure that her three daughters (Mitzi Gaynor, Julie Newmar, Leslie Parrish) are married—pronto and suitably. For supposed contrasting characterizations, Gaynor was the brainy head of a motivational research laboratory, Newmar a moronic physical culture enthusiast, and Parrish a far-out patroness of avant-garde arts. Mama Ritter seems to be determined to see Gaynor marry playboy Gig Young, but at the finale when the three girls (all blondes) have been matched and wed, including Gaynor to Douglas, Thelma collects her wager on the church steps from her dumb detective employee William Bendix. All along, she had been rooting for Gaynor and Douglas to hit it off well together.

Thelma was definitely out of place in this forced froth, which badly needed the slick talents of Cary Grant to carry off the thin comedy. That rugged, ungenteel Thelma could possibly breed three such luscious daughters was but one of the more incongruous points of the feature. Judith Crist (*New York Herald-Tribune*) was of the opinion: "Miss Ritter, begowned and bejeweled, but still her rasp-voiced self, is delightful as the lady who knows just what money can buy and where to place her bets, . . ." A more realistic appraisal of her performance was offered by the *New York Times*: "They [Thelma and Gig Young] perform with an air of condescension that makes me suspect how bored they are." *For Love or Money* did adequately at the box office.

Hardly any better was Thelma's next lighthearted foray, *A New Kind of Love* (DeMille and Coronet Theatres, October 30, 1963). Mannish career girl Joanne Woodward, with a knack for adapting sleek Parisian dress creations into inexpensive ready-to-wear models, flies to Paris with her gruff employer George Tobias and efficient store buyer Thelma. At least this time Thelma was cast in a more probable role, as a hardworking New Yorker type. On the trip over, Thelma snaps about the posh plane salon: "If Lindbergh could

With Mitzi Gaynor in *For Love or Money* (Universal, 1963).

have looked into the future on that lonely night in 1927 he'd have said 'To hell with it.' " (Her other dialogue in this feature was equally flat in its punchlines.)

Once in Paris, Woodward is easy prey for wolfish newspaper reporter Paul Newman, and it is not long before she undergoes an incredible transformation into a chic woman. Unsure of Newman's feelings for the real her, she poses as a glamorous and expensive whore and eventually learns that he really does care for her. Meanwhile, Thelma has kept up a brave front as she watches her beloved boss Tobias foolishly flirt with the store's French buyer, Eva Gabor. When Gabor leaves Tobias flat, Thelma is right there to eagerly accept contrite Tobias's matrimonial bid, thus making the symmetry of the movie comedy work out nicely. Neither the guest appearance of Maurice Chevalier, nor the bits of indulgent fantasy helped to bridge the credibility gap

With Eva Gabor, George Tobias, and Joanne Woodward in *A New Kind of Love* (Paramount, 1963).

in this dreary film where everyone was trying too hard to be funny and innovative. Thelma was given the benefit of doubt by many reviewers. ". . . [she] illuminates her every moment" (*New York Herald-Tribune*). ". . . [not even] several fashion shows or Thelma Ritter can get it out of its Miami Beach sands" (*Washington Post*).

Thelma's final 1963 release was *Move Over Darling* (Astor Theatre, December 25, 1963). This project was begun the previous year as a remake of Irene Dunne's *My Favorite Wife,* entitled *Something's Got to Give.* But star Marilyn Monroe was undergoing emotional problems at the time, and it was not long before production was shut down and after Monroe's death (August 5, 1962), it was hastily revamped as a Doris Day picture.

Move Over Darling opens five years after Day and her lawyer husband James Garner have been in a plane crash. Garner's lifeboat was rescued, but Day's raft had drifted out of sight. After waiting the statutory five-year period, Garner petitions the court to have Day declared legally dead and then promptly marries neurotic but nice Polly Bergen. Day, of course, reappears to complicate matters, undecided whether she intends wooing back her errant husband or not. As Garner's vinegary mother, Thelma wore well-tailored outfits, although she seemed incapable of ever appearing chic. There was actually little screen time given to her lovable curmudgeon portrayal of a mother-in-law. She was around to toss caustic wisecracks at Bergen, bemoan her befuddled son's inability to handle the domestic situation more gracefully, and to coach Day in ways and means to regain her former legal and romantic status with Garner. Her dialogue bits were just functional. (i.e., "Tell me, I want to know everything." "For heavens

With Doris Day in *Move Over, Darling* (20th-Fox, 1963).

sake, what did you do to build such a fire under Nick?" "Better think of something else." (More importantly, the scripters had forgotten that by the 1960s there was very little left for a backseat observer to do in a film. No longer was it necessary for a Thelma Ritter or Eve Arden to wisecrack about subjects and sentiments that the leading players would not dream of verbalizing. The era of more realistic screenfare had slowly but surely arrived, and now the stars could spout forth nearly anything that popped into their heads.

Thelma was well paid for her work in *Move Over Darling.* Day and her producer husband Martin Melcher obviously realized how much Thelma had contributed to *Pillow Talk* and had offered attractive terms to have her grace this new venture. Audiences were satisfied with the obvious humor Thelma's screen character presented, and the critics were still ready to compliment her for ". . . injecting sure-fire wit into the zany goings on" (*New York Daily News*). But the real savior of *Move Over Darling* was veteran character actor Edgar Buchanan as the folksy, nasal-toned judge who handles both Garner's missing person petition and the later hearing to determine whether Day or Bergen is legally married to Garner. His peppery comments on the action were the one joy in this labored farce, which could not decide whether it should be slapstick or sophisticated comedy. One memorable moment occurs when it is revealed it was Thelma who instigated the matrimonial determination hearing. Wry Buchanan mumbles soto voce to the harassed Garner: "I'd remember that come Mother's Day."

While in Hollywood, Thelma had some comments to make on screen directors: "Some of the new directors are damn good, but a lot of them think they're teaching acting. Alfred Hitchcock, on the other hand, is one of our best directors and you hardly hear from him.

"If Hitchcock looks as if he's going to throw up after you've finished a scene then you know it's no good and you'll have to do it over. He has eyes like a camera and doesn't miss a thing but he doesn't jump all over the place picking at everyone."

About her future: ". . . I doubt if I will ever do another musical. I couldn't take it physically anymore. Those 18-hour days of rehearsals and tryout shows out of town can really knock you out.

"That's one reason why I would never want to become involved in a TV series. Those things really put you on a treadmill. They tell you about all the millions you'll make but about all that will get you is a corner room with cross ventilation in a swanky sanitarium."

Thelma was more than happy to return to New York and her family and lead the leisurely life of a well-situated housewife. It was another two years before she returned to Hollywood to take sixth billing in *Boeing-Boeing* (Forum and Guild Theatres, December 23, 1965). This broad bedroom farce had been a huge hit in the original French version and in Continental editions, but had quickly folded in its Broadway outing. The picture's casting gimmick was having Jerry Lewis play his first full-fledged screen characterization with supposedly no reliance on his customary bag of sight gag tricks. The sex farce found Lewis and Tony Curtis as rival American correspondents in Paris. Lewis arrives as the uninvited houseguest at Curtis's bachelor apartment, throwing into chaos the latter's well-organized romantic life in which he maintains a revolving relationship with three airline stewardesses, each having a different off-duty schedule.

In a direct recap of her *Pillow Talk* role, although this time she was not an alcoholic, Thelma played the long suffering cook-housekeeper of Curtis. It is her task to rearrange—with split second timing—the flat to suit the various international tastes of each gal coming to the apartment so that none of them knows of the other's past visits. Thelma's Bertha takes a jaundiced view of her employer's gymnastic sex life, but interestingly enough, she is less upset by her boss's triple standards than by the naiveté of the shapely misses. With such an assortment of cheesecake in view, there was ample opportunity for double takes and salty remarks from down-to-earth Thelma regarding the physical attributes of the various feminine guests. At times, she finds herself at a loss, trying to keep up with the change of ambience and cuisine required to match each girl's nationality (i.e., Miss Air France, Miss Lufthansa, Miss British Airways) and tossing off salutations in the guest's native

language. Her prize line is when she socks out a sarcastic "Wunderbar" to the German miss who has become something of a trial.

Said the *New York Times* of Thelma in *Boeing-Boeing:* ". . . it's that Brooklyn buzzsaw, good old Thelma Ritter who steals the picture—what there is of it."

". . . Miss Ritter as might be expected has the tangiest lines and she makes the withering most of them." The *New York Daily News* in its three-star review announced: "Lucky for you, lucky for me, lucky for the Paramount comedy, there is Thelma Ritter, bless her, as Tony's grumbling maid. She provides the only amusing moments in it."

Back in New York, Thelma was persuaded by her friend Nancy Walker to join the cast of James Kirkwood's two-act comedy *UTBU (Unhealthy to Be Unpleasant)* (1965), which Walker had been signed to direct. It focused on a bizarre organization which employs blind Alan Webb and other agents to right the world's wrongs by eliminating any and all nasty people. Webb's weapons are a shin-banging cane and an assortment of time bombs. Tony Randall plays a middle-aged egomaniac actor, a relic of the theater of fifty years ago, who plans a great stage comeback. His balmy mother (Thelma), however, refuses to back his foolhardy production. Randall is trying hard to kill her, but UTBU has other plans for him. Others entangled in the chaos are the dyspeptic maid Margaret Hamilton and a caricature stage mother (Constance Ford).

The slim vehicle played heavily on farce and snappy reading of potentially flat lines, and required above all, an audience most indulgent to a novice playwright and overly fond of the starring members of the cast. In short, the show was fighting impossible odds.

Thelma was handed a role that much better suited the talents of Ruth Gordon a la *Where's Papa*. She was the eccentric matriarch—"ninety-four and I haven't broken my hip yet"—who was wavering between shrewdness and senility. She never could keep straight which members of her family were dead or alive. When she misses her son Randall at breakfast one morning, she puts on widow's weeds and rushes off to Campbell's Funeral Home, assuming he has died. In one scene Thelma wears a lace trimmed fuddy-duddy dress with a bow in her hair, in another she is dressed in a 1910-style bathing suit, and later on she is dressed in western garb, brandishing six-shooters. The whole world seems to be her target. To maintain her shaky sanity, she drinks herself silly, which allows for a replay of all the gambits she employed in *Pillow Talk*. (When inebriated, she is apt to act like a child with arms spread-

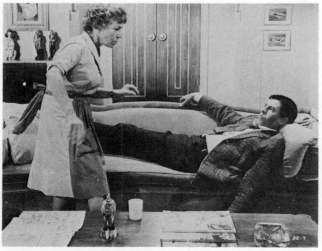

With Jerry Lewis in *Boeing-Boeing* (Paramount, 1965).

With director Nancy Walker, Alan Webb, and Tony Randall in *UTBU* (1965).

eagle descending stairs like a glider plane.)

UTBU first tried out in Boston (Wilbur Theatre, November 29, 1965). The *Boston Globe* reported: "The main delight of the evening is Miss Ritter. Wisp-haired, ashen-faced and dressed in various shades of shroud, she is a perfect image of senility. She is so lunatically right that it is sometimes painful just to look at her. Unfortunately, however, except for a mild drunk scene in the second act, Miss Ritter's character is gradually diminished in importance as the comedy clutters onward." The show next moved to Philadelphia (Walnut Street Theatre, December 15, 1965) to unpromising results. The *Philadelphia Inquirer* noted: "Miss Ritter seems to have the choicer lines, but then again her

With Tony Randall and Alan Webb in *UTBU*.

laconic delivery and miming instincts could make her sound hysterical asking the right time."

UTBU made its New York City bow at the Helen Hayes Theatre, January 4, 1966. The *New York Times* wrote: "There are such phenomena as intrinsically funny people and Thelma Ritter is one. By any logic of expectation, she ought now to be less funny because there are few surprises left in her appearances. But all she need do is apply that umpire's voice and gravelly innocence to the most pallid of lines and it seems more humorous. With a good line she is irresistible. . . ." *Variety* evaluated Thelma's role: "It's actually not much more than an incidental character but she makes it credible and frequently diverting." The *Village Voice* noted: "I had no idea that slangy old Thelma Ritter

With Tony Musante, Martin Sheen, Gary Merrill, Diana Van Der Vlis, Ed McMahon, Kathleen Smith, Jack Gilford, Victor Arnold, Donna Mills, Jan Sterling, Mike Kellin, Robert Bannard, and Beau Bridges in *The Incident* (20th-Fox, 1967).

possessed such reserves of genuine sweetness."

One critic referred to *UTBU* as "*U*nnecessary *t*rivia, *b*adly *u*sed." The show folded after 7 performances, at a loss of $125,000 on a $110,000 investment.

The next year Thelma made *The Incident* (Victoria and Plaza theaters, November 5, 1967), which afforded her a chance to demonstrate solid dramatics, even if her role was badly truncated in the final print and lacked dimension. Based on a television drama *Ride with Terror* performed on the "DuPont Show of the Week" (December 1, 1963), the black and white movie was filmed on a low budget on location in New York City. It was a stark study of human apathy, focusing on sixteen people aboard the Jerome Avenue subway traveling from the Bronx to Manhattan at 2 A.M. On the express train are Jan Sterling, a sex and money-starved housewife; Mike Kellin, her mild-mannered husband; Victor Arnold, a sexually aggressive guy; Donna Mills, his timorous date; Gary Merrill, a desperate reformed drunk; Robert Fields, a shy homosexual attracted to Merrill; Henry Proach, a derelict; Ed McMahon, an overly concerned husband driven frantic by his need to support his family; Diana Van Der Vlis, his materialistic wife; Kathleen Smith, their sleepy daughter; Ossie Davis, a black trying to make his respectable way in a white world; Ruby Dee, his proud wife who merely tolerates the race barriers; Jack Gilford, an elderly Jewish man full of complaints about his seemingly ungrateful son; Thelma, his patient wife; Beau Bridges, a soft-spoken soldier with a broken arm on leave in New York; and Robert Bannard, his army pal who has invited Bridges home to stay with his parents. Having just committed a robbery, Martin Sheen and Tony Musante, two crazed cool hoods high on drink, jump on the train and begin to taunt the passengers.

The import of the drama was to point out the cowardice of people in contemporary society, who will sit back in feigned indifference in order to avoid becoming involved in problems that are not their own. The action reaches a climax when Bridges, caring enough about his own integrity and the other passengers' well-being, confronts the obnoxious thugs and is stabbed in the stomach. Not even then do the other passengers appreciate his efforts, and at the Times Square exit they move away quickly, leaving the wounded Bridges and his pal to cope with his wound.

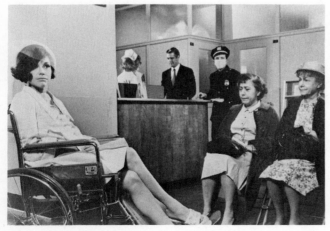

With Mary Tyler Moore, George Peppard, Morty Gunty, and Eda Reiss Merin in *What's So Bad about Feeling Good?* (Universal, 1968).

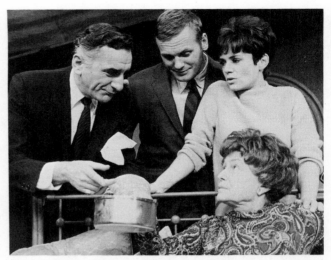

With Woody Ronroff, Tab Hunter, and Monica Moran in *Barefoot in the Park* (1968).

The film received mild reviews, and due to its socially critical nature and the low-key publicity campaign utilized by Twentieth Century-Fox, came and went quickly at the box office. Thelma was only mentioned in the context of the cast as a whole.

When George Seaton returned to on-location shooting in New York for his far-out comedy *What's So Bad about Feeling Good?* (Trans-Lux Theatre, May 24, 1968), he requested Thelma to provide an unbilled cameo for the film. She agreed. The picture's premise had a rare tropical toucan bird spreading a virus of love and charity over Fun City (New York), upsetting the normal routine as everyone falls prey to the germs. Included in the epidemic are Madison Avenue dropout George Peppard and his hippie-styled girl friend Mary Tyler Moore. Peppard and Moore become accidental custodians of the bird and attempt to hide it from stuffy, shocked presidential aide Dom DeLuise who it out to trap the whimsical creature. In a sequence in which Moore sneaks the bird into Beekman Hospital for medication, Thelma can be seen as Mrs. Schwartz, a talkative woman in the clinic waiting room. "This pinheaded comedy . . ." (*New York Times*) was pretty much of a dud in theatrical release and was quickly relegated to the television late show circuit.

This film cameo and a later brief appearance on Jerry Lewis's television show (ABC) were among her last professional appearances. In February, 1968, she costarred with Tab Hunter and her daughter Monica in a stock edition of *Barefoot in the Park* which played at the Papermill Playhouse, New Jersey. Except for these outings, she stuck to her guns about living the life of a retired matron. Offers still came, but nothing tempting enough to bring her out of her enforced rest, required particularly by recurring poor health.

After being stricken at her Forest Hills home with a heart attack on January 27, 1969, she was admitted to Queens Hospital, where she died from another attack on February 5, 1969, at 12:45 A.M. She was survived by her husband, himself in failing health, her two children, and the grandchildren.

The most fitting tribute to Thelma was written by playwright Paddy Chayefsky in a *New York Times* piece:

> The fact is, she was never properly publicly recognized as an actress. She was blessed—or cursed—with a tough urban wit and voice to match and so she got all the gravelly Tenth Avenue parts. But anyone who saw her as Burt Lancaster's rigidly obsessed mother in *Birdman of Alcatraz* got an idea of what this woman could do.

> . . . Her acting emotion had first to filter through that urban crust of hers before it exhibited itself externally. Her power as an actress was consequently one of depth. Even her sketchiest roles had this substance of human embattlement. . . . she revealed to her audience the tragedy of the human condition, which is the definition of great acting. She was a supreme comedian, a consummate technician, and a kind and gentle woman who was esteemed by everyone who ever worked with her.

> In the end, that has to be, I suppose, the final tribute to an artist. She had become archetypical in her own profession; for many years now, there has been a wide range of women roles described by casting directors as 'a Thelma Ritter type.' She was a character actress, which means only that they don't write many starring parts for middle-aged women. The point is, she was a great character actress, the best we had, and she was not expendable.

FILMOGRAPHY: THELMA RITTER
FEATURE FILMS

MIRACLE ON 34th STREET (20th Century-Fox, 1947) 96 M.

Producer, William Perlberg; director, George Seaton; story, Valentine Davies; screenplay, Seaton; art director, Richard Day, Richard Irvine; camera, Charles Clark; editor, Robert Simpson.

Maureen O'Hara (Doris Walker); John Payne (Fred Gailey); Edmund Gwenn (Kris Kringle); Gene Lockhart (Judge Henry X. Harper); Natalie Wood (Susan Walker); Porter Hall (Mr. Sawyer); William Frawley (Charles Halloran); Jerome Cowan (District Attorney Thomas Mara); Philip Tonge (Mr. Shellhammer); James Seay (Dr. Pierce); Harry Antrim (Mr. Macy); Thelma Ritter (Peter's Mother); Mary Field (Girl's Mother); Theresa Harris (Cleo); Alvin Greeman (Alfred); Anne Staunton (Mrs. Mara); Robert Hyatt (Thomas Mara, Jr.); Richard Irving, Jeff Corey (Reporters); Anne O'Neal (Sawyer's Secretary); Lela Bliss (Mrs. Shellhammer); Anthony Sydes (Peter); William Forrest (Dr. Rogers); Alvin Hammer (Mara's Assistant); Joseph McInerney (Bailiff); Ida McGuire (Drum Majorette); Percy Helton (Santa Claus); Jane Green (Mrs. Harper); Marlene Lyden (Dutch Girl); Walden Boyle (Judge's Clerk); Patty Smith (Alice); Jean O'Donnell (Secretary); Snub Pollard (Mail-Bearing Court Officer).

CALL NORTHSIDE 777 (20th Century-Fox, 1948) 111 M.

Producer, Otto Lang; director, Henry Hathaway; story, James P. McGuire; screenplay, Jerome Cady, Jay Dratler; art director, Lyle Wheeler, Mark-Lee Kirk; camera, Joe MacDonald; editor, J. Watson Webb, Jr.

James Stewart (McNeal); Richard Conte (Frank Wiecek); Lee J. Cobb (Brian Kelly); Helen Walker (Laura McNeal); Betty Garde (Wanda Skutnik); Kasia Orzazewski (Tillie); Joanne de Bergh (Helen Wiecek-Rayska); Howard Smith (Palmer); Moroni Olsen (Parole Board Chairman); John McIntire (Sam Faxon); Paul Harvey (Martin Burns); George Tyne (Tomek Zaleska); Richard Bishop (Warden); Otto Waldis (Boris); Michael Chapin (Frank Jr.); E. G. Marshall (Rayska); John Bleifer (Jan Gruska); Addison Richards (John Albertson); Eddie Dunn (Patrolman); William Post, Jr. (Police Sergeant); Lionel Stander (Corrigan); Robert Karnes (Photographer); Henry Kulky (Bartender—Drazynaski's); Wanda Perry, Ann Staunton (Telephone Operators); Rex Downing (Copy Boy); Stanley Gordon (Prison Clerk); Truman Bradley (Narrator); J. M. Kerrigan (Bailiff); Samuel S. Hinds (Judge Charles Moulton); Thelma Ritter (Woman).

A LETTER TO THREE WIVES (20th Century-Fox, 1948) 103 M.

Producer, Sol C. Siegel; director-screenplay, Joseph L. Mankiewicz; based on the story *A Letter to Five Wives* by John Klempner; art director, Lyle Wheeler, J. Russell Spencer; music, Alfred Newman; camera, Arthur Miller; editor, J. Watson Webb, Jr.

Jeanne Crain (Deborah Bishop); Linda Darnell (Lora May Hollingsway); Ann Sothern (Rita Phipps); Kirk Douglas (George Phipps); Paul Douglas (Porter Hollingsway); Barbara Lawrence (Babe); Jeffrey Lynn (Brad Bishop); Connie Gilchrist (Mrs. Finney); Florence Bates (Mrs. Manleigh); Hobart Cavanaugh (Mr. Manleigh); Patti Brady (Kathleen); Thelma Ritter (Sadie); Ruth Vivian (Miss Hawkins); Stuart Holmes (Old Man); George Offerman Jr. (Nick); Ralph Brooks (Character);

Joe Bautista (Thomasino); James Adamson (Butler); Carl Switzer, John Venn (Messengers).

CITY ACROSS THE RIVER (Universal, 1949) 90 M.

Producer-director, Maxwell Shane; based on the novel *The Amboy Dukes* by Irving Shulman; adaptation, Shulman; screenplay, Shane, Dennis Cooper; music, Walter Scharf; camera, Maury Gertsman; editor, Ted J. Kent.

Stephen McNally (Stan Albert); Thelma Ritter (Mrs. Cusack); Luis Van Rooten (Joe Cusack); Jeff Corey (Lt. Macon); Sharon McManus (Alice Cusack); Sue England (Betty); Barbara Whiting (Annie Kane); Richard Benedict (Gaggsy Steens); Peter Fernandez (Frank Cusack); Al Ramsen (Benny Wilkes); Joshua Shelley (Crazy Perrin); Tony Curtis (Mitch); Mickey Knox (Larry); Richard Jaeckel (Bull); Anabel Shaw (Jean Albert); Robert Osterloh (Mr. Bannon); Al Eben (Detective Kleiner); Sara Berner (Selma); Sandra Gould (Shirley); Bert Conway (Mr. Hayes); Frank Cady (Shirley's Partner); Duke Green (Giotta); Joseph Turkel (Shimmy); John Pickard (Detective); Don MacCraken (Gallagher); Myron Welton (Phil); Harry Wagner (Janitor); Ronnie Ralph (Jerry); Billy Snyder (Cab Driver); Chuck Hamilton (Clerk); Drew Pearson (Foreword).

FATHER WAS A FULLBACK (20th Century-Fox, 1949) 84 M.

Producer, Fred Kohlmar; director, John M. Stahl; based on the play by Clifford Goldsmith; screenplay, Aleen Leslie, Casey Robinson, Mary Loos, Richard Sale; music, Cyril Mockridge; camera, Lloyd Ahern; editor, J. Watson Webb, Jr.

Fred MacMurray (George Cooper); Maureen O'Hara (Elizabeth Cooper); Betty Lynn (Connie Cooper); Rudy Vallee (Mr. Jessop); Thelma Ritter (Geraldine); Natalie Wood (Ellen Cooper); James G. Backus (Professor Sullivan); Richard Tyler (Joe Burch); Buddy Martin (Cheer Leader); Mickey McCardle (Jones—Football Player); John McKee (Cy—Football Player); Louise Lorimer, (Mrs. Jones); Ruth Clifford (Neighbor); Charles J. Flynn (Policeman); William Self (Willie); Joe Haworth (Reporter); Rodney Bell, Wilson Wood, Don Barclay (Grandstand Coaches); Forbes Murray (College President); Bill Radovich (Football Player); Bob Patten (Manager); Bess Flowers (Woman).

PERFECT STRANGERS (Warner Brothers, 1950) 87 M.

Producer, Jerry Wald; director, Bretaigne Windust; based on the play *Ladies and Gentlemen* by Charles MacArthur, Ben Hecht; adaptation, George Oppenheimer; screenplay, Edith Sommer; music, Leigh Harline; camera, Peverell Marley; editor, David Weisbart.

Ginger Rogers (Terry Scott); Dennis Morgan (David Campbell); Thelma Ritter (Lena Fassler); Margalo Gillmore (Mrs. Bradford); Anthony Ross (Robert Fisher); Howard Freeman (Arthur Timkin); Alan Reed (Harry Patullo); Paul Ford (Judge Byron); Harry Bellaver (Bailiff); Frank Conlan (John Brokaw); George Chandler (Lester Hubley); Marjorie Bennett (Mrs. Moore); Edith Evanson (Mary Travers); Frances Charles (Eileen Marcher); Sumner Getchell (John Simon); Ford Rainey (Ernest Craig); Paul McVey (District Attorney); Whit Bissell (Defense Attorney); Sarah Selby (Mrs. Wilson); Alan Wood (Court Clerk); Ronnie Tyler (Newsboy); Creighton Hale, John Albright, Frank Marlowe, Ed Coke (Reporters); Ned Glass (O'Hanlon); Joseph Kerr (Doctor); Art Miles (Sheriff); Richard Hartell (Weather Man); Hugh Murray (Minister); Frank Pat Henry (Doctor); Lou Marcelle (Television Announcer); Joleen King (Nurse); Dick Kipling (Autopsy Surgeon).

ALL ABOUT EVE (20th Century-Fox, 1950) 138 M.

Producer, Darryl F. Zanuck; director, Joseph Mankiewicz; based on the story *The Wisdom of Eve* by Mary Orr; screenplay, Mankiewicz; music, Alfred Newman; art director, Lyle Wheeler, George W. Davis; camera, Milton Krasner; editor, Barbara McLean.

Bette Davis (Margo Channing); Anne Baxter (Eve Harrington); George Sanders (Addison de Witt/Narrator); Gary Merrill (Bill Sampson); Celeste Holm (Karen Richards); Hugh Marlowe (Lloyd Richards); Thelma Ritter (Birdie); Marilyn Monroe (Miss Caswell); Gregory Ratoff (Max Fabian); Barbara Bates (Phoebe); Walter Hampden (Dinner Speaker); Eddie Fisher (Stage Manager); Steven Geray (Captain of Waiters); Randy Stuart (Girl); Craig Hill (Leading Man); Leland Harris (Doorman); William Pullen (Clerk); Eugene Borden (Frenchman); Helen Mowery (Reporter); Barbara White (Autograph Seeker); Bess Flowers (Well Wisher); Claude Stroud (Pianist).

I'LL GET BY (20th Century-Fox, 1950) 82 M.

Producer, William Perlberg; director, Richard Sale; story, Robert Ellis, Helen Logan, Pamela Harris; screenplay, Mary Loos, Sale; music director, Lionel Newman; choreographer, Larry Ceballos; songs, John LaTouche, Ted Fetter, and Vernon Duke; Bud Green and Michael Edwards; Mack Gordon and Harry Warren; Ted Koehler and Harold Arlen; Gordon and Josef Myrow; B. G. De-Sylva, Irving Caesar and George Gershwin; Sammy Cahn and Jule Stune; Roy Turk and Fred Ahlert; Shamus O'Connor and J. J. Stamford; camera, Charles G. Clarke; editor, J. Watson Webb, Jr.

June Haver (Liza Martin); William Lundigan (William Spencer); Gloria DeHaven (Terry Martin); Dennis Day (Freddy Lee); Harry James (Himself); Thelma Ritter (Miss Murphy); Steve Allen (Peter Pepper); Danny Davenport (Chester Dovley); Reginald Gardiner, Jeanne Crain, Dan Dailey, Victor Mature (Guest Stars); Tom Hanlon (Announcer); Peggy O'Connor (U.S.O. Girl); Harry Seymour (Stage Manager); Charles Tannen (Director); Erno Verebes, John Trebach (Waiters); Vincent Renno (Headwaiter); Tom Greenway (Moving Man); Thomas F. Martin (Sound Engineer); Carol West (Mitzi Maloo); Harry Lauter, Don Hicks, (Assistant Directors); John Butler (Man by Fireplace); Dick Winslow (Cooky Myers); Alan Block (Commentator).

THE MATING SEASON (Paramount, 1951) 101 M.

Producer, Charles Brackett; director, Mitchell Leisen; screenplay, Brackett, Walter Reisch, Richard Breen; music, Joseph J. Lilley; art director, Hal Pereira, Roland Anderson; camera, Charles B. Lang, Jr.; editor, Frank Bracht.

Gene Tierney (Maggie Carleton); John Lund (Val McNulty); Miriam Hopkins (Fran Carleton); Thelma Ritter (Ellen McNulty); Jan Sterling (Betsy); Larry Keating (Mr. Kalinger, Sr.); James Lorimer (George C. Kalinger, Jr.); Gladys Hurlbut (Mrs. Conger); Cora Witherspoon (Mrs. Williamson); Malcolm Keen (Mr. Williamson); Ellen Corby (Annie); Billie Bird (Mugsy); Samuel Colt (Colonel Conger); Grayce Hampton (Mrs. Fahnstock); Stapleton Kent (Dr. Chorley); Jean Ruth, Laura Elliot (Bridesmaids); Charles Dayton (Best Man at Wedding); Bob Kortman (Janitor); Jean Acker, Sally Rawlinson, Tex Brodus, Bob Rich (Party Guests); Franklyn Farnum, Richard Neill, Sam Ash, Jack Richardson (Board of Directors) Beulah Christian, Kathryn Wilson, Beulah Parkington, Margaret B. Farrell (Board of Directors' Wives); Beth Hartman (Receptionist); Mary Young (Spinster); Gordon Arnold, John Bryant (Ushers at Wedding); Bess Flowers (Friend at Wedding).

AS YOUNG AS YOU FEEL (20th Century-Fox, 1951) 77 M.

Producer, Lamar Trotti; director, Harmon Jones; story, Paddy Chayefsky; screenplay, Trotti; music, Cyril Mockridge; camera, Joe MacDonald; editor, Robert Simpson.

Monty Woolley (John Hodges); Thelma Ritter (Della Hodges); David Wayne (Joe); Jean Peters (Alice Hodges); Constance Bennett (Lucille McKinley); Marilyn Monroe (Harriet); Allyn Joslyn (George Hodges); Albert Dekker (Louis McKinley); Clinton Sundberg (Frank Erickson); Minor Watson (Cleveland); Wally Brown (Gallagher); Rusty Tamblyn (Willie); Ludwig Stossel (Conductor); Renie Riano (Harpist); Roger Moore (Saltonstall); Dick Coogan (Benson); Charles Conrad (Information Clerk); James Griffith (Cashier); Charles Cane (Rogell); Billy Lechner (Mail Boy); William Frambes (Bellboy); Carol Savage (Librarian); Helen Brown (Clancy); Don Beddoe (Head of Sales); Raymond Greenleaf (Vice President); Emerson Treachy (Public Relations Head).

THE MODEL AND THE MARRIAGE BROKER (20th Century-Fox, 1951) 103 M.

Producer, Charles Brackett; director, George Cukor; screenplay, Brackett, Walter Reisch, Richard Breen; art director, Lyle Wheeler, Don De Cuir; music director, Lionel Newman; camera, Milton Krasner; editor, Robert Simpson.

Jeanne Crain (Kitty); Scott Brady (Matt); Thelma Ritter (Mae Swazey); Zero Mostel (Wixted); Michael O'Shea (Doberman); Helen Ford (Emmy); Frank Fontaine (Johannson); Dennie Moore (Mrs. Gingras); John Alexander (Mr. Perry); Jay C. Flippen (Chancellor); Bunny Bishop (Alice); Kathryn Card (Mrs. Kuschner); Maude Prickett (Delia Seaton); Athalie Daniell (Trudy); Dennis Ross (Joe); Ken Christy (Mr. Kuschner); Shirley Mills (Ina Kuschner); Eve March (Miss Eddy); Tommy Noonan (Young Clerk); Jacqueline French, Edna May Wonscott, June Hedin (Miss Perrys) Nancy Kulp (Hazel); Frank Ferguson, Harris Brown (Conventioneers); Mae Marsh (Woman); Joyce MacKenzie (Doris).

WITH A SONG IN MY HEART (20th Century-Fox, 1952) 116 M.

Producer, Lamar Trotti; director, Walter Lang; screenplay, Trotti; music director, Newman; vocal director, Darby; new song, Newman and Eliot Daniel; Ken Darby; camera, Leon Shamroy; editor, J. Watson Webb, Jr.

Susan Hayward (Jane Froman); Rory Calhoun (John Burn); David Wayne (Don Ross); Thelma Ritter (Clancy); Robert Wagner (G.I. Paratrooper); Una Merkel (Sister Marie); Helen Westcott (Jennifer March)); Richard Allan (Dancer); Max Showalter (Guild); Leif Erickson (General); Lyle Talbot (Radio Director); Stanley Logan (Diplomat); Eddie Firestone (U.S.O. Man); Frank Sully (Texas); George Offerman (Muleface); Ernest Newton (Specialty); Harry Carter (Chauffeur); Donald Kerr (Cab Driver); Frank Kreig (Waiter); Dick Winslow (Conductor); Jewel Rose (Laboratory Technician); Rosa Marie Monteiro, Carol Savage, Adele Longmire (Nurses); Albano Valerio (Priest); Robert Easton (Kansas); Maude Wallace (Sister Margaret); William Slack (Texan); Douglas Evans (Colonel); Dick Ryan (Officer); Shirley Tegge (Cigarette Girl).

TITANIC (20th Century-Fox, 1953) 98 M.

Producer, Charles Brackett; director, Jean Negulesco; story-screenplay, Brackett, Walter Reisch, Richard Breen; art director, Lyle Wheeler, Maurice Ransford; camera, Joe MacDonald; editor, Louis Loeffler.

Clifton Webb (Richard Sturges); Barbara Stanwyck

(Julia Sturges); Robert Wagner (Giff Rogers); Audrey Dalton (Annette Sturgis); Thelma Ritter (Maude Young); Brian Aherne (Captain Smith); Richard Basehart (George Healey); Allyn Joslyn (Earl Meeker); James Todd (Sandy Comstock); William Johnstone (John Jacob Astor); Charles FitzSimons (Chief Officer Wilde); Harry Bernard (First Officer Murdock); Harper Carter (Norman Sturges); Edmund Purdom (Second Officer Lightoller); Christopher Severn (Messenger); James Lilburn (Devlin); Frances Bergen (Mrs. John Jacob Astor); Guy Standing, Jr. (George D. Widener); Hellen Van Tuyl (Mrs. Straus); Roy Gordon (Mr. Isidor Straus); Marta Mitrovich (Mrs. Uzcadum); Ivis Goulding (Emma); Merry Anders, Gloria Gordon, Melinda Markey (College Girls); Mae Marsh (Woman); Donald Chaffin, Ralph Green, Owen McGiveney (Stewards); David Thursby (Seaman); David Hoffman (Tailor); Gordon Richards (Manager); Anthony Eustrel (Pelham Sanderson); Ivan Hayes (Officer); Harry Cording (Engineer); Eugene Borden (Dock Official); Charles Keane (Stoker).

THE FARMER TAKES A WIFE (20th Century-Fox, 1953) 80 M.

Producer, Frank P. Rosenberg; director, Henry Levin; based on the novel *Rome Haul* by Walter D. Edmonds and the stage play by Frank B. Elser, Marc Connelly; screenplay, Walter Bullock, Sally Benson, Joseph Fields; songs, Harold Arlen and Dorothy Fields; choreographer, Jack Cole; camera, Arthur E. Arling; editor, Louis Loeffler.

Betty Grable (Molly); Dale Robertson (Daniel Harrow); Thelma Ritter (Lucy Cashdollar); John Carroll (Jotham Klore); Eddie Foy, Jr. (Fortune Friendly); Charlotte Austin (Pearl); Kathleen Crowley (Susanna); Merry Anders (Hannah); May Wynn (Eva); Noreen Michaels (Amy); Ruth Hall (Abbie); William Pullen (John); Juanita Evers (Miss Kranz); Mort Mills (Floyd); Lee Turnbull (Andy); Howard Negley (Governor Fish); Joanne Jordan (Boatwife); Gene Roth (Ethan McCarthy); Mel Pogue (Abner Green); Gordon Nelson (Race Official); Ralph Sanford (Quack); Martin Deane, Bobby Haytt, Brad Mora, (Boys); Ed Hinton, Max Wagner, John Close, Fred Aldrich, Paul Kruger, Ralph Montgomery (Boaters); Don Garrett (Cab Driver); Jack Harris (Militia Officer); Kermit Maynard (Driver); Lee Phelps (Bartender); Ted Jordan (Driver); Donald Kerr (Jacob).

PICKUP ON SOUTH STREET (20th Century-Fox, 1953) 83 M.

Producer, Jules Schermer; director, Samuel Fuller; based on a story by Dwight Taylor; screenplay, Fuller; music, Leigh Harline; art director, Lyle R. Wheeler, George Patrick; camera, Joe MacDonald; editor, Nick DeMaggio.

Richard Widmark (Skip McCoy); Jean Peters (Candy); Thelma Ritter (Moe); Murvyn Vye (Captain Dan Tiger); Richard Kiley (Joey); Willis B. Bouchey (Zara); Milburn Stone (Winoki); Henry Slate (MacGregor) Jerry O'Sullivan (Enyart); Harry Carter (Dietrich); George E. Stone (Clerk at Police Station); George Eldredge (Fenton); Stuart Randall (Police Commissioner); Frank Kumagi (Lum); Victor Perry (Lightning Louie); Maurice Samuels (Peddler); Payel Baer (Stranger); Jay Loftin (Librarian); Virginia Carroll (Nurse); Roger Moore (Mr. Victor); Clancy Cooper (Lean Man); John Gallaudet (Campion); Wilson Wood (Driver); Ray Montgomery, Ray Stevens (F.B.I. Men); Ralph Moody (Captain); George Berkeley (Customer); Emmett Lynn (Sandwich Man).

REAR WINDOW (Paramount, 1954) 112 M.

Producer-director, Alfred Hitchcock; based on novelette by Cornell Woolrich; screenplay, John Michael Hayes; assistant director, Herbert Coleman; costumes, Edith Head; music, Franz Waxman; set director, Hal Pereira, Joseph McMillan Johnson, Sam Comer, Ray Mayer; special effects, John P. Fulton; camera, Robert Burks; editor, George Tomasini.

James Stewart (Jeff); Grace Kelly (Lisa Fremont); Wendell Corey (Thomas J. Doule); Thelma Ritter (Stella); Raymond Burr (Lars Thorwald); Judith Evelyn (Miss Lonely Hearts); Ross Bagdasarian (Song Writer); Sara Berner (Woman on Fire Escape); Frank Cady (Fire Escape Man); Jesslyn Fax (Miss Hearing Aid); Rand Harper (Honeymooner); Irene Winston (Mrs. Thorwald); Harris Davenport (Newly Wed); Marla English, Kathryn Grant (Party Girls); Alan Lee (Landlord); Anthony Warde (Detective); Benny Bartlett (Miss Torso's Friend); Fred Graham (Stunt Detective); Harry Landers (Young Man); Len Hendry, Mike Mahoney (Policemen); Jenni Paris, Sue Casey (Sunbathers); Bess Flowers (Woman with Poodle); Barbara Bailey (Choreographer); Jerry Antes (Dancer); Nick Borgani (Man); Jack Stoney (Ice Man); Georgene Darcy (Miss Torso).

DADDY LONG LEGS (20th Century-Fox, 1955) 126 M.

Producer, Samuel G. Engel; director, Jean Negulesco; based on the novel by Jean Webster; screenplay, Phoebe and Harry Ephran; art director, Lyle Wheeler, John De Cuir; assistant director, Eli Dunn; choreographer, Fred Astaire, David Robel; ballet director, Roland Petit; music, Alfred Newman; ballet music, Alex North; songs, Johnny Mercer; camera, Leon Shamroy; editor, William Reynolds.

Fred Astaire (Jervis Pendleton); Leslie Caron (Julie); Terry Moore (Linda); Thelma Ritter (Miss Pritchard); Fred Clark (Griggs); Charlotte Austin (Sally); Larry Keating (Alexander Williamson); Kathryn Givney (Gertrude); Kelly Brown (Jimmy McBride); Ray Anthony & Orchestra (Themselves); Steven Geray (Emile); Percival Vivian (Professor); Sara Shane (Pat); Numa Lapeyre (Jean); Ann Codee (Mme Sevanne); Joseph Kearns (Guide); Larry Kent (Butler); Charles Anthony Hughes (Hotel Manager); Ralph Dumke (Mr. Bronson); Damian O'Flynn (Larry Hamilton); Kathryn Card (Miss Carrington); Helen Van Tuyl (College Dean); George Dunn (Deliveryman); Janice Carroll (Athletic Girl Dancer); Virginia Hunter, Eileen Maxwell (College Girls); David Hoffman, Paul Bradley (Jewelers); Guy Des Rochers (French Lieutenant); Carleton Young (Commission Member); Ivis Goulding (Dignified Woman); William Hines (Army Sergeant).

LUCY GALLANT (Paramount, 1955) 104 M.

Producer, William H. Pine, William C. Thomas; director, Robert Parrish; based on the novel *The Life of Lucy Gallant* by Margaret Cousins; screenplay, John Lee Mahin, Winston Miller; art director, Hal Pereira, Henry Bumstead; music director, Van Cleave; camera, Lionel Lindon; editor, Howard Smith; assistant director, William McGarry; songs, Jay Livingston and Ray Evans.

Jane Wyman (Lucy Gallant); Charlton Heston (Casey Cole); Claire Trevor (Lady MacBeth); Thelma Ritter (Molly Basserman); William Demarest (Charles Madden); Wallace Ford (Gus Basserman); Tom Helmore (Jim Wardman); Gloria Talbott (Laura Wilson); James Westerfield (Frank Wilson); Mary Field (Irma Wilson); Edith Head (Herself); Governor Allan Shivers (Himself); Joel Fluellen (Summertime); Louise Arthur (Sal); Jay Adler (Station Master); Frank Marlowe (Nolan); Roscoe Ates (Anderson); and: Howard Negley, Jack Pepper, Bill Hunter, Barbara Stewart, Edmund Cobb, Gene Roth, Max Wagner, Frank Hagney, Jack Shea, Robert Williams, Joey Ray, Ben Burt, Charles Regan, Beatrice Maude, Fern Barry, Emily Getchell, Mary Boyd, Elizabeth Cloud-Miller.

THE PROUD AND PROFANE (Paramount, 1956)
111 M.

Producer, William Perlberg; director, George Seaton; based on the novel *The Magnificent Bastards* by Lucy Herndon; screenplay, Seaton; assistant director, Frank Baur; art director, Hal Pereira, Earl Hedrick; music, Victor Young; camera, John F. Warren; editor, Alma Macrorie.

William Holden (Lt. Col. Colin Black); Deborah Kerr (Lee Ashley); Thelma Ritter (Kate Conners); Dewey Martin (Eddie Wodcik); William Redfield (Chaplain-Lieutenant Holmes); Ross Bagdasarian (Louie); Adam Williams (Eustace Press); Marion Ross (Jean—Red Cross Worker); Theodore Newton (Bob Kilpatrick); Richard Shannon (Major); Peter Hansen (Lt. (J.G.) Hutchins); Ward Wood (Sgt. Peckinpaugh); Geraldine Hall (Helen—Red Cross Worker); Evelyn C. Cotton (Beth—Red Cross Worker); Ann Morriss (Pat—Red Cross Worker); Nancy Stevens (Evvie—Red Cross Worker); LoRayne Brox (Sissy—Red Cross Worker); Don Roberts (Lt. Fowler); Taylor Meason (Marine); Freeman Morse (Paul); Frank Gorshin (Harry); Mickey Finn (Naval Officer); Terry Macrea (Lt. Dean); Richard H. Tyler (Ralph); Ruth Rickaby (Hostess, R.C. Club); James Ogg (Jerry); Elizabeth Slifer (French Woman); Genevieve Aumont (Lili Carere); Claude Akins (Big Soldier); Joseph Moran (Marine).

A HOLE IN THE HEAD (United Artists, 1959) 120 M.

Producer-director, Frank Capra; based on the (television) play by Arnold Shulman; screenplay, Shulman; music, Nelson Riddle; art director, Eddie Imazir; songs, Sammy Cahn and Jimmy Van Heusen; camera, William H. Daniels; editor, William Hanbeck; assistant director, Arthur S. Black, Jr., Jack R. Berne; costumes, Edith Head.

Frank Sinatra (Tony Manetta); Edward G. Robinson (Mario Manetta); Eleanor Parker (Mrs. Rogers); Eddie Hodges (Ally Manetta); Carolyn Jones (Shirl); Thelma Ritter (Sophie Manetta); Keenan Wynn (Jerry Marks); Joi Lansing (Dorine); George DeWitt (Mendy); Jimmy Komack (Julius Manetta); Dub Taylor (Fred); Connie Sawyer (Miss Wexler); Benny Rubin (Mr. Diamond); Ruby Dandridge (Sally); B. S. Pully (Hood); Joyce Nizzari (Alice); Pupi Campo (Master of Ceremonies).

PILLOW TALK (Universal, 1959) 105 M.

Producer, Ross Hunter, Martin Melcher; director, Michael Gordon; story, Russell Rouse, Clarence Greene; screenplay, Stanley Shapiro, Maurice Rachin; songs, Buddy Pepper and Inez James; Joe Dubin and J.J. Roth; Elsa Dora and Sol Lake; music, Frank DeVol; art director, Alexander Golitzen, Richard Riedel; costumes, Jean Louis; assistant director, Phil Bowles, Carl Beringer; camera, Arthur E. Arling; editor, Milton Carruth.

Rock Hudson (Brad Allen); Doris Day (Jan Morrow); Tony Randall (Jonathan Forbes); Thelma Ritter (Alma); Nick Adams (Tony Walters); Julia Meade (Marie); Allen Jenkins (Harry); Marcel Dalio (Pierot); Lee Patrick (Mrs. Walters); Mary McCarty (Nurse Resnick); Alex Gerry (Dr. Maxwell); Hayden Rorke (Mr. Conrad); Valerie Allen (Eileen); Jacqueline Beer (Yvette); Arlen Stuart (Tilda); Perry Blackwell (Entertainer); Robert B. Williams (Mr. Graham); Don Beddoe (Mr. Walters); Muriel Landers (Fat Girl); William Schallert (Hotel Clerk); Karen Norris (Miss Dickenson); Lois Rayman (Jonathan's Secretary).

THE MISFITS (United Artists, 1961) 124 M.

Producer, Frank E. Taylor; director, John Huston; screenplay, Arthur Miller; music, Alex North; assistant director, Carl Beringer; art director, Stephen Grimes, William Newberry; camera, Russell Metty; editor, George Tomasini.

Clark Gable (Gay Langland); Marilyn Monroe (Roslyn Taber); Montgomery Clift (Perce Howland); Thelma Ritter (Isabelle Steers); Eli Wallach (Guido); James Barton (Old Man in Bar); Estelle Winwood (Church Lady); Kevin McCarthy (Raymond Taber); Dennis Shaw (Young Boy in Bar); Walter Ramage (Old Groom); Philip Mitchell (Charles Steers); Peggy Barton (Young Bride); J. Lewis Smith (Fresh Cowboy in Bar); Marietta Tree (Susan); Bobby LaSalle (Bartender); Ryall Bowker (Man in Bar); Ralph Roberts (Ambulance Driver).

THE SECOND TIME AROUND (20th Century-Fox, 1961) 99 M.

Producer, Jack Cummings; director, Vincent Sherman; based on the novel *Star in the West* by Richard Emery Roberts; screenplay, Oscar Saul, Cecil Dan Hansen; song, Henry Mancini; music, Gerald Fried; art director, Jack Martin Smith, Walter M. Simonds; sound, Alfred Brizlen, Frank W. Moran; assistant director, Jack R. Berne; makeup, Ben Nye; camera, Ellis W. Carter; editor, Betty Steinberg.

Debbie Reynolds (Lucretia); Steve Forrest (Dan Jones); Andy Griffith (Pat Collins); Juliet Prowse (Rena); Thelma Ritter (Aggie); Ken Scott (Sheriff John Yates); Isobel Elsom (Mrs. Rogers); Rudolph Acosta (Rodriguez); Timothy Carey (Bonner); Tom Greenway (Shack); Eleanor Audley (Mrs. Trask); Blossom Rock (Mrs. Collins); Tracy Stratford (Cissie); Jimmy Garrett (Tobey); Lisa Pons (Mrs. Rodriguez); Nicky Blair (Mr. Stone); Tom Fadden (Feed Store Owner); Duane Grey, Joe Yrigoyen (Bonner's Pals); Pat Moran (Hardware Store Owner); Jack Orrison (Newspaper Editor); Felipe Turich (Bartender); Pilar Arcos (Cook); John Paxton, Leonard Baker, Tex Lambert (Bandits); Chester Hayes (Hurdy Gurdy Man); Margie Duncan (Rascal); Hane Moebus (Railroad Conductor); Joe Hamilton (Old Prospector).

BIRD MAN OF ALCATRAZ (United Artists, 1962)
147 M.

Executive producer, Harold Hecht; producer, Stuart Millar, Guy Trosper; director, John Frankenheimer; based on the book by Thomas E. Gaddis; screenplay, Guy Trosper; assistant director, Dave Silver; music, Elmer Bernstein; art director, Ferdie Carrere; sound, George Cooper; camera, Burnett Guffey; editor, Edward Mann.

Burt Lancaster (Robert Stroud); Karl Malden (Warden Shoemaker); Thelma Ritter (Elizabeth Stroud); Neville Brand (Bull Ransom); Betty Field (Stella Johnson); Telly Savalas (Feto Gomez); Edmond O'Brien (Tom Gaddis); Hugh Marlowe (Roy Comstock); Whit Bissell (Dr. Ellis); Craham Denton (Kramer); James Westerfield (Jess Younger); Leo Penn (Eddie Kassellis); Lewis Charles (Chaplain Wentzel); Adrienne Marden (Mrs. Woodrow Wilson).

HOW THE WEST WAS WON (MGM, 1963) 165 M.

Producer, Bernard Smith; director, John Ford (The Civil War); George Marshall (The Railroad); Henry Hathaway (The Rivers, The Plains, The Outlaws); suggested by a series of articles in *Life* magazine; screenplay, James R. Webb; art director, George W. Davis, William Ferrari, Addison Hehr; assistant director, George Marshall, Jr., William McGarry, William Shanks, Robert Saunders, Wingate Smith; music, Alfred Newman; songs, Newman and Ken Darby; Newman and Johnny Mercer; Newman and Sammy Cahn; camera, William H. Daniels, Milton Krasner, Charles Lang, Jr., Joseph LaShelle; editor, Harold F. Kress.

Carroll Baker (Eve Prescott); Lee J. Cobb (Marshal); Henry Fonda (Jethro Stuart); Carolyn Jones (Julie Rawlings); Karl Malden (Zebulon Prescott); Gregory Peck

(Cleve Van Valen); George Peppard (Zeb Rawlings); Robert Preston (Roger Morgan); Debbie Reynolds (Lilith Prescott); James Stewart (Linus Rawlings); Eli Wallach (Charlie Gant); John Wayne (General Sherman); Richard Widmark (Mike King); Brigid Bazlen (Dora); Walter Brennan (Colonel Hawkins); David Brian (Attorney); Andy Devine (Peterson); Raymond Massey (Abraham Lincoln); Agnes Moorehead (Rebecca Prescott); Harry Morgan (General Grant); Thelma Ritter (Agatha Clegg); Mickey Shaughnessy (Deputy); Russ Tamblyn (Reb Soldier); Spencer Tracy (Narrator); Kim Charney (Sam Prescott); Bryan Russell (Zeke Prescott); Tudor Owen (Harvey); Barry Harvey (Angus); Jamie Ross (Bruce); Mark Allen (Colin); Lee Van Cleef (Marty); Charles Briggs (Barker); Jay C. Flippen (Huggins); Clinton Sundberg (Hylan Seabury); James Griffith, Walter Burke (Gamblers); Joe Sawyer (Ship's Officer); John Larch (Grimes); Jack Pennick (Corporal Murphy); Craig Duncan (James Marshall); Claude Johnson (Jeremiah); Rodolfo Acosta (Henchman).

FOR LOVE OR MONEY (Universal, 1963) 108 M.

Producer, Robert Arthur; director, Michael Gordon; screenplay, Larry Markes, Michael Morris; art director, Alexander Golitzen, Malcolm Brown; music, De Vol; music supervisor, Joseph Gershenson; sound, Waldon O. Watson, Corson Jowett; assistant director, Joseph Kenny; camera, Clifford Stone; editor, Alma Macrorie.

Kirk Douglas (Deke Gentry); Mitzi Gaynor (Kay); Gig Young (Sonny Smith); Thelma Ritter (Chloe Brasher); Julie Newmar (Bonnie); Leslie Parrish (Jan); William Bendix (Rogel); Richard Sargent (Harvey Wofford); Elizabeth MacRae (Marsha); Willard Sage (Orson Roark); Jose Gonzales Gonzales (Jaime); Billy Halop (Elevator Operator); Alvy Moore (George); Frank Mahony (Red Beard); Alberto Morin (Maitre D'); Theodore Marcuse (Artist); Ina Victor (Nurse); Nydia Westman (Martha); Don Beddoe (Milo); Phil Chambers (Captain Crab Boat); Karen Norris (Ava); Sean MacGregor (Seymour); John Morley (Helicopter Pilot); Vince Townsend, Jr. (Guard); Charles Thompson (Uncle Ben); John Indrisano, Ted Fish (Pugs); Claudia Brack, Susan Counter, Evelyn Dutton (Bridesmaids); Bess Flowers (Bewildered Woman).

A NEW KIND OF LOVE (Paramount, 1963) 110 M.

Producer-director-screenplay, Melville Shavelson; art director, Hal Pereira, Arthur Lonergan; costumes, Edith Head; makeup, Wally Westmore; assistant director, Arthur Jacobson; music, Leith Stevens; additional themes, Errol Garner; sound, John Cartier; camera, Daniel Fapp; editor, Frank Bracht.

Paul Newman (Steve Sherman); Joanne Woodward (Samantha Blake); Thelma Ritter (Lena O'Connor); Eva Gabor (Felicianne Courbeau); George Tobias (Joseph Bergner); Marvin Kaplan (Harry Gorman); Robert Clary (Albert Sardou); Jan Moriarty (Suzanne); Joan Staley (Airline Hostess); Robert F. Simon (Chalmers); Maurice Chevalier (Himself); Ted Mapes (Floor Walker); Eva Janey (Midinette); Lomax Study (Hansom Cab Driver); Jacqueline May (French Waitress); Albert Carrier (Gendarme); June Smaney, Audrey Betz, Irene Chapman (Amazons); Armand A. Archerd (Onlooker); Christian Kay (Model with Pearls); Allyson Daniell (Lingerie Model); Sandra Downs (Stewardess); George Nardelli (Waiter); Audrey H. Swanson, Kay Armour, Paul Micale (Shoppers); Ralf Harolde (French Waiter); Trude Wyler, Eva Jancy (Midinettes); Helen Marler (Cardin Model); Jimmy Starr (Sports Writer); Peter Canon (Soccer Referee); Suzanne Dadolle (French Columnist).

MOVE OVER, DARLING (Twentieth Century-Fox, 1963) 103 M.

Producer, Aaron Rosenberg, Martin Melcher; director, Michael Gordon; based on the story by Bella and Samuel Spewack, Leo McCarey and the screenplay *My Favorite Wife* by the Spewacks; screenplay, Hal Kanter, Jack Sher; assistant director, Ad Schaumer; art director, Jack Martin Smith, Hilyard Brown; song, Joe Lubin and Kanter; sound, Alfred Bruzlin, Elmer R. Raguse; special camera effects, L. B. Abbott, Emil Kosa, Jr.; camera, Daniel I. Fapp; editor, Robert Simpson.

Doris Day (Ellen Wagstaff Arden); James Garner (Nick Arden); Polly Bergen (Bianca Steele Arden); Thelma Ritter (Grace Arden); Don Knotts (Shoe Salesman); Fred Clark (Codd); Elliott Reid (Dr. Herman Schlick); Edgar Buchanan (Judge Bryson); John Astin (Clyde Prokey); Max Showalter (Desk Clerk); Eddie Quillan (Bellboy); Alvy Moore (Waiter); Pami Lee (Jenny Arden); Leslie Farrell (Didi Arden); Chuck Connors (Stephen Burkett); Rosa Turich (Maria); Harold Goodwin (Bailiff); Alan Sues (Court Clerk); Pat Moran (Drunk); Bess Flowers (Woman); Mary George (Maid); Rachel Roman (Injured Man's Wife); Kelton Garwood, Joel Collins (Ambulance Attendants); Ted Jacques (Pool Attendant); James Patridge (Skipper); Bing Davidson (Ensign J.G.); Jack Sahakian (Ex. Officer, J.G.); Billy Halop, Mel Flory (Seamen); Stan Richards (Officer); Michael Romanoff (Floorwalker); Joe Mell (Stock Clerk); John Harmon (Cab Driver); Sheila Rogers (Secretary); Jimmy Bays (Doorman); Pat Harrington, Jr. (District Attorney).

BOEING-BOEING (Paramount, 1965) 102 M.

Producer, Hal B. Wallis; associate producer, Paul Nathan; director, John Rich; based on the play by Marc Camoletti; screenplay, Edward Anhalt; art director, Hal Pereira, Walter Tyler; music, Neal Hefti; assistant director, Daniel J. McCauley; costumes, Edith Head; camera, Lucien Ballard; editor, Warren Low, Archie Marshek.

Jerry Lewis (Robert Reed); Tony Curtis (Bernard Lawrence); Christiane Schmidtmer (Lisa Berger); Dany Saval (Jacqueline Grieux); Suzanne Leigh (Vicky Hawkins); Thelma Ritter (Bertha); Lomax Study (Pierre); Eugene Borden, Peter Camlin, Roger Etienne, George Dee (Cab Drivers); Francoise Ruggieri (French Taxi Driver); Robert Tafur (Elegant Gentleman); Nai Bonet (Air India Hostess); Mimi Dega (Wife); Victor Dunlop (Husband); Lucien Lanvin (French Waiter); Albert d'Arno, Maurice St. Clair (Maitre D's) Louise Lawson, Julie Parrish (Pretty Girls).

THE INCIDENT (20th Century-Fox, 1967) 107 M.

Producer, Monroe Sachson, Edward Meadow; director, Larry Peerce, based on the television play *Ride with Terror* by Nicholas E. Baehr; screenplay, Baehr; music, Terry Knight; assistant director, Steve Barnett, Alex Hapsas; makeup, Herman Buckman; costumes, Muriel Getlinger; sound, Jack Jacobsen, Richard Vousek; camera, Gerald Hirschfeld; editor, Armand Lebowitz.

Tony Musante (Joe Ferrone); Martin Sheen (Artie Connors); Beau Bridges (Pvt. Felix Teflinger); Jack Gilford (Sam Beckerman); Thelma Ritter (Bertha Beckerman); Brock Peters (Arnold Robinson); Rudy Dee (Joan Robinson); Ed McMahon (Bill Wilks); Diana Van Der Vlis (Helen Wilks); Mike Kellin (Harry Purvis); Jan Sterling (Muriel Purvis); Gary Merrill (Douglas McCanon); Robert Fields (Kenneth Otis); Robert Bannard (Pvt. Philip Carmatti); Victor Arnold (Tony Goya); Donna Mills (Alice Keenan); Kathleen Smith (Wilks's Daughter); Henry Proach (Derelict); Neal Hynes (Change

Booth Attendant); Ben Levi (Man Who Gets Mugged); Marty Meyers (Pool Hall Owner); Don De Leo (Mr. Carmatti); Ted Lourie (Host); John Servetnik (Bartender); Ray Cole, Barry Del Rae (Young Men); Nico Hartos (Policeman); Macine McCrey (Black Woman); Nina Hansen (Mrs. Carmatti).

WHAT'S SO BAD ABOUT FEELING GOOD? (Universal, 1968) 94 M.

Producer-director, George Seaton; based on the novel *I Am Thinking of My Darling* by Vincent McHugh; adaptation-screenplay, Seaton, Robert Pirosh; assistant director, Donald Roberts; music, De Vol; art director, Alexander Golitzen, Henry Bumstead; camera, Ernesto Caparros; editor, Alma Macrorie.

George Peppard (Pete); Mary Tyler Moore (Liz); Don Stroud (Barney); Susan Saint James (Aida); Dom De Luise (Monroe); Nathaniel Frey (Conrad); John McMartin (The Mayor); Charles Lane (Dr. Shapiro); Jeanne Arnold (Gertrude); George Furth (Murgatroyd); Sgt Gunty; Joe Ponazecki (Officer Ponazecki); Emily Yancy (Sybil); Frank Campanella (Captain Wallace); Joey Faye (Zoo Keeper); Thelma Ritter (Mrs. Schwartz); Donald Hotten (Sam); Robert Moore (Board Member); Gilliam Spencer (The Sack).

Eileen Heckart

5'7"
131 pounds
Brown hair
Brown eyes
Birth sign: Aries

While other top character stars have relied on the wisecrack to gain audience approval, Eileen Heckart has made a specialty of the pathetic lonelyheart whose heartrending sadness pulls at the viewer's sympathy. Occasionally, she shifts her focus to the penultimate nagging Jewish mother image, as in A Family Affair *and* Butterflies Are Free *on stage and* No Way to Treat a Lady *on screen.*

*Eileen made her reputation on Broadway in the 1950s (*Picnic, The Bad Seed, The Dark at the Top of the Stairs*) as a consummate dramatic player, who in a short scene or two could steal the limelight from most any seasoned star. During that same decade, she was a frequent television performer, where her woebegone look and plaintive, deep voice soon became synonymous with the best of that medium's golden age of live drama.*

Although she has only made a dozen motion pictures to date, Eileen, who won a Best Supporting Actress Oscar for Butterflies Are Free *(1972), has long been firmly established as a prime screen character star, one of the few to emerge since the mid-1950s.*

Anna Eileen Herbert was born March 29, 1919, in Columbus, Ohio, the second child of a struggling dry cleaning shop owner. From the time of her birth, Eileen's parents were embroiled in domestic squabbles. Mr. Herbert threatened to take his wife Esther Stark (Purcell) Herbert to court because Eileen was not being reared as a Catholic. When Eileen was two years old, her parents divorced and to protect Eileen's welfare, she was adopted as a foster child by her mother's stepfather, John W. Heckart, a well-to-do building contractor. Eileen's brother Robert would live with his father until the latter died in 1930.

Eileen remembers: "My mother loved movies. . . . Before I could walk, she would take me with her. I cut my teeth on Joan Crawford movies. Joan Crawford was always so rich, so beautiful, so lavishly dressed, and she dragged a mink stole better than anyone else."

About her show business ambitions: "I made up my mind when I was eight that I was going to become an actress. I was attending Girl Scout camp at the time, and one of the Scout leaders told me I had talent. Once, I played in a camp play. I don't remember a thing about it except that the audience laughed. The audience enjoyed me. I smelled blood. That start was enough to keep me going for the rest of my life."

Eileen's mother did not receive much financial support from her own stepfather, and while she was preoccupied with earning a living, Eileen was often shuttled back and forth between her grandparents, a Ping-Pong existence which left its mark on Eileen.

But life was not always tense in the money-strained household. Eileen's mother was a bit of a character herself: "I remember she raised canaries and it was my job as a kid in Columbus, Ohio, to come home after school and help her clean out the cages. Then, one year, at Thanksgiving, she fell in love with a Spitz puppy and we found ourselves in the Spitz puppy business."

By the time Eileen was in high school, her foster parent had taken the notion that she was not serious about her education, and he withdrew any meaningful financial support. She took an after school job to help with the family budget. She would have graduated from local Bexley High School with the class of 1937, but in her senior year she contracted whooping cough and was home sick so often that she had to repeat the year. Another of her disappointments in the final year at Bexley was: "I didn't even get a part in the senior class play. It broke my heart."

Eileen entered Ohio State University in Columbus in the fall of 1938. (By then her mother had remarried; there would be two daughters from that union.) Eileen, the maturing young adult, was still hooked on show business: "I decided almost at the start to be a character actress or a comedienne. I knew I had to be some kind of actress, and since I wasn't beautiful, I knew I could never expect to become a leading lady. But I knew with everything in me that I could act."

She majored in English and speech at Ohio State, planning to obtain a teacher's certificate to support herself until she made good on the stage. She claims she was just an average student. Years later, Eileen would jovially relate: "I was aggressive in those days. I belonged to five community drama groups and two on campus, and whenever I was in trouble in a course I'd just see that the professor had two tickets to the play I was in currently. That way I got through." Among her curriculum, were three advanced courses in Shakespeare. ". . . from them [I] gained only the courage to say I still didn't like him."

The daily eight-mile streetcar trek to and from the college campus was not the only distraction from Eileen's studies. She had a job at Lazarus, a Columbus department store. There she was a salesgirl in the "hot-items" bargain section.* Another of her duties at her seven dollars weekly Lazarus post was to perform makeup demonstrations for Max Factor cosmetics. To earn additional money, Eileen performed commercials ($3.50 weekly) for local radio stations (which eventually led to her obtaining dramatic work on these Columbus outlets), booked fashion shows into campus sorority houses ($5 weekly), and distributed samples of Philip Morris cigarettes to fellow students ($10 monthly plus free cigarettes). Of her marathon job-hopping, Eileen has said: ". . . [it] was a hardship, but I was determined to graduate. I felt that if I had that degree I could get any kind of job I wanted. . . . When your family doesn't have money, you try to prepare yourself to do anything. I knew from the beginning that in acting so many start and so few succeed, I wanted a cushion."

Energetic Eileen "found" time during her college years to be socially active. At Phi Beta sorority she was pledge president her first year, later rush chairman, and in her senior year, president of the sorority. And of course, there was Eileen's extracurricular participation in college dramatics. Her first lead role was in the George S. Kaufman-Edna Ferber drama *Stage Door,* followed by a juicy part in George Brewer-Bertram Block's *Dark Victory,* and subsequent parts in a cycle of Broadway rehashes. "In school you play everything and believe you're at your best."

---

* I was good at selling—very fast, very persuasive, very sure of myself. Even now [1963], when I go shopping I want to grab the sales slip out of the salesclerk's hand and make it out myself."

Eileen received her B.A. degree from Ohio State University in the spring of 1942. She had work offers from Max Factor to demonstrate and sell cosmetics in Hollywood or on the road, and Lazarus asked her to become a book or candy buyer. She rejected both possibilities, having her heart set on coming to New York to prepare for a professional theatrical career.

She arrived in New York with a bankroll of $142. Her auditions as a stock performer for both CBS and NBC radio were rejected, but within five weeks of arriving in Manhattan she obtained a spot doing commercials on Gertrude Berg's *The Goldbergs,* the popular Jewish-oriented domestic comedy show. This radio work was performed on her lunch breaks from McCreary's where she had a full daytime job. At night, she worked in a recreation center, and sometimes she earned extra money by calling time for badminton players at the Hotel Shelton. Her combination jobs earned her $75 weekly: ". . . [I was] enormously wealthy, but I was so busy working, I didn't even have a chance to buy a dress."

Making the rounds of theatrical agents and casting offices was a vital part of Eileen's activities. She got no nibbles, save for being accepted by the Blackfriar's Club, a Catholic off-Broadway type group, for some of their showcase productions. She appeared in *Tinker's Dam* and in *Moment Musical,* a revue show offered on May 31, 1943. But for Broadway-minded Eileen: "The Blackfriars were amateurs. I wasn't satisfied."

While in the Stroller Players at Ohio State, Eileen had performed in Clifford Odets's *Golden Boy* with a fellow student, John Harrison Yankee (of Swedish extraction, the family name was originally Yanku). They fell in love but decided to wait to get married. Eileen came to New York just before Yankee enlisted in the Navy. On June 26, 1943, they were married in Jacksonville, Florida, where he was stationed. He would spend most of his World War II duty years on a base in Attu, Alaska.

Eileen returned to New York in time to participate in the activity for the 1943–1944 theatrical season. It was still a time when there were 97 productions mounted each year for the main stem (twice the number of today's Broadway output), and entertainment World War II audiences were eager for almost any passable divertissement.

Eileen's first breakthrough occurred with a featured role in an Equity Library Theatre showcase production of Philip Barry's *Holiday.* Her performance was dramatic enough to win her an audition and a post as understudy-assistant stage manager in the John Van Druten romantic comedy *The Voice of the Turtle* (Morosco Theatre, December 9, 1943). After six

Eileen Heckart in 1943.

In *Moment Musical* (1943).

months of being the standby for Audrey Christie, who had the role of morally loose actress Olive Lashbrooke,* Eileen persuaded Christie to call in sick one matinee, so she would have the opportunity to perform in front of a Broadway audience. It was an experience Eileen never forgot, and she in turn has always attempted to be equally understanding to her understudies once she attained stage success.

Eileen had a busy year in 1944. She was heard on such radio shows as *Gangbusters* and *True Story* (in minor roles, never in a capacity that would win her audience identification with her voice), had a small assignment in a City Center revival of *Our Town*, played in a brief tour of the comedy *Janie*, and for the U.S.O. performed in a production of *Over Twenty-One*.

In late 1944, Eileen accepted an acting post with the Shorewood Players in Milwaukee, remaining with them throughout part of 1945 and then playing repertory

---

* In Warner Bros.' filmization of *The Voice of the Turtle* (1947), contract character star Eve Arden portrayed the chic, nosy Olive Lashbrooke. It was the first of many subsequent occasions when Arden and Eileen, both angular but far different in human approach to a characterization, would "share" the same stage and/or film part.

stock in Boston and Cambridge. When actress Ruth Chatterton organized a road company of *Windy Hill*, a three-act comedy by Patsy Ruth Miller, co-producer-director Chatterton starred Kay Francis and Roger Pryor in the vehicle, with Eileen being cast in a subordinate assignment. The show opened September 20, 1945, at the Shubert Theatre, New Haven, and would play through the following May. Eileen left the tour to accept an understudy's part in *Brighten the Day* (Lyceum Theatre, December 12, 1945), a short-lived play (29 performances) by John Cecil Holms about the concept that money is only good if it is spent. It starred Charles Butterworth, Lenore Lonergan, Phyllis Avery, and Gene Blakely.

By now, Eileen's husband was out of the navy, and he joined her in New York where he eventually entered the insurance brokerage field, an occupation he still pursues. Eileen now embarked on acting courses at the American Theatre Wing to sharpen her talents. Among her instructors were Peter Frye, Joseph Anthony, William Hansen, and Herbert Berghof. Part of her drive for a more perfect technique was a matter of gaining the professional confidence that her work to date had not provided. Eileen has explained: "You do need something in this business to lean, something to help you help yourself and accept yourself. All of us in this business know each other so well, and yet it's still possible to get hurt, and get hurt often. The meek may inherit the earth, but the strong survive in the theater. Acting is not entirely inborn. Only to a certain degree is it inborn. Anyone can become a good technician, become proficient, and have a fairly good life in the theater. The difference between anyone and a great actor is made up of those moments in the life of some actors in which they kindle a spark—something that makes a moment so real that what they are doing becomes great acting."

In the spring of 1947, Eileen made her debut on television on the "Kraft Theatre" (May 14, 1947, NBC) in a small role. It was a medium that would provide tremendous creative opportunities for Eileen, not to mention salary checks. She would later observe: "In a television studio you don't dare go beyond yourself when you're acting. There's no trial space and no audience reaction. Television is the greatest showcase in the world, but it does not, in itself, provide an actor with the proper background."

In the summer of 1947 Eileen would be cast in a stock version of *Made in Heaven*, a marital mixup comedy. Also for her there was a pre-Broadway revival tour of the evergreen *Burlesque*. The following year was not very encouraging. There was a summer tour of *Blind Alley*, a psychological drama in the same vein as *The Desperate Hours,* and a four-day run in Edward Caulfield's comedy *Waltz Me Around Again* (Brighton Theatre, Brooklyn, September 19, 1948) which starred Nancy Walker.

It was in 1948 that Eileen agreed to assist fellow actor Will Hare with an audition at the Actors Studio. She sufficiently impressed the staff and was asked to return to audition for director Martin Ritt. She performed a sequence from *Golden Boy* and flunked the chance to become part of the acting workshop that was gaining such a big reputation in the theater world and would have opened many doors to Eileen if she had become a member. Eileen recalls: "I didn't know the *Golden Boy* scene, but I think I played it well. I'm not ashamed of that audition. People like you or they don't. If everybody likes you, there's something wrong."

Eileen was an understudy in the revival of Sidney Howard's Pulitzer Prize-winning drama *They Knew what They Wanted* (Music Box Theatre, February 16, 1949), starring Paul Muni and featuring Carol Stone, Edward Andrews, and Henry Jones. This edition lasted a modest 61 performances. Then on May 6, 1949, Eileen replaced Jean Hagen (who was off to Hollywood and filmmaking) in a small featured role in Herman Wouk's *The Traitor* (48th Street Theatre, March 31, 1949). This play dealt with an atomic scientist (Wesley Addy) who trades secrets with a foreign country, involving naval intelligence officer Lee Tracy and professor Walter Hampden. The *New York Times* decided ". . . [it is] second-rate melodrama about a first-rate subject." It folded after 67 performances, but at least it presented Eileen with a full-fledged Broadway role, more than the unsuccessful pre-New York tryouts of *The Stars Weep* or Joe Miller's farce comedy *Trial Honeymoon* had the previous year.

It was also in 1949 that Eileen made her first appearance on "Suspense," a live video half-hour thriller series which debuted on March 1, 1949, on CBS. In Eileen's initial assignment on the new program, she spoke two lines in a subway scene. Before the series concluded on August 15, 1954, Eileen would have appeared a total of 35 times on the show. The combination of her homebody looks and midwestern demeanor was just right for her assorted dramatic characterizations, effective but not so starkly outstanding that audiences would tire of seeing her so aften.

Eileen suffered a miscarriage in 1950, but it was in that year that she had the chance to create her first original Broadway characterization. It was the first time she was not inheriting a hand-me-down role. Samson Raphaelson's *Hilda Crane* (Coronet Theatre, November 1, 1950) was the vehicle. Originally the prestigious Theatre Guild organization had optioned

to produce the show, but when Joan Fontaine, Margaret Sullavan and June Havoc proved unavailable for the star part, the Guild dropped its sponsorship. Arthur Schwartz became the drama's producer, with Jessica Tandy in the lead role and her husband, Hume Cronyn, directing.

The plot of *Hilda Crane* focused on thirty-three-year-old Tandy returning home to Winona, Illinois, planning to wed for a third time. Her future mother-in-law (Evelyn Varden) dreads the thought of her forty-three-year-old son (John Alexander), a lawnmower manufacturer, wedding Tandy who has not yet outgrown her notions of grandeur and who has made a well-reported mess of her New York years. Eileen was on hand as Nell Bromley, wife of real estate man Richard McMurray. The function of her stage character would prove to be a prototype of her stage work for the next several years: that of a plain Jane soul who longs for the fulfillment of marriage and the dignity of being important to others in multi-level relationships. Usually, as here, Eileen's stage alter ego would be warmhearted, sincere, and tremendously willing to be helpful in her ineffectual way. Because of her typically reserved demeanor, her outbreaks of occasional raucous vulgarity (as in this play in which she portrays a bubbly bride hungry to taste the full fruits of sexual satisfaction), and her energetic candor about male-female relations give her character a refreshing slant. Playwrights have long ago found that the delineation of average-looking, good-hearted females who are frustrated by a range of emotional unfulfillment make for entertaining theatrics. These plain Janes also provide a necessary reality bridge to a drama or comedy's lead players who more often than not possess an overabundance of supercharged character traits with which the playgoer has difficulty in fully empathizing.

The critics were generally unenthusiastic about Raphaelson's dramatics, which *New York Herald-Tribune*'s Otis L. Guernsey, Jr. felt were showcase in a too ". . . frail and wavering context." Eileen's cameo-sized role evoked little lasting notice, although one reviewer commented she did a "gay job" as the carefree bride.* *Hilda Crane* closed after 70 performances.

Most of 1951 and 1952 was spent by Eileen in emoting on television, in such dramatic series as "Robert Montgomery Presents," "Ford Theatre," "Lucky Strike Hour," and "Kraft Theatre." One of her more publicized appearances was on "Philco Playhouse"'s *The Best Laid Schemes* (May 4, 1952, NBC) with Joseph Buloff.

---

* When Twentieth Century-Fox made the unimpressive film version of *Hilda Crane* (1956), Peggy Knudson inherited Eileen's role as the friend of lead Jean Simmons.

In the summer of 1952, Eileen, age thirty-three, gave birth to her first child, Mark. That fall, she obtained her next Broadway role, when during the September, 1952 Boston tryouts of *In Any Language,* she was hired to replace Anna Minot in the featured role of Valerie McGuire. The Edmund Beloin-Henry Garson drama had been having more than its share of out of town problems, Jeffrey Lynn already having been replaced by Walter Matthau as the airline-owning husband of Uta Hagen. The latter had the lead as a fading Hollywood movie musical star who has come to Rome to make a comeback bid in an arty Italian-made feature. Eileen's part called for her to be Hagen's practical but wisecracking secretary.

In Any Language debuted on Broadway at the Cort Theatre (October 7, 1952). Despite director George Abbott's efforts to bolster the farce, the brief appearance of former silent screen vamp Nita Natali as an unexplained marchessa and the presence of shapely Gloria Marlowe as an Italian actress, the play received qualified reviews. The authors were blamed for ". . . stretching a fifteen minute revue sketch into a full-length farce." Most of the kudos went to Hagen for her energetic uplifting performance as the Betty Grable-type screen star, for it was an atypical assignment for the actress who had gained her stage reputation in such heavy dramatics as *The Country Girl.* Eileen for the first time received more than token critical notice. The *New Yorker* magazine commended her for performing ". . . as one of those wry and sardonic secretaries who are seldom absent from works of this nature, . . ." Robert Coleman (*New York Daily Mirror*) observed: "She's a most promising comedienne." *In Any Language* died after 45 performances.

After a decade of pounding the Broadway beat, Eileen found it easier to gain the proper attention at play auditions. She read four times for director Joshua Logan before she was given the role of Rosemary Sidney in William Inge's *Picnic* (originally titled *Front Porch*). The drama is set in smalltown Kansas on a warm Labor Day in the mid-1930s. A stud (Ralph Meeker), friend of wealthy localite Paul Newman, wanders into town and has a remarkable influence on some of its womenfolk, who, until his arrival, had been more concerned with the pending annual picnic. Widow Peggy Conklin finds her sullen younger daughter (Kim Stanley) infatuated by the road-traveler, and her older girl (Janice Rule) soon forgets about rich but stolid Newman because of her budding love for the virile vagrant, which causes her to run away with him. Along the way, Conklin's star boarder, spinster schoolteacher Eileen, is so aroused by Meeker's blatant sensuality that she makes a drunken pass at him at the picnic, which so

With Janice Rule, Ralph Meeker, Peggy Conklin, and Arthur O'Connell in *Picnic* (1953).

later embarrasses her that her pride disappears and she begs her long-time beau, befuddled hardware man Arthur O'Connell, to marry her.

Because of *Picnic*'s thematic orientation and since Columbus, Ohio, was so far from critical Broadway

With Arthur O'Connell in *Picnic.*

eyes, it was decided to test the show at the profession-ally-sized and run Hartman Theatre there (January 15, 1953). It must have been a rare moment of professional and emotional satisfaction for Eileen to have a juicy role in an important production that was playing her home-town. She was living up to her demanding ambitions, much more than could probably be said for most of her high-toned college "pals." *Variety* reported of Eileen's performance in *Picnic* at the Hartman Theatre: ". . . [she] has the plum role as the schoolteacher and handles it beautifully."

With glowing word-of-mouth, *Picnic* moved on to St. Louis, Cleveland, and Boston before arriving on Broadway at the Music Box Theatre (February 19, 1953). Richard Watts, Jr. (*New York Post*) wrote of Inge's second produced stage work: ". . . [it] revealed the power, insight, compassion, observation and gift for looking into the human heart that we had all ex-pected of him. . . ." The drama, which had a 477-per-formance Broadway engagement, would earn Inge the Pulitzer Prize and the N.Y. Drama Critics' Circle Award.

Eileen's high-keyed role offered her a tremendous acting range in a part that any sensitive playgoer could easily empathize with, a strong factor in creating the tremendous rapport between Eileen's Rosemary and audiences. Rosemary is the physically unimpressive everywoman schoolteacher of decades ago, the minor career woman who ekes out a livelihood teaching man-ners and force-feeding education to everyone else's children. This situation obviously rankles when all she really wants in life is a chance to marry and have children. Behind the resignation to her robot-like ex-istence, there is still the spark of a young woman. It is spinster Eileen who insists to attractive Rule: "I had boys callin' me all the time. But if my father had ever caught me showing off in front of the window he'd have tanned me with a razor strap. 'Cause I was brought up strict by a God-fearing man."

At the Labor Day outing, Eileen's Rosemary has a few drinks too many, and the mere thought of returning the next day to the odious regimen of teaching another batch of children is almost too much for her to accept. The fact that good old Arthur O'Connell has still not proposed to her after all these years of courtship pushes Rosemary into further despair. The sight of alarmingly masculine Meeker triggers her breaking point. At the deserted dance pavillion she saddles up to Meeker: "Dance with me, young man. Dance with me. I can keep up with you. You know what? You remind me of one of those ancient statues. There was one in the school library until last year. He was a Roman glad-iator. All he had on was a shield. A shield over his arm.

That was all he had on. All we girls felt insulted havin' to walk past that statue every time we went to the library. We got a petition and made the principal do something about it. You know what he did? He got the school janitor to fix things right. He got a chisel and made the statue decent. Lord, those ancient people were depraved."

Later the distraught Rosemary falls to her knees and begs the confused O'Connell: "Oh, God. Please marry me, Howard. Please. Please . . . please." By the end of the play he has consented, still not sure why or how, and the jubilant Rosemary and her man are off on a honeymoon to his cousin's tourist camp in the Ozarks.

Eileen received full appreciation for her touching portrayal of the husky-voiced, frustrated single woman. She was rated "superlative" (*New York Journal Ameri-can*), "admirable" (*New York Daily News*), "tremen-dously effective" (*New York Daily Mirror*). The *New York Herald-Tribune* reported Eileen ". . . makes her passionate drunkenness terrifying."

For her *Picnic* emoting, Eileen received the Outer Circle Award and a Daniel Blum citation, giving her at last some official recognition as a Broadway per-former. But the preparation for her characterization was not snap work for Eileen. She later explained: "Actually I played the part for eight months before I felt that I really understood it and gave a good per-formance. I didn't know what I was doing. I didn't think I was any good. I was unhappy. I kept telling myself to respect myself in the part. It seemed to me that others in the cast didn't like what I was doing. I was in a hit, but the kicks were fewer than they should have been. . . . Logan kept trying to tell me I was having my first success—I was a pro: I couldn't act for a kind of pleasure only; I had to go out there and win. I received two awards for my performance in *Picnic,* but the main thing I learned from it was not to rip myself apart over a role. I'm not a natural-born co-medienne, like Lucille Ball or Vicki Cummings. I don't have that kind of timing or sense of comedy. My comedy comes from a situation."

When *Picnic** went on national tour in 1954, Eileen declined to be part of the package (Louise Larabee was substituted). One reason that Eileen refused was that she was pregnant, and later in the year she would give birth to her second son Philip. Another factor was

---

* Columbia filmed *Picnic* (1956) with Joshua Logan again directing, and it was decided that the Rosemary role required a big marquee name, so the part was enlarged to accommodate Rosalind Russell. Her exaggerated theatrics were just one of the many problems with the screen version. In 1965, a musical adaptation of *Picnic* entitled *Hot Spell* tried out and closed in Boston. Lovelady Powell enacted Eileen's part.

that she felt she had given all she could offer to the role and wanted new acting challenges.

During the Broadway run of *Picnic,* Eileen continued with her television work. One of her more remarkable performances was on "Philco Playhouse" 's *The Haven* (November 1, 1953, NBC), scripted by Tad Mosel, who would provide Eileen with some of her best video assignments, and produced by the series' Fred Coe, a long-standing champion of Eileen's talents. Others in the cast were Bart Burns, Gloria Kelly, Charles Taylor,

and Fred Herrick. The simply-etched story concerned a chance human revelation at a summer camp, which induces the rejuvenation of a disintegrating marriage. So penetrating was Eileen's acting in *The Haven,* that the usually reticent Marlene Dietrich who happened to see the telecast was so impressed that she sent Eileen a bouquet of white orchids and geraniums.* The video industry itself would grant Eileen the Sylvania Award as the best character actress of the season. Eileen's reaction at the time was: "It's so fantastic to think that

With Patty McCormack and Luella Gear in *The Bad Seed* (1954).

---

* In *Marlene Dietrich's ABCs* (1962), the living legend would write under the letter H about Eileen: "If she were acting in Europe, she would be Queen of the Boards. In America, the typecasting barbarism deprives the world of her true talents."

in one performance . . . you play to 20 million people? I could stay with *Picnic* for twenty years and not be seen like that."

Eileen went from one long run hit to another, Maxwell Anderson's *The Bad Seed* (46th Street Theatre, December 8, 1954), a thriller directed by Angela Lansbury's stepfather, Reginald Denham. Based on the novel by William March, the macabre tale deals with the descendant (Nancy Kelly) of a long dead mass murderess, who discovers her seemingly sweet and graceful child (Patty McCormack) has inherited all of her grandmother's murderous traits. Her horror mounts as she pieces together the facts that her amoral girl has drowned a young classmate at a school picnic, merely because he won the penmanship medal she thought she deserved. As the eight-year-old commits other homicides, the mother finds herself with no other alternative but to kill herself and, hopefully, her child. William Hawkins (*New York World-Telegram*) characterized the play: "As purely purposely diversion it ranks with *Dracula,* and sometimes sets your spine to as much tingling." In the mid-1950s when the public's mind was not yet accustomed to the wanton malice of juvenile delinquency, the impact of such an innocent-looking

In *The Bad Seed.*

human package being an emotionless killer was tremendous. Today's blasé audience would shrug "so what" at the whole affair.

Eileen had two small but telling scenes in the one-set play. As Mrs. Daigle, the floosey wife of Wells Richardson and the mother of the drowned boy, she drags Joan Croyden, her late son's schoolteacher to Kelly's apartment to learn more details about the mishap. As she enters the apartment, she slobbers: "There's something funny about the whole thing. I've said so over and over to Mr. Daigle. He married quite late you know. In his forties. 'Course I wasn't exactly what the fellows call 'a spring chicken' either. We won't have any more children. No more." Then she slithers drunkenly to the point of her visit, which obviously is embarrassing her meek husband. He tries to calm her to no effect. "Rest. Sleep. When you can't sleep at night, you can't sleep in the daylight. I lie and look at the water where he went down. There's something funny about the whole thing, Christine [Kelly]. I heard that your little girl was the last one who saw him alive. Will you ask her about the last few minutes and tell me what she says? Maybe she remembers some little thing. I don't care how small it is! No matter how small! You know something, Miss Fern dyes her hair. She knows something and she won't tell me. Oh, my poor little Claude! What did they do to you."

In her hysterical, inebriated state, there is a strange blend of her normal gossipy nature and the recent tragedy which has cut off the only hope for meaning in her life, motherhood. She babbles to Kelly: "It was no accident. You can wear such simple things, can't you? I never could wear simple things. I couldn't even buy 'em. When I got 'em home they didn't look simple. He was such a lovely dear little boy. He said I was his sweetheart. He said he was going to marry me when he grew up. I used to laugh and say, 'You'll forget me long before then. You'll find a prettier girl, and you'll marry her!' And you know what he said then? He said, 'No, I won't because there's not a prettier girl in the whole world than you are.' If you don't believe me, ask the girl who comes in and cleans. She was present at the time."

Finally, her husband persuades her to go. She exits saying: "It's a pleasure to stay drunk when your little boy's been killed. Maybe I'd better lay down."

Later in the play, Eileen's Mrs. Daigle returns to Kelly's apartment, still convinced McCormack knows something about the drowning. Neither the calculating girl nor Kelly, who knows now that her daughter is a murderess and is revolted at her part in transmitting the bad seeds to her child, will say much to Mrs. Daigle, who has been reduced to a pathetic mass of trauma and drunkenness. The woman leaves the apartment, her nerve fibers at the breaking point: "Oh my God, oh my God, it's time to go home! Oh, Christine, Christine, you know something! You know something and you won't tell me!"

The role seemed tailor-made for Eileen. Once again her character was functioning not only to progress the plot, but to add a needed touch of tragic humanity to soften the focus on the show's lead players. Little Patty McCormack, who was known to the public as the sweet little aunt on television "I Remember Mama," became the juvenile toast of Broadway. Eileen received an appropriate share of critical applause. ". . . [Her] free-swinging execution of the play's fat part, that of the bereaved but alcoholic mother, is uncompromising as she alternates between comic and the pathetic" (Henry Hewes, *Saturday Review of Literature*). ". . . added kudos to Eileen Heckart for those two compelling drunk scenes." (John McClain, *New York Journal American*). "Miss Heckart plays them [the two scenes] magnificently—never losing the private agony of the mother in the rush of drunken conversation." (Robert Coleman, *New York Daily Mirror*). It was William Hawkins (*New York World Telegram And Sun*) who perceived the theatrical nature of Eileen's tragic-comic relief part in *The Bad Seed:* "Eileen Heckart has a showy role as the drunken mother of a little boy who has suspiciously drowned on a picnic. It won her two huge hands last night. This seems to me curious, except that drunks often excite audiences to loud encouragement. The role should be heartbreaking, and Miss Heckart is apparently directed to play it for laughs."

Eileen received the Donaldson Award for her performance in *The Bad Seed*. The show would run 334 performances, but Eileen would leave the hit play in mid-1955, replaced by character actress Pert Kelton, who was as short and rotund as Eileen was tall and angular. Of her *Bad Seed* assignment Eileen would comment: "Every role I've ever played has been somewhat outside me and my life with my husband and little boys. If feeling is real, it's no longer acting. I was strongly affected in myself by only one part—the mother of a child who is murdered, in the Broadway production of *The Bad Seed*. I was happy to leave that play; it made me feel sick."

It seemed every season had a memorable performance by Eileen on television. This year it was *My Lost Saints* (March 13, 1955) on "Goodyear TV Playhouse" (NBC). It presented Eileen as Kate, a domestic servant, who for the past eighteen years has been the loyal maid to Barbara Robbins and Richard Keith. She is such an efficient soul that she has effectively taken over super-vision of the household and its inhabitants' personal affairs. Then Eileen's mama (Lili Darvas), a Polish farm woman, comes for a visit, and suddenly Eileen finds her loyalties sharply divided. Arthur Penn directed the sixty-minute play which had been written especially for Eileen by Tad Mosel. J.P. Shanley (*New York Times*) wrote: "A performance of rare skill was contributed by Eileen Heckart. . . . her conception of the housekeeper, as a generous, warmhearted woman faced with a crisis in which she apparently had to choose between her duty to her mother and her own welfare was a moving and entirely believable characterization."

Director Martin Ritt, who had vetoed Eileen's Actors Studio audition seven years before, had a completely different attitude about the now seasoned performer who tried out for the Arthur Miller double-bill of long one-act plays. She was selected to be Van Heflin's co-star in *A Memory of Two Mondays* and *A View from the Bridge* (Coronet Theatre, September 29, 1955).

A Memory of Two Mondays is a chronicle of the daily life of men and women working in the shipping room of a dingy, barren auto parts warehouse in the New York of the 1930s. In spirit and flavor it seemed typical of the Clifford Odets material turned out for the Group Theatre in those Depression years. This curtain raiser presented J. Carrol Naish as a hard-drinking, lecherous, foreign-born foreman; Russell Collins, his compassionate assistant; Heflin as an ambitious salesman; Biff McGuire, a poetry-spouting Irish idealist, who is beaten down by the grime of the job and poverty; Leo Penn as a self-educated apprentice; Gloria Marlowe as a flirtatious tootsie; and Eileen as the spinsterly switchboard operator, a pal to everyone, and completely lonesome.

Both critical and audience attention was riveted on the second and longer work, *A View from the Bridge*. Set within view of the Brooklyn waterfront, it traces the traumas of longshoreman Eddie (Heflin) who is alienated from his loving but drab and unimaginative wife Beatrice (Eileen) and too horrified to admit to even himself that he has become enamored of his orphaned niece (Marlowe). Because he is so jealous of the girl's attachment to Eileen's cousin (Dick Davalos) who has been smuggled illegally into the country, he is first led to taunt the boy as a homosexual and later to commit the cardinal sin of reporting him to the immigration authorities. The culmination of the domestic tragedy makes the drama ". . . a must for anyone who is at all interested in what the contemporary American theater is thinking about" (Walter Kerr, *New York Herald-Tribune*).

Eileen's projection as the alarmed stevedore's wife was greatly overshadowed by Heflin's powerful lead role and by the craftsmanlike work of Naish as the attorney-narrator. In fact, said Brooks Atkinson (*New York Times*): "Everyone knows that Eileen Heckart is a talented actress. But she plays Eddie's wife like a bundle of nerves. There is little warmth or domesticity in her portrait of an Italian homemaker."* The show ran for 149 performances and was not a commercial success in its original format.

Meanwhile, Eileen finally had the opportunity to make her screen debut. If she were not the typical stage ingenue, she certainly was far from the accepted cinema lead, and had to await the opportunity for a suitable character role that would take advantage of her ability to combine pathos and comic warmth. Warner Bros. *Miracle in the Rain* (Loew's State Theatre, April 1, 1956) proved to be the vehicle, and her fifth-billed role as Grace Ullman the part. This film was shot on location in New York in mid-1955. It was a rare sojourn for her into the woman's picture-tearjerker genre, seemingly at this period the special province of movie stars Jane Wyman and Susan Hayward.

Miracle in the Rain, set in 1942 Manhattan, finds mousey Wyman working as a secretary at the Excelsior Shoe Manufacturing Company with lecherous Fred Clark as her boss. When her daily work is done, she always trots home to her neurotic mama (Josephine Hutchinson), a self-oriented creature who has not recovered from her husband (William Gargan) walking out on her ten years before. There are rare occasions when Wyman slips out and sees a movie with drab fellow employee Eileen. One day after work, Wyman is

With Jane Wyman in *Miracle in the Rain.*

laden down with bundles. When it begins to rain, a brash soldier, Van Johnson, comes to her rescue, and it is not long before he requests a date. She timidly agrees, but only if Eileen goes along as an informal chaperone. Later, Wyman and Johnson become engaged, but then he is shipped overseas to active duty. When he is reported killed in action, Wyman loses her desire to live, although each day she prays for Johnson to the statue of St. Andrew at St. Patrick's Cathedral. Not taking care of herself, a cold turns to pneumonia, and it is Eileen and the Cathedral priest who find the girl collapsed on the church steps. She is clutching the very same Roman coin she had given Johnson before he went away and swears she has heard Johnson's voice tell her that "Love never dies."

It may have been difficult for realistic audiences to emotionally accept the "miracle," but the sudsy yarn, filmed in realistic black and white, did respectably in the film market, thanks to the conviction of the cast who carried off the hokey story. Eileen's small role came across nicely, providing a believable characterization of a lonesome office chum. The *New York Times* evaluated: ". . . [she] adds a few touching bits as Miss Wyman's spinster office pal." The *New York Herald-Tribune* listed Eileen as among the "experts" who added fine support to the production. Eileen had made the transition to motion pictures painlessly.

Somebody Up There Likes Me (Loew's State Theatre, July 5, 1956) was also filmed largely on location in Manhattan. In the tradition of *I'll Cry Tomorrow,* it adopted a cliché, contrived method to present the rags to semi-riches career of boxer Rocky Graziano. Paul Newman, who had also had a featured role with Eileen in the stage version of *Picnic,* gave a resounding performance in his second movie. In contrast to Humphrey

With Van Johnson and Jane Wyman in *Miracle in the Rain* (WB, 1956).

---

* This one-act drama would later be expanded into a full length play. When it was picturized in 1962, Maureen Stapleton would inherit Eileen's part.

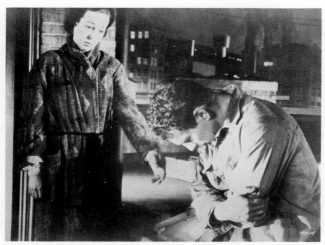

With Paul Newman in *Somebody Up There Likes Me.* (MGM, 1956).

Bogart's *The Harder They Fall,* which focused only on the seamier side of the sport, *Somebody Up There Likes Me* was a fighter's success story detailing how a crude Lower East Side punk could make something of his existence and become an inspiration to others. This picture was one of the more impressive 1956 releases, thanks to the aggressive direction of Robert Wise (who had delved into the subject before in the grimy *The Set-Up*) and to the vital, manly performance of youthful Newman.

Eileen was billed fourth as Ma Barbella, Newman's downtrodden mother, oppressed by her drunken dreamer of a husband's (Harold J. Stone), illness and the unrelenting squalor of her surroundings. She seemingly has little faith in the future of her juvenile delin-

With Paul Newman in *Somebody Up There Likes Me.*

quent son. After a stretch in the reformatory then some time in the penitentiary, and later in an army prison (for going A.W.O.L.) Newman embarks on a new life in the boxing field, emerging as the middleweight champion of the world.

The critics were impressed by Eileen's short part as the drabbly dressed, accented creature. ". . . [she] is sensitive as Rocky's mother, a dolorous woman weighed down by misfortune" (William K. Zinsser, *New York Herald-Tribune*). *Daily Variety* rated her "exceptionally fine," and *Time* magazine observed: "Eileen Heckart adds a wirethin hysteria to the role of the mother." Despite her impressive emotion, Eileen had come and gone from the screen early on in the story, dimming the memory of her performance, particularly in contrast to Everett Sloane as the fierce fight manager and Pier Angeli as the gentle, loyal wife of crude Newman.

Eileen's third release of 1956 was *Bus Stop* (Roxy Theatre, August 31, 1956). This is the Marilyn Monroe film of which the *New York Times* announced in its review: "Hold onto your chairs everybody, and get set for a rattling surprise. Marilyn Monroe has finally proved herself an actress in *Bus Stop*. She and the picture are swell!"

Bus Stop was based on William Inge's screenplay of his 1955 Broadway success and was directed for the screen by Joshua Logan, both of whom were very familiar with Eileen's acting proficiency and agreed to her coming to Hollywood to handle the assignment. The screenplay expanded the stage version to a degree, but it maintained a good deal of the intimacy and character exploration that had made the Broadway edition so popular. In the movie, innocent cowboy Don Murray is brought from his Montana ranch to a Phoenix, Arizona, rodeo by his pal Arthur O'Connell. At the Blue Dragon Cafe, he champions disreputable chanteuse Monroe, whose act is being ignored by the boisterous, rude customers. Murray determines on the spot to wed the girl who has just given him a kiss in kindness. She in turn is dismayed to think Murray may be serious. She attends the local rodeo with her plain Jane waitress pal Eileen only to discover that Murray intends to marry her that day. Later Eileen helps Monroe pack her belongings so she can make a hasty escape out of her dressing room window to catch a bus for Los Angeles. But the dumb songstress is waylaid by Murray who rather forcibly insists she join him and O'Connell on a trek back to Montana. They board a bus which, due to a snowstorm, is forced to stay put overnight at Betty Field's roadside diner, and by morning, Monroe has determined that Murray really loves her.

Once again, the whole focus of the picture was so far away from Eileen's rather extraneous role (it is non-

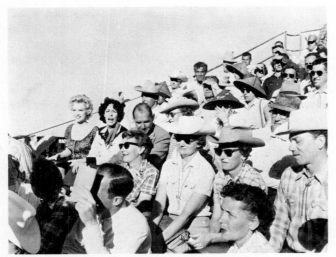

With Marilyn Monroe in *Bus Stop* (20th-Fox, 1956).

film that two or more endings were shot, one having the girl live, another showing her killed on the old wharf (as in the play), and so forth. There was much publicity that Warner Bros. would release the picture in some locations with one conclusion and in other markets with an alternate climax. *The Bad Seed* did exceedingly well in distribution and grossed more than $4.1 million, the only substantial film hit Eileen would appear in until *Up the Down Staircase* more than a decade later.

In *The Bad Seed,* Nancy Kelly and Patty McCormack recreated their roles as mother and daughter respectively. Eileen's brief scenes which had been a satisfying mixture of sadness-crudeness on stage, was switched to a more pathetic interpretation for the screen rendition, as she and her meek husband (Frank Cady) visit Kelly's apartment to question little McCormack about the

existent in the stage version) that her presence was pleasant but unessential. The *New York Times* reported: "Eileen Heckart is droll as the chippie's friend."

It was Eileen's fourth picture of 1956 (a rather amazing quantity for her first year in films) that offered her a meaty role. She was among the Broadway cast members utilized in the Mervyn LeRoy-directed screen version of *The Bad Seed* (Astor Theatre, September 12, 1956). For the wide screen, the drama was scenically opened up, which if anything dissipated the permeating sense of doom that had been a keynote of the stage edition. In fact, every flaw of the play became exaggerated in the picturization, particularly playwright Anderson's failure to really delve into the thesis that any family can develop bad seeds. LeRoy opted for a shock approach in his direction, which proved to be an easy but unsatisfactory handling of his subject. In fact, he and the studio were so uncertain how to conclude the

With Nancy Kelly in *The Bad Seed* (WB, 1956).

drowning of their son. Garbed in a straight-lined skirt and simple white blouse, with a hangdog expression on her somewhat horsey face, Eileen was a realistic but jarring note in a strident production. As Bosley Crowther in the *New York Times* explained: "As for Eileen Heckart's performance as the grief-torn mother of the boy who is drowned, it is badly confused." William K. Zinsser in the *New York Herald-Tribune* went a step further: ". . . Eileen Heckart is fine as the dead boy's bibulous mother (though her two long scenes are almost superfluous)."

For her showy performance, Eileen was nominated for her first—and to date only—Academy Award. Like Patty McCormack, another nominee in the same best supporting actress category, she lost to Dorothy Malone, who won for her nymphomaniac part in *Written on the*

With Marilyn Monroe in *Bus Stop*.

With Nancy Kelly and Frank Cady in *The Bad Seed*.

Wind. It was a long-standing Hollywood maxim that whenever two people were nominated from the same picture, and particularly in the same category, they canceled out one another's votes.

Meanwhile, Eileen continued to be an active video performer. On "Kraft Theatre" (NBC), she played the lead in Bob Crean's *Anna Santonello* (August 8, 1956), a tale of a middle-aged woman, who after her tyrannical father's death, finds that her three brothers (Will Kuluva, Simon Oakland, Joe Campanella) expect her to slave for them in the same fashion. But a chance meeting with Irish-American repairman James Gregory changes Eileen's outlook. The *New York Journal American* reported: ". . . [she] delivers another of her customary fine, sensitive and endearing solid portrayals."

Eileen was among those who graced "Hallmark Hall of Fame"'s production of Lillian Hellman's *The Little Foxes* (December 16, 1956). For offbeat casting, stately Greer Garson was hired to play the bitchy Regina, with Eileen as Birdie, Sidney Blackmer as Benjamin Hubbard, and E.G. Marshall as Oscar Hubbard. *Variety* observed: "Eileen Heckart, as Birdie, a sister-in-law, gave the play heart for in human terms she told the meaning of a sensitive, good hearted individual, albeit immature, who is caught in the vortex of an unconscionable, money-grubbing family. Hers was a most moving scene when she attempts to warn and protect Miss Garson's daughter from her own weak-willed, brutal son." Eileen seemed to enjoy her portrait of a retarded southern matron with a gooey Dixie diction, a distinct change from her Italian-accented wife in *A View from the Bridge*.

No License to Kill, an episode on "Alcoa Theatre" (February 3, 1957, NBC), was an unusual presentation in that it was produced in cooperation with the Con-

necticut State Police and the Aetna Casualty and Surety Company. It was the story of a fatal automobile accident, the people involved in it, and the methods utilized by the police to reconstruct the events. The cast included Hume Cronyn, Jack Klugman, Edward Binns, Maureen Cassidy, Eileen, and Carl Betz as her husband.

It was on CBS's "Studio One" that Eileen had one of her most satisfactory video roles, that of Evie Jackson in Tad Mosel's *The Out-of-Towners* (May 6, 1957), as the smalltown postmistress who comes to New York for a convention and finds love with greeting card salesman E.G. Marshall.*

By now, Eileen was so established on Broadway that her special brand of stage pathos had become a defined type. It was little wonder that she was selected to portray Lottie Lacey in William Inge's *The Dark at the Top of the Stairs* (1957), directed by Actors Studio exponent Elia Kazan. Set in 1920s Oklahoma, the yearning drama of human fear revolves around harness salesman Pat Hingle finding it less difficult to adjust to thoughts of a new profession (mass produced automobiles have made his calling outmoded) than the emotional turmoil he faces at home. His over-restrained wife (Teresa Wright) is overwhelmed by her need to be better than her neighbors in all ways, even to over-

With Charles Saari, Frank Overton, Teresa Wright, Timmy Everett, and Judith Robinson in *The Dark at the Top of the Stairs* (1957).

---

* It would be seven years before the touching drama was turned into the film *Dear Heart,* starring Geraldine Page in Eileen's role. Ironically, by that time the much praised video version would have been so forgotten that the movie was nominated for a best original screenplay, until it was belatedly pointed out that it had been done first on television.

In *The Dark at the Top of the Stairs.*

caring for their oddball mama's boy son (Charles Saarl) and their extremely introspective daughter (Judith Robinson).

Distraught, she sends for her sister Eileen who arrives in Act II from Oklahoma City with her meek dentist husband (Frank Overton) in tow. Dressed as a matronly flapper, Eileen's Lottie is a loud-mouthed bigot (her favorite word is "honey"), filled with all sorts of prejudices. She is patronizing to her niece's Jewish military school date, but her full wrath is saved for ". . . the Catholics [who] keep the basements of their churches filled with guns and all kinds of ammunition." She derides her husband's admiration for movie actress Norma Talmadge ("Norma Talmadge, Norma Talmadge. I don't see what you see in her. Besides, she's a Catholic."). In fact, she denounces all screen actresses in one fell swoop: "I hear they're all a bunch of trollops." But being a bundle of emotional contradictions, she herself has a mad crush on actor Rudolph Valentino, a commonplace experience for women her age, which she cannot bear to admit: "Those eyes, that seem to be laughing at you, and all those white teeth, I think it's a sin for a man to be as pretty as he is. Why, I'd be scared to death to let a man like him touch me."

It is not long before Eileen's Lottie admits: "I talk all the time just to convince myself that I'm alive. . . . Nothing ever really happened to me while it was going on." With her husband offstage, she confesses to Wright that it has been three years since her husband even touched her in bed. "Something inside him just got up and went for a walk, and never came back." Surveying Wright's supposedly tumultuous relationship with Hingle, a man she has always criticized in the past, Eileen reveals: "I wish to God someone loved me enough to hit me."

The Dark at the Top of the Stairs had its world premiere at the Shubert Theatre, New Haven, November 7, 1957. The play was endorsed by the local critics. *Variety* reported of Eileen: ". . . [she] strikes a wide range of emotional chords, all with bell ringing effect." When the show premiered on Broadway at the Music Box Theatre (December 5, 1957), the accolades for the play and cast was such that a long run was insured.

As the bossy, overly loquacious soul who inwardly is terrified, Eileen received some of her best stage reviews ever. "There is a grand performance by Eileen Heckart as a woman who must remain a stranger to her husband—an expertly shaded performance which ranges from broad humor to pitiable loneliness" (John Chapman, *New York Daily News*). "Miss Heckart, noisily picking the meat out of cracked walnuts and even more noisily pretending that all is well with her own love life, grips a wicker rocker with her fist, instructs the world in intolerance . . . , and lavishes her secretly shattered heart on the youngsters around her in a run-on, non-stop, piercingly desperate performance that is simply stunning. Beneath the busy, showy, wantonly generous activity there is a secret, and a hidden simplicity. When she gets to it, when her fingers hide her mouth and she speaks as softly and as honestly as she can, the dazzling pattern irises down to a sharp, chilling, blindingly clear focus. Miss Heckart can bring tears by the harsh expedient of cutting off her own." (Walter Kerr, *New York Herald-Tribune*).

A few years ago, Eileen stated: "The best Broadway work I've done was as Lottie Lacey in *The Dark at the Top of the Stairs.* But the part was beautifully written, and allowed for a full characterization. That helped. And Elia Kazan, the director, had four ideas for me for every one I had. I usually cross out the author's stage directions. Authors should write the words and leave the rest to us."

At the time of her casting in *The Dark at the Top of the Stairs,* Eileen, while grateful for the role, had some words on being the stage's new professional neurotic: "Just once before I get too old, I'd like to play an attractive, normal uncomplicated woman. I've never played a pretty woman in my life.

"I guess I started out my career in the wrong shoes. I used to go on interviews, with unglamorous saddle shoes. I can't tell you how many times producers said to me 'Sorry, you're not attractive enough for the part.'

"I've played so many women with problems, but I personally don't understand how I escaped being a little sick myself.

"In the world of beautiful people, shapes and faces like Brigitte Bardot come and go, but talent improves with age. The tragedy of so many glamor girls is that they depend on their beauty and fail to develop other more sustaining qualities."

*The Dark at the Top of the Stairs** would run for 468 performances, with Eileen leaving the cast December 1, 1958, replaced by Audrey Christie, an ironic change from fifteen years prior when Eileen had been Christie's understudy in *The Voice of the Turtle.* For her performance as Lottie Lacey, Eileen was awarded the N.Y. Drama Critics Award as best supporting actress of the year.

While in *The Dark at the Top of the Stairs,* the ever-experimenting Eileen agreed to perform in ANTA's Theatre Matinee Series in their March 11, 1958 program at the Theatre De Lys. She accepted the virtuoso part of Mrs. Rowland in Lamont Johnson's *Before Breakfast,* a one-act play written in 1916, in which she played the nagging wife of an unsuccessful village poet. The offstage voice for the gin-drinking spouse was performed by Anthony Ray. The *New York Times* reported: "In her fifteen minute portrait, she growls with fury, snivels with self-pity, shouts with outrage, and finally, gags with horror. It is an extraordinary vignette." When an international theater festival was held at Congress Hall in West Berlin in 1959, Eileen repeated her *Before Breakfast* performance. Other American actors in the junket who played in one-act shows were Ethel Waters, Lillian Gish, Burgess Meredith, and Thornton Wilder.

Before going into *The Dark at the Top of the Stairs,* Eileen had gone to Hollywood to perform in *Hot Spell* (Guild Theatre, September 17, 1958). This Hal B. Wallis production for Paramount release was one of Shirley Booth's rare cinema excursions, in a role reminiscent of *Come Back Little Sheba.* The film's thesis was aimed at destroying America's concept of the institution of motherhood, but Daniel Mann's direction was

---

* When Warner Bros. filmed *The Dark at the Top of the Stairs* (1959), Eileen's role was given to Eve Arden. Under Delbert Mann's direction, Arden mistakenly offered an arch Miss Brooks-type performance, destroying the concept of the complicated sister-in-law.

With Shirley Booth in *Hot Spell* (Paramount, 1958).

so pat and bland that the potential barb was all but vitiated.

In *Hot Spell,* Booth is a dowdy, small southern town housewife completely unaware of her failure as a wife or mother. Her twenty-five year marriage to volatile Anthony Quinn is falling apart. He has turned to a nineteen-year-old chippie for consolation. It is the self-centered Quinn who botches his relationship with his children: he refuses to set up his older son (Earl Holliman) in business; gives his daughter (Shirley MacLaine) bad advice which costs her the love of boyfriend (Warren Stevens); and in a bid to communicate to his younger son (Clint Kimbrough), takes him to the pool hall to teach him the facts of life, but soon alienates the youth. Booth's Alma Duval blots out the present, dreaming of bygone days when she was the belle of New Paris, Louisiana. Her only concession to the domestic disharmony is to bake a chocolate cake, give out gifts at a birthday party, and continually spout empty cheery clichés. In the rash of frazzled emotions supercharged by the "hot spell," Quinn takes off for Florida with his gal and is killed in a car crash. Benign Shirley gathers together her brood and departs for New Paris, Louisiana, to bury Quinn at the local cemetery. At the funeral, she finally comprehends that one cannot substitute delving into the past for coping with the present or future.

Eileen appeared in *Hot Spell* in a brief part as a forlorn neighbor, who herself has lost her man many years before. In a pathetically amusing sequence, this confidant of lower-middle-class Booth attempts to teach her unsophisticated friend how to sublimate her inadequacy feelings with the help of a cigarette and a belt of whiskey. Raspy-voiced Heckart reasons that if Booth becomes worldly she can compete with Quinn's now

With Shirley Booth in *Hot Spell.*

generation tart. The sad sight of the two misguided women vainly attempting to be seasoned ladies is the one memorable moment of the picture, even granting Bosley Crowther's (*New York Times*) observation that it was ". . . a rather cheap and inconsistent drinking scene."

It was more than coincidence that Eileen, who along with Geraldine Page and Maureen Stapleton is one of the stage's leading portrayers of vulnerable, uncomely women, should be cast in a picture with Booth. This picture greatly helped to pave the way in the 1950s for new audience interest in the screen adventures of ordinary females. The Booth image was of a woman, who now may be middle-aged, but always lacked the one ingredient so long valued by society, obvious physical beauty. It was a factor that the blessing of money, charm, or ingenuity could not very well disguise.

Before a few more astute film executives in the 1950s and later years realized that there was a huge potential audience of ordinary women interested in empathizing with fellow "blighted" creatures, the cinema followed quite a different course when presenting screen adventures of the unconventional woman. If the lead role were to be nonglamorous, there were specific reasons for it. Sylvia Sidney was bedraggled in a score of 1930s features, but it was the lack of money and the forces of society that weighed her down. She was never a plain Jane even in tattered rags with a dirt-smudged face and tenement filth all about her. The star might be grandly neurotic or the patient saint like Bette Davis in *Now, Voyager,* or Olivia de Havilland in *Devotion,* or a striking woman blemished by a physical defect as Joan Crawford in *A Woman's Face,* or Jane Wyman in *Johnny Belinda.*

Whenever a nonpretty female was presented in the

typical pre-1950s feature, it would be in a subsidiary role, given very little screen time or character deliniation. They might be young, broad comedy foil stereotypes as played by Joan Davis, Judy Canova, Virginia O'Brien, Cass Daley, and others, who laughingly admitted they could not land an attractive male, shrugged their shoulders, and made the best of the situation. If they were the arch, acid-tongued variation a la Eve Arden, there would generally be little rationale for the character's failure to cope with her loneliness. Or on the other hand, the screenplay might pass the woman off on the generally unappealing second male lead, himself usually a buffoon variation of the virile man. If the part called for a Marie Dressler-Marjorie Main type, they would be presented as raucous, middle-aged rural gals generally well-adjusted to life, with little explanation given as to how they coped with society when young women.

It was the rare exception for filmdom to examine the emotions of a marriage-hungry, youthful spinster, with Agnes Moorehead's "poor Aunt Fanny" in *The Magnificent Ambersons* an excellent example, even if the plot of this movie was set in noncontemporary times. Fanny became neurotic simply from the overwhelming frustrations of being so plain and so quickly relegated by everyone to a voyeuristic, old maid's life. She yearned for the same fulfillment that every ordinarily attractive woman could expect to attain.

By the 1950s, with the downfall of the Hollywood studio system and the glamour and sparkle that accompanied it, the movie industry began to examine on occasion the humdrum life of those not blessed with surface allure. There was Jane Wyman trapped in the mama's girl syndrome in *Miracle in the Rain* and her December–May love relationship with Rock Hudson in *All That Heaven Allows.* These two films, however, conceded too easily to Hollywood unreality. It remained for Shirley Booth in *Come Back Little Sheba, About Mrs. Leslie,* and *Hot Spell* to break the trend by following the example of the Italian neo-realistic cinema which had presented big-boned Anna Magnani in *The Open City.* Magnani in her Continental pictures and later in America (*The Rose Tattoo, Wild in the Wind, The Fugitive Kind*) would demonstrate that beneath the workhorse exterior of some women there often exists seething sexual passion and tremendous compassion.

Thus by the mid-1950s there could be a full-blown screen treatment of the withdrawn young woman as played by Geraldine Page in *Summer and Smoke,* which helped pave the way for her role in *Dear Heart.* Her role capitalized on the almost-homely type Eileen had been playing on television and stage throughout the

Eileen Heckart, circa 1960.

1950s. Finally, there would be Maureen Stapleton who in her varying degrees of plumpness and stark drabness has portrayed a series of screen roles examining the innermost nature of lonely, unpretty misses. She may be married to Raf Vallone in *A View from the Bridge,* Walter Matthau in *Plaza Suite* or Van Heflin in *Airport,* but in each case she is extremely vulnerable because she knows she cannot compete in the market of surface beauty. In the "Among the Paths to Eden" episode from *Trilogy* she is the pitiable lonelyheart, craving a man's company so desperately she haunts cemeteries, hoping to spark a bereaved widower on an emotional rebound.

All of which is by way of saying that *Hot Spell,* although it failed in its purpose, was a remarkable step forward in the American cinema's handling of the common, everyday woman and that both Shirley Booth and Eileen, by choice and/or accident, have been tremendous forces in this dramatic progression.

Eileen was relatively inactive in the professional world of 1959, save for a Hollywood visit to film *Heller in Pink Tights* (Capitol Theatre, March 16, 1960). She was billed fifth as Lorna Hathaway in this

color spoof of a traveling theater company in the West of the 1880s. Anthony Quinn's acting troupe has a hard time surviving in good times, but they are burdened with a voluptuous leading lady (Sophia Loren) who has an insatiable attraction for finery. Consequently, she and Quinn are constantly in debt, forcing the company to skip from town to town. Boss Quinn hopes to settle the group in Cheyenne, but there Loren become embroiled in a poker game, offering herself as the stake and losing to Steve Forrest who demands his prize. Later Loren leads Forrest into the town of Bonanza where she retrieves a long-standing debt owed him by town boss Ramon Novarro. She promptly invests the funds into a permanent headquarters for Quinn's show. After a final skirmish between Forrest and Novarro's henchmen, Quinn's company settles into its own home at last, and hopefully for keeps.

In *Heller in Pink Tights,* Eileen functioned as the over-seasoned, red-wigged, cigar-smoking second leading lady of the troupe. She refuses to admit her ingenue daughter (Margaret O'Brien) is twenty-one and not sixteen and will not let anyone forget she once had a "promising" stage career. Her film highlights here include such bits as selling photos of O'Brien to admirers at fifty cents apiece, or she and O'Brien sneaking out of their hotel room, unable to pay the bill, dressed with multi-layers of clothing (all the costuming they own) in hopes of passing by the desk clerk unnoticed. Later during an Indian raid on Quinn's wagon Eileen is ever so reluctant to leave behind her daughter's teenaged finery for the savages. As the clucking mama and theatrical ham, Eileen received her critical due: ". . . [she] just about steals the whole shootin' match. . . . It's really comedy and Miss Heckart carries it off with polish." (*Variety*). The George Cukor-directed film was not a money-winner, lacking that gutsy approach needed to give the proceedings some life of their own.

It was in 1960 that Eileen gave birth to her third son, Luke. By this time, she and her family were well-established residents of New Canaan, Connecticut, having purchased a rambling 1840 farmhouse. It was also the year Eileen voluntarily embraced Catholicism and decided to bring her three sons up in that faith.

Although she adored being a wife and mother and demanded of herself complete devotion to her home responsibilities, she needed her professional career for total fulfillment. As she would explain in 1963: "I couldn't devote my life to keeping house. I don't have that much creativity in the kitchen. Cooking bores me. When I'm onstage, playing a character other than myself, I feel I'm creating. I enjoy it. I go out there to play seriously—play to win. I loathe amateurs. It gives me chills to think of myself as part of an amateur actors'

With Anthony Quinn and Margaret O'Brien in *Heller in Pink Tights* (Paramount, 1960).

With Margaret O'Brien, Anthony Quinn, and Sophia Loren in *Heller in Pink Tights.*

suburban group, laughing and gossiping. Even when I play bridge, I play to win. Once, on location for *Heller in Pink Tights,* I stayed up four nights in a row playing bridge, because I was determined to improve my game. I played seriously. I wouldn't be acting if I weren't acting seriously."

This was the year of acting experimentation for Eileen. She performed in a limited tryout engagement of *The Shemansky Affair* at Masillon, Ohio, and then accepted an offer to star in Bertolt Brecht's *Mother Courage* for John Houseman's theater group at U.C.L.A. Eileen remembers: "The material is so big and specific. The part of Mother Courage should be played by a European. I'm too American. But I had a rapport with that woman and with her strength. I had a lot to give that role, and I've never worked harder. Brecht says to cut off all emotion in a performance, and to Method actors *that's* news. We're always trying to turn on emotion and to deal with it onstage. When Brecht confronts Mother Courage with her dead son, he tells you to drain yourself of all feeling and expression. I worked on that scene through three bad performances, but for the last four performances, the scene, the whole play worked. To play Mother Courage emotionally and to feel those audiences responding in a way I'd never before experienced was unforgettable. Those four performances were the most gratifying of my life."

Even Eileen's appearance in the Theatre Guild's big 1960 production was offbeat for her. Arthur Laurents's *Invitation to a March* was a modern fable based on the sleeping princess tradition. Here, well-to-do Jane Fonda, the daughter of gooey southern matron Madeleine Sherwood, is to be married to the highly eligible Tom Hatcher at an exclusive Long Island wedding. But whenever he converses with Fonda about their safe and predictable future, she starts to yawn and soon falls asleep. It is when plumber James MacArthur kisses her that Fonda really comes to life, questioning the complacency of her society's materialistic values. All this leads to a tug of war between Hatcher's mama (Eileen) and MacArthur's mother (Shelley Winters). It develops that MacArthur is illegitimate and that his father was the lover of both Winters and Eileen.

With Laurents directing, the social comedy tried out in Columbus, Ohio, in September, 1960, where it underwent substantial refinements, but it was evident to all that top-featured player Eileen (billed under Shelley Winters) had been dealt the best of the cutting dialogue. By the Boston tryout, Winters was so upset by the critical and public attention being heaped on Eileen's candid bitch, that she left the show and Celeste Holm substituted. *Invitation to a March* debuted at the Music Box Theatre, October 29, 1969, to better than average notices. The *New York Times* labeled it a ". . . crisp, wise-cracking Broadway-style comedy," but failed to indicate that the show sacrificed any real characterization for its Restoration-style pungent wit.

Eileen received the lion's share of the notices. ". . . it is Eileen Heckart, with blue hair and a fabulous collection of Capri pants, who steals the show as the rich, acidulous, jaded daughter of a fishmonger. After all, she's got the best lines and knows what to do with them" (Robert Coleman, *New York Daily Mirror*). "Miss Heckart's worldliness is continually amusing and her timing is electronic" (John Chapman, *New York Daily News*).

Never had Eileen's physical appearance and costuming received so much attention in the reviews. Here she was the complete opposite of the drab figure she usually portrayed: ". . . [she] first moves onto the stage as though she were being served for dessert with a cigarette-holder no longer than a piccolo, wearing jacket and trousers scarcely more scarlet than a jungle pool after a stag-fight. But her temperance does not last long, and before the first act is over she is back with a fragrant cheroot gripped in her very firm teeth, her icy form turned out as a purple toreador" (Walter Kerr, *New York Herald-Tribune*).

It was Kerr who later in his review noted one of the play's prime structural faults: "But we have by this time become so fond of Miss Heckart's conformist tartness, and just suspicious enough of Miss Holm's peach-melba phrases, to want to put the laurel wreath where it doesn't belong. Miss Holm gives the battle everything, including the whoosh of her elbows, but the message is somehow too soft to win. At best, a draw."

Eileen would later say: "In *Invitation to a March,* I was confused during the rehearsals and din't hear half of what was being said on the stage. I had a talk with the young man who played my son, and we tried to find some way of making our relationship more real, in order to strengthen the performance. Every actor tries to do this." After the show had come and gone, Eileen would reflect on her progression as an actress: "But I know how to tune in to an audience. . . . I'd get a hand [in *Invitation to a March*] just for the cross— going from one side of the stage to the other in tight purple slacks. Audiences vary. Timing comes from them, not from you. Any time you press to reach for an audience, you lose it."

Invitation to a March ran only 113 performances, closing at a financial loss. One reason Eileen accepted the role in the prestigious, well-mounted production was that her casting was an obvious change of pace: "Deedee's a happy neurotic. She's got more than she thought she'd get out of life and doesn't suspect she's missing love."

One of Eileen's more intriguing television appearances in 1960 was on the noteworthy syndicated "Play of the Week" series, in Federico Garcia Lorca's *The House of Bernardo Alba* (June 6, 1960). The two-hour telecast was directed by Boris Sagal. Anne Revere starred as the stern Spanish matriarch obsessed with family honor. Widowed as the play opens, she informs her five daughters (Eileen being one of them) that they must enter the traditional eight-year period of cloistered mourning. The inability of one of them to live up to the strictures creates the dramatic tension.

The following year, Eileen was well represented on television by her performance in "Coming, Mama" (April 11, 1961), an episode of "Alfred Hitchcock Presents" (NBC). The 26½-minute drama offered her a rare opportunity to portray a woman driven to desperate means and then entirely unrepentant about her antisocial act. She plays a self-sacrificing middle-aged daughter who fears she will be unable to wed suitor Don DeFore because her supposedly invalid mother is so demanding on her life. In despair she poisons her mother and marries DeFore, only to learn he has been hiding the fact from her that he, too, has the same sort of mama. Having once created her own freedom, Eileen is now an expert in such matters. The show closes with her being overly sweet to her mother-in-law, telegraphing to the viewer that the elderly woman is not long for this earth.

In the City Center revival (June 1, 1961) of the Richard Rodgers-Lorenz Hart musical *Pal Joey,* Eileen agreed to portray Melba Snyder, the hardbitten newspaper woman who has five minutes of stage dialogue and one song. But the one song "Zip" was a showstopper. The *New York World Telegram and Sun* reported Eileen's strip number ". . . brought pandemonium to City Center. . . ." For Eileen, who had never professionally sung before, "It was pretty scary getting out there and doing a thing like that." The producers tried to induce Eileen to allow them to star bill her in the production, but she refused since her role was a featured part at best, explaining that the billing would throw the production out of whack. Audience reception to *Pal Joey* was so outstanding that the run was extended to five weeks.

Eileen's natural penchant for playing the eccentric led her to John Patrick's comedy *Everybody Loves Opal* (Longacre Theatre, October 11, 1961). It was a bizarre outing by the author of *The Hasty Heart, The Teahouse of the August Moon,* and *The Curious Savage,* which even a neophyte play producer should have predicted would not be Broadway commercial. Its broad plot had Opal Kronkie (Eileen) as a middle-aged recluse who lives in a rundown mansion next to the town dump. Her only companion is Mr. Tanner, the cat. Being an inveterate collector of anything and everything she can drag home on her little red cart, her abode is an unbelievable junk heap. When three con artists (Stubby Kaye, Brenda Vaccaro, Donald Harron) take refuge from the law in her house, optimistic Opal showers them with kindness and friendly advice, not knowing they have decided to heavily insure her, name themselves the beneficiaries, and then eliminate her. No matter what scheme they concoct (backing a car into her, dousing her with kerosene and setting a fire, dropping the ceiling on her), the fates seem to be on Opal's side, with the finale revealing the house to be crammed full of money. All the guests had to do was just ask!

The critics were unimpressed by Patrick's whimsy, directed by drawingroom-comedy-expert Cyril Ritchard. The *New York Times* thought Patrick's ". . . characters are lifeless and his treatment of them has hardly a vestige of freshness." But everyone seemed to love Eileen: "For a long time, Miss Heckart has been famous for coming on in a presumably minor role and stealing the show, and, now that she has the center of the stage to herself, she remains beautifully in command of it. Her Opal, shabby, seemingly scatterbrained and relentlessly guileless, is genuinely endearing and entirely believable. For all the dangerous temptations she faces, she is never saccharine or cloying, and she gives the role an indomitable spirit and a gallant humor that makes her heroine a woman deserving of respect" (Richard Watts, Jr., *New York Post*).

Eileen certainly gave her all to *Everyone Loves Opal.* Her costuming itself was something to behold. Wearing

With Donald Harron, Stubby Kaye, and director Cyril Ritchard in *Everybody Loves Opal* (1961).

a black union suit, several layers of tatters, topped by four or five ragged overcoats and red earmuffs, she was indeed the queen of the Raggedy Anns. Her Opal was eccentric, to say the least. Being a tremendous tea-lover,

In *Everybody Loves Opal.*

she hangs clotheslines across the living room, so she can use a tea bag, then hang it up to dry, ready at a moment's notice to be yanked off and dunked again. When the insurance doctor (James Coco) arrives to examine Opal, it is revealed that she has six toes on one foot. Coco expresses concern about the effect it has on her walking, but Eileen assures him "It helps." She is the one whose philosophy is "Everybody collects something: I collect everything." When moll Vaccaro reveals her reluctance to marry one-lunged Harron, Eileen chirps: "Look at it this way, honey. Between you, you'll have three." There is nothing Eileen's Opal will not do for anyone. When Coco mentions he has a crick in his

Brenda Vacarro, author John Patrick, and Eileen Heckart at cast party for *Everybody Loves Opal.*

neck, she volunteers her remedy, leaping through the air at him in a flying tackle that would do any chiropractor full justice.

Everyone Loves Opal, which certainly would not be a suburban housewife's matinee delight, closed after 21 performances. It would have better success as a staple on the summer stock circuit where it was used as a vehicle for such assorted types as Nancy Walker, Martha Raye, and Zasu Pitts.

Eileen once said, "I still think that as a Spanish or an Italian, I'm a little like Mickey Rooney, trying to play Romeo. But I must prove to myself I can play more than neurotic women." Perhaps it was this rationale that led Eileen to play the first of her several stage Jewish mothers, in *A Family Affair* (Billy Rose Theatre, January 27, 1962). One quipster tagged the show the Hebrew *Father of the Bride.* The James Goldman-John Kander-William Goldman musical is set in Chicago, where Rita Gardner is about to wed nice young Jewish lawyer, Larry Kert. Everything seems simple. But Kert's parents, garrulous, gossipy Eileen and her furrier-husband Morris Carnovsky, suddenly find themselves in strong conflict with orphan Gardner's bachelor uncle Shelley Berman (in his Broadway debut), each side insisting they know exactly how the wedding is to be engineered. Even with the hiring of a marriage consultant (Bibi Osterwald), there is chaos. What was to have been "a family affair" takes place at a ritzy country club.

A Family Affair had had more than its share of trouble on the road. In Philadelphia, Hal Prince was called in to doctor the show, and he replaced Ward Baker as director. Critical reaction to the show was less than satisfactory. The *New York Times* evaluated: ". . . [it] is not strong on taste; it resorts to the clichés of Jewish domestic attitudes. Nor is it fresh in style; it often has the air of a busy, good-humored borrower from various musical-comedy sources. Since some of these sources are first-rate, some numbers are lively."

In this ethnic melee, Eileen plays the ultimate Jewish mother stereotype (that is, until her role in the film

With Morris Carnovsky and Shelley Berman in *A Family Affair* (1962).

No Way to Treat a Lady came along). She refers to her husband as "the intellectual furrier" and is constantly advising her son on how to be a good husband: "Remember always be firm and yielding." When it comes to making arrangements for the wedding party, Eileen, who seemingly has a horde of relatives, demands invitations for every last one of them, or else. Even when confronted by steadfast Osterwald, who has been hired to arbitrate the catered affair, Eileen raises herself to her full height and exclaims, "I'm not afraid of you."

It was in *A Family Affair* that Eileen was called upon to be a song-and-dance lady. She had to solo "Summer Is Over," sing in trio "I'm Worse Than Anybody," and join in the female chorus number, "My Son the Lawyer." John McClain in the *New York Journal American* well summed up Eileen's musical comedy shortcomings: "Miss Heckart is, of course, a superb comedienne and even indulges in a few small dances with good effect, but she should hardly be entrusted with a song. Her voice [husky contralto] is small, with almost no register, and she has not mastered the Rex Harrison technique of projecting a monotone to give the effect of singing, more's the pity." For her characterization, Eileen fared much better: ". . . [she] brings her biting style of humor [to the role] . . . ." (*New York Daily Mirror*).

A Family Affair would straggle along for 65 performances and then close on March 25, 1962, at a loss of its $420,000 investment, plus the twenty per cent overcall. The United Artists LP original cast album soon became a leftover item in record stores.

Although Eileen had been the star of *Everybody Loves Opal,* it was with difficulty that the producers of *A Family Affair* persuaded her to accept top costarring billing with Berman. Her rationale was: "I didn't want it because of the responsibility. I mean, who knows how many tickets I'm going to sell?" On another occasion, she explained in more detail:

. . . the producers said that the show would be thrown out of focus if my name didn't appear above the title, with Shelley Berman's. I agreed with them, but I am still a character actress. The billing just meant that the two leads were equally important to the show. A star has to watch herself every second. When she shows herself to the public, she has to be sure the public sees her as a nice human being. As the star of a show, furthermore, you have to carry the entire responsibility for the show, and every other member of the cast is dependent on you. Being what I am, I have the freedom to accept any role that appeals to me. And my little boys need me to be what I am. I want them to become good citizens. I can spend my time with them, instead of doing all the things a star has to do to keep herself in front of the public—all those things that have nothing to do with acting but that you are obliged to do to keep the public from forgetting you. Stars have to be seen. They have to go to openings of plays that they care nothing about. They have to appear on television panel shows. They have to keep themselves in demand—in demand by all those people somewhere in Kansas who can see them only in movies and on television. They have to do all that extra work, while I'm lounging around in blue jeans with my three little boys.

The following year, Eileen was in the revival of *Too True to Be Good* (54th Street Theatre, March 12, 1963). The George Bernard Shaw play, first produced in 1931, had an impressive cast for the new presentation. Besides Eileen there was Lillian Gish, Glynis Johns, Robert Preston, Cyril Ritchard, David Wayne, Ray Middleton, and Cedric Hardwicke. *Too True to Be Good,* written late in Shaw's life, finds the playwright at a loss to understand or sympathize with the new values humanity is substituting for the vanishing old set of moral guidelines. As Preston, the atheist son of Hardwicke, who has secretly become a clergyman and a burglar, addresses the audience at the play's end: "I must have affirmations to preach. If I could only find them!" As Howard Taubman observed in the *New York Times:* ". . . [it] is hardly prime Shaw, but are there any second-class Shaws around to comfort us in these arid days?"

In *Too True to Be Good,* Eileen, a nurse at a mental hospital (who does not mind increasing the institution's mortality rate), joins forces with burglar Preston in scampering around the world with wealthy patient Johns. Along the way, they encounter Johns' distracted mother (Gish), Preston's authoritarian father (Hardwicke), a T.E. Lawrence-like army private (Wayne), a pious sergeant (Middleton), and an ineffectual Colonel (Ritchard). Dressed in her guise as a countess, replete with black, bat-styled eyeglasses and a red inverted flying saucer on her head, Eileen was rated ". . . broadly droll as a common sort. . . ." (*New York Times*) and one of the eight stars whose ". . . performance adds to the brightness" (*New York Post*). The show ran for 96 performances, proving that New Yorkers were not culture-conscious, but also that there was more interest in the drama than when originally presented on Broadway where it lasted only 56 showings.

Meanwhile, Eileen's first movie in three years, *My Six Loves,* opened on Broadway (Paramount Theatre, April 3, 1963). This sappy Debbie Reynolds feature, blandly directed by Gower Champion, causes one to question what persuaded Eileen to accept her fourth-billed part. Certainly it was not her once-voiced ra-

In *My Six Loves* (Paramount, 1963).

tionale about her movie work (i.e., "I like good little gems"). This family trade concoction finds overworked musical comedy star Reynolds hiking off to Connecticut for a long rest, accompanied by her secretary Eileen. Before long, six children in need of a parent attach themselves to Reynolds, and the film bogs down in Reynolds's inability to decide whether to wed manly Broadway producer David Janssen or to hitch herself to godly minister Cliff Robertson and adopt the sextet. One guess what she does? The Paramount executives must have known how soft an hors d'oevre *My Six Loves* was, for they laced the picture with the expertise of seven comedy experts. Besides Eileen there was Jim Backus, Hans Conried (as a harried playwright), Mary McCarty, Alice Pearce, Alice Ghostley and John McGiver (as the judge). Judith Crist (*New York Herald-Tribune*) sized up this mawkish cinema exercise in broad comedy and coy sentimentality: "It is only when Eileen Heckart, as a latter day Eve Arden type really sweats at it. . . .that you are made aware of the morass of marshmallow enveloping you." It is not a picture anyone, except Reynolds, cares to remember.

In 1964, Eileen performed in a summer tour of *The Time of The Cuckoo,* playing the role of Leona Samish which Shirley Booth had originated on Broad-

With Debbie Reynolds in *My Six Loves*.

way (for years, critics had been calling Eileen the young Shirley Booth). In July, 1964 there was a mild rhubarb when Eileen was imported to "star" as Regina Giddens in *The Little Foxes* at the Stadium Theatre in Columbus, Ohio. The gesture of Eileen's hometown to honor her in this starring vehicle almost did not come to pass when some forces involved in the presentation thought it unfair that a Broadway figure should be brought in at the expense of some true local talent. Actors Equity Association was forced to arbitrate the matter, and settled in favor of Eileen. (There was no controversy involved whatsoever when Eileen was invited to attend graduation ceremonies at Ohio State University in 1970 to accept the college's Centennial Award for outstanding achievement.)

And Things That Go Bump in the Night (Royale Theatre, April 26, 1965) was a milestone in Eileen's career. Not only was this the most bizarre stage production she has yet appeared in, but it proved conclusively to one and all that the lady had a large sized coterie of followers, albeit mostly unmarried males who would champion her marathon-style performance in most any type of vehicle.

Terence McNally's avant garde drama had first been

produced at the Tyrone Guthrie Theatre in Minneapolis in February, 1964, with Leuren McGrath, Robert Drivas, and Ferdi Hoffman starring in an elongated study of a strange family who have barricaded itself away in a cellar, seeking refuge from the sinister world outside. On Broadway, under Michael Cocoyannis's direction, Eileen starred as Ruby, the brood mother, who like a Promethean creature has set her course and cannot be persuaded to change. She does not perceive that by negating every value of mankind, one by necessity eradicates one own's reason for being. Eileen's Ruby has decided to wait out the finality of the world's destruction within the confines of her Manhattan home basement shelter. She has caused an electric-charged fence to be erected around the house and has established evening curfews for her family. The play opens with Fa (Clifton James) reading in the newspaper that "It is coming" and then falling into a stupor for the remainder of the play. Grandpa (Hoffman), a former Shakespearean actor confined to a wheelchair, would rather meet his end elsewhere, and vicious, homosexual son Drivas who has brought home a pickup (Marco St. John) and the amoral young daughter (Susan Anspach) are not too sure of mad Ruby's rationale but are positive they wish to avoid death. Death seems to be only an abstraction to them even when St. John, after a bout of entertainment with Drivas, is humiliated and chased out of the basement, only to be electrocuted on the fence.

And Things That Go Bump in the Night was critically roasted. John McClain in the *New York Journal American* noted: ". . . in point of credibility it makes [*Tiny*] *Alice* seem like a literal dramatization of *Rebecca of Sunnybrook Farm*." Norman Nadel in The *New York World-Telegram and Sun* was of the opinion: ". . . [it] is a cacophonous statement of silly and superficial ideas, and a remarkably bad play." The other critics, when not reviewing the "Halloween-like audience" or the confusion of ideas in this Charles Addams-ish monster marathon, managed to write a few words about Eileen's performance. As the former diva who is the focal force of this mad offering, she screems at the play's end, "What will happen to us? Nothing. But we will continue. We will continue." Eileen was rated "arresting" by the *New York Post*. The *New York Journal American* reported: "Too bad for the cast, especially Eileen Heckart, a fine actress; . . ." The *New York Daily News*'s John Chapman described Eileen as ". . . in a couple of fright wigs, [she] seems to be looking for two helpers so she can start cooking soup for *Macbeth*."

The show was not Broadway fare by any standards in either content or structure. But the producers (including movie mogul Joseph E. Levine) refused to give up the ghost. Two days after the opening, the play reduced all tickets to $1 each and struggled on through May 8, 1965. Eileen was quoted as saying before the Broadway opening: "I don't know what will happen. It's a marvelous and very strange play. But I told my husband no matter what happens it will be worth all the love and care and effort I will have put into it."

As a decided contrast to this venture, on September 20, 1965, Eileen replaced Mildren Natwick as the zany mother in Neil Simon's long-running success, *Barefoot in the Park,* and remained with the show until May 23, 1966, when Ilka Chase succeeded her.

It was in 1965–1966 that reporters began tagging Eileen the suburban commuter star. A typical interview at the time had Eileen saying: "I'm so suburban I catch the 11:10 to Norwalk every night. Today is matinee day so I came in, had a singing lesson because you never know when a musical will come along. . . ." In fact, one well-known columnist tagged along with Eileen after an evening performance to see how she maneuvered from the theater down to Grand Central Station in such a short time span. He was breathless, but not Eileen, who talked almost non-stop all along the way.

Some of Eileen's press remarks at this period are facetious, but offer insight into her personality:

My husband is proud and bored with my career. He really couldn't care less about the theater, but he's great on opening night. He's such a layman about acting that I get good advice from him.

I can cry on stage, big tears, by thinking of something sad. I'm the best crier in the business. But one day I discovered that my laugh was terrible. Shirley Booth is the best with laughter. She can laugh in every key. Making *Hot Spell* with her, I asked how she did it. She told me that she had practiced hours a day with a metronome. We got a metronome and she gave me instructions. I got to laugh in two keys but Shirley gave me up as a bad job.

When I get a new script, I begin by spending days reading and re-reading it and thinking about it. I have no idea, at first, how to play the part. Some actors begin with nothing and gradually build a role. I would rather make a decision after a fifth reading and have it be bad than remain uncertain. I make notations in the script of how I am going to act as the director makes his suggestions to me during rehearsals. I write it all down. Then I have a mental picture of what I'm going to do. But I can't see it until we start the out-of-town tryouts. My greatest satisfaction in acting is that I am able to give of myself. It's difficult, but I like it. And because I like it, it becomes an indulgence. The money is attractive, too. It wasn't at first, but now I don't turn up my nose at money. Also, it takes years of involvement to learn just a little bit about acting,

and I'm happy about having learned something. These days, a lot of actors go in for psychoanalysis, because they think it will make them understand their own feelings better and thus help them become better actors. Actors work on emotion all the time. But actors who think psychoanalysis will make them better actors are misguided.

On television, Eileen and co-star Maureen Stapleton won New York Emmy awards for their performances on *Save Me a Place at Forest Lawn* on "New York Television Theatre" (March 7, 1966, WNDT). In Lorees Yerby's drama, which also had an off-Broadway run in 1963 of 38 performances, Eileen was Clara and Stapleton Gertrude, two elderly widows who meet each day at a local cafeteria to discuss their grandchildren, the good old days, and their only future, death. It may have been contrived drama and filled with the acting tricks of both stars, but it emerged as compelling entertainment.

Later in 1966, Eileen appeared again on the "New York Television Theatre" (October 3, 1966, WNDT) in a forty-five-minute version of Paul Zindel's *The Effects of Gamma Rays on Man-in-the Moon Marigolds.* The drama had been first presented at the Alley Theatre in Houston (June, 1965) with Chris Wilson starring. Then the play tried out for one performance at the White Barn Theatre (August 21, 1966) in Connecticut with Irene Daley in the lead role. It would later open off-Broadway (Mercer-O'Casey Theatre, October 7, 1970) with Sada Thompson as the mother, replaced in October, 1971, by Joan Blondell. Eileen herself would appear in a Cambridge, Massachusetts version of the drama in 1971.

As the alcoholic, disillusioned mother who is so frustrated by her own life of disappointment, Eileen won critical plaudits. Jack Gould of the *New York Times* wrote: "The absorbing interest of the forty-five minutes was merely to watch the actress [Eileen] subtly and perceptively register the contrasting stages of the widow's bitter journey to defeat.

"In the recollection of a childhood experience, Miss Heckart was radiant with a contagious wonder. In her loathing of her environment, she was the embodiment of the broken human. In a moment of pride, she would have been off for lunch at the Colony. In her final alcoholic detachment from reality, her eyes had the proverbial glazed overcast of those who cannot bear to see more. And it was all done so effortlessly, so beautifully."

Eileen was back on Broadway in the ultracommercial success, Robert Anderson's *You Know I Can't Hear You When the Water's Running* (Ambassador Theatre, March 13, 1967). Starring Eileen, Martin Balsam,

George Grizzard, and featuring Melinda Dillon, each of the four playlets concerned some facet of sex, and the thesis was that physical love should be a natural, easy thing. Richard Watts, Jr., writing in the *New York Post,* expressed the view: "They are notably fine comic and dramatic episodes, written with skill and insight, and their brilliant playing in widely diverse roles demonstrates how expert American acting can be when it is given the proper opportunity."

Eileen was not in the first divertisement *The Shock of Recognition* (in which auditioning actor Balsam strips naked to show he could play the role in question). In *The Footsteps of Doves,* Eileen and Balsam, a married couple of twenty-five years, come to a department store to select a new bed (should it be a single or a double?). Effete salesman Grizzard is not much help, but Balsam receives unexpected comfort from Dillon who has come to buy a big bed because she is all alone. In *I'll Be Home for Christmas,* spouses Eileen and Balsam have a difference of opinion in their discussion of the sex education issue with their almost adult children, but a letter arrives from the son stating he is going to explore life on his own. The final vignette, *I'm Herbert,* finds Eileen and Grizzard as two very elderly people sitting on a porch in rocking chairs and recalling the confused events of their individual pasts, often forgetting who their companion of the moment is.

Balsam emerged the most versatile of the performers, with Eileen running a close second. Walter Kerr reported in the *New York Times:* "She is also brilliantly frustrated in the occasion's most serious piece, a friendly family quarrel called *I'll Be Home for Christmas.* Here she pins her hopes on keeping the children well-informed about their sex lives, hers, everybody's. And the tight little tug at the corner of her mouth as one of the youngsters takes off on his own is marvelously ambiguous. She's meant so well, and where did she miss it?"

Eileen remained with the hit (which chalked up 756 performances) until February 27, 1968, when she was replaced by Irene Dailey. In the London edition, Rosemary Murphy had Eileen's roles.

During July 1966, Warner Bros. had filmed Bel Kaufman's best-selling *Up the Down Staircase* (Radio City Music Hall, August 17, 1967) on location in New York, largely at the Margaret Knox Junior High School at 100th Street and First Avenue. Since Tad Mosel scripted the drama, it was more than coincidental that his "protégée" Eileen should be just right for the role of Henrietta Pastorfield, the slightly frantic member of the mythical Calvin Coolidge High School.

The picture starred a miscast Sandy Dennis as the idealistic young miss, who with a college degree and an abundance of enthusiasm, is assigned as an English teacher to a multi-racial school located in a Manhattan slum area. In the unfolding of the many episodes that befall her in the 1966-style *Blackboard Jungle,* she receives kindly advice from mellow older teacher Ruth White, words of expedience from bachelor educator Eileen, and almost total disillusionment from her observations of callous English instructor Patrick Bedford, thoughtless disciplinarian Roy Poole, and stolid principal Sorrell Brooke. After one of her students attempts suicide over puppy love for Bedford, a black youth nearly drops out, and a punk makes advances to her, she is ready to call it quits, but she realizes her pupils really appreciate her, and therefore she must carry on.

Up the Down Staircase was slickly directed by Robert Mulligan and grossed over $5 million. In its Pollyanna way, it was just as phony as the British school-oriented *To Sir with Love,* since none of the Calvin Coolidge High School teachers were more than caricatures of familiar types, from Eileen who teaches punctuation with games and has a lonely yen for her mature male pupils to the folksiness of Jean Stapleton. There were few viewers of this film who did not already know that a teacher's lot was filled to the breaking point with endless paper work and administrative problems, and that it was a tough job to communicate with pupils and stimulate their minds with meaningful education.

It was in 1968 that Eileen received her first bad film notices, in *No Way to Treat a Lady* (Forum and Tower East Theatre, March 20, 1968). Filmed on location in New York in the summer of 1967 by director Jack Smight (*Harper*), the suspense thriller focused on psychotic theatrical producer Rod Steiger, a man so overburdened by a mother complex (his dead mother had been a great stage actress) that he is driven to murdering lonely women and daring the police to catch him. Steiger's elaborate homicide methods included intricate disguises: as an Irish priest, a Jewish cop, a German handyman, a homosexual hairdresser, a hefty bar girl, and an Italian waiter. Along the way, Steiger fastens on Jewish police detective Morris Brummel (George Segal), who happened to comment to the press that he considered the crimes well executed. Bcause Steiger telephones Segal at home and at the precinct to comment on past and upcoming crimes he has or will commit, the police plant a false murder story, naming Steiger the suspect. They hope this will enrage him, and he will talk long enough on the phone to Segal so the call can be traced. The gimmick backfires when Steiger decides this is foul play and retaliates by selecting Lee Remick, a Lincoln Center guide and Segal's

With Sandy Dennis in *Up the Down Staircase* (WB, 1967).

girlfriend, as his next victim. He nearly succeeds before the final confrontation between Steiger and Segal occurs.

In this mixture of black comedy and the farce, with a few borrowings from *The Boston Strangler*, Eileen was presented as Mrs. Brummel, Segal's possessive upper-middle-class Yiddish mama with whom he lives on Manhattan's upper West Side. Director Smight must have intended Eileen's exaggerated performance to be a balance to the tour de force presence of Steiger, but it just did not work. This was due primarily to the bulk of Eileen's scenes being only with Segal, who had already proven his ability to portray the contemporary Jewish schlemiel in *Bye, Bybe Braverman* and knew the value of understatement. Thus, there was no accord between Eileen's over-indulged, cartoon strip emoting and Segal's subdued comic restraint.

Eileen's Mrs. Brummel appears decked out in matronly finery (including mini-skirts) and sporting a powdered gray wig. For a constant nibbler she is too thin, but age and makeup gave her face a Molly Goldberg look. She is a bundle of ethnic clichés, from her

exaggerated accent to the abundance of gesticulations to the sing-song delivery of her corny dialogue. Since one of her sons (Franklin) has become a respectable doctor, she is still aghast to believe that her other boy (Segal) could remain a policeman. But if that is her cross to bear, she will suffer, and suffer she does. When she is not nagging her thirty-five-year-old son to eat a little something, she is deriding his profession. When Segal first mentions his interest in Remick and describes her to mama, Eileen retorts: "Of course, she's short, blonde and beautiful . . . She'll break your heart." But Eileen has not reckoned with smart cookie Remick, who when she comes to meet mama, handles the situation beautifully, mimicking Eileen's own put-down of Segal. Before long, Eileen is won over completely. She coos to Segal: "That girl is a gem. An absolute gem. She reminds me of me!"

One of the biggest loopholes in Eileen's characterization as the archetypal Jewish mother is her complete indifference to the potential dangers her son undergoes in his profession. When Segal is taken off the Steiger

In *No Way to Treat a Lady* (Paramount, 1968).

case at one point, Eileen holds up a newspaper to the nonlistening Segal: "Look at that. Look at that. Announcements to the world my son was fired." Eileen's Mrs. Brummel cannot fathom that Steiger is a menace; it is outside her province of interest. When he calls Segal at home, she calls her son to the phone with a continual casualness that vitiates the growing tension of the Steiger murder spree. *Variety* criticized: "All supporting performances are fine except for Eileen Heckart's heavy hamming of a 'typical' Jewish mama." *Cue* noted: ". . . [the] routine of using Eileen Heckart in the nagging Jewish mama bit is tired. . . ." Another reviewer penned that Mrs. Brummel was ". . . so extravagantly played by Eileen Heckart that she might drive George Jessel to seek asylum in Syria—and her son to matricide." The *British Monthly Film Bulletin* was more kindly to Eileen: "And if there is too much of the Yiddisher Momma in Eileen Heckart's performance, her timing and the genuinely comic dialogue allotted to her are more than enough to smooth it over."

If Eileen's performance in *No Way to Treat a Lady* was a technical step in the wrong direction, it still proved that at the age of forty-nine she was an established entertainment commodity that could be presented to the public in almost any package and, hopefully digested mindlessly. Like other top character stars, she

was often called upon to bolster production with both her marque name and her particular brand of theatrics.

For "CBS Playhouse," an expensively mounted but unsatisfying series of television specials, Eileen appeared in *Secrets* (May 15, 1968), directed by Paul Bogart. It was Eileen's seventh appearance in a Tad Mosel teleplay. Originally Eileen had been scheduled to play the wife of Arthur Hill, but when Kim Stanley bowed out of the show, Barbara Bel Geddes was hired to replace Eileen, and Eileen took on Stanley's nine-minute role of an aging, possessive actress whose homosexual son takes her to court for attempting to murder him. Staid, middle-aged businessman Hill is brought into the proceedings as a potential juror who fears Eileen may be the actress with whom he once had an affair, and that the trial could reveal the sordid alliance. Despite the network hoopla over *Secrets* being an important dramatic event, it was rather ordinary. In the golden age of television, it would have been passed off as just one more craftsmanlike production.

When asked why she had never become involved in a video series, Eileen replied: "You have to sign one of those seven-year contracts, and I can't see uprooting our home to go and live in California." She went on to explain that she regarded most female stars of television series as castrators. "They've got to be. If they have their own show, then they are really the heads of million dollar corporations, and they have to function on all cylinders—overseeing the writing, costuming, production, and preserving their image. Where is there time for anything else? For some women it's the worst thing that could happen."

The following year did not begin on a creatively satisfying level for Eileen. She allowed herself to be

With George Segal in *No Way to Treat a Lady.*

talked into starring in Jerome Weidman's *The Mother Lover* (Booth Theatre, February 1, 1969). The mishmash was a mess from the start. During rehearsals Kenneth Mars quit, and director Larry Blyden took over the assignment.

Author Weidman evidently had been overly impressed by the prior *Oh Dad, Poor Dad, Mama's Hung You in the Closet and I'm Feelin' So Sad,* because he structured his play in the same alternating dream-reality fantasy mode. The plot has certified public occountant Blyden visiting his Jewish mama in Queens every Sunday morning. She is a landlady, and Valerie French is her new boarder. Blyden falls for her, and decides it would be nice to get married. If he killed mama he would have so much more free time and money ("the taxi fares alone"), and the couple could afford a live-in maid and all. The balance of the black comedy deals with Blyden's efforts to drive Eileen crazy and then to her death.

The Mother Lover, co-produced by Leland Hayward and Joseph E. Levine's Avco-Embassy film company, sputtered in tryouts before its delayed opening and closed after one performance. The kindest thing said of the production was that it was "shoddy." Donald J. Mayerson in The *Villager* put it best about Eileen. "Eileen Heckart, one of my favorite actresses, must have a penchant for playing Jewish mothers. It doesn't work. She has none of the large breasted, suffocating qualities needed for the part, and no amount of Yiddish inflection or reading from *The Forward* can convince me that Miss Heckart is anything less than goyish."

Another example of artistic bad judgment on Eileen's part was her participation in the independently produced film *The Tree* (72nd Street Playhouse, June 9, 1969). It was her tenth film to date and indicated how much Eileen still regarded herself as a growing actress who must experiment in even shaky vehicles if it will provide an acting experience for herself. Since her *Picnic* success in 1953, she doubtlessly could have found many more film roles to showcase her talents, but she rarely ventured on the screen, save when the production was shot in New York, so that she could remain close to her first love, the stage.

Produced-written-directed-released by Robert Guenette, *The Tree* was filmed on location in Paterson, New Jersey, in late 1967 at a cost of $153,000. Its fuzzy plot focused on Jordan Christopher, a psychotic Vietnam veteran who kidnaps a six-year-old girl and hides out with Eileen, who had been the former mistress of his late father. Needless to say, kindly Eileen takes neurotic Christopher to bed for comfort sake. The story, as such, weaves back and forth between the past and present, revealing Christopher's hatred of his pos-

sessive mother (Ruth Ford) and his unnatural love for his sister (Gale Dixon). It develops that he had once raped his sister and therefore the kidnapped girl might be his own child. By now, Dixon is dead, having killed herself when her husband deserted her, and Christopher, unable to cope with the world, hangs himself on the symbolic tree.

With all of its pretentions, *The Tree* did boast a seasoned cast, proving that Guenette must have had far more intriguing ideas than appeared in the release print. And unlike many other self-indulgent movies made in the 1960s, it did see a release, albeit a brief one at the art house dead end (72nd Street Playhouse). The reviews were enough to suffocate any potential audience interest, left over after bad word-of-mouth reports on the film. But the cast emerged from the fiasco with dignity. Of the "paper-thin, Peyton Place characters," *Cue* magazine noted: "There is sincerity with the cast members, including Eileen Heckart and Jordan Christopher, going about their business as though in a film of stature." *Variety* reported: "A usual fine performance from Eileen Heckart."

A fine commercial turn of events was Eileen's starring role in Leonard Gershe's *Butterflies Are Free* (Booth Theatre, October 21, 1969). It was based on the real life adventures of Harold Krents, a blind boy who went on to become a Harvard law student, with the kookie ingenue derived from Gershe's appreciation of actress Mia Farrow. The comedy had originally tried out at the Westport Playhouse (August 26, 1969) with Maureen O'Sullivan in the mother role, but by the time it reached Broadway, Eileen had taken over the assignment.

With Keir Dullea in *Butterflies Are Free* (1969).

With Edward Albert in *Butterflies Are Free* (Columbia, 1972).

In *Butterflies Are Free*, blind boy Keir Dullea has moved out of his Scarsdale home and taken a studio apartment in Greenwich Village, determined to break away from his mother's apron strings and develop on his own, perhaps as a musician (he plays the guitar and composes songs). It is not long before his next-door neighbor, a shallow, callow nineteen-year-old (Blythe Danner) named Jill, a would-be actress who was once married to a Jack for six days, has introduced herself. She takes an unusually compassionate interest in Dullea. Having gone to bed together and deciding to unbar the connecting door to their adjoining rooms, things look bright for Dullea and Danner, but then there is a knock on the door, and lo and behold, there stands Eileen, the suburban matron who has promised to give her son another month to adjust on his own but just cannot resist interfering in his life. With the words "Hello Mother!" act I comes to a close, having given the audience a brief glimpse of Eileen and what is to come.

In a minute Eileen has sized up Danner as the thoughtless creature she is (a girl who meant to enroll at U.C.L.A. but could not find a parking place that day) and confronts her in a tug-of-war for Dullea's loyalty and well-being. Danner accuses her of deliberately hurting her son: "I can't. I can only irritate him. You can hurt him. The longer you stay, the harder it will be for him when you leave. Let him come with me and you go have your kicks with someone who won't feel them after you're gone."

Throughout the light comedy, there is a sprinkling of funny lines, most of them evolving from Eileen's characterization of the predatory widowed Jewish mother, herself an intellect of sorts and not a creative dunce. (She had a successful series of children's books

based on the imaginary adventures of a blind super-child.) Due to some scripting contrivance, it dawns on her that she perhaps has not given her son what he needs. Humbled, she is willing to alter her outlook, but not her values. Thus when Danner returns late that night, having forgotten a dinner date with Dullea, Eileen has sarcastic words for her and her new play-wright lover (Michael Glaser) whom Danner has dragged home to help her move to his flat.

Eileen engages in an amusing interchange with Glaser, each propounding their views on the establish-ment, particularly the suburban housewife set. Eileen's Mrs. Baker says: "Well, I wouldn't count on the giddy little matron, and I don't intend to pay money to see nudity, obscenity and degeneracy."

Glaser: "Mrs. Baker, these things are all a part of life."

Eileen: "I know, Mr. Austin. . . . So is diarrhea, but I wouldn't classify it as entertainment."

Butterflies Are Free emerged a hit. ". . . [it] is an enormously entertaining light comedy which can al-ways be called a commercial manufacture if you are persuaded that every time you enjoy yourself in the theater someone is playing a dirty trick on you, . . ." (Walter Kerr, *New York Times*). Dullea was ranked sympathetic and professional, and Eileen got a *healthy* round of ovations. "Every time she opens her mournful mouth she is winding up for a haymaker. You know that, you expect it, you delight in it. Miss Heckart can say as little as 'Oh, Jill,' turning 'Jill' into a three-syllable knifing down under cover of a ceasefire, and rock the house with it. Horrendous mothers are not that funny each time out in life. This is the stylization that says they ought to be if they are going to be around at all, and Miss Heckart offers the controlled statement superbly." But it was Danner who was touted the ingenue find of the season and grabbed the lime-light from all. In fact when she and Eileen were both nominated for Tony awards for their *Butterflies Are Free* performances, it was Danner who won!

Nevertheless, Eileen enjoyed her stay with the show, which substantiated her reputation as a top character stage star. "It didn't surprise me when it became a sellout. I was so sure of it I had a telephone installed (in the dressing room) before the opening. The only other time I did that was before *You Know I Can't Hear You When the Water's Running*. Then I even ordered furniture for my dressing room."

On October 14, 1970, after a year with the show, Eileen was replaced by Rosemary Murphy, so the former could prepare for the London version of the play (Apollo Theatre, November 4, 1970). It was Eileen's British stage debut, and unfortunately it fell

In *The Effect of Gamma Rays on Man-in-the-Moon Marigolds* (1971).

flat. The English critics thought the comedy, starring Eileen, Dullea, and Barbara Ferris was "soggy," but they were kinder to Eileen. ". . . [she] plays the tigress mother with a glittering, drawled astringency which almost masks the sugar of her last gooey scenes." (London *Observer*). The British had little interest in the rather specialized subject of Jewish momism. The show folded after a few weeks.

If the London debacle was a grave disappointment to Eileen, the subsequent history of *Butterflies Are Free* must have given her pause to reconsider the vagaries of show business. After the successful Broadway launching of the show, a national company was organized with Eve Arden in the lead, giving the role a more Gentile, less warm interpretation. Then in one of the casting amazements of the decade, seventy-two-year-old Gloria Swanson was persuaded to take over for Arden on the road, where she did exceptionally well. Critics were mindful of her perhaps too grand and chic portrayal of Mrs. Baker, but they all agreed it was fine to see Swanson back on the stage, and that she had perfected her comedy timing. Then on September 7, 1971, she took over the Broadway version of *Butterflies Are Free* and injected new box office life to the show, which had been surviving on two-fers. Her glamorous but thoughtful and ever-so-energetic performance captivated the critics anew and made many reviewers and playgoers rethink their initial evaluation and appreciation of Eileen's handling of the star assignment. This situation might well have prompted Eileen to accept the lucrative offer of Mike Frankovich to costar in his Columbia Pictures screen version of *Butterflies Are Free* with Oscar-winner Goldie Hawn. Milton Katselas, who directed the stage hit, was brought in to direct the film, which began principal photography in Hollywood on September 27, 1971.

Meanwhile on television, Eileen appeared in an offbeat bit of casting in an episode of "Gunsmoke" (CBS), in the episode "The Innocent." She played Athena Royce, a greenhorn missionary teacher on route to her first assignment. Now that Eileen had reached the top ranks of character stardom, there were fewer and fewer video offerings that appealed to her or for which she was suitable without sacrificing her standing in the profession.

Although Eileen had been unavailable to play the lead part in *The Effect of Gamma Rays on Man-in-the Moon Marigolds,* she jumped at the chance to again play Beatrice when the show was mounted for an engagement at the New Theatre in Cambridge, Massachusetts (April 13, 1971). "The play has a universal truth. Forgive me if I sound pompous. I don't mean to, but I could see so many qualities in his portrait of this woman. She was a born loser. Any real moment of pride in her life's been denied to her. I've known this woman. Paul writes with a sense of beauty and truth." The Melvin Bernhardt-directed production received favorable Boston notices.

Eileen dug deeply into the characterization of the middle-aged alcoholic who has given up on life and people. Living in a slum railroad flat apartment with her two daughters and an aged boarder (for $50 weekly), she can find no reason for her existence: "Half-life! If you want to know what a half-life is just ask me. You're looking at the original half-life! I got stuck with one daughter with half a mind, another one who's half a test tube; half a husband—a house half-full of rabbit crap, and half a corpse! That's what I call a half life, Matilde! Me and cobalt 60! Two of the biggest half-lifes you ever saw!"

By the end of the drama, Eileen's Beatrice, who in her own school days was known as Betty the loon, has alienated herself from any possible link with salvation. She has kicked out the boarder, killed her older daughter's pet rabbit, refused to attend her younger daughter's one moment of triumph at school (winning the science fair prize for growing radioactively treated marigolds), and torn the junky apartment to shreds, half-heartedly believing she might convert the premises into a tea shop. In total hopelessness, she shouts out "I hate the world. Do you know that Matilda? I hate the world."

When Eileen left *Marigolds* in July, 1971, to go to Hollywood to make *Butterflies Are Free,* Betty Field took over the mammoth role. Meanwhile, the original production was still running in New York with business revitalized by the hiring of Joan Blondell in October, 1971, to take over the Beatrice part. And the screen rights. . . . They had been sold to Paul Newman as a projected cinema project for his wife, Joanne Woodward. (Filmed in 1972 by Twentieth Century-Fox).

In this period, Eileen passed up the opportunity to appear in the Broadway rendering of *And Miss Reardon Drinks a Little* (Morosco Theatre, February 25, 1971). This Paul Zindel drama had first been presented at Mark Taper's Forum in Los Angeles in 1967 and after revisions was prepared for New York. Eileen was approached to costar with Julie Harris and Estelle Parsons, as the third school teacher sister, the one ostensibly successful member of the family, but really an uptight hypocrite. But the producers and Eileen could not agree on billing (third), and so Eileen withdrew and Nancy Marchand was substituted. She might well have offered the contrived theatrics a touch of sympathetic pathos so obviously missing from the show.

In July 1971 she performed with Joanne Woodward, Richard Kiley, and Pat Hingle in Tad Mosel's *All The*

Way Home, adapted from James Agee's *A Death in the Family.* This Toronto-filmed teleplay for the "Hallmark Hall of Fame" was televised on December 1, 1971. Had the video drama been done a decade or so back, it would have been an exceptional event within the medium. But in the 1970s it was just another remake of a remake, and garnered no particular audience enthusiasm or enduring critical raves. Woodward was the straightlaced wife who matures through the tragic death of her husband (Kiley), with Hingle emoting as the wayward brother-in-law, and Eileen as the staunch aunt. Her craftsmanlike work went unheralded.

Columbia Pictures' rendition of *Butterflies Are Free* premiered at Radio City Music Hall on July 6, 1972 and did the expected big summertime business. While producer M.J. Frankovich claimed the only essential change wrought upon the stage show was transposing the setting from New York to San Francisco, there were many more unfortunate alterations, most essential being the shift of plot emphasis from the blind boy (Edward Albert) to the kookie antics of his next door neighbor Goldie Hawn. This pandering to commercialism—after all did not Miss Hawn win an Oscar for similar dumb blonde posing in *Cactus Flower?*—was understandable if not entirely forgiveable. But the performance offered by Eileen was her worst ever on screen. Whatever spontaniety she had possessed on Broadway had disappeared in the intervening months. Oh, Eileen was still the same pushy suburban mother who proves to be selfless enough when the chips are down, but her cinema Mrs. Baker was pasty in looks and robot-like in performance. Eileen tossed out her lines of dialogs with such unenthusiasm that she lost nearly every laugh her part had garnered on stage. Part of the blame can be traced to the uninspired direction of Milton Katselas who helmed the Broadway version, but for some unexplainable reason Eileen at best could only summon up a spiritless shell of her stage performance. (Ironically, it would be for this less than excellent screen performance that Eileen would win her first Academy Award, beating out such other Best Supporting Actress contenders as Shelley Winters, Geraldine Page, Jeannie Berlin, and Susan Tyrell. At the April, 1973 Oscar ceremonies, Eileen seemed just as surprised as the studio audience that her performance won the prize.)

While *Butterflies Are Free* was racking up big coins around the country (over $7 million in domestic gross rentals in 1972), and Edward Albert was being heralded as the new screen find of 1972, Eileen had returned to the summer theater circuit in *Remember Me,* an alleged pre-Broadway melodrama that floundered along the straw hat circuit in mid-1972. No one can dispute that the premise of the Ronald Alexander play was not unique (Eileen is a vicious dame who appears out of the past into the ritzy home of Robert Stack, the weak-willed man who was her porno-circus partner twenty years before he escaped to a rich marriage to Marian Seldes.) Needless to say the bizarre opus was later shelved for "rewrites." Eileen returned to the lucrative field of guest starring on television, such as an episode of the "Streets of San Francisco" (ABC, September 24, 1972). The new celebrity returned to Hollywood to co-star with Gene Hackman and Liv Ullmann in *Zandys Bride,* a Warner Bros. film, and then in the fall of 1973 jaunted back to her beloved Broadway to co-star with Arthur Kennedy in Ira Levin's suspense thriller, *Veronica's Room.*

Eileen has traveled a long professional course since 1958 when she stated: "I am not a star, nor do I want to be one. Let's say that I don't think I will ever be one." Solidly established in the entertainment world, she can now state: "I love to act. Of course, it's been helpful to have a husband who supported me. That way, I didn't have to take a part unless I really loved it. We've been married twenty-eight years [as of 1971], so I've never had to retire from the theater. I was able to pick and choose only what I wanted to do." On another occasion, the contented Eileen admitted: "I've had no particular pressures about combining a personal life and a career. It is amazing how much you can find time for. And, of course, I've had a wonderful nurse for my children. . . ." Eileen is level-headed enough to admit: "To my sons, my profession isn't anything special. Of course, they come to all my openings, but they really think to themselves, 'There's my mother up there on the stage hollering at everyone just like she hollers at everyone at home!' "

As for her future, Eileen says: "Retirement? Never! An actress is out in the world. The very aliveness of acting makes it attractive to me. I'll never retire."

FILMOGRAPHY: EILEEN HECKART
FEATURE FILMS

MIRACLE IN THE RAIN (Warner Brothers, 1956) 107 M.

Producer, Frank P. Rosenberg; director, Rudolph Mate; based on the novel by Ben Hecht; screenplay, Hecht; music, Franz Waxman; song, Ray Heindorf, M.K. Jerome, and Ned Washington; assistant director, Mel Dellar, Lee White; art director, Leo K. Kuter; camera, Russell Metty; editor, Thomas Reilly.

Jane Wyman (Ruth Wood); Van Johnson (Arthur Hugenon); Peggie Castle (Millie Kranz); Fred Clark, (Stephen Jalonik); Eileen Heckart (Grace Ullman); Josephine Hutchinson (Agnes Wood); William Gargan (Harry Wood); Marcel Dalio (Waiter); George Givot (Head Waiter); Barbara Nichols (Arleene Witchy); Halliwell Hobbes (Eli B. Windgate); Paul Picerni (Young Priest); Alan King (Sgt. Gil Parker); Irene Seidner (Mrs. Hamer); Arte Johnson (Monty); Marian Holmes (Mrs. Rickles); Minerva Urecal (Mrs. Canelli); Frank Scannell (Auctioneer); Walter Kingson (Narrator); Jack Lomas (Auctioneer's Assistant); Anna Dewey (Elderly Woman); Charles Meredith (Receptionist, N.Y.T.); Grandon Rhodes (Mr. Baldwin); Norbert Schiller (Dr. Zero); Harry Harvey, Jr. (Boy In N.Y.T.); Michael Vallon (Italian Flower Man); Paul Smith (Dixie Dooley); Glen Vernon (M.C.); Malcolm Atterbury (Messenger); Ray Walker (Salesman); John Connoughton (Altar Boy); Lucita (Accordionist); Chalo Alvarado (Italian Count); Darlene Fields (Girl with Count); Jess Kirkpatrick (Andy—Bartender); Paul Maxey (Stout Man); Tony Hughes (55 Year Old Man); Roxanne Arlen (Cathy Wicklow); Rose Allen (Elderly Woman).

THE BAD SEED (Warner Brothers, 1956) 129 M.

Producer-director, Mervyn LeRoy; based on the play by Maxwell Anderson and the novel by William March; screenplay, John Lee Mahin; art director, John Beckman; music, Alex North; assistant director, Mel Dellar; camera, Hal Rosson; editor, Warren Low.

Nancy Kelly (Christine); Patty McCormack (Rhoda); Henry Jones (LeRoy); Eileen Heckart (Mrs. Daigle); Evelyn Varden (Monica); William Hopper (Kenneth); Paul Fix (Bravo); Jesse White (Emory); Gage Clarke (Tasker); Joan Croydon (Miss Fern); Frank Cady (Mr. Daigle).

BUS STOP (20th Century-Fox, 1956) 96 M.

Producer, Buddy Adler; director, Joshua Logan; based on the play by William Inge; screenplay, George Axelrod; art director, Lyle R. Wheeler, Mark-Lee Kirk; music, Alfred Newman, Cyril J. Mockridge; song, Ken Darby; assistant director, Ben Kadish; camera, Milton Krasner; editor, William Reynolds.

Marilyn Monroe (Cherie); Don Murray (Bo); Arthur O'Connell (Virgil); Betty Field (Grace); Eileen Heckart (Vera); Robert Bray (Carl); Hope Lange (Elma); Hans Conreid (*Life* Photographer); Casey Adams (*Life* Reporter); Henry Slate (Manager of Night Club); Terry Kelman (Gerald); Linda Brace (Evelyn); Helen Mayon (Landlady); Lucille Knox (Blonde on Street); Kate MacKenna, George Selk (Elderly Passengers); Phil J. Munch (Preacher); Mary Carroll (Cashier); Fay L. Ivor (Usher); Richard Culvert Johnson, William Schub (Messengers); G.E. Dunlap (Orville); Jim Katugi Noda (Japanese Cook).

SOMEBODY UP THERE LIKES ME (MGM, 1956) 113 M.

Producer, Charles Schnee; associate producer, James E. Newcom; director, Robert Wise; based on the autobiography of Rocky Graziano, written by Rowland Barber; screenplay, Ernest Lehman; assistant director, Robert Saunders; music, Bronislau Kaper; song, Sammy Cahn; art director, Cedric Gibbons, Malcolm Brown; camera, Joseph Ruttenberg; editor, Albert Akst.

Paul Newman (Rocky); Pier Angeli (Norma); Everett Sloane (Irving Cohen); Eileen Heckart (Ma Barbella); Sal Mineo (Romolo); Harold J. Stone (Nick Barbella); Joseph Buloff (Benny); Sammy White (Whitey Bimstein); Arch Johnson (Heldon); Robert Lieb (Questioner); Theodore Newton (Commissioner Eagan); Robert Loggia (Frankie Peppo); Judson Pratt (Johnny Hyland); Matt Crowley (Lou Stillman); Donna Jo Gribble (Yolanda Barbella); Robert Easton (Corporal Quinbury); Ray Stricklyn (Bryson); Michael Dante (Shorty); Harry Wismer, Sam Taub (Announcers); John Rosser, Frank Campanella (Detectives); Steve McQueen (Fidel).

HOT SPELL (Paramount, 1958) 86 M.

Producer, Hal B. Wallis; associate producer, Paul Nathan; director, Daniel Mann; based on the play *Next of Kin* by Lonnie Coleman; screenplay, James Poe; assistant director, Michael D. Moore; art director, Hal Pereira, Tambi Larsen; music, Alex North; special effects, John P. Fulton; camera, Loyal Griggs; editor, Warren Low.

Shirley Booth (Alma Duval); Anthony Quinn (Jack Duval); Shirley MacLaine (Virginia Duval); Earl Holliman (Buddy Duval); Eileen Heckart (Fan); Clint Kimbrough (Billy Duval); Warren Stevens (Wyatt); Jody Lawrence (Dora May); Harlan Warde (Harry); Valerie Allen (Ruby); Irene Tedrow (Essie Mae); Anthony Jochim (Preacher); Elsie Weller (Librarian).

HELLER IN PINK TIGHTS (Paramount, 1960) 100 M.

Producer, Carlo Ponti, Marcello Girosi; associate producer, Lewis E. Ciannelli; director, George Cukor; based on the novel *Heller with a Gun* by Louis L'Amour; screenplay, Dudley Nichols, Walter Bernstein; art director, Gene Allen; music, Daniele Amfitheatrof; assistant director, C.C. Coleman, Jr.; camera, Harold Lipstein; editor, Howard Smith.

Sophia Loren (Angela); Anthony Quinn (Tom Healy); Margaret O'Brien (Della Southby); Steve Forrest (Clint Mabry); Eileen Heckart (Mrs. Lorna Hathaway); Ramon Novarro (DeLeon); Edmund Lowe (Manfred Montague); George Mathews (Sam Pierce); Edward Binns (Sheriff McClain); Warren Wade (Hodges); Frank Silvera (Santis); Robert Palmer (McAllister); Leo V. Matranga, Taggart Casey (Gunslingers); Cal Bolder (Goober); Howard McNear (Photographer); Frank Cordell (Theodore); Taylor "Cactus" McPeters (Williams); David Armstrong (Achilles); Alfred Tonkel (Calchas); Paul T. Salata, Robert Darin (Servants); Bryn Davis (Venus); Cathy Cox (Juno); Syl Lamont, Riza Royce, Ruth Barnell, Allan Paige (Peasants); Amanda Randolph (Maid); Richard Shannon (Man at Desk); Harry Chesire (Poker Player); Bernard Nedell (Double for Edmund Lowe); Iron Eyes Cody, Rodd Redwing, Chief Yowlachie, Eddie Little Sky (Indians); Dean Williams (Kansas Sheriff); Lorraine Crawford (Madam); Bob Adler (Stage Coach Driver).

MY SIX LOVES (Paramount, 1963) 105 M.

Producer, Gant Gaither; director, Gower Champion; story, Peter V.K. Funk; screenplay, John Fante, Joseph Calvelli; assistant director, Michael Caffey; costumes, Edith Head; music, Walter Scharf; song, Sammy Cahn and James Van Heusen; sound, Hugh Grenzbach, John Wilkinson; camera, Arthur E. Arling; editor, John Woodcock.

Debbie Reynolds (Janice Courtney); Cliff Robertson (Jim Larkin); David Janssen (Alvin Bliss); Eileen Heckart (Ethel); Hans Conreid (Kinsley Cross); Mary McCarty (Doreen Smith); John McGiver (Judge Harris); Max Showalter (B.J. Smith); Alice Ghostley (Selina); Alice Pearce (Bus Driver); Pippa Scott (Diane Soper); Claude Stroud (Dr. Miller); Darlene Tompkins (Ava); Leon Belasco (Mario); Billy Hughes (Lee); Jim Backus (Sheriff); Barry Livingston (Sherman); Deborah Price (Dulcie); Teddy Eccles (Sonny); Sally Smith (Brenda); Colleen Peters (Amy); Pat Moran (Studio Executive); Leon Tyler (Columnist); Yvonne Peattie (Lady Columnist); Ted Bergen, Bill Hudson, Ted Quillin (Reporters); Maurice Kelly (Man With Mike); Larry Alderette, Paul Rees, Robert Cole, Robert Karl, Cass Jaeger, Frank Radcliff, Terry Terrill (Photographers); Georgine Cleveland, Molly Dodd (Women); Sterling Holloway (Oliver Dodds); William Wood (Judge's Clerk); Gary Getzman (Bus Driver's Son); Thomas Thomas (Stage Manager); Richard Fitzgerald (Actor); Mimi Dillard (Receptionist); Tommy Farrell (Studio Representative); Victor Biono (Fat Man).

UP THE DOWN STAIRCASE (Warner Brothers, 1967) 120 M.

Producer, Alan Pakula, Robert Mulligan; director, Mulligan; based on the novel by Bel Kaufman; screenplay, Tad Mosel; art director, George Jenkins; assistant director, Don Kranze; music, Fred Karlin; camera, Joseph Coffey; editor, Folmar Blangsted.

Sandy Dennis (Sylvia Barrett); Patrick Bedford (Paul Barringer); Eileen Heckart (Henrietta Pastorfield); Ruth White (Beatrice Schracter); Jean Stapleton (Sadie Finch); Sorrell Booke (Dr. Bester); Roy Poole (McHabe); Florence Stanley (Ella Friedenberg); Jeff Howard (Joe Ferone); Ellen O'Mara (Alice Blake); Jose Rodriguez (Himself); John Fantauzzi (Ed Williams); Vinnette Carroll (The Mother); Janice Mars (Miss Gordon); Loretta Leversee (Social Studies Teacher); Robert Levine (Mr. Osborne); Elena Karam (Nurse Eagen); Frances Sternhagen (Charlotte Wolf); Salvatore Rosa (Harry A. Kagan);

NO WAY TO TREAT A LADY (Paramount, 1968) 108 M.

Producer, Sol C. Siegel; director, Jack Smight; based on the novel by William Goldman; screenplay, John Gay; art director, Hal Pereira, George Jenkins; assistant director, Terence Nelson; song, Stanley Myers and Andrew Belling; camera, Jack Priestley; editor, Archie Marshek.

Rod Steiger (Christopher Gill); Lee Remick (Kate Palmer); George Segal (Morris Brummel); Eileen Heckart (Mrs. Brummel); Murray Hamilton (Inspector Haines); Martine Bartlett (Alma Mulloy); Barbara Baxley (Belle Poppie); Irene Dailey (Mrs. Fitts); Doris Roberts (Sylvia Poppie); Ruth White (Mrs. Himmel); Val Bisoglio (Det. Monahan); David Doyle (Lt. Dawson); Kim August (Sadie); Michael Dunn (Mr. Kupperman); Joey Faye (Superintendent); Patricia Ripley (Woman #1); P. Jay Sidney (Medical Examiner); Don Blair (Reporter); Bob O'Connell, Tony Major, Glen Kezer (Officers); Tom Ahearne (Father O'Brien); Vincent Sardi, J. Molinski (Themselves); Richard Nicholls (Man in Sardi's); R. Bernard (Indignant Man); John Gerstad (Dr. Shaffer); Bill Fort (Staff Editor); Al Nesor, Sam Coppola, Louis Basile (Customers); Zvee Scooler (Old Man); Eddie Philips (News Vendor); John Dutra (Man With Dog); Burr Smidt (Detective Sgt.); Linda Canby (Teenage Girl); Jim Dukas (Police Artist); Don Koll (Detective).

THE TREE (Guenette, 1969) 92 M.

Producer, Robert Guenette; associate producer, Robert Wood; director-screenplay, Guenette; music, Kenyon Hopkins; production design, Frances Gudermann; camera, Jess Paley; editor, Howard Milkin.

Jordan Christopher (Bucky Gagnon); Eileen Heckart (Sally Dunning); George Rose (Stuey Moran); James Broderick (Detective McCarthy); Ruth Ford (Mrs. Gagnon); Fred J. Scollay (Alex); Kathy Ryan (Terry); Alan Landers (Jim Wisiewski); Gale Dixon (Lorry); Ed Griffith (Detective Gorman); Tom Ahearne (Joe); Billy King (Delivery Boy); Bess Gerard (Waitress); Alan Zemel, Glenn Scimonilli (Boys On Bikes).

BUTTERFLIES ARE FREE (Columbia, 1972) 109 M.

Producer, M.J. Frankovich; director, Milton Katselas; based on the play by Leonard Gershe; screenplay, Gershe; production designer, Robert Clatworthy; costumes, Moss Mabry; music, Bob Alcivar; songs, Stephen Schwartz; John Denver, Bill Danoff, and Taffy Nivert; Alcivar and Randy McNeill; assistant director, Ivan Volkman; makeup, Karl Silvera; technical advisor, Harold Krents; public relations, Charles M. Powell; camera, Charles B. Lang; editor, David Blewitt.

Goldie Hawn (Jill); Edward Albert (Don Baker); Eileen Heckart (Mrs. Baker); Michael Glaser (Ralph); Mike Warren (Roy).

ZANDYS BRIDE (Warner Brothers, 1974)

Producer, Harvey Matofsky; director, Jan Troell; screenplay, Marc Norman; assistant director, Miles Middough; production designer, Al Brenner; sound, Charles Knight; camera, Jordan Cronenweth; editor, James Benson.

With: Gene Hackman, Liv Ullmann, Eileen Heckart, Susan Tyrell, Joe Santos, Frank Cady, Harry Dean Stanton, Alf Kjellin.